Electronic and Computer Music

Peter Manning

OXFORD
UNIVERSITY PRESS

2004

OXFORD
UNIVERSITY PRESS

Oxford   New York
Auckland   Bangkok   Buenos Aires   Cape Town   Chennai
Dar es Salaam   Delhi   Hong Kong   Istanbul   Karachi   Kolkata
Kuala Lumpur   Madrid   Melbourne   Mexico City   Mumbai   Nairobi
Sao Paulo   Shanghai   Taipei   Tokyo   Toronto

Published by Oxford University Press, Inc.
198 Madison Avenue, New York, New York 10016

www.oup.com

Oxford is a registered trademark of Oxford University Press

Library of Congress Cataloging-in-Publication Data
Manning, Peter, 1948–
Electronic and computer music / Peter Manning.—
Rev. and expanded
edition.
p. cm.
Includes bibliographical references and index.
Discography
ISBN 0-19-514484-8; 0-19-517085-7 (pbk.)
1. Electronic music—History and criticism. 2. Computer
music—History and criticism. I. Title.
ML1380 .M36 2003
786.7'09—dc21   2002155278

2   4   6   8   9   7   5   3   1

Printed in the United States of America
on acid-free paper

To Liz, Clare, and David

Preface

Since the publication of the first edition of this book, the medium of electronic and computer music has expanded at a breathtaking pace. Back in 1985 the era of MIDI was in its infancy, and few even then could have accurately predicted the true extent of the digital revolution that ensued, bringing increasingly powerful audio synthesis and processing resources to individual users via the personal computer and the Internet. Whereas a single chapter on computer music seemed adequate at that time, this section had already expanded to four chapters for the second edition in 1993. The exponential nature of developments since then is reflected in the expansion of the equivalent section in the new edition to a total of twelve chapters.

The material of computer music retained from the second edition has been substantially rewritten to reflect changing perceptions and experiences of the world of computers and digital engineering in general. In so doing, I firmly prepared the ground for the new material that follows. Many aspects of the technology that were still in their infancy at that time have now achieved their potential, in turn unlocking yet further avenues of exploration and discovery that need to be critically assessed. The expanded perspective takes these issues fully into account, charting developments to the dawn of the new millennium and beyond.

The situation regarding the associated musical repertory is perhaps less certain, for reasons that will become clear in due course. Whereas a close correlation between key technical developments and associated works that fully exploit their creative potential can be maintained up until the early 1980s, the sheer diversification and expansion of activities that occurred subsequently make it impossible to sustain this approach. The perspective thus shifts in emphasis at this point in the chronology more specifically toward the functional characteristics of these technologies, viewed in ways that will facilitate independent study. There is undoubtedly a need for a book devoted exclusively to the repertory of the medium from its birth to the present day, but this is a project yet to be completed.

Viewed in retrospect, it is interesting to note that many of the issues discussed in the earlier editions have achieved new levels of importance. The revival of interest in vintage analog synthesizers is a striking case in point. The growing desire to simulate the functional characteristics of such devices or indeed reproduce the technology itself has generated a demand for information that is no longer generally available. The retention of the original chapter on voltage-control technology in the new edition is thus clearly of more than simply historical value, providing important information for those wishing to revisit this fascinating world of analog synthesis for themselves.

A number of key issues still remain to be resolved, demonstrating that advances in technology do not necessarily result in concomitant improvements in their creative value. There is, for example, no universal language for expressing musical ideas in a format that has a direct equivalence with the technical resources necessary to realize them. This creates many context-specific difficulties that have yet to be adequately addressed.

At the most fundamental level it is the nature of the working relationships established between composers and performers and their sound-producing tools that holds the ultimate key to failure or success. These relationships are ultimately dependent on the modes of communication and interaction that can be facilitated by new technologies, relating the worlds of creativity and subjectivity with the highly objective environment of electronic engineering. It is this point of intersection that provides a constant point of reference throughout this account, and the intention is to provide the reader with a perspective that connects these interdisciplinary strands in the pursuit of common goals within this diverse, complex, and intriguing medium of creative expression.

Contents

V. Digital Audio

VI. MIDI

VII. Desktop Synthesis and Signal Processing

VIII. The Expanding Perspective

Photo gallery follows page 132.

Electronic and Computer Music

The Background to 1945

Buried among the records of the United States patent office for the year 1897 is a rather unusual entry, no. 580.035, registered in the name of Thaddeus Cahill. The invention described has long since passed into obscurity, but in several respects it was to prove as significant a landmark for electronic music as the more celebrated phonograph patents of Edison and Berliner registered some twenty years previously.

Cahill's entry described an electrically based sound-generation system, subsequently known as his Dynamophone or Telharmonium, the first fully developed model being presented to the public early in 1906 at Holyoke, Massachusetts. As the former title suggests, the machine was essentially a modified electrical dynamo, employing a number of specially geared shafts and associated inductors to produce alternating currents of different audio frequencies. These signals passed via a polyphonic keyboard and associated bank of controls to a series of telephone receivers fitted with special acoustic horns.

The Dynamophone was a formidable construction, about 200 tons in weight and some 60 feet in length, assuming the proportions of a power-station generator. The quoted cost, some $200,000, provides another startling statistic. For all its excessive proportions and eccentricities the machine offered sound-production features that were entirely new and flexible to a degree not equaled by subsequent designs for some considerable time. Cahill saw his invention not merely as a substitute for a conventional keyboard instrument but as a powerful tool for exploring an enlarged world of pitched sounds. He believed it would become possible to produce the notes and chords of a musical composition with any timbre. This claim highlighted the ability of the performer to vary the musical quality of the selected sounds in terms of the relative strengths of each of the primary harmonics associated with a particular note. Such a facility necessitated the use of separate inductors for each overtone, adding greatly to the complexity of the system.

News of Cahill's work traveled far, attracting the attention of no less a composer than Ferruccio Busoni. In an extended essay entitled *Sketch of a New Esthetic of Music* (1907),[1] he championed the Dynamophone as a powerful tool for exploring new concepts of harmony.[2]

Sadly, however, Busoni did not choose to pioneer investigations himself. Cahill, and the New England Electric Music Company that funded the venture, intended to sell production models of the machine to large cities and towns throughout America for the transmission of "Telharmony" to hotels, restaurants, theaters, and private homes via the local telephone exchange. This visionary quest to provide a music broadcasting network for the nation was not to become a reality, however, for in addition to the excessive capital outlay required, it was discovered that the machine seriously interfered with other telephone calls. Faced with such impossible commercial odds the venture ran into financial difficulty, and eventually failed in 1914, just before the outbreak of the First World War in Europe.

Advances in the newly established field of electronics were, nevertheless, preparing the way for less costly and more compact approaches to the generation of synthetic sound. The direct current arc oscillator appeared in 1900, and by 1906, the same year as the first demonstration of the Dynamophone, Lee De Forest had patented the vacuum-tube triode amplifier valve. Progress was slow but steady, and by the end of the war, with the industry well established, several engineers were able to investigate the possibility of using the new technology for the construction of electronic musical instruments. The primary motivation behind most of these designs was a desire to create additions to the conventional orchestral range, with an underlying hope that composers could be persuaded to provide a suitable repertoire. The devices that emerged were thus intended primarily to satisfy traditional ideas of musical writing. Some indeed, such as the Neo-Bechstein Piano (1931), were little more than modified acoustical instruments, using special pick-ups to capture naturally produced vibratory characteristics for the processes of electronic amplification and modification. The best-known modern example of this class of instrument is the electric guitar.

The majority relied on an electronic method of sound generation, for example, the Thérémin (1924), the Sphärophon (1927), the Dynaphone (not to be confused with the Dynamophone) (1927–8), the Ondes Martenot (1928), and the Trautonium (1930). Most were keyboard-oriented, providing a single melodic output and an ancillary means of controlling volume, usually taking the form of a hand-operated lever or a foot-pedal. The Thérémin was a notable exception, having no keyboard at all. Instead, two capacitor-based detectors were employed, one a vertical rod, the other a horizontal loop. These controlled pitch and amplitude, respectively, by generating electrical fields that altered according to the proximity of the hands of the performer.

Electronic instruments of this type flourished briefly during the interwar period. Despite contributions from composers such as Hindemith, Honegger, Koechlin, Milhaud, and Messiaen, only a limited repertory of works was produced. More sustained interest was shown by writers of film music until the emergence of more modern synthesizer technology, but outside this particular sphere of activity these instruments failed to establish any lasting position of significance. Today, the Ondes Martenot is the only example of these original designs still encountered on the rare occasion in concert use, its position being sustained by works such as Messiaen's *Turangalîla* symphony and *Trois Petites Liturgies*.

The Givelet (1929), soon to be overshadowed by the Hammond Organ (1935), heralded a rather different and commercially more successful line of development, for these instruments were polyphonic rather than monophonic, designed in the first instance as competitively priced replacements for the pipe organ. The Givelet combined the principles of the Pianola or "player piano" with those of electronic sound generation, for it could also be controlled via a prepunched tape. The Hammond Organ, although a more conventional instrument from the performer's point of view, gained a reputation for its distinctive if not entirely authentic sound quality. This was largely due to the method of tone generation employed, involving the rotation of suitably contoured discs within a magnetic field in a manner reminiscent of the Dynamophone. The potential of the Givelet and the Hammond Organ as substitutes for the piano in the field of popular music was quickly recognized and exploited. Applications such as these, however, contributed very little to an appreciation of the artistic potential of this new medium of sound production, and it was perhaps inevitable that the first excursions into such an unknown sphere should be so closely modeled on traditional instrumental practice. There were, nevertheless, a few pioneers who were anxious to explore the possibilities of an expanded sound world in a less restricted manner.

One of the earliest attempts to employ nontraditional sound-generation techniques as part of a communicative art form arose from the activities of the members of the Futurist movement. This was initiated by the Italian poet Filippo Marinetti in February 1909 with the publication of his *Manifesto of Futurist Poetry*.[3] The musical objectives of the movement were outlined by Balilla Pratella in the *Manifesto of Futurist Musicians*, published in October 1910. Echoing the revolutionary spirit of the movement, this document called for "the rejection of traditional musical principles and methods of teaching and the substitution of free expression, to be inspired by nature in all its manifestations."[4]

Five months later to the day, Pratella suggested in the *Technical Manifesto of Fu-*

turist Music that composers should "master all expressive technical and dynamic elements of instrumentation and regard the orchestra as a sonorous universe in a state of constant mobility, integrated by an effective fusion of all its constituent parts."[5] Further, he considered that their work should reflect "all forces of nature tamed by man through his continued scientific discoveries," for example, "the musical soul of crowds, of great industrial plants, of trains, of transatlantic liners, of armored warships, of automobiles, of airplanes." Exactly two years later another Futurist, Luigi Russolo, published a related manifesto entitled *The Art of Noises* as an open statement to Pratella.[6] This document proposed the composition of works based entirely on the use of sound sources from the environment:

> Musical sound is too limited in qualitative variety of timbre. The most complicated of orchestras reduce themselves to four or five classes of instruments differing in timbre: instruments played with the bow, plucked instruments, brass-winds, wood-winds and percussion instruments. . . . We must break out of this narrow circle of pure musical sounds and conquer the infinite variety of noise sounds.[7]

This document is notable for its appreciation of the relevance of acoustic laws to the generation of musical structures from noise sources:

> We must fix the pitch and regulate the harmonics and rhythms of these extraordinarily varied sounds. To fix the pitch of noises does not mean to take away from them all the irregularity of tempo and intensity that characterizes their vibrations, but rather to give definite gradation of pitch to the stronger and more predominant of these vibrations. Indeed noise is differentiated from musical sound merely in that the vibrations that produce it are confused and irregular, both in tempo and intensity. Every noise has a note—sometimes even a chor—that predominates in the ensemble of its irregular vibrations. Because of this characteristic pitch it becomes possible to fix the pitch of a given noise, that is, to give it not a single pitch but a variety of pitches without losing its characteristic quality—its distinguishing timbre. Thus certain noises produced by rotary motion may offer a complete ascending or descending chromatic scale by merely increasing or decreasing the speed of motion.[8]

The practical manifestations of his proposal involved the construction of specially designed noise instruments, Intonarumori, in collaboration with the percussionist Ugo Piatti. The first public performance of the "Art of Noises" took place in June 1913 at the Teatro Storchi, Milan, barely three months after the publication of the manifesto, and with only some of the Intonarumori completed. A second altogether more successful performance using the full complement of instruments was given as part of a concert of Futuristic music, presented by Marinetti and Russolo at the Teatro dal Verne, Milan, in April 1914.

The historical interest in this venture lies not so much in the acoustical design features of the Intonarumori themselves, instruments that in any event have long since been destroyed, but more in the motivation that led to their construction. The Futurist movement did not succeed in its attempt to produce a major revolution in the path of new music, but its challenging of traditionally accepted relationships between the science of acoustics and the art of musical sound production was to prove singularly prophetic.

Busoni had already attacked traditional nineteenth-century musical practices in his *Sketch of a New Esthetic of Music*, advocating a reappraisal of the whole language of music "free from architectonic, acoustic and aesthetic dogmas."[9] This book caught the attention of a young French composer, Edgard Varèse, who, having rebelled against the traditional outlook of the Paris Conservatoire, was eager to explore new concepts of musical expression. Varèse, perhaps more than any other composer of his time, pioneered in his instrumental music the aesthetics that were necessary for the acceptance of electronic sound-processing techniques in musical composition. It is thus particularly tragic that it was not until the 1950s, toward the end of his life, that he gained access to the facilities he so fervently desired.

As early as 1916 he was quoted in the New York Telegraph as saying: "Our musical alphabet must be enriched. . . . We also need new instruments very badly. . . . In my own works I have always felt the need for new mediums of expression."[10] He was quick, however, to deny suggestions that his efforts were directed toward the Futurist movement.

> The Futurists (Marinetti and his noise artists) have made a serious mistake. . . . Instruments, after all, must only be a temporary means of expression. Musicians should take up this question in deep earnest with the help of machinery specialists. . . . What I am looking for are new technical means which can lend themselves to every expression of thought.[11]

Varèse had become acquainted with the electronic designer René Bertrand in May 1913, and this marked the start of a long and lasting friendship.[12] In 1922, during the composer's first stay in America, he declared in an interview for the *Christian Science Monitor*: "What we want is an instrument that will give us continuous sound at any pitch. The composer and electrician will have to labor together to get it. . . . Speed and synthesis are characteristics of our own epoch."[13]

During the 1920s, Varèse continued his search for new sound textures, but without the aid of any suitable technical facilities. His work with natural instrumental resources in his first published compositions was nevertheless singularly prophetic, for he was concerned to use procedures that were to become primary characteristics of electronic sound processing: analysis and resynthesis. He experimented, for example, with altered attack characteristics for brass instruments, where the initial transient would be suppressed by making the entry of a sound piano, and its central portion or body heavily accentuated by means of a rapid crescendo. Such an effect is remarkably similar to that achieved by playing recordings of normally articulated notes backward, the decay thus becoming the attack. He was also particularly concerned to use instruments as component building blocks for sound masses of varying quality, density, and volume, in contrast to their traditional roles as sources of linear counterpoint.

His philosophy of musical expression, to use his own term, was based on the concept of "organized sound," with no prior restrictions as to the choice or use of the component sound sources involved in the process of synthesis. Percussion instruments figured prominently in his works. *Ionisation* (1930–1), for example, is scored entirely for instruments of this family. With the aid of effects such as sirens, whips, a lion's roar, and sleigh-bells, he struggled to develop a compositional art that integrated the natural sounds of the environment with more traditional sources of musical expression. This was not the somewhat crude Futurist "Art of Noises" exploring the exotic, but an attempt to extract an artistic perspective from the universe of sound.

Varèse was not immune from imitators. The American composer George Antheil required the use of car horns, airplane propellers, saws, and anvils in his *Ballet mécanique,* first performed in Paris in 1926, and again in New York in 1927. The work of Joseph Schillinger is also of interest in this context. Schillinger, a Russian composer and theorist, advocated the development of new musical instruments based on electrical principles in a similar vein to Varèse as early as 1918. A decade later he traveled to America in response to an invitation from the American Society for Cultural Relations with Russia, remaining in the United States until his premature death fifteen years later. Soon after his arrival he embarked on a collaborative venture with his countryman Thérémin, designing a domestic version of the Thérémin for commercial manufacture by RCA. As an aid to promotion Schillinger composed his *Airphonic Suite for RCA Thérémin and Orchestra*, the work receiving its first performance at Cleveland, Ohio, in November 1929, with Thérémin as soloist. His interest in fostering the creative application of science for musical ends is illustrated by the following extract from an article entitled "Electricity, a Musical Liberator," which appeared in *Modern Music* in March 1931:

> The growth of musical art in any age is determined by the technological progress which parallels it. Neither the composer nor performer can transcend the limits of the instruments of his time. On the other hand technical developments stimulate the creation of certain forms of composition and performance. Although it is true that musicians may have ideas which hurdle these technical barriers, yet, being forced to use existing instruments, their intentions remain unrealized until scientific progress comes to the rescue. . . .
> If we admit that the creative imagination of the composer may form musical ideas which, under the specific conditions of a given epoch, cannot be translated into sounds, we acknowledge a great dependence of the artist upon the

technical position of his era, for music attains reality only through the process of sound.[14]

During the remaining years of his life he became increasingly preoccupied with aspects of music theory, producing a set of twelve books describing *The Schillinger System of Musical Composition* (1946),[15] followed two years later by a monumental treatise, *The Mathematical Basis of the Arts*.[16] Neither of these volumes, unfortunately, was published until after his death. Despite some rather curious aspects, including the use of statistical data as a basis for measuring the degree of stylistic consistency displayed by major classical composers, and the formulation of a set of compositional rules based on empirical analyses of musical structures, his theories contain some features of particular interest. In particular, his attempt to analyze sounds in music-acoustic terms, using such identifying features as melody, rhythm, timbre, harmony, dynamics, and density anticipated the type of methodology to be applied from many quarters in the search for a morphology to describe the elements of electronic music.

Varèse, unlike Schillinger, continued to press actively for practical facilities. Toward the end of 1927, he became restless to learn more about the possibilities of electronic instruments, and contacted Harvey Fletcher, the director of the acoustical research division of Bell Telephone Laboratories, with a view to acquiring a laboratory for research in this field. Fletcher took an interest in his proposals but could not offer the funds necessary for such a venture. In desperation, Varèse departed for Paris in the autumn of 1928 to ascertain from Bertrand what potentially useful technical developments had taken place in his absence. One product of his visit was the formulation of a project to develop what might have become the first sound synthesis studio, and an associated school of composition. Although details were never officially published, his biographer, Fernand Ouellette, managed to obtain a copy of this document from Ernst Schoen, Varèse's first pupil. The proposal ran as follows:

> Only students already in possession of a technical training will be accepted in the composition class. In this department, studies will concentrate upon all forms required by the new concepts existing today, as well as the new techniques and new acoustical factors which impose themselves as the logical means of realizing those concepts.
>
> Also under Varèse's direction, with the assistance of a physicist, there will be a working laboratory in which sound will be studied scientifically, and in which the laws permitting the development of innumerable new means of expression will be established without any reference to empirical rules. All new discoveries and all inventions of instruments and their uses will be demonstrated and studied. The laboratory will possess as complete a collection of phonographic records as possible, including examples of the music of all races, all cultures, all periods, and all tendencies.[17]

The scheme was not to materialize, for Varèse was unable to find an adequate source of finance. On 1 December 1932, while still in Paris, he wrote again to Fletcher requesting access to the facilities of the Bell Telephone Laboratories in return for his services to the company: "I am looking to find a situation where my collaboration would have value and pecuniary return."[18] Varèse was so eager for laboratory facilities that he was even prepared to sacrifice his career as a composer, at least for a time. He also applied to the John Simon Guggenheim Memorial Foundation for a grant towards his work. In response to a request for more details, he wrote again to the Foundation on 6 February 1933 offering the following proposal:

> The acoustical work which I have undertaken and which I hope to continue in collaboration with René Bertrand consists of experiments which I have suggested on his invention, the Dynaphone. The Dynaphone (invented 1927–8) is a musical instrument of electrical oscillations somewhat similar to the Thérémin, Givelet and Martenot electrical instruments. But its principle and operation are entirely different, the resemblance being only superficial. The technical results I look for are as follows:
>
>   1. To obtain absolutely pure fundamentals.
>   2. By means of loading the fundamentals with certain series of harmonics to obtain timbres which will produce new sounds.
>   3. To speculate on the new sounds that the combination of two or more interfering Dynaphones would give if combined in a single instrument.
>   4. To increase the range of the instrument so as to obtain high frequencies which no other instrument can give, together with adequate intensity.
>
> The practical result of our work will be a new instrument which will be adequate to the needs of the creative musician and musicologist. I have conceived a system by which the instrument may be used not only for the tempered and natural scales, but one which also allows for the accurate production of any number of frequencies and consequently is able to produce any interval or any subdivision required by the ancient or exotic modes.[19]

This application, unlike his previous proposal, laid down for the first time the acoustical principles that would serve as the basis for a program of research, investigating the musical applications of electronic sound synthesis. The Dynaphone, despite his assertions, did not differ significantly from its relatives. Its ability to generate timbres in an additive manner using harmonic stops, for example, was matched by a similar facility within the Ondes Martenot. Nevertheless, since Varèse was well acquainted with its designer, he was aware of the potential of developing its circuits to produce not merely an enhanced electronic instrument, but a versatile sound synthesis system serving a wide variety of compositional demands.

The Guggenheim Foundation, unfortunately, did not understand the purpose of Varèse's proposal, and despite repeated requests Varèse failed to win financial support from this quarter. Similarly, despite a certain degree of interest, and a willingness to support his Guggenheim applications, Harvey Fletcher was unable to grant him facilities at Bell Telephone Laboratories. It is ironic to note that the latter institution, twenty years later, was to pioneer research into a revolutionary new area of sound generation, computer synthesis.[20]

Despite these setbacks, some progress was being made in other quarters. The 1900s had seen the birth of the commercial 78 r.p.m. gramophone record and the 1920s the development of electrical recording systems as a sequel to broadcasting, making generally available a technique not only for storing sound information, but also for effecting certain alterations to its reproduction. Darius Milhaud realized that changing the speed of a recording varies not only the pitch but also the intrinsic acoustical characteristics of the material, and during the period 1922 to 1927 carried out several experiments investigating vocal transformations. Percy Grainger performed similar experiments during the 1930s, paying particular attention to the use of piano sounds as source material.

During 1929–30, Paul Hindemith and Ernst Toch carried out rather more detailed operations on phonograph recordings at the Rundfunk-Versuchsstelle Hochschule für Musik in Berlin. Hindemith was primarily interested in testing his theories of acoustics and the analysis of harmonic structures, later outlined in his treatise *The Craft of Musical Composition* (1937).[21] A by-product of this period of scientific investigation was a collaborative venture with the scientist Friedrich Trautwein, leading to the invention of the Trautonium, and the composition of his *Concerto for Solo Trautonium and Orchestra* (1931).

Hindemith, however, did not choose to explore the creative possibilities of synthetic sound production for himself beyond the specific limits of instrumental imitation. The time was still not ripe for any general acceptance of processes of musical composition that extended beyond the traditional orchestra. Varèse, nonetheless, was not to remain quite so isolated in his specific endeavors, for the climate of musical opinion was slowly beginning to change. A prophetic address was given extemporaneously by the conductor Leopold Stokowski to a meeting of the Acoustical Society of America on 2 May 1932, entitled "New Horizons in Music."[22] Stokowski, as a keen conductor of contemporary music, devoted much effort to bringing young composers into contact with as large a public as possible, and he appreciated the importance of establishing, even on a general level, a sustained dialogue between scientists and artists in an increasingly technological society. His address included not only a discussion of the artistic implications of the uses of technology as an aid to communication through the media of the radio and the phonograph but also some interesting predictions regarding the future use of electronic synthesis devices as compositional tools.

Another vista that is opening out is for the composer, for the creator in music. . . . Our musical notation is utterly inadequate. It cannot by any means express all the possibilities of sound, not half of them, not a quarter of them, not a tenth of them. We have possibilities in sound which no man knows how to write on paper. If we take an orchestral score and reproduce it, just mechanically perfect, it will sound mechanical. It won't have the human element in it. Also there would be so much that the composer was trying to express, that he conceived but couldn't write down because of the limitations of notation. . . . One can see coming ahead a time when the musician who is a creator can create directly into TONE, not on paper. This is quite within the realm of possibility. That will come. Any frequency, any duration, any intensity he wants, any combinations of counterpoint, of harmony, of rhythm— anything can be done by that means and will be done.[23]

Stokowski's predictions were based at least in part on a knowledge of some interesting technical developments that were taking place at the time. Hindemith's experiments with phonograph records had caught the attention of several members of the Bauhaus movement, including László Moholy-Nagy, Oskar Fischinger, and Paul Arma. These artists became absorbed with the physical shapes of recorded sounds and carried out their own investigations during the period 1930–2. Initially they attempted to alter the acoustical content by running the recordings backward against the stylus to scratch new patterns. The results, however, were largely unsatisfactory, and their attention soon turned toward the more interesting possibilities of manipulating optical soundtracks, a recording method developed for use with moving film.

Optical recording involves the transfer of sound information onto film in the form of patterns of varying densities, which may subsequently be detected and reproduced acoustically via a photocell detector. Physical alterations to the shaded contours will thus affect the sound reproduction. The German inventor Rudolf Pfenninger pioneered research in this field, discovering in 1932 that analysis of the shapes on an optical soundtrack elicited sufficient information for the synthesis of a wide range of musical timbres in terms of handdrawn patterns.

This work was important, for despite many practical limitations it resulted in the first really flexible system of communication between the composer and his synthesis tools. Investigations continued in Ottawa, where Norman McLaren completed a series of films employing "drawn" soundtracks,[24] and in Leningrad, where Yevgeny Sholpo developed four versions of his Variophone, a machine for graphically encoding sound information. The latter acted as models for the ANS (photoelectric optic sound synthesizer) developed at the Moscow Experimental Studio, later expanded into the Scriabin Museum Laboratory in 1961.

The relentless march of technology, nevertheless, was already signaling the demise of optical recording techniques in favor of another medium, magnetic tape. Magnetic recording systems had been in existence since 1898, when the Danish scientist Valdemar Poulsen invented his Telegraphone, a machine employing steel wire that could be permanently magnetized by an electromagnet. The quality of reproduction, however, was very poor and the system as a whole decidedly cumbersome. Poulsen made some improvements to his machine during the early 1900s and launched a series of companies to market the device, but these soon ran into financial difficulties and the venture collapsed.

The development of magnetic recording then remained almost dormant until a German, Dr. Kurt Stille, began filing patents during the early 1920s. His work led to the development of a synchronized sound system for films using magnetized steel tape. Stille sold the rights of his machine to Ludwig Blattner, who marketed the first commercial version, the Blattnerphone, in 1929. A model was bought by the British Broadcasting Corporation in 1931 and installed at the Savoy Hill studio. During the early 1930s the firm of Marconi bought the manufacturing rights and began marketing a less cumbersome machine, the Marconi-Stille recorder. Steel tape, however, was still employed as the recording medium and this created many practical difficulties. Erasure of previously recorded signals was now possible, but the tape was awkward to splice, requiring welded joints. It was also extremely heavy and liable to sheer dangerously when spooled at high speed.

A major breakthrough occurred in Germany in 1935 when the firm of AEG produced the Magnetophon, a machine that utilized a plastic tape coated with fine ferrous particles. This invention was a notable improvement on the steel tape recorder and heralded the start of a series of technological developments, which led by the end of the Second World War to a compact and versatile recording system, soon to rival the direct disc-cutting methods of the previous era. The primary advantages of the new medium were the facility to reuse the recording tape, the ease of editing, and the ability to record two or more discrete tracks of recorded information simultaneously on the same piece of tape. Magnetic recording soon displaced its optical rival, mainly as a result of the superior quality of reproduction. This process of change was inevitably self-perpetuating, for engineers were diverted from the task of improving the characteristics of optical sound transfer, and as a result one important recording technique, of considerable interest to electronic sound synthesis, lost the support of commercial development.

Magnetic tape systems supply no direct means of contact between the composer and the component characteristics of recorded sounds, for the wave patterns are not visible to the eye, nor may they be usefully modified by any direct physical action. Little importance was attached to such a disadvantage for some considerable time, for very few of the studios that emerged during the 1950s and early 1960s incorporated any visual means for specifying or altering material. For the most part, designers concentrated on the keyboard, the slider, and the rotary knob as the primary control facilities for their systems, pending the development of digital technology and the computer graphics terminal, the precursor of the modern video interface used by all personal computers.

Once again it was Varèse who prophesied the advent of such an important synthesis facility well before it true potential was generally recognized. During the late 1930s he entered a period of deep personal crisis regarding his whole language of composition. His own experiments with phonograph records led to increasing frustration with the limitations of this experimental medium, and he soon abandoned this line of investigation, spending the next three years attempting a rationalization of his ideas for a new sound world. As a result of this period of reflection he delivered one of his most important lectures to the University of Southern California during 1939. This included the following pertinent observations:

> When you listen to music do you ever stop to realize that you are being subjected to a physical phenomenon? Not until the air between the listener's ear and the instrument has been disturbed does music occur. . . . In order to anticipate the result, a composer must understand the mechanics of the instruments and must know just as much as possible about acoustics. . . . We composers are forced to use, in the realization of our works, instruments that have not changed for two centuries. . . . Personally, for my conceptions, I need an entirely new medium of expression: a sound-producing machine (not a sound re-producing one). . . . Whatever I write, whatever my message, it will reach the listener unadulterated by "interpretation." It will work something like this: after a composer has set down his score on paper by means of a new graphic, similar in principle to a seismographic or oscillographic notation, he will then, with the collaboration of a sound engineer, transfer the score directly to this electric machine. After that anyone will be able to press a button to release the music exactly as the composer wrote it. . . . And here are the advantages I anticipate from such a machine. Liberation from the arbitrary, paralyzing tempered system; the possibility of obtaining any number of cycles or if still desired subdivisions of the octave, consequently the formation of any desired scale; unsuspected range in low and high registers, new harmonic splendors obtainable from the use of sub-harmonic combinations now impossible, new dynamics far beyond the present human power orchestra; a sense of sound projection in space by means of the emission of sound in any part or in as many parts of the hall as may be required by the score.[25]

Many of the more ambitious predictions could only be matters of speculation at that time, from both a technical and a musical viewpoint. Composers faced major problems of specification, particularly in equating the subjective world of the creative musician to the highly objective characteristics of the new technology, a situation that is still not wholly resolved today. By the end of the 1930s, nevertheless, scientific advances had produced the basic theories for the design of sound synthesis systems, and advocates of such technologies were able to predict with some confidence the likely course of future developments.

The writings of both Stokowski and Varèse on the potential uses of electronics in musical composition at that time were endorsed by John Cage, a composer who in most other respects subscribed to a very different school of aesthetics. Speaking to a meeting of a Seattle Arts Society in 1937, he postulated:

> I believe that the use of noise . . . to make noise . . . will continue and increase until we reach a music produced through the aid of electrical instruments . . . which will make available for musical purposes any and all sounds that can be heard. Photoelectric film and mechanical mediums for the synthetic production of music . . . will be explored. Whereas, in the past, the point of disagreement has been between dissonance and consonance, it will be, in the immediate future between noise and so-called musical sounds.
>
> Wherever we are, what we hear is mostly noise. . . . We want to capture and control these sounds, to use them not as studio effects but as musical instruments. Every film studio has a library of "sound effects" recorded on film. With a film phonograph it is now possible to control the amplitude and frequency of any of these sounds and to give it rhythms within or beyond the reach of the imagination. . . . Many inventors of electrical musical instruments have attempted to imitate eighteenth and nineteenth century instruments just as early automobile designers copied the carriage. . . . .When Thérémin provided an instrument with genuinely new possibilities Théréministes did their utmost to make the instrument sound like some old instrument giving it sickeningly sweet vibrato, and performing upon it, with difficulty, masterpieces of the past. . . . The special function of electrical instruments will be to provide complete control of the overtone structures of tones (as opposed to noises) and to make these tones available in any frequency, amplitude and duration. . . .The composer (organizer of sound) will be faced not only with the entire field of sound but also with the entire field of time. The "frame" or fraction of a second, following established film technique, will probably be the basic unit in the measurement of time. No rhythm will be beyond the composer's earth.[26]

In the event, these commentaries proved to be more than mere conjecture. Collectively they established pioneering artistic principles well in advance of any practical means for realizing them. The subsequent birth of the electronic music studio was thus to take place in a climate where many of the problems encountered in relating such technology to the language of music had already been identified, if not actually solved.

On 9 December 1939, Cage performed his *Imaginary Landscape No. 1* in Seattle, employing a muted piano, cymbal, and two variable-speed turntables playing RCA Victor test recordings of fixed and variable frequencies. In 1942, he produced *Imaginary Landscape No. 2* for percussion quintet and amplified coil of wire, and

Imaginary Landscape No. 3 for percussion sextet, tin cans, muted gong, audio frequency oscillators, variable-speed turntables for the playing of frequency test recordings, buzzer, amplified coil of wire, and marimba, amplified by a contact microphone. Interest in the medium had thus already extended to the use of live electronic techniques, and the stage was set for the first properly equipped studios, and their associated schools of composition.

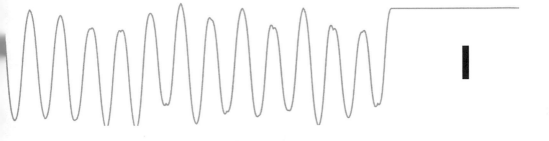

Developments from 1945 to 1960

2

Paris and *Musique Concrète*

The revival of the arts after the Second World War took place in an environment altogether more favorable for the development of electronic music. The rapid advances in technology as a result of the war, an upsurge of interest from many quarters in new sound techniques, and a generally expansionist economic climate provided sufficient incentives for institutions to provide support.

In Europe two broadcasting networks, Radiodiffusion Télévision Française (RTF) in Paris, and Norwestdeutscher Rundfunk (NWDR)[1] in Cologne, took up the initiative. Both of these established studios of considerable importance, in the first instance pursuing radically different objectives. Movements toward new paths in musical composition during the second half of the century tended, at least initially, to polarize around select groups of activists with a strongly defended identity, and these studios were no exception. The Paris group, which will be considered first, became dedicated to the advancement of *musique concrète*, while the Cologne group championed the cause of *elektronische Musik*.

Intense disagreements developed between the studios and these were aired in public on a number of occasions, notably at the summer European festivals of contemporary music that were then approaching their zenith in terms of their international significance. The reasons for this overt hostility were not merely a matter of patriotism, although understandably this factor played a part. They lay more fundamentally in marked differences of outlook as regards acceptable practices of electronic composition.

To talk of a group when considering the early years of the Paris studio is a little misleading, for the initiative and leadership for the project came from a single pioneer, Pierre Schaeffer. Schaeffer, an electronic engineer, served his apprenticeship with the RTF during the 1930s after initial training at the Paris Polytechnic. His technical skills led to rapid promotion, and by 1942, at the age of only thirty-two, he was able to persuade the corporation, then under the control of the German occupying forces, to initiate research into the science of musical acoustics with himself as director. From very modest beginnings as a Studio d'Essai this venture gradually gathered momentum, the more familiar name Club d'Essai being substituted in 1946. In the course of his research Schaeffer's attention was drawn toward the use of recording techniques as a means of isolating naturally produced sound events, and in 1948 he started to consider how such material might be used as a basis for composing.

Schaeffer's preliminary investigations, inspired to some degree by an interest in the Futurists, were concerned with an exploration of the properties of percussion sounds. His recording equipment was very basic, consisting of a simple direct disc-cutting lathe, with all its attendant limitations. Taping facilities were introduced in due course, but not before a considerable quantity of work had been carried out using the former facility. During the first four months of 1948, he studied the effect of striking a number of percussion instruments in different ways. This led him to observe that any single musical event is characterized not only by the timbre of the main body of the sound, but also by the nature of its attack and decay. On 21 April he carried out experiments recording bell tones on to disc, where by operating a volume control inserted between the microphone and the cutter he was able to eliminate the natural attack of each note. Two days later he speculated whether an instrument might be constructed to produce the sounds of an orchestral instrument by means of a bank of previously recorded events. This idea anticipated the Mellotron, an early precursor of the digital sampler introduced in 1963. This device plays prerecorded loops of tape, triggered individually via a conventional music keyboard.

Having made a superficial study of the attack, body, and decay of isolated sound events, and also the effects of playing recordings backward, Schaeffer turned his attention toward the task of resynthesis. His first work, *Étude aux chemins de fer*, was constructed from recordings made at the depot for the Gare des Batignolles, Paris. These included the sounds of six steam locomotives whistling, trains accelerating, and wagons passing over joints in the rails. The piece was constructed for the most part from successive rather than overlaid extracts of material, and this drew particular attention to the repetitive characteristics of the sounds. Schaeffer quickly realized that sources retaining a significant proportion of their identifying characteristics after processing created major problems of association. As a result, the piece was more an essay on the activities of a seemingly schizophrenic goods yard than the intended creative study in sound.

In an attempt to overcome this difficulty he reverted to more conventional sources of musical sounds, investigating the effects of playing recordings at different speeds. This led to the discovery that such alterations affected not only the pitch and overall duration of individual events, but also their amplitude envelope (attack-body-decay). Such interdependence made it impossible to vary one of these characteristics without affecting the others. A further study of the relationships between these intrinsic features led to a series of short *Études*, realized during the early summer of 1948.

The *Étude pour piano et orchestre* endeavoured to combine the sounds of an amateur orchestra tuning up with a spontaneous piano improvisation played by Jean-Jacques Grunenwald. The result was largely unsatisfactory in musical terms, for there was no coherent dialogue between the areas of sound material, creating the impression that two apparently unconnected pieces had been crudely mixed together. This early discovery of the problems of integrating dissimilar sources was an important one, for it identified a major stumbling block for composers of electronic music. Two of the studies, *Étude au piano I* and *Étude au piano II*, were based on sounds derived from the piano alone. Schaeffer had considered the possibility of a *piano à bruits* from a very early stage in his investigations, unaware at the time of similar experiments by John Cage in America. His provisional conclusions, however, led him to reject live performance on a modified piano as little more than a simple extension of the normal characteristics of the instrument, and these studies were created instead by manipulating recordings of traditionally produced sonorities. Pierre Boulez created the source textures, the intention being to reflect different musical styles, for example, classical, romantic, impressionistic, or atonal. Schaeffer then endeavored to achieve a degree of continuity by careful juxtaposition of the selected material, but once again the fragmentary nature of the latter proved problematical.

The first public presentation of these pieces took the form of a broadcast entitled *Concert à bruits*, transmitted by the RTF on 5 October 1948. The reactions of the unsuspecting listeners were fiercely divided, developing into a spirited controversy both in musical circles and the general press. Further developments, however, had to wait for several months, for Schaeffer was posted abroad until the spring of 1949 as an official representative at a number of symposia on recording and broadcasting. On his return, he approached the RTF with a view to gaining the funds necessary for supporting a team of assistants. In response, they appointed the composer Pierre Henry as co-researcher, and as studio technician seconded the sound engineer Jacques Poullin, who had already expressed an interest in Schaeffer's work. During the summer of 1949, Schaeffer began to reappraise the role of natural instruments as sound sources, carrying out experiments that retraced much of the ground covered by Varèse some twenty years previously. His next piece, *Suite pour quatorze instruments*, is of particular significance, for it provided the starting point for his work on a syntax for *musique concrète*.

His main preoccupation at this time was the possible parallels that might be drawn between the processes of conventional and *concret* composition. This led to the identification of two distinct methods of approach. On the one hand, composers may choose to start the creative process by developing a clear concept of the sound structures they wish to achieve. Such a picture then requires rationalization and modification in terms of the available practical facilities, leading in the case of *concret* work to a precise set of studio routines, which may then be executed. On the other hand, composers may wish to start with a selection of potential sound sources, offering a range of characteristics with which they may experiment, building up from the results of such investigations the elements for a complete composition.

These distinctions were to prove important not only for Schaeffer, but for the development of electronic music in general, for they highlight important procedural difficulties encountered in relating the subjective world of musical creativity to the objective, scientific world of the sound studio. It will be seen in due course how the former approach requires provision of a versatile specification language, capable of translating a variety of musical ideas into equivalent studio procedures. The latter approach, by contrast, involves a less complex dialogue between the composer and the system, built around the functional characteristics offered by the devices themselves, or in the case of *concret* material the intrinsic characteristics of the chosen sources. Classical ideas of an "orchestra" and a "score" may thus be pursued, electronic devices, where appropriate, taking the place of traditional instruments.

In practice most composers have drawn upon aspects of both approaches and Schaeffer was quick to recognize the existence of a dichotomy. His earlier pieces had for the most part proceeded from a general idea of the desired result to an attempt at its realization by the selection of suitable material and processes. In the *Suite* he experimented with almost the reverse approach, studying the intrinsic characteristics of instrumental music and then applying suitable *concret* procedures to produce a new musical work. Each of the five movements highlighted one particular aspect of this compositional method. The Courante, for example, was a monody assembled from the juxtaposition of short extracts drawn from the entire library of source material. The Gavotte, in contrast, used interpretations of one short musical phrase on different instruments, juxtaposed to create a set of variations. Extensive use was made of pitch transposition, effected by playing the source recordings at different speeds.

Schaeffer was not happy with the musicality of the results, and not without cause. The latter movement suffered particularly badly from its reliance on a single phrase, which despite many interpretations and transpositions retained many of its original characteristics. As a result the primary impression gained was one of monotonous repetition with little sense of shape or direction. These difficulties provoked him to carry out closer analyses of the nature of sounds, leading to a preliminary definition of an *objet sonore*; a basic sound event, which is isolated from its original context and examined in terms of its innate characteristics outside its normal time continuum. He asserted that the abstraction of such events from natural sound sources to provide components for the regeneration of musical material required processes compatible with the principles of post-Webern serialism (this was later to be challenged fiercely by the German school of *elektronische Musik*).

Schaeffer tried to establish why his transformation procedures failed to remove or materially alter many of the distinctive characteristics of his sound sources. He concluded that techniques such as playing recordings at different speeds or in reverse, and the use of elementary montage, did not produce anything essentially new. The use of musical instruments, musical habits, and musical structures had conditioned the way in which he had carried out his processes of analysis and resynthesis, and it thus seemed appropriate to return to his original starting point, the world of noises, as a more basic source of sound information. Such a move, however, did not remove the problems of association, as he had already discovered in preparing *Étude aux chemins de fer*, and it proved necessary not only to examine the nature of sounds in more detail but also to perfect an expanded range of transformation techniques.

Taking sound events of varying lengths and degrees of complexity as sources, Schaeffer began to study them not only on a "macro" level as before, identifying the primary characteristics of the structures as a whole, but also on a "micro" level. The latter approach involved examining the inner detail of the characteristics themselves, for example the way in which an attack developed, or the changes in timbre occurring during the body of a note. Such exercises, however, did not offer any major solutions to the problems already posed. At one extreme, the "micro" elements were still of sufficient duration for the retention of distinctive characteristics that would survive processes of juxtaposition and transposition. At the other extreme, the division of sound events into too short a series of extracts led all too quickly to the isolation of meaningless "blips."

Despite these setbacks, Schaeffer decided that his investigations had reached a stage where he was ready to embark on a major piece of *musique concrète*, and in collaboration with Henry commenced work on *Symphonie pour un homme seul*. During the early stages of formulating his ideas, Schaeffer encountered considerable difficulty in selecting suitable sources of material. Two lines of development were uppermost in his mind at this time: (1) the extension of the possibilities of instrumental sources by means of new technical aids, and (2) the development of his principles of *objets sonores*, and their rules of composition.

His quest for an area of sound material that would prove sufficiently rich to sustain a major composition led him to select a source which in many respects offered connections with instrumental material and noises; the sounds of a man. His initial idea was to select sound material solely from noises that could be produced naturally by the man, for example breathing, walking, and whistling. These sources, however, proved too limiting and this selection was soon extended to include sounds drawn from the man's communication with the world via his actions, for example, the production of percussive sounds, or the playing of orchestral instruments. The inclusion of a prepared piano in the latter category was inconsistent with his earlier views on such devices, and this element of ambivalence suggests that Schaeffer had still some way to go before achieving a thorough consolidation of his ideas. In this instance, the influence of Henry clearly served to widen his artistic outlook, resulting in a less dogmatic approach to the use of technology as a compositional tool. The final catalogue of sounds selected as sources was as follows:

Human sounds	Nonhuman sounds
Various aspects of breathing	Footsteps, etc.
Vocal fragments	Knocking on doors
Shouting	Percussion
Humming	Prepared piano
Whistled tunes	Orchestral instruments

The work is divided into eleven movements, some of which are modeled loosely on classical structures, for example, Partita, Valse, and Scherzo. The rhythmic pattern of the spoken word or phrase acts as the central theme, highlighted by the use of repeated loops and the juxtaposition of extracts with complementary fragments of instrumental and percussive patterns. The mood is light and humorous, contrasting sharply with the rigid structures of the early pieces of *elektronische Musik*.

During the winter of 1949–50, Schaeffer and Henry turned their attention towards staging the first public concert of *musique concrète*, finally presented in the hall of the École Normale de Musique, Paris, on 18 March, the *Symphonie* providing the central feature. Schaeffer was at last able to investigate how the characteristics of a concert auditorium might best be exploited, and accordingly designed and built a complete live performance system incorporating several sets of turntables, loudspeakers, and mixing units. The performance did not go as smoothly as expected, for the routines involved in mixing and projecting the sounds around the hall were under-rehearsed, and the complexities of creating live montages from unwieldy turntables proved at times overwhelming.

The concert, nevertheless, was well received by many of those who attended, and was followed by further public recitals on a more modest scale in the Club d'Essai, where the equipment of Schaeffer's studio could be utilized more conveniently. The critic Roger Richard, writing in the magazine *Combat*, 19 July 1950, noted that:

A public not especially prepared or warned to be on their guard readily accepts the impact of this extraordinary music. . . . *Musique concrète* is ready to leave the laboratory. It is time musicians exploited it. When musicians and musicologists such as Roland Manuel, Olivier Messiaen and Serge Moreaux express interest in it we can trust in this departure.[2]

After a short period of absence, Schaeffer returned to his studio in the autumn of 1950 to find Henry working on two of his own compositions, *Concerto des ambiguïtés* and a *Suite*. Henry had encountered considerable difficulty in devising an acceptable method of notation for his construction score. Accordingly, Schaeffer became preoccupied with the task of creating a practical syntax for *musique concrète*, using these two works as experimental models. The characteristic source phrases in the *Concerto* had been notated traditionally whilst the material for the *Suite* consisted of a series of graphic drawings. The structure of the *Concerto*, however, rapidly rendered the use of conventional scoring unsatisfactory, for the principal sound source was a prepared piano, producing acoustic results that differed significantly from the note/events suggested by the original score.

After much thought he concluded that it was necessary to assemble a *solfège* for the *objets sonores* that would classify sounds in terms of hierarchies of tessitura, timbre, rhythm, and density. A provisional system of scoring was adopted, closely modeled on the classical Western music system. Using conventional five-line staves for each sound element, a page of the score was divided into four areas: (1) living elements such as voices, (2) noises, (3) prepared instruments, and (4) conventional instruments. The time scale was linear, drawn along the bottom of the score in seconds, with a vertical dashed line every five seconds. For natural instruments and vocal sources normal clef and notational symbols were employed, excepting that the duration values of the individual pitches had to be modified to conform to the time axis. For *concret* sounds, elements of standard notation were combined with extra graphical symbols to give an approximate indication of the events' pitch characteristics with respect to time. Schaeffer appreciated that the method suffered from several disadvantages, for example, the use of the vertical axis to represent pitch precluded any clear indication of timbre. This method of representation was nevertheless a distinct improvement.

The year 1951 was to prove extremely important from a technical point of view, for the RTF agreed to provide Schaeffer with a new studio. This development led to the introduction of the tape recorder as the principal recording medium in place of the ageing disc cutters. The effect was considerable, for the whole philosophy of *musique concrète* was based on the simple manipulation of microphone recordings, the use of electronic sound sources and electronic processing devices being expressly forbidden. The initial reaction was singularly unenthusiastic, for the long and close association with the old equipment had fostered a methodology such that its limited facilities had become a major part of the musical process. Familiarization with the enhanced capabilities of tape, however, gradually dispelled such prejudices, although it was some time before the disc cutters were totally abandoned.

In addition to a set of conventional tape recorders, including, however, one capable of registering five independent tracks of sound, three special versions were also installed. One of these, known as a Morphophone, was fitted with a row of twelve playback heads instead of the usual one. Each head in turn thus reproduced the sounds captured via the recording head, producing delayed echoes that could be mixed to create a pulsed type of reverberation.[3] The two other machines, known as Phonogènes, were designed to play prerecorded tape loops via a single replay head at different speeds. One provided a continuously variable range of tape speeds while the other, controlled by a twelve-note keyboard with a two-position octave switch, provided twenty-four tempered pitch transpositions.

Poullin had been particularly concerned with the problems of sound distribution in an auditorium ever since the experience of the first public concert of *musique concrète*.[4] The ability to record five sound channels on a single reel of tape provided the basis for a well-ordered system of multichannel distribution, and this inspired him to develop a sound projection aid known as a *potentiomètre d'espace*.[5] It is important to appreciate that very little was known about the practical applications of multichannel recording in the early 1950s. The monophonic long-playing record, with its extended fidelity, was only just beginning to pose a serious challenge to the old 78s, and the stereophonic groove had yet to leave the research laboratory. Poullin's enhancement of a multichannel playback system was thus quite remarkable for its time, offering composers the opportunity to explore spatial projection as an added dimension for *musique concrète*. Four loudspeakers were employed to reproduce discretely encoded sound information, recorded on four of the five available tracks. Two loudspeakers were positioned at the front of the auditorium on either side of the stage, a third in the center of the ceiling, and the fourth half way along the back wall.

The effects of off-axis listening, arising from the impossibility of seating an entire audience at a point equidistant from all the loudspeakers, were minimized by employing specially designed units that concentrated their energy in a 60° cone, thus increasing their power of direct sound projection. This arrangement had one major advantage over the more usual four-channel convention of a loudspeaker in each corner, for the use of a ceiling loudspeaker made it possible to create illusions of vertical as well as horizontal movements, adding an extra spatial dimension to the diffusion of sound. The fifth tape track supplied an additional channel of information, to be distributed between the four loudspeakers by a concert performer operating the *potentiomètre d'espace* itself. The latter consisted of a small hand-held transmitting coil, and four wire receiving loops arranged around the performer in a tetrahedron, representing in miniature the location of the loudspeakers in the auditorium. Moving the coil about within this receiving area induced signals of varying strengths in the loops, this information being applied to electronic amplitude controls, regulating the distribution of the fifth track between the four channels.

The new studio led to a considerable expansion of activities. Schaeffer and a growing number of associates adopted the title "Groupe de Musique Concrète, Club d'Essai." This organization was subsequently renamed "Groupe de Recherches Musicales" (GRM) in 1958, and formally adopted by the RTF as part of "Service de la Recherche de l'ORTF" in 1960. During 1951 Schaeffer and Henry worked intensively on the first *opéra concret*, *Orphée 51*. Many practical problems arose in the construction of a score, and Schaeffer found his visions of a grand opera greatly tempered. After a less than satisfactory premiere in Paris the work was revised and considerably expanded as *Orphée 53* for a performance at Donaueschingen in October 1953.[6]

The difficulties encountered in sketching *Orphée* forced Schaeffer to develop still further his ideas regarding a *solfège* for *musique concrète*. This led him to formulate the idea of an *orchestre concret*, based on the observation that certain sounds would continue to display specific characteristics whatever the degree of transformation effected, within the perceptual limitations of the human ear. The persistence of these characteristics resulted in these elements being treated as "pseudo" instruments, notated in the realization score in a manner similar to that accorded to conventional instruments.

Schaeffer also felt it necessary to prepare two entirely different types of score. These were: (1) *la partition opératoire*, concerned with registering the technical procedures invoked within the studio, and (2) *la partition d'effet*, concerned with indicating the development of musical ideas in terms of parallel staves, each associated with an element of the *orchestre concret*. To an outside observer an idea of the structure of the work could only be given by the second representation, this taking the form of the provisional score discussed earlier. The notational system, however, was still far from adequate, and the problems of sound classification greatly retarded his progress throughout 1951. These frustrations precipitated a deep personal crisis, exacerbated by the discovery that his colleagues were more interested in developing musical ideas within the constraints of the existing studio than with the task of pioneering new techniques and developing an associated morphology. This conservatism disturbed him greatly, for he could foresee not merely disagreements but more serious conflicts arising between musicians and scientists over the future of the medium.

His morale was boosted considerably by the appointment of the scientist André Moles as a research member of the team during the summer. Moles had become interested in the study of perception and had written a thesis on the physical structure of recorded sounds. His results closely concurred with the observations of Schaeffer,[7] and a further study of the relationships between composers and their sound worlds led to analyses of psychoacoustic phenomena that were to prove invaluable in the quest for a *solfège*. He was also acutely aware of the problems of communication encountered in using an electronic medium for composing. Accordingly he also advocated the design and development of machines that could record and display acoustical features in a graphic form.

It was during 1951 that the previously mentioned disagreements between the proponents of *musique concrète* and *elektronische Musik* began in earnest. Schaeffer and Henry's *Symphonie pour un homme seul*, broadcast on radios Cologne (NWDR), Hamburg, Baden-Baden, and Munich, was received with considerable hostility by those who preferred the German approach. The Summer School at Darmstadt, the Internationale Ferienkurse für neue Musik, took up the controversy by organizing a symposium on the subject of sound technology and music. The French and the Germans disagreed violently and the Swiss criticized both for describing their work as "music."

Schaeffer returned to his studio to spend several months in a further period of consolidation, determined to defend and expand the aesthetic principles in which he believed. His diary at this time reflects the conflicts that arose at Darmstadt. In particular, he criticized the concepts of *elektronische Musik* for providing no obvious key to thes problems of communication associated with contemporary music. He also denied the suggestion that *musique concrète* had no connection with the musical languages of Schoenberg and Stravinsky, saying that it had a middle role to play, between the polarities represented by the two composers. In support of this view Schaeffer equated techniques of montage and tape looping with the polytonal and polyrhythmic structures of Stravinsky. He also suggested that the *objet sonore* provided a basis for an extension of Schoenberg's *Klangfarbenmelodie*, reaching beyond the concept of a melody of timbres derived from a series of pitches to include more comprehensive structures derived from other acoustical features.

In 1952, Schaeffer finally published a definitive syntax for *musique concrète* in the form of a treatise entitled "Esquisse d'un solfège concret." This appeared as the last section of a book, *A La recherche d'une musique concrète*,[8] which outlined the events of the previous four years. The treatise is divided into two main sections. The first consists of a set of twenty-five provisional definitions for use in the description of *objets sonores*, and the basic processes that might be applied to them, while the second is concerned with the application of these definitions to create an operational language for the synthesis of *musique concrète*.

The twenty-five provisional definitions may be summarized as follows:[9]

1. *Prélèvement*, concerned with the initial action of creating a sound and then recording it on to disc or tape.

Any such sound event (*objet sonore*) is then classified in two ways, each associated with its own set of definitions:

A. 2. *Classification matérielle des objets sonores*, the material classification of sounds prior to any aesthetic or technical analysis. This classification is based on the temporal length of each sound and its center of interest. Three classes are identified:

3. *Échantillon*, a sound lasting several seconds or more with no clearly defined center of interest.

4. *Fragment*, a sound lasting one or perhaps a few seconds with a clearly defined center of interest.

5. *Éléments*, short extracts isolated from a sound, for example the attack, decay, or part of the main body of the event.

B. 6. *Classification musicale des objets sonores*, value judgments on the nature of sounds, in particular their degree of complexity. Four classes are identified:

7. *Monophonie*, concomitant elements isolated by the ear from an accompanying texture. Schaeffer draws a parallel with the subjective ability to identify a melody within a polyphonic texture.

8. *Groupe*, a *monophonie* of some significance lasting many seconds, which may be studied for its internal development or repetitions. A *groupe*, by definition, is constructed from *cellules* or *notes complexes*:

9. *Cellule*, thick sound complexes with no overall shape, involving rapid changes of rhythm, timbre, or pitch, or complex combinations of notes that cannot easily be discerned.

10. *Note complexe*, any element of a *monophonie* that displays a sufficiently clear envelope (attack, body, and decay) to be equated to a musical note. Schaeffer adds a rider to the effect that the element also must be of a simple nature.

11. *Grosse note*, a *note complexe* in which the attack, the body, or the decay is of a significant duration. Beyond certain limits, a *grosse note* must be treated as a *groupe*.

12. *Structures*, the ensemble of material with which the composer starts his examination. This may consist not only of *cellules* or *notes complexes* but also of ordinary notes, prepared or not, obtained from classical, exotic, or experimental instruments.

The next group of definitions identifies the operations involved in processing the sound prior to the main task of composition:

13. *Manipulations*. Three types are identified:

14. *Transmutation*, any manipulation of the material that leaves the form essentially unaltered.

15. *Transformation*, any manipulation that alters the form of the material, rather than its content.

16. *Modulation*, any manipulation that is not clearly a *transmutation* or a *transformation*, but a variation selectively applied to one of the three attributes of pitch, intensity, or timbre.

17. *Paramètres caractérisant un son* leads on from definition (16) to propose

parameters for the analysis of *concret* sounds. In place of the classical notions of pitch, intensity, and duration, Schaeffer substitutes the idea of:

18. Three *plans de référence*, which describe the evolution of each of these quantities as a function of one of the others: pitch/intensity, pitch/duration, and intensity/duration.

The importance of these *plans* merits a close examination of their characteristics, and these will be returned to in due course.

The next group of definitions describes the primary processes involved in realizing a piece of *musique concrète*:

19. *Procédés d'execution*. Six operations are identified, the last three being concerned with the spatial organization of the material in its final realization:
20. *Préparations*, the use of classical, exotic, or modern musical instruments as sound sources, without any restriction as to the mode of their performance.
21. *Montage*, the construction of *objets sonores* by simple juxtaposition of prerecorded fragments.
22. *Mixage*, in contrast to *montage*, involves the superimposition of *monophonies*, to create polyphonic textures.
23. *Musique spatiale*, all music that is concerned with the projection of *objets sonores* in space during a public performance.
24. *Spatialisation statique*, the projection of clearly identifiable *monophonies* from specific locations. This feature arises from the use of different channels on the multitrack tape recorder for the distribution of information at the time of *mixage*.
25. *Spatialisation cinématique*, the dynamic projection of *objets sonores* during performance using the *potentiomètre d'espace*.

These definitions by their very nature could only serve as generalizations of the various processes involved in the earlier stages of *musique concrète*. The whole *solfège* was subjected to significant change as Schaeffer's work continued, and ultimately consolidated in a formidable work, *Traité des objets musicaux*, which appeared in 1966.[10] This synopsis nevertheless gives a useful insight into the philosophical principles applied during the period of its gestation. Indeed, the three *plans de référence* have a more lasting significance that extends well beyond the limited sphere of *concret* composition, for they are germane to any psychoacoustic study or synthesis of sound material.

Schaeffer defined his *plans* as follows:

1. *Plan mélodique ou des tessitures*, the evolution of pitch parameters with respect to time.
2. *Plan dynamique ou des formes*, evolution of intensity parameters with respect to time.

3. *Plan harmonique ou des timbres*, the reciprocal relationship between the parameters of pitch and intensity represented as a spectrum analysis.

These three *plans* may be combined as follows:

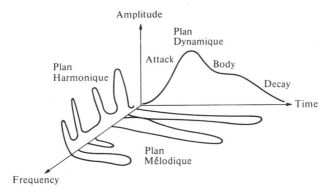

Figure 1

The result highlights the problems encountered in creating a visual representation of sonic events. Although several attempts have been made to improve on this model over the years, the impossibility of reducing such detail to a single two-dimensional graph has proved a major stumbling block. The model cannot be expanded to embrace multiple *objets sonores*, and is in itself only capable of limited accuracy. The *plan harmonique*, for example, only provides an accurate indication of timbre at one selected instant during the course of the event. If this spectrum changes significantly several extra *plans harmoniques* might be required to represent the timbre at different stages in the evolution of the *objet sonore*.

Schaeffer was only too well aware of these difficulties. His solution was to construct a syntax that was based on a limited number of descriptive criteria for each *plan*. This involved a rationalization of the seemingly infinite range of sonic possibilities into categories that were neither too specific nor too vague. His approach was based on the following line of reasoning: In the strictest sense, it is impossible to give a simple description of the evolution of pitch with respect to time unless the sound under examination is exceptionally pure. As noted earlier, a thorough description would demand the superimposition of the *plan harmonique* both on the *plan mélodique*, to obtain a frequency/time graph of partials, and also on the *plan dynamique*, to obtain an amplitude/time graph of partials. Such an outcome destroys the whole purpose of the simplified analytical model.

Fortunately, the psychology of perception offers a viable compromise, for the brain, when evaluating the quality of a sound at a selected instant, takes into account the acoustic phenomena that immediately precede it. Indeed, there is a minimum sampling time necessary for the comprehension of any sonic event. Experiments have shown that sufficient information is contained in extracts of the order of about one twentieth of a second for the brain to identify any center or centers of pitch interest with some degree of certainty. Lengthening the analysis interval permits the ear to study the changes in these centers with respect to time.

Schaeffer's approach is of considerable significance, for it focuses attention on aspects of psychoacoustics that are an essential part of any study or manipulation of sound material, whether natural or electronic in origin. He made an important distinction between two very different elements regularly encountered in *objets sonores*: (1) the complex spectrum associated with a sharp attack or an abrupt change in content, and (2) the more ordered, slowly changing spectrum usually associated with the body and the decay. The latter characteristic is particularly clear if the *objet* is a note with a definite pitch center. The former characteristic is often described as a transient response, an important feature in many natural musical sounds. One of the major problems of all-electronic synthesis even today is the difficulty encountered in creating satisfactory transients, and this key aspect will be returned to in due course.

During attack transients the spectrum table is extremely complex, so much so that a *plan harmonique* drawn during this particular stage of a sound would be most misleading, for its content will be undergoing rapid changes only partially comprehended by the ear. The spectral elements are in many instances so disordered that the result is a semicontinuous spectrum of noise, indicated on the *plan mélodique* by a wide shaded band or bands of frequencies. The body and the decay, by contrast, are often sufficiently stable for a much narrower band or bands to be drawn, in particularly clear cases reducing to a line. Schaeffer thus proposed that a single *plan harmonique* for an *objet sonore* should be drawn during the body of a note, at the point where the spectrum reaches its greatest state of development. The preceding diagram illustrates the use of the three *plans* to identify the salient features of a sound of moderate density, displaying three predominant areas of partials after an initial transient. It also reveals that the decay is characterized by a more rapid attenuation of higher partials relative to their lower counterparts.

Five principal criteria were proposed for evaluating the *plan mélodique,* to be associated specifically with the pitch characteristics displayed during the body of the *objet sonore*. These were: (1) *stable*, displaying a fixed pitch characteristic; (2) *cyclic*, displaying a pitch vibrato of about 5 to 6 Hertz (Hz); (3) *continuous ascent;* (4) *continuous descent;* and (5) *discontinuous*, where the pitch flickers in a complex fashion.

Suggestions for subsidiary criteria included a variation on (2), *spinning*, to describe sounds that fluctuate more rapidly about a central pitch, and a variation on (5), *indistinct*, to describe the pitchless quality of uniform noise.

The principal criteria for the *plan dynamique* were divided into four groups, one for the attack, two for the body, and one for the decay. Three principal criteria are specified for the attack: (1) *plucked,* (2) *percussive*, and (3) *aeolian*.

Two subsidiary criteria were suggested for use in describing the artificial types of attack encountered in the use of *concret* techniques: (1) *stepped*, to describe an

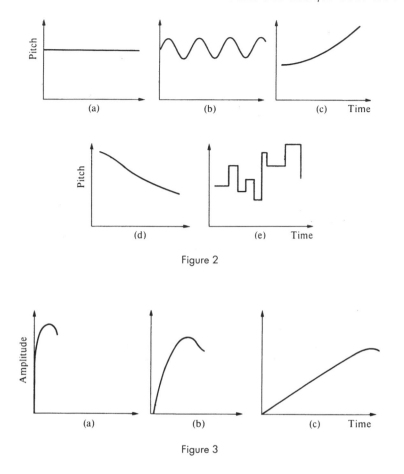

Figure 2

Figure 3

attack that develops as a succession of terraced levels, and (2) *pulsed*, to describe an attack that develops in successive waves.

The decision to provide two complementary sets of principal criteria for the body of the sound requires some explanation. Schaeffer clearly felt it desirable to classify not only the nature of the body itself but also the way in which it develops out of the attack. Six principal criteria were proposed under the latter heading. These were: (1) *shock*, no sustaining into a body at all; (2) *natural resonance*, the sound sustained by a smooth natural reverberation; (3) *artificial resonance*, the same effect created by artificial overlaying; (4) *drubbing*, a beating continuation of the attack impetus; (5) *pulsation*, sustaining by repetition of the attack either sequentially or by partial overlaying; and (6) *artificial*, a synthetic sustaining characteristic produced by a montage of various elements.

Five principal criteria were proposed for the body itself, with the intention that these should be treated as complementary to the criteria for the *plan mélodique*,

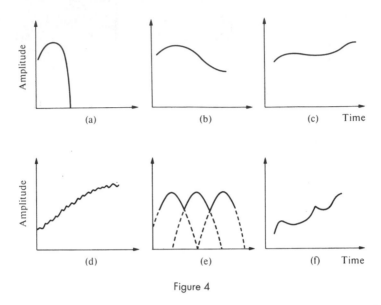

Figure 4

discussed above. These were: (1) *stable*, steady intensity; (2) *cyclic*, continuous amplitude vibrato of about 1 to 5 percent; (3) *continuous crescendo;* (4) *continuous decrescendo;* and (5) *discontinuous*, for example, stepped or pulsing.

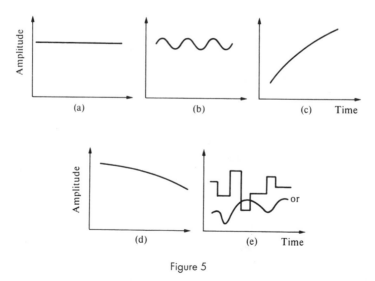

Figure 5

The decay of a sound, concerned with the gradual dissipation of the accumulated energy, was accorded five principal criteria. These were: (1) *cut dead*, rapid decay with almost no reverberation; (2) *normal reverberation*, a natural exponential decay; (3) *artificially extended reverberation*, generally involving a subsidiary peak of reverberant energy; (4) *artificially discontinuous reverberation*, sharp interruptions to the natural decay characteristic; and (5) *artificially cyclic reverberation*, superimposition of an amplitude vibrato onto the decay.

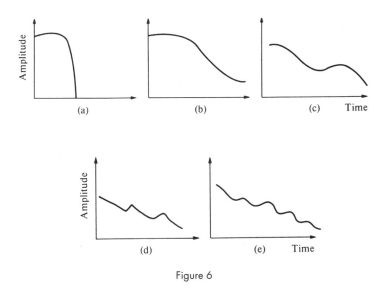

Figure 6

The *plan harmonique*, as already observed, provided an analysis of the timbre spectrum of an *objet sonore*, most suitably at the peak of its development. Schaeffer's approach was slightly different for this *plan*, for he divided his principal criteria into three complementary groups, concerned respectively with density, richness, and coloration. Four principal criteria of density were proposed: (1) *pure*, a single fundamental tone; (2) *blurred*, a less distinct fundamental; (3) *thick*, an identifiable primary area of frequency, but with no clear fundamental; and (4) *white*, no distinct frequency area.

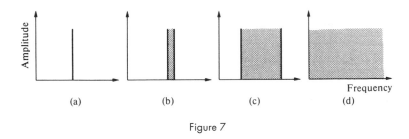

Figure 7

Two principal criteria of richness were identified: (1) *rich timbre*, displaying many partials; and (2) *poor timbre*, displaying few partials.

Three principal criteria of coloration were identified, intended to provide a qualitative assessment, as a counterpart to the more quantitative assessment provided by the criteria of richness. These were: (1) *dark*, few partials, rapidly falling

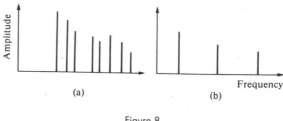

Figure 8

in intensity up the spectrum; (2) *clear*, few partials, but with a more evenly distributed energy spectrum; and (3) *brilliant*, a similar energy distribution to that shown in a clear sound, but with a greater number of upper partials forming more concentrated groups.

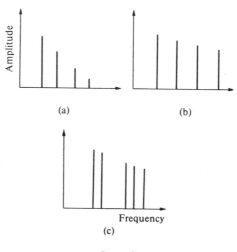

Figure 9

These thirty-three criteria, for all their generalities, provide for some 54,000 different combinations of sonic characteristics, a daunting indication of the scale of the task facing any prospective morphologist. The "Esquisse d'un solfège concret" was only intended as a preliminary treatise, designed to serve the needs of a particular school evolving around the philosophy of *musique concrète*. It is pertinent, nevertheless, to note that this pioneering attempt to study the nature of sound in relation to the electronic studio provided a major point of reference for those who have subsequently sought to pursue this important area of psychoacoustic research.

The year of publication could not have been more auspicious. During the rebirth of the arts after the Second World War, Paris had become increasingly important as a focal point for developments in new music. Composers who worked in the studio at this time included Jean Barraqué, Pierre Boulez, Michel Philippot, and Hermann Scherchen. Others to visit the facilities included Yves Baudrier, Marcel Delannoy, Henri Dutilleux, Karel Goeyvaerts, Jean-Jacques Grunenwald, André Jolivet, Olivier Messiaen, Darius Milhaud, and Karlheinz Stockhausen. The compositional ideas of the period influenced the way in which *concret* techniques were developed, particular interest being paid to the application of serial or similar determinate procedures for the specification of duration, pitch, dynamics, and timbre. Messiaen, for example, produced a short study, *Timbres-durées,* and Boulez employed a precise plan for both duration and pitch in his *Étude I sur un son,* using the Phonogènes to give chromatic intervals and octave transpositions of a single sound source. Neither of these composers, however, sustained more than a passing connection with Schaeffer's studio, discouraged perhaps by the inevitable lack of refinement at this time.

Stockhausen's brief association with the studio arose during his year's study with Messiaen at the Paris Conservatoire. Goeyvaerts had drawn his attention to the synthesis possibilities of the sine wave generator, and the recording facilities at the Club d'Essai attracted him for reasons that were distinctly counter to Schaeffer's ideas. Stockhausen nevertheless completed a short piece of *musique concrète,* a short rhythmic study entitled *Étude* (Electronic Composition 1953 no. 1) before returning to Germany in early 1953 to start his long association with developments at Cologne. In 1954, Milhaud produced a work entitled *La Rivière endormie* for mezzo soprano, two actors, orchestra, and tape, and Varèse visited the studio to produce the first version of the tape part for his piece *Déserts,* an important event that will be returned to in a later chapter.

Toward the end of the decade the principles of *musique concrète* became far less proscriptive, more elaborate electronic processing techniques gaining gradual acceptance. Natural rather than electronic sound sources, however, were to remain the primary interest for many composers. During 1957–8, the Greek-born composer Iannis Xenakis produced his first major studio work, *Diamorphoses* (revised 1968), in which he applied principles of mathematical organization to the processes of composition with *concret* sounds. The mechanistic influence on the modern world is reflected in the choice of sonic material, for example jets, bells, and the sounds of physical destruction.

Over the same period, Schaeffer began a major reorganization of both his methods of composition and also the studio itself, and the term *musique concrète* was replaced by the far more universal description *experiences musicales.* Schaeffer's two major compositions of 1958, *Étude aux allures* and *Étude aux sons animés,* also demonstrated a significant change in his creative outlook. Instead of concentrating on the manipulation of material extracted from naturally generated sound sources, he placed considerable emphasis on the reverse technique of additive synthesis, building up rich timbres from simple electronic components. This approach reflected the philosophies of the Cologne and Milan studios, both to be discussed shortly. Henry departed to found his own studio Apsome elsewhere in Paris, and Luc Ferrari and Francois-Bernard Mâche joined Schaeffer's team, the group renaming themselves "Groupe de Recherches Musicales" (GRM), as noted earlier.

Diversification of ideas and techniques was by then leading to very new pastures for some. Xenakis, for example, having worked with sounds of both natural and electronic origin, began to experiment with computers, first as normal data-processing machines and then as sources of synthetic sounds themselves. By the early 1960s, work inspired by Schaeffer's studio was merging with other lines of development to create a rapidly expanding medium of electronic music; the age of isolated pioneering was coming to an end.

3

Cologne and *Elektronische Musik*

Elektronische Musik, unlike *musique concrète*, was pioneered not as the result of the efforts of a single individual, but as the result of a collaborative venture between several interested parties, drawn from both musical and technical backgrounds.

During 1948, Dr. Werner Meyer-Eppler, at that time director of the Department of Phonetics at Bonn University, was visited by Homer Dudley, a research physicist at Bell Telephone Laboratories in New Jersey. Dudley brought with him a newly developed machine called a Vocoder (Voice Operated reCOrDER), which could operate both as a speech analyzer and also as an artificial talker. In the former capacity, the instrument operated by detecting the energy levels of successive sound samples measured over the entire audio frequency spectrum via a series of narrow band filters, the results being displayed graphically as functions of frequency energy against time. The relative levels detected by these filters thus produced a dynamic analysis of the changing timbres. Synthesis, the reverse process, was achieved by scanning graphs displaying shaded representations of selected timbres and supplying the characteristics to the feedback networks of the analytical filters, suitably energized from a noise generator to produce audible spectra.

Although the fidelity of the machine was limited, its purpose being primarily to process speech rather than music, Meyer-Eppler was considerably impressed by its functional characteristics. During 1949, he published an account of the history and design of electronic musical instruments entitled *Elektrische Klangerzeugung*, which included a description of the vocoder.[1] In the same year, he used the resynthesis capabilities of the vocoder to illustrate a lecture on electronic sound production, given at the North West German Music Academy, Detmold. By good chance the audience included Robert Beyer from Nordwestdeutscher Rundfunk. Beyer had already shown a keen interest in the musical uses of electronic technology. As early as 1928 he had published an article on "The Problems of the 'Coming Music'" in the periodical *Die Musik,* which included a discussion on the use of electronic instruments in musical composition.[2]

Both scientists felt the interest shown at Detmold warranted further public exposure, and they both presented lectures on "The Sound World of Electronic Music" at the 1950 International Summer School for New Music at Darmstadt. Beyer concentrated on the design principles employed in the manufacture of electronic musical instruments and Meyer-Eppler outlined the state of research in the field of speech synthesis. The composer Herbert Eimert expressed particular interest in their ideas and the three men agreed to enter into an informal association, with the object of furthering the development of *elektronische Musik.*

During the autumn of 1950, the design engineer Harald Bode delivered one of his Melochords, an electronic solo instrument not unlike the Trautonium, to Meyer-Eppler at Bonn. This was used to prepare a number of *Klangmodelle*, simple studies in the production of electronic sounds created by layering recordings of selected tones. The results of these preliminary investigations were presented by Meyer-Eppler at Darmstadt in July 1951 in a lecture entitled "The Possibilities of Electronic Sound Production." Beyer contributed a paper on "Music and Technology" and Eimert discussed "Music on the Borderline." Schaeffer attended Darmstadt that year, and as noted earlier, this public confrontation provided a sharp impetus to the growing differences between French and German philosophies of electronic music.

On 18 October 1951, the radio station at Cologne broadcast an evening program entitled "The Sound World of Electronic Music," which consisted of a forum held between Eimert, Beyer, and Meyer-Eppler, using the *Klangmodelle* as illustrations. On the same day a special committee consisting of the three participants, the technical director of Cologne Radio, Fritz Enkel, and a number of his assistants, agreed to establish an electronic music studio "to pursue the processes suggested by Meyer-Eppler and compose directly on tape."[3] Work began on the studio that autumn, but it was to take nearly two years for the system to become fully operational, an occasion marked by the formal appointment of Eimert as artistic director.

Throughout the intervening period, interest in the project continued to grow. In December 1951, Meyer-Eppler lectured on "New Methods of Electronic Tone Generation" to an audience of nearly a thousand at a meeting of technologists in Bonn. During the first half of 1952, the composer Bruno Maderna produced a piece entitled *Musica su due Dimensioni* in association with Meyer-Eppler at the Institute of Phonetics, Bonn. This work was presented at the ensuing Darmstadt Summer School to an audience that included Goeyvaerts, Bengt Hambraeus, Giselher Klebe, Gottfried Michael Koenig, and Stockhausen, all of whom were subsequently to become involved in the composition of *elektronische Musik* at Cologne. Viewed in retrospect, the scoring of Maderna's piece for flute, percussion, and a loudspeaker reproducing a tape of electronically generated material is of some interest stylistically. This integration of natural and electronic sounds conformed neither to the principles of *musique concrète* nor to the early manifestations of *elektronische Musik*, anticipating, perhaps unwittingly, a time when the application of electronic techniques to processes of musical composition would cease to be subjected to such rigid distinctions.

Beyer and Eimert, with technical assistance from Enkel, composed their first all-electronic compositions while the studio was still under construction: *Klang im unbegrenzten Raum* (1951–2), *Klangstudie I* (1952), and *Klangstudie II* (1952–3). Toward the end of 1952, the studio became partly operational as a self-contained system, permitting work to be transferred in stages from the laboratory bench to more congenial surroundings. During the first half of 1953, Beyer and Eimert composed *Ostinate Figuren und Rhythmen*, and Eimert alone composed *Struktur 8*. These pieces are characterized by the strict application of serial procedures to the processes of tone selection and processing. *Struktur 8*, for example, is derived entirely from a restricted set of eight tones related by intervals.

In June of the same year, these first complete pieces of *elektronische Musik* were premiered in Paris, ironically for Schaeffer, during a Festival of New Music organized by the Centre de Documentation de Musique Internationale in association with Nordwestdeutscher Rundfunk.[4] Eimert and Meyer-Eppler subsequently presented extracts from this program at the 1953 Darmstadt Summer School. Through the autumn, work at the studio gathered momentum. Goeyvaerts composed *Compositie nr. 5 met Zuivere Tonen*, and Eimert composed *Glockenspiel*. The latter piece consisted of twice-sixty sounds of a bell-like quality using calculation tables, which arranged bell timbres derived from natural bells in series of increasing and decreasing density.

It was at this point that Stockhausen began his long and influential association with the Cologne studio, realizing *Studie I* (Composition 1953 no. 2), quickly followed by *Studie II* early in 1954.[5] These last two pieces provide a useful focal point for an assessment of the musical characteristics of this early era, but first account must be taken of the technical and philosophical climate in which they were produced.

The early 1950s have already been identified as a time characterized by powerful crosscurrents in the search for new horizons in musical composition. The Germans held the work of the Second Viennese School in high esteem, and many became avowed disciples of the cause of furthering the principles of serialism. An increasing desire to exercise control over every aspect of musical composition led to a keen interest in the possibilities of electronic synthesis, for such a domain eliminated not only the intermediate processes of performance but also the need to accept the innate characteristics of natural sound sources. The acquisition of such power, however, was to precipitate a major crisis in this movement toward total determinism, for it proved extremely difficult to create culturally acceptable alternatives for these essential characteristics of traditional music.

Musique concrète, for all its limitations and shortcomings, retained a reassuring degree of familiarity by virtue of its derivation from the sonic resources provided by the natural sound world. The early advocates of *elektronische Musik* not only restricted themselves to entirely synthetic means of sound production but also were at pains to dissociate their work from the imitative qualities of electronic musical instruments. A continuing interest in phonetic research under the direction of Meyer-Eppler, however, was to exert a major influence on this quest for a "pure" electronic serialism, working entirely from first principles of sound synthesis. In due course, a growing interest in the subtleties of manipulating and synthesizing formants led to the integration of natural voice sounds with electronic sources, thus opening the door to the creative possibilities of manipulating other material of a natural acoustic origin.

Such a broadening of horizons was ultimately irreconcilable with the highly formalistic principles associated with the early compositional aesthetics of the studio, which were thus to prove unsustainable. Eimert's attitude in this regard was particularly pointed. In an article published in *Die Reihe*, vol. 1 (1955), he declared:

> In electronic serial music . . . everything to the last element of the note is subjected to serial permutation. . . . Examination of the material invariably leads one to serially ordered composition. No choice exists but the ordering of sine tones within a note, and this cannot be done without the triple unit of the note. A note may be said to "exist" where elements of time, pitch, and intensity meet; the fundamental process repeats itself at every level of the serial network which organizes the other partials related to it. . . . Today the physical magnification of a sound is known, quite apart from any musical, expressionist psychology, as exact scientific data. It cannot, however, be the function of electronic music to make the sine tone the living parasite to feign similarity where disparity exists. Talk of "humanized" electronic sound may be left to unimaginative instrument makers.[6]

Such confidence in the potential of *elektronische Musik* did not escape contemporary criticism. In the same volume of *Die Reihe* H. H. Stuckenschmidt, writing on the aesthetics of electronic music, observed that:

> [Eimert] is opposed to all metaphorical synaesthetic interpretation, that is he is opposed to the idea of composition and interpretation by association and reference.

Aesthetic understanding of the new art is not facilitated by this attitude. It cannot be denied that the associative effect, which the initiator denies as being of any relevance, has been the principal reaction of the majority of listeners faced for the first time with electronic music. There appears to be a considerable discrepancy between postulation and reception, a discrepancy which must be of the very nature of the new art form. . . . in that nothing pertaining to electronic music is analogous to any natural existent phenomenon of traditional music, associations have to be evoked from elsewhere. Instead of being integrated, they remain an ever-increasing conglomeration of mentally indigestible matter. Thus the listener's reaction in broad outline corresponds to his relationship to a humanly transfigured world.[7]

One year previously, Eimert, writing in the technical handbook of Nordwest-deutscher Rundfunk, had himself drawn attention to a major difficulty: "A far reaching, still unsolved question is whether electronic music as a universal source of all sounds possesses any coherent form-sustaining force corresponding to tonality— a self-sustaining system of timbres."[8]

The desire to exercise total control over the processes involved in specifying timbres led, after some deliberation, to the selection of the sine wave oscillator as the most suitable source of electronic material. From the world of mathematics, Fourier's principles of waveform analysis established that periodic sound material could be broken up into basic sinusoidal components of different frequencies, amplitudes, and phases.[9] The key to complete flexibility in the reverse process of resynthesis lay in the provision of facilities capable of generating each of these components individually. A single sinusoid is a geometric derivation of simple harmonic motion, a natural example of which is the oscillatory movements of a clock pendulum. The resultant function, if plotted on a sheet of graph paper or displayed electronically on a cathode ray oscilloscope, reveals the distinctive wave characteristic ⌒⌣, where the speed of repetition determines its frequency and the degree of oscillation its amplitude. Initially the Cologne studio was only equipped with a single, high precision sine wave oscillator and just three other electronic sound sources. Two of these, despite Eimert's avowed dislike, were electronic musical instruments: a Melochord and an Electronic Monochord, used primarily by other users in the production of background music for radio plays. The remaining source consisted of a simple noise generator.

The Monochord was specially commissioned from Trautwein, taking the form of a modified concert Trautonium. Trautwein, however, failed to complete the instrument on time, and it was left to Enkel to finish its construction in the studio workshop. The Melochord, it will be recalled, had already been used for the synthesis of Meyer-Eppler's pioneering *Klangmodelle*.

Both instruments were equipped with a pair of keyboards, each providing an independent monophonic output. The Melochord generated pitches derived from the traditional equal-tempered twelve-note scale, octave transposition switches extending the range of the thirty-seven keys from three octaves to seven. A foot-pedal was employed to regulate the overall volume level, individual notes being shaped by an electronically operated attack and decay envelope function, automatically triggered each time a key was depressed. The keyboard system for the Monochord was more flexible, for both the interval step size and also the general compass could be varied using separate controls. Again, a foot-pedal volume control was provided, but in place of an electronic enveloping facility both keyboards could be set to produce a dynamic response, which varied according to the pressure exerted on each key.

The keyboard oscillator produced a sawtooth characteristic $\wedge\!\!\wedge\!\!\vee$, one of the three most basic harmonic wave shapes offered by electronic oscillators, the other two being the triangle wave $\wedge\!\!\wedge\!\!\vee$ and the square wave $\sqcap\!\sqcup\!\sqcap$. The harmonic structures of these compound waves are determined by the application of simple mathematical algorithms. The sawtooth, or ramp wave contains a complete series of harmonics such that the amplitude of each component relative to the fundamental is the reciprocal of its numerical position in the series. If the fundamental frequency, F, is given an amplitude of x, the second harmonic, $2F$, will have an amplitude of x/2, the third harmonic, $3F$, an amplitude of x/3, and so forth. In contrast both triangle and the square waves are composed of odd harmonics only. In the case of the triangle wave the amplitude of each component decreases in proportion to the squared reciprocal of its position in the harmonic series. The frequency components F, $3F$, $5F$, $7F$, and so on, are thus associated with amplitudes in the proportions x, x/9, x/25, x/49, and so on. In the case of the square wave the relative amplitude of each component is the simple reciprocal of its position in the series. The components F, $3F$, $5F$, $7F$, and so on, are thus associated with amplitudes in the proportions x, x/3, x/5, x/7, and so on.

In their raw state these three sources are aurally quite disappointing, for they produce fixed timbres lacking in distinguishing characteristics. Despite their functional differences in mathematical terms, the very regularity of their overtone series makes it hard to distinguish between these sources subjectively. A square wave may easily be mistaken for a sawtooth wave, and a triangle wave often appears to be simply a less strident version of either. Their true potential as sources of distinctive timbres only becomes significant when these functions are processed electronically. The most useful technique involves the application of filters to highlight certain harmonic components and attenuate others. Such shaping facilities were incorporated in both the Melochord and the Monochord, but limited in application to a general smoothing of higher-order harmonics. The resulting timbres offered a consistency of quality appropriate to a performance instrument but were to prove unduly restrictive in scope when applied to the compositional aims of elektronische Musik.

Engineering expediencies such as the above to provide simplified methods for creating synthetic sound lead inevitably to some sacrifice of flexibility.[10] For the early Cologne composers, the only acceptable solution to this dilemma was the rejection of any technique imposing such constraints in favour of much more basic methods of sound synthesis, however arduous and time-consuming.

As noted earlier, just one other electronic source was initially available, a white-noise generator. "White" noise consists of a concentrated succession of random frequency elements evenly distributed throughout the audio spectrum to produce a bland "hiss." As the antithesis of the single sine wave such a characteristic was to prove of considerable interest, for it is possible by means of highly selective filters to isolate bands of frequencies so narrow that the results are to all intents and purposes single tones. Under these conditions, varying the tuning of each filter produces a result almost identical to that obtained by turning the frequency dial of a sine wave oscillator. Progressive widening of the filter creates a gradually expanding timbre, for the single tone is transformed first into a cluster of closely adjoining frequencies either side of a central focus of interest, and then into a widening spectrum of "colored" noise, displaying an ever-decreasing sensation of a central pitch.

Within limits imposed by the number of generators available, and the practicalities of overlaying a number of recordings, a similar effect may be achieved by mixing together a sufficient number of sine tones of suitable amplitudes to span the desired frequency band. Using this technique, it is possible to manipulate the individual generators to produce interesting deviations from the gradual progression into noise spectra associated with the former method. For example, instead of increasing the number of sine tones to span an ever-increasing bandwidth with a consistent density, the existing components may be retuned to provide a more structured representation of the frequency spread, the individual elements becoming recognizable as individual spectral components. These so-called note mixtures became a major feature of *elektronische Musik*, for they provided a useful basis for creating a flexible and controllable continuum between noiselike spectra and pure tones.

The term "note mixture" (a more accurate description in translation would have been "tone mixture") was reserved for combinations of sine tones where the constituent frequencies are not related harmonically to a fundamental pitch. This attempt to distinguish between harmonic and inharmonic spectra was not entirely successful, for the subtleties of transformation that are possible between these two types of timbre create a very uncertain boundary area between these two states. The pieces *Studie I* and *Studie II* provide interesting illustrations of this morphological feature. Stockhausen considered all four possible sources in the Cologne studio before selecting the sine wave generator as the sole source for both pieces. The possibilities of synthesizing noiselike spectra from sine tones, however, were to manifest themselves in *Studie II,* a prelude to a more thorough working-out of the tone/noise continuum in his more substantial composition *Gesang der Jünglinge* (1955–6).

The timbres for *Studie I* were derived from a special frequency table, calculated in turn from a series of harmonic ratios. Taking the pitch of 1920 Hz as a starting point, he first obtained a series of six frequencies, successively dividing by the following proportions:

12/5   4/5   8/5   5/12   5/4

This produces the following values:

1920 Hz   800 Hz   1000 Hz   625 Hz   1500 Hz   1200 Hz.

Each of the five new frequencies was then subjected to the same sequence of proportional divisions, and the process repeated on each of the new values obtained to the point where the frequency of 66 Hz was reached, this value being declared as the lower limit. A mirror process folding values upward from 1920 Hz was then applied to provide a complementary series. The selection of timbres was determined by first dividing the table vertically into groups of six frequencies and then marking off sequences of one to six elements in the following order, the columns being read off left to right:

4   5   3   6   2   1

This technique can best be illustrated by reference to the first section of the lower half of the table:

Without knowledge of the method of derivation, and an ability to recognize harmonic ratios calculated in inversion, the casual observer might be forgiven for deducing that the groupings just illustrated are composed of inharmonic partials. A normal harmonic series, for example, derived from a fundamental of 100 Hz, would follow the sequence:

100,   200,   300,   400,   500,   600,   700,   etc. Hz

No such lowest common multiple exists for the sequence

325,   417,   521,   625,   781,   1000   Hz

All the ratios, however, are calculated in whole-number proportions (to simplify matters the above figures have been rounded to the nearest Hertz) by virtue of their method of calculation. Aurally the simpler ratios have a recognizable harmonic coherence. 325 to 781, for example, satisfies the ratio 5/12, perceived as a perfect (nontempered) minor tenth. The more complex ones, however, focus attention on harmonic relationships that are not so familiar. 781 to 1000, for example, satisfies the ratio 25/32, not quite approximating to a perfect fourth.

These sounds display remarkably bell-like qualities, particularly in the upper registers, and their closely structured relationships create an air of timbral stability. The uncertain boundary between these harmonic timbres and note mixtures may readily be demonstrated by tuning a bank of oscillators to any of the larger groupings and then detuning them slightly to achieve indisputably inharmonic ratios. The effect is a subtle shift in timbre and the introduction of more pronounced beating between components, but there is no feeling that a major morphological transformation has occurred.

The selection of groupings and the specification of their duration values and dynamics were all determined serially. During the piece the entire sequence of frequencies repeats six times. For each pass the members of each source group of frequencies were allocated unique amplitude values in the proportions n decibels, $n-4$ dB, $n-8$ dB, $n-12$ dB, $n-16$ dB, and $n-20$ dB.[11] The value n corresponded to the standard reference studio level, subjectively associated with a healthy fortissimo. After each pass the allocations within each group were rotated by one step so that each frequency in turn became the strongest timbre element. For example, see table 3.1:

Table 3.1 Table of Amplitudes

First pass		Second pass	
1920 Hz	n dB	1920 Hz	$n-20$ dB
800 Hz	$n-4$ dB	800 Hz	n dB
1000 Hz	$n-8$ dB	1000 Hz	$n-4$ dB
625 Hz	$n-12$ dB	625 Hz	$n-8$ dB
1500 Hz	$n-16$ dB	1500 Hz	$n-12$ dB
1200 Hz	$n-20$ dB	1200 Hz	$n-16$ dB

After these elements had been further partitioned into their groupings as outlined earlier, the constant reference level n in each selection was modified by a further series of attenuation ratios to provide a greater degree of dynamic structuring. Finally one of six envelope patterns was superimposed on each selection according to yet another series of permutations. Three of these patterns involved the addition of a little coloration from an echo chamber, an interesting method of timbre modification to feature more prominently in *Studie II*.

The duration of events was determined by the strongest frequency in each selection. In the lower half of the table (1920 Hz down to 66 Hz), this value was divided by ten to produce a figure that served as the physical tape length of the recorded sound, measured in centimeters. Frequency and duration were thus directly proportional, the lower the predominant frequency the shorter the sound. Given a recording speed of 76.2 cm/sec (30 in/sec) this created a scale of duration values ranging from about 2½ sec at 1920 Hz to about 1/11 sec at 66 Hz.

For the upper half of the table, a mirror characteristic was extrapolated, duration values becoming progressively shorter with ascending frequency centers. Procedurally, this was achieved by using prerecorded complementary selections from the lower half of the table and subjecting them to variable speed transposition. A doubling of the tape speed, for example, led to a doubling of each component frequency and a halving of the associated duration.

Three tape machines were available for the construction of this piece: one single-track recorder, one four-track recorder, and one variable-speed recorder. The first two machines provided the primary means for assembling the timbres by montage from the single sine wave generator and the process was inevitably laborious. Up to four tones could be independently recorded on the multitrack machine, the result being mixed down on to the single-track machine and, where appropriate, copied back on to one track on the former machine, releasing the other three tracks for the recording of further tones. The variable-speed recorder was an old AEG model, one of the very first production series, specially converted to provide a continuous range from about 9 cm/sec to 120 cm/sec, allowing pitch transposition over about 3¾ octaves.

Variable-speed processing was to prove a very powerful tool for the composer of electronic music as the years advanced, and its potential was well appreciated by the schools of *elektronische Musik* and, as already noted, *musique concrète*. In the serially orientated sphere of the former the very consistency of the process, imposing proportional change on all the recorded characteristics, provided the greatest attraction. In contrast, it will be recalled, it was this very degree of permanence that presented Schaeffer with some of his greatest compositional problems. Doubling the playback speed not only halves the overall duration of the recorded events but also smaller-scale variations in amplitude and frequency characteristics such as vibrato, and the attack and decay. As Schaeffer was quick to discover, subjecting recordings of natural sounds to different playback speeds could produce some interesting effects. The sharp attack of a trumpet note, for example, will be perceived as a noisy and irregular succession of noise elements if played at a fraction of the original recording speed. The permanence arises from the impossibility of manipulating such features independently of all the other aspects of the sound. The apparent transformations are the result of our subjective reactions to a scientifically determined process, which affects the material as a whole.

The techniques of electronic synthesis from first principles, however, provide

the composer with the option of avoiding these fixed relationships between envelope, pitch, and duration, at least during the initial stages of material preparation.
If dynamic shaping is applied to an electronic source prior to variable-speed processing the situation is no different from that which would apply to a natural source.
If, however, a source offering a stable spectrum is first subjected to variable-speed
processing and then dynamically shaped, any desired envelope characteristic may
be specified for the transposed material.

The use of echo enhancement in *Studie I* was followed by a more significant use
of reverberation in *Studie II*. In this piece, the selected pitch series for the source
tones resulted in true note mixtures, for the frequencies were derived from a scale
of 81 tones employing the constant interval $25\sqrt{5}$. This provided steps of approximately 1/10 of an octave, starting from a lowest frequency of 100 Hz. Instead
of being combined into sets of different sizes, five element groupings were employed throughout. Once again, Stockhausen used a serial procedure for selecting
the frequency components for each source, a simple algorithm providing a pattern
of frequencies as follows:

Unlike *Studie I* the amplitudes of the components for each group were of equal volume. Instead of combining components to produce a direct recording of each mixture, short extracts of each tone were spliced in ascending frequency order and

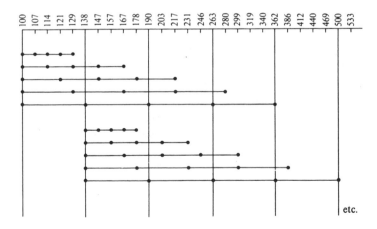

Figure 10

then joined end to end to make a loop. Short bursts of these loops, which produced rapid and repeating arpeggios of the constituent frequencies, were then fed
into a reverberation chamber, and the results were recorded on tape. This technique resulted in sounds that were remarkably "alive" by virtue of the overlapping
effect of the numerous reflections and the natural exponential decay of the events
from their initial sharp attack. The basic envelope of each sound ⌐⌐⌐ was then
lengthened or shortened as required by varying the reverberation time, and the

mirror characteristic of an exponential growth and a sharp decay ⌐ created by the simple expedient of playing the recordings backward.

A structured montage of these shaped events provided the compositional building blocks. The first section, for example, consists of successions of chords of similar density, based on pairs of events arranged to give smooth arched envelope shapes, ⌒. The second section, in contrast, highlights discontinuous montages of chord complexes, created by overlapping several forward or backward envelopes, for example: ⌇. The third section features rapid, staccato sounds, the fourth long chord complexes, and the fifth a fusion and transformation of the material presented in the earlier sections.

These two examples of *elektronische Musik* illustrate the type of processes involved in relating contemporary principles of structuralism to the early facilities for electronic synthesis at Cologne. So far, however, only passing reference has been made to the electronic processing facilities incorporated in the system, and an appreciation of their role demands an excursion into the realms of elementary electronic theory.

Filters have already been identified as devices that attenuate specific frequencies in applied sound spectra, this subtraction serving to highlight those that remain. In general terms these devices may be divided into four distinct types: high-pass, low-pass, band-pass, and band-stop (notch). High-pass filters act to eliminate all applied frequencies below a specific point, known as the frequency cutoff. Low-pass filters, conversely, act to eliminate all applied frequencies above a specific point. Band-pass filters may be considered as combinations of high- and low-pass filters with overlapping ranges, connected in series to eliminate frequencies either side of a selected region. Band-stop filters offer the inverse response characteristics to band-pass types, attenuating a specific region of frequencies but passing all others.

To the electronic engineer ideal filters should be capable, at an extreme setting, of providing a sharp transition between the two states of signal pass and signal reject. Such conditions would result in the following response diagrams for the four principal types (the shaded areas indicate the frequency regions permitted to pass by the units concerned):

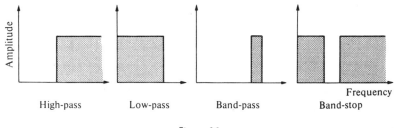

Figure 11

In practice it is not possible to design filters that change so abruptly from a pass state to a reject state. Furthermore, the discontinuity thus introduced results in a "ringing" type of distortion that is highly undesirable. A more gradual characteristic from one state to the other is thus engineered, taking the form of an attenuation curve that may be of varying severity according to the filter design. In certain configurations this response may be varied by the user, in others it is fixed at the construction stage. The following examples illustrate the types of response that may be associated with a band-pass filter:

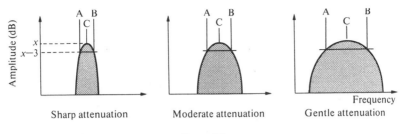

Sharp attenuation   Moderate attenuation   Gentle attenuation

Figure 12

The band-pass filter provides the most comprehensive range of characteristics for isolating frequency areas within a rich source spectrum. The following features are significant for the musical user:

1. the center frequency of the pass band (C in the above diagrams);
2. the effective width of the pass band, the limits being defined as the points at which the energy levels have fallen by 3 dB from the energy levels at the center of the band (A to B in the above);
3. the flatness of the response within the pass band, and the associated rate of attenuation either side.

If such a filter is constructed from a pair of high-pass and low-pass units, as described above, the bandwidth and the rate of attenuation may be made independently adjustable:

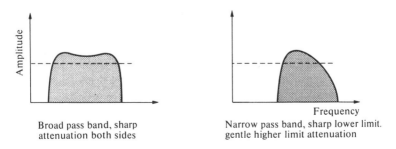

Broad pass band, sharp   Narrow pass band, sharp lower limit.
attenuation both sides   gentle higher limit attenuation

Figure 13

If the filter is of an integrated type, however, the bandwidth and the response characteristics are usually interdependent, the steeper the response the smaller the effective bandwidth. The sharpness of such a filter's setting is described either in terms of decibels of attenuation per musical octave deviation from the center frequency, for example, 12 dB per octave, or as a "Q" factor, a measure of the curve's exponential characteristic with respect to the center frequency. The penultimate set of diagrams above, representing Qs of about 2 to 80, are typical of the responses obtainable from this type of variable, band-pass filter. The effect of applying noise as an input signal to such a unit and increasing the Q is thus the isolation of a progressively narrower band of frequencies. This process of increasing resolution is not infinite, however, for according to the quality of the design there comes a point when the filter circuitry cannot be prevented from becoming self-oscillatory, generating a sine wave at the center frequency without any external excitation.

The Cologne studio was equipped with a variable center frequency, center Q, band-pass filter unit that also offered a high-pass or a low-pass mode of operation according to the position of a selector switch. This facility, however, was somewhat limited in its functionality, as only one shaping characteristic could be produced at a time. More elaborate manipulations of a number of areas of the applied spectrum require the use of several band-pass units tuned to different frequencies, each receiving its own direct feed of the source and passing its processed output to a mixing unit. This arrangement of a series of filters connected parallel is commonly referred to as a filter bank. In permanently wired units, the center frequencies of the component filters are usually fixed at the design stage, the most commonly employed settings being derived from the frequency divisions associated with the tempered scale, for example spaced an octave, third-octave, or semitone apart. In a typical unit each filter is fitted with an attenuator allowing the overall gain at the centre of the pass band to be varied from zero to unity gain.

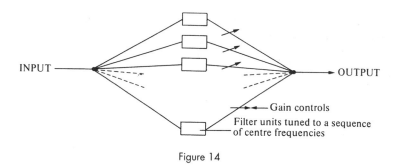

Figure 14

The Q response, like the center frequency, is normally fixed so that two adjacent filters set to the same through gain will combine to produce a flat response over the enclosed frequency region.

The reasons for this arrangement become clearer when the effect of setting all the filters to the same through gain is considered. In this situation, the combination of filter characteristics ensures an even amplitude response throughout the

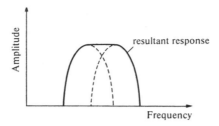

Figure 15

frequency range of the bank, all components of the applied spectra thus being passed unaltered in terms of their intensity. Variations from this norm introduce elements of timbre variation in a suitably progressive manner, the variety of choice being determined by the spectral nature of the source and the number of filters assigned to each octave. "White" noise would appear to provide the most versatile source of input for such a bank in view of its uniform spectral density.

A filter bank tuned to musical octaves or divisions thereof, however, does not divide the audio spectrum into equal frequency bands, for musical pitch follows a logarithmic characteristic, not a linear one. Octaves from a starting frequency of 55 Hz, for example, follow the series 110, 220, 440, 880, and so on, Hz. The absolute bandwidth of each filter thus increases in proportion up the bank, doubling every octave. The use of "white" noise, supplying constant energy per unit frequency division, will thus bias the output of any shaping characteristic selected via the bank toward the higher frequency regions. To overcome this drawback many studios provide a "pink" noise generator as an alternative source. This provides a constant density of spectral energy per musical interval, exactly matching the bandwidth characteristics of the above types of filter bank. Patterns of attenuation settings thus match the perceived result. For example:

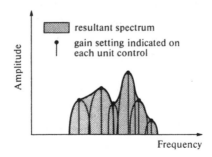

Figure 16

Lack of funds limited the Cologne studio to a single, octave filter bank in the first instance, consisting of eight filters tuned to center frequencies of 75, 150, 300, 600, 1200, 2400, 4800, and 9600 Hz respectively. In due course, when considering how the range of studio facilities could be most usefully expanded, some thought was given to the possible advantages of designing nonstandard filter banks. It was suggested, for example, that instead of dividing the audio spectrum into octave or part-octave divisions, center frequencies could be better spaced to reflect the more linear distribution of partials commonly associated with conventional musical pitch sources.

Harmonics, for example, as simple multiples of a fundamental frequency, become increasingly closer together in terms of intervals as the series is ascended. A consistent measure of control over the selection of components from any such source would thus demand a bank of evenly spaced filters, perhaps every 100 Hz or so, depending on the frequency of the fundamental. The number of units required, however, made such an approach totally impracticable. One of the engineers at Cologne radio, Karl-Heinz Adams, suggested the following compromise, incorporating a facility to switch the center frequencies of the units to a number of different settings:[12]

> One filter with three settings, covering the range 25–100 Hz in 25 Hz steps.
>
> Three filters with twelve settings, covering the range 100–1000 Hz in 75 Hz steps.
>
> Three filters with thirteen settings, covering the range 1000–5000 Hz in 307 Hz steps.
>
> Three filters with ten settings, covering the range 5000–15000 Hz in 1000 Hz steps.

Despite the flexibility of operation provided by this arrangement, composers made relatively little use of this subsequent addition to the studio facilities. Such an outcome provides an interesting early example of the dilemma facing equipment designers in the 1950s, during an era almost entirely dependent on manually operated equipment. On the one hand, the need to exercise such direct control over every aspect of the synthesis and signal processing environment placed the composer in the closest possible proximity to the technology itself. On the other hand, the amount of work involved in crafting sound material cannot be understated, and it was rapidly becoming clear that even the most serially motivated composer, seeking to further the doctrines of Eimert, generally preferred to limit the complexities of the technical process to the bare minimum required.

One important area of sound processing that has so far received little explanation concerns the use of modulation techniques. Two of these processes, based on amplitude and frequency modulation, were subsequently to be identified with the voltage-controlled synthesizer, commercial versions of which first appeared during the mid-1960s. Despite the less developed state of studio electronics during the previous decade, devices offering these characteristics were incorporated in the designs of early studios such as Cologne. One special type of modulator, known as a ring modulator, survived the advances of technology virtually unaltered. This is a device that accepts two separate input signals, performs a simple arithmetic operation on the constituent frequency components, and presents the results as a single output. The products of this modulation are known as sum and difference tones in view of the interaction of the applied signals. If a frequency, F_1, of 400 Hz is presented to one of the inputs and a frequency, F_2, of 300 Hz is presented to the other input, the products are a sum tone F_1+F_2, and a difference tone F_1-F_2. (If the latter result produces a negative value, the sign may be ignored, since it is the *difference* value that determines the resulting frequency.) In the above instance, the result will be a sound consisting of two tones, one of 700 Hz, the other of 100 Hz. If one (or both) of the inputs is complex, then each component is subject to modulation. A sound consisting of the three harmonics 300, 600, and 900 Hz, modulated with a tone of 75 Hz, for example, will produce a spectrum consisting of the sum tones 375, 675, and 975 Hz, and the difference tones 225, 525, and 825 Hz.

The mathematical nature of the process results in a very distinctive range of timbres, for the products obtained will be nonharmonic unless the source tones are related in specific whole-number ratios. By way of an illustration, a tone of frequency F modulated with a tone of frequency $4F$ will generate modulated tones of $5F$ and $3F$. The ability to transform harmonic spectra into nonharmonic spectra (consider the earlier example of a note consisting of the components 300, 600, and 900 Hz modulated with a tone of 75 Hz) provides an interesting compositional procedure. The usefulness of the technique, however, is restricted by its very nature, for the ratios are fixed determinates. The composer may vary the sources, but not the way they interact. This modulation process is particularly conducive to the production of bell-like sounds, amenable to further modification via devices such as filters.

With regard to other modulation devices available at Cologne, the basis for one type of amplitude modulator existed in the electronic enveloping facility attached to the Melochord. If such a circuit is made self-triggering, the attack/decay characteristic will automatically recycle, setting up a regular modulation of amplitude. As an integral part of a much-disliked electronic musical instrument, however, this particular facility received little attention from the composing community. Instead, a technique was developed whereby a ring modulator could be transformed into an electronic "gate," alternately blocking and passing an applied signal. This involved the following arrangement:

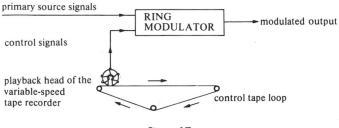

Figure 17

The tape loop consisted of a prepared pattern of impulses; short bursts of a signal alternating with short periods of silence. The ring modulator, it will be recalled, is a device that requires two input signals to operate. If one of these is removed, the other cannot pass. The use of an audio frequency signal for the control impulses in the above arrangement would result in corresponding bursts of a ring-modulated sound at the output, assuming that the primary source was of a continuous nature. By using a control-impulse frequency well above the audio range, however, the normal functioning of the device was inhibited. Some generation of sum and difference tones would occur, safely above the upper limit of hearing, but the main effect was a leaking of the primary source signals directly to the output of the modulator whenever the control signal was also present.

The use of this technique required care, for variations in the playback speed affected the pitch of the recorded control signals. This problem was partly overcome by selecting a tone for the original recording that transposed to the required frequency on playback at the new speed. Little scope existed, however, for varying the speed of an existing control loop. Cologne set the standard control frequency at 30 kHz, right at the upper limit of the playback response of their machine. Any increase would have led to the disappearance of the control tone altogether, and any significant decrease would have resulted in the reappearance of difference tones at the upper end of the audio spectrum.

The studio incorporated another amplitude-processing facility, which permitted the timbre of a sound to be varied dynamically via the octave filter bank. Each of the eight output lines could be switched on or off via an associated relay and level detector driven in turn by a very narrow band-pass filter tuned to a unique center frequency between 1000 and 5000 Hz. The inputs to these drivers were connected in parallel to create a frequency-operated control network, capable of decoding multiple patterns of activating tones, recorded individually and mixed down onto a single tape track.

One other device was available for dynamic shaping. This consisted of a photo-resistor and a constant light source positioned either side of a moving strip of transparent film. By using a paintbrush and a quick-drying opaque varnish, varying proportions of the strip width could be masked, leading to fluctuations in the light levels reaching the resistor. The corresponding changes in the value of the latter were then harnessed to control the gain of an associated amplifier.

Reference has already been made to the use of echo and reverberation in the preparation of Stockhausen's *Studie I* and *Studie II*. The differences between these two types of sound coloration frequently give rise to considerable confusion, and some clarification is appropriate before discussing the techniques involved in more detail. In examining the subjective response of the ear to sounds of different frequencies the lower limit of pitch recognition is identified as the point at which repetitions of a wave become individually perceived. This phenomenon occurs at about 10 to 15 Hz. Our ability to detect these repetitions, however, is influenced by the nature of the wave characteristic itself. If the shape is extremely smooth, for example, a sine wave, the function is perceived as a gentle pulsing, felt rather than heard. If the contours are sharper, for example, a sawtooth wave, the abrupt changes in shape are perceived as sharp, regular clicks. Increasing the repetition rate of the latter leads to a blurring of the clicks and an increasing sensation of pitch. What is happening in neural terms is that new clicks are being detected before the brain has finished processing their predecessors, hence a growing sensation of continuity. This persistence factor is an important auditory feature, for as the above study has shown the ear displays a response time of the order of 100 milliseconds (1/10 sec) at the lowest boundary point.

Echo and reverberation both involve the generation of successive reiterations of a sound source. Echo enhancement is generally associated with either single or multiple repetitions such that each reflection may be distinguished as a distinct event. Unless the sound is extremely short, or the delay between repetitions particularly long, the sounds and their echoes will overlap to some degree. This feature will not mask the echo effect providing that the time between repetitions is no shorter than the boundary interval of 100 milliseconds and the envelopes of the individual sounds are sharply focused. Should the sounds display particularly smooth envelope characteristics, however, the value of this boundary as a discriminator between echo and reverberation becomes less certain, for repetitions spaced considerably further than 100 milliseconds apart may become indistinguishable.

Reverberation is generally associated with successive reiterations occurring less than 100 milliseconds apart, for our auditory responses will be acting to blur the repetitions into a smooth extension of the original sound. At Cologne, the facilities for this type of enhancement consisted initially of a room with highly reflecting surfaces, equipped with a loudspeaker for broadcasting signals and a microphone for capturing the resultant response. Acoustic chambers such as this have the potential to generate by far the most natural type of reverberation. The complex reflections set up under such conditions ensure that multiple reiterations are generated at intervals considerably less than 100 milliseconds. Furthermore, each new element of source information is subject to a smooth exponential decay, caused by the steady loss of energy on each new reflection. The main disadvantages encountered are: (1) the physical space required, (2) the cost of lining the surfaces with suitably nonabsorbent materials, and (3) the practical difficulties encountered in subsequently making any alterations to these materials to alter the reverberation time. (The latter is defined scientifically as the time taken for a sound to decay to one-millionth of its original intensity, equivalent to an attenuation of 60 dB.)

Such limitations hampered the work of composers at Cologne, and attention quickly turned toward other methods of producing reverberation, in particular the reverberation plate, developed by the German firm EMT. This device, widely used by the recording industry until the early 1980s, consists of a highly tensile sheet of metal carefully suspended in a long wooden box, and heavily screened from external noise and vibration. At one end an electromechanical transducer is attached, converting incoming electrical signals into equivalent mechanical vibrations that excite the plate. Shock waves are thus created that travel in various directions through the sheet, setting up reflections at the edges similar to those created in an acoustic chamber. Another transducer at the other end, which converts the reflected waves back into an electrical form, detects these reflections. The elasticity of the medium permitted the production of long reverberation times, typically in the order of eight seconds or more. This operational characteristic could be progressively reduced to as little as a fraction of a second via a variable damping system.

Such versatility and convenience is not achieved without some sacrifice, for all mechanical reverberation devices introduce their own particular element of artificiality. Cheaper designs, usually based on a coiled spring rather than a plate, were particularly troublesome in this respect, often producing a pronounced and uneven coloration due to the existence of a number of resonant frequencies in the spring itself. Plate reverberation units are far less prone to such distortions, but nevertheless still impart their own distinctive quality to the treated sound. For all the early dogma over the use of totally specifiable synthesis techniques, many of the works to emerge from Cologne carry this clearly identifiable coloration. Reverberation, nonetheless, was to prove a valuable tool for creating feelings of warmth and depth to the more clinical world of all-electronic sounds, and the desire for such a tempering clearly outweighed the resultant compromise of principles.

Echo facilities were provided by a tape delay system. In order to understand the principles involved here it is necessary to consider the tape head layout of a conventional recorder. In the case of professional machines, three independent heads are normally employed. During recording the first head, the erase head, carries a very high frequency signal acting to randomize the magnetic particles embedded in the tape coating. Any signals left on the tape as a result of a previous recording are thus removed in preparation for the new recording, imprinted by the second head. The third head provides the reverse function to the record head, translating the magnetic imprint back into electrical signals. Although the signal from this replay head may be ignored when making a recording, listening to its output provides an immediate check of the quality of the magnetic imprint.

The significant feature here is the delay that results between the magnetic imprint leaving the record head and its arrival at the replay head. The distance between the two heads and the speed of the tape determines this interval of time. If, for example, the heads are ¾ in (1.9 cm) apart, and the tape is traveling at 7½ in/sec (19 cm/sec), the delay will be 1/10 sec (100 msec). Monitoring the source signal and the recorded signal simultaneously will thus produce a single repetition, which may just be distinguished from its origin. Halving or quartering the tape speed will increase this delay to 200 or 400 milliseconds, resulting in a clearly discernible echo. If the output from the replay head is passed back into the recording channel, multiple echoes will result:

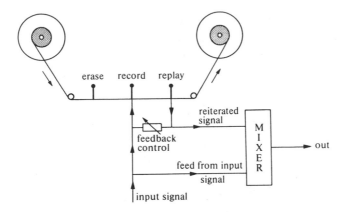

Figure 18

If the feedback control is set to unity gain, the reiterations will recycle at constant amplitude, continuing theoretically to infinity. In practice the increasing degradation of quality with each rerecording limits the useful life of the recycling process. It is more usual therefore to set the feedback control to a less-than-unity gain, giving rise to an exponential decay in the amplitude of successive reiterations. This technique may be modified to provide a form of reverberation by shortening the tape delay to less than 100 milliseconds. Subjectively, however, the quality of this enhancement leaves much to be desired. In addition to a growing risk of spurious interference from the recording circuitry the constant repetition time results in a very rigid prolongation, lacking all the subtleties of natural or even plate reverberation.

An extension of this technique that partially overcomes this drawback was introduced into the Cologne studio in due course. This took the form of a special tape recorder fitted with several replay heads, positioned in a row to provide successive reiterations of signals presented to the record head. In addition to manipulating separate gain controls for each output, the delay pattern could be varied by adjusting the spacing of the heads. The conventional reel-to-reel transport was replaced with a single recirculating loop, allowing the machine to operate without interruption for extended periods. This device was almost identical to Schaeffer's Morphophone, outlined earlier, and it is pertinent to note that the techniques of tapehead echo were already very familiar to composers of *musique concrète*, albeit in the world of natural, rather than electronic, sound sources.

A modification of the erase-record-replay head arrangement permitted the addition of reiteration to an existing recording on the same piece of tape. By adding an extra replay head prior to the erase head prerecorded information could be recovered before the tape was wiped clear, the signals passing electrically to the record head for rerecording. Mixing of the output from the normal replay head with this feed could then be applied to provide the desired degree of enhancement. Direct superimposition of echo/reverberation, achieved by switching off the erase head while leaving the record head live is a most unsatisfactory alternative, for the new magnetic field causes partial erasure of the original imprint. The need for an extra replay head may be avoided by playing the source tape on one machine, and feeding the information to another, set in playback mode. This approach, importantly, preserves the original tape for another attempt, should the first operation prove unsuccessful. With tape recorders at a premium in the early 1950s, however, this four-head arrangement on a single machine provided a significant saving on resources.

The play-erase-record section of the latter arrangement provided another synthesis technique explored notably by Stockhausen in subsequent works such as *Kontakte* (1959–60). Here the output from the normal playback head is disregarded, and a tape loop of a suitable length is substituted for the normal reel-to-reel arrangement. Information recorded onto this loop from an external source then recirculates to the preerase replay head after a delay, which is determined by the length of the loop and the tape speed. If this information is then fed electronically to the record line for rerecording a powerful means of building up complex spectra is created, offering a considerable flexibility over the time that elapses between reiterations.

The spatial projection of sounds was another compositional feature that received particular attention as the studio developed. In addition to versatile monitoring facilities within the electronic studio itself, a multichannel loudspeaker system was installed in the main recording studio. During the early years, special attention was paid to three-channel sound projection, using up to eighteen loudspeakers arranged in three groups. Two of these groups were situated in the front corners of the studio, and the third at the midpoint of the back wall. Driving this system from the four-channel tape machine left one channel free to carry further information that, if so desired, could be superimposed on any of the loudspeaker groups via a set of three frequency-controlled switches and an associated control tape loop or reel-to-reel recording. In a concert situation, the latter facility could be employed to create some degree of live performance, although adherence to the compositional practices advocated by Eimert would have demanded strict control over its operation. This approach to spatial projection contrasted sharply with that associated with Poullin's *potentiomètre d'espace,* where the distribution of sound events was freely influenced by the physical movements of a visible performer.

Attention has already been drawn to the sensation of depth associated with a reverberated sound. In the natural sound world, the distances of sources from a listener are only partially deduced by their perceived amplitudes. The ratio of directly to indirectly radiated information is far more important, the greater the distance, the greater the degree of environmental coloration. In planning the projection of electronic sounds the addition of varying degrees of reverberation to selected elements is an important factor, for the inherently dry characteristics of electronic sources all too readily create a very shallow landscape of sound. Pierre Boulez, writing in the first volume of *Die Reihe,* made the following pertinent observations:

> A final obstacle linked with "interpretation" is the continuity of projection of a work in space. . . . We are here faced with definite limitations; the attraction of an "objective" work is speedily dissolved, for the psychological reactions of an audience to which music is fed by loudspeakers can hardly be avoided where the audience is deprived of the possibility of associating a sound with a gesture. Thus the arrangement in space becomes a structural necessity and represents considerably more than an appropriate setting for a more or less spectacular exhibition.[13]

The possibility of introducing dynamic alterations to the location of sounds brought a new dimension to the compositional process, for hitherto ideas of utilizing space in musical performance had almost always been associated with static distributions of players and their instruments. The movements of opera singers on stage might be considered an exception, but these are largely improvised as a visual characterization of the written drama, and have little bearing on the music itself. It is perhaps ironic that sudden movements in stereophonic recordings of such works can prove at times quite disconcerting for the listener, denied any visual contact with the dramatic action.

The position of images in a stereo- or multiphonic system is determined by the relative distribution of energy between the channels. Stereophony permits the creation of a structured spread of sound between two loudspeakers, situated ideally a few feet away from the listener on axes radiating at 45 degrees from either side of a central point. Wider angles are possible, but these lead to an increasing lack of spatial definition for more centralized images. If a sound is fed exclusively to one of the channels the image will be identified as coming from a bearing coincident with the position of the associated loudspeaker. Its distance, as already noted, will be determined by the degree of coloring achieved through reverberation, as well as its perceived amplitude. Progressive redistribution of the signal from this channel to its counterpart will cause the image to move across the listening area, a central position being established when the energy is shared equally between the two loudspeakers.

The generation of images fully surrounding a listener requires a minimum of three channels, the angles between the loudspeakers of necessity increasing from 90 degrees to 120 degrees. Image location, however, is considerably improved by increasing the number of channels to four, allowing retention of the 90° axes. The engineers at Cologne soon realized the desirability of the latter arrangement and quadraphonic projection soon became established as the preferred extension of stereophony, pending the development of other multichannel formats.

The decision to locate the fourth speaker in the ceiling for Poullin's system in

Paris was notable for its introduction of vertical movement into the location of sound images. Such an arrangement, nevertheless, is rarely employed today, mainly as the result of pressure from the commercial recording industry which has favored a two-dimensional approach to surround-sound presentation, not least on the grounds of practicality in the domestic environment.

In a modern studio, a variety of techniques are employed for moving sound sources between channels, both mechanical and electronic. A simple rotary control is all that is required to pan a single sound between two channels. Rotation between three or four channels is a more complicated task, involving the manipulation of several control functions simultaneously. One popular arrangement presents the user with a joystick, which is used to steer the sound image over the entire listening area.[14] One ingenious method for automated panning was devised at Cologne during the late 1950s. Four microphones were positioned at 90° intervals around a rotating table, the latter supporting a single loudspeaker with a particularly directional horn. Sounds fed to the latter could then be passed from one microphone to the next in either direction, the captured signals being distributed to the appropriate output channels.

The practical problems encountered in using a single sine wave generator as the exclusive source of electronic material led to considerable frustration, especially amongst the younger composers at Cologne, who were less inclined to follow the strict doctrines of Eimert. Their resultant reappraisal of the potential of other sound sources generated the first major challenge to the establishment. It seemed clear to the new school that there were no overriding reasons for always resorting to first principles when embarking on an electronic composition. Where existing spectra from harmonic generators could usefully serve particular synthesis routines there was little purpose in increasing the complexity of the technical process unnecessarily.

Clearly the sheer diversity of compositional ideas precluded the possibility of a single unified aesthetic for electronic music. There was a marked tendency, however, to adopt hierarchical procedures in preparing and structuring sound material, such that the processes of composition became increasingly concerned with the manipulation of earlier defined complexes, or "macros." In traditional music-writing, individual instruments are in a sense treated as macros, for they offer a specific range of functional characteristics determined at the point of their construction. Eimert's doctrines are to be commended for their challenge to the assumption that the "instrument" provided the only philosophical basis for musical composition. Few composers, however, were willing to reject the basic concept of a composite sound source, offering a suitably structured range of functional characteristics. The wind of change, thus, was directed toward a more flexible environment for studio working, where composers might be free to define their own terms of reference, freely drawing upon an expanded range of basic resources.

The electronic source that attracted the greatest interest at this time was the square wave generator, for it transpired that a simple development of its circuitry transformed the device into a powerful source of compound timbres. In essence, a conventional square wave consists of an electronic timing circuit that switches a steady voltage supply on and off at regular intervals, the speed of switching determining the frequency of the resultant note:

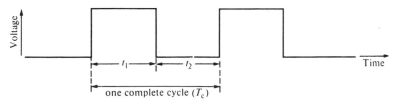

Figure 19

By varying the proportions $t_1 : t_2$, such that the overall cycle time T_c $(t_1 + t_2)$ remains constant, a change in timbre may be produced without any alteration to the fundamental pitch of the note, for example, an increase of t_2 at the expense of t_1 could lead to the following:

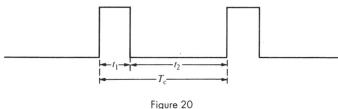

Figure 20

Aurally, the effect on the raw sound is a squeezing out of the strong lower-order harmonics, to leave their weaker higher relatives increasingly exposed. At the extreme case of $t_2 = T_c$, where $t_1 = 0$, the sound disappears altogether. The possibilities of different timbres increase significantly if the generator provides control over groups of impulses, rather than single pulse cycles. A double impulse generator provides the simplest example of this development:

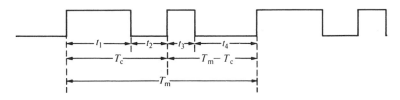

Figure 21

T_c (the first complete on/off cycle) no longer determines the fundamental pitch of the note, for there is a new master-cycle time T_m. T_c thus becomes a secondary centre to T_m, with a complement $T_m - T_c$. Further, the timbres of these pitch components are determined by the ratios of $t_1 : t_2$, and $t_3 : t_4$. A facility to adjust t_1, t_2, t_3, and t_4 independently thus creates a versatile source of compound spectra. Triple- or multiple-impulse generators merely require the addition of further timing circuits into the oscillator loop. One version, favored at Cologne, is known as a burst generator. This consists of a modified square wave generator that may be interrupted at regular intervals to create pulse trains, for example:

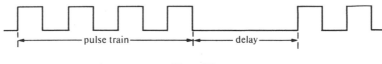

Figure 22

One special feature associated with the production of square waves and their derivatives has so far escaped attention. All the other electronic wave shapes discussed produce functions that are constantly changing in value with respect to time. When these are transformed into acoustical waves via a loudspeaker the cone of the latter is continuously moving in or out, pushing or pulling the surrounding air to set up pressure patterns that radiate to the ears of the listener. In the case of a square wave, the function is merely an alternation between two steady voltage states. This causes the loudspeaker cone to jump in and out between two static points of displacement. The air is thus energized by the transient act of switching, no information being transmitted during the intervening time intervals.

If the repetition rate is sufficiently fast the static periods are of little consequence. At lower speeds, extending down into the subaudio range, however, an interesting possibility arises. Instead of alternating between fixed voltage levels and applying these directly to the loudspeaker, the switching process itself may be used as a treatment for other signals. The alternate blocking and passing of an audio signal is an important studio technique, already demonstrated in discussing the tape-controlled ring and timbre modulators installed at Cologne. Direct electronic switching merely awaited development of the appropriate technology. Although this may be classified under the general heading of amplitude modulation its special characteristics have merited the descriptive term "gating." At subaudio speeds the ear will follow the periodicity of the gating function as a rhythmic articulation. As the speed is increased, the transient characteristics become progressively more significant, first merging with, and then masking, the source signal.

The significance of these processes was discovered during the middle and late 1950s, powerfully enhancing the range of synthesis techniques. In addition to electronic impulse generation and signal gating, similar procedures involving the manipulation of magnetic tape were explored in earnest. Cutting out selected sections and substituting equivalent lengths of blank tape leads to a physical gating of a recording. Playing the modified versions at different speeds will then vary both the rate of gating and the overall pitch of the processed material. Alternating between fragments of two different sounds, or juxtaposing extracts of several sounds, spliced into a loop, opens up further possibilities, for the resultant timbres are influenced both by the merging of the components and also by the pulse characteristic produced by the transition from one sound to another. Such a technique, it will be recalled, had been used for generating the source material for Stockhausen's *Studie II*. The primary drawbacks were the considerable time required in preparation and the impossibility of changing the gating characteristics dynamically. Nevertheless, the process could be serially organized, if so desired, and the loops once prepared proved powerful sources of material.

The increasing desire for compositional flexibility eventually forced a move away from "cut and stick" techniques for material preparation. The play-erase-record head arrangement for building up sound complexes on tape loops was a significant break with this tradition, for such a technique of necessity involved a human performance element, reacting to and controlling the aggregation of events. Stockhausen's *Gesang der Jünglinge* (1955–6) proved to be a major turning point in the artistic development of the studio, for against all the teachings of the establishment at this time the piece was structured around recordings of a boy's voice, treated and integrated with electronic sounds.

Stockhausen's interest in phonetics stemmed from his earlier contacts with Meyer-Eppler, who, as noted earlier, had continued to research into the characteristics of speech and aural perception. The innate characteristics of such material inspired a fascination with its potential as compositional material, and he accordingly set to work to create a continuum between electronic imitations of phonemes and naturally recorded speech. Cutting up progressively shorter extracts of the latter produced most interesting results, for the events thus isolated displayed remarkably stable spectral features, some approximating to tones, others to noise. Such elements provided a meeting point with electronically produced sounds, and the possibility of synthesizing speech characteristics or developing new structures around specific elements.

Thus his electronic sources were no longer treated as static, totally determined quantities, for the need to inspire living qualities into the material demanded the use of techniques that produced dynamically variable and conveniently malleable spectra. Macro-generating procedures such as impulse generation and modulation were thus of primary importance. The use of naturally produced source material was taken a stage further in Ernst Krenek's *Pfingstoratorium—Spiritus Intelligentiae, Sanctus* (1955–6). This piece freely combined electronic note mixtures and noise spectra with both spoken and sung material, the latter clearly echoing the era of plainsong and modal polyphony. It was Stockhausen's *Kontakte* (1959–60), however, which provided the most important turning point in the studio's development, for the piece combined an all-electronic tape with live parts for piano and percussion.

Stockhausen was at pains to develop a strong sense of integration between the electronic sounds and the resonant qualities of the live instruments. This demanded the infusion of an even greater feeling of naturalism into his synthetic textures, to an extent where the intrinsic barrier between the two spheres became essentially transparent. Such an objective was not achieved by resorting to the crude technique of electronic imitation so detested by Eimert. On the contrary, the integrity of the tape part is such that it functions, and may indeed be performed on its own without any obvious exposure of its links with the chosen instruments. The points of "contact" are far more subtle, built on common acoustical features that act to unify the dissimilar elements when they become integrated as a single aural experience.

Impulse techniques figure prominently in this piece. In an apparent contradiction to the trend suggested earlier in a piece such as *Gesang der Jünglinge* the synthesis procedures were meticulously specified throughout, little being left to chance interactions of electronic devices. A closer examination of the construction score (no such document exists for *Gesang der Jünglinge*) reveals that considerable experimentation took place during the early stages of composition, subjective assessment thus playing a primary role in determining the generative routines. Further, the application of his concepts of "moment form" led to a self-regulated freedom of material within the overall ordered structure. Sounds thus could evolve as if part of a separate existence, evaluated for their instantaneous value rather than as consequences of and antecedents to surrounding events.

From the philosophical angle *Kontakte* illustrates very clearly the powerful continuum that may be created between the duration structures of events and the timbre of the events themselves. In discussing impulse generation a little earlier a basic relationship was established between the timing of components in a cyclic pattern and the resultant quality of the sound produced. At subaudio speeds, the components become events in their own right, the "atomic" structure thus being revealed as a rhythmic force.

About seventeen minutes into the piece a passage occurs in which the interdependence of these two aspects is dramatically demonstrated: both piano and percussion fall silent, heralding the appearance, like an airplane falling out of the sky, of a rasping, twisting stream of sound. This strident intruder spirals down until its pitch characteristic becomes transformed into an ever-slowing succession of sharp clicks, the very components of the original sound.

Initially these clicks are very dry, producing a sound similar to that obtained from a wood block when struck with a hard object. These clicks are then smoothed and extended by gradually adding an element of reverberation, resulting in a growing sense of a pitch based on the note E below middle C, which happens to be the "wolf" or most resonant frequency of a grand piano. This pitch is then echoed by the piano and the xylophone, the resultant merging of timbres providing perhaps the most poignant point of contact in the whole work. This process of gradual transformation is not yet finished, however, for as the pulses blur into one another a fresh stream of sound is heard emerging from the background, echoing the higher resonant frequencies of the former like a ringing cluster of finely filtered noise components.

Other composers have rarely approached such a thorough mastery of the techniques of sound synthesis. The dangers of allowing technology to dominate creativity rather than the reverse have already been hinted at, and this piece provides a useful point of reference when evaluating the benefits of the increasingly sophisticated technical resources that were to follow.

By the early 1960s, several composers had contributed to the artistic output of the Cologne studio. In addition to the works already discussed, the following are of note, all associated with the first decade of operation: Herbert Brün, *Anepigraphe* (1958); Eimert, *Etude über Tongemische* (1953–4), *Fünf Stücke* (1955–6), *Zu Ehren von Igor Stravinsky* (1957), *Variante einer Variation von Anton Webern* (1958), *Selektion I* (1959–60), *Epitaph für Aikichi Kuboyama* (1960–2), and *Sechs Studien* (1962); Bengt Hambraeus, *Doppelrohr II* (1955); Hermann Heiss, *Elektronische Komposition 1* (1954); Mauricio Kagel, *Transición I* (1958–60); Gottfried Michael Koenig, *Klangfiguren I* (1955), *Klangfiguren II* (1955–6), *Essay* (1957–8), *Suite* (1961), and *Terminus I* (1961–2); Gyorgy Ligeti, *Glissandi* (1957) and *Artikulation* (1958); and Henri Pousseur, *Seismogramme I und 11* (1954).

The very titles of these pieces give an indication of the strong interest in serially ordered procedures in sound synthesis. The desire to adopt more flexible approaches to compositional procedure, however, fueled the earlier-noted move away from the strict dogma of the earliest years. Eimert was not unmoved by this pressure, his *Epitaph für Aikichi Kuboyama,* for example, followed the vogue for exploring the use of phonetics by including a part for a speaker, complementing the use of speech sounds for the tape itself. More radical changes in outlook, nevertheless, heralded the time for a change in directorship, and in 1963 Stockhausen replaced Eimert as head of the Cologne studio. Work began immediately on a long-overdue reconstruction of the studio, the most major change being the expansion of facilities into two interlinked production rooms, one equipped with the sound-generation and processing devices and the other with a comprehensive range of recording and playback facilities. The latter arrangement permitted live material to be recorded in suitable surroundings without recourse to one of the main production studios, otherwise heavily committed to tasks of day-to-day broadcasting. In practical terms, at least, the techniques of *musique concrète* and *elektronische Musik* thus became formally recognized as complementary facets of electronic music.

4

Milan and Elsewhere in Europe

The breaking down of the dogmatic barriers established between the Cologne and the Paris studios was underpinned by the establishment of another important studio at Milan in 1955 by Radio Audizioni Italiane (RAI), co-founded by Luciano Berio and Bruno Maderna. This center, although clearly influenced by the design of the Cologne studio, was created to serve the needs of the Italian schools of composition, reflecting far more catholic tastes than those associated with either of its forebears. The majority of composers thus paid little attention to the philosophical implications of using or avoiding the use of microphones in the production of material, for they were far more interested in the perceived characteristics of sound structures than the formalistic principles by which they were obtained.

Berio, writing in the periodical *Score* (March 1956), noted that:

> Thus far the pursuit of the other Studios has been classified in terms of *musique concrète* and "electronic music" which have become debatable definitions from today's armchair perspective since they seem to have been coined partly from retarded-futuristic pioneerism, partly to be "dissociated from the rabble" and partly from a simple and legitimate desire to identify the objects of our daily discourse. In the long run, what really counts is the approach itself in its purest conception: it establishes an element of continuity in the

general picture of our musical culture and is not to be identified only with its technical means but also with the inner motivation of our musical evolution.[1]

The pieces produced in this studio during the late 1950s and early 1960s included Berio, *Mutazioni* (1955), *Perspectives* (1957), *Thema-Omaggio a Joyce* (1958), *Différences* (1958–60), *Momenti* (1960), and *Visage* (1961); Maderna, *Notturno* (1956), *Syntaxis* (1957), and *Continuo* (1958); Luigi Nono, *Omaggio a Emilio Vedova* (1960); André Boucourechliev, *Etude I* (1956) and *Texte 1* (1958); Pousseur, *Scambi* (versions I and II) (1957); and John Cage, *Fontana Mix* (1958–9). A predominant feature in these works is an overriding preoccupation with texture and sonority. In an almost surreal manner sound clusters built both from conglomerations of sine tones and streams of filtered noise become the very life force of the compositional process, defining their own structures and relationships to one another.

This freedom of expression provided a powerful connection with contemporary styles of Italian instrumental composition, concerned likewise with the exploitation of color and sonority. The Milan school provided cogent answers to the problems of the early Cologne works and the naïveté of the first excursions into *musique concrète*. Berio's *Différences* illustrates how the natural sound world can be subtly enlarged by the skilful use of electronic processing. The piece is a quintet for flute, clarinet, harp, viola, and cello, to which is added a part for tape, consisting of a manipulation of previously recorded instrumental material. The latter appears after an exposition by the instruments alone, acting as a powerful force in the development of sonorities as the piece unfolds. Speed transposition, modulation, and the use of filtering to make textures more remote thus become primary features of the electronic process.

Speech, too, became a primary source of interest to composers at Milan. Particular attention was paid to the continuum that may be created between the rich but unintelligible timbres obtained from treated phonemes (the smallest units of speech) and the sharply structured and meaningful groupings of untreated phonemes that create words and phrases. The ability to play on the processes of human understanding by regulating the degree of perceptive consciousness provided a primary means of sharpening the ear of the listener to explore and evaluate the unfamiliar world of electronic sound. The immediacy of this approach broke free from the structuralism of the early Cologne school in a manner that was most appealing.

Berio's *Thema* is based entirely on a manipulation of a short text taken from James Joyce's *Ulysses*.[2] After an unaltered reading of the entire passage lasting just under two minutes, the piece develops as a growing dissolution of the original text by fragmentation, overlaying, and variations of the vocal timbre via processes of filtering. The text readily lent itself to a manipulation of onomatopoeic elements such as "chips," "smack," "trilling," and "hiss," considerable play being made on the noise quality associated with "s" sounds. Alliterative elements, too, provided a tantalizing focus of attention: for example, "a veil awave," "blew, blue, bloom," and "jingle, jaunted, jingling." His *Visage* went several stages further, technically, integrating phonemes with streams of filtered noise and amalgams of oscillator tones, enhanced by the application of modulation processes. Here the play on our perceptive skills is all the more intriguing, for with the exception of the Italian word "parole" (word), which emerges from ghostly mutations only on the rarest of occasions, no semantically meaningful combinations of phonemes are used. Syllables such as DA, ST, FER, and SA abound, combining to produce nonsense speech, which merges with nonverbal sounds of human communication such as gabbles, laughs, moans, and sobs. Such constant inferences of human emotions form a powerful central theme. The work contrasts sharply with Schaeffer and Henry's *Symphonie pour un homme seul*, where the expression of such characteristics is for the most part masked by the immediacy of the described actions. In the stage version of *Visage* the original vocalist, Cathy Berberian, added a visual aspect by dressing as an old woman in gray rags, initially huddled in a heap in almost total darkness. As the piece unfolds, a cold light grows around her, and, as if in the guise of a supernatural apparition, the body untwists until the face is revealed for an instant before descending to the gloom from whence it came.

Pousseur's *Scambi* is an example of an electronic work that may be varied in its mode of performance. The tape is split up into several sections that may be freely permuted. The sole source of material is white noise, treated to subtractive synthesis via filters. The resulting frequency bands are then gated and overlaid as a montage, creating agitated mobiles of sound.

The technical facilities at Milan were extensive for this time, and for a short period this studio was to be the most comprehensively equipped in Europe. It was clear both to Berio, as director, and the system designer, Alfredo Lietti, that commercial electronic equipment was not always ideally suited to musical applications, and as a consequence the majority of the devices were custom-designed. Lietti, writing in the periodical *Elettronica* in 1956, noted that:

> The engineer who is to design the equipment must first of all consult with the musician so as to obtain a clear picture of the various requirements. Here certain characteristics must be overcome which arise from the different trainings received by engineers and musicians respectively, and the different terms they normally employ.
>
> Consider electronic music, for example. The musician may have a clear idea of the sound he desires to obtain, but, of course, it is a musical idea. The engineer, however, is interested in the physical data of the sound and whether it can be produced electronically. Obviously the difficulty can only be resolved by an effort at mutual understanding.[3]

The electronic sound sources consisted of nine high precision sine-wave generators, a white-noise generator, an impulse generator, and a modified Ondes Martenot. The provision of nine sine-wave generators was a considerable improvement over the single master generator offered at Cologne, for it permitted live manipulation of frequency complexes, a facility very much to the advantage of the composer. Special fine-tuning controls were fitted to facilitate accurate frequency selection, and the amplitude of each generator could be adjusted from a central control panel. A cathode ray oscilloscope was also available to provide a graphic display of the synthesized material.

The manipulation of material was greatly enhanced by the provision of a generous array of mono, stereo, and four-track recorders. The treatment devices consisted of ring modulators, amplitude modulators, a reverberation chamber, a tape-head echo unit, two oscillator-controlled variable-speed tape recorders, various high-pass/low-pass/band-pass filters, and an octave filter bank connected to a wave analyser. The latter device not only provided a visual display of the frequency components present at the output, it also could be employed as an extremely powerful band-pass filter in its own right, reducing octave-filtered sound material to bandwidths as narrow as 2 Hz.

The two variable-speed tape recorders were each fitted with special devices that permitted not only normal pitch/duration transpositions but also, within certain limits, the variation of either of these basic characteristics independently. This modification was developed by Springer at the firm Telefonbau und Normalzeit and later became commercially available as the Springer Machine or Tempophon.[4] The basis for this system was a rotating arrangement of four playback heads set at 90 degrees to each other, forming the periphery of a special capstan.

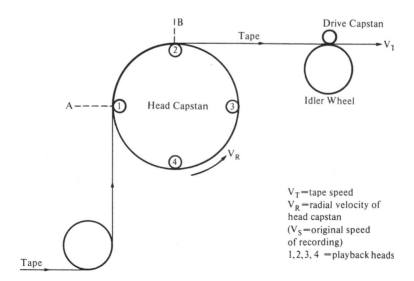

V_T = tape speed
V_R = radial velocity of head capstan
(V_S = original speed of recording)
1, 2, 3, 4 = playback heads

Figure 23

If the drive capstan and the head capstan are both rotated, information from the original material will be reproduced as a series of consecutive samples drawn from each of the playback heads in turn. For the output to appear continuous a certain degree of overlapping between samples is required, and as may be seen from the diagram opposite the transport is arranged so that at the point of changeover the succeeding head makes contact with the tape just before the preceding head drops out.

It is possible to arrange for the head capstan to remain stationary, that is, $V_r = 0$. If V_t is thus set equal to V_s, the pitch and duration content of the original material will be reproduced exactly. If the drive capstan and the head capstan are varied such that $V_t + V_r = V_s$, the speed of the heads relative to the tape will remain constant while the absolute speed of the tape itself and the duration of the recorded material will be altered. The rotating heads thus extract "snapshot" samples of sound from the traveling tape and reproduce these at their correct pitches. The machine also may be employed in a more extreme fashion by varying the speeds of both drives quite independently, changing both pitch and duration. If the tape is stationary and the heads rotated, for example, the information recorded on a small section of tape (between A and B in the diagram) may be frozen as a continuous sound, varying in pitch as a direct function of the capstan speed.

The fidelity of sound produced from this device was unfortunately rather poor, for the head design limits the frequency response and the process of breaking up analog sound into discrete segments often results in considerable distortion at the point of changeover from one head to the next. The machine, nevertheless, usefully served the requirements of a number of composers at Milan and elsewhere, anticipating far more sophisticated approaches to the same processes of time compression and expansion offered by modern digital technology. The Cologne studio, among others, purchased a Springer machine in the late 1950s, and Eimert used the instrument extensively in preparing his composition *Epitaph für Aikichi Kuboyama*.

The Milan studio, like those at Paris and Cologne, continued to exert a major influence on the artistic development of the medium throughout the 1960s. The veritable explosion of activity during this decade, however, was to divert attention from the uniqueness of these institutions and encourage a cross-fertilisation of ideas, both compositional and technical. Already by the beginning of this period a number of centres had been established, not only in Europe but also in Russia and Japan. Developments in America and Canada, too, were well under way, and these will be studied in the next chapter. Some of these studios had only a relatively short life, for example Geneva (1959–62), Eindhoven (1957–60), and Munich (1957–66). The majority, however, became centers of lasting significance, for example, APELAC, Brussels (1958), Berlin (1962), Gent (1962), Stockholm (1964), Tokyo (1956), Warsaw (1957), and Utrecht (1961).

Developments were few and far between in Great Britain during the 1950s and early 1960s. The establishment of a Radiophonic Workshop by the British Broadcasting Corporation (BBC) in London in 1958 could have provided a major focal point for British electronic music. The unenlightened artistic policy of the Music Department at the BBC, however, was to direct otherwise, for the studio was required to serve the day-to-day needs of the radio and television drama groups, leaving little time for serious composition. The principal composing members of the studio staff, Daphne Oram, Desmond Briscoe, and Delia Derbyshire, thus experienced a working environment quite different from that enjoyed by their continental counterparts, and with the notable exception of Roberto Gerhard, few other composers were granted access to the facilities. Artistic advance was thus left largely in the hands of a few spirited pioneers such as Tristram Cary, struggling with little or no financial help to establish private studios of their own.

These barriers to creative development were finally circumvented with the advent of voltage control technology, a revolution in which British imagination and entrepreneurial skills were to play an important part. The initiative for this development, however, was to come from America, and it is to activities on that side of the Atlantic that attention must now be turned.

America

Events in America after the Second World War followed quite different paths from those in Europe, primarily because of a lack of institutional support during the early years. Indeed, until the mid-1950s, no major systems of lasting significance were constructed, many so-called studios consisting merely of a collection of tape recorders and interconnecting wires assembled in a back room or, at best, commercial recording systems leased for experimentation. Despite this general lack of resources, several composers managed to investigate the creative possibilities of manipulating sounds recorded on tape.

In 1948, two recording engineers working in New York, Louis and Bebe Barron, began to experiment with the medium, playing recordings of instruments backward and forward and investigating the effects of splicing out selected elements and juxtaposing others. John Cage became interested in their work and in 1951 gathered together a group of musicians and technical advisers for the purpose of making music directly on to tape. The composing members of the group consisted of Cage, the Barrons, Earle Brown, Morton Feldman, David Tudor, and Christian Wolff, and for the next two years they worked in the Barrons's studio developing a project that became known as "Music for Magnetic Tape."

Apart from *Heavenly Menagerie* (1951), *For an Electronic Nervous System No. 1* (1953), and some background music for films prepared by the Barrons themselves, the only complete works produced during this period were: Cage, *Imaginary Landscape No. 5* (1951–2) and *Williams Mix* (1952), and Wolff, *For Magnetic Tape* (1952–3). These compositions explored many of the techniques associated with *musique concrète* and to a certain extent *elektronische Musik*, but musically they were motivated by rather different aims. Cage in particular was concerned with exploring principles of indeterminacy: *Williams Mix* and *Imaginary Landscape No. 5* were based on "I Ching" chance operations, involving an elaborate series of tape-splicing and looping routines.

The source material for the former work consisted of about six hundred recordings prepared from six categories of sounds: basic electronic sounds, manually produced sounds including instrumental sources, wind-produced sounds including singing, city sounds, country sounds, and quiet sounds amplified to levels comparable with the rest of the material. The resultant succession of haphazard events creates a powerful impact on the ear of the unsuspecting listener. The intention was to provoke a positive reaction to such a kaleidoscope of disorder, shaking the protective assuredness of traditional musical tastes and expectations and impelling the listener to search actively for plausible associations amongst the diverse events. In complete contrast to the early Cologne works, *Williams Mix* forces a level of communication by its very assault on traditional values, without any pretence to provide an alternative aesthetic that may be safely assessed from a distance. This challenge to the normal detachment of audiences is made all the more pointed by the inclusion of cheers, jeers, and applause toward the end of the piece, as if the composer is assessing the performance of the listener, rather than vice versa.

The project terminated in 1953 and the composers went their separate ways. Brown and Feldman continued their investigations for a time at the Rangertone Studios, in Newark, New Jersey, producing *Octet 1* (for eight loudspeakers) and *Intersection* respectively in the same year. Only Tudor failed to produce a work at this time. Brown subsequently traveled to Paris and continued his work there. Cage continued to work at various private studios in New York, traveling to Milan and producing *Fontana Mix* in 1959 before settling down to work both at Brandeis University and at Stony Point, New York, where in collaboration with David Tudor he became preoccupied with the use of electronic equipment in live performance.

Fontana Mix in many respects was a direct consequent of *Williams Mix*, the elements of indeterminacy being derived from graphic designs rather than detailed computations of chance routines. Speech sounds played an important part in the compositional process, and the technical sophistication of the Milan studio facilitated an altogether more compelling piece. Two subsequent works were based on *Fontana Mix*, both signifying Cage's progression toward live improvisation techniques and away from the permanence of studio-based compositions. *Aria with Fontana Mix* completed at Milan in the same year adds a part for a live vocalist. The score for the latter consists of indeterminate arrangements of phonemes from five languages (English, French, Italian, Armenian, and Russian) with the addition of several extramusical sounds such as cheek slapping and finger-clicking. Ten different vocal styles are demanded, indicated in the score by colors. The choice of these styles is left to the performer, adding further to the indeterminacy of the result. *Fontana Mix-Feed* (New York, 1964) belongs more properly to a discussion of live electronic music. The work uses a group of percussion instruments fitted with contact microphones, the signals from the latter being amplified to such an extent that they feed back from the loudspeakers to the microphones via the instruments. The result is an effect similar to the "howl around" feedback of a badly adjusted public address system.

Music for Magnetic Tape existed for only a limited period as an artistic movement before diversifying into a series of individual objectives beholden to no particular studio philosophy, but freely drawing from, and contributing to, the increasing ferment of ideas.

While Cage and his associates were experimenting in the Barrons's studio, Vladimir Ussachevsky, shortly to be joined by Otto Luening, was pursuing another line of investigation. Superficially their experiments, which became generally known as "Tape Music," closely related to those of Music for Magnetic Tape, for both approaches were based on the use of the tape recorder as a tool for registering and manipulating sound material. Closer examination reveals a marked difference in musical outlook, for both Luening and Ussachevsky were far more conservative in their attitude toward composition. In particular, they saw the tape recorder as a means of extending traditional ideas of tonality and instrumentation, rather than as a tool for creating a totally new sound world.

During 1951–2, Ussachevsky carried out a series of experiments, preparing five studies entitled *Transposition, Reverberation, Experiment, Composition,* and *Underwater Valse*. These were presented at a Composers' Forum given on 9 May 1952 in the McMillin Theater, Columbia University.[1] *Transposition* was a simple study in octave transposition using piano notes as sources. *Reverberation* was based on the application of tapehead echo, and the other pieces were arrangements of instrumental material, subjected to similar simple processes of modification. Their performance attracted considerable attention, and the composer Henry Cowell wrote an encouraging review in the *Musical Quarterly* (October 1952):

People who work experimentally with new sounds seem to have trouble in distinguishing between the material of musical composition and the compositions themselves. They are apt to rush their new sounds prematurely into pieces that are hardly creative work in the generally accepted sense, and that are easily identified as vehicles for new sounds rather than works in which these sounds form an integral part. . . . It is therefore refreshing when a composer offers his experiments frankly by that name, without confusion. Vladimir Ussachevsky did just this. . . . These were not compositions and no attempt was made to call them so. But the sounds are certainly a possible resource for composers.[2]

Luening attended the Forum and invited Ussachevsky to present his experiments at a conference of composers in Bennington, Vermont, during August 1952. Luening studied with Busoni in Zurich, Switzerland, from 1918 until 1920 and had become interested in the study of musical acoustics and instrumental design. At Bennington, Ussachevsky experimented with violin, clarinet, piano, and vocal sounds using an Ampex tape recorder, and Luening began to prepare a tape composition using a flute as the source of material. News of their work came to the attention of Oliver Daniel, who invited them to prepare a group of short compositions for inclusion in a concert to be promoted by the American Composers' Alliance at the Museum of Modern Art, New York, under the direction of Leopold Stokowski. The invitation was accepted, and Luening and Ussachevsky departed for the home of Henry Cowell at Woodstock, New York, where, using borrowed tape recorders, they prepared pieces for the first public concert of Tape Music on 28 October 1952. Four pieces were performed: Ussachevsky, *Sonic Contours*; Luening, *Invention in 12 Notes*, *Low Speed*, and *Fantasy in Space*, the last work being the product of his earlier experiments with flute sounds at Bennington.

Again the critics were encouraging in their accounts. The audience included Luciano Berio, who was especially impressed with *Sonic Contours*. These pieces made considerable use of tape techniques such as overlays (montage), tapehead echo, extreme changes of speed, and splicing, but their structures retained many recognizable tonal characteristics such as simple chords, scales, and arpeggios. The attention accorded to this recital overshadowed the work of Cage and his associates. *Williams Mix,* for example, had to wait for two years before receiving its first public performance before an unsympathetic audience at the 1954 Donaueschingen Festival, Germany. Examples of Tape Music had already been presented in Europe alongside *musique concrète* during the festival promoted by Radiodiffusion Télévision Française in Paris in April 1953. This contrast in fortunes illustrates the value of institutional support during the pioneering era, whether from universities or broadcasting organizations, both in terms of studio resources and also the acquisition of status. Acceptance of the medium as a credible art form within the broader music community proved very much harder for those who worked outside these important spheres of influence.

After their early successes, Luening and Ussachevsky began exploring the possibilities of using prepared tapes in conjunction with performing instruments. Late in 1953, Luening received a commission from the Louisville Orchestra to write a work for them, and this he accepted on the condition that he could share the venture with Ussachevsky. Permanent studio facilities were still not available, and the equipment had to be gathered together from a variety of sources. A small equipment grant from the Rockefeller Foundation facilitated the purchase of one tape recorder, but the others had to be borrowed or purchased privately. After a trial performance of *Rhapsodic Variations,* for tape recorder and orchestra at the Bennington Composers' Conference, the work was performed in public by the Louisville Orchestra on 20 March 1954 under the direction of Robert Whitney. Another commission soon followed, this time for the Los Angeles Orchestra. The work, *A Poem in Cycles and Bells*, took the form of a paraphrase of their earlier works *Fantasy in Space* and *Sonic Contours*, and in musical terms was altogether more successful, a better sense of textural integration being achieved between the instrumental parts and the prepared tape. The publicity accorded to Tape Music inspired several private studios to begin experimenting with the medium, but for the most part their activities were directed toward commercial ends, providing the background effects for films, radio, and television.

So far no mention has been made of Varèse's contributions to this embryonic phase of developments in the United States. His determined but nonetheless unsuccessful lobbying for studio facilities during the interwar period led to a deep personal crisis, starting during the late 1930s and extending for the whole of the following decade. After *Densité 21.5* for solo flute (1936), the only work produced during this period was *Étude* (1947), scored for two pianos, percussion, and mixed chorus. This was intended to form part of *Espace*, a project of immense proportions involving simultaneous performances from all the capitals of the world, mixed and coordinated via a specially arranged linkup of broadcasting stations. Sadly, this vision of a universal hymn to humanity was not to become a reality despite several attempts to attract financial and practical support.

The postwar upsurge of interest in electronic music also occurred well toward the end of his life. In 1950, for example, when he started composing again in earnest, he was already sixty-seven. It is thus hardly surprising that at such a late stage in a career characterized by continual disappointment and disillusionment with the Establishment, he should now choose to leave others to carry on the crusade for studio facilities and concentrate only on the realization of his own compositional ambitions. In a modest way, nevertheless, his parallel explorations into the possibilities of electronics made a contribution that was far more significant musically than the much-publicized early efforts of Luening and Ussachevsky.

During the late 1940s, Varèse had been formulating an idea for a piece that would interpolate passages of sound material organized on magnetic tape with live instrumental performance, and by the beginning of 1950 an outline of the work, *Déserts*, had been prepared. In the summer, he began composing the instrumental parts, completing them toward the end of 1952. During 1953, with the aid of a technical assistant, he began gathering together recordings of iron mills, saw mills, and various other factories in Philadelphia with the object of assembling material for use in the construction of the taped sections. Gradually he built up a comprehensive library of sound material, in his own private way carrying out investigations just as detailed as those of Schaeffer, working unaided with a very modest collection of taping equipment in his house in Greenwich, New York.

Boulez visited America in the winter of 1952–3, presenting *musique concrète* to New York for the first time at a special concert for the Composers' Forum, Columbia University. During his stay, the two composers met for the first time, and Boulez was thus able to give an informed account of his work on *Déserts* on return to Paris. Rumours of Varèse's work had spread to Paris some time previously, and Schaeffer himself made a rather inaccurate reference to him in his book *À la recherche d'une musique concrète* (1952):

> Varèse has dedicated himself to that poor relation of the orchestra, the percussion section. He has promoted it to orchestral status. He has added to it various effects supplied by American studios. I do not know the details: more or less electronic "Varinettes," produced I know not how, but occasionally similar to ours.[3] Varèse crosses France without stopping. This Frenchman has not had our misfortune to be a prophet in his own country. He is listened to and revered in Germany. Soon he will return to New York where he is considered Maestro.[4]

The reference to Germany concerns a series of lectures Varèse presented to the 1950 Darmstadt Summer School at the invitation of Wolfgang Steinnecke, and *Déserts* would naturally have been uppermost in his mind at this time. The association of this work with *musique concrète* is not particularly appropriate for his approach to organized sound was far more liberal, including elements that might equally be attributed to *elektronische Musik*, or Music for Magnetic Tape, or Tape Music: common to all, yet restricted by none.

In 1954, Varèse received an invitation from Schaeffer to complete the tape parts for *Déserts* in his Paris studio. In the absence of any comparable opportunities in America this was accepted, and he departed for France in late September. At the Club d'Essai he worked remarkably quickly, completing the work in barely two months. His enlightened approach to principles of sound organization took Schaeffer by surprise, for Varèse would frequently indulge in elaborate transformations, investigating whatever electronic techniques the engineers could devise.[5] The studio was ill-equipped for such operations; the use of extensive filtering or ring modulation, for example, was foreign to the still-strict doctrines of *musique concrète*.

The results were not wholly satisfactory, a combination perhaps of three factors: the relatively short period spent in preparation, the limitations of the equipment, and the immense practical problems that confront any composer encountering a complex studio system for the first time. Varèse, indeed, was to spend the next eight years trying to improve the tape, creating no fewer than four different versions. The first performance of Déserts took place in the Théâtre des Champs-Elysées on 2 December 1954, conducted by Hermann Scherchen. Forty years previously this hall had been the venue for the riotous first performance of Stravinsky's Rite of Spring, and the audience for Déserts was quite ready to demonstrate that noisy public disapproval was not quite a phenomenon of the past. Matters were made worse by the fact that the RTF were making a live transmission of the concert, which also included works composed by Mozart and Tchaikovsky. The considerable adverse publicity that followed was positive in at least one respect: the use of electronics in music was now attracting the attention of a wide if often unsympathetic audience.

After two rather more successful performances in Hamburg and Stockholm conducted by Bruno Maderna, Varèse remained in Paris for a while, returning to the United States in the spring of 1955. During May of the same year he attended an arts conference at Bennington, Vermont, presenting a lecture on his work on the 16th, and supervising the first American performance of Déserts, given in the National Guard Armory the following day. The first major presentation of the work took place on 30 November 1955 in the Town Hall, New York, and on the whole was well received. This performance could not have occurred at a more appropriate time, for the interest of institutions in supporting electronic music was just being kindled.

In June 1955, Luening and Ussachevsky had obtained a further grant of nearly $10,000 from the Rockefeller Foundation, funded through Barnard College, to investigate the state of studio facilities both at home and abroad. During a six-week tour of Europe they visited Schaeffer in Paris, Meyer-Eppler in Bonn, Eimert in Cologne, and Berio and Maderna in Milan. They were thus able to piece together a very thorough account of the work being carried out at these major centers. In Canada they discovered that developments were also well advanced. Hugh le Caine, working with the support of the Canada Research Council, had established a studio at Ottawa University in 1954, and Norman McLaren was making also useful advances in the use of optical sound-generation techniques.

By comparison, only limited progress could be identified in America. One or two universities were willing to consider giving some support to suitable ventures, but none had yet made a commitment to a major, long-term program of development. Milton Babbitt, working at Princeton University had been interested in the possibilities of electronic sound production for a number of years, instigating a series of experiments into the possibilities of handdrawn sound. A lack of support, however, led to the initiative in this field passing to Norman McLaren in Ottawa.[6] At Illinois, however, they learned of a project that was to hold a particular significance for the future, for an investigation had been started into the possible uses of computers in musical composition. This research, headed by Lejaren Hiller and Leonard Isaacson, was concerned in the first instance with the use of mathematical procedures to generate data for conventionally notated instrumental scores, but this was to herald the use of the computer itself as a means for generating sound.[7] In the latter context Luening and Ussachevsky discovered that one of the programs of research at Bell Telephone Laboratories, New Jersey, was directed toward the development of techniques for both the analysis and the synthesis of sound. These investigations were concerned not only with conventional analog approaches but also with the possibility of developing computer-based methods. This organization, as will be seen in due course, was subsequently to pioneer digital sound synthesis under the direction of Max Mathews.[8]

The work at Bell Telephone Laboratories proved to be unique. Apart from Ampex, which was involved in the design and manufacture of recording and amplification equipment, most industrial concerns were not willing even to consider supporting research and development in this field unless they could expect immediate commercial benefits.

Luening and Ussachevsky decided to take the initiative and make a formal approach to the authorities of Columbia University, with a view to establishing an electronic music studio within the Department of Music. The idea was well received, leading to a small grant for an experimental laboratory. By this stage their approaches to electronic composition were extending beyond the operational restrictions imposed by only using the tape recorder and microphone. Ussachevsky's *Piece for Tape Recorder*, produced early in 1956, for example, integrates both electronic and natural sound sources, although only limited use is made of the former.[9] The piece also incorporates two extracts from his earlier work *Sonic Contours*.

In fulfillment of their Rockefeller grant requirements, Luening and Ussachevsky prepared a comprehensive report on the state of electronic music in Europe and America. In essence they had come to the view that the development of electronic music in their country could best be assisted by directing financial support toward the university sector, where research and development could be fostered in an environment free from commercial pressures. Their recommendations were accepted in principle, and protracted discussions commenced over the most suitable course of action. Developments were to take an unexpected turn, however, for on 31 January 1956 the Radio Corporation of America demonstrated a fully self-contained sound synthesizer to a meeting of the American Institute of Electrical Engineers in New York. RCA's interest in the medium was, not new, for it had attempted to market a commercial version of the Thérémin during the 1930s. The sudden appearance of such an advanced machine was nevertheless a complete surprise, the product of rather a curious line of development that merits closer scrutiny.

The RCA synthesizer was quite different from any of the systems so far discussed, for it offered a programmable means of controlling the functions of the various devices. Ussachevsky, in particular, was keen to acquire the synthesizer for use as the basis of a studio at Columbia University, and preliminary approaches were made to several RCA executives. It soon transpired that Milton Babbitt, at Princeton University, was also interested in gaining access to the machine, and they agreed to collaborate by preparing a joint application. RCA responded by granting access to the machine, which was, at least for Babbitt, conveniently situated at their Princeton Laboratories.

The stage, meanwhile, was being set for an electronic composition that was to be of the greatest musical significance, Varèse's *Poème électronique*. In 1956, the electronics firm of Philips, based at Eindhoven, Holland, began to consider their plans for the World Fair to be held in Brussels in 1958. The company decided to construct a special pavilion and invited the distinguished architect Le Corbusier to prepare the design. Le Corbusier immediately seized on the idea of combining technology and the arts by creating not merely a building, but an environment of sound, color, and structure, reflecting the creative role that electronics and associated sciences could play in contemporary society. He collaborated with Xenakis over the preparation of mathematical models for the construction of the building itself and invited Varèse to provide the music in the form of a prepared tape, leaving the composer completely free to approach the world of sound in whatever manner he should choose.

It was thus that Varèse was finally rewarded for his years of struggle, with an opportunity to compose an electronic work that explored the projection of sound in space, an area of investigation that had inspired his ill-fated project *Espace* twenty years previously.

Like *Déserts*, the realization of this piece was to take Varese to Europe, on this occasion to the Philips Laboratories at Eindhoven. Here he enjoyed a range of facilities without precedent at that time, for a complex studio system was especially assembled for this composition, backed by a team of highly skilled electronic engineers and advisers. The resulting work reflects a style of electronic composition unique to the composer, tied in no way to any established studio conventions. The source material includes machine noises, the sound of aircraft, bells, electronically generated sounds, singers, and piano and organ sounds, subjected to elaborate processes of pitch transformation, filtering, and modification of their attack and decay characteristics. The projection of sound was achieved by employing a three-channel tape system, distributed across eleven different groups of loudspeakers, positioned in the ceiling alcoves and the walls. Visual effects, associated with the movement of sounds, were created by means of a comprehensive lighting system, which produced changing patterns of colored images.

The World Fair opened to the public on 2 May 1958 and by the time it finally closed its doors at the end of the year over two million people had visited it. *Poème électronique* was thus accorded a vast audience drawn from all over the world. News of this achievement naturally spread back to the United States, and shortly after his return to New York in the autumn of the same year a performance of the work was given in his honor in Greenwich Village. This concert, unfortunately, fell short of expectations, for when relayed in a small theater over single loudspeakers, devoid of any lighting effects, the work lost a considerable proportion of its original grandeur. This occasion was also to result in yet another disappointment. The concert was preceded by a lecture at the end of which Varèse proudly announced that the firm of Bogen-Presto, a division of the Seigler Corporation, had offered to provide him with a studio so that he could continue with his work. News of this received widespread coverage the next day in both the local and the national press, but the firm changed its mind and the offer was withdrawn.

Luening and Ussachevsky's quest for a fully equipped studio proved more successful. During 1957–8, firm proposals drawn up jointly with Babbitt were submitted to the Rockefeller Foundation requesting financial support for the establishment of a permanent center for electronic music. Initially they suggested that a University Council for Electronic Music should be established, consisting of representatives drawn from all the institutions that were already interested or involved in working in this field. The Foundation, however, did not wish to create a situation in which it might find itself faced with the prospect of sponsoring a large number of different projects, each consequently being eligible for only a small share of the total grant. The final application thus drew up a plan for a single electronic music studio to be set up between Columbia and Princeton Universities only, outlining in detail equipment and staffing requirements for a five-year initial period, after which the universities would be expected to meet recurrent expenses.

The proposal was accepted, and a grant of $175,000 was advanced in January 1959 for a Columbia-Princeton Electronic Music Center, to be situated at Columbia University, and based on the RCA synthesizer, which was to be purchased from the manufacturers. Delivery of the original Mark 1 version was soon arranged, pending its replacement by an improved Mark 2 version, delivered later in the year.

The origins of the RCA synthesizers may be traced back over a decade to the late 1940s. At this time two electronic engineers, Harry F. Olson and Herbert Belar, both employed by the company at its Princeton laboratories, became interested in the possibility of developing technological systems for both the composition and the realization of musical works. The company was sufficiently far-sighted to realize that such investigations might lead to useful advances not only in communication theory but also in areas of acoustical research, and accordingly gave them official support for their ventures.

The publication of the *Mathematical Theory of Communication* by Shannon and Weaver in 1949 inspired the engineers to embark on an elaborate project to construct a machine for musical composition, based on a system of random probability.[10] Although the acoustic output of the device was limited to the production of a monophonic progression of tones, the operating system is of some interest for it attempted to rationalize some of the creative principles involved in the processes of musical composition into a programmed series of electromechanical functions.

The basis for the composing system lay in a statistical study of the characteristics of twelve Stephen Foster folk songs. In the first instance, the occurrences of two- and three-note pitch sequences were tabulated to provide a probability table. By providing random selection routines, weighted in accordance with the probability table, pitch sequences could then be generated as the basis for synthesized tunes. Seemingly unaware of the limitations of their analytical procedures and the inadequacies of such a limited sample of data the authors surmised that a composing machine might be developed that would produce new music similar to that of Stephen Foster songs, and proceeded to build it.[11]

Doubts about the soundness of their theories are strengthened by the superficial consideration afforded to the rhythmic structure of the songs. Olson and Belar regarded this characteristic to be of secondary importance, merely incorporated into a succession of notes to make a "satisfactory" melody, and accordingly provided their own probability table for bars in 3/4 and 4/4 meter, offering just seven variations each. In an age when the computer had yet to make its mark the implementation of the system demanded the construction of an elaborate network of relays and associated valve electronics capable of assessing and interpreting logic states. The block diagram of the machine was as follows:

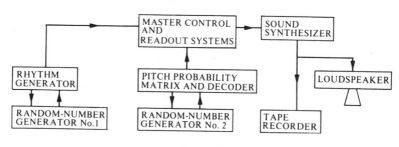

Figure 24

The output from each of the random-number generators consisted of four control lines. Each line could be set either to an "on" state (a steady voltage present) or an "off" state (no voltage present). As table 5.1 shows, a total of sixteen patterns may be generated from a group of four such lines, and providing a means of decoding is available these may be used to select sixteen different functions elsewhere in the system. This technique illustrates a simple application of binary logic, the basis of all digital computer systems:

Table 5.1   Binary Logic Table

Function Selection	Binary State of the Lines (0 = off, 1 = on)			
	1	2	3	4
1	0	0	0	0
2	0	0	0	1
3	0	0	1	0
4	0	0	1	1
5	0	1	0	0
6	0	1	0	1
7	0	1	1	0
8	0	1	1	1
9	1	0	0	0
10	1	0	0	1
11	1	0	1	0
12	1	0	1	1
13	1	1	0	0
14	1	1	0	1
15	1	1	1	0
16	1	1	1	1

The decoding system consisted of a four-element relay tree arranged as in figure 25. This diagram shows all four relays in the "off" position, providing a through connection between input no. 1 and the output. Turning any relay on causes all the switches connected to the associated relay line to change over to their alternate setting. Only one through path, however, will still be available, selected according to table 5.1.

Two such trees were required to operate the composing machine, one controlling selections from the rhythm generator, the other operating the probability matrix and decoder. In the case of the rhythm generator, a preliminary choice had to be made between 3/4 and 4/4. For each meter, seven different patterns were available for selection. Matching up the seven associated lines of control with the sixteen available function selections was achieved by connecting two or more selections to certain pattern generators, biasing the probability of choice. Assigning two selection lines to the same pattern, for example, would double the chances of that pattern being selected to odds of 2 in 16.

Operation of the probability matrix and decoder was altogether more complicated, for the selection of pitches required a dynamically changing bias in accordance with the earlier mentioned analyses of two- and three-note sequences in the source songs. As a matter of convenience, all of the latter were transposed to D major before examination. This rationalization reduced the number of possible

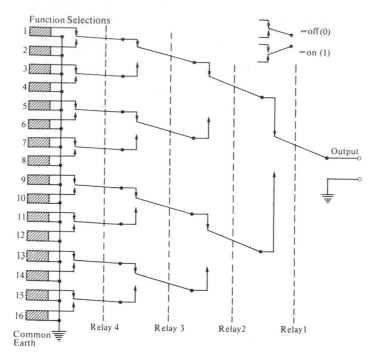

Figure 25

pitches to twelve, ranging diatonically from [musical notation] to [musical notation] with the addition of G♯ to accommodate the occasional modulation to the dominant.

All the possible two-note sequences were first identified, and recorded as key entries in a table, fifty in all. Treating each entry as the first two elements of a three-note sequence, an analysis was then made of the pitches completing the sequence on every occurrence in the source material. The statistics thus derived were tabulated as a list of pitch alternatives, along with the proportional frequency of their choice expressed in sixteenths.

Application of this table was implemented via a fifty-position stepper switch, each position being uniquely assigned to one of the fifty possible two-note sequences. On arriving at a new setting in response to the preceding cycle, the hardwired matrix would route the sixteen function-selection lines to appropriate pitch generators in accordance with the probability data. Random-number generator no. 2 would then be permitted to activate one of the lines, the pitch selection thus made being output for a duration determined by the rhythm generator. The cycle would finish by changing the two-note reference setting to the note just generated and its predecessor, ready for the next cycle.

By way of an example, if the current two-note sequence happened to be

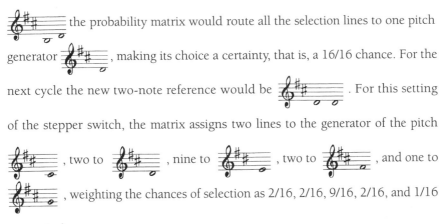 the probability matrix would route all the selection lines to one pitch generator , making its choice a certainty, that is, a 16/16 chance. For the next cycle the new two-note reference would be . For this setting of the stepper switch, the matrix assigns two lines to the generator of the pitch

, two to , nine to , two to , and one to

, weighting the chances of selection as 2/16, 2/16, 9/16, 2/16, and 1/16 respectively.

Such a machine offered considerable potential as a tool for experimenting with statistically based compositional procedures. Although today such a system can be readily simulated in computer software, at the beginning of the 1950s the digital revolution had barely begun, and in its time the Olson and Belar machine offered a unique system for creating pitch sequences. The premises on which the whole project was based cannot be allowed to pass without further comment, however, for they provide a clear example of the consequences of a serious breakdown in communication between scientists and artists concerning the essential characteristics of their respective disciplines.

Olson and Belar misunderstood the creative processes of musical composition in one important respect, for they assumed that objectively expressed characteristics derived from an analysis of a selection of a composer's output of scores could supply all the information necessary for a simulation of the intuitive processes that inspired them. Disciples of compositional theory will recognize that the machine would have been of interest to composers wishing to explore aspects of probability theory as part of their musical language, providing, of course, it could have been modified to allow easy reprogramming of the probability matrices. Such an application is quite different from that intended by Olson and Belar, for it does not presuppose the machine's capabilities to act as a substitute for the composer himself.

Coincidentally, the completion of the machine in late 1950 neatly bisects the time between completion of Schillinger's *The Mathematical Basis for the Arts* and the publication of the first few chapters of *Musiques formelles* by Xenakis, a treatise that expounds the virtues of stochastics as a basis for composing.[12] The errors of judgment displayed by Olson and Belar, however, provide a salutary warning as to the dangers that can befall the unwary experimenter in applying probability theory to the art of musical composition. Leonard Meyer, writing on the nature and limits of critical analysis in his book *Explaining Music,* succinctly pinpoints the primary reasons for the failure of the machine to synthesize "typical" melodies by Stephen Foster:

> To understand a composer's choices is to envisage the psychological-stylistic alternatives open to him at a particular point in the composition. . . . Even in the long run our most confident surmises about routes and goals may prove wrong. This is because given the particular style within which he works the composer is a *free agent*. He invents and shapes his initial musical substance—his themes, harmonic progressions, textures and the like. These have implications for subsequent events. But they do not *determine* them. . . . Determinism is a mistaken notion applied to works of art not only because implications are plural, but also because, within the style he employs, the composer may at any particular point in a piece be absolutely arbitrary. That is, he may invent and use a musical idea or relationship which has nothing to do with—was in no way implied by or dependent upon—preceding events in the piece.[13]

On the simplest level of analysis it must be clear that the composing machine was incapable of synthesizing even a songlike structure, let alone a song in the style of a particular composer. The probability mechanism, working from note to note, could not accommodate such basic considerations as tonality and the strophic structure of phrases. These conceptual shortcomings, fortunately, did not apply to their next venture, the first RCA synthesizer. Although the machine was not presented to the public until 1956, work on its construction began in early 1951, and there is evidence to suggest that the synthesizer was at least partly operational in 1952. The overall design of the completed Mark 1 version is illustrated in figure 26.

Two identical but functionally independent synthesis channels were provided by the system, each sharing a common bank of sound sources. The latter consisted of a white-noise generator and twelve electrically driven tuning-fork oscillators, designed to generate the twelve tempered pitches of the musical scale between

F♯/G♭: and F: in the form of sine tones. Selection of these

these sources and control of subsequent operations was achieved via a set of relay trees, of an identical design to those used in the composing machine. Instead of random-number generators, however, the source of control lay in a prepunched paper tape, and an associated group of brush sensors (fig. 26).

The first programmable function in each synthesis channel involved the selection of a sound-source generator via a sixteen-element relay tree, decoding the patterns contained in four punched tape columns. The three spare relay tree connections were available for the selection of additional external sources, should these

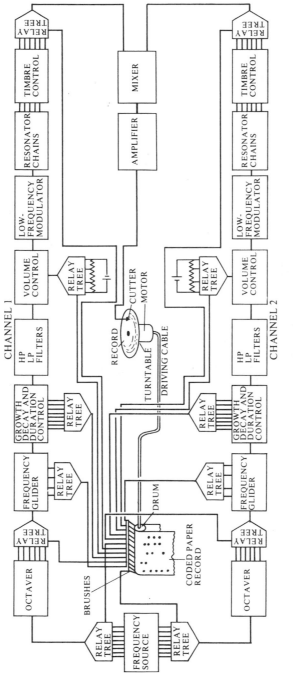

Figure 26

be required. The diagram of the frequency-selection network for one channel shows clearly how the control system was derived from its ancestor:

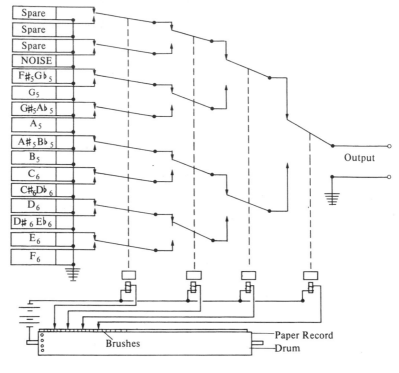

Figure 27

The next stage in the synthesis process involved the use of an octaver, bypassed only when the white noise generator or the external inputs were selected. This device, operated by an eight-element relay tree and an associated three-column punched tape record, accepted a frequency from the oscillator bank, converted the sine wave electronically into a square wave, and passed it on to a set of octave multipliers and dividers. The latter, in a manner similar to that employed in electronic organs, acted to transpose the pitches to any one of eight octave ranges in accordance with the control code, extending the range of the synthesizer from F♯/G♭:

 to F: . The wave was finally converted from a square function (composed of odd harmonics only) to a sawtooth function (composed of both odd and even harmonics).

The output of the source bank/octaver could, optionally, be connected to another device, a frequency glider, which permitted a smooth transition to be made from one pitch selection to another. Although to the user this unit appeared to act directly on the incoming sawtooth wave, in electronic terms it consisted of another self-contained sawtooth generator, directly controlled by the incoming wave through a feedback network, which could be adjusted to respond to the changes in applied frequency in different ways. Normally the glider was not connected to the punched tape control system, and a single characteristic set manually via preset controls on the device for the duration of a synthesis run. By disconnecting one of the other control functions, however, a total of eight different types of glide could be programmed via a relay tree and three punched tape columns. The following are typical of the types of frequency glide obtainable, ranging from a progressive pitch change to a damped oscillatory pattern:

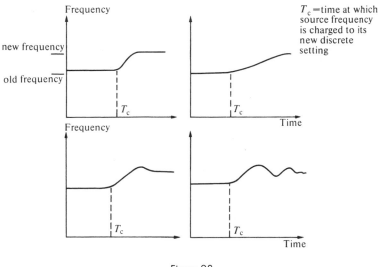

Figure 28

The frequency glider functioned as the last device in the generation section of the synthesis chain, all signals then passing to the processing stages. The first device in the latter chain consisted of an envelope shaper, triggered and controlled via the control tape. Up to eight different attack and decay patterns could be selected via a relay tree and three punched tape columns. Each selection involved a different set of time constants, creating attack times that varied from 1 millisecond to 2 seconds and decay times ranging from 4 milliseconds to 19 seconds.

In addition to the production of simple attack and decay functions based on exponential characteristics, for example:

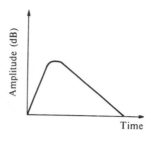

Figure 29

Functions of a more artificial nature also could be specified. Furthermore, by changing the punched tape code during the course of an envelope the functions could be combined to produce hybrid responses:

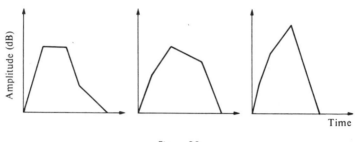

Figure 30

The next device in the processing chain consisted of a pair of filters supplying high-pass, low-pass, or in combination band-pass characteristics according to the position of a manually operated selector switch. These suffered from one particular disadvantage, for they could not be made to track the incoming signal automatically. Consequently, it was not possible to provide a consistent shaping for a sequence of different pitches.

The output from these filters passed to a programmable, general amplitude control system. This device provided a total of sixteen different degrees of attenuation via a relay tree and four punched tape columns. Presets regulated the attenuation range over which the device operated, and the circuits were designed to produce equal steps of intensity between the two selected limits.

The next stage in the processing chain provided a facility for the production of low-speed modulation. The device consisted of an amplitude modulator operating at a frequency of between 6 and 7 Hz with a shallow modulation pattern approximating to a square wave. This inclusion of a vibrato generator in the RCA synthesizer is indicative of Olson and Belars's original intention, to provide a machine capable of imitating conventional instrumental sounds, rather than a more flexible system for the exploration of new timbres.

The last device in the processing chain consisted of a bank of eight resonators, employed to augment the timbre-shaping facility offered by the earlier described pair of filters. Each resonator consisted of an amplifier fitted with a regulated feedback loop that could be tuned to respond to excitation at a particular frequency. The effect on any applied signal was to boost frequency components at or very close to the point of resonance, creating a band-pass type of response. By reducing the overall gain of the amplifier so that the output emerged at a more normal system level, the circuit acted as an attenuator for frequencies outside the resonance area, the sharpness of the response being determined by the degree of feedback. By means of a toggle switch the resonator response could be inverted to produce a band-reject characteristic, attenuating instead of boosting the frequency band. The frequency of resonance itself for each unit could be set manually to a range of settings in steps of approximately one third of an octave. Selection of the units was programmed via a relay tree and four punched tape columns, permitting the manipulation of up to sixteen different preset combinations.

The master control system provided the primary means of communication between the composer and the synthesizer in the realization of a work. It is clear from the preceding description that manual adjustments to device controls were necessary at several strategic points in the processing chain. These, however, were essentially preoperative functions, determining the range of functional characteristics on which the programmed sequence of instructions would draw.

The punched tape was 15 inches wide, carrying device control information coded in thirty-six columns, eighteen for each channel, as follows:

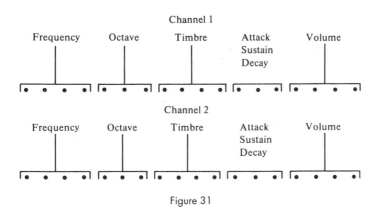

Figure 31

The tape was perforated on both edges to engage with matching teeth on a circular drum, the latter being linked to a motor with a variable-speed drive that transported the tape at speeds ranging from two to eight inches per second. A key punching system permitted the composer to enter his instructions as a sequence of punched-hole patterns. Duration thus became a function of distance measured along the paper tape, according to the speed at which it was played. The punching system ensured that the holes were spaced equidistantly, the tape advancing a fixed distance after each complete row of punches had been entered.

The tape-reading system consisted of a set of spring-loaded brushes, which pressed down on to the surface of the paper. When a hole passed under a brush, the latter made electrical contact with the drum beneath, activating the relay line assigned to that particular column. Several springs were connected to each brush to ensure that electrical contact was maintained until the tape had moved to the position for the next punched row. If a new hole was detected the circuit remained complete. If no hole was encountered, however, electrical contact was broken and the associated relay returned to its "off" state.

The output from the two synthesis channels could be monitored via a pair of loudspeakers and also recorded directly on to disc. The choice of such a cumbersome recording medium, where a groove once cut could not be reused, contrasts sharply with the programming flexibility of the punched tape input system. The Radio Corporation of America, however, as a company with an extensive investment in the gramophone industry, was naturally interested in the development of specially designed disc-cutting equipment for the synthesizer. It also should be appreciated that the use of the tape medium was still undervalued in many branches of the recording industry at this time, and there was a tendency to cling to and seek improvements in traditional techniques rather than explore new ones. Another factor also may have influenced this choice: the use of a gramophone turntable, with its comparatively low speed of rotation and high inertia, facilitated the use of a direct-drive system, powered via a flexible cable from the motor employed to transport the punched tape. This simple linkage between the control and the recording systems ensured accurate mechanical synchronization between the sequential instructions supplied by the former and the acoustical product registered by the latter.

The cutting lathe employed a 16-inch lacquer rotated at 33⅓ revolutions per minute. Instead of a single groove, six concentric tracks could be cut, each providing a maximum of about 3 minutes' recording time. A second cutting lathe, driven by the same motor, provided a means of blending the six channels together as a single track on a new lacquer, using a set of six playback pickups and a mixing system. By repeating this process, this secondary lacquer could be used to record thirty-six channels of information, supplied from six primary lacquers. Similarly, six secondary lacquers could be employed to provide an aggregate of 216 channels on a single tertiary lacquer.

The 3 minutes of recording time per channel available on each disc compared slightly unfavorably with a maximum control tape time of about 4 minutes, when the latter was run at its slowest speed. The assembly of complete pieces involved the playing of a sequence of completed lacquers alternately on the two drives, considerable manual dexterity being required to ensure smooth joins between sections.

Despite the mechanical ingenuity of the RCA engineers the lathe cutting system proved wasteful on lacquers and extremely cumbersome for the user, and it was unfortunate that the Mark 2 version of the synthesizer delivered to the Columbia-Princeton Electronic Music Center in 1959 still employed the same system of recording. Action was quickly taken to overcome this shortcoming, and within a matter of months the engineers at Colombia had replaced the direct-drive disc cutter with an electronically synchronized four-channel Ampex tape recorder.

The design of the Mark 2 version was clearly influenced by the experience gained in using its predecessor for serious musical composition, rather than the synthesis of popular tunes. Four channels of synthesis were provided, doubling the voice output capabilities of the machine. The sound-source bank was also considerably enlarged. In addition to a set of twelve tuning fork-based oscillators producing a master octave of tempered pitches, and a noise generator, two sets of twelve variable-frequency oscillators were provided. Each of the latter could be tuned to any desired frequency setting between 8130 and 16180 Hz, a range slightly larger than the revised master octave tunings of C = 8372 Hz: and B = 15804 Hz: . Used together, these sources could be used to provide an octave scale with thirty-six divisions. An enlarged octaver, required now only to act as a divider, provided a ten-octave range of pitches extending down to C = 16.3 Hz: . Two relay trees were provided to control generator and oc-

selection routines for each channel as before. The availability of a ten-octave dividing network, however, necessitated the provision of a four-bit coding system, leaving four selections completely unused. Despite the provision of twenty-four extra oscillators no change was made to the size of the relay system controlling the selection of the generators. Each synthesis channel could thus only call on sixteen of the sources at any one time, the selection being allocated manually via a special switchboard.

The frequency glider, envelope, and volume control systems were retained without major alteration. The low-frequency modulators, however, offered a slightly wider range of amplitude modulation speeds, ranging from 5 to 10 Hz. The facilities for shaping timbre, too, were rearranged to achieve greater flexibility. Two sets of resonators were included for each channel, and the high- and low-pass filters were fitted with relay control facilities. Selection of all these options was centralized via a comprehensive patch panel.

One general feature is particularly notable. The layout of the Mark 2 version took full account of the need to provide a system which is essentially modular in construction, for no restrictions were imposed regarding the way, or the order, in which the individual devices are used. In the case of all the synthesis channels, the routing of signals from the source bank to the output thus became entirely a matter of choice, problems of different signal levels being minimized by the addition of buffer amplifiers to the input and output stages of each device.

Two mechanically linked paper tape drives were used for performance control, each providing information for a pair of synthesis channels. The standard designation of punched columns to relays, with the addition of an extra column for the octaver, was identical to that used in the Mark 1 model. It was the clear intention, however, that interchanging the plug connections to the sensors could freely alter these designations. Furthermore, the destinations of the individual lines activated by the relay trees could be interchanged or even paralleled, in the latter case weighting particular device functions and bypassing others. An alternative input system using continuous lines in place of punched holes, drawn with a felt-tip pen and read by an optical scanner, was introduced during the 1960s.

The use of a punched tape control system for the RCA synthesizers created a landmark in the development of systems for the production of electronic music. Despite the inevitable shortcomings of an all-mechanical approach, the ability to program an entire sequence of operations opened up modes of operation hitherto time-consuming at best and impracticable at worst. The construction of a sequence of enveloped and rich pitches from the single sine-wave generator at Cologne, for example, required an extensive series of practical routines, turning knobs, and cutting and splicing tape. Punching a control tape for the RCA synthesizers for similar ends took a mere fraction of the same time. The availability of such a facility, however, did not eliminate all the problems encountered in specifying sounds, and indeed created many of its own.

Olson and Belar, as in the case of their random probability machine, overestimated the potential of the synthesizers. In particular, they failed to realize that despite the sophistication of their source bank and control systems, the devices themselves could not be programmed to synthesize many important characteristics of natural sound production, let alone supply satisfactory alternatives. It has already been seen how filter and resonator networks acting on a sawtooth wave source may be used to produce a number of different timbres. The discussion of waveform synthesis in connection with the Cologne studio, however, has shown how such general shaping procedures cannot be compared to the totally controllable techniques of additive synthesis from individual sinusoidal sources. In claiming that the machine could simulate instruments such as the clarinet, saxophone, oboe, or violin the designers also overlooked the problem of generating realistic attack transients. The availability of a single envelope shaper for each channel, operating on a fixed source spectrum, was quite inadequate for such purposes. However, the machine was capable of providing novel renditions of popular tunes such as "Obelin," "Sweet and Low," and the "Old Folks at Home." Olson and Belar even ventured into the classical repertoire, reproducing such works as Brahms's Hungarian Dance no. 1 "in the gypsy style" and Bach's Fugue no. 2 from book 1 of the *Well-Tempered Clavier*.

Despite these practical drawbacks and the narrowness of musical vision displayed by the designers, the relocation of the RCA synthesizers to Columbia University ensured that considered attention could be paid to their true musical potential. The "note/event" orientation of the programming system naturally imposed a considerable influence over the way in which the machines were employed; hence the common interest both of Luening and Ussachevsky, and also of Babbitt. The Electronic Music Center provided a major focus for composers both at home and from abroad, and the level of activity was intense right from the start. Two inaugural concerts were given in the McMillin Theater, Columbia, on 9 and 10 May 1961 before an invited audience, in a blaze of publicity. The programs included Bulent Arel, Stereo Electronic Music no. 1; Babbitt, Composition for Synthesizer; Mario Davidovsky, Electronic Study no. 1; Halim El-Dabh, *Leiyla and the Poet*; Luening, *Gargoyles*, for violin solo and synthesized sounds; and Ussachevsky, *Creation: Prologue*.

Babbitt's *Composition* was the fruit of a seemingly effortless transition from a strictly ordered style of instrumental writing to an electronic equivalent. The piece is made all the more approachable by its particularly clear pitch and rhythmic articulation, allowing considerable emphasis to be placed on elements of repetition and symmetry. Ussachevsky's *Creation: Prologue* consisted of a choral setting of Latin and Babylonian texts, punctuated by the occasional passage of electronic sounds, again for the most part used in an orchestral manner. There is some unease in the relationship between the forces, the inevitably clinical nature of the electronic outbursts contrasting sharply with the nuances of human voices. The same unease permeates Luening's *Gargoyles* for much the same reason, that is, the lack of a satisfactory continuum between two sharply contrasting sources of sound material. El-Dabh's *Leiyla* explored the potential of spoken texts in a manner not unlike that adopted by Berio for his *Visage*. Passages for two male voices are integrated with simple oscillator sounds from the synthesizer, and examples of mid-Eastern music performed on flute, string, and percussion instruments. Davidovsky and Arel were the only composers seriously to seek a new sound world beyond the traditions of instrumental writing. Of the two works, the Davidovsky *Study* makes the deeper excursion into the subtleties of textural manipulation, in a manner reminiscent of that adopted by composers associated with the Milan school.

The publicity accorded to Columbia/Princeton at this time overshadowed several other important developments that were taking place elsewhere in America, and over the border in Canada. The pioneering work of Hugh Le Caine at Ottawa, for example, was attracting national interest through a series of short pieces starting with *Dripsody* (1955), a study based on the sound of water drops. In 1958, the composers Gordon Mumma and Robert Ashley had established a private studio at Ann Arbor, Michigan, followed the next year by studios at the University of Illinois under the direction of Lejaren Hiller and the University of Toronto under the direction of Arnold Walter. The establishment of another private venture also took place in 1959, that of the San Francisco Tape Music Center, under the direction of Ramon Sender and Morton Subotnick. With the turn of the decade the medium entered an era of escalating activity, with a proliferation of studios throughout the world.

The scale of this expansion was greatly influenced by an important development during the mid-1960s: the introduction of the commercially marketed voltage-controlled synthesizer. Overnight, facilities for electronic music became available in the form of neat self-contained packages, operational from the moment of being switched on. The effect on the evolution of the medium was truly dramatic. On the positive side, many thousands of composers of all abilities were able to experiment with the medium for the first time. On the negative side, questions of aesthetics and compositional methodology were frequently swept aside by the surfeit of mediocre works that poured forth from many quarters.

Extracting and highlighting the more notable developments is no easy task, for the sheer diversity of activities demands the adoption of an increasingly selective approach, with the division of the medium into a number of different genres. Before consideration is given to the musical output of the 1960s and beyond, however, attention must first be turned to the new technology itself, the subject of the next chapter.

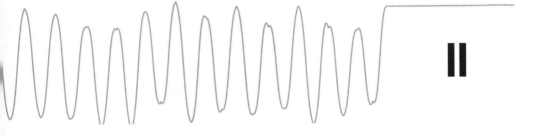

New Horizons in Electronic Design

6

The Voltage-Controlled Synthesizer

The birth of the transistor in the late 1950s heralded a major turning point in the development of facilities for electronic music. Hitherto the evolution of devices had been governed by the characteristics of thermionic valves. Problems of heat dissipation, fragility, and the sheer size of these components thwarted efforts to design systems that were both versatile and compact. The new technology suffered from none of these disadvantages and generated remarkably few of its own.

One of the first engineers to grasp the significance of this technological revolution for electronic sound synthesis was Harald Bode, the inventor of the Melochord. In 1961, he published an article on transistor-based devices, drawing particular attention to the advantages of modular design.[1] Such a concept was new indeed, for with the advent of miniaturization it had become possible to envisage the production of easily transportable system packages, containing customized selections of self-contained and mutually compatible units such as oscillators, filters, and modulators.

The new designs were to prove revolutionary in another respect. Hitherto uniquely assigned knobs or sliders had controlled the functional characteristics of most studio devices. Connections between these units were thus concerned solely with the passing of audio signals from one stage in the synthesis chain to another. The versatility of transistor-based electronics made it possible to design any number of devices that could be controlled by a common set of voltage characteristics. These could be supplied either internally via manually operated regulators, or externally, from any suitable voltage source. The former mode of operation was little different from that employed for traditional studio equipment. The latter, however, introduced an entirely new dimension: the passing of control information from device to device via a secondary chain of interconnections.

Despite Bode's interest, the primary initiative passed elsewhere. In 1964, Robert Moog, an American engineer working in New York, constructed a transistor voltage-controlled oscillator and amplifier for the composer Herbert Deutsch. This led to the presentation of a paper entitled "Voltage-Controlled Electronic Music Modules" at the sixteenth annual convention of the Audio Engineering Society in the autumn of the same year, which stimulated widespread interest.[2]

Similar developments were taking place on the West Coast. Sender and Subotnick had become increasingly dissatisfied with the limitations of traditional equipment at the San Francisco Tape Music Center, and their quest for new devices led to an association with another engineer, Donald Buchla. Like Moog, Buchla appreciated the musical possibilities of transistor voltage-control technology, and proceeded to develop his own prototype modules. On the strength of their early successes both engineers, quite independently, decided to establish their own manufacturing companies, launching the first commercial versions of the Moog Synthesizer and the Buchla Electronic Music System almost simultaneously in 1966. During 1964–5, a third engineer, Paul Ketoff, designed and built a portable voltage-controlled synthesizer, known as the Synket, for the composer John Eaton. Although interest in its capabilities, especially as a live performance instrument, led to the construction of a number of copies, this synthesizer was not developed as a commercial product.

By the end of the decade, two further manufacturers had entered the market, Tonus, marketing under the trade name ARP in America, and EMS Ltd., pioneered by Peter Zinovieff in England. For several years these four companies competed as the market leaders for a share of a highly lucrative and rapidly expanding market for voltage-controlled synthesizers, until eventually succumbing to the competition provided by a new generation of manufacturers, not least from Japan.

The effects of such commercialism have already been alluded to at the end of the previous chapter, in particular the rapid proliferation of studios, both private and institutional. The growing accessibility of system packages was to prove a mixed blessing, for in many instances the ease of device interaction led to a fascination with the technology for its own sake, rather than the musical premises for its use. Manufacturers were naturally keen to publicize the more novel features of their individual products, leaving unsuspecting composers to discover for themselves the practicalities of using such equipment for creative purposes.

In order to evaluate the musical characteristics of voltage-controlled systems it is advantageous to understand the general principles on which they operate. Although much of the original technology is now consigned to synthesizer museums, a growing interest in what has become known as "retro-synthesis," where such characteristics are either reproduced using modern analog circuits or simulated digitally, requires a clear understanding of the underlying operational principles.

Except in the rarest of circumstances, every voltage-controlled device offers one or more adjustable characteristics. Oscillators, for example, are usually controllable in terms of both frequency and amplitude. Even a ring modulator usually incorporates an amplifier to regulate the level of signals appearing at its output. If the system is voltage controlled, manually operated knobs or sliders fitted on the front of each device act as potentiometers, regulating the level of voltage supplied to the associated internal circuitry from a common power supply, typically +5 volts (V). Despite their integral construction it is helpful in the initial stages of study to view these potentiometers as separate from the devices themselves. The frequency and amplitude controls for an oscillator may be represented thus:

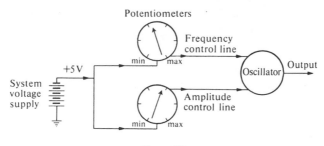

Figure 32

Inserting optional breakpoints in each control line, across which an additional voltage from another source may then be applied, usefully modifies such an arrangement. If the internal potentiometer for a device function is set to supply +2 V along its control line, and an external source supplies an extra +1 V across the breakpoint, a potential of +3 V will be delivered to the device.

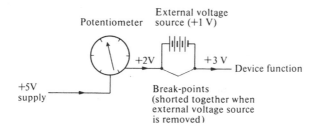

Figure 33

At this point, the concept of *negative* voltage must be introduced. If the external voltage source is unipolar, that is, only capable of generating positive potentials, it will always add to the internally supplied value. If the source is bipolar, however, capable of delivering both positive and negative potentials, the internally supplied voltage may be treated as a reference level, which may be increased or decreased as required. A supply of −1 V from the external voltage source in the above illustration, for example, will reduce the voltage arriving at the device from +2 to +1 V.

The response characteristics of the device functions themselves vary from one design concept to another. In the majority of cases, however, both frequency and amplitude control circuits are designed to operate logarithmically rather than linearly. Equal steps in voltage are thus conveniently associated with equal changes in musical interval or sound intensity throughout the operating range. Typical response values are 0.3 or 0.5 V per octave, and 0.3 or 0.5 V per 10 dB.

Keyboards have proved especially popular as control devices, attached to any device function across its associated control line breakpoint. Their voltage outputs are usually bipolar, the null point of 0 V being associated with a specific key at or near the middle of the range. Playing a succession of keys upward from this point thus generates a stepped series of voltages that increase in positive potential. Playing a scale downward generates the reverse, a stepped series of voltages that increase in negative potential. The step size itself is usually adjustable by means of a sensitivity control, expanding or contracting the voltage range of the keyboard either side of the null point.

The most obvious, and in practice the commonest, use of a keyboard is to control the frequency of an oscillator, the two devices combining to form a monophonic melody generator. Tuning involves two adjustments, one to the internal potentiometer of the oscillator to link the null key on the keyboard to the required pitch, the other to the keyboard sensitivity control to ensure that the voltage step size generates tempered semitones between adjacent keys. The ability to transpose the keyboard range upward or downward by means of the former control helps to overcome the practical limitations of the short, three- or four-octave keyboards favored by several manufacturers. Nonstandard tempered pitches are obtainable by resetting the voltage step size. Halving the sensitivity, for example, will result in quarter-tones between adjacent keys. Reducing this factor further permits the production of tempered microtones.

Chords or more complex aggregations of pitches may be manipulated by connecting a keyboard across the breakpoints of several oscillators, the latter being tuned in the first instance to the desired pitch intervals relative to one another via their internal potentiometers. The logarithmic response of the frequency circuits will ensure that the oscillators will track together upward or downward in response to applied keyboard voltage steps, preserving the interval relationships.

The use of a keyboard control for parallel tracking need not be limited to signal sources. If the audio output from a square, ramp, or triangle oscillator is passed for modification to a tunable low-pass filter, the latter device may be made to track the former by connecting the keyboard output across both frequency control breakpoints. The advantage of this arrangement is a consistent modification of timbre no matter which pitch is selected.

Some keyboards provide two output voltage functions with individually adjustable sensitivities. In the example just given, applying one such function to the oscillator and the other to the filter with different sensitivity settings will cause the two devices to track key selections with different results. If the filter control steps are larger than those applied to the oscillator the frequency settings of the former will increase more rapidly as ascending keys are selected. As a result, the tonal quality will steadily brighten as fewer oscillator harmonics are subject to attenuation. If the filter steps are smaller the reverse effect will occur, the effects of attenuation increasing with higher key selections.

The idea of using keyboard voltage control for functions other than those associated with frequency may seem a little unusual. There are many instances, however, where a facility for generating a range of easily selectable steps for any number of device characteristics has proved an invaluable aid to synthesis operations. As a regulator of amplitude, for example, the keyboard provides a useful means of controlling sound levels as a series of accurately specified gradations of intensity. In essence, therefore, a voltage-controlled keyboard may be viewed as a manually operated device for the sequential control of a discrete chain of events.

Some designs of voltage-control keyboards incorporate circuits to provide yet another output characteristic, by making each key touch-sensitive. A similar facility, it will be recalled, was incorporated in the Monochord supplied to the Cologne studio in the early 1950s. In some versions, the keys generate a voltage proportional to the pressure exerted upon them. In others, the time taken for each key to be depressed is measured electronically and converted into a corresponding voltage, which is sustained until the next key is struck. The faster the key action, the greater the voltage generated. If the touch characteristic is fed to the amplitude control line of an oscillator while the normal keyboard output is fed to the frequency control line, both dynamics and pitch may be directly controlled by the performer. One further output facility is normally provided: a trigger voltage generated each time a key is depressed. This, as will be seen shortly, may be used to "fire" the timing circuits of an associated signal-processing device such as an envelope shaper.

Keyboards were not the only manual control aids to find favor with designers of voltage-controlled systems. The joystick proved to be a popular alternative, permitting the operator to manipulate two functions simultaneously with one hand. The device consists of a lever protruding upward from a central bearing, which may be freely moved in any direction within a circular outer limit determined by the mechanics of the bearing mounting. The spatial positioning of the lever end is decoded by a series of linkages under the unit into two coordinates: x_1-x_2, and y_1-y_2:

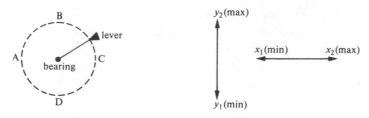

Figure 34

The movements from one lever position to another, measured in terms of these coordinates, are used to change the voltage outputs of two associated potentiometers. Moving the lever from position A to position C, for example, varies the output from the x potentiometer from its minimum setting to its maximum. Because the joystick maintains a midpoint position along the axis $y_1 - y_2$, the output from the y potentiometer remains constant at its median voltage value. Moving the lever from position D to position B produces the converse response: the x potentiometer delivers a constant median voltage, while the output from the y potentiometer increases from minimum to maximum. All other joystick trajectories will involve simultaneous adjustments to both potentiometers.

Unlike keyboards, joysticks are not suitable for specifying accurately predetermined sequences of discrete control voltage steps. As interactive, continuously variable performance aids, however, they provide the composer or performer with a flexible tool for intuitive control over selected device functions. One or two designers have attempted to extend the versatility of the joystick control still further by suspending the bearing itself in a flexible mounting, permitting a third voltage output to be generated by movements in the vertical plane. Considerable skill, however, is required to achieve even generally focused changes in all three functions simultaneously.

Most joysticks are constructed to provide a bipolar output, 0 V being associated with a dead-center position. Sensitivity controls regulate the degree of voltage variation obtained when the joystick is moved to the extremes of its travel in each plane. Variations on the joystick principle include a touch sensitive pad, which decodes the position of a finger on a grid to similar effect.

Despite such improvements in the choice and availability of manually operated facilities for device control, the primary fascination with voltage-control technology arose from the ability to utilize the dynamically varying outputs of devices such as oscillators as control inputs for others. A sine wave oscillator, for example, generates a constantly recycling voltage function. The range of voltage variation within each cycle determines its amplitude, and the number of complete cycle repetitions per second determines its frequency. In a synthesizer, oscillator circuits are frequently designed to give bipolar characteristics, where the associated function will fluctuate either side of a zero voltage reference:

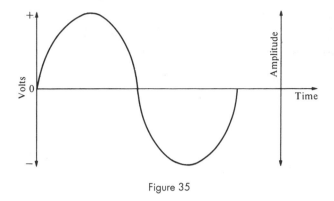

Figure 35

If such a voltage source is applied across one of the control breakpoints for another oscillator, its fluctuating output will modulate the selected function about the voltage level set via the internal potentiometer.

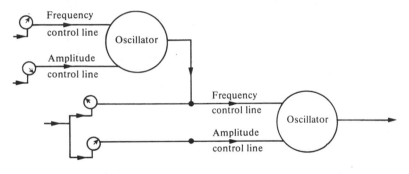

Figure 36

The first oscillator thus adopts the role of a frequency control voltage source for the second, the output of the latter providing the audio product. Once again numerous permutations and combinations of control connections are possible. Feeding the output of one oscillator to both the frequency and the amplitude control lines of a second, for example, will produce a linked modulation of both characteristics. Alternatively, separate oscillators may be connected to each control line to generate an altogether more complex, asynchronous modulation of frequency and amplitude. Chaining several oscillators in series may produce even more elaborate characteristics. Sheer complexity, however, in no way guarantees musical value, and overenthusiastic or ill-informed experimentation will frequently prove counterproductive. Even the simplest arrangement illustrated above is capable of producing a multiplicity of timbres that demand some understanding of the constituent functions that are involved in such an application.

The novice electronic composer of the late 1960s and 1970s, experimenting with such device arrangements for the first time, was often impressed by the ease with which a single audio oscillator is transformed into a rich sound source. Such a reaction, however, was usually tempered by the discovery that the relationships between parameter settings and the perceived results are far from straightforward.

The acoustical products of both frequency and amplitude modulation are governed by mathematical considerations concerning the characteristics of both the modulated and the modulating waves. The wave shapes themselves are important elements in these equations, for each harmonic component contributes to the resulting timbre. In the interests of clarity, consideration is thus restricted in the first instance to the modulation of one sine wave oscillator by another.

If the output of one such oscillator, delivering a low-frequency wave of small amplitude, is connected across the frequency control breakpoint of a second, the output of the latter will be subject to gentle pitch vibrato. The frequency of the control wave determines the speed of this vibrato, and the amplitude determines the depth. Increasing the output level of the control oscillator will thus increase the depth of the vibrato without altering its speed. If both the speed and the depth are sufficiently gentle the ear will be able to follow the changes in frequency without difficulty. If the depth of modulation is particularly pronounced, or the speed exceeds about 11 to 12 Hz, however, it becomes impossible to track the changes as a function of time. The persistence factor of the human ear ensures that modulating speeds greater than this boundary figure result in a blurring of these frequency changes, the sound becoming transformed into a seemingly stable complex of timbres.

This transformation may be analyzed in terms of three determining components. These are (1) c, the carrier (= original) frequency of the second, audio oscillator; (2) m, the modulating frequency of the control oscillator; and (3) d, the depth of modulation created, measured in terms of the maximum frequency deviation obtained either side of the carrier. Two series of side bands will be introduced either side of the carrier frequency, drawn from the progressions $c-m$, $c-2m$, $c-3m$ . . . and $c+m$, $c+2m$, $c+3m$. . . . If the audio oscillator is generating a carrier frequency of 1000 Hz and the control oscillator a modulating frequency of 150 Hz, for example, side bands at 850 Hz, 700 Hz, 550 Hz, etc., and 1150 Hz, 1300 Hz, 1450 Hz, and so on, may be generated in addition to the carrier.

The outer limits of the side bands and the relative amplitudes of the frequency components between these extremes are regulated by I, the modulation index. The value of I is calculated by dividing the frequency of deviation by the frequency of modulation, d/m. In the previous illustration, if the modulating wave produces a deviation of 300 Hz either side of the carrier frequency, $I = 300/150 = 2$.

The distribution of energy for different values of I may be calculated from mathematical tables, known as Bessel functions, one for each matching pair of side bands. The carrier itself enters into the distribution equations, responding to its own zero order function. The functions themselves are complex, creating wavelike patterns for each order of side band. In essence, as the value of I increases, a fluctuating quantity of energy is "stolen" from the fundamental and distributed among an increasing number of side bands. The following diagrams give an approximate indication of the characteristics of some representative modulation indices:

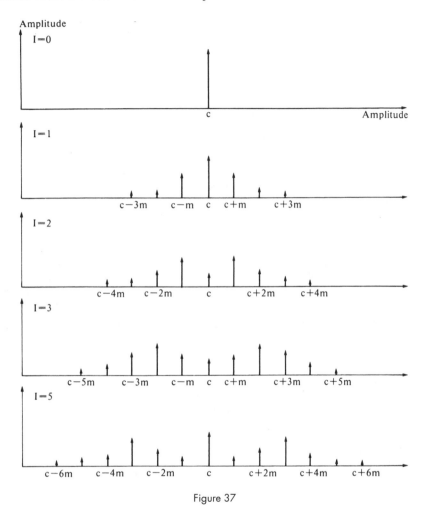

Figure 37

Viewed as diagrammatic representations these characteristics reveal some fascinating responses for different degrees of modulation. Their musical significance, however, is far from straightforward, for there are no easily definable relationships between the perceived nature of frequency-modulated sounds and their scientific determinates. Modifications to c, m, or d will indeed often result in elaborate sonic transformations. These characteristics, nevertheless, are determined by the process itself, which may only be regulated in terms of three interdependent variables. Composers, thus, have limited scope for tailoring the resultant range of sounds to their particular needs. Instead, they must accept or reject a predetermined morphology, relying on subsequent signal-processing techniques such as filtering to produce any modifications to these mathematically ordered timbre characteristics. Further consideration of the characteristics of frequency modulation will be given in a later chapter.[3]

Amplitude modulation results in an altogether simpler set of side-band characteristics, providing once again the process is restricted to the modulation of one sine wave oscillator by another. When the output of one such generator is applied across the amplitude control breakpoint of a second, the amplitude of the former wave determines the degree of amplitude variation generated in the output of the latter, and its frequency the speed of modulation. At low modulation speeds, less than about 11–12 Hz, the modulating function will be clearly perceived as a variation of amplitude with respect to time. This effect may be varied from a gentle pulsing to a complete cyclic enveloping of the sound. The latter effect will be produced if the amplitude of the control wave is increased sufficiently to ensure that the greatest negative voltage swing generated during each cycle is sufficient to cancel out entirely the steady "carrier" level supplied by the internal amplitude potentiometer of the second oscillator.

At higher modulation speeds, above the 11–12 Hz boundary, variations in amplitude blur into a continuous spectrum. The resultant timbre is composed of three frequency components: the carrier frequency c and two complementary side bands, one a summation of the carrier and the modulating frequency, $c+m$, the other the difference frequency, $c-m$. The amplitude of the modulating wave determines the strengths of the pair of side bands to the carrier. Thus, the greater the depth of modulation the stronger the side bands.

A distinct similarity may be noted between the characteristics of amplitude modulation and those of ring modulation. The latter process, it will be recalled, involves the use of a special circuit that acts on two separate frequency sources, F_1 and F_2, to produce a summation frequency $F_1 + F_2$ and a difference frequency $F_1 - F_2$. If F_1 is viewed as a carrier frequency and F_2 as a modulating frequency the products of ring modulation are identical with those generated by amplitude modulation. In the latter case, however, the carrier frequency is always present in the output, whereas in the former both input frequencies are firmly suppressed. Ring modulation may thus be considered a rather special form of amplitude modulation, although the electronic processes involved are in engineering terms quite different.

Frequency and amplitude modulation of complex signals involves similar processes of multiplication to those encountered in ring modulation of such sources. Each frequency component in the carrier wave is subject to modulation by each frequency component in the modulating wave, the amplitude of these elements affecting the characteristics of each set of side bands.

Voltage-control technology facilitated a further type of signal modulation known generally as spatial or location modulation. It will be recalled that the left-to-right positioning of a stereo sound image is determined by the proportional distribution of its signal elements between two playback channels. Movement of the image in response to a single control voltage function demands a circuit arrangement that is capable of adjusting the amplitude of both channels simultaneously, a gain on one channel being automatically matched by an equivalent loss on the other. Such a function may be derived from a pair of voltage-controlled amplifiers (VCA), an inverter to reverse the polarity of the applied voltage being inserted in the control line of one of the units:

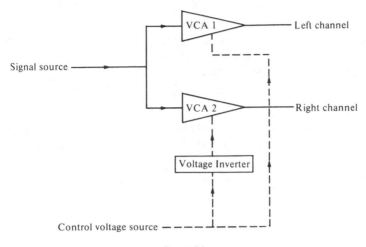

Figure 38

When the control voltage supply is set to its maximum value VCA 1 will be set fully on, and VCA 2 fully off. As the voltage is reduced, the resultant fall in the output of VCA 1 will be matched by a corresponding rise in the output of VCA 2, the former level falling to zero and the latter rising to a maximum at the other extreme.

Application of a control wave from an oscillator will result in a modulation of incoming audio signals between the two channels. The spatial movements become increasingly blurred as the oscillator speed is increased, leading to the production of amplitude modulation side bands. Alternatively, a joystick may be employed as a manual panning control by applying the single voltage output associated with movements of the lever along one of its axes.

A simple extension of this principle allows the use of both voltage outputs to control the distribution of a sound image between the four output channels of a quadraphonic playback system. The composer may then "steer" the sound image freely about the listening area, the joystick movements manipulating the relative amplitudes of all four components simultaneously. The capacitor-based detectors used for the Thérémin and the *potentiomètre d'espace* provide interesting precedents for the latter method of spatial control.

A number of other device characteristics are particularly amenable to external voltage control. Reference has already been made to the control of filter tunings via a keyboard. Most synthesizer manufacturers developed voltage-controlled re-verberation units, usually of the simpler and more portable spring type, where an applied voltage may be used to control the depth of enhancement.

Envelope shapers figure prominently in voltage-controlled systems, offering several functional characteristics that may be manipulated by other devices. These amplitude processors have proved especially popular in view of their ability to provide a semi-automatic dynamic shaping of events. Simpler versions provide three basic variables: an attack time, during which an applied sound is allowed to grow from zero intensity to a preset amplitude; a sustain or "on" time during which this amplitude is maintained; and a decay time during which the signal level fades away to zero. The attack and decay functions are often fixed features, providing exponential amplitude curves.

Although all three segments may usually be varied manually, many commercial designs restrict the provision of an external voltage-control breakpoint to just the decay characteristic. The range of duration values that may be specified for each segment varies considerably from manufacturer to manufacturer, but the follow-ing characteristics are typical: attack time 2 milliseconds to 1 second, sustain time 0 second (= no sustain) to 2.5 seconds, and decay time 3 milliseconds to 15 sec-onds. As these specifications suggest, a wide variety of envelope shapers may be created, using different combinations of segment settings, for example:

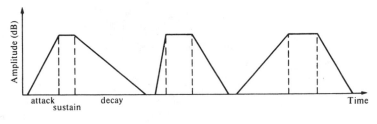

Figure 39

Many designs offer, in addition, an "off" delay that may be switched in to allow automatic recycling of the shaper after a specified interval. This segment provides a timed period of silence between the end of each decay and start of the next at-tack, which may be varied typically from 0 second (= immediate attack) to about 5 seconds. If this recycling facility is switched out, the envelope shaper must be activated by a trigger voltage pulse supplied either internally via a manual push-button or externally from a device such as a keyboard. If the duration of this pulse is extended by holding down the button or a key it is normal for the sustain seg-ment to be prolonged until the point of release, the chosen decay characteristic then completing the envelope. Similarly, interrupting an envelope with a fresh trig-ger pulse will reactivate the attack-sustain-decay characteristic, the attack segment being truncated to the portion necessary to restore the amplitude to its maximum level. In the extreme case of one key selection being immediately followed by another selection, a continuous level of amplitude will be maintained.

The following connections between a keyboard, oscillator, and envelope shaper will create a simple monophonic instrument, responding to key selections with a succession of dynamically shaped pitches:

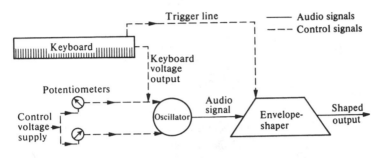

Figure 40

Some versions offer a level detection facility, which may be used to trigger the envelope function as soon as the incoming audio signal reaches the chosen amplitude. The electronic circuit employed for this purpose is known as a threshold detector or Schmitt trigger. This consists of an amplitude-sensitive switch, which closes to create an "on" state only when an applied signal exceeds a preset value. This state is then maintained until the signal falls back below the threshold level, whereupon the switch opens again.

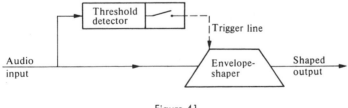

Figure 41

In this particular application of threshold detection only the "off" to "on" trigger pulse is required to activate the envelope shaper, the reopening of the switch being ignored. More complex applications will be discussed in due course.

External voltage control of segment timings is restricted, in practice, to low-frequency control waves, or the output of manual devices such as joysticks. Modulating the decay time will only produce a detectable ripple in the decay characteristic if the modulation speed is significantly less than 11 Hz, and the internally preset "carrier" decay time is sufficiently long to allow several repetitions of the control wave before the signal dies away, for example:

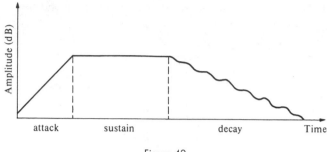

Figure 42

Very slow control waves with cycle times of the order of seconds may be used to produce sequences of dynamically changing envelopes, with the shaper set to recycle automatically. The following illustrates the effects of slowly modulating the decay time under these conditions:

Figure 43

One popular application of envelope shapers set in a recycling mode is the extraction of "snapshot" samples of sound from a source that is dynamically changing in frequency or timbre. If the attack and decay segments are set to their minimum values, adjustments to sustain and recycle delay segments will regulate the on/off characteristics of what has now become a simple electronic "gate." Enveloping of a slowly oscillating frequency in this manner will extract a pattern of pitches, which is a permutation of the gating speed and the cycle time of the source signal. More sophisticated designs of envelope shapers known as ADSRs (Attack-Decay-Sustain-Release) provide an extra feature in the form of an initial decay characteristic, inserted between the attack and sustain segments. This addition permits an extra emphasis to be placed on the attack itself, in a manner much more akin to the transients of many naturally generated sounds. Various electronic techniques have been employed to achieve such a response within the voltage control domain. One of the commonest involves the use of two envelope shaper circuits connected in parallel. One supplies the primary three-segment attack-sustain-decay envelope. The other supplies a secondary two-segment attack-decay envelope that fires simultaneously with the first. Providing the attack times of both circuits are set equal, regulating the maximum gain and the decay time of the secondary shaper will produce different initial peaks and decays.

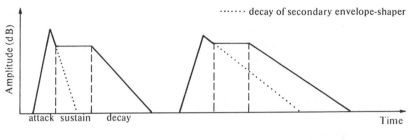

Figure 44

Voltage-controlled envelope shapers, despite such enhancements, are still subject to a number of practical limitations. In particular, they can only shape the dynamics of the entire sound applied to their inputs, and not the individual spectral elements. Most natural sounds exhibit extremely complex envelope characteristics with numerous independently evolving components. In addition, the common restriction of fixed exponential attack and decay characteristics precludes the possibility of generating envelopes with more flexible shapes, for example an attack that tails off rapidly in its sharpness, or a decay that begins quickly and ends gently:

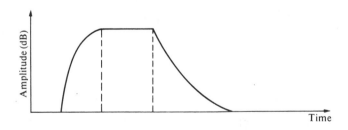

Figure 45

In an analog, as opposed to a digital, domain the opportunities for refining techniques of envelope shaping are extremely limited. Two solutions exist for the problem of generating a dynamic variation in timbre during the course of each shaped event. The first, applicable specifically to the synthesis of material from a bank of sine wave oscillators, involves the provision of an envelope shaper for each generator, shaping each frequency component before any subsequent processes of Fourier addition.

Voltage-controlled synthesizers, however, rarely provided sufficient oscillators or sufficient envelope shapers for any useful application of this technique. Manufacturers placed a higher priority on the use of frequency and amplitude modulation methods of timbre generation, which only required a small number of oscillators and the most basic range of electronic wave forms: sine, square, ramp, and triangle. Further, any prospect of achieving accurate Fourier synthesis by combining generators was usually overshadowed by problems of frequency stability. Standards of reliability and accuracy were all too frequently sacrificed in favor of commercial design economies, not always serving the interests of more serious composers.

The second solution to the problem of achieving timbre variation during enveloping involves using the envelope shaper itself as a control voltage source. In generating the segments of an envelope a composite electronic voltage function is produced to operate an internal amplifier. If this voltage, described by some manufacturers as a trapezoid function, is made available externally, it may be applied to other devices in a synthesis chain, for example a variable frequency low-pass filter. The latter will then track the envelope function, the frequency of cutoff rising with the attack and falling with the decay. Suitable settings of both filter and envelope shaper will then allow applied sounds to grow in brightness as their intensity increases, a feature associated with many instrumental sounds.

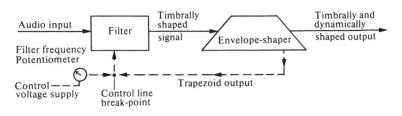

Figure 46

Larger voltage-controlled synthesizers provide a number of ancillary amplitude-processing devices based specifically on the properties of the Schmitt trigger. Similarities may be noted between some of these and the standard envelope shaper. The differences arise in the greater degree of versatility afforded. The simplest application is that of an electronic "gate," which acts directly to block or pass applied audio signals depending on the state of the associated trigger. The latter may be activated either by the incoming signal itself or by any other suitable external voltage source. If the gating circuit responds instantaneously to trigger signals the resultant abrupt switching of the audio level may result in shocks to the human auditory mechanism, which are perceived as clicks. These become particularly noticeable if the voltage of the gate control signal fluctuates rapidly about the threshold setting. Introducing special attack and decay circuits, which slew the switching response slightly, may reduce such unwanted side-effects:

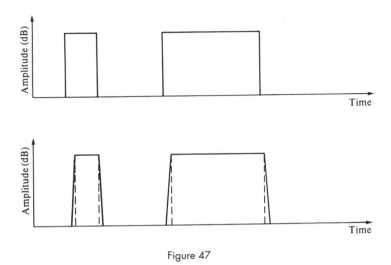

Figure 47

More comprehensive designs offer both a variable trigger threshold control and also adjustable slew rates. The characteristics of one audio signal may be used to shape another directly by using two gate circuits. The first is set in a self-triggering mode, the trigger response being additionally output as a control signal for the second unit.

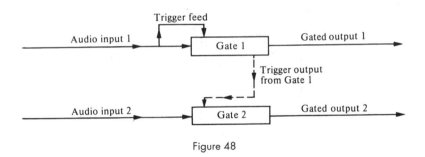

Figure 48

In the arrangement just mentioned, audio signal 2 will only pass when audio signal 1 is activating its own gate. A useful variation of this technique involves the insertion of a voltage inverter in the control line between the two gates. This reverses the response of the second gate such than an "on" state in gate 1 generates an "off" state in gate 2, and vice versa. Using this arrangement, the audio signal fed to gate 2 will pass unhindered except when the audio signal fed to gate 1 triggers itself, whereupon the former is suppressed.

The Schmitt trigger provides the basis for another signal processor known as a limiter.[4] Although originally intended as a recording and broadcasting aid to remove unwanted peaks from applied signals, this device is of special value in an electronic music system, where the opportunities for generating unexpected overloads in signal lines abound. Further, the resultant modifications of attack transients can lead to marked transformations of the sound events themselves. The threshold setting determines the maximum level at which an applied signal passes through the unit unaltered. As soon as a signal exceeds this setting the trigger fires, switching in attenuation circuits that flatten out the overshoot. This effect may best be explained in the form of a diagram, comparing a steadily increasing input level with the regulated output:

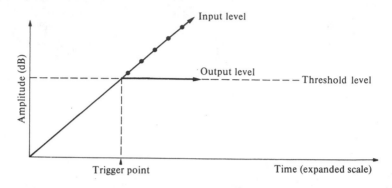

Figure 49

As in the case of the gate, useful modifications to the trigger response may be introduced by adding attack and decay slew circuits, acting to delay the reaction of the attenuator to changes in the trigger state. Rapidly increasing input amplitudes, for example, may be allowed to overshoot the threshold level for an instant before the attenuator comes fully into operation:

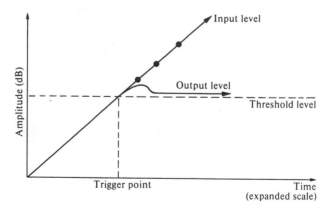

Figure 50

This modification generates artificial transients, the shorter the rise time of the input signal, or the longer the delaying effect of the attack slew circuit, the more pronounced the initial overshoot. The decay setting provides a matching effect when the input signal falls back again below the threshold level.

A useful development of the limiter, sometimes known as a sustain unit, incorporates amplifying circuits that act on signals below the threshold setting. In this mode, the latter acts as a reference level to which incoming signals are automatically adjusted. Such a facility is often used to highlight subtleties of timbre otherwise masked by fluctuations in amplitude.

The Schmitt trigger is also incorporated in several versions of a complementary pair of amplitude processors known as compressor/expanders or companders. A trigger-based compressor differs from a limiter in the behavior of the attenuation circuits to signals that exceed the threshold setting. Instead of flattening the overshoot, the characteristic is merely rounded, the degree of compression being fixed or variable according to the design.

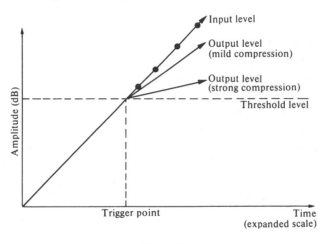

Figure 51

Expanders in the opposite manner, increasing the gain of signals above threshold setting.

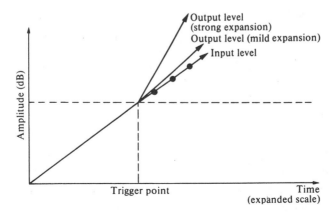

Figure 52

In both cases, the introduction of attack and decay circuits modifies the response to signals that cross the threshold by the reaction of the amplitude processors.

In outlining the basic features of voltage-controlled systems it has become apparent that the potential advantages of such facilities for the composer are tempered by the very elementary provision of resources for programming the operation of the control networks. The need for some form of electronic storage mechanism for registering sequences of device control values was quickly appreciated, and by the end of the 1960s most synthesizer manufacturers were incorporating such a facility in their more advanced models.

The basis for a link between digitally orientated control facilities and analog devices arose in the first instance from the on/off voltage patterns created by pulse generators. These devices, it will be recalled, were commonly employed in "classical" studios such as Cologne as direct sources of audio material. The transistor-based versions originally developed for synthesizers operate on very similar principles.

One special type of multiple-pulse generator developed for voltage-controlled systems is based on a modified Schmitt trigger, the pulse patterns being made dependent on the characteristics of an external voltage source. The threshold detector functions in the normal way, firing the trigger whenever the input voltage reaches its preset value. Instead of the trigger signal being applied internally, it is fed directly to the output of the unit, producing a positive voltage pulse. Two options are available at this stage, depending on the particular design. The trigger either remains on, or switches on and off repeatedly at an adjustable rate until the input voltage falls back again below the threshold level. Application of a fluctuating voltage to the input will thus result in the generation of asymmetric pulse patterns.

A refinement of this triggering system was employed in the design of a device known as a timing pulse generator. Three operating modes are normally provided. These are: (1) "single shot" manual firing via a push button, one pulse only being produced each time the button is depressed; (2) repetitive mode firing, where the trigger fires repeatedly at a rate proportional to an applied voltage; and (3) pulse burst firing, where the trigger starts and stops firing at a selected rate in response to externally applied pulses. If the pulse patterns are generated at audio speeds, highly complex timbres may often be produced.

The use of two fixed-voltage levels to determine the information content of an audio or control signal forms a useful parallel with the basic techniques employed in digital information processing. Here all the operational instructions and data are specified in terms of binary numbers, the digit 0 being used to indicate an "off" state and the digit 1 to indicate an "on" state. The digital equivalents of gating circuits are derived from a series of four basic logic functions known mnemonically as AND, NAND, OR, and NOR. Each of these functions examines the states of two digital inputs, and generates an output pulse if particular on/off logic conditions are detected. An AND gate will switch on if both inputs are activated simultaneously. A NOR gate, conversely, will switch on if neither input is activated. The other gates are essentially extensions of the above, responding additionally to the possibility of just one input line being activated. Thus an OR gate will switch on if either one or both inputs are activated, and a NAND gate will switch on if neither or just one of the inputs is activated, but not both. These characteristics may best be illustrated diagrammatically as a truth table:

Inputs			Logic gate type		
A	B	AND	OR	NAND	NOR
				✕	✕
	#		✕	✕	
#			✕	✕	
#	#	✕	✕		

\# = Input active
✕ = Output active

Figure 53

Pulses, by their very nature, cannot directly supply variable control voltage characteristics. They may, however, be usefully employed for controlling the operation of special voltage-generating systems known as sequencers. The latter title is a little misleading, for it may more generally be applied to a number of studio devices. A voltage-controlled keyboard, for example, is a manually operated sequencer since its output consists of a series of voltage steps that may be used to control the production of a continuous progression of discrete events. In larger studios, however, the term was normally reserved for devices that produce a sequential output of voltage levels under electronic control.

The first generation of commercial sequencers designed for voltage-control applications appeared during the late 1960s. These devices consisted of a set of constant voltage supplies, each of which may be individually regulated, and a switching system that connects each supply in turn to an output line. Many circuit designs offer a unipolar series of output voltage steps, ranging in value from 0 volts to +5 or +10 volts. Bipolar responses, by contrast, are obtained by applying a negative voltage bias to the entire output, typically at half the maximum output value, to make the overall range symmetrical about zero volts. The earliest prototypes used an electromechanical switching system consisting of a relay-activated rotary switch. This was quickly superseded by electronic switching techniques that are less cumbersome in terms of physical design and also capable of much faster speeds of operation.

The total number of individual voltage steps that may be produced varies from one design to another. Some smaller models provided as few as eight elements. More comprehensive designs were capable of sequencing fifty or even upward of a hundred successive events. Three modes of operation are normally provided. These are: (1) single step, where the switching system may be manually advanced one position at a time; (2) single run, where in response to suitable clock control pulses the sequencer will step itself through the bank of voltages once only; and (3) repetitive mode, an extension of mode (2), where, on encountering the last position in the bank, the sequencer will automatically loop back to the beginning and continue to recycle until the source of control pulses is switched off. Many versions permit the operating length of the sequencer to be truncated via an adjustable last location marker. This feature allows the composer the freedom to program any specified number of voltage steps up to the maximum available before termination or repetition.

The switching systems of the next generation of sequencers, manufactured from the early 1970s to the early 1980s, were designed using a precursor of modern digital technology, based on the characteristics of the switch register. This consists of a digital counter, operating on a bank of binary storage locations wired in series:

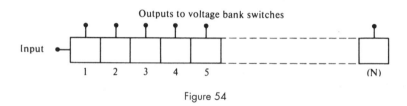

Figure 54

Each location may either be deenergized "off" (indicated below by the number 0) or energized "on" (indicated by the number 1). Initially the register is cleared so that all locations are deenergized. At the start of a sequence the register accepts an "on" pulse from the input, which energizes the first location. This results in a switching pulse at the output, which is used in turn to effect a connection from the first position in the voltage bank to the output of the sequencer.

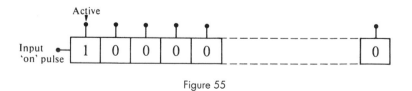

Figure 55

Subsequent pulses fed to the input have the effect of displacing the start pulse location by location along the register. Since the object is to step through the sequencer bank one voltage location at a time these stepping pulses must be of a de-energized (= "off") type, otherwise two or more locations will be switched on simultaneously.

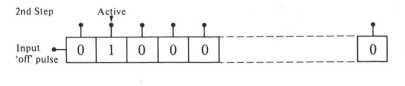

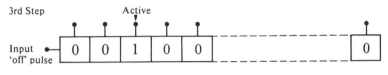

Figure 56

On reaching the last location the "on" pulse will either halt the sequencer automatically or recycle to the first location, depending on the operational mode selected.

These early digital sequencers were not necessarily restricted to the production of just a single series of stepped voltage functions. Some models provide two or even three parallel banks with independent outputs. Normally, however, they made use of a common switching system, ensuring that the step-by-step changes in each bank occur simultaneously. This facilitates synchronous control of two or more device functions, for example, frequency from one bank and amplitude from another. The stepping operation itself, as noted earlier, may be controlled manually, or by a clock pulse generator. For maximum flexibility the latter must be capable of offering a wide and continuously variable range of pulse rates. Some sequencers included a provision for manipulating the clock speed electronically via an external control voltage. A slowly repeating wave from a sine oscillator, for example, may be employed to vary the step rate continuosusly between two selected speeds. A more involved step-rate pattern may be produced from a sequencer with two or more output channels by connecting the voltage output from one of the banks directly to the clock input. Under these conditions, the time of each successive step may be individually programmed.

From a musical standpoint the primary value of a sequencer is its ability to realize a programmed series of instructions. Sequencers of the type just described suffered from one important limitation, however, for they could not provide a continuous variation in voltage. If, for example, an attempt is made to create a smooth glissando using a sequencer to control the frequency-control input to an oscillator, almost the entire resources of a hundred-element bank may be required to ensure that the individual frequency steps are too small to be individually detected.

Further, each voltage level had to be set painstakingly by hand. Such an operation proved extremely time-consuming for an effect that could, with care, be achieved by a single sweep of a manual joystick control.

The ability to program step functions is of particular value when the object is to generate sequences of discrete "note/events," for these involve simple and precise specifications of pitch, duration, envelope, and timbre. This approach to electronic synthesis has already been highlighted in discussing the characteristics of the RCA synthesizers, and the elementary digital sequencer was well suited to such applications as the provision of simple control data for imitative instrumental textures, and the realization of serially based ideas.

One other application of this type of sequencer meriting attention in this context was its use in some circumstances as an audio wave generator in its own right. This was achieved by programming a single wave function as a series of voltage values, setting the sequencer in repetitive mode, and then significantly raising the speed at which the values are polled, the fundamental frequency being determined by the number of cycles completed every second. In so doing, the device was transformed into an elementary digital oscillator, anticipating a design revolution that will be studied later in more detail within the broader context of computer music.[5] By way of an illustration, the output of twenty-four voltage steps in a bipolar mode might be set to create the following approximation to a sine wave:

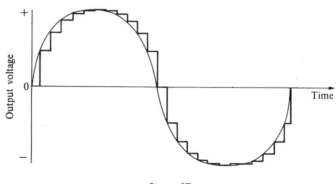

Figure 57

The general characteristic of this wave, as may be seen from the previous diagram, is approximately sinusoidal, and will be perceived aurally as a note with a clearly defined fundamental frequency. The stepped irregularities, however, introduce a considerable amount of spectral distortion, perceived as a harsh "buzz." Such unwanted side effects can only be reduced by increasing the number of voltage steps available for each cycle is increased, and in the case of lower frequency tones it was discovered that upward of five hundred such steps often were required to achieve an acceptable degree of purity.

Practical considerations such as the above tempered the practical value of this step function technique when applied in an unmodified form. Some designers, however, managed to reduce the problems of step distortion by incorporating a special circuit known as an integrator, which will electronically interpolate between steps to produce a gradient. This enhancement enabled the composer to achieve more accurate approximations to continuous curves with far fewer elements. Contrast a sine wave constructed out of twelve voltage steps with one constructed out of twelve gradients:

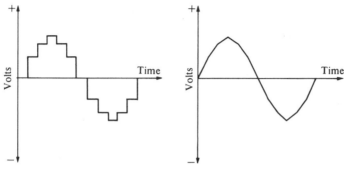

Figure 58

The gradient technique clearly produces a better approximation, and in many applications only twenty-four elements are required to achieve a sine function of adequate purity. Such a facility also enhanced the use of these sequencers as sources of continuously varying control voltages.

Earlier discussions have drawn attention to the problems encountered in attempting additive syntheses in an electronic music studio, in particular the number of individual sine wave generators required, and the high degree of tuning accuracy and frequency stability demanded of each unit. The direct specification of wave shapes, by contrast, provided a powerful degree of freedom in the construction of stable harmonic spectra, within the practical constraints referred to above. Altering the clock rate will shift the entire spectrum upward or downward in frequency, preserving the wave shape exactly.

Where the object was to achieve dynamic changes in timbre, however, composers had no option but to return to the techniques of additive synthesis, for it is not practicable to restructure wave shapes dynamically by hand in these circumstances. Even a simple idea such as progressively adding a second harmonic component to a pure sine wave would require complex adjustments to be made to all the individual voltage-bank settings simultaneously, an impossible task if undertaken manually.

One feature lacking in the types of sequencer so far described is a facility for registering and storing control voltage functions produced elsewhere in the system. The basis for such a device became known as a sample-and-hold processor.

In its simplest form this consists of an analog voltage-detection circuit that will sample the instantaneous value of an applied voltage function, the timing of this action being determined by a control pulse. The information thus obtained is retained as a steady voltage until replaced by a new value, sampled in response to the next control pulse. Providing a regular succession of pulses is applied, the device will produce a step pattern approximation to the applied voltage function, translating the characteristic into a succession of discrete values.[6]

Storage of these values demands the addition of a memory facility. Some early designs incorporated arrays of analog storage circuits capable of directly recording voltage steps in the form of electrical charges. Digital memories, however, were to prove more versatile, and as the years advanced this new technology became more reliable and significantly cheaper. The conversion of analog voltages into binary numerical equivalents, and the reverse procedure, the generation of analog voltages from binary data, are subjects that merit close attention for such operations are axiomatic not only to control voltage registration and recovery but also to all computer-based techniques of sound synthesis. Although a detailed study of digital technology is reserved for later chapters, some useful preparatory ground can be covered in the current context.

The principles of binary number coding have already been outlined in discussing the control systems for the RCA synthesizers. Their application in digital electronics is to all intents and purposes identical, each possible permutation of "on" and "off" states in a given group of binary elements being associated with a unique numerical value. In a digital memory the organization of binary locations or "bits" into groups or "words" involves two key considerations, the total number of words available, and the number of bits constituting each word. The former factor determines the total number of voltage samples that may be stored, and the latter the accuracy of their representation.

Each word in a digital memory is assigned a unique address by which it may be referenced via a pointer, the latter being manipulated by the control system. In a computer the associated memory may be randomly accessed via a pointer that may be freely moved from one location to any other. A simple first-generation memory sequencer, however, lacked the sophisticated programming capability of the computer, and was usually restricted to serial access only, where the pointer is only able to move sequentially along the memory bank, location by location.

A reset button is provided to initialize the pointer to the first location in the memory, and the effective working length of the memory can usually be adjusted using a special "last location" flag. Incrementing of the pointer itself is controlled via a variable rate clock pulse generator, the last location marker either terminating the operation or looping the pointer back to the first location, to repeat its progression.

Two modes of operation are usually possible. The sequencer may be set either to store new values, obtained via the sample-and-hold processor and an associated analog-to-digital converter, or to reproduce previously stored values, via a matching digital-to-analog converter. In the former mode the process proceeds as follows: at the first clock pulse the instantaneous value of an applied voltage is sampled and temporarily registered as a steady voltage. The analog-to-digital converter reads this value and generates an equivalent binary bit pattern. The control system then "writes" this pattern into the word location addressed by the pointer. Once this operation has been completed the sequencer waits for the next clock pulse, which increments the location pointer and reactivates the sample-and-hold processor to obtain a new value for the next conversion and storage operation.

The alternative mode of operation, used to recover previously stored voltage step values, is a reversal of this process, with two important differences. At the first clock pulse the control system "reads" the contents of the location currently addressed by the pointer and passes this information to the digital-to-analog converter. The location itself, however, is unaffected by this procedure, for only an image of its contents is transferred. This permits the stored value to be reproduced any number of times, as a result of either memory looping or a succession of separate scans. The digital-to-analog converter translates the pattern image into an equivalent voltage level, which is sustained until it receives a new pattern as a consequence of the next control pulse, which automatically moves the pointer to the next memory location. In both cases synchronization of the various processing stages is achieved by deriving all control pulses from a single clock.

If the system clock speed is freely adjustable, different sampling rates may be employed according to the nature of the voltage function to be registered. Too low a sampling rate for a rapidly fluctuating voltage will result in step approximations that are too crude. Increasing the sampling rate will improve the sampling accuracy but reduce the period over which the sequencer may be operated, for the end of the memory bank will be reached more quickly. Advancements in digital technology, however, notably the falling price of memory, ameliorated this problem with the passage of time, and by the late 1970s, as the era of voltage control technology drew to a close, most manufacturers were providing high capacity sequencers of this type at a reasonable cost.

Sampling a voltage function at one clock speed and reproducing it at another allows the step rate to be freely varied without altering the step values themselves. Studio control characteristics may thus be speeded up or slowed down without affecting their content. The interdependence of frequency and duration characteristics when sounds are subjected to variable-speed tape processing is a limitation that has been discussed earlier. Using a memory sequencer in the manner just described to control the generation of frequency functions allows such features to be manipulated separately, providing all the material is generated within the confines of the voltage-control system itself.

The accuracy of step approximation depends not only on the frequency of their occurrence, referred to as the sampling rate, but also, when digitized, on the resolution of the numerical equivalents, referred to as the accuracy of quantizing.[7] As noted earlier, the total number of values available for encoding voltages between the operating limits of the system is determined by the word size itself. Early memory sequencers generally employed word lengths of between eight and twelve bits. Although higher order resolutions were theoretically possible, the costs of manufacturing analog-to-digital and digital-to-analog converters to higher specifications were prohibitive. Each extra bit of resolution involved a quantum leap in cost, and sixteen bits, to all intents and purposes, was to mark the upper limit of attainable converter accuracy in hardware terms for many years to come.

It will be recalled that a three-row punched code in the RCA synthesizers permitted a total of $2^3 = 8$ different binary patterns to be created. Similarly, a four-row code permitted $2^4 = 16$ different patterns. A memory sequencer employing an eight-bit word length will thus permit coding of $2^8 = 256$ different numerical values. Assuming that the associated analog-to-digital and digital-to-analog converters offer a linear response, and that the synthesizer operates over a total control voltage range of 6 V, each digital increment will correspond to a voltage change of 6/256 = approximately 0.023 V.

The acceptability of such a minimum voltage step size depended on the device function to which it was applied. As a control of amplitude levels, or the duration characteristics of an envelope shaper, for example, such a resolution will normally prove satisfactory. As a control of frequency, however, such a step size will generally prove too large. If the voltage response characteristic is 0.3 V per octave, for example, a rather unusual tempered scale with almost thirteen divisions to the octave will result. Although it is possible, with the addition of an analog sensitivity regulator, to increase the basic step size in such a situation to a more useful semitone, the device will still be restricted to the registration of conventionally tempered pitches. Any attempt to register and subsequently reproduce a smooth glissando will simply result in the production of a chromatic scale.

It may thus be appreciated that the simulation of acceptably smooth glides in frequency demands a much higher degree of step resolution. Ten-bit sequencers allowed division of the voltage into $2^{10} = 1024$ discrete steps. Similarly, twelve-bit designs provided $2^{12} = 4096$ different steps. In the situation discussed earlier, the latter degree of resolution will provide voltage gradations sixteen times finer than those obtainable from an eight-bit converter. Pitch may thus be manipulated in steps of 1/208 of an octave, an interval size sufficiently small to provide an apparently continuous change of frequency.

The consequences of the decisions taken at the design stage as regards word length and memory size were to prove very significant for the user. Some small voltage-controlled synthesizers were equipped with very basic memory sequencers, offering as few as sixty-four words of storage, at a resolution of eight bits. More comprehensive designs offered 512 or more memory locations of higher resolution, sometimes organized into parallel banks to provide simultaneous registration and control of several voltage functions. Even the larger systems, however, almost invariably lacked one highly desirable facility: the ability to program the memory locations directly. Such facilities did not become generally available until the mid-1970s, signaling an important new era in electronic design facilitated by the invention of the microprocessor, an important development to be discussed in a later chapter.

Voltage-control technology unquestionably provided the primary driving force behind developments in studio design during the late 1960s and most of the 1970s. It would be erroneous, however, to suggest that all the major advances in electronic music during this period were intimately connected with the activities of commercial companies. Or, for that matter, that the compositional philosophies built up around the more traditional technology of the 1950s became irrelevant in the new era of studio design. Indeed, many of the works produced in leading studios during the 1960s and early 1970s made relatively little use of few voltage-controlled devices.

The impact of mass marketing, nevertheless, was without precedent, leading to artistic trends that were not wholly advantageous to the artistic development of the medium as a whole. It has been noted that the operational characteristics of a particular synthesizer exert a considerable influence on the range and type of compositional operations that may be satisfactorily executed. A proliferation of news studios equipped with identical synthesizers thus dictated a single design philosophy to all potential users. While modularity in some, although by no means all, commercial designs permitted an element of choice, it was rare for commercial systems to be developed in direct response to a specific set of artistic requirements.

Such an environment contrasts sharply with the continuous dialogue that was sustained between the engineers and the composers in centers such as Paris, Cologne, and Milan during the pre–voltage-control era. Studios such as these took only a modest interest in commercial equipment, choosing for the most part to research those aspects of the new technology that were of particular relevance to their needs and develop their own items of equipment. The studio founded at the Institute of Sonology, Utrecht, in 1961 provides a particularly notable example of a major center that decided to develop an extensive and unique voltage-controlled system designed entirely to its own requirements.

Individual design pioneers, often working with extremely limited resources, made some useful contributions to this technology. Reference has already been made to the work of Paul Ketoff in developing his voltage-controlled Synket. His interest in live rather than studio-based synthesis focused attention sharply on the problems of immediate and effective communication between a composer and his tools. It was the latter problem, perhaps the greatest stumbling block throughout the evolution of the medium, which inspired a most remarkable private enterprise, Oramics, developed by Daphne Oram in England at Fairseat, Kent, starting in 1959.[8]

As noted in the previous chapter, developments in England during the 1950s outside the closed doors of the BBC Radiophonic Workshop were few and far between. Oram's association with this institution during its formative years provided a major inspiration for her own ideas, which were to bear fruit in her private studio. The attraction of Oramics lay in its use of visual communication as the basis for sound specification. "Drawn sound" techniques were by no means new to the medium. Reference has already been made to Norman McLaren's manipulation of optical sound tracks in Ottawa, and the work of Yevgeny Sholpo in Leningrad.[9] Projects such as these, nevertheless, remained isolated from the mainstream of technical advance, not least as a result of their geographical remoteness.

In Oramics, a rationalized system of drawn shapes and neumes was employed to control sound production in terms of the primary characteristics of frequency, timbre, amplitude, and duration. The specification medium consisted of ten perforated 35 mm clear plastic strips of film, mounted in parallel and transported synchronously by a central drive system from right to left over an array of photocells. Each of the latter was illuminated from above by a steady light source. The composer operated the system by adding shadow masks or neume patterns to the strips of film, which modulated the light intensity as they passed over the photocells. The latter translated these fluctuations into voltage functions, used to control associated studio devices.

In such an environment, time thus becomes a linear function of distance measured along the strips according to their speed of transport, which was normally set at 10 cm/sec. The strips were divided into two banks of five, the upper bank being employed for discrete control specifications, and the lower bank for continuously variable characteristics. This distinction was reflected in the construction of the photocell system. In the case of the lower bank one photocell was provided for each strip, measuring the overall contour of the shadow masks. For the upper bank, four narrow-aperture photocells were mounted in parallel under each strip, their positions being indicated by a faint four-line stave engraved on the film. These acted as light-sensitive switches activated by rectangular neumes drawn on the stave lines. Although this coding system does not follow normal binary conventions a clear parallel may be drawn with the punched tape control systems of the RCA synthesizers.

The main purpose of the upper bank was to provide pitch control information, entered across three of the strips of film. A fourth strip could be used to operate switches within the system, and the remaining strip was available as a control facility for switching functions associated with any ancillary equipment that might be attached to the system from time to time.

In its normal mode of operation, the pitch control system could be used to generate a tempered chromatic scale from 𝄢 to 𝄞 (8ve). The whole range, however, could be externally transposed downward via a master regulator to start as low as 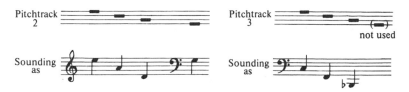 and upward to finish as high as . Continuously

variable adjustment on this control allowed accurate fine-tuning of the pitch. Neumes on each line on the three pitch tracks were associated with a specific element of the coding system. In normal mode, the lower two tracks provided coarse divisions of the frequency range, tuned in fifths as follows:

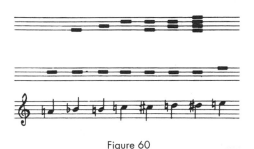

Figure 59

The lines on the top pitch track were used in combination with these primary tunings to provide tempered semitones by means of a frequency addition process. For example:

Figure 60

Pitches above required more complicated combinations of neumes

across the pitch tracks. The pitch generators themselves consisted of a bank of four synchronized photomultipliers, which continuously scanned shadow masks of hand-drawn wave forms, the pitch control system determining the rate of repetition. Up to four different timbres could thus be specified and blended in amplitude using the lower optical tracks, the fifth track in this bank being normally reserved for the control of a reverberation facility.

The ability to draw the dynamic shaping of pitched events not only allowed a readily assimilated audiovisual correlation of specifications, it also overcame the rigid attack and decay characteristics of conventional analog envelope shapers. One further shaping facility was offered: hand-drawn control over pitch vibrato, achieved by reassigning one of the lower optical control tracks to the time-base generator for the photomultipliers. A fluctuating mask characteristic then could be used to modulate the repetition speeds specified via the pitch control system.

Oramics was only capable of generating a monophonic output, in common with many of the voltage-controlled synthesizers that were soon to follow. Polyphonic textures had thus to be generated one strand at a time, the individual layers being built up through the processes of tape multitracking. Despite this procedural drawback, the flexibility afforded over the nuances of sound production provided the composer with a specification facility that had few rivals at the time.

Analog technologies reached their zenith during the mid-1970s. As the decade drew to a close, the seeds were already being sown for their impeding decline during the 1980s in the face of the digital revolution inspired by the invention of the computer. Before progressing to this new era in the history of the medium, the rich legacy of creative work that dates from the 1960s and early 1970s deserves some critical attention. This period of creative development marks an important watershed in electronic music, where the distinctiveness of individual endeavor, channeled for the most part through established studios and performing groups, begins to become submerged within a much broader culture of general accessibility and increasing affordability. Thus the exclusiveness of the Paris, Cologne, or Milan studios was eventually to be undermined by products and technologies available to all via the high street store and, more recently, the Internet, but not before the realization of some highly significant artistic achievements, to which attention is now turned.

1 Ondes Martenot

2 Leon Thérémin in 1927

3 Pierre Schaeffer at work in his studio in the early 1960s

4 Stockhausen at work in the Cologne
studio, c. 1960

5 Peter Zinovieff playing the Synthi 100

6 Philips Pavilion at the 1958 World Fair

7 RCA synthesizer

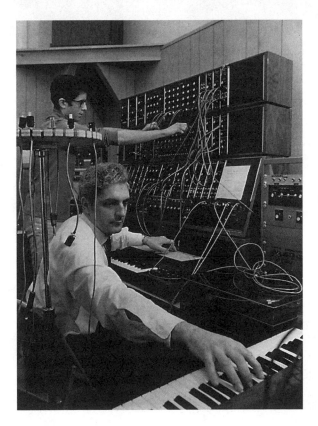

8 Robert Moog and Jon Weiss working with a Moog modular system

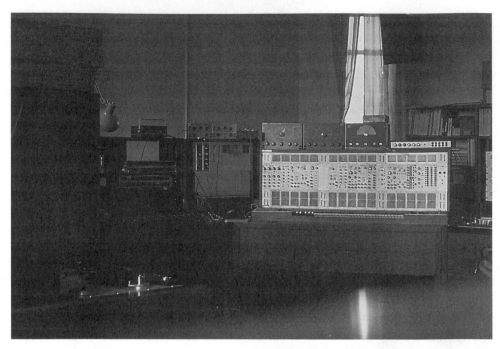

9 ARP 2600 synthesizer

10 Daphne Oram in her Oramics studio

11 Joel Chadabe seated at the Coordinated Electronic Music Studio System,
State University of New York at Albany in 1970

12 The electronic music studio, University of Toronto

13 Merce Cunningham's Variations V, with John Cage, David Tudor, and Gordon Mumma

14 E-mu systems emulator, c. 1982

15 IRCAM musical workstation

16 GROOVE system, Bell Telephone
Laboratories, c. 1970

17 Buchla Series 200 modular system,
late 1960s

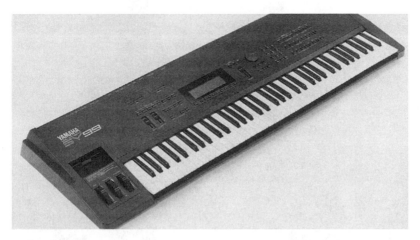

18 Yamaha SY99

19 Jon Appleton playing the Synclavier in 1978 while
Cameron Jones, one of its developers, stands by

20 Pierre Henry performing spatialization at the pupitre d'espace in 1952 in Paris

Photographs are reproduced by kind permission of the following:

(1) Thomas Bloch, www.chez.com/thomasbloch; (2) Electronic Music Foundation;
(3) Archives INA GRM; (4) Universal Edition (London) Ltd.; (5) Electronic Music
Foundation; (6) Philips Company Archives; (7) RCA, New York; (8) Electronic Music
Foundation (photo Joel Chadabe); (9) Electronic Music Foundation (photo Joel Chadabe);
(10) Daphne Oram, Wrotham, Kent; (11) Electronic Music Foundation (photo Carl Howard);
(12) Dennis Patrick, Electroacoustic Music Studio, University of Toronto; (13) Electronic
Music Foundation (photo Herve Gloaguen); (14) Electonic Music Foundation; (15) Philippe
Gontier; (16) Bell Laboratories, Murray Hill, NJ; (17) Electronic Music Foundation;
(18) Yamaha-Kemble Music (UK) Ltd.; (19) Electronic Music Foundation (photo Joel
Chadabe); (20) Fairlight Instruments Pty, Sydney.

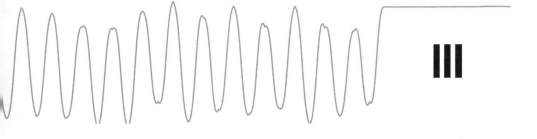

The Electronic Repertory from 1960

7

Works for Tape

The continuing work of the established studios provides a useful starting point for a general perspective of the more significant electronic works to be produced during the 1960s and 1970s. Major centers such as Cologne, Paris, Milan, and Columbia/Princeton remained primarily concerned with the production of tape works. A growing interest in live electronics, however, foreshadowed by the activities of Cage and his associates, gave rise to a sphere of activity that is sufficiently distinctive to demand consideration in its own right in the next chapter. Yet a third category must be added to take account of the birth and development of electronic techniques in the fields of rock and popular music, for it is in this sphere that the characteristics of electronic synthesis have attracted and sustained the greatest public attention.

The studio at Milan was to suffer mixed fortunes as the years advanced, resulting in a major decline in its importance during the 1970s. After *Visage*, Berio lost interest in the studio, moving away to work first at Columbia/Princeton and then briefly at the RTF studio in Paris.[1] With his departure, attention focused on the work of his contemporary, Luigi Nono.

Nono was highly motivated by the principles of socialism, and this conviction is strongly reflected in his compositions. His first excursion into the electronic medium, *Omaggio a Emilio Vedova* (1960), shows an unexpected familiarity with electronic techniques, arising from his preoccupation with texture in his instrumental works. *La fabbrica illuminata* (1964) for soprano and tape is an aggressive commentary on the plight of the industrial worker, constructed from electronically treated recordings of factory sounds and choral singing. Over this scenario the soprano sings an impassioned protest against the tyranny of human exploitation. *Ricorda cosa ti hanno fatto in Auschwitz* (1965) is a harrowing recollection of the horror of the concentration camp. Nono treats this emotive subject with a degree of directness and integrity that is compelling and highly communicative. The effect is that of a terrible dream remaining throughout one step removed from the rational, controllable state of human consciousness.

A floresta é jovem e cheia de vida (1966), a work for four actors, soprano, clarinet, copperplates, and tape, is dedicated to the National Front for the Liberation of Vietnam. The texts, compiled by Giovanni Pirelli, consist of eleven extracts from speeches and writings made by activists during the course of the anti-imperialist struggle. Nono concentrates here on an analysis and re-synthesis of their meaning rather than the linguistic components, thus differing noticeably from the techniques adopted by Berio in works such as *Thema* and *Visage*.

Contrappunto dialettico alla mente (1967–8) by contrast shows a much closer indebtedness both to Berio and also to Stockhausen, a much-valued mentor during the 1950s. The piece consists of a rich interplay between vocal fragments and electronic sounds, highly reminiscent of Stockhausen's *Gesang der Jünglinge*. *Non consumiamo Marx* (1969) and *Y entonces comprendió* (1969–70) are both strongly expressed reflections on the political unrest inspired in part by the Paris student riots in 1968. Recordings of Fidel Castro and the sounds of street demonstrations permeate *Y entonces comprendió*, creating a powerful eulogy for those who perished in the cause. One of his last major works to have been composed at Milan, *Como una ola de fuerza y luz* (1971–2), explored the potential of electronic tape as a resource for use in conjunction with large orchestral forces. Here rich electronic textures are integrated with fluid mobiles of instrumental sound to create a work of considerable stature.

Creative work at the RTF studio in Paris polarized around the principal members of the Groupe de Recherches Musicales, in particular François Bayle (later to become its director), Luc Ferrari, Ivo Malec, and Iannis Xenakis. Schaeffer devoted his time increasingly to theoretical matters, culminating in an exhaustively researched book *Traité des objets musicaux* (1966). His only studio works of note consisted of a reworking of *Symphonie pour un homme seul* (1966) and *Étude aux objets* (1959, revised 1967).

Bayle, although firmly committed to the principles of *musique concrète*, gradually introduced electronic elements into his works, writing both for tape and for tape plus instruments. One of his first major studio pieces, *Vapeur* (1963), developed from an earlier study, *Lignes et points* (1961, in turn revised 1966), is based on the sounds of a bass clarinet, double bass, harp, and cymbals. As the work evolves, initially unaltered recordings of these sources undergo progressive electronic transformations, extending the compass and variety of timbres extracted from the instrumental material. Another all-tape work, *L'Oiseau-Chanteur* (1964), combines electronic sources with recordings of a French horn, oboe, and harpsichord. In this instance, the instrumental material remains unmodified, the processing of the other sounds serving to highlight and extend the spectral content of the former.

Ferrari showed a particular disposition toward methods of rhythmic organization in his electronic works. After a series of preliminary studies, he produced a series of more substantial works including *Tautologos I* and *II* (1961) and *Presque rien No. 1* (1970). In both *Tautologos I* and *Tautologos II*, the structure is created by regulating timbre in terms of the frequency and density of the component events, organized into complex rhythmic patterns. *Presque rien No. 1* is an excursion into the sphere of organized collage using a wide variety of natural environmental sources such as birds, footsteps, seaside sounds, and children's voices. As the work progresses, the source elements, which remain largely untreated in themselves, become submerged under a growing stream of noise components that grow in density, eventually masking the environmental elements completely.

Malec pursued a compositional philosophy closely allied to that of Ferrari, structuring his work in terms of articulated changes of density and timbre. His works, however, were especially short in duration, typically between 2 and 7 minutes. Such brevity demanded meticulous attention to detail so that the processes of sound manipulation could be adequately articulated as a structural feature. *Reflets* (1961) and *Dahovi* (1961), for example, both highlight the evolving timbres of a succession of individually articulated sounds, prolonged where appropriate by the judicious addition of reverberation.

Xenakis stands out as perhaps the most unusual member of the original Groupe de Recherches Musicales. His early association with the Paris studio dates back to the mid-1950s, and a continuing development of his mathematical theories of musical organization placed his electronic compositions in a class of their own. Rejecting any allegiance whatsoever to established schools of composition, he furthered the principles of stochastics, an essentially self-styled description of an original and highly involved approach to probability calculus.[2] Mathematical organization of this order quickly led him to the computer, in the first instance generating numerical data for use as the basis for both instrumental and electronic compositions. Computer-assisted sound synthesis was thus but a step away from a reality, and this important area of activity will be returned to in due course. Other aspects of technology were also to become part of his creative art. His training as an architect inspired the use of visual as well as aural means of communication in his works, for example, holography and the projection of laser light beams. Such excursions into wider spheres of scientific development were motivated by a desire to develop an art of the universe in all its cosmic manifestations, thus pursuing in a highly individual way ideas very close to those of Varèse.[3]

Such an integration of very different facets of the medium defies any attempt to divide his electronic works into specific categories. A later tape piece such as *Persepolis* (1971), for example, owes as much to the computer as to the electronic studio in its conception. His most concentrated period early of activity, 1957–62, nevertheless resulted in a group of pieces that are clearly identifiable with the ideals of the Paris studio at that time. *Concret P.H.* (1958, revised 1968), realized directly after *Diamorphoses*, was produced for the Philips pavilion at the Brussels exhibition as a counterpart to Varèse's *Poème électronique*. The entire piece was realized from a single *concret* source, the sounds of burning charcoal, which are processed to produce expansive sweeps of sound that reflected the curved construction of the auditorium.

Orient-Occident (1960, revised 1968) is characterized by rich expansive sonorities derived from both *concret* and electronic sources. The former material consisted of resonant spectra produced by drawing a cello bow across the edges of metal rods, tam-tams, and cardboard boxes. The electronic sounds were derived from radio signals, demodulated into an audio form and transposed to produce high and low frequency tone clusters, linked by glissandi. Articulation is enhanced by using percussive material from a recording of an earlier orchestral work, *Pithoprakta* (1956), played at a reduced speed.

Bohor (1962) is perhaps the most notable contribution of Xenakis to the Paris school of composition. His choice of source material, a Laotian wind instrument and some items of oriental jewelry, recalls the early studies of Schaeffer. The methods of manipulation, however, are more refined, involving slow transformations of repeating sounds, the resultant ostinati acting to sharpen the ear to the inner changes of detail.

The continuing reputation of the RTF studio attracted other composers during the 1960s, notably Earle Brown and Luciano Berio. Despite his earlier association with Cage's "Music for Magnetic Tape," Brown's later works show a stronger affinity with developments in Europe, not least the mature manifestations of *musique concrète*. His *Times Five* (1963), for example, for flute, violin, cello, trombone, harp, and tape, uses recordings of instruments to extend both the perceived size of the live ensemble and also the range and variety of instrumental characteristics.

Berio's work at the studio culminated in *Laborintus II* (1965) for two sopranos, contralto, speaker, chorus, chamber ensemble, and tape, produced in response to a commission to commemorate the 700th anniversary of Dante's death. The origins of this work may be traced back to an earlier sketch, *Esposizione*, realized at Milan in 1962 just before his departure for the United States. Although further work at the Columbia/Princeton Center during the same year led to a preliminary version of *Laborintus II*, the final version owes a great deal to the major revisions he carried out in Paris. The texts for the piece, compiled by Edoardo Sanguineti, are drawn from Dante's *Divine Comedy*, *Convicio*, and *Vitta Nuova*, biblical sources, and the writings of Eliot, Pound, and Sanguineti himself. The live vocal elements predominate throughout, Berio's technique of fragmentation and collage acting to develop relationships between phonetics and musical structure as the basis for this extended piece of music theater.

As noted in an earlier chapter, the Cologne studio began to change direction under the increasing influence of Stockhausen during the late 1950s and early 1960s, culminating in his appointment to the directorship in 1963. The degree of polarization that followed became so intense that to all intents and purposes the studio became a personal laboratory for the composition of both his live and recorded electronic works. By the date of Stockhausen's succession to the directorship most of his early associates had either left for pastures new or ceased to compose electronic music altogether. After a series of live electronic pieces, Stockhausen completed one further major tape work at Cologne: *Hymnen* (1967). In the previous year, however, during a visit to Japan, he had completed another work in the same genre, *Telemusik*, at the studio of NHK Radio, Tokyo, to which attention must first be turned.

Japan might seem an unlikely country to have made a significant contribution to the development of electronic music by the mid-1960s. The initiative came from the establishment of an avant-garde in Japanese composition soon after the Second World War, inspired at least in part by the rapid development of communications with the Western world. Two composers, Toshiro Mayuzumi and Makoto Moroi, were instrumental in introducing the new medium to a totally unsuspecting public long before many Western nations had even begun to consider its potential.

During the autumn of 1954, a group of technicians and producers at NHK Radio began some elementary experiments in electronic sound generation using an array of laboratory oscillators and tape recorders. Early in 1955, this group of pioneers received details of facilities installed at Cologne, and using these as a basis began work on constructing a studio system to an almost identical specification. Moroi visited the Cologne studio in the autumn of the same year, and on his return commenced work with Mayuzumi on the production of the first pieces of Japanese electronic music in the newly completed NHK studio.

Inspired by their encounter with serialism, they found that mathematics provided a primary structural basis for their compositions. In *Variations on the Numerical Principle of 7* (1956), the influence of the Cologne school is especially evident, for the piece was based on a tuning scale of $49\sqrt{7}$, recalling the proportional approach to pitch specifications employed by Stockhausen in his *Studie II*.

By this time, other Japanese composers were becoming attracted to the medium. One group, known as *Jikken Kobo* (Experimental Laboratory) was granted access to recording facilities owned by the Sony Corporation and began to produce a series of simple *concret* pieces under the leadership of Toru Takemitsu. His personal contributions included the tape works *Relief Statique, Vocalisme AI,* and *Clap Vocalism* (1956). In 1960, this group transferred their activities to a new studio at the nearby Sogetsu Art Centre, which continued in operation until 1966.

In the meantime, activities at the NHK studio continued apace. In 1957 Mayuzumi realized an interesting precedent for Stockhausen's Telemusik. This work, entitled *Aoi-no-Ue,* is a partially electronic realization of an eighteenth-century Noh play, oscillators being substituted for the flutes, and noise and pulse generators for the percussion. In a similar vein, *Campanology* (1959) explores the recorded sounds of Buddhist bells, thus integrating *concret* elements with his compositional processes.

Stockhausen's visit to the NHK studio in 1966 undoubtedly influenced the subsequent course of Japanese electronic music, for many of the works that followed showed a more subtle approach to the medium, particularly with regard to the manipulation of timbre. Moroi's *Shosange* (1968) is based on modulations of traditional temple instruments including the triton, shakuhachi, and shamisen. Mayuzumi's *Mandala* (1969) is a reflection on the cosmic philosophy of the Buddhist religion, in which pure electronic sounds are complemented by manipulations of human voice sounds.

The musical contrast between *Telemusik* and *Kontakte* is very strong, for over the intervening six years a marked change in Stockhausen's compositional outlook had taken place, not least from an acquaintance with the music of Varèse. The universality of *Poème électronique* inspired a growing interest in other cultures, hence the motivation to travel to Japan to investigate at least one of these national traditions at first hand.

The sound sources for the work consist of electronic sine and triangle wave generators, function (impulse) generators, temple instruments, and a kaleidoscope of folk and religious music recordings from Bali, Japan, Vietnam, Hungary, Spain, Russia, the Amazon, the Sahara, and Brazil. The processes of amplitude and ring modulation are widely employed, resulting in transformations of the national sources that are so extreme that the original characteristics are only occasionally discernible, such instances providing powerful vistas of the familiar in a sound world that is predominantly synthetic.

The work is divided into thirty-two sections, each introduced by the recorded sound of a Japanese temple instrument. These signals mark the passage of time, heralding a change in material, and a new set of modulation processes. In some instances they stand out in isolation, in others they become extended and treated as an integral part of the section itself. The choice of temple instrument on each occasion has a direct bearing both on the length of the section it introduces, and also on the temporal ordering of the work as a whole. Strokes on the *keisu* at the start of sections 11 and 22 divide the work into three primary parts, approximately in the duration ratios 5 : 7 : 9. The use of this metal plate chime reflects its tradi-

tional role as a means of signifying a change of ritual during the Buddhist cere-
mony of worship.

Each part is subdivided by the higher-pitched *rin* bell, which announces the
start of sections 8, 16, and 24. The majority of the remaining sections are announced by strokes on one of a family of three wood blocks. The deep-sounding
mokugio introduces every sixth section, starting with section 3. Within this overall
framework the middle-sounding *bokusho* introduces a total of eight sections starting with the first, and the high-sounding *taku* a total of twelve sections, starting
with the second. Section 31 stands out as a major exception to this arrangement.
Following a fusion of transposed and modified *bokusho*, *mokugio*, *rin*, and *keisu* elements in section 29, this penultimate section is heralded and dominated by a gentle
chorus of four large temple bells.

A marked degree of mathematical organization is evident, not only in the proportions used for the duration of each section, clearly derived from a Fibonacci series,[4] but in the meticulous specifications used for the modulation and filtering
procedures that recall the tightly ordered organization of works such as *Studie II*
and *Kontakte*. The choice of material, and the refinement of its handling, results in
a piece that flows with an apparent timelessness that surpasses even *Gesang der
Jünglinge*. The piece is thus not a collage of disparate events but a delicately colored perspective, which owes much to the Japanese Noh drama.

Hymnen is a *tour de force* lasting almost two hours. The choice of material, the
national anthems of countries drawn from all over the world, and electronic sounds
both from studio generators and also from the ether, shows a clear affinity with the
sources used for *Telemusik*. The methods of organization and transformation,
however, result in a work that is significantly different.

The use of shortwave receivers to capture many of the anthems not only empha-
sizes the characteristics of radio communication as a means of linking nations, but
it also introduces a recognizable process of initial transformation. This is achieved
in terms of filtering and atmospheric interference, the severity of which depends
on the distance of the transmission and the general reception conditions. Such an
international perspective strongly echoes the concepts that lay behind Varèse's ill-
fated project, *Espace*.

The work is divided into four regions, each of which is dedicated to a particular composer. Within each region there are a number of centers that usually consist of a pointed reference to a particular anthem or group of anthems. Between
these centers the processes of development and metamorphosis act to build linking bridges in an architecture that aims to unify all the constituent elements as
parts of an ordered universe.

The first region, dedicated to Boulez, has two such centers: the Internationale
and the Marseillaise. The piece starts with a mêlée of short-wave radio sounds, obtained by rapidly tuning from station to station. This chaotic assault on the ear,

augmented by hissing sounds, roars, and distorted glissandi, moves erratically toward a semblance of order, provided by the two centers mentioned earlier. During this journey the listener is made aware of other electronic elements and anthems (notably that of the German Federal Republic)[5] and also shadows of an underlying harmonic structure derived from the anthems themselves. Further elements appear, with a disruptive effect on the main progression of events. Four times the flow is completely broken by the ghostly calls of a casino croupier. Another digression is created by a 2-minute polyphonic recitation on the various shades of red available in Windsor and Newton's artists' watercolors.

The disintegration of the first region leads to an extended bridge passage of floodlike sounds that rush up the audio spectrum to become the chatter of birds before descending once more into the depths, heralding the second region, which is dedicated to Pousseur. This has four centers, the first, the anthem of the German Federal Republic already alluded to, proving the most significant. After a cavernous, almost unrecognizable echo of the Marseillaise, achieved by playing the recording at an eighth of the correct speed, the great hymn by Haydn boldly bursts forth. This is immediately dislocated by a barrage of interruptions that include the juxtaposition of hymn fragments, sporadic gating of the sound, freezing of motion in the form of an extended chord that subsequently slides outward pitchwise in both directions, and finally the superimposition of different strands to create a polyphony.

Under such an assault the anthem suddenly vanishes, fleeting reappearances becoming submerged in the bridge to the second center, a compilation of African national anthems. These in turn become amalgamated with a synthesized version of the opening of the Soviet anthem to create a third center. The flow is then dramatically interrupted by a studio recording of a conversation between Stockhausen and his assistant during the preparation of the piece. Stockhausen refers to this as his own personal center where time (future, past, and present) becomes reduced to a single dimension.

The African anthems then resume their dialogue with the Soviet anthem as before, only to dissolve away as the music moves toward the third region. This section, dedicated to Cage, continues with a meditation on the Soviet anthem, which steadily develops into a full center. The use of synthetic rather than natural sounds gives an unearthly feel to this exposition, the harmonic flow becoming increasingly disrupted as the processes of amplitude and frequency modulation become dominant features, culminating in another "frozen" chord. The center then gently dissolves by means of a slow transposition of the chord downward, in semitone steps, fading away into a background of Morse signals. These sounds from the ether form the bridge to the second center, based on the American national anthem.

The latter enters brightly, only to become victim to extensive fragmentation, created by the interpolation of extracts drawn both from other anthems and from popular songs. The British anthem makes a few brief appearances here. Although never accorded a center in its own right, this anthem is heard fleetingly on a number of occasions during the piece, including, perhaps a little perversely, the bridge to the African center. The dissolution of this center advances on several levels. The background of radio interference increases in intensity as if to suggest a worsening of reception conditions. Concurrently the pitched material becomes fragmented, only to polarize as yet another "frozen" chord is in turn subjected to spatial modulation as if encapsulating the sound universe. The chord and the rest of the fragments, then abruptly disappear, leaving the background mush of static to form a bridge to the next center.

With the sudden intrusion of another studio conversation, this time remarking on the need to jump from America to Spain in a few seconds, the music plunges into the third center, a wild fresco reflecting the colorful nature of the Spanish nation. Successive multitracks of the Spanish anthem spiral upward to become high-pitched streams of sounds that finally fade into the distance. After a short pause these return to descend into deep, resonant sounds, marking the start of the fourth region.

This last region, dedicated to Berio, is the most economical in terms of material. It is also the most monumental, marking the fusion of elements into coherent pillars as the last steps on the path to unity. The first center, the Swiss national anthem, sung, not played, has been ghosted in short fragments as far back as the end of the Spanish center in the previous region. These interjections become stronger and more recognizable before themselves becoming caught up in the process of transformation toward mobile streams of sound.

The second and final center is an amalgam of three elements: a slow pedal of deep rumblings, the reverberated cries of voices, and a rich downward spiral of electronic tones. The first of a further three interjections by the croupier leads to the development of a massive downward-moving timbre cadence, an idea foreshadowed in Krenek's *Pfingstoratorium-Spiritus Intelligentiae, Sanctus*, where frequencies sliding off the bottom of the spectrum are replaced by new elements entering at the top. A slow duet for electronic tones over a continuing pedal leads, after the second and third croupier interjections, to a brief recapitulation of ideas from earlier regions. During this process the sounds or a single man breathing in his sleep become apparent, providing the final bridge into silence. The slow recitation of the word "pluramon" as a final element of this center identifies it as the Utopian realm of *Hymunion in Harmondie under Pluramon*, the name being a play on *hymn union*, *harmonia mundi*, and *plurism monism*.

Two other versions of *Hymnen* exist: *Hymnen mit Solisten* (1966–7) and *Hymnen mit Qrchester* (1969). The former involves the whole of the electronic tape with an added part for a small group of soloists. The latter uses only part of the tape, from the third center in region two to the end of region three. In both cases the score is notated in terms of written instructions and simple signs. Unlike *Kontakte*, these instrumental augmentations were added as options subsequent to the production of the main tape, and in no way detract from the conception of the original version as a complete work in its own right.

The reasons for describing *Hymnen* in such detail are threefold. First, the work is arguably one of the most important "classical" tape pieces to emerge from the 1960s. Second, its large-scale integration of synthetic and natural sound material provides an excellent example of the marrying of ideas and techniques gestated in the schools of *elektronische Musik* and *musique concrète*, in a manner anticipated by Varèse in his *Poème électronique*. Stockhausen's mature and perceptive handling of the *objet trouvé* provided all the necessary ingredients for a music drama worthy of Wagner, a comparison that he himself has acknowledged. Third, the work owes almost nothing to the voltage-control revolution, which was gaining momentum in the commercial sector at the time of its production. *Hymnen* was painstakingly constructed using procedures that were for the most part manually controlled, refining techniques that had been developed during the 1950s. The piece, nevertheless, was in no sense dated by the traditional manner of its composition. The musical ideas and the quality of their expression looked forward to the next decade, pointing to the earlier-mentioned dichotomy between increasing sophistication in voltage-control technology and the artistic shortcomings of electronically controlled processes.

With the expansion of interest in electronic music during the 1960s other studies began to grow in importance. Henry, it will be recalled, had left Schaeffer's studio in 1958 to found his own private studio, Apsome. His output continued to be prolific, well over fifty works being produced during the first ten years of this studio's existence. In addition to concert works, he has composed tapes for film, theater, and dance. His ballet *Le Voyage* (1961–2), choreographed by his close friend Maurice Béjart, describes the journey from death into reincarnation, as told in the *Tibetan Book of the Dead*.

La Reine verte (1963), again choreographed by Béjart, utilizes both electronic and natural sources, the latter consisting of a piano, percussion, and textless vocalization from a group of singers. Great pains were taken to establish a strong continuum of timbre between these elements, shaped by the natural formants of the vocal sounds.

Variations pour une porte et un soupir (1963) is his most overtly *concret* piece of the period. Three basic sources were employed: the sigh of breathing, both inhaling and exhaling, pitched sighs obtained by playing a musical saw in a variety of ways, for example, bowing or rubbing, and the squeaks and groans of rusty door hinges. The degree of transformation applied is for the most part kept to a bare minimum. It is the character of the sources, and the skillful juxtaposition of the resultant recordings, which structure the work. Henry's Catholicism led him to compose several works with a religious setting. In 1964–5, for example, he composed four electronic interludes based on the Gospels according to Matthew, Mark,

Luke, and John. These were followed by *Messe de Liverpool* (1967) and *Messe pour le temps present* (1970).

Pousseur worked at the APELAC studio in Brussels during the 1960s before moving on to take up the directorship of the University studio at Gent. Two of his works stand out as being of particular significance: *Trois visages de Liège* (1961) and *Jeu de miroirs de votre Faust* (1966). The former is a more refined work than his earlier *Scambi*, completed at Milan. The style, however, is strongly derivative of Cologne works from the middle and late 1950s. It employs a text, a group of short poems by Jean Séaux, reflecting the industrial and social life of the city. The other source material is predominantly electronic, filtered noise bands and both ring and amplitude modulated tones providing rich sonorities, frequently the subject of glissandi. The voice transformations are relatively mild, simple collage and reverberation adding a mobility to the recitation of text without destroying its intelligibility. *Jeu de miroirs de votre Faust* is an electronic commentary on his full-scale opera, *Votre Faust,* a work that he took almost six years to complete (1961–7). Once again vocal elements, both spoken and sung, predominate, with only minor transformations being applied to their content.

Yet another protégé of Cologne, Bengt Hambraeus, returned home to work primarily in the Swedish Radio studio at Stockholm.[6] After composing a series of short background pieces for radio and television during the late 1950s, he produced a major concert work, *Tetragon,* in 1965. The style is strongly reminiscent of the more mature electronic works of Luening and Ussachevsky. A variety of instrumental sounds are subjected to simple tape manipulation techniques such as multilayering, variable-speed processing, and head echo bounced from channel to channel to produce a powerful reworking of conventionally scored material.

The Munich studio proved an active center during the 1960s, despite major changes in its administration, culminating in a complete removal of the system to the Hochschule für Gestaltung, Ulm, in 1966. Much of the original equipment was built and paid for by the successful electronics firm Siemens. This resulted in a studio of some sophistication, differing markedly from its European counterparts in the use of a punched tape control system. While strongly reminiscent of the RCA synthesizers, this programming facility proved altogether more flexible, mainly as a result of the enhanced range of controllable synthesis and treatment devices.

Despite the advanced state of design, the studio was intended first and foremost as a facility for producing background soundtracks for radio and television, thus restricting the scope for the production of concert works. In 1964 Mauricio Kagel produced a realization of Cage's *Imaginary Landscape No. 3* for electronic tape and percussion, a testament to a composer who proved a major inspiration for his own compositional style. Herbert Brün also spent some time at Munich before moving to the University of Illinois in 1963, completing a short piece, *Klänge unterwegs,* in

1961. Yet another expatriate of Cologne, Ernst Krenek, visited the studio during 1966–7 to produce a tape for a short television opera, *Der Zauberspiegel*.

The university studio at Berlin achieved some importance, mainly as a result of the activities of Boris Blacher. Blacher, very much the elder statesman, had established a considerable reputation with the German public over many years, particularly in the field of opera. His excursions into the electronic medium occurred at a very late stage in his career, and were restricted for the most part to the preparation of taped interpolations for inclusion in large-scale choral and orchestral works. These included a full-scale opera, *Zwischenfälle bei einer Notlandung* (1964–5), scored for voices, orchestra, and tape, to a libretto by Heinz von Cramer.

The Warsaw studio made a significant contribution to the flowering of contemporary Polish music after the 1956 uprising, sustaining a level of activity second to none. These achievements, unfortunately, passed almost unnoticed outside Poland itself, for few of these electronic works have ever been heard in Western Europe or America. Krzysztof Penderecki took an active interest in the studio, exploring its capabilities as a tool for generating and manipulating new tone colors in works such as *Psalmus* (1961) and *Brygada smierci* (1963). Instrumental writing, nevertheless, remained his main means of expression, but he frequently employed performance techniques that are closely allied in their effect to the characteristics of electronic composition. By the middle of the decade the studio was attracting composers from other countries. One of the first, François-Bernard Mâche, an affiliate of the RTF studio in Paris since 1958, visited Warsaw in 1966 to complete a short *concret*-inspired piece, *Nuit blanche*, to a text by Artaud.

The use of solo instruments with prerecorded tape features prominently in the works of Andrzej Dobrowolski. His *Music for Magnetic Tape and Oboe Solo* (1965), *Music for Magnetic Tape and Piano Solo* (1972), and *Music for Magnetic Tape and Double Bass Solo* (1977) all display a deep preoccupation with the interplay of rich electronic textures with an extended palette of live instrumental sounds.

Studios were also established in Denmark (Copenhagen, 1956) and Norway (Oslo, 1961) by the respective state broadcasting corporations. Although the output from these studios was relatively modest during these early years the contributions of Per Norgaard and Arne Nordheim should not be overlooked. Norgaard gained a considerable reputation within Denmark as a strongly avant-garde composer, pursuing post-Webern techniques of serialism, and his work at Copenhagen stimulated considerable interest in the potential of the electronic medium. His pieces include *Dommen* (1961–2), an extensive work for tape, soloist, and orchestra, and *Labyrinten* (1966–7), a short opera. Nordheim's work at Oslo resulted in a number of works, the first, *Katharsis* (1962), taking the form of a ballet for orchestra and tape. His style is less formalized than that of Norgaard, displaying a more developed sensitivity toward nuances of timbre. The manipulation of naturally produced music material on tape as a restrained enhancement to live performance proved a particular attraction. His *Epitaffio* (1963) for orchestra and tape, for example, uses the latter part only sparingly, mainly to introduce montages of choral singing to which the instruments respond.

The "closed door" policy of the BBC Radiophonic Workshop, and the continuing lack of support from other quarters, severely retarded developments in Britain during the 1960s. Indeed, Roberto Gerhard was the only established composer from the broader community to be granted reasonable access to the BBC facilities during the decade. This permitted him to produce a number of pieces, primarily for radio, working both at the BBC and at his own private studio in Cambridge. Most notably, *The Anger of Achilles* (1963), for orchestra and tape, won the Italia prize for composition in 1965.

Tristram Cary continued to work in his own private studio, first in London, and then from 1963 until his departure for Australia in the early 1970s at Diss, Norfolk. The majority of his compositions have been written for radio, television, and film rather than concert-performance. *The Little Island* (1958), for example, is a cartoon with an electronic sound track, which is integral to, and not merely background for, the visual action.

Daphne Oram continued to develop her Oramics system at Fairseat, producing, like Cary, a succession of film scores. Music for theater works also figured prominently, including *Rockets in Ursa Major* (1962), *Hamlet* (1963), and *Purple Dust* (1964). Another private studio was founded in London during the late 1950s by Ernest Berk to provide electronic music for the Modern Ballet Group, an experimental venture that continued for well over a decade.

The general lack of facilities in Britain led several composers to improvise in a manner strongly reminiscent of the early struggles of Luening and Ussachevsky in America more than a decade previously. One result was the establishment of a special studio by Brian Dennis specifically designed to integrate electronic elements into music for schoolchildren.

Perhaps the most significant development in this sphere was the formation of a collective during the mid-1960s between the composers Hugh Davies, Don Banks, Anthony Gilbert, David Lumsdaine, and the flautist Douglas Whittaker. This group stimulated considerable interest in the medium among the younger British composers via seminars given for the Society for the Promotion of New Music (SPNM). These activities drew the electronic engineer and composer Peter Zinovieff into the circle. Zinovieff, who was in the process of establishing his own studio at Putney, London, sensed the potential for developing commercial voltage-controlled equipment to satisfy a growing demand, and thus it was that EMS, London, was born.

By the end of the decade, a few institutions in Britain, principally universities, were at last beginning to respond to the growing interest in the medium. After one short-lived attempt to establish a studio at the University of Manchester, permanent studios were established at the Universities of Cardiff, Goldsmiths' College

London, York, and Durham in quick succession with others soon to follow during the early 1970s. Electronic music had at last become accepted as a legitimate area of study in U.K. education and research.

Utrecht, the last of the second-generation European studios to be considered here, proved to be especially important to the development of the medium during the 1970s. As the Institute of Sonology within the University of Utrecht, this center was able to make advances on several fronts, both in scientific research and development and also in the theory and practice of composition. The early acquisition of a computer opened up new avenues of investigation, complementing and augmenting a sophisticated custom-built voltage-controlled system that had been constructed during the late 1960s.

Although this studio officially dates from 1960, composers such as Henk Badings, Dick Raaijmakers, and Tom Dissevelt had carried out some preliminary work at Eindhoven during the late 1950s, using items of equipment supplied by the electronics firm Philips, the entire operation being subsequently transferred to Utrecht. It was the appointment of Gottfried Michael Koenig as artistic director in 1964, however, which heralded the start of a full-scale research and development program. The introduction of a comprehensive course in sonology attracted students from all over the world, providing a powerful theoretical base for the production of works by both established and up-and-coming composers.[7]

The voltage-controlled equipment was constructed to an exacting specification, thus ensuring that the control networks functioned reliably and predictably. Until the introduction of direct computer-based control facilities in the mid-1970s, sequencers provided the primary means for programming events. Despite the introduction of this new digital technology the studio retained its older "classical" equipment for those who wished to work in a more traditional manner.

Electronic synthesis governed by strict syntactical considerations became a major feature of the studio's creative output at this time, aided in due course by the mathematical capabilities of a digital computer to produce music data from sets of algorithms. This trend diverged sharply from the freer, more intuitive compositional directions pursued by Stockhausen at Cologne during the 1960s, aligning itself more closely to the mathematical approaches of Xenakis, while sustaining a strong regard for the post-Webern tradition of serialism.

Koenig's *Terminus II* (1966–7) is characterized by a continuous variation of timbre, all the sounds being derived from an initial complex of sliding oscillator tones. Continuity is achieved by presenting the sounds in the order of their derivation, tending to a generative process of transformation. The use of mathematically determined procedures becomes more apparent in his next series of compositions entitled *Funktion Grün* (1967), *Funktion Orange* (1968), *Funktion Gelb* (1968), and *Funktion Rot* (1968), leading in turn to *Funktionen Blau, Indigo, Violett,* and *Grau* (1969). These were all derived from a series of composing programs entitled PROJECT 1, first conceived at the Mathematical Institute of Bonn University during a visit in 1963–4. In the absence of direct computer control of studio equipment at this stage analog control tapes were used in place of the sequencer, voltages being encoded as frequency functions via a pair of modulators and demodulators.

Chants de Maldoror (1965–6, revised 1968–9) by Rainer Riehn makes a virtue of the normally unwanted electronic distortions that can inadvertently occur when operating a studio, for example hiss, mains hum, and overenergized feedback. These sources are subjected to elaborate juxtaposition and montage to create a piece of rich, fast-moving sonorities.

In America, work at the Columbia/Princeton Center continued apace during the 1960s The RCA synthesizer Mark 2 proved highly attractive to the East Coast schools of composition, which for the most part shared a common interest in transferring "note/event" styles of writing to the electronic medium. There were some, however, who shared the European bias toward less restricted concepts of sound structure and transformation, and the limitations of the synthesizer in this respect led in due course to the introduction of additional synthesis and treatment facilities, including some voltage-controlled modules.

Babbitt continued to work extensively with the RCA synthesizer during the early part of the decade. *Vision and Prayer* (1961) combines a part for live soprano, based on a text by Dylan Thomas, with an all-electronic tape. The techniques employed contrast sharply with those of a work such as Berio's *Visage*. The scoring of the voice part remains distinctively conventional throughout, the synthesized material, highly instrumental in nature, being restricted to particular sections of the work. With no attempt being made to relate these elements in terms of any continuum of timbre the dialogue is distinctly uneasy, highlighting the artificial nature of the electronic sounds.

Philomel (1963–4), based on a setting of a poem by Hollander on the *Metamorphoses* of Ovid, is a more integrated piece, again written for soprano and tape, the latter combining electronic sounds with manipulations of the voice part. The text is a scenario describing the metamorphosis of the tongueless Philomel into a nightingale. Such an effect demanded a conscious interplay between the natural and electronic elements, the latter being employed to produce rich polyphonic textures suggesting the atmosphere of the forest in which the event takes place. His *Ensembles for Synthesizer* (1963), a wholly electronic piece, is more complexly ordered than its earlier counterpart, *Composition for Synthesizer*. Babbitt here was particularly concerned to explore further the manipulation of complex textures, unobtainable in live instrumental performance.

Mario Davidovsky's association with the studio proved to be long and productive. After some preliminary experimentation with all-electronic sounds he turned his attention to the use of electronic sounds in combination with live instruments, composing a group of pieces. *Synchronisms 1 to 6*. In *Synchronisms No. 1* (1963) for flute and tape, *Synchronisms No. 2* (1964) for flute, clarinet, violin, cello, and tape, and *Synchronisms No. 5* (1969) for cello and tape, the source material is worked in a highly sectionalized manner. The constant changes in format from instrumental sounds alone, to instrumental sounds plus tape, or to tape alone highlight the wide variety of natural and artificial timbres obtainable from these resources through the processes of juxtaposition. In *Synchronisms No. 4* for boys' voices or mixed chorus and tape, *Synchronisms No. 5* (1969) for percussion and tape, and *Synchronisms No. 6* (1970) for piano and tape, Davidovsky adopts a more flexible approach to compositional procedures, integrating rather than contrasting the live and electronic resources.

Ílhan Mimaroğlu also made extensive use of the Columbia/Princeton facilities, displaying like Davidovsky a keen interest in the integration of electronic and instrumental sounds. His style of composition, however, despite the sophistication of the facilities at his disposal, recalls the traditional "cut and stick" approaches of the 1950s. Such meticulous attention to detail greatly enhances the essentially dramatic nature of much of his writing, which is rich in contrasts of timbre and dynamics. Rather than integrate live and recorded material in performance he has preferred to create works for tape alone, manipulating natural sound sources in a manner highly reminiscent of musique concrète. *Bowery Bum* (1964), for example, is based entirely on the sounds of a plucked rubber band, subjected to simple filtering and tape manipulation. The visual arts, in particular painting, provided a major stimulus for his compositions. *Bowery Bum*, for example, was influenced by Dubuffet, and *Le Tombeau d'Edgar Poe* (1964), based on the text of the same name by Mallarmé, is reminiscent of Davidovsky's early *Synchronisms* in its use of juxtaposition. The treatment of the text here is strongly reminiscent of the techniques used in Berio's *Thema*, involving elements of filtering, montage, fragmentation, and reverberation.

The influence of Berio also may be detected in *Prelude XII*, the last of a set of *Preludes* composed during 1966–7. Here a setting of a poem in Turkish by Orhan Veli Kanik is clearly influenced by phonetic considerations, the speech formants influencing the electronic background in a manner that recalls the synthetic speech components of Berio's *Visage*. This penchant for vocal transformation reveals itself again in the last movement of a later work: *Music for Jean Dubuffet's "Coucou Bazar"* (1973).

The work of Mimaroğlu contrasts sharply with the more esoteric styles of composition pursued by Babbitt and his followers. Such diversity from a single studio, however, is a compliment to its wide-ranging artistic policy, a reflection of the more universal approach to electronic music composition generally fostered during the 1960s and 1970s.

Jacob Druckman's association with the studio commenced in 1966. His style of composition, although clearly identifiable with the East Coast avant-garde, shows a particular regard for the larger-scale manipulation of timbre and texture. *Animus I* (1966) for trombone and tape, is characterized by a strong sense of association between the electronic and instrumental sounds, the links being strengthened by the inclusion of trombone material and transformations thereof in the tape part. In *Animus II* (1967–8), for mezzo-soprano, percussion, and tape, the voice provides a bridge to the electronic material, the latter including a collage of speech fragments, complementing the text-less vocalization of the mezzo-soprano in a manner owing much to the influence of Berio.

In *Animus III* (1969), for clarinet and tape, the instrumental part is particularly demanding, requiring the production of an extended range of timbres. The tape part includes both clarinet and vocal elements, the latter being matched by the live shaping of formants achieved by varying the mouth excitation of the reed. A further performance element is added by the incorporation of a feedback loop to produce delayed repetitions of the clarinet part, almost qualifying the piece for inclusion under the heading of live electronic music. The animation of the electronic material evokes a powerful dialogue with the clarinet, creating an impression that all the electronic sounds are somehow a live reaction to the antics of the performer.

A later work, *Synapse* → *Valentine* (1969–70), for double bass and tape, finds Druckman yet again attempting to throw a new perspective on the integration of live and electronic elements. In sharp contrast to his earlier works, this two-movement work treats the two components as entirely separate forces, exploring the qualities of contrast and opposition rather than unity. This dualism is extensively developed, the bass player being required to execute virtuoso feats of rapid pizzicatos, double stops, trills, and tapping of the instrument, combined with a vocal contribution of speech fragments, both sung and spoken.

Perhaps the most significant piece to emerge from Columbia/Princeton during the 1960s was *Time's Encomium*, composed in 1969 by Charles Wuorinen. Wuorinen, a former pupil of both Luening and Ussachevsky, had been a student at Columbia before joining the staff of the music faculty in 1964. *Time's Encomium* was a commission from Nonesuch Records, who had recognized the talent of this promising young composer from his wide-ranging output of traditionally scored music. The piece received instant and widespread acclaim, leading to the award of the 1970 Pulitzer Prize for music. The source material was generated entirely from the RCA synthesizer, further treatment in the form of reverberation, filtering, and ring modulation being applied in one of the Center's analog studios.

The opening sequence of contrasted chords shows a keen awareness of the textual refinements that may be derived from electronic sources, the progression into motivic fragments and thence to a slowly evolving complex of sustained and individually enveloped pitches providing a framework ripe for development. The influence of his teachers is unmistakable: one of the recurring motives, a "galloping" sequence of pitches, for example, directly recalls the opening of Luening's *Gargoyles*. Wuorinen's deep regard for considerations such as larger-scale shaping and organic growth, however, ensures that such clearly identifiable fragments do not become reduced to mere patterns.

Developments in the Experimental Studio at Illinois proceeded on an altogether

broader front. Luening and Ussachevsky, it will be recalled, had discovered Lejaren Hiller and Leonard Lsaacson employing the computer as a means of generating compositional data during their 1955 international tour of studios. It was
thus but a small step to the substitution of electronic devices in place of conventional instruments, to create a hybrid system. The direct use of the computer for
the digital synthesis of sound was another application that rapidly gained importance during the 1960s, providing a tempting alternative to the new voltage-control
technology. Many composers, nevertheless, continued to prefer analog methods of
synthesis, sustaining a significant level of output for this category.

Hiller composed a number of electronic works before turning more specifically
to computer sound synthesis. These included *Machine Music* (1964) for piano,
percussion, and tape, and *Suite* (1966) for two pianos and tape. *Machine Music* reflects the style of Bartòk both in its use of incisive rhythms and in the adoption of
an archlike structure. The work is divided into eleven sections each using one or
a specific combination of the three primary forces in a symmetrical structure of
densities, pivoting around the sixth movement. The tape part employs a wide variety of sound sources both live and electronic, subjected to extensive treatment in
terms of filtering and all three primary methods of modulation. Ring modulation
in particular features prominently, the resultant spectra complementing the inharmonic resonant frequencies obtained naturally from the tuned percussion.

The *Suite* is part of a much larger multimedia piece, *A Triptych for Hieronymus*
(1964–6), requiring a performance area for dancers and actors, encircled by groups
of instrumentalists and loudspeakers. A focal point for the action is provided by
the projection of film slides on to a screen. The tape part for this three-movement
extract is derived from a colorful mixture of natural and electronic sources, this
aural kaleidoscope being combined with the live instrumental material to create a
spatial perspective that is closely integrated with the visual action.

The electronic works of Salvatore Martirano delve even further than the works
of Lejaren Hiller into the possibilities of sound theatre. His works are imbued with
a strong sense of vitality and drive, creating contrasts of color and style that cleverly
conceal highly organized methods of composition. Jazz has proved a major influence in his output. *Underworld* (1964–5), scored for tenor saxophone, two double
basses, four percussionists, and tape, indeed, is almost entirely based on a jazz
idiom, elevating the prerecorded electronics to a role that appears as alive in its
synthesis as the instrumental performance.

L's GA (1967–8) is a full-scale electronic dramatization of Lincoln's Gettysburg
Address, the political nature of the text providing the motivation for an almost
grotesque excursion into the world of the surreal. The work starts with deep organlike sounds, created by pumping low-frequency sine tones from loudspeakers
down large tubes of cardboard, normally intended for storing carpets, the results
being recorded by microphones. The reading of the Address is similarly subjected
to a live process of transformation by the inhalation of helium gas, causing the voice

of the reader to rise uncontrollably in pitch to a childlike gabble. The accompanying collage of electronic and instrumental sound elements rises to a crescendo, the tension being released by the banal outpourings of an electronic organ with full vibrato, caricaturing the inimitable style of American electioneering.

Herbert Brün's move to Illinois provided a useful influence on the studio's output from a more European perspective. His earlier work at Cologne had inspired a particular interest in linguistics, leading him to explore parallels between musical and verbal communication. *Futility* (1964) consists of an alternation between wholly electronic passages and recorded fragments of a self-composed poem, a sense of continuity being created by shaping the synthetic material to match the natural inflections of the spoken part. Later works such as *Soniferous Loops* (1965) and *Non Sequitur VI* (1966) translate these processes of shaping formants into the sphere of live instrumental writing, used in combination with electronic tape.

The works of Kenneth Gaburo are amongst the most significant to emerge from Illinois during the 1960s. Like Brün, he took a keen interest in phonetics, exploring vocal transformations in a manner owing much to the influence of Berio. *Antiphony III* for chorus and tape (1962) and *Antiphony IV* for voice, piccolo, bass trombone, double bass, and tape (1967) both involve elaborate treatment of phonemes. The former involves a lively interplay between the live vocalists, uttering speech elements rich in sibilants and plosives such as "k," "s," and "t," and the tape part, which consists of similar material subjected to extensive juxtaposition, transposition, and reverberation. *Antiphony IV* calls on a wider range of resources, the instrumental elements, used in both live and tape parts, extending and characterizing further the pitched inflections of the vocal material.

Jazz elements, too, figure prominently in some of his works, for example, *Lemon Drops* (1965), *Exit Music II: Fat Millie's Lament* (1965), and *For Harry* (1966). *Lemon Drops* is a short all-tape work derived entirely from an electronic tone generator, the incisive rhythms and clearly articulated keyboardlike sounds developing in a manner appropriate to a jazz improvisation. *Exit Music II* commences with two gentle and repeating rhythmic patterns, which slowly change in content. The quiet entry of an untreated excerpt from a big-band piece seems to evolve naturally from the opening texture, growing in volume to become the dominant feature before fading again into the background. *For Harry,* Gaburo's last piece to be composed at Illinois before he relocated to the University of California at San Diego, is a tribute to the composer Harry Partch. The latter's rejection of the conventional in terms of musical instruments and tuning systems led him to pursue in isolation the cause of new acoustic instruments and associated timbres, in his own way developing concepts not unconnected with the expanded sound world of electronic music. Gaburo's tribute delicately explores the world of microtones and subtle rhythmic combinations, creating a captivating aura of timbres.

The San Francisco Tape Music Center relocated to the Tape Music Center at Mills College, Oakland, in 1966. The studio's two founders, Ramon Sender and Morton

Subotnick, however, did not accompany this move. Sender chose instead to continue his activities at Donald Buchla's private studio at Berkeley, California, concentrating increasingly on techniques of improvisation. Subotnick moved to New York University to develop another studio, based on a Buchla system, for the Intermedia Program at the School of Art. Although his previous compositional output at SFTMC had been extensive, it was for the most part concerned with incidental music for plays. His later work at New York led to more substantial pieces realized using a Buchla synthesizer. *Prelude No. 4* (1966) for piano and tape reveals a highly instrumental approach to electronic writing. *Silver Apples of the Moon* (1967), a commission from Nonesuch Records, demonstrates even more clearly his adherence to "note/event" methods of organization. A wide variety of timbres and intricate duration structures are employed, the latter assisted to no small extent by the use of a sequencer.

The Wild Bull (1968), also a commission from Nonesuch, is characterized by more elaborate applications of sequencer control, resulting in intricate and imaginative shapes derived from a single sound source, a sawtooth oscillator. The rapid interplay between different dynamics and timbres generates a strong rhythmic drive, which at times creates the feel of a free jazz improvisation. *Laminations* (1969–70), for orchestra and tape, utilizes large instrumental forces. With such a powerful reserve of live sounds, heavy demands were placed on the synthetic material, for the directly communicative quality of the various instruments made them naturally dominant.

Gordon Mumma and Robert Ashley's private venture at Ann Arbor, Michigan, the Cooperative Studio for Electronic Music, proved highly influential in establishing a major movement in the sphere of live electronics, a development to be discussed in the next chapter. Their studio work during the early part of the 1960s involved the production of pieces not only for tape alone and tape plus instruments, but also what might be described as an intermediate category, tape plus instruments plus live electronics.

Their styles of composition show a considerable indebtedness to the techniques of jazz, albeit of a somewhat progressive nature. The very names of their work suggest a less than academic attitude towards electronic composition, borne out by the colorful, freely structured nature of their content, for example *A Slice of Life* (1961) and *Eimert Plays Basie* (1961) by Ashley, and *Commodious Means* (1962) by Mumma.

The years 1964–6 marked the peak of their creative activities at Ann Arbor. Ashley's *The Wolfman* (1964) exists in two versions, one for jazz trio and tape, the other for amplified voice and tape. The former version, prepared for the Bob James Trio, involves a performance of a blues song in conjunction with a tape of heavily modulated speech components, the latter elements at times completely swamping the live instruments. In the second version, the voice replaces the instruments with a mimic of the tape, taking the form of a succession of sustained vocal sounds that are subjected to rich distortions by the application of live acoustic feedback between the performer's microphone and his loudspeaker. *Untitled Mixes* (1965) was also written for the same jazz trio, the instrumentalists being required to imitate the tape material with a variety of plucking, sliding, and exotic percussion effects.

Mumma's *Peasant Boy* (1965) is a similar piece to *Untitled Mixes,* scored for the same jazz trio and tape, again with the intention that the instrumentalists should imitate the tape sounds. Neither piece, however, is entirely successful in achieving a cohesive integration of live and electronic elements. The solutions to these problems of relating instrumental and electronic material for Mumma and Ashley lay in eliminating the need for a prerecorded tape part, thus cultivating a more interactive environment for the realization of their compositions.

Steve Reich founded his own private studio in San Francisco toward the end of 1963, moving it to New York in 1966. His two major tape works, *Its Gonna Rain* (1965) and *Come Out* (1966), both use short verbal phrases as the starting point for progressive transformations. The basic processes involved were essentially very simple. In *Come Out,* the fragment "Come out and show them" is initially presented as an untreated repeating loop for almost 30 seconds. This in itself creates a developing musical experience, for the ear becomes increasingly aware of the inner acoustical detail of the fragment in terms of pitch, inflection, and rhythm. Transformation then proceeds by using two identical loops of this source simultaneously, starting in perfect unison and then slowly slipping out of synchronization. This phasing effect gradually introduces echo effects for the shorter elements such as "c" and "t," while the longer ones become extended. As the slippage progresses, juxtaposition and overlay ensue, creating new formants. Subsequent multiple combinations of the loop channels to produce four, eight, or even more loops ensure that the original sense is completely lost in an ever-extending montage of rhythmic and timbre elements. Such a process was readily translatable to live performance; hence his subsequent interest in applying this special technique of transformation to ensembles of instruments, both acoustical and electronic.

Several other American composers developed a preference for electronic musical instruments on the concert platform, notably Terry Riley and Philip Glass, and these activities will be considered in the next chapter. Riley, however, like Reich, worked on studio pieces while developing his own style of instrumental composition. During 1961, he spent a short while at the San Francisco Tape Music Center, producing a number of sketches, including an electronic version of his *In C,* normally performed live with any combination of instruments that might be available. His works *Poppy Nogood and the Phantom Band* (1968) and *A Rainbow in Curved Air* (1969), based on electronic keyboards, augmented in the case of the former work with a saxophone, could not have been performed live in view of the use of elaborate multitracking and tape feedback. To ears conditioned by more modern pop music techniques, the effects merely suggest recordings of particularly versatile performances, from some viewpoints a considerable virtue.

Electronic composition in Canada remained strangely isolated from developments in America and Europe at this time. The oldest studio, run by the National Research Council in Ottawa, continued in operation under the direction of Hugh Le Caine. István Anhalt completed a series of pieces, *Electronic Composition Nos. 1 to 4*, between 1959 and 1961, which received performances in America alongside works from better-known composers such as Wuorinen, Luening, and Ussachevsky. The fourth piece, indeed, was completed at the Columbia/Princeton Center. Anhalt's style contrasts significantly with many of the East Coast American composers, showing a greater affinity with the subtleties associated with European schools of composition, notably Milan. His treatment of timbre and pitch organization is most sensitive, displaying a coherence that arises naturally out of the sound shapes themselves, rather than some predetermined formalistic structure.

The main impetus to developments in Canada, however, stemmed from the founding of a studio at the University of Toronto in 1959, initially under the directorship of Arnold Walter. Walter collaborated with Myron Schaeffer and Harvey Olnick in a number of ventures, including two electronic tapes for television films, *Summer Idyll* (1960) and *Project TV* (1962), and one for a ballet, *Electronic Dance* (1963). Pauline Oliveros visited the studio in 1966, producing a wealth of compositions, including *I of IV, II of IV, III of IV, IV of IV*, and *NO MO*. Many of these works were the products of simple sound generation and treatment processes, resulting in a performance style of electronic composition that could be transferred to the live concert platform.

The Toronto studio was initially equipped with a number of custom-built devices. These included a Hamograph, a special form of reverberation unit constructed from a spiral of steel mesh, an adapted keyboard controlling a bank of tunable oscillators and band-pass filters, and a multiple-head tape recorder. The Hamograph was a device capable of controlling the amplitude of up to twelve different channels of sound, each driven via a tape control loop and an associated on/off gate activated via a Schmitt trigger and an associated level detector. Tape-recorded signals thus provided a primary means of process control until the advent of voltage- and digital-control technology in the mid- to late-1960s.

During the decade, other universities in Canada established studios: McGill (Montreal) and Vancouver in 1964, Simon Fraser in 1967, and Laval a year later. The work of Murray Schafer first at Montreal and then at Simon Fraser is notable for its emphasis on electronic music for schools and colleges. Like Brian Dennis in England, he concentrated on the presentation of the medium as a creative tool accessible to all without recourse to complex technological procedures. Such a desire to achieve a directness of contact with the tools of synthesis has only to be taken one stage further to enter the sphere of live electronics.

8

Live Electronic Music

Live electronic music or, to be more specific, compositions wholly or largely based on live synthesis, became a major sphere of activity during the 1960s. There are many antecedents that can be cited, stretching back to Cahill's Dynamophone and the subsequent proliferation of electronic musical instruments during the interwar period. A more positive antecedent, however, lies in the compositions of John Cage during the 1940s and 1950s, which introduced a far less stylized approach to live electronic sounds. Instrumental imitation forms but one aspect of the developments to be discussed under this heading, for the latter were primarily motivated by a desire to transfer studio procedures to the concert platform in a manner that was not limited to traditional performance practice. Schaeffer's ill-fated attempt to generate the final stages of his works live at the first public concert of *musique concrète* is perhaps the most interesting early excursion into this type of composition.

Cage's growing interest in live electronics provided the catalyst for the birth of a number of live electronic ensembles in America that, with some justification, considered themselves the pioneers of a new art form that embraced aspects of progressive jazz and even rock. It is to Europe, however, that attention is first turned, for it was here that the most coherent transition from established studio techniques to live synthesis occurred.

Kagel's *Transición II* (1959) for piano, percussion, and two tape recorders has been claimed as the first example of the use of a tape recorder as a live performance aid. The percussionist plays on the soundboard, strings, and rim of the piano while the pianist plays the keys. One tape recorder reproduces material recorded prior to the performance while the other is used to record extracts of the performance itself to be cut into loops and reproduced as an echo of events past. Stockhausen's interest in live first clearly surfaced 1964. For the next two years he worked intensively in the Cologne studio, composing three pieces for the genre: *Mikrophonie I* (1964), *Mixtur* (1964), and *Mikrophonie II* (1965).

Mikrophonie I uses a large tam-tam as the sole sound source for the entire work.[1] Two microphones are held on either side of the instrument, each connected to an amplifier and loudspeaker via an adjustable band-pass filter. Six performers are required, two activating the tam-tam, two varying the positioning of the microphones, and two controlling the settings of the filters and associated amplifiers. The score specifies the production of a wide variety of sounds from the tam-tam. These include vocal-like resonant frequencies, generated by rubbing the surface with cardboard tubes, deeply reverberant sounds from soft mallet-strokes, sharp percussive effects from striking the surface with hard rods of wood, metal, or plastic, and effects such as atmospheric noise, achieved by scraping or brushing. The microphones and filters act to highlight and modify timbre features that can only be detected very close to the surface of the instrument.

Mixtur is an altogether more complicated work technically, requiring five orchestral groups, four ring modulators, and associated sine-wave generators. The original version required large groups of woodwind, brass, pizzicato strings and harp, bowed strings, and percussion. A later version (1967) was scaled down to a more modest ensemble of instruments. Only the percussion group is not subject to any processes of modulation, the sounds of the tam-tam being highlighted via a contact microphone and amplification system. The sounds from each of the other four groups are captured via microphones and fed to one side of a ring modulator, a sine tone being fed to the other to provide a modulating frequency.

The electronic processes in this work differ from those used for *Mikrophonie I* in one important respect. Whereas the latter work is based on subtractive synthesis, using filters to isolate and highlight components in an already complex sound, *Mixtur* features additive synthesis, using modulating frequencies to generate additional partials in the form of sum and difference tones. The frequency settings of the oscillators at times drop into the subaudio range, unbalancing the ring modulators to the point where the wave function acts as an amplitude modulator for the instrumental material. Once again a sectionalized structure is employed, resulting in twenty "moments," each incorporating a simplified notation to specify textural effects rather than exact scoring.

Mikrophonie II is perhaps the most significant of this trilogy of pieces, scored for Hammond organ, choir, four ring modulators, and tape. The tape consists of short extracts from three former works. Two are scored for instruments, *Carré* (1959–60) and *Momente* (1961−4), and one is electronic, *Gesang der Jünglinge*. Despite the inclusion of these recorded passages, the work is based predominantly on live electronic techniques. The quotations from *Gesang* and the use of a text drawn from *Einfache grammatische Meditationen* by Helmut Heissenbüttel highlight Stockhausen's continuing interest in the study of phonetics in relation to electronic music.[2] The choir comprises twelve singers: two groups of three sopranos and two groups of three basses. The sounds from each group are fed to one side of a ring modulator via microphones, the Hammond organ replacing handtuned sine wave oscillators as the frequency source for the complementary inputs. Modulation thus occurs only when a choral group and the organ sound together. At all other times these sources are perceived naturally, the organ adopting a very low profile relative to the vocal parts. This increased flexibility of ring modulation results in elaborate transformations, foreshadowing the complex timbres incorporated in both *Telemusik* and *Hymnen*.

Stockhausen's next live electronic work, *Solo* (1966), was prepared during his visit to the NHK Studio in Tokyo. *Solo*, as the title suggests, is a work for any single melody instrument, originally either a flute or a trombone, and a complex tape feedback system regulated by four assistants. A single tape loop is stretched between a stereo tape recorder, which records incoming signals, and a tension pulley several feet away. As the loop passes from recorder to pulley, six playback head assemblies detect these signals, the latter components being mounted on stands that may be adjusted in a horizontal plane. The positioning of the heads is critical, for precise delays are specified between sounds being fed to the record head and their reproduction at each of the playback heads. Microphones are employed to pick up source information from the instrument. The outputs from the playback heads are fed to a mixing desk at which the assistants regulate both their distribution between four loudspeakers and also the level of direct feedback to the record lines. The cumulative effect of this looping process is a permuting series of patterns, which merge eventually into a stream of continuous sound. The latter is then punctuated by cutting off the feedback gain completely for short intervals, creating new blocks of sounds, which similarly permute. A heavy onus is placed on the partnership skills of the instrumentalist and his assistant. The score offers a choice of six formal schemes, each demanding very precise actions on the part of the performers.

After *Hymnen*, Stockhausen returned to live electronics with an increasing interest in developing improvisation techniques for ensembles, working from scores involving a minimal amount of notation. Improvisation, however, is in many respects a misnomer, for the very minimalism of the material demands the most disciplined of interactions between the players if the composer's intentions are to be satisfactorily fulfilled. It became clear to Stockhausen that such performance demands could only be fulfilled by forming his own ensemble of players who work together over an extended period of time towards a coherent realization of his compositional objectives. This ensemble drew together a group of distinguished composers and performers, including Alfred Alings, Harald Bojé, Johannes Fritsch, Rolf Gelhaar, and Alfons and Aloys Kontarsky.

His next composition for the genre, *Prozession* (1967), is an intricately programmed series of processes based on a scheme of + (more), − (less), and = (same) signs. These control the change in state of features such as pitch and amplitude, and also larger aspects of form such as the number of repetitions or the number of sections. The content is derived from fragments of earlier works assigned to particular instruments: *Mikrophonie I* for the tam-tam, adaptations of *Gesang der Jünglinge, Kontakte,* and *Momente* for the viola, *Telemusik* and *Solo* for the Electronium,[3] *Piano Pieces I–XI* (1952–6) and *Kontakte* for the piano. The electronic element, apart from the electronium, is provided by two microphones, two filters, and amplitude regulators, which are controlled by an additional performer.

Kurzwellen (1968) for piano, Electronium, tam-tam, viola, and four shortwave radios is more readily identifiable as a descendant of *Hymnen*. Once again, two microphones and filters provide an active means for modifying the sounds electronically, an extra dimension being added by the use of a contact microphone to amplify the viola. Each instrumental player uses his own short wave radio to select source material from the ether, these elements providing the basis for instrumental enhancement and electronic modification. This greater freedom of choice is countered by a stricter degree of control over the processes of development and interaction, still using the same system of +, −, and = signs.

Aus den sieben Tagen (1968), although not specifically a composition requiring electronics, has frequently been performed with their use. Scored for an unspecified ensemble, the work consists of fifteen texts that are interpreted collectively by the performers. Despite this apparent move into the sphere of free improvisation, the work, through its texts, demands the expression of ideas in a manner requiring the highest qualities of discipline and rationality from the individual.

In *Spiral* (1968) for a soloist with shortwave receiver, the electronic processes are reduced merely to the level of selection from a ready-made source of material, with no further application of processing. *Mantra* (1970), however, exhibits a return to a more involved use of electronics, which inspired a number of imitators. The work is scored for two pianists, a shortwave radio or a tape of shortwave sounds, two ring modulators, two oscillators, woodblocks, antique cymbals, and sound projection, the latter aspect being controlled by an assistant.[4] This return to the individual performer and a detailed score results in a piece that is strongly reminiscent of a much earlier style of composition.

The suggested scoring for *Ylem* (1972) signaled the adoption of a slightly freer attitude toward live electronic devices. No fewer than four of the nineteen elements making up the ensemble are wholly or partially electronic. At the first performance these consisted of an Electronium, an amplified cello fitted with a foot-operated filter, a keyboard synthesizer, and a VCS 3 synthesizer manufactured by

EMS, London, used to process the amplified sounds of a saxophone/bassoon.[5] The variety of facilities offered by the synthesizers presented considerable scope for live synthesis as well as treatments. The score instructions, however, restrict their role primarily to the production of a web of timbres around a selected group of sounds, providing links for the other players.

Stockhausen's ensemble at Cologne Radio was soon to undergo a change of personnel. After a difference of opinion in 1970 both Fritsch and Gelhaar left his group to form an independent ensemble, Feedback, in association with David Johnson, John McGuire, and Michael von Biel, among others. With no overriding allegiance to Stockhausen they became free to develop other aspects of live electronic music using ideas generated by the group members.

The live electronic ensembles that emerged elsewhere in Europe during the 1960s concentrated for the most part on group improvisation. Franco Evangelisti established one of the earliest ensembles, Gruppo di Improvvisazione Nuova Consonanza, in Rome in 1964, attracting a wealth of composer participants over the years. These included Mario Bertoncini, Aldo Clementi, Roland Kayn, and Ivan Vandor from Europe, and Larry Austin and John Eaton from America. Their works were essentially group efforts, based predominantly on traditional instruments and voice. Their primary objective lay in the development of performance techniques that would produce sounds of an electronic nature from these natural sources, for example, high squeaks from wind and brass instruments and bowed percussion. Electronic sources nevertheless were used from time to time, principally an electronic organ and a group of oscillators. Filters and ring modulators provided the primary means for sound processing. Toward the end of the decade their improvisations began to include passages for prerecorded tape, introducing a more formal element into the shaping of their compositions.

A group consisting for the most part of expatriate American composers founded a rival ensemble, Musica Elettronica Viva, in Rome during 1966. These included Allan Bryant, Alvin Curran, Jon Phetteplace, Frederic Rzewski, and Richard Teitelbaum. MEV established a well-equipped studio of their own to assist in the development of their resources for live synthesis, and this led, as a by-product, to the production of one or two pieces for voices or instruments and prerecorded tape. The bulk of their activities, nevertheless, were directed toward live performance and their compositions steadily developed in the opposite direction, from pieces with a well-defined format to increasingly freer styles of improvisation.

The specifications for their earlier works give an indication of the variety of resources they employed. *Variations IV* (1966), for example, is scored for instruments, voice, transistor radios, Volkswagen bus, garden hose, pebbles thrown on auditorium roof, wooden chairs, stone floor scraped with various materials, and magnetic pickups used with loudspeakers to create feedback. This piece was an adaptation of Cage's *Variations IV* (1964), performed simultaneously with *Solo for Cello.*

Later works displayed an increasing use of electronic equipment, including tape-delay systems, contact microphones, Moog synthesizer modules, neurological am-plifiers and associated electrodes to decode alpha waves generated by the brains of selected performers, and photocell mixers. The latter, developed by Rzewski, were controlled using light pens, the latter providing a powerful resource for sound projection via multichannel amplification systems.

The concerts given by groups such as MEV caused a considerable stir in musi-cal circles, not least for the highly theatrical nature of their presentation. Whereas Stockhausen's partially improvised works imposed the discipline of a score or set of instructions on the players, the works of MEV concentrated more specifically on the individual motivations of the players as the basis for a structure, respond-ing to, rather than interpreting, ideas for an overall plan. Pieces such as *Spacecraft* (1967–8), *Free Soup* (1968), and *Sound Pool* (1969), largely conceived by Rzewski, extended the participatory element to the audience themselves, the latter being encouraged to react to and influence the evolution of the works. In *Spacecraft* the primary objective was the liberation of the performer from his environment, start-ing with his own musical tastes, and proceeding through the processes of inter-action with others toward a communal art of music making. This development of a social art led in *Sound Pool* to the integration both of teaching and performance skills, the more able musicians being directed to organize and assist weaker players in their endeavors to contribute ideas to the general flow.

Similarities exist between MEV and the British Group AMM, founded in 1965 by Lou Gare, Keith Rowe, and Eddie Prevost in association with Cornelius Cardew and Christopher Hobbs. This combination of jazz and avant-garde musicians led to an interesting fusion of musical ideas. In the early years, the group concentrated upon the search for new sounds and performance techniques, using contact micro-phones and a variety of electromechanical aids. Their musical outlook, however, became first narrowed and then confused by increasingly extreme political ideas, leading to the formation of a breakaway group known as the Scratch Orchestra in 1969 under the leadership of Cardew, Michael Parsons, and Howard Skempton. Gare and Prevost continued to run AMM for several years, directing it toward a more conventional type of jazz ensemble with a decreasing emphasis on electronics.

A growing interest in live electronic music in Britain toward the end of the 1960s led to the formation of other ensembles, notably Gentle Fire and Naked Software. Both groups benefited considerably from the skills of Hugh Davies. His gifts for designing unusual transducers out of materials such as scraps of metal and wood, rubber bands, and coils of wire attached to suitable electrical pickups such as contact microphones, provided them with a wealth of cheap and versatile per-formance aids.

Two Cambridge research fellows, Roger Smalley and Tim Souster, formed a group called Intermodulation in 1969, which specialized in the performance of works for instruments and live electronics. Smalley's first piece to involve live elec-tronic modulation, *Transformation I*, was scored for piano, two microphones, ring modulator, and filter and completed early in the same year. The similarities in scoring with Stockhausen's *Mantra* become all the more striking when it is appreciated that Smalley's piece appeared a year earlier. The parts for both the pianist and the electronics operator are precisely notated, although the score allows some flexibility in the synchronization of its various layers.

With Smalley's departure for Australia in 1976, Souster restyled the group under the new name of *0 dB*, concentrating on works that incorporated strongly rhythmic features drawn from both the music of Africa and Western rock, for example, his own *Afghan Amplitudes* (1976) and *Arcane Artefact* (1976). Rock and jazz influences, albeit of a progressive type, also figured prominently in the works of David Bedford and Barry Guy. In the late 1970s, contemporary jazz entered into a period of revolution, following paths very similar to those pursued by the more "traditional" avant-garde some ten years previously. Live electronics became an integral part of this quest for new styles not only in Britain but also elsewhere in Europe and America.

John Eaton's own venture promoting the Synket as a concert instrument led him to compose a number of pieces for live performance. The presentation of his *Songs for RPB* for soprano, piano, and Synket at the American Academy in Rome in 1965 is the first recorded occasion on which a portable synthesizer was used on stage. Eaton was particularly interested in the use of quarter-tone intervals, and these feature in many of his works. His *Concert Piece for Synket and Symphony Orchestra* (1967) matches the Synket against two orchestral groups tuned a quarter-tone apart. The ability to vary the tunings of the synthesizer accorded it a powerful role as an intermediary, generating rich timbres to complement the variety of textures obtainable from combinations of instruments. *Blind Man's Cry* (1968) for soprano, Synkets, and Moog synthesizer initiated a trend toward works for ensembles of synthesizers, the increased resources permitting a more versatile approach toward scores for live electronics. His *Mass* (1970) is scored for soprano, speaker, clarinet, three Synkets plus a derivative known as a Synmill, Moog synthesizer, and tape delay system. This shows an even greater preoccupation with the development of connections between live and electronic sounds, the high shrieks of the soprano and clarinet blending into clusters of sine tones while the Synkets imitate percussion and string instruments.

In Japan, Takehisa Kosugi entered the field of live electronic music as early as 1961 with *Micro I*, a piece for solo microphone. His association with the Sogetsu Art Centre led to the formation of a collective, Group Ongaku, which devoted itself to live improvisation. Toshi Ichiyanagi, having completed a number of studio compositions at the NHK Studio from 1962 onward, turned his attention toward live electronics, like Kosugi associating himself with the Sogetsu Art Centre. The use of sound in association with sculpture provided a particular fascination for him. In 1964, he constructed a system for an art gallery in Takamatsu, where an exhibition of sculpture was accompanied by sounds generated by arrays of photocell-controlled oscillators, operated by the movement of passers-by. In 1966, he constructed a similar system for a department store in Tokyo, this time for an exhibition of kinetic sculptures. Environmental music, controlled or at least influenced by the audience, was not unique to Japan, however. Tristram Cary, for example, constructed a six-oscillator system for an escalator at the 1967 EXPO exhibition, controlled by the movement of passengers.

The development of live electronic music in America during the 1960s was dominated by performance ensembles, in some instances of a collective type, concerned with the development of group projects, in others firmly led by a specific individual. Cage's group at Stony Point, New York, clearly belonged to the latter category, although the subsequent migration of several members of his ensemble to live electronic music groups based all over the world suggests a strong fermentation of the former approach. His performers included David Tudor, who remained a close associate for many years, David Behrman, Toshi Ichiyanagi, Alvin Lucier, Gordon Mumma, Pauline Oliveros, and Christian Wolff.

Cage's *Music for Amplified Toy Pianos* and *Cartridge Music*, both composed in 1960, marked an auspicious start to the decade. In the former piece, a single performer plays any number of toy pianos to which contact microphones have been fitted. In the latter, gramophone cartridges, into which all manner of objects have been inserted, and contact microphones attached to any responsive surface, provide a rich, if somewhat unusual, source of material. To the casual observer, the results are an instant, if at times unpleasant, type of *musique concrète*. Because the sounds are entirely the products of performance actions, however, any comparison with the output of the Paris studio is, to say the least, misleading. Cage had moved away from such predetermined orderings of material manipulation toward an electronic art that was truly live.

In 1961 he produced an electronic version of *Winter Music*, a work originally scored for one to twenty pianos in 1957. This may be performed simultaneously with his next piece, *Atlas Eclipticalis* (1961–2), for chamber or orchestral ensemble, with contact microphones, amplifiers, and loudspeakers operated by an assistant. The instrumental format is variable, up to eighty-six parts, and the work may be played complete, or in any part thereof. The score is distinctive for its notational detail. Most of Cage's compositions from this period are laid out graphically, leaving much to the interpretative skills of the performers. The material for *Atlas Eclipticalis*, however, is largely the product of indeterminate selection, resulting in a colourful if perplexing constellation of sounds.

Indeterminacy and variable instrumental formats are primary characteristics of a series of pieces entitled *Variations I–VIII*, composed between 1958 and 1968. *Variations II* (1963) for any number of players using any sound-producing means calls on contact microphones or any other suitable transducer to amplify the vibrating characteristics of the selected sources. David Tudor gained a reputation for his performances of the work using a piano fitted with contact microphones to the frame and soundboard, and gramophone cartridges to the strings. Later *Variations* employed more bizarre resources. *Variations V* (1965), for example, calls for film, slides, prerecorded tapes, and dancers, the latter triggering the audiovisual elements by breaking light beams focused on photoelectric cells. Robert Moog designed special distance-sensitive antennae as additional controlling devices. This work was specially written for the Merce Cunningham Dance Company, a troupe that enjoyed a long and fruitful association with Cage and his associates.

Cage's boundless enthusiasm for pastures new led him into the field of computer-assisted composition in 1969 with *HPSCHD,* a joint project with Hiller.[6] A discussion limited to his electronic works, however, gives a very narrow vista of this pluralistic composer. It is this very quality that recognizes no boundaries to means of artistic expression that has influenced so many composers and elicited a grudging respect even from those who find his work perplexing, frustrating, or annoying in the extreme.

Although Tudor became known primarily as a performer of other composers' works of live electronic music, he also contributed several pieces of his own to the genre. *Fluorescent Sound* (1964), written for Stockholm's Museum of Modern Art, utilized the resonant sounds of fluorescent light tubes, amplified and distributed via loudspeakers. *Rainforest* (1968) incorporates a system of specially designed loudspeakers, consisting of electromagnetic coils with their moving parts attached to a variety of resonators instead of the normal paper cones. These transducers added rich harmonics, distorting the electrical signals passed to them for acoustic output, in this instance generated from a bank of oscillators manipulated by two performers.

Behrman, after a short spell working in the studio at Brandeis University, Waltham, set up his own experimental studio in New York during 1966. His piece *Wave Train* (1966) relies significantly on controlled acoustic feedback between guitar pickups attached to the strings of the piano and the monitor loudspeakers to which these signals are fed. Considerable skill is required in setting the gains of these pickups: too high a level results in a permanent and unpleasant feedback, while too little merely amplifies the damped, basic characteristics of the strings. A median setting produces richly reinforced textures, as the excitement of the strings becomes self-perpetuating.

Behrman was a member of the Sonic Arts Union, an influential group of live electronic music composers and performers, formed in 1966. The other members were Robert Ashley, Alvin Lucier, and Gordon Mumma. Ashley and Mumma, it will be recalled, had established the Cooperative Studio for Electronic Music at Ann Arbor, composing several tape compositions before turning almost exclusively to the live medium. Lucier's contact with studio electronics started in 1965 subsequent to his appointment at Brandeis University. Tape compositions, however, were very few, the facilities being used primarily for developing his performance ideas.

Mumma's first major work of live electronic music, *Medium Size Mograph,* was completed in 1963. This piece for piano, four hands, and "cybersonic" equipment used custom-built, portable electronics both to modify the piano sounds and also to translate the latter into control functions for the electronic generators. In *Mesa* (1966) for cybersonic metal reeds, a member of the accordion family is wired up to an arrangement of transducers, modulators, and filters, acting to transform simple melodic phrases into complex successions of sounds, rich in nonharmonic partials. The controls for the electronics, as in all these pieces, are contained in a box slung around the performer's neck. Alterations to device settings may thus be made while performing the instrument. In later works such as *Cybersonic Cantilevers* (1973), the audience became a source of control information for the work, recalling the participation pieces of Musica Elettronica Viva.

Ashley developed a particular interest in the use of live electronics in music theatre. In 1965, he composed *Lecture Series,* a piece for speaker, public address system, electronic processing equipment, and related "events." This interest in speech, which stems back to his tape piece *The Wolfman,* was developed further in *Purposeful Lady Slow Afternoon,* the first part of a larger work entitled *The Wolfman Motor City Revue* (1968). This piece is built around an amplified reading of a woman's first sexual experience and the aftermath. A discreetly associative visual element is supplied by two sequences of film slides projected simultaneously on different screens.

Lucier was the most adventurous member of the group. *Music for Solo Performer* (1965) is the first live electronic piece to have used amplified alpha brain waves, here combined with resonating percussion instruments, gating devices, and pre-recorded tapes of electronically processed waves. *North American Time Capsule* (1967) was written in response to an invitation from Sylvania Electronic Systems to compose a work using a prototype for a new design of vocoder, which employed digital sampling techniques.[7] The score consists merely of a set of instructions, thus leaving much to the imagination of the performers. Eight vocoders are required, processing the sounds of a chorus who are free to describe aspects of their civilization through speaking or singing, in any language, to the future discoverers of the time capsule deep in space. Additional sonic aspects of contemporary life also may be incorporated, for example, the sounds of vacuum cleaners, electric shavers, motor cars, or aircraft, along with the sounds of musical instruments.

Later works are even more theatrical in their staging. *Vespers* (1968) requires several performers to walk about a darkened stage carrying electronic location detectors that respond to the presence of a number of solid objects positioned strategically within the performance area by clicking at different rates, the nearer the object, the faster the clicking.

In *I am Sitting in a Room* (1970), Lucier returned to a simpler technology, using a chain of microphones, tape recorders, and loudspeakers on stage to generate cumulative reiterations of a source text reading. The use of acoustic linking from recording to recording adds an extra dimension to the progressive transformations, for the resonant frequencies set up by the room enhance the sound as it radiates from loudspeaker to microphone.

Reich's live electronic music shows a marked preference for keyboards, used in a conventional performing role alongside more traditional instruments. Pattern-generating procedures continued to form the basis of his works, for example, *Phase Patterns* and *Four Organs*, both written in 1970. Terry Riley followed a similar path as regards choice of instruments, but with a greater emphasis on improvisation. *Persian Surgery Dervishes* (1971), for example, received remarkably different performances as a result of the considerable freedom he accorded to the performers in terms of their interpretation.

La Monte Young and Philip Glass developed ensembles much in the same vein as those of Reich and Riley. Glass cultivated a more popular image, concentrating, with works such as *Contrary Motion* and *Music in Fifths* (1969), on slowly changing timbres and harmonies produced from electronic musical instruments.

The percussionist Max Neuhaus produced notable realizations of Brown's *Four Systems* (1964), Sylvano Bussotti's *Coeur pour batteur* (1965), and Cage's *Fontana Mix-Feed* (1965) before concentrating more specifically on his own compositions. The scores for these three works gave ample scope for instrumental interpretation. *Four Systems*, for example, consists merely of a series of horizontal lines differentiated in thickness and length. Amplification and controlled feedback from loudspeaker to microphone provided the primary means of electronic enhancement, inducing resonating instruments such as cymbals and gongs to vibrate with rich timbres.

The general growth of interest during the decade led to the First Festival of Live Electronic Music at the University of California in 1967, followed five years later by a spectacular international collaboration, ICES 1972, held in London. The latter festival, which included as a special event the chartering of a train for performers and audience, which ran between London and Edinburgh, brought together composers and performers on a scale that is never likely to be equaled again. ICES included several rock concerts, a strong portent of the gathering strength of popular electronic music, to which attention must now be turned.

9

Rock and Pop Electronic Music

Electronic jingles and related sound effects have invaded the lives of millions every day via the media of radio and television since the mid-1960s. These ephemera, while familiarizing the general public with the nature of synthesized sounds, have generally debased such sources to the level of an advertising aid. Such a widely recognized application, however, is only one step removed in the public consciousness from the culture of rock and pop music, which uses electronic material as a matter of course to advance a culture with broad appeal. For the last fifteen to twenty years of the twentieth century, the commercial digital synthesizer dominated the medium, serving in many instances both the serious and the popular music sectors with equal success. As a result, the primary distinctions became increasingly those of application rather than those of technology, and these circumstances still hold true as the new millennium unfolds.

These conditions differ from those associated with the pioneering era of rock and pop music, and these processes of evolution merit closer scrutiny. This formative period reached a peak of activity during the late 1960s and early 1970s with the development of the voltage-controlled synthesizer. Here experimentation by several leading artists with new methods of sound production inspired a range of technical developments that were to prove highly influential on the creative evolution of the electronic medium as a whole.

During the late 1960s, rising expenditure on basic electronic mixing and amplification equipment by the commercial music sector led to the acquisition of increasingly sophisticated studio and stage resources. A growing curiosity with the synthesis and processing of sound led a number of major rock and pop groups to acquire state-of-the-art resources, offering them creative opportunities that far exceeded those available to most noncommercial composers. The resulting rapid growth of activity within this sector was not an entirely new phenomenon, however, and it is important to take account of some key antecedents.

Popular music has made use of electronic devices since the 1920s. Indeed, it was not unknown for dance bands of the period to make regular use of simple amplification, and by the end of the following decade the Hammond organ was in regular use.[1] It was the growth in popularity of the electric guitar during the 1950s, however, that heralded the start of major developments in this particular sphere. Initially this instrument was equipped with a pickup at or near the bridge, an amplifier, and a loudspeaker, the system producing a bright but essentially faithful reproduction of the string sounds. Over the years, a number of electronic sound-processing devices were added in an effort to improve the versatility of the instrument. Some of these are adaptations of equipment originally engineered for the electronic music studio. Others have been more specifically engineered as enhancements for the guitar.

Facilities for tonal modifications were originally limited to simple bass and treble controls integral to the amplifier. In due course, more flexible filtering facilities were added, these providing additional control over the important middle-frequency areas. Reverberation and echo quickly proved popular means of enhancement, such effects being generated either via a spring delay unit or sometimes an alternative device known as a Copycat.[2]

The former facility suffered from an unevenness of response, resulting from the various frequencies of resonance associated with the component springs. Because reverberation plates were both expensive and far from portable, considerable pressure was exerted on manufacturers to produce better-quality spring units, sometimes incorporating three or more coils in an attempt to even out these resonant frequencies. The Copycat, a direct descendant of Schaeffer's Morphophone, was a compact tape loop delay system providing, normally, between three and five playback heads, suitably spaced to provide an irregular pattern of delays. Careful regulation of the component playback levels and the degree of feedback supplied to the record head allowed an acceptably smooth prolongation of all but the most percussive of guitar sounds. Thus it was that pioneering techniques such as those developed by Stockhausen at Cologne were to be quickly replicated within the commercial sector, albeit for somewhat different ends.

Tremolo was another treatment that proved popular during the formative years. This characteristic effect is derived from the Hammond organ, produced by a special amplitude regulator that modulates the amplitude gain of applied signals by a few decibels at a repetition speed of about 7–11 Hz. Pitch vibrato, by contrast, could not be generated electronically except with extreme difficulty until the introduction of suitable digital signal-processing devices toward the end of the 1970s, the presence of frets on the fingerboard restricting the performer's ability to produce such an effect directly via the string. The Hawaiian guitar provided the only practical alternative, its hand-operated lever acting to adjust the tension, and hence the tuning, of the strings.

More marked manipulations became possible with the introduction of the wah-wah and fuzz-tone effects. The wah-wah consists of a variable frequency low-pass filter coupled to an amplitude regulator, the device normally being controlled via a foot pedal. The effect of linking an increase in amplitude with a rising frequency of cutoff is very similar onomatopoeically to a "wah-wah" sound, the brightness of timbre rising and falling with the gain. The fuzz-tone generator is a special type of frequency multiplier, like a ring modulator, which transforms the guitar into a harsh and aggressive sounding instrument by adding rich and complex partials to each note. Special limiters also were introduced as sustaining devices, artificially prolonging the duration of individual notes or chords by automatically compensating for the loss in gain that occurs during the decay portion of each envelope. If a limiter is also used to round the initial attack transients, the result is a smooth organlike sound, facilitating an extremely legato style of playing.

The terms "phasing" and "flanging" have variously been applied to a number of processing techniques that introduce very small time delays into applied signals. If these delays are then mixed with their sources a complex interaction occurs, resulting in an amplification of certain frequencies and a cancellation of others. The effects become particularly marked if the time delay is varied dynamically, for this leads to a modulation of the interactions, perceived as a complex "squeezing" of the sound, as if shaped by an unseen hand reaching through the constituent spectrum of timbres. If the source and processed signals are fed to separate speakers, the characteristics of frequency cancellation and amplification are set up as a result of acoustic interactions in air, creating strange illusions of spatial movement.

A variety of methods were employed for the generation of such delays. One of the simplest required two tape recorders operating at the same speed and set in record mode, both receiving a common feed from the source signal. Providing the distance between the record and playback heads is identical both recorders will reproduce the source simultaneously. If a pencil is inserted between the heads on one of the machines and pushed against the tape, the deflection of the latter increases the effective distance the tape has to travel by a fractional amount, delaying its arrival at the replay head, relative to the other machine. An alternative approach, resulting in a slightly different flanging characteristic, requires the transport speed of one machine to be modulated very gently.

Both techniques proved very difficult to regulate, and were in due course replaced by analog delay lines that could achieve the desired effects electronically.

By the mid-1980s, the technology associated with almost all of the effects described above had been entirely reengineered in the digital domain as a series of digital signal processing functions, often consolidated in a single effects unit. Such devices are still used extensively in live performances today, offering a versatility that hitherto could only rarely be achieved. The subtleties of timbre possible with most of these devices, however, can still only be fully explored in the more disciplined environment of a studio.

The electric guitar was not the only instrument to benefit from electronic improvements over the years. Electronic keyboard instruments were subject to similar modifications, in some instances being developed into comprehensive synthesizers in their own right. This trend led to a progressive blurring of the boundary between instruments designed for use on stage and resources intended primarily for the studio. One or two instruments, nevertheless, were to retain their identity against this tide of technological change. The electronic piano, for example, remained popular with many bands and groups, well into the 1980s, its artificial sound gaining a status of its own. By far the most unusual design to survive almost as long is the Mellotron.[3] The development of the digital sampler, however, was finally to seal the fate of these relics from an earlier era.

The steady integration of electronic devices with more traditional rock and pop instruments established an important link on a purely technical level with the main genres of electronic music, one that has largely remained unbroken to the present day. Artistic links, however, have proved far more tenuous, for the philosophical and stylistic differences have not proved easy to bridge. Furthermore, excursions into new sound worlds by rock and pop musicians have often lacked any sustained development. Many a group in search of a distinctive identity has experimented with the more exotic possibilities of synthesizers and associated devices during the early stages of its career, only to return to more traditional sound repertoires as the years have advanced.

One early style of popular electronic music to establish a partial bridge across this cultural divide was that launched by Walter (now Wendy) Carlos in 1968 with the album *Switched on Bach*. This compilation, and its sequel, *The Well Tempered Synthesizer*, issued the following year, consists entirely of electronic realizations of selected works by Bach, created using a Moog synthesizer. The response of the popular market at this time was without precedent, resulting in sales of these records that quickly surpassed the entire market worldwide for conventional interpretations of the works of Bach. This evident interest in electronic versions of the classics soon encouraged others to follow suit. The Japanese composer Isao Tomita achieved particular success with his electronic arrangements, starting with the album *Snowflakes are Dancing* (1974), based on the piano works of Debussy. These realizations, however, are concerned less with the overt sensationalism of Carlos and more with a considered exploration of the subtleties of texture that can be derived from electronic orchestrations.

Extracts from classical works, either synthesized or performed conventionally in association with electronic elements, were to appear in a number of rock pieces produced during the 1970s, although not always to good effect. The inclusion of the Hallelujah Chorus from Handel's *Messiah* in "The Six Wives of Henry VIII" by the group Yes (*Yessongs*, 1973), for example, serves to confuse rather than consolidate an already convoluted collage of musical fragments. Emerson, Lake, and Palmer adopted a more considered approach to the integration of classical material into a popular idiom, carefully preserving the spirit of the sources in their own recordings. *Pictures at an Exhibition* (1971) provides a striking example of their skills in this regard, unaltered quotations from the original Mussorgsky score and elaborate synthesized manipulations providing the outer extremes of a carefully constructed framework of rock and classical styles.

Although the proactive use of electronic techniques in rock and pop music first became prominent during the mid-1960s, isolated examples may be traced back to the previous decade. These include the use of speeded-up recordings of voices to create high-pitched and childlike twitters by the Chipmunks in both "Witch Doctor" (1957) and "The Chipmunk Song" (1958). It was the Beach Boys, however, who provided the main stimulus for the sector with their use of vocal tape transformations and the sounds of a Thérémin in "Good Vibrations" (1966) and "She's Goin Bald" (1967). The Tempophon is also employed extensively in these pieces, providing progressive transpositions of pitch without alteration to the tempo.

The Beatles, after preliminary experimentation with simple tape loops and reversed playback of recordings in "I'm Only Sleeping" and "Tomorrow Never Knows" from their album *Revolver* (1967), incorporated a number of more elaborate tape transformations in their next record, *Sgt. Pepper's Lonely Hearts Club Band* (1967). The song "A Day in the Life," for example, incorporates multitracking techniques that could never have been realized live, and was indicative of an important trend at that time in rock toward the greater flexibility of studio-engineered music, rather than straight reproductions of concert pieces. Live performance, however, remained the primary interest of most rock groups, leading in turn to an increasing demand for more sophisticated performance facilities.

Prerecorded tapes provided one solution to the problems of managing stage presentations. In the album *Anthem of the Sun* (1967–8), the group Grateful Dead introduced a tape interlude between two songs that incorporated elaborate transformations of vocal, percussion, piano, and electronic sounds in the form of a montage. In *Aoxomoxoa* (1969), electronic treatments feature extensively in the songs themselves, particular use being made of phasing, modulation, filtering, and multitracking via a tape delay system. Several of these effects were nevertheless generated entirely live, in an effort to reduce the dependence on prerecorded material. One motivation for the use of electronic techniques in rock pieces from the late 1960s onward was undoubtedly a desire to evoke the twisted and blurred imagery associated with the act of drug taking. *Their Satanic Majesties Request* (1967) by the Rolling Stones, for example, is permeated with electronic distortions of the instrumental source materials that verge on the bizarre.

Frank Zappa and the Mothers of Invention used electronics in several of their albums, moving from studio-produced treatments in *Uncle Meat* (1967–8) to synthesizers in live performances for release such as *Roxy and Elsewhere* (1974). Considerable skills were demanded of their keyboard player, George Duke, in performing both on conventional instruments and also on synthesizers during the piece. The challenge of this new performance art was pursued by several other rock musicians, including Rick Wakeman of Yes, Brian Eno of the Matching Moles and Roxy Music, and Keith Emerson, of Emerson, Lake, and Palmer.

Yes paid particular attention to the use of extended electronic interludes in their songs, often creating works of symphonic proportions. In "Close to the Edge" (1972) Wakeman exhibits a considerable feat of dexterity, manipulating synthesizer, organ, Mellotron, and piano for long periods in this four-movement work. Brian Eno displays similar virtuosity in albums such as *Little Red Record* and *Roxy Music* (1972). Eno, perhaps more than any other instrumentalist of his time, attempted to forge close links between rock and avant-garde styles of composition. His solo work *Discreet Music* (1975) might equally well have been included in the earlier discussion of studio electronic works, for the procedures employed show a close affinity to the tape works of Steve Reich. Two melodic lines provide the sole sources of material, subjected to tape echo, tape delay, and simple filtering. The structure of the piece is that of a continuous process of transformation, based on a series of repeating and permuting patterns that slowly change in complexity and texture.

Emerson's skills have already been alluded to in considering *Pictures at an Exhibition*. Similar feats of performance are evident in *Toccata*, a work based on the fourth movement of Ginastera's first piano concerto from the album *Brain Salad Surgery* (1973). Here the services of the Mellotron are dispensed with completely, synthesizers being used instead to imitate orchestral instruments.

Soft Machine provides an example of a British group, which having originally specialized in the composition of avant-garde jazz, developed a rock image through the use of electronics. Their earliest works, *Soft Machine* (1968) and *Soft Machine II* (1969) display an imaginative use of "wah-wah" effects on both guitar and vocal material. Their later albums, involving the use of synthesizers were less distinctive in this regard, mainly as a result of a more elementary use of these devices simply as keyboard substitutes.

More novel applications of electronic techniques are to be found in the earlier recordings of groups such as Pink Floyd and, to a lesser extent, Velvet Underground and Jimi Hendrix. Pink Floyd have made extensive use of synthesizers and prerecorded tape in their works, frequently exploring more exotic effects of sound transformation applied to a variety of *concret* sources. Albums such as *Atom Heart Mother* (1970), *Meddle* (1971), and *Dark Side of the Moon* (1972–3) exhibit strong sociocultural characteristics in the integration of instrumental material with environmental sounds. The latter include the mooing of cows, footsteps, frying eggs and bacon, football crowds, clock chimes, and the mechanical clatter of cash registers.

Works such as these differ markedly from many that drew on similar material in the mainstream of electronic composition, for the instrumental parts display a strong adherence to traditional rock orchestration and principles of tonal organization. "Echoes," which occupies the entire second side of *Meddle,* is especially notable for its sensitive and coherence use of electronic material in this context. This is most evident in an extended central section, which effects a subtle transformation from the regular pulsing of a percussion backing pattern to a ghostly timeless world of distant cries and undulating moans and back again. A debt to ideas pursed by Stockhausen is evident from time to time, especially in the closing section, which incorporates an upward-moving timbre continuum of successive vocal glissandi.[4]

The music of Velvet Underground shows some affinity with the words of La Monte Young and Riley, for their violist, John Cale, had migrated to rock after playing for both musicians. Although the use of cyclic variation anticipates similar techniques employed by Eno, the style is wilder and altogether more adventurous. The group was originally formed by Andy Warhol for a multimedia show entitled "Exploding Plastic Inevitable," staged in a New York nightclub during 1965. Music from this production formed the basis of the album *Andy Warhol's Velvet Underground Featuring Nico* (1967–9). The use of electronics contrasts sharply with that of Pink Floyd, with an emphasis on heavy modulation or even sheer distortion. This aggressive rock style was also pursued by guitarist Jimi Hendrix, who displayed a particular predilection for the fuzz-tone generator in albums such as *The Jimi Hendrix Experience* (1967–8).

In term of building bridges across the cultural divide that separates rock and pop music from the central, albeit sometimes highly experimental core of electronic and computer music, the activities of several German groups merit special attention at this time. The resulting movement, known as Krautrock, was to prove highly significant, exerting an influence that is still reverberating today. The origins of Krautrock can be traced to Can, a group established by a quartet of classically trained musicians in 1968, in the first instance seeking to explore the possibilities of improvisation. What set the group apart from many other experimental groups of the period was their desire to develop a fusion style between pop and jazz, based on the pulsing background beat of rock music. Works such as *Tago Mago, Future Days* and *Soon over Babaluma* released in the early 1970s went much further than the output from groups such as Velvet Underground or Jimi Hendrix in throwing away conventional ideals. The result was a new art form that could freely draw on such seemingly different aesthetics as those associated with a jazz artist such as Miles Davis, and the music of the electronic avant-garde.

Other groups were soon pursuing the ideas pioneered by Can. In 1969 the classically trained musicians Florian Schnieder-Esleben and Ralf Hütter founded a group that came subsequently to be known as Kraftwerk, forging even stronger links across the cultural divide through the extensive use of synthesizers and associated processing devices, including the vocoder. Notable works as *Autobahn* (1974) and *Trans-Europe Express* (1977) led to what is arguably their peak period of influence with the albums *The Man Machine* (1978) and *Computer World* (1981). Kraftwerk, perhaps more than any other group associated with Krautrock, established the foundations for a new and rapidly expanding genre, known as electronic dance music.

While the medium of rock retained a strong preference for tonal harmony, texture provided the primary key to this important development, demanding a more versatile use of electronics. The German group Tangerine Dream, formed by Edgar Froese in the mid-1970s, proved one of the most adventurous exponents of Krautrock in terms of exploring the creative possibilities of synthesizers. Froese had become aware of the advantages of studio multitracking facilities in preparing his own solo album *Aqua* (1973–4) and *ngc 891* (1974) and the characteristics of carefully ordered montage are evident in releases such as *Rubycon* (1975) and *Cyclone* (1978).

The group's concern with the manipulation of timbre was emphasized by their distinctive choice of instrumentation, drums, percussion, and guitar figuring far less prominently than is usual in most rock music of the period. Synthesizers, electric piano, and the Mellotron provided the primary instrumental resources, augmented at times by the use of solo woodwind instruments such as flute, cor anglais, and clarinet. A very close sense of integration between these diverse components is achieved in many of their pieces. Toward the end of "Madrigal Meridian" from *Cyclone,* for example, the perceptual boundary between the natural and synthetic sound worlds is completely confused by the use of a string-tone synthesizer, which creates an astonishingly realistic impression of the natural instruments.

By the late 1970s, this pioneering all-analog phase of electronic rock and pop music had run its course. Individuality was being replaced by a growing degree of uniformity in both technical and creative terms as commercial manufacturers flooded the market with low cost synthesizers offering broadly similar characteristics. This in turn inspired a culture that found much value in mediocrity, in which sales figures rather than artistic innovation becomes the driving force. Beneath this outer mantle, however, forces were at work developing new ideas and applications for this constantly evolving technology. Although a comprehensive account of the history of popular music and its culture is beyond the scope of this book, some key features closely associated with the subsequent development of the electronic medium as a whole merit further consideration in the current context.

One outcome of the maelstrom of ideas and technologies stirred up during the late 1960s and early 1970s concerns the stratification of creative activities into a series of related but nevertheless distinct typologies. Aside from Krautrock, these have included in particular Disco, Hip-Hop, Ambient, and Techno. Although the boundaries between some of these movements are not always easy to define, and the characteristics of Techno in particular were to become especially diffuse as the years advanced, these identities provide some useful points of reference.

Disco exerted an influence on the popular music idiom from 1974 to about 1983, providing an alternative to the more aggressive tendencies of rock and creating one of the foundation stones for Techno. It embraced the sound world of the analog synthesizer, albeit often uncritically, content to exploit the expanding repertory of commercial resources dating from this pre-MIDI era as a cheap substitute for acoustic instruments, starting with songs such as "Never Can Say Goodbye" by Gloria Gaynor, and "Waterloo" by ABBA.

In 1975, Donna Summer burst on the scene with "Love To Love You Baby," in turn preparing the ground for works such as "Stayin' Alive" (1977) by the Bee Gees, for the film *Saturday Night Fever*. The zenith of Disco came in 1978 with works such as "You Make Me Feel" by Silvester and "Y.M.C.A." by Village People, from which point onward the movement gradually lost momentum and became submerged in the general movement of dance music. The true significance of Disco lies not so much with the memory of such well-known works but with the efforts of the producers who fostered these groups by introducing them to the possibilities of electronic sound production. Here the work of pioneers such as Jean-Marc Cerrone and Giorgio Moroder deserve special recognition.

Hip-Hop emerged primarily from the activities of Afrika Bambaataa and Grandmaster Flash. The culture of Hip-Hop embodies Rap, the art of reciting text in rhythmically modulated manner against a pulsating background of music, which in turn has origins in the music of Africa. In the early 1970s a Jamaican disc jockey, Kool Herc, working in the Bronx, New York, started to develop a new style of Rap based on a percussive background of short extracts taken from existing recordings. These were generated from a pair of turntables by lowering the styli into the grooves of the records at selected points, the latter being then rotated backward and forward in brisk movements entirely by hand. At a stroke, one of the fundamental techniques of early *musique concrète* was reborn, creating a new art form in its own right, based on rhythmic transformations of the acoustic wave content of the groove.

Afrika Bambaataa, another disc jockey from the Bronx, took an interest in this form of Rap during the late 1970s, bringing Hip-Hop to the attention of the world with his record *Planet Rock*, released in 1982. The work fused the rhythmic structures of Hip-Hop with the expanded electronic sound world of Krautrock, notably that associated with Kraftwerk, and established his credentials as a foremost exponent of the style. Grandmaster Flash, also from the Bronx, formed a Hip-Hop group known as the Furious Five, which launched its career with *Superrappin'* (1979), followed by two major successes, *Freedom* (1980) and *The Birthday Party* (1981).

The legacy in terms of the many artists that have followed in the footsteps of these pioneers is considerable, as are the performance skills that have evolved from this very distinctive art of acoustic sampling. Hip-Hop, however, was to face a very real threat from the invention of the digital sampler during the 1980s, which, as will be seen in due course, provided a means of imitating the characteristics of record scratching in a relatively facile manner. The demise of the long-playing record was also to limit the opportunities for rapping, certainly as far as the use of new recordings was concerned. Notwithstanding these practical threats to the art of what is some times known as turntablism, many performing artists continue to use this distinctive technique of resynthesis to the present day.

The origins of what has generally become known as Ambient music have already been discussed in considering the music of Brian Eno, and it will be clear from this earlier account that there is a strong affinity here with the techniques of studio-based electronic composition. Indeed, *Discreet Music* and *Another Green World*, both produced in 1975, can be regarded as key foundation stones for this particular style. A fundamental concept of Ambient music is the need to listen closely to sounds that are familiar part of daily life, but which rarely if ever are given the attention they deserve. The movement as a whole is bound by a common concern that music should not be driven by any obtrusive pulse or beat if this disturbs the ability of the inner ear to detect the detail of individual sounds and their transformations.

This art of listening has strong resonances with many aspects of electronic and computer music, and provides a major bridge across the underlying cultural divide. Unfortunately, Ambient music, by its nature was to remain largely overshadowed by more forceful styles of rock and pop music for much of the 1980s. One artist in particular, Aphex Twin, managed finally to elevate its status to the mainstream consciousness of the general public with a series of electronic ballets entitled *Selected Ambient Works '85–'92*, and a subsequent album *Classics*, released in 1995. Other leading exponents have included The Orb and KLF.

It is with Techno, the final movement to be considered here, that the greatest practical links have been forged with the core activities of electronic and computer music. The term itself has been subject to a number of interpretations over the years, principally because it has become synonymous with dance music, which relies almost entirely on electronic synthesis. Its origins can be traced to Detroit, at a time when the city had entered a period of high unemployment as a result of a rapid decline in its core manufacturing industries. There was thus a strong imperative to seek inspiration from more modern technologies, and this permeated the world of popular music.

The three pioneers of Detroit Techno were Juan Atkins, Derrick May, and Kevin Saunderson. Atkins is generally regarded as being the originator of the first genuine Detroit Techno work, *No UFOs*, part of a project known as *Model 500*, released in 1985 before the three associates set off to Europe where they discovered the world of Kraftwerk. It was May, however, who was to prove the most adventurous of these pioneering artists in terms of the use of synthesizers with a highly influential series of records issued between 1987 and 1991, including such celebrated numbers as *Nude Photo* and *Strings of Life*.

The most important feature of Techno has been its extensive use of electronic music technology, moving from the world of analog devices to the most recent digital products. Later manifestations such as Minimal Techno and Trance, Listening Techno, and Hardcore are all linked by the use of synthesizers, samplers, and signal processors as the primary means of sound production. The ramifications of these developments have been profound for the medium as a whole, since the demands of popular music have become the dominant driving force in the development of new commercial products.

This trend has forced fundamental changes in the working relationship between the creative artist and his tools, not least as the result of an increased dependence by composers, both popular and serious, on the characteristics of systems designed for the many rather than for the few. The course of these developments has been affected by fundamental and far-reaching changes to the technology itself in moving from an analog to a digital domain, and it is the evolution of the latter that is now to be studied in some depth.

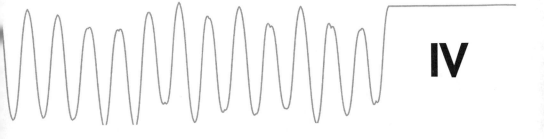

IV

The Digital Revolution to 1980

The Foundations of Computer Music

The term "computer music" has been associated with a number of creative activities facilitated by the emergence of computer technology, ranging from the computation of data for use in composing conventionally notated scores to the direct synthesis of sound within the computer itself. The processes of transition from analog to digital modes of working were to have profound consequences for the evolution of medium as a whole, and both the nature of the new technologies and the manner of their implementation constitute important areas of study.

Here we finally engage with the synthesis and signal processing techniques that underpin the powerful range of digital facilities in general use today. These fundamental changes in the nature of the underlying technology have materially altered the working environment for both composers and performers. The effects on their art and practice, however, has been more evolutionary in its nature, taking advantage of new techniques whenever appropriate, but at the same time retaining many of the practical and philosophical principles associated with the earlier analog era.

During the early phase of computer development, the only tools available to the pioneers of computer music were mainframe machines, large and expensive items of equipment designed in the first instance as self-contained systems for scientific and commercial data processing. By the end of the 1960s, however, advances in system design were encouraging the development of more compact and less expensive computers for an expanding market, thus widening the opportunities for access and engagement in creative research. As will be seen in due course, this facilitated a trend toward self-sufficiency in the computer music sector, an activity that was to gather considerable momentum during the 1970s in both Europe and America.

The key to progress in this regard lay in a new generation of even cheaper minicomputers, providing facilities that not only greatly expanded the range of computer applications but also began to undermine the primary manufacturing sector occupied by high-cost mainframe machines. With the invention of the microprocessor in 1972 the foundations of an even more far-reaching technical revolution were soon established, leading in due course to the scientific workstation and its increasingly powerful rival, the personal computer. By the early 1990s these systems were acquiring multimedia capabilities, enhanced yet further by the development of the Internet as a fast and accessible means of communicating with other computers anywhere in the world.

The computing environment today is thus radically different to that encountered by the early pioneers. Indeed, it is hard especially for younger readers even to imagine the conditions that prevailed during the birth and early development of computer music. Software tools during the formative years were very limited in their scope, and as a result developers of applications had to engage directly with the core processes that regulated the inner workings of the computer. This "hands on" approach demanded considerable technical proficiency, resulting in a high dependence on those with advanced skills in computing and electronic engineering.

To put these matters in an appropriate perspective it is necessary to step back to the birth of the electronic computer, an event owing a great deal to the technical demands of the Second World War. In 1942, two researchers in the School of Electrical Engineering at the University of Pennsylvania started work on a machine that would facilitate the calculation of data for the design and development of new military weapons. Although not completed until 1946, the resulting machine, known as ENIAC (ElectroNic Integration And Calculation) had much in common with an even earlier prototype, albeit of a much simpler construction, developed during the late 1930s by John Antanasoff at Iowa State College. It was ENIAC, however, that provided the all-important springboard for work that would transform the principles of automated calculation into an architecture that was fully programmable by means of software, rather than hardware reconfiguration for different tasks.

Credit for the latter is largely due to the work of a mathematician, John Von Neumann, who established the basic principles of the stored program, which takes complete control of the associated hardware. These concepts attracted the attention of several business equipment manufacturers who started to investigate the potential of computer technology, notably Remington Rand, leading to an experimental model, the 409, released in 1949. The first truly commercial computer, the UNIVAC (UNIVersal Automatic Computer) entered production in 1951, establishing a market that was gather further momentum in 1953, with the release of IBM's first model, the 701.

Although internal design features were to change markedly over the next two decades, many key operational characteristics of these pioneering mainframe computers were to remain essentially unaltered, resulting in some significant constraints that merit closer scrutiny. A typical computer of the 1950s or 1960s incorporated the following basic items of hardware:

1. An operational control system, known as the central processing unit or CPU.
2. A bank of programmable digital storage locations, known as the memory.
3. An input device, usually a punched card reader or paper-tape reader, used to pass externally prepared information to the system.
4. An output device, usually a printer or a teletypewriter, used to recover information from the system in a readable form.[1]
5. One or more ancillary magnetic tape or disk drive units, used to store bulk information in a digitally coded form for rapid system access.

Prior to the late-1960s, most data preparation tasks were carried out away from the computer, using special mechanically driven data preparation machines that translated manual keystrokes on an alphanumeric keyboard into equivalent patterns of binary code, punched onto a deck of cards or a roll of paper tape. Complete tasks or jobs were then submitted to the machine and queued according to their priority for processing.[2] Such an environment, known as batch mode processing, provided no opportunity for any direct interaction between the programmer and the computer while the program was executing.

In due course improvements in machine architectures allowed the development of systems capable of distributing the processing power between several tasks, thus allowing a number of independent users to communicate directly with the computer via a network of desktop terminals. This sharing of computing power was achieved by multiplexing the processor between the various tasks so rapidly that it would appear totally committed to the requirements of each user. In truth this illusion was more a goal than a reality, and the inability to provide truly continuous processing for individual tasks was to create a number of operational problems, not least in the case of applications concerned with the input and output of sound information.[3]

The principle of a central computing resource accessed by a number of users is still widely used today, where groups of workstations or personal computers are connected to a common server, the latter facility providing additional computing resources to those provided locally by each machine. The Internet, indeed, may be viewed as a central computing resource in its own right, immediately accessible from any computer equipped with an Internet browser and a suitable electronic link to the information highway.

Today personal computers can accommodate many music applications as a matter of course, including tasks as demanding as high quality audio synthesis and signal processing. This was certainly not the case during the early years of computing, and the practical hurdles faced by the pioneers of computer music in this context were considerable. In operational terms the performance of three of the primary hardware components identified above have proved especially significant in shaping and constraining the development of applications. These are (1) the CPU, (2) the memory available to service the requirements of programs and data, and (3) the capacity and accessibility of ancillary digital storage devices.

The primary restraints on CPU performance are determined by the basic speed of the processor and the nature and scope of the instructions available to program its functions. Since most computing tasks were initially processed one by one as part of a single batch stream run in the background, the speed of the processor was not in itself the ultimate constraint on the nature of the tasks that could be executed. Computationally more intensive tasks would simply take longer to complete. CPU time, however, was invariably at a premium, and the demands of users often exceeded the available capacity, even when these facilities were operating twenty-four hours a day. Demanding applications such as digital synthesis were invariably treated as a low priority, resulting in considerable delays and major restrictions on what could be realistically attempted.

Memory was also expensive, a finite resource in programming terms, and initially difficult to manage in large configurations for reasons largely to do with the restricted addressing capabilities of early mainframe CPUs. The memory of a computer is organized in a manner similar to that of the digital memory sequencer, in which each memory location is assigned a unique physical address by which it may be referenced, the number of bits per location depending on the architecture. Early computers fixed the content of each memory address, ranging from eight to twelve, sixteen, eighteen, or even twenty-four bits per location. Over the years a slightly different method of memory organization gained favor, based on a principle known as byte addressing. Here each memory address contains eight bits (one byte), but the addressing mechanism allows the CPU to treat a group of bytes as a single, composite data location.

The high cost of memory imposed major constraints on the early development of the computer, and it was not until the mid-1960s that the initial goal of a dollar-per-byte was finally bridged. During the early 1970s, the downward trajectory in price started to accelerate, and by the early 1980s equivalent memory had become available for less than a hundredth of this amount. This rapid reduction in cost continued more or less unchecked until the dawn of the new millennium, when problems of global supply and demand started to constrain further progress in this regard. Whereas memory capacities of 128 megabytes (128,000,000 bytes) or more for personal computers were by this point far from exceptional, such resources would have been unimaginable to the pioneers of computer music, limited to perhaps one or two megabytes of memory at the very most. Even these resources would have been regarded as generous by those who were subsequently to work with the first generation of minicomputers, providing perhaps no more than 64 kilobytes (64,000) and sometimes as little as four kilobytes (4,000 bytes) of memory in total. Once again, it was demanding applications such as digital synthesis that required large quantities of memory space, and these operational restrictions were to prove of material significance.[4]

The limited data capacity of early ancillary digital storage devices, especially random access disk drives, also posed major problems for digital synthesis, given the considerable quantities of data required to represent even a single second of high quality audio information. Although magnetic tapes were far cheaper than comparable hard disks and also offered a reasonably generous storage capacity per reel, information could only be written and read sequentially by the computer, making the medium entirely unsuitable for any interactive applications that demanded rapid random access to the data.[5]

The CPU itself acts as the administrative and operational heart of a computer. In addition to controlling the memory and the peripherals its primary purpose is to process digital information. The sequences of instructions that control the operation of the CPU are organized into a program, loaded in the first instance into the memory from a suitable input device. Since these programs are nonpermanent and easily altered, they are known collectively as software.

A distinction can be made between two types of program. The first type, traditionally described as applications software, consists of programs designed to carry out specific computing tasks, such as the calculation of a payroll or word processing. The second, known as the operating system, is a special program or set of subprograms that has to be loaded into memory as soon as the computer is switched on. Its purpose is to control the various functions of the computer, such as loading and supervising the use of applications programs, and managing the storage of data and program files on disk. Since key parts of the operating system have to remain loaded at all times the amount of free memory available for user programs is correspondingly reduced. In situations in which memory has been at a premium this further constraint severely tested the ingenuity of programmers.

With the birth of the microcomputer the initial booting of computers was simplified by adding a special memory chip known as the BIOS (Basic Input/Output System), which holds a permanent record of key components of the primary operating system, automatically accessed as soon as the machine is switched on. Such memory is generally known as ROM (Read Only Memory) to distinguish it from RAM (Random Access Memory), a term used to describe conventional memory, which can be overwritten with new information at any time. Prior to this important technical development the task of starting or restarting a computer required a special deck of punched cards or tape, known as the bootstrap.

Direct specification of instructions for a computer is known as machine-level programming. In its most primitive form, rarely if ever encountered today, this involves entering each instruction as a number, which is then translated directly into a binary-coded equivalent. Such code is both difficult to prepare and very hard to check. To overcome these difficulties a more practicable method, known as assembly programming, was quickly devised. This involves entering the instructions in a syntactic form, using simple mnemonics, which are more easily recognized by a programmer. These are then translated internally into equivalent machine instructions by a special interpreter program, supplied by the computer manufacturer.

Programming in assembler code allows the selection of the most efficient sequence of instructions to achieve a particular objective, and in earlier situations when processing power in terms of speed and available memory was severely restricted such a facility was often an essential feature of software design. From a programmer's point of view, however, there are a number of drawbacks associated with this low-level approach to writing applications. In particular, such direct control of a computer's processing functions remains extremely complex, error-prone, and very time-consuming in terms of writing new code. As a result, even the simplest mathematical operations require the use of several assembler statements.

A more serious, longer-term disadvantage that was materially to affect the development of early computer music software is the dependence of such programs on the host computer architecture. Although the industry today is generally concentrating on a very small range of different processor architectures, such stability was unknown until the early 1990s. In the past, therefore, the replacement of a computer or the transfer of work to a different machine invariably necessitated much laborious reprogramming before such software could be successfully ported.

To overcome such difficulties, a repertory of high-level programming languages was developed during the mid-1950s, and it is the modern equivalents of these that are used by most software developers. These employ simpler directives that are semantically more powerful, in many instances a single command replacing an entire sequence of assembler instructions. Most important, these programs are for the most part machine-independent, allowing the software to be transferred from one computer architecture to another with a minimum of difficulty.

This portability is achieved via special compilers, which act to translate these higher-level instructions into the machine code appropriate for the particular computer. During the 1960s and 1970s, languages such as ALGOL, COBOL, and FORTRAN were in common use, the latter being especially popular with scientists. By the early 1980s, other languages had gained in importance, for example, BASIC, Lisp, Pascal, and C, the latter in particular becoming especially significant as an all-embracing tool for the design both of operating systems, notably UNIX, and also applications-specific software.[6]

Although these high-level languages have greatly simplified the task of programming, such features involve some sacrifice in terms of the efficient use of computer resources. Again, whereas the power of present-day computers is such that this tradeoff is of little or no material significance, this was certainly not the case during the pioneering era. Here the combination of much slower processors, less memory, and far less efficient compilers greatly impaired their use for writing computationally intensive and time-critical applications. It is against this background of an earlier and very different world of computing, significantly constrained in the range and nature of its applications by the technology of the period, that the birth and early development of computer music can now be studied.

The first attempts at harnessing the computer as a tool for synthesizing sound date from the mid-1950s. During this period the acoustic research division of Bell Telephone Laboratories, New Jersey, became interested in the possibilities of transmitting telephone conversations in a digitized form, converting the analog signals into equivalent patterns of numerical samples at one end of the line, and performing the reverse process at the other. The complexities encountered in multiplexing several conversations together down a single line, and then separating them again at the other end, led to the use of the computer as a development aid. The conventional telephone line only required a relatively modest frequency bandwidth, concentrated toward the lower end of the audio frequency spectrum. The research team, however, quickly realized that despite some major technical obstacles, there was a distinct possibility that full bandwidth transmission systems could be developed, capable of handling broadcast-quality music.

It was in such a visionary climate of investigation that one of Bell's research engineers, Max Mathews, began exploring the use of the computer as a means of synthesizing sound from first principles, using mathematical principles of waveform calculation.[7] His first attempts consisted of two experimental programs: MUSIC I, which appeared in 1957, followed by MUSIC II in 1958. MUSIC I was exceedingly basic, limited to the generation of a single triangle-wave function. MUSIC II was a little more flexible, allowing four functions to be manipulated simultaneously, drawn from a repertory of sixteen different waveforms.

The computer employed for MUSIC I was an IBM 704, the immediate successor to IBM's very first computer, the 701. In common with all first-generation computers of the time it was based on slow and often unreliable valve technology. The introduction of transistor-based circuits in the late 1950s held the vital key to more efficient computer architectures, and by the end of the decade an entirely new family of machines entered production. Bell Telephone Laboratories took delivery of one of these second-generation computers, an IBM 7094, just in time for Mathews to adapt and complete his work on MUSIC II. Assisted by Joan Miller, he then embarked on a much-expanded version of this program offering a variety of synthesis and signal processing functions, MUSIC III, completed early in 1960.

By now a number of people were showing an interest in the project, not least the director of the acoustical research group, John Pierce. In 1961, James Tenney also became directly involved with developments at Bell, soon to be followed Hubert Howe, Godfrey Winham, and Jim Randall, working at Princeton University, New Jersey. With further assistance from Joan Miller, Mathews completed the next version of his program, MUSIC IV, in1962. It was this version that provided the basic model for an extensive family of derivatives, subsequently made available to growing numbers of prospective users across the world. As will be seen in due course, one derivative in particular, CSOUND, remains in widespread use today, now directly accessible as freeware via the Internet for use on a variety of computing platforms.

The earlier mentioned differences between high- and low-level programming techniques are of some importance in tracing the evolution of these versions. MUSIC IV, like its predecessors, was written almost entirely in assembler code, in this instance specifically for the IBM 7094. Since Princeton, conveniently, had purchased just such a machine shortly after Bell, a copy of this program could thus be quickly implemented with a minimum of difficulty. Several improvements were introduced at Princeton, and the new version of the program was renamed MUSIC IV B. Particular attention was paid to improving the intelligibility of the program for use by composers rather than scientists, a consideration that had not previously been regarded as a major priority.

Developments in computer technology, however, were already sealing the fate of both versions. With the advent of integrated circuits, providing a means of incorporating several miniaturized transistors within a single molding, a third generation of computers was born, launched by IBM in 1965 with the System 360 series. The increased capabilities of these machines were accompanied by radical alterations to the internal machine functions, demanding in turn an entirely different interpreter for low-level programming. Programs such as MUSIC IV and IV B would thus have had to be completely rewritten using the new code, and this daunting prospect caused the pioneers at Bell and Princeton to rethink their strategy.

In an attempt to avoid short-term obsolescence and to make MUSIC programs more generally available to centers not equipped with IBM machines it was considered prudent to prepare versions that were written in FORTRAN. The first of these, MUSIC IV F, was written by Arthur Roberts in 1965, soon to be eclipsed by a more comprehensive version, MUSIC IV BF, written by Howe at Princeton during 1966–7 and subsequently improved by Winham. Portability, however, was achieved at a price, for these compiler-generated programs were inevitably less efficient than versions written directly in assembler code. The primary consequence was a significant increase in the time taken to process synthesis tasks, making computer music composers particularly unpopular with computing centres.

Mathews, meanwhile, continued to develop his own versions at Bell Telephone Laboratories, completing an all-FORTRAN version, MUSIC V, in 1968. This program was partially successful in overcoming the inefficiencies of the compiler through a major reorganization of the component synthesis functions, taking into account the internal functional characteristics of the compiler itself. The result was an altogether simpler program, more readily understood by composers with little or no prior experience of computer operation, but lacking nevertheless a number of potentially very useful refinements, notably filters. A number of computer music centers, however, chose this version as the starting point for the development of their own custom-designed versions, in some instances materially different to the original MUSIC V.

Despite these developments, the advantages of low-level programming were not neglected. In 1968, Barry Vercoe, while working at Princeton, developed a very fast and efficient assembler version of MUSIC IV B, entitled MUSIC 360, specifically for the corresponding IBM range of third-generation machines. This extra investment of time and effort was based on the premise, as it turned out correct, that IBM was unlikely to change its basic machine architecture yet again for at least a decade, thus ensuring a reasonable life span for the program. After moving to the Massachusetts Institute of Technology (MIT) in the early 1970s, he developed another assembler version, this time for the PDP 11, manufactured by the Digital Equipment Corporation. This program, MUSIC 11, is of particular significance, for as a result of major efficiency gains in terms of processing demands and the use of memory space MUSICn-based direct synthesis techniques finally became generally available to an expanded community of users. Further, at MIT itself, major advances were made in developing new input facilities for composers, including such useful communication aids as an interactive computer graphics system and a conventional music keyboard.

Another version, MUSIC 10, designed specifically for the larger PDP 10 series of computers, was completed in 1975 by John Chowning and James Moorer at Stanford University, California, further improvements being implemented in due course both at Stanford and also IRCAM in Paris. Recognition of the increasing importance of the programming language C led Richard Moore in 1985 to develop CMUSIC, an expanded version of MUSIC V at the Computer Audio Research Laboratory (CARL), located at the University of California, San Diego (UCSD). In a similar move, Barry Vercoe translated MUSIC 11 into a C version at MIT in 1986.[8] Thus it was that CSOUND was born, its subsequent release into the public domain ensuring wide dissemination and continuing popularity of the program as a comprehensive and easily extensible software resource both for composing and research.

With a lineage stretching almost to the midpoint of the previous century, these MUSICn programs have undergone extensive development over the intervening years, taking full advantage of the quantum increases in processing power and versatility of the underlying technology. Despite these changes, many of the original features employed in their design have been retained, the most significant of these being the principles of wavetable synthesis.

If a sequence of sounds is to be synthesized digitally entirely from first principles the computer must be programmed to calculate the corresponding pressure-wave characteristics in terms of discrete numerical samples, the later being passed for conversion into equivalent voltage steps by a digital-to-analog converter. A particularly versatile and extremely powerful technique is known as additive synthesis, where a number of different sinusoidal components are dynamically mixed together. In order to minimize the processing demands on the CPU, and at the same time reduce the number of control variables that have to be specified by the composer, it became common practice to use a modified version of this technique. Here a specific repertory of timbres is identified before the main processes of synthesis commence, constructed from groups of sinusoidal components that are fixed at the outset in terms of their harmonic ratios and relative amplitudes. Such conditions allow the use of a single composite waveform for each timbre, calculated mathematically and stored in memory as a wavetable function.[9]

It will be recalled that the primary compound waveforms employed by analog synthesizers included the square wave, the triangle wave and the sawtooth wave, all of which may be reduced to component sinusoids with fixed harmonic and amplitude ratios. In the digital domain the possibilities of mathematical calculation allow the number of individual sinusoids and their component harmonic and amplitude ratios to be freely specified, resulting in a variety of composite waveforms, each associated with a distinctive timbre. To avoid excessive computation, blocks of memory, typically 512 words (or equivalent byte groupings) long, are set aside for the storage of individual wave functions, taking the form of numerical tables that record the successive values required to represent one complete cycle. A continuous function may then be generated by repeatedly scanning through these values in a cyclic fashion. Such a technique shows a strong similarity to that previously discussed in considering the use of a sequencer to generate control functions for a synthesizer.

The fundamental frequency of cyclic function produced by this technique is dependent upon the speed at which samples are subsequently output to the converter, and the number of samples used to represent each fundamental cycle. Applying a sample rate of 10,000 samples per second in the above instance would result in a sine wave of 10,000/512 = 19.5 Hz, approximately. Doubling this rate to 20,000 samples per second would increase the frequency in proportion to about 39 Hz. It thus becomes evident that one method of providing control over the output frequency is via a proportional variation of the sampling rate itself. A conventional computer, however, operates using a fixed clock rate, making it impracticable to implement such a superficially advantageous solution.[10]

A different method of extracting wave-form samples from the associated memory blocks had thus to be evolved, where the frequency of repetition would be determined by modifying the number of samples used to represent each cycle, whilst keeping the sampling rate constant. To return to the example cited earlier, at a sampling rate of 10,000 (10 kHz) the output frequency could be doubled from 19.5 Hz to 39 Hz merely by reading every second sample in the memory block. The entire wave would then be scanned after 256 steps instead of 512. Reading every fourth sample will quadruple the frequency, and so forth. Since the memory block is read as a continuous loop, location 1 following location 512, no problems are encountered in extracting sample values at intervals that do not repeat an exact number of times within a table length, for example, every third or every fifth sample in the above instance.

Although this basic technique permits the generation of multiples of 19.5 Hz, or subdivisions thereof by multiple readings of each sample in turn, it does not allow the production of any other frequency values. This difficulty is overcome by the application of simple routines to estimate function values that lie between adjacent elements in the wave table, either by rounding to the nearest table value or, for better fidelity, approximating an intermediate value. Although this additional calculation stage increases the time required to compute the result, even the more accurate methods of interpolation that are sometimes employed in this context are less time-consuming than calculating each sample value entirely from first principles.

Notwithstanding the improvements in synthesis efficiency that could be achieved by using techniques such as wavetable synthesis, the demands of even the simplest of tasks were sufficient to render live sound generation all but impossible during the pioneering years. In such a situation, the only feasible way of overcoming this hurdle is to allow the computer to calculate all the output values over whatever period of time proves necessary, accumulating the samples in the first instance on an auxiliary storage device such as a magnetic disk or tape. As a subsequent process the resulting audio data sample values are then recovered sequentially and passed to a digital-to-analog converter at the required sampling rate.[11]

In the early days it was rarely possible to attach a digital-to-analog converter directly to a mainframe computer. Instead, a tape containing the digitized audio data had to be transported to a laboratory that specialized in data conversion, perhaps many miles away. Problems of both synthesis and subsequent conversion were further exacerbated by the growing desire to generate information in stereo rather than mono. Since each channel requires its own set of samples, both processing and storage requirements are thus doubled. In practice samples are usually interleaved, requiring the control system for the associated pair of converters to operate at twice the speed of mono in terms of data transfer, dividing up the audio samples correctly between left and right channels.

In terms of processing overheads, the delays that composers encountered in working with such systems were often considerable, and the ultimate goal of a real-time environment for a comprehensive range of software synthesis tools was not to be easily achieved. Even a relatively powerful mainframe computer dating from the early 1970s required upward of 10 or 20 minutes of CPU time to synthesize the samples for just a minute of high quality sound. If the synthesis instructions were especially complex it was not unknown for this ratio to increase by several orders of magnitude.

In view of these heavy demands, and the fact that mainframe computers were shared resources, composers invariably encountered significant delays, perhaps extending to many hours, between submitting synthesis tasks to the computer operators and collecting the resulting data stored on tape or computer disk, ready for audio conversion. Such a working environment contrasted sharply with the immediacy of response offered by an analog studio, and this proved a powerful disincentive for established electronic composers wishing to explore the potential of computer music. The compensations lay in the range and flexibility of the synthesis facilities that could be provided for the more demanding user, in particular the ability to specify refined and precisely ordered sounds via a musically orientated syntax.

A central concept of the MUSICn family of programs is the division of synthesis tasks into two components, the "orchestra" and the "score." The "orchestra" is constructed from statements that define a network of unit generators and processors, in the first instance simulating standard analog studio devices such as oscillators, filters, envelope shapers, and reverberation units. In due course a number of new unit generators were added as a by-product of investigations into new algorithms for generating and manipulating sound material, and some of the more significant of these will discussed in a later chapter.[12] Since all these devices are software simulations the only absolute limit on the number and variety of unit generators in use at any one time is the maximum workspace available in memory.

The "score," as its title suggests, provides performance data for the orchestra. Suitable sequences of control information must be provided for each unit generator, including such key details as the starting time and duration of each event. Each oscillator wavetable is specified via function-generating routines, which translate basic variables such as the relative strengths of individual harmonic components into a composite function before the main processes of synthesis begin.

The need to specify all aspects of the synthesis process in advance, coupled with the subsequent delays in processing, left no opportunity for any interactive experimentation. Such conditions encouraged a highly didactic approach toward the compositional process itself. Indeed, an interesting parallel can be drawn with

Stockhausen's early electronic works *Study I* and *Study II*, where the decision to explore the possibilities of serial composition at the level of describing every event in terms of individual sinusoids led to an equally quantitative and predetermined method of working.

Thus it was that compositional principles with a strong mathematical content became the dominant influence on much of the early creative output produced using MUSICn software at Bell Labs and elsewhere. This characteristic is strongly reflected in the titles of works such as *Variations in Timbre and Attack* (1961) and *Five Against Seven—Random Canon* (1961) by John Pierce, or *Noise Study* (1961) and *Five Stochastics Studies* (1962) by James Tenney. A radical departure from such methodology and a signpost for important developments in digital synthesis of a rather different nature was pioneered by Mathews himself with *Bicycle Built for Two* (1962). This early example of speech synthesis achieved some notoriety in the public domain, inspiring in turn a wider research interest in this important aspect of communication technology.

The quantity of information required for additive synthesis is often considerable, even when extensive use is made of compound wave functions. Working at this level of detail is also far removed from the notion of a traditional instrument with a more familiar and rational set of performance characteristics, and this soon encouraged the development of alternative synthesis methods that could be more easily comprehended and practically managed. The origins of one particularly significant technique to be developed during the early stages of computer music have already been discussed in the context of analog systems. Here the special characteristics of voltage-controlled synthesizers make it possible to apply the output wave characteristics of one oscillator to modulate the frequency and/or amplitude control characteristics of a second oscillator. Since the control of an input to one unit generator oscillator by the output data flow of another requires no more than a simple link statement within the orchestra, such techniques are relatively easy to implement in MUSICn programs and leave ample scope for experimentation.

The work of John Chowning, at Stanford University, was to prove important in this context. During the late 1960s, he began detailed investigations into the characteristics of frequency-modulated sounds using the computer as a synthesis source. He discovered that the application of frequencies of deviation greater than the carrier frequency itself led to the production of unusual acoustic phenomena. Such modulation conditions, when studied mathematically, suggest an oscillation that deviates into a negative frequency region for part of its cycle. A wave of 150 Hz subject to a deviation of 200 Hz would thus be modulated between 350 Hz and −50 Hz. The ear, however, does not recognize negative frequency components as a downward extension of the normal audio spectrum. Instead, they are perceived as positive frequencies, but with an inverted waveform or phase. The modulation characteristic will thus appear as follows:

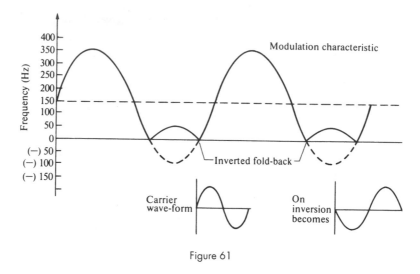

Figure 61

Identical effects occur to the side bands generated by the process of modulation itself, those bands that lie below 0 Hz being folded back into the audio spectrum. It will be recalled that under normal conditions frequency modulation results in a symmetrical distribution of side bands either side of the carrier frequency, the spacing and number of side bands generated from a particular carrier being regulated by the frequency of modulation, and the deviation. If negative side bands are generated, however, the distribution ceases to be symmetrical. Consider, for example, the results of modulating a carrier of 200 Hz with a frequency of 70 Hz, such that the amplitude of the latter produces a peak deviation in the carrier of 250 Hz. In these circumstances theory predicts the generation of side bands of varying amplitudes at 270, 340, 410, 480, and 550 Hz above the carrier, and 130, 60, −10, −80, and −150 Hz beneath, the negative values being folded back into the audio spectrum with an inversion of phase. This latter characteristic was to prove especially significant in terms of the spectral characteristics that could thus be created.

The aural effects become especially meaningful if such characteristics are varied dynamically. If the modulating wave is changed from 70 Hz to 73 Hz in the above instance, the spacing of the upper side bands increases proportionally to 273, 346, 419, 492, and 565 Hz. The lower side bands, however, will change in frequency to 127, 54, −19, −92, and −162 Hz. The negative components, on fold-back, thus gain in frequency, moving in the opposite direction from their positively generated counterparts. The interactions between crossing side bands radically alter the perceived characteristics of the modulated sounds. In particular they exhibit a remarkably "alive" quality as they permute, because of the complex phasing relationships that occur between the components. Within the precise domain of digital synthesis, control over these characteristics may be accurately exercised via the three basic variables of the carrier frequency, c, the modulating frequency, m, and the deviation, d.

During the 1970s, with assistance from James Moorer, Chowning continued his research into FM techniques, paying particular attention to the possibility of synthesizing instrumental timbres by suitable combinations of c, m, and d values. Bell and brass sounds proved particularly productive avenues of exploration, sometimes necessitating the use of double or triple modulators with multiple carriers. Only very minor modifications to the internal sample generation routines of MUSICn synthesis programs were necessary to accommodate the specification of negative frequency components, and Chowning's models soon became widely used and extremely popular with computer music composers. His own early FM works *Sabelithe* and *Turenas* (an anagram of "natures"), written in 1971 and 1972 respectively, convincingly demonstrate the richness and variety of timbres that may be produced by such a technique. Most significantly, his exploration of timbre transformation, in which one sound is changed internally into another, signaled an important new area of synthesis that many others were later to explore.[13]

In terms of signal processing facilities the use of filter units in MUSICn programs results in complex and potentially very time-consuming calculations during the sample generation process. As part of his attempts to improve the computing efficiency of these programs, Max Mathews had omitted filters altogether in the original version of MUSIC V, and this forced composers to control changes in timbre by manipulating the wave-generation functions directly. This restriction seriously impeded the creative use of this program, and explains why so many centers subsequently modified the FORTRAN code to overcome this limitation. Barry Vercoe's decision not to compromise functionality in the quest for greater computing efficiency in his own versions was particularly auspicious. It not only ensured that MUSIC 360 provided possibly the most comprehensive range of facilities of any MUSICn program of its time but also laid the best possible foundations for its notable derivative, CSOUND.

The inclusion of reverberation facilities further extended the versatility of MUSICn programs, and given the rather clinical nature of the musical output produced by more basic scores and orchestras the temptation to use such a resource to add an element of warmth to the overall sound often proved irresistible. The initial reverberation algorithms were rather elementary in their construction, a reflection of the high overheads encountered in this type of signal processing, both in terms of memory requirements and also processing requirements. Later versions were more sophisticated, leading to a number of derivatives that explore the possibilities of projecting sounds in an enlarged acoustic space.

The pioneering work carried out at Bell Telephone Laboratories, MIT, Princeton, and Stanford encouraged other centers throughout the world to establish facilities for computer music. By the end of the 1970s, enthusiasts had installed

MUSICn programs in centers as far apart as Melbourne in Australia; Ontario and Waterloo in Canada; Marseilles and IRCAM in France; Durham, Glasgow, and London in Great Britain; and Padua in Italy. In America, similar facilities were also to be found in many universities, including Columbia, Illinois, Indiana, Michigan, New York at Buffalo, and Queen's College, New York. Computer music had finally come of age.

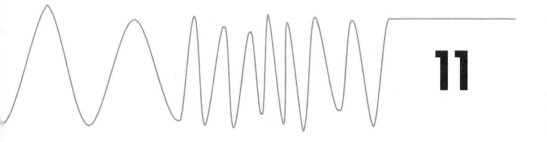

11

From Computer Technology to Musical Creativity

Software Synthesis and Computer-Assisted Composition

The pioneering phase of computer music, spearheaded by the development of the MUSICn series of programs, came to an end with the diversification of technologies that led to cheaper and ultimately more versatile alternatives to the mainframe computer. Although these programs could still not be executed in real time, improvements in processing power were steadily reducing the time delay between submitting tasks and auditioning the results. Composers, accordingly, became more adventurous in their use of these programs, highlighting in turn the drawbacks of relying on a basic alphanumeric coding system for the input of score data.

Leland Smith, working at Stanford University, pioneered a notable improvement in this regard. Using MUSIC V, he produced a music-based syntax for specifying details of pitch and rhythm via a subprogram entitled SCORE (1971). In addition, routines were included for applying processes of transposition and transformation, creating in effect a simple composing facility.[1]

Mathews had briefly turned his attention to auxiliary input methods during the mid-1960s, developing a graphical interface for the entry of simple score details to MUSIC IV in association with Leonard Rossler. This project, however, came to a premature end with the removal of the IBM 7094 computer from Bell Telephone Laboratories. No further significant progress was made in this context until Barry Vercoe developed a simple graphical input system for MUSIC 11 almost a decade later.[2] Although by the mid-1970s the design of facilities for communicating with computers had advanced significantly, leading manufacturers generally took the view that graphical facilities were only of interest to a small minority of their clients. As a result very little was invested in the development of suitable tools to support this mode of data input.[3]

In assessing the significance of these software synthesis programs, one feature in particular distinguishes them from alternative methods of generating or processing sound information, both past and present. This is their exceptional capacity to function as development tools for creating comprehensive and versatile resources for composers to explore and develop new ideas. Modern versions of programs such as CSOUND are richly equipped with enhanced synthesis and signal processing tools of immense power and versatility, and many of these enhancements have been developed by members of the CSOUND community as an extension of their own research into new techniques and refinements. Such an open agenda, making the results of such investigations freely available to other users, contrasts very sharply with the essentially closed and competitive environment associated with commercially manufactured synthesizers, samplers, and signal processors.

Jean Claude Risset, another early pioneer of software synthesis techniques, also made a number of important contributions to the creative development of the medium at this time. Having trained as a scientist in Paris he became a member of Mathew's research team in 1964. During his time at Bell Labs he carried out extensive research into the nature of sound using MUSICn resources, preparing an important catalogue of practical scores and orchestras for the simulation of musical instruments, notably members of the brass and wind families. Having completed a seminal work at Bell, *Suite for Computer Little Boy* (1968), exploring the grouping of harmonically derived timbres, Risset returned to his native France to further technical and musical developments both at Marseilles and at IRCAM. During the 1970s he produced a number of pieces including *Dialogues* (1975) for flute, clarinet, piano, percussion, and computer-generated sounds, and *Songes* (1978), an essay in transformations from natural violin and flute sounds to the complex timbres of frequency-modulated tones.

Risset's intense preoccupation with the nature of timbre and the continuum that can be established between natural and synthetic sounds opened up powerful new avenues of creative exploration, extending to digital processing of acoustic sources as well as the synthesis of material entirely from first principles. At IRCAM, modifications were made to MUSIC V and MUSIC 10 to allow the input of short extracts of externally generated source material. Special algorithms were also added to allow the acoustic content to be analyzed, generating the data necessary for subsequent resynthesis. At this point, modifications could be introduced, thus creating a powerful compositional tool.

Digital signal processing has become an increasingly important technique for composers, for it facilitates the integration of natural and synthetic sound worlds in ways that cannot be achieved by purely analog means. It will be recalled that analog systems offer a number of useful techniques for processing natural sound sources, including filtering, modulation, reverberation, and tape manipulation. The scope of such transformations is nevertheless limited, as it is not possible to extract certain key features of the sounds themselves. For example, the components of pitch and duration cannot be satisfactorily isolated one from another in the analog domain. Variable-speed processing results in proportional changes to both components, and the "snapshot" sampling mechanisms of the Tempophon provide a very poor quality of reproduction.[4] In the digital domain, where each second of sound is quantified in terms of many thousands of discrete numerical samples, the full force of mathematical analysis techniques can be brought to bear on the data, allowing the constituent components of frequency, amplitude and time to be accurately isolated.

Work on the programming routines necessary for such complex operations began at Bell Telephone Laboratories, stimulated by the arrival of Risset. Credit for the transformation of this computational minefield into a musically understandable set of procedures, however, must be given in the first instance to James Moorer, working at Stanford University. During the 1970s, he produced a number of miniatures to illustrate the use of such techniques, including *Perfect Days* (1975) and *Gentlemen Start Your Engines* (1977). Both of these incorporate speech sources and make extensive use of asynchronous pitch and duration manipulations. *Perfect Days* also employs an interesting process known a cross-synthesis, in which the spectral characteristics of one sound are used to control the articulation of another.[5]

The basis for the latter technique can be traced back to the analog vocoder. This device, it will be recalled, provides a dynamic analysis of the frequency spectrum of an applied sound via a bank of band-pass filters. If the amplitude functions thus derived are used to control the operation of another identically tuned bank of filters, these characteristics may be superimposed on any sound applied to the input of the second bank. In the analog domain, the control data consists of a series of voltage functions, each varying in a different way as a function of time. In the digital domain, the spectral content can be analyzed in greater detail and the features thus extracted may then be manipulated using powerful digital algorithms. In *Perfect Days*, for example, speech elements are used to articulate selected components within the sound of a solo flute, resulting in a degree of animation that touches on the surreal.

Speech generation and manipulation techniques feature in the works of Charles Dodge, a composer closely involved with the development of synthesis facilities at both Columbia and Princeton universities. His strong commitment to serial principles of musical organization reflected the dominant compositional philosophies being furthered at both institutions at this time, and resulted in a style of composition that contrasts sharply with the freer methods of expression adopted by many West Coast and also European composers, including Risset. In *Speech Songs* (1973), for example, the phonemes of his text are subject to strictly ordered permutations within a strongly sectionalized, formal scheme.

Such indebtedness to the teachings of Babbitt are evident in his other computer-generated works written during this formative period, for example, *Changes* (1969), *Earth's Magnetic Field* (1970), *Extensions for Trumpet and Tape* (1973), and *In Celebration* (1975). The choices of texture are predominantly instrumental in nature, the precision of the computer being exploited to provide a refined measure of control over the processes of synthesis. The work *Changes* evolves as a textural interplay between three contrasting elements: percussion-like sounds, pitch sequences, and chords. Some instrumental sounds are clearly identifiable, for example, the insistent tapping of a side drum located toward the beginning of the composition and the interjection of brass notes reminiscent of a horn or trombone. A consistent mobility of timbre, however, prevents such associations from acquiring any sense of permanence. The entire piece is given a strong sense of propulsion by its jazz-orientated organization of rhythm. *In Celebration*, like *Speech Songs*, incorporates synthetic vocal material, the extensive use of cross-synthesis leading to a convincing parody of vocal part-singing.

A number of composers worked with MUSIC programs at Princeton during the formative years, including Benjamin Boretz, Jim Randall, Barry Vercoe, and Jonathan Harvey, and the emerging repertory did much to establish the credibility of computer music at a time when the primary focus of attention lay elsewhere. Boretz was a committed disciple of total serialism, and thus made full use of the quantitative characteristics of the composing medium. *Group Variation II* (1973), for example, is a taut, pointillistic composition built on a strictly organized scheme of "note/events." Randall was also heavily influenced by these compositional principles in early works such as *Quartets in Pairs* (1964), which is a brief contrapuntal study. *Mudgett: Monologues by a Mass Murderer* (1965) combines entirely synthetic material with a prerecorded tape of a soprano, introduced in the second movement in a manner strikingly reminiscent of Schoenberg's expressionist period.

Jonathan Harvey, one of the most influential members of the British avant-garde, realized an early piece entitled *Time Points* during a year's residency 1969–70.[6] This study was conceived as a manipulation of a series of fixed timbres, articulated in terms of their pitch, duration, dynamics, and vibrato. Such an economy of means resulted in a clear and well-defined aural perspective, which highlights the inner nature of the chosen types of sounds. A later work, *Mortuos Plango, Vivos Voco* realized at IRCAM in 1980 became an important point of reference for many composers seeking to explore the possibilities of digital signal processing. This piece is based on the sounds of the great tenor bell at Winchester Cathedral, and the voice of Harvey's own son, Dominic, who was a chorister from 1975 to 1980. Its title is taken from the inscription around the bell, the full text providing the source material for the boy. The pitch and time structure of the work is based entirely on the rich irregular harmonic spectrum of the bell. The eight sections are each based on one of the principal eight lowest partials. Chords are constructed from the repertoire of thirty-three partials, and modulations from one area of the spectrum to another are achieved by means of glissandi. Constant transformations between the sounds of the boy's voice and that of the bell act to unify the contrasting sources of material.

Synthesism (1969–70) by Barry Vercoe displays more than a passing affinity with the sounds and methods of organization employed by Stockhausen at Cologne during the 1950s. Streams of filtered noise are blended with sounds built out of distinct tones, using a tuning principle that divides the octave into sixteen equal parts. *Synapse* (1976) for computer tape and viola, another work realized at MIT, shows a sensitive regard for the performance characteristics of the live instrument in terms of the accompanying synthetic material and its articulation.

Whereas the importance of MUSICn software in shaping the foundations of computer music must not be underestimated, other lines of research and development in related areas were pursued from an early stage, signaling the birth of a considerably enlarged spectrum of activities within the genre. One important area focuses on the use the computer as an aid to the compositional process itself.

The use of the computer as a tool for generating music data structures from higher-order specifications may be traced back to the pioneering work of Lejaren Hiller and Iannis Xenakis in the 1950s, in both cases initiated before Max Mathews had started work on the MUSICn series of programs.[7] Both composers were concerned in the first instance with the production of conventional computer output in the form of alphanumeric data, subsequently transcribed by hand into a standard score format for performance by acoustic instruments.

In the case of Hiller, it was a collaboration with John Cage over the composition of HPSCHD (1969) that launched computer-assisted composition firmly into the public domain.[8] Many of the composing subroutines and processes used for this work were derivatives of those used first in the *Illiac Suite* (1956)[9] and subsequently in the *Computer Cantata* (1963). In the *Illiac Suite*, assisted by Leonard Isaacson, Hiller experimented with the automation of a number of stylistic models. The first movement is concerned with the production of tonal melody and harmony in two- and four-part counterpoint. The second movement restricts the latter element entirely to note-against-note principles of organization, highlighting the diatonic nature of the interweaving melodic lines. In the third movement, a more progressive style is suggested by using the computer to manipulate serial note rows. Finally, in the fourth movement probability theory, rather than structural rules of tonal and rhythmic organization, is used to determine the evolution of the material, thus creating a distinctly radical idiom.

The *Computer Cantata*, composed in association with Robert Baker, was his first piece directly to employ computer-generated sounds, used in association with more traditional electronic and natural sound sources, including the voice.[10] The pitches, duration values, amplitudes, and timbres were all determined via random probability programs, operating on the distribution of pitches contained in a short extract from *Three Places in New England* by Charles Ives.

In the case of HPSCHD, similar techniques were applied to extracts derived from piano works by Mozart, Beethoven, Chopin, Schumann, Gottschalk, Busoni, Schoenberg, Cage, and Hiller. Cage had become preoccupied with the use of chance elements in musical composition, in particular adaptations of principles described in the ancient Chinese book of *I Ching*, and the computer provided an ideal means of automating these processes of data generation. The work is of indeterminate length, from one to seven harpsichords and one to fifty-one tapes of computer-generated sounds. The score consists of the tapes and seven solo parts for the players, each of these elements lasting 20 minutes. In performance, HPSCHD thus lasts a minimum of 20 minutes, with no upper limit on its maximum duration, for the performers are at liberty to start any solo or any tape at any time. In the version released as a commercial recording, computer-generated instructions are provided for manipulating the volume, bass and treble controls of a conventional hi-fi system, thus involving the listener directly in the act of performance.

The synthesized material for the tapes was created using routines specially adapted from Mathews's MUSIC IV B program. Each note specification consisted of a simple timbre selected from a choice of sine wave, sawtooth, or square wave characteristics. This timbre was then allocated an attack time, a decay time, an overall duration, and a maximum amplitude, all details being supplied directly by the composing program. In this regard, thus, the processes of composition and synthesis by means of a computer became fully integrated.

The achievements of Xenakis at this time were also notable. His critical attitude toward the electronic medium as a whole is revealed in an essay titled *New Proposals in Microsound Structure*, first published in 1968 and subsequently added to his extensive treatise, *Formalised Music*.

> Since the war all "electronic" music has [also] failed, in spite of the big hopes of the fifties, to pull electroacoustic music out of its cradle of the big cradle of the so-called electronic pure sounds produced by frequency generators. . . . Only when the "pure" electronic sounds were framed by other "concrete" sounds which were much richer and much more interesting (thanks to Edgard Varèse, Pierre Schaeffer and Pierre Henry) could electronic music really become powerful. The more recent attempts to use the flower of modern technology, computers coupled to converters, have shown that in spite of some relative successes,[11] the sonorous results are even less interesting than those made ten years ago in the classic electroacoustic studios by means of frequency generators, filters, modulators and reverberation units.[12]

This harsh indictment of wholly synthetic sound production whether by analog or digital means goes to the very heart of philosophical issues that are as relevant today as they were in the 1970s. His specific reference to the notion of "electroacoustic" music as opposed to "electronic" or "computer" music suggests an emphasis on what is heard rather than the technology that lies behind its creation. At the same time, a subtle and yet crucially important distinction is being made in terms of the values that should be applied in judging the success or otherwise of the creative experience.[13]

Xenakis started to experiment with the computer as a compositional aid in 1956, using an IBM 7090. The first fruits of his labors, *ST/10-1, 080262*, a work for instrumental ensemble, received its first performance on 24 May 1962 at the headquarters of IBM France. The program used to prepare this work, written in FORTRAN, embodied an automated version of theories first explored in an earlier work, *Achorripsis*, for twenty-one instruments (1956–7). These were based on the use of a minimal structure to control the generation of data according to the laws of probability. Factors such as the time of occurrence, the type of timbre, the choice of instrument, the gradient of glissando, the duration, and the dynamic of each component sound are thus governed by large-scale determinants, which bias the probability weightings used in the data-generation process.

Several compositions were produced using modifications of the *ST/10* program, including *ST/48-1, 240162* for large orchestra, *Atrées* for ten solo performers, and *Morsima-Amorsima* for piano, violin, cello, and double bass, all three pieces being completed in 1962. In 1966 Xenakis founded EMAMu (renamed CEMAMu, the Centre d'Études de Mathématique et Automatique Musicales in 1972), researching computer music techniques and producing a number of multimedia works. These included *Polytope de Cluny* (1972–4) and *Diatope* (1977), each composed and controlled in performance via the computer, using two special programs prepared in collaboration with Cornelia Colyer. *Polytope de Cluny* is an automated light/sound composition employing six hundred electronic flashes, three lasers, and a seven-track electronic tape, first staged in the Cluny Museum, Paris. *Diatope* takes these technologies a stage further, employing sixteen hundred electronic flashes, four lasers, and a twelve-track tape.[14]

Others were soon to follow the lead of Hiller and Xenakis. Gottfried Michael Koenig had become interested in computer-assisted composition while working at the WDR studio, Cologne, during the early 1960s, and on appointment to the Institute of Sonology, Utrecht, in 1964 he developed two composing programs, starting with PROJECT 1, 1964–7, and followed by PROJECT 2, 1968–70.

PROJECT 1 was closely modeled on traditional principles of serial composition and offered only a limited measure of control over the processes of data generation. Like the ST programs of Xenakis, it was conceived solely as a personal composing system. PROJECT 2, in contrast, was intended for general use by composers at the Institute, and consequently offered a more flexible range of facilities. This program incorporates a set of probability functions, which may be utilized to control the selection of numerical values from a table of possibilities via a random-number generator. Various types of weighting are offered. A function called ALEA, for example, will make entirely random selections from a table of values, each element once chosen remaining eligible for reselection. Another, called SERIES, will remove values from the table after selection to prevent repetitions occurring. When all the available elements have been used up the function may be programmed with a fresh copy of the table.

A different type of selection procedure is provided by a function called TENDENCY. This allows the composer to apply "masks" to the random-number generator, dynamically adjusting the range of values from which it may make choices. The selection and control of functions and their associated data tables and the production of musical score characteristics from their output is carried out via three subprograms concerned respectively with the three basic parameters of pitch, time, and dynamics.

Koenig used PROJECT 1 to generate two instrumental works: *Project 1-Version 1* (1966) and *Project 1-Version 3* (1967), both for instrumental ensemble. Having launched PROJECT 2 with a piece entitled *Uebung fuer Klavier* (1970), he commenced work on a number of functional improvements to the software, extending the range of options available and adding facilities for interactive specification. This latter development signaled an important shift in emphasis facilitated by the enhanced capabilities of the studio's computer, a PDP 15. Although it was still the case that no version of MUSICn could yet operate in real time, it proved possible to develop a basic repertory of freestanding synthesis algorithms that generate sound directly with reasonable fidelity, using a digital-to-analog converter connected to the computer. Attention thus started to focus on novel methods of sound generation that could generate rich and varied audio spectra with minimum overheads in terms of computation.

Koenig's encouragement of other researchers at Utrecht to use PROJECT 2 as real-time control facility for their various synthesis experiments was thus to reap a number of dividends. The Canadian composer Barry Truax took a particular interest in the structure of PROJECT 2, notably the use of stochastic procedures and tendency masks to generate and control the production of audio spectra, the more detailed the specifications the more predictable the final result. The latter characteristic encourages what has become known as a "top-down" approach to composition, where the large-scale determinants are established first and the inner details supplied at a later date. These investigations were to lead to the start of an important research project, continued at Simon Fraser University, British Columbia, on his return to Canada in 1974.

His initial series of PODn (Poisson Distribution) programs demonstrated the creative possibilities of working with sound fragments or grains, rather than continuous waveforms, in the first instance synthesized from first principles either by additive synthesis (POD 5) or FM synthesis (POD 6). In due course, Truax extended these principles to the granulation and manipulation of externally generated sound material, creating a powerful, fully interactive synthesis and signal processing system.[15]

Nautilus, for solo percussion and four computer-synthesized soundtracks, composed in 1976, provides an impressive early example of the versatility of his POD system. His use of tendency masks to control the frequency and density of the FM spectra lead to subtle shadings of texture and a strong sense of organic development within the sounds themselves. Spatial location receives particular attention, the elements being subjected to rotation in both directions. The careful addition of reverberation leads to an illusion of nearness when the movement is rapid and an illusion of distance when the images become almost stationary.

A strong sense of identification with nature through sound is evoked in the works of another POD composer, Jean Piché. His *Heliograms* (1978), for example, is a representation of four solar photographs taken outside the earth's atmosphere. An analog mix-down of thirty-two different tracks of sound information, incorporating both additive and FM techniques results in a work of powerful proportions, taking full advantage of the spatial characteristics of granular synthesis.

One other pioneering synthesis system developed at Utrecht during the 1970s deserves special attention in this context. During 1973–4, Werner Kaegi, a specialist in phonetics, designed a software model for the production of quasi-speech sounds, leading to the development of a significantly faster hardware version by Stan Templaars known as VOSIM, completed in 1978. Kaegi's researches showed that a considerable number of speechlike sounds could be generated by the skillful manipulation of a pair of oscillators programmed to generate pulsed trains of single waves. Although the control specifications for these pulse trains are relatively complex, the basic principles of operation are relatively straightforward. The wave characteristic consists of a sine-squared function, the primary variables being the duration of each cycle and the delay before its repetition.

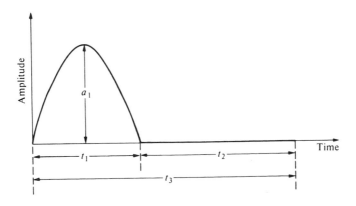

Figure 62

The fundamental pitch of the output is determined by t_3, this being the sum of the period of the wave pulse itself, t_1, and the delay before its repetition, t_2. In addition a strong formant is generated at the frequency $1/t_2$. The nature of the sounds thus generated becomes of particular interest when the time constants are dynamically varied. Random variation of t_2 will introduce significant noise elements, variation of t_1 while t_3 is kept constant produces diphthongs, and progressive changes to t_3 will result in glissandi. Control over the amplitude of the sounds simply requires suitable adjustments to a_1.

By this stage, vocal synthesis techniques were being investigated by a number of researchers, attention turning to the possibilities of simulating the characteristics of the singing voice as well as those of speech. The subsequent work of Xavier Rodet and Gerald Bennett at IRCAM, was to prove especially significant in this context, and developments such as these will be studied in due course.[16]

By the early 1970s, the nature and range of activities embraced by the term "computer music" were extending well beyond what reasonably might be considered an initial, exploratory phase of research and development. Individual activities such as those identified at Utrecht were beginning to multiply in number, each project in its own way expanding the knowledge base of this steadily expanding medium of composition. Herbert Brün, for example, also chose to write his own synthesis software, believing—like Truax—that his compositional objectives could only be fully realized if he maintained total control over all aspects of the creative process. His works are somewhat enigmatic, exploring ideas that lie much closer to those of John Cage than his earlier associates in Cologne and Munich. In 1963 he joined the staff at the University of Illinois, taking a keen interest in the work of Lejaren Hiller, in particular his interests in algorithmic composition, resulting in a set of composing routines known collectively as MUSICOMP.

Having used these resources for early works such as Soniferous Loops (1965) and Infraudibles (1968), Brün developed a special synthesis program entitled SAWDUST, which permitted him to work with the smallest parts of waveforms, linking, mingling, or merging such components to create composite shapes. The latter were then treated either as periodic waves by means of cyclic repetition, or as passing moments of orientation in a predetermined process of gradual transformation. This led to the composition of a trilogy of works, entitled Dust, More Dust, and Dustiny (1976–7).

The attractions of software-based approaches to sound synthesis and signal processing, not least the degree of flexibility afforded, led to increasing expectations and in some quarters a growing sense of frustration. The ultimate goal of designing digital facilities that could match the immediacy and interactive response of analog systems was to remain remarkably elusive. It was still the case, even at the end of the 1970s, that the computing power available to all but the most generously endowed studios was not sufficient to sustain more than a very limited range of live synthesis applications. This continued to place computer music at a serious disadvantage to its analog counterpart, encouraging a number of pioneers to explore an alternative approach, drawing on the most attractive features of both technologies.

Hybrid Synthesis

The principal antecedents for this alternative approach, known as hybrid synthesis, have already been discussed in considering the evolution of the RCA synthesizers and the development of digital sequencers for use with voltage-controlled systems. The common factor here is the notion that the performance of an analog synthesizer can be greatly enhanced by the addition of a programmable digital control system. It soon became clear that the scope and quantity of information required in this operational context, even for quite complex control functions, was considerably less than that required to synthesize and process the sound material itself. This led to a number of important initiatives in this context, which reached their zenith in the early 1970s. Although these systems have long since passed into obscurity, the experiences gained in their development and creative exploitation have proved invaluable in the design and use of all-digital systems. For this reason, their characteristics are worthy of close study.

One of the earliest investigations into hybrid synthesis was initiated by James Gabura and Gustav Ciamaga at the University of Toronto during 1965–6, resulting in an experimental real-time control system, PIPER 1, for two Moog voltage-controlled oscillators and two custom-built amplitude regulators using an IBM 1620 computer. In 1967 Lejaren Hiller and James Beauchamp attempted to obtain sufficient funds from the National Science Foundation for the construction of an elaborate hybrid system at the University of Illinois. Sadly, the application was turned down both on this occasion and again in 1969 when resubmitted by Hiller in a revised form, subsequent to his move from Illinois to the State University of New York at Buffalo.

Given these echoes of Edgard Varèse's earlier ill-fated attempts to secure funding from Bell Telephone Laboratories it somewhat ironic that yet again it should fall to Max Mathews to pioneer the first fully developed hybrid system in America, at Bell Labs. On this occasion he was assisted by F. Richard Moore, who acted as his programming assistant, the results being first presented to the public in a paper delivered to a conference on "Music and Technology," organized by UNESCO in Stockholm in 1970.[17]

This system, known as GROOVE (Generated Real-time Output Operations on Voltage-controlled Equipment), utilized a Honeywell DDP-224 minicomputer, which was for its time both fast and in programming terms extremely versatile. To this was attached a large auxiliary disk drive, a digital tape drive, an interface for the analog device incorporating twelve eight-bit and two twelve-bit digital-to-analog converters, and sixteen relays for switching functions. An additional pair of converters provided the horizontal and vertical coordinates for a cathode ray display unit, displaying visual representations of the control instructions provided by the composer. The software generated a linear time-scale along the horizontal axis, the sensitivity of which could be varied by the composer. This span, typically 10 seconds, acted as a basic timing-block or page, the screen automatically clearing at the end of each page to display the next. Up to ten different functions could be displayed without undue overcrowding.

The inclusion of a graphical monitoring system is of particular interest, for such a comprehensive visual representation of the device control functions, linked to a real-time generation system, brought the composer into intimate contact with the processes of digital synthesis. Thus the first major steps were taken on the road to the modern WIMPS (Windows, Icons, Mouse, Pointers, Systems) graphics interface, which is now a standard resource for all personal computers.[18] Device commands were entered via a conventional typewriter terminal, using a mnemonic code, and translated by the computer into sequential control values for the analog device interfaces. Several ancillary input devices were provided specially for the purpose of varying selected device functions during the performance of a computer score of control data. These consisted of a twenty-four-note keyboard, four rotary knobs, and a three-dimensional joystick, the voltage outputs from the knobs and joystick being multiplexed to a single analog-to-digital converter for registration by the computer. The keyboard was connected directly to a twenty-four-bit binary register, each key controlling the state of a uniquely assigned bit.

The output of control data to the studio interfaces was regulated via a variable-rate clock pulse generator. Because the computer acts as a control device in a hybrid system and not as a direct source of audio signals, adjustments to the clock rate vary the rate of change of events, not the nature of the events themselves. The performance of a composition could be halted at any point by depressing a special key, allowing the control functions to be studied in detail via the graphical display, alterations made, and the instruction sequence run forward or backward for a short distance to assess the effects of such changes.

The analog section of the system was notable for its modular construction. In addition to a basic configuration of twelve voltage-controlled oscillators, seven voltage-controlled amplifiers, and two voltage-controlled filters, a variety of signal-processing functions could be selected from an array of seventy-two different circuits mounted on plug-in cards. Fifty fine-resolution potentiometers were provided for the manual specification of basic control values associated with these circuits. Interconnections for the entire audio system were routed via a five-hundred-element central patch field.

Clearly, in a hybrid system, where the synthesis of sound is entirely dependent on hardware analog devices, little scope exists for developing input methods that are not specifically tied to the functional characteristics of the devices themselves. In truth similar restrictions apply to most freestanding synthesizers, including the all-digital designs that dominate the commercial sector today. Back in 1970, however, the ability to interact directly with the processes of sound generation in this manner, calling on the enhanced control capabilities of a digital computer, created a new and highly attractive environment for developing and evaluating compositional ideas.

The degree of interaction permitted by such systems varied considerably from one design to another. In GROOVE, Mathews clearly intended the composer to work with traditional programming techniques in the first instance, leaving interactive modifications to be applied during performance. As the following extract from his paper delivered at Stockholm demonstrates, he viewed his system as an instrument which, once configured, could be freely influenced in its performance in the manner described above:

> The composer does not personally play every note in a score, instead he influences (hopefully controls) the way in which the instrumentalists play the notes. The computer performer should not attempt to define the entire sound in real time. Instead the computer should contain a score and the performer should influence the way in which the score is played. . . .The mode of conducting consists of turning knobs and pressing keys rather than waving a stick, but this is a minor mechanical detail. . . .The program is basically a system for creating, storing, retrieving and editing functions of time. It allows the composition of time functions by turning knobs and pressing keys in real time; it stores time functions on the disk file; it retrieves the stored functions (the score), combines them with input functions (the conductor functions) in order to generate the control functions which drive the analog synthesizer and it provides for facile editing of time functions via control of "programme" time.[19]

GROOVE remained operational for almost a decade, its fate being sealed by the withdrawal of the Honeywell computer in 1978. Although use of the system was strongly directed toward research applications a small group of composers was granted regular access, notably Joseph Olive, Emmanual Ghent, and in due course Laurie Spiegel. Perhaps the best-known piece to be realized via GROOVE is Ghent's *Phosphones* (1971). This is essentially two pieces, a tape work that may be performed alone, and a light composition, stored as control instructions for a dimmer unit on perforated paper tape. In a full performance, these two parts are synchronized with each other, and with the movements of dancers, originally choreographed by Mimi Garrard. Ghent went on to compose other multimedia works for Garrard, developing further the notion of automated computer control of both sound and lighting, for example, *Dualities* (1972). Indeed, his increasing preoccupation with automation led him to explore the possibilities of computation as an integral part of the composing process itself, thus echoing the work already discussed in the context of other algorithmic composers such as Xenakis.

While Mathews was developing GROOVE at Bell Telephone Laboratories, another major hybrid system, MUSYS III, was under construction in London under the direction of Peter Zinovieff. For its time this system was perhaps the most attractive computer facility available anywhere, certainly one of the cheapest in terms of capital costs. The venture was all the more remarkable for being a private one, well established before any useful contributions could be made from the profits of his commercial company, EMS (London).

Zinovieff started the construction of his studio in 1962, basing it initially on traditional, analog, and entirely manually controlled sound-generation and signal processing devices. By the time this system had become operational in 1963, he was already carrying out preliminary investigations into the possibilities of voltage control, slightly ahead of Moog, Ketoff, and Buchla, and over the next few years the studio gradually expanded to accommodate new devices based on this design principle. This in turn generated the need for a more sophisticated control system, answered in the first instance by the construction of an elaborate sequencer during the period 1966–8. The project, however, was to prove a major disappointment, for the resultant device incorporated over seven hundred different controls, presenting the composer with formidable practical difficulties.[20]

It was a suggestion by an associate, Mark Dowson, that the computer might provide a more viable method of sequential control that led to the purchase of first one, and then a second PDP 8 minicomputer, and the commencement of work on a hybrid synthesis system.[21] By the end of 1969, most of the hardware interfaces had been designed and assembled by David Cockerell and Zinovieff, and within a few months MUSYS III was operational, using software written by Peter Grogono.

The decision to use two small computers instead of one larger machine is of some interest, as it allowed the control program to be divided into two sections. One section was concerned with the translation of higher-level arithmetic and logic instructions into time-ordered sequences of device commands, the other with the orderly transference of these commands to the associated interfaces. A small hard disk unit provided an intermediate data storage facility, accessible by both computers.

The analog system consisted of three types of devices, classified as follows: (1) devices equipped with integral digital-to-analog converters; (2) voltage-controlled devices that could be connected to the computing system via a set of general-purpose converters; and (3) devices restricted to manual operation only. In the first category the primary sound source consisted of a bank of 252 oscillators, divided into three groups of 84. Each group provided a seven-octave range of tempered pitches with the choice of sine or square waveforms, or a combination of both. Such a large bank of analog oscillators, however, posed significant problems in terms of frequency drift with respect to time. These were largely overcome by a special tuning program that automatically checked and adjusted the oscillator outputs relative to a reference crystal-clock frequency whenever called upon to do so. The remaining digitally controlled sound sources consisted of four sine/square oscillators offering both audio and control-wave modes of operation, a fifth high-resolution sine/square/triangle oscillator, and two noise sources.

Powerful filtering facilities were provided in the form of a bank of sixty-four band-pass filters tuned a semitone apart, where both the Q factor and the through gain of each unit could be directly controlled via the computer. This facility could function in a number of modes. As a general resource for shaping timbres it could be used to process audio signals either generated within the system or input from an external source. In addition, the bank could be transformed into an audio source in its own right by selecting the sharpest Q settings and applying "pink" noise to the inputs.[22] Under these conditions the filters resonated to produce almost pure sine tones at their center frequencies. Less acute Q settings led instead to the generation of narrow noise bands.

The filter bank also could be used as a signal analyzer by monitoring the high Q responses of each unit to applied signals and storing the information digitally on disk. The line spectra thus extracted could then be studied either as a numerical printout or as a graphic display, using the oscilloscope. Reversing this process permitted the use of vocoder techniques or, with skillful data processing, a restricted form of cross-synthesis between sources. Additional filtering facilities were supplied in the form of a secondary bank of twelve tunable filters and two further band-pass/band-reject units, all digitally controlled.

Amplitude-shaping facilities consisted of three basic attack/decay modulators and a master envelope shaper. The latter device consisted of a special integrator, used to regulate the gain of an associated amplifier. Because the computer directly controlled the rate of integration in both the attack (positive) and the decay (negative) phases, a variety of envelope characteristics could be generated. Three other digitally controlled integrators, each generating a voltage function and a network of four digital-to-analog converters provided a means of linking the computers at a control level with devices associated with the second category. These consisted initially of a small voltage-controlled synthesizer and four separate voltage-controlled oscillators. The synthesizer, known as the VCS 4, provided six voltage-controlled oscillators, two envelope shapers, two ring modulators two variable Q tunable filters, two spring reverberation units, four output amplifiers, and a pair of four-octave keyboards.[23] In due course the VCS 4 was replaced by the much larger Synthi 100 synthesizer, the flagship commercial product of EMS (London).

The third category of devices, not controllable by the computer, provided a broad range of auxiliary analog processing facilities, including ring modulators, filters, limiters, reverberation units, amplifiers, and auxiliary colored noise sources. In addition, both two- and four-track recording facilities were provided. From the composer's point of view such a range of device characteristics afforded considerable flexibility. At one end of the scale, the computer could be used to control every aspect of a synthesis task, using a comprehensive program of operational instructions entered via a teletypewriter. At the other, an entirely "classical" approach was possible, operating all the devices manually.

In designing MUSYS, particular attention was paid to the practical problems encountered in interacting with the computers themselves. In hybrid synthesis, it will be recalled, the primary task of the control system is to transfer information to and from the device interface registers at clock-controlled intervals. At the very lowest and most detailed level of specification, the composer has to supply the computer with a complete set of register values for each clock pulse. In MUSYS, such information could be entered using either a conventional teletypewriter or a specially constructed console. The latter provided quick access to each of the device registers via a panel of pushbuttons, the contents of the selected register being displayed as a binary pattern of lights. New values could then be entered directly into the register by depressing buttons individually to change their associated light states, the effects on the associated device function being immediately perceived both visually and aurally.

Sequences of register values could be transmitted for storage or retrieval via a spin-wheel that increased or decreased the timing pulse counter setting according to the direction of rotation, the counter acting directly on the internal array pointers. Although this technique facilitated a step-by-step assembly of entire control programs, its primary value was as an interactive aid to composition at higher levels of device specification, involving the use of macro-programming statements entered via the teletypewriter. The device data generated from these statements could then be performed under computer control, and modified where necessary by stopping the program and making adjustments in console mode. This flexibility of operation within a system that fully integrated all aspects of the synthesis process at the control level provides an interesting template for assessing the functional characteristics of modern, all-digital systems, the subject of subsequent chapters.

During 1970, a number of composers attended a short inaugural course on MUSYS. These included Don Banks, Edward Cowie, Anthony Gilbert, Jonathan Harvey, David Lumsdaine, and Keith Winter. The commercial nature of the studio and a lack of external funding, however, severely restricted access to others subsequently, and the system was dismantled in 1979. Nevertheless, a number of notable works were produced using these facilities, especially during the earlier part of the decade. In 1971, Harrison Birtwistle composed *Chronometer*, an extensive work based almost entirely on the manipulation of clock sounds. The sophistication of the MUSYS system permitted Birtwistle to employ subtle processes of timbre shaping and transformation, focusing attention on the inherent variety of characteristics that may be derived from such rich and aurally complex sources. These techniques were further extended in *Orpheus* (1976), one of the last major works to be completed at the studio.

Hans Werner Henze also used the studio on a number of occasions, completing one all-electronic work, *Glass Music* (1970), and tape parts for two orchestral works, *Violin Concerto No. 2* (1971) and *Tristan* (1973). In the *Concerto* the tape part is restricted to a recitation that undergoes a number of transformations in a manner reminiscent of the electronic works of Berio. In *Tristan,* a similar treatment of a reading of part of the Tristan story is combined with large blocks of electronic sound, the latter being used to heighten the tension of the orchestral climaxes.

A third major hybrid system was completed at the Elektronmusikstudion (EMS), Stockholm, in 1972. Work on a studio had been initiated as early as 1964 under the direction of Karl-Birger Blomdahl, the newly appointed head of music for Swedish Radio. His premature death in 1968 forced the corporation to reconsider its commitment, and after negotiations with the government the project continued in association with the Ministry of Education.

The original brief was most exacting and ambitious, demanding: (1) an instantaneous response from the composing system, (2) that the control system should be so simple that virtually no composer should encounter difficulties using it, and (3) that the quality of synthesis should meet the highest expectations. No expense was spared in designing devices to meet the last requirement. As a result, the stability and accuracy of the analog oscillator bank, for example, was second to none. The first requirement, too, was more than adequately met as a result of state-of-the-art engineering at a control level. The biggest challenge proved to be the second requirement, a Utopian vision that for all the power and sophistication of modern technology is just as elusive today as it was in the 1970s.

The range of facilities provided was extensive, comprising twenty-four oscillators with a choice of seven different waveforms, a noise generator offering both "pink" and "white" characteristics, two third-octave filter units of twenty-eight channels each, three ring modulators, two amplitude modulators, four reverberation units, two general-purpose amplifiers, and four output-channel amplifiers. In due course, a bank of digital oscillators was added to augment the analog oscillator bank, a significant first step toward the development of an all-digital hardware system. All the necessary interfaces for the application of digital control were built into the analog devices themselves. A very bold decision was taken at the outset to eliminate all traditional means of external control such as sliders and knobs, a special numerical dialing system being substituted for manual operation of the studio. Each device function was associated with a set of split metal contacts consisting of pairs of flat metal plates inlaid with a number, for example:

Figure 63

By means of a metal brush a numerical value could be selected and transmitted to the associated interface by shorting the contacts of suitable combinations of digits. The system provided visual verification of the selection by illuminating the values from underneath. Connections between devices were made via a similar system of shorting studs. It was possible, therefore, to play the studio in real time by manually selecting devices, settings, and interconnections, and then experimenting with static sound building blocks in a manner not unlike that facilitated by the button control panel provided for MUSYS. Dynamic composition, however, required the introduction of a programmable control system, and thus ultimately the services of a computer.

The studio first became operational in 1966 using an elementary digital control system that allowed step-by-step sequences of device settings to be assembled on magnetic tape. Such a system was little more than an electronic version of the punched tape system used by the RCA synthesizers and was cumbersome to use and prone to errors that were difficult to correct. The first steps toward the provision of computer control were taken in 1968 when landlines were installed to connect the studio to an external machine in the University of Stockholm.

This situation was far from ideal, for the operating facilities were as remote as those commonly endured by early users of MUSICn programs. A journey across the city was therefore necessary to punch out specifications in a very basic format on cards, for execution at the convenience of the computing center. The administrative changes that occurred during the same year, however, led to the injection of new funding and the placing of an order for a PDP 15 computer from the Digital Equipment Corporation. This was installed late in 1970, and the first software package, EMS 1, became available for use in the spring of 1972.

EMS 1 provided the composer with an exceedingly powerful specification language. Opinions were sharply divided, however, on its ease of use, illustrating a major problem in this regard, as some electronic composers naturally conceive their ideas in a mathematical formulation, whereas others work far more intuitively. EMS 1 placed the latter group of users at a severe disadvantage, because in its original version no provision was made for entering or modifying data directly via the studio console. Entire sections of a work had thus to be precoded in the form of a complete set of programming statements, any alterations requiring the use of a separate editing program and a complete recompilation of the instructions before the effects could be monitored aurally. Later versions of EMS were to provide greater flexibility in this respect.

Although EMS 1 was to remain the primary control language for the system during the 1970s, some interesting alternatives were developed with the specific aim of improving the functionality of the system. The primary architect and director of the EMS project, Knut Wiggen, quickly became aware of the limitations of the initial software. Accordingly, he encouraged the development of composing programs, including his own MUSIC BOX, which accepted musical ideas in the form of mathematical procedures or rules, and generated corresponding control data for the devices.

The requirements of more intuitive composers were addressed by Michael Hinton, who developed IMPAC, a control program that embodied random probability functions that could be manipulated in a "top-down" manner not unlike that explored by Barry Truax for his POD programs. Indeed, it was a visit by Truax to EMS in 1972 that provided a major stimulus for his own investigations in this context. Perhaps most crucially, programs such as IMPAC demanded effective user interfaces for real-time control. Thus it was that several auxiliary devices were introduced, for example, joysticks and a handheld tablet, which could be moved over a sensor pad in a manner similar to the movements of the modern computer mouse. The Hungarian composer Tamas Ungvary also played a major role in developing such resources, producing his own composing program COTEST in the mid-1970s.

The remoteness of Stockholm from the rest of Europe tended to limit the production of works to Scandinavian and East European composers. Occasional visits by leading composers from more western climes, however, provided the opportunity for a useful exchange of cultural ideas and for one brief period following the resignation of Knut Wiggen in 1976, the studio was directed by the American composer John Appleton. Aside from Tamas Ungvary the most significant Swedish composers to work at the studio at this time were Lars-Gunner Bodin, Sten Hanson, and Knut Wiggen.

Wiggen's works such as *Resa* (1970) and *Sommarmorgan* (1972) are notable for their rich and sensitively shaped textures, whereas Bodin concentrated on more traditional modes of writing in works such as *Toccata* (1969). Ungvary's *Axionell II* (1978) for flutes and computer-generated sounds is a mature example of the composer's use of the medium. It is based on two primary ideas; progression from the extreme polarities of electronic and instrumental music toward a homogeneous musical unity, and development of the flute's inner tension, which gives rise to a more lyrical and ornamental mode of expression.

By the middle of the 1970s, the development of computer music had thus expanded to embrace not only software synthesis and computer-assisted composition but also a variety of hybrid synthesis applications. The complexities of digital technology and the associated expense still concentrated activities in hands of the few, for the most part enjoying support from well-endowed institutions and organizations. Although this exclusivity was slowly beginning to erode, the longer-term development of the medium was still highly dependent on the activities of leading research institutions.

Two major centers established during the 1970s deserve special recognition in this context. The first of these, the Center for Computer Research in Music and Acoustics (CCRMA) was established in 1976 at Stanford by Chowning and Leland Smith, a development helped to no small extent by a growing commercial relationship between the university and the manufacturer Yamaha.[24] This connection, however, in no way inhibited the consequential rapid expansion of research activity, the results of which have been generously shared with the computer music community.

The second center, IRCAM (Institut de Recherche et Coordination Acoustique/ Musique), was established in Paris by Pierre Boulez in 1970. Unlike CCRMA, however, this was an entirely new enterprise requiring the construction of a purpose-built research center and performance area. The resources available for this project were without precedent at the time, rivaling the very best available in the USA. IRCAM also cooperated particularly closely with both Bell Labs and Stanford during the early 1970s, with the added benefit of Max Mathews as senior consultant.

One factor, perhaps above all others, ensured that the productivity of these centres was not only considerable but also to be of lasting significance. This was their ability to bring musicians and technologists together in ways that have encouraged the pooling of expertise and the thorough testing of new concepts, both in technical and artistic terms. With the commercial sector poised to enter the field the balance of opportunities at the end of the decade was set to change, in a manner not dissimilar to that associated with the introduction of the first commercial voltage-controlled synthesizers during the previous decade. The foundations of computer music had been securely established, but the development of the microprocessor was about to transform its destiny.

12

The Microprocessor Revolution

The foundations of computer music had been predicated on the development of applications to synthesize and process sound material, either directly by the computer itself or indirectly by programming the computer to control a network of analog devices. In terms of immediacy of response and scope for interactive working, only the latter approach could adequately fulfill such a brief, the main disadvantage being that analog equipment offered a finite repertory of functional characteristics that could only be modified by physically altering the configuration of the devices themselves. Direct synthesis methods, by contrast, offered the converse situation, in which flexibility in terms of software simulations was achieved at the expense of interaction. The more complex the processes specified the longer the likely delays before the results could be accessed and evaluated. The quest for a true middle course, drawing on the strengths of both approaches within the digital medium, still lacked the technology necessary to achieve it.

Back in the 1970s, there was no immediate prospect of a solution to this impasse. From today's perspective, where the raw computing power now at the disposal of personal computer users is many orders of magnitude greater than that provided by even the largest mainframe computers of this era, the significance of this situation is a little hard to grasp. Voltage control electronics had facilitated a burgeoning commercial synthesizer industry where the economics of competition and mass-production constrained the market price. Conditions were still very different in the computer industry, and the high-cost culture remained a serious impediment to those seeking to establish the creative credentials of the digital domain.

Three primary phases of development have already been identified in studying the evolution of the computer from birth to early maturity. It will be recalled that the early development of computers based on valve technology was followed by a second generation of smaller and faster machines during the late 1950s, based on transistor-based circuit boards. These in turn were replaced by a third generation of machines in the mid-1960s, based on integrated circuits. It was the technology developed for the latter devices that held the all-important key to more affordable computing architectures.

Second-generation computers still used many components developed directly from the world of analog engineering. Although the initial savings in space and cost brought about by the move from valves to transistors was clearly impressive, it was still necessary to wire together thousands of individual parts in order to create a fully operational system. The real breakthrough came with the discovery of the electrical properties of silicon, whereby first tens, then hundreds, and then thousands of logic gates could be fabricated as part of a single wafer of silicon, in some circumstances physically no larger than a square centimeter. These integrated devices were soon to revolutionize the design of computers, allowing the miniaturization of many circuits, from memory components to the interfaces that control the flow of instructions and data to and from the outside world.

The ultimate design goal was the central processing unit itself. Here the fabrication of suitable chips proved to be a much greater challenge. Unlike the ordered arrays of gates required for a conventional memory bank, a conventional CPU involves highly complex arrangements of logic circuits and cross-connections that cannot be easily reproduced within the physical constraints of a single two-dimensional wafer of silicon. For this reason, the CPUs of most third generation computers only achieved a partial integration of the component logic circuits, requiring a network of chips each concerned with a particular subset of the processor's architecture.

Despite these obstacles, by the end of the 1960s a number of manufacturers had turned their attention to the possibility of fabricating a complete computer, or at least its operational core, within a single silicon chip. In technical terms the key to such a challenging design revolution lay in the manufacture of moldings containing not one but several wafers of silicon, allowing electrical connections to be made between layers as part of a three-dimensional matrix, thus overcoming the problem of interlaced connections. This architecture became known as VLSI (Very Large Scale Integrated) technology.

The functional characteristics to be satisfied for such a device to qualify as a true microprocessor became a matter of heated debate between competing designers, but some measure of agreement was reached over the minimum criteria to be met in order to qualify for such a descriptor. Such a device had to be able to process both text and numbers in conventional digital code and directly address a memory bank of sufficient capacity to hold both a program and its associated data. In addition, it had to provide an instruction set sufficient in scope and versatility to execute the standard logical and arithmetic operations associated with a conventional computer, and also be capable of communicating with a variety of input and output devices.

A true microprocessor, thus, has to offer all the basic functions of a traditional CPU, linked to a conventional memory bank and standard peripherals such as a disk drive, an alphanumeric keyboard, and a visual display unit or printer. In practice, many microprocessors have been used for dedicated applications of a far more restricted nature, for example, the control of a specific manufacturing process or such routine aspects of everyday life as the management of traffic signals, car engines, or washing machines. In such situations, the software to control the microprocessor is highly specific, and is often coded permanently by means of special read-only memory chips, or ROM. Over the years, a number of distinctive applications have justified the fabrication of special processors, known generically as ASICs.[1] One such family of devices, classed as signal processors, has proved particularly significant for computer music applications, and their special characteristics will be studied further in due course.

Intel manufactured the first true microprocessor, identified as the 4004, in 1971. By today's standards, this device was extremely slow and hard to program, difficulties in the latter context being compounded by the fact that only four bits of data or programming code could be handled at a time. The 4004 microprocessor was followed in 1972 by the 8008, which was able to address eight-bit data blocks or bytes directly. This embryonic technology received a major boost in 1974 when Intel released the 8080. This processor was not only much faster than its predecessors but also supported by a much more versatile instruction set. By the end of 1975 many leading digital component manufacturers had added eight-bit microprocessors to their product ranges. Motorola, for example, introduced the 6800 processor, Zilog introduced the Z-80, an improved derivative of the 8080, and MOS Technology introduced the 6501, forerunner of a highly successful derivative, the 6502.

Some firms, such as Texas Instruments, concentrated on producing their own versions of popular processors such as the 8080. As a result, a market that was already becoming competitive now became fiercely so, driving prices steadily downward. Intersil set an interesting precedent by producing a low-cost microprocessor that emulated the central processing unit used at the heart of Digital Equipment Corporation's first general-purpose minicomputer, the eight-bit PDP 8, thus starting a new and ultimately successful line of attack on the traditional high-cost sectors of the computer market.

The expanding market for microprocessors encouraged entrepreneurs to start manufacturing do-it-yourself microcomputer kits, consisting of a single printed circuit board containing a microprocessor, a small memory bank, and a simple interface. The increasing availability of such products quickly established a new pastime as a home computer hobbyist, and a growing public awareness of the potential of computer technology within the domestic environment. Software was almost nonexistent at this stage, and as a result prospective users were generally left with little more than a brief description of the basic instruction set, information on how to connect a suitable power supply, and their ingenuity. The formation of self-help groups and the establishment of the first magazines for home computer users, however, soon began to address the growing need for technical support and advice.

Despite the relatively primitive nature of these early single-board microcomputers, a number of enthusiasts began to explore applications of a musical nature, in particular the construction of elementary control systems for analog synthesizers, communicating data values via a simple low resolution digital-to-analog converter. One product that appeared in 1976, the 6502-based KIM-1 board manufactured by Commodore, attracted particular attention in this context, not least for being significantly cheaper but essentially no less functional than many of its rivals. Notwithstanding the programming challenges faced in such a task, entering each machine code instruction via an elementary keypad and LED display, the rewards in terms of the measure of control that could be exercised over voltage functions were extensive.

Early pioneers of this new art of microprocessor-controlled music included David Behrman, co-director of the Center for Contemporary Music at Mills College 1975–80. In addition to a continuing involvement with the Sonic Arts Union, he toured as a composer and performer with the Merce Cunningham Dance Company during the period 1970–6, and in so doing became aware of the considerable practical problems encountered in controlling real-time performances of electronic music. His first work involving the KIM-1, *Figure in a Clearing* (1977), used the microprocessor to control the time intervals between chord changes. His second work, *On the Other Ocean* (1978), was based on control functions derived from a set of six pitches. Whenever the improvisations of the two synthesizer performers selected these pitches, special trigger circuits sent a message to the KIM-1. The program would then respond to each event signal by transmitting altered pitch information to the synthesizers, in so doing creating an interactive feedback loop.

Other composer/performers who worked with the KIM-1 at Mills College include George Lewis, and Jim Horton, a founder member of the League of Automatic Music Composers (1978–82), an organization that devoted itself to the advancement of microprocessor-generated music. The membership of the League was to include John Bischoff, Tim Perkis, and Rich Gold, as well as Behrman himself, and in the true spirit of their adopted role models in the field of experimental music such as John Cage their performances courted considerable publicity. Less evident, but cumulatively no less significant, were the experimental activities of many other individuals, both amateur and professional, who acquired cheap microprocessor boards such as the KIM-1 and discovered for themselves the musical possibilities of this new technology.

Stimulated by the success of these experimental microprocessor boards, manufacturers soon turned their attention to the design of fully integrated microcomputer systems. These provided a basic operating system, a range of software tools including a BASIC language compiler,[2] and a communications interface consisting of a standard alphanumeric keyboard and a VDU. In 1977 three of these systems were released in quick succession, the Commodore PET, based on a 6502 processor, the Radio Shack TRS-80, based on a Z-80 microprocessor, and the Apple II based on a 6502. By the end of the decade several other manufacturers were entering the microcomputer market with rival products. The early 6502-based 400 and 800 series of machines from Atari emulated a number of functional characteristics associated with the Apple computer, and the release of these models marked the start of a fierce competition between the two manufacturers.

Eight-bit microprocessors dominated the microcomputer industry until the early 1980s, when a new generation of much more powerful, sixteen-bit microprocessors was launched. The first mass-produced sixteen-bit microprocessor was the LSI 11/03, which appeared in 1978, manufactured by Western Digital. This product, as in the case of the eight-bit Intersil chip described earlier, emulated the central processing unit of a standard DEC minicomputer, in this case the highly successful sixteen-bit PDP 11. In due course this microprocessor and even more versatile derivatives such as the LSI 11/23 completely displaced the older CPU architecture, cheaper LSI-based machines eventually replacing the entire range. In 1978 Intel introduced the 8086, a sixteen-bit version of its 8080, and within a matter of months Zilog followed suit with a sixteen-bit Z-8000, matched by Motorola in 1979 with a sixteen-bit 68000.

By 1980 microcomputers were being manufactured in relatively modest but steadily increasing quantities for a market still dominated by educational and research institutions, but with a new and burgeoning domestic sector. Industry and commerce had yet to be tempted away from systems supplied by more traditional computer manufacturers, who were naturally keen to preserve the considerable profit margins associated with large multiuser mainframe installations. This segmentation of activities was upset dramatically in 1981 when the computing giant IBM entered the microcomputer market with the launch of the IBM PC, based on a sixteen-bit 8088 microprocessor, a specially modified version of the 8086. Despite a number of practical shortcomings, especially when compared with the functional characteristics of the alternative architectures, IBM steadily secured a growing share of the market.

The association with IBM itself finally provided the necessary pedigree for attracting potential purchasers from all quarters, including those associated with core wealth-producing activities worldwide. A subtle but important change of perspective helped establish the status of the new technology, the more experimental and potentially inferior connotations associated with the term "microcomputer" and the activities of the home hobbyist being gradually replaced by the more assured and individually empowering term, "personal computer."

These developments were to have a significant impact on the computer industry, and key characteristics will be studied closely in due course. Many smaller companies either ceased production or turned instead to the manufacture of cheap clones of the IBM PC itself, a development that IBM chose largely to ignore, confident, as it found out to its cost, in the lasting appeal of its own machines. The company's loss of control over the destiny of its personal computer was boosted further by a decision to entrust the development of system software to Microsoft, the consequences of which are known to all.

Notable exceptions to this trend were companies such as Apple, Atari, and Commodore, who managed to secure and retain a significant customer base by developing new and highly competitive product ranges. One sphere of activity that showed particular resilience to the growing influence of the IBM PC was the games and general entertainment sector. Here budget-priced machines such as the Sinclair Spectrum (based on a Z-80) and the Commodore 64 and 128 (both based on the 6502) maintained their position as market leaders for a number of years. IBM attempted to penetrate this lucrative market with a version of the PC known as the PC Junior, but this product was not a commercial success and was soon withdrawn.

A unique collaboration between the British Broadcasting Corporation (BBC) and the microcomputer manufacturer Acorn resulted in the BBC Micro, a product based on the 6502 microprocessor that dominated the U.K. educational market during the early 1980s. In Japan, the desire to serve national rather than international interests in the first instance extended to the world of business and commercial computing, firms such as NEC limiting the penetration of foreign manufacturers such as Apple and IBM for many years.

The design revolution signaled by the fabrication of circuits in silicon was to affect the development of computer music systems in an even more fundamental way, as it facilitated the construction of custom-built devices devoted exclusively to audio applications. The efficiency gains achieved by using optimized hardware were of sufficient magnitude for the execution of a number of real-time synthesis and signal processing functions in real time, facilitating the development of hardware digital synthesizers. One of the first systems to use this architecture, VOCOM, was produced by David Cockerell and Peter Eastty for Peter Zinovieff at his private London studio in 1972.[3] This consisted of an array of hardware digital oscillators and filters, controlled by the same pair of PDP 8 minicomputers used for the hybrid system, MUSYS.[4] In the same year, EMS, at Stockholm, completed the installation of its custom-designed all-digital oscillator bank, controlled via the studio's main computer, a PDP 15.

In thus moving from a hybrid environment, where computers are used to control analog synthesis and signal processing devices, to one involving the use of purpose-designed digital hardware, a new design principle was established. Known generically as mixed digital engineering, this approach was to prove highly influential in shaping the development of real-time computer music resources during the latter part of the twentieth century. Crucially, it provided a viable basis for establishing a commercial synthesizer industry based on digital rather than analog technology.

It was with this prospect in mind that John Appleton, Sydney Alonso, and Cameron Jones entered into a collaborative partnership at Dartmouth College, New Hampshire. Within the space of two years, a working prototype had been completed for an all-digital synthesizer, based entirely on a network of integrated circuits linked to an integral microprocessor. In 1976 they established the New England Digital Corporation and started to manufacture production versions of their system, marketed as the Synclavier.

The main synthesis engine of the Synclavier consists of a bank of timbre generators, each providing a choice of twenty-four sinusoidal harmonics for each voice. The total number of voices provided varies from a basic bank of eight generators to upward of thirty-two, according to the options purchased or subsequently added. The user can configure these generators directly using a pushbutton console, and thus requires no detailed knowledge of the programming code used internally by the synthesizer. Although the designers originally intended the Synclavier to be primarily a performance instrument, interest in the use of proprietary software for voice editing and programmed control led quickly to the addition of a VDU and an alphanumeric keyboard. Disk storage facilities for programs and data were initially restricted to a single floppy disk unit, but these were subsequently expanded to include a hard disk drive.

The control system is based around a specially designed sixteen-bit microprocessor known as ABLE and an associated memory bank, the latter being used primarily as a multichannel sequencer for the storage of performance data. The primary input device for registering and performing sound events consists of a five-octave keyboard, which may be split functionally into two sections, each controlling a separate voice or group of voices. Envelope characteristics for each key selection are entered via pushbuttons with a facility to program both the overall envelope and also the envelope of individual harmonics for each note. Fine tunings of pitches, time constants, and amplitudes are specified via a continuously adjustable knob, coupled to group of function buttons and a digital display, which gives a numerical reading of the current settings.

One or a pair of foot-pedals may be connected as auxiliary performance aids, one controlling volume, the other any other selected variable, for example, the overall duration of note envelopes. A touch-ribbon permitting continuous pitch variations is also available as an alternative to the music keyboard, copying a principle first explored in the Ondes Martenot.[5] As an alternative to additive synthesis the Synclavier offers frequency modulation facilities for each voice. A very distinctive FM timbre characteristic is generated by a special option that allows up to four voices to track pitch changes synchronously. Later versions of the Synclavier provide enhanced graphics facilities for the display and manipulation of synthesis data such as wave-shape and envelope characteristics, and a signal processing facility for externally generated sound material, input using analog-to-digital converters.

Although key segments of the original control software were hidden from general view, New England Digital made it possible for the composer Joel Chadabe to develop a special interactive performance program known as PLAY in 1978, in association with Roger Meyers. This permits a performer to superimpose continuous variations on a preprogrammed sequence of events, fed to the synthesizer as control information from a specially prepared disk file. For his own Synclavier-based compositions such as *Solo* and *Playthings* (1978), Chadabe added two capacitor-based field detectors as motion-sensing aids. These were modern equivalents of Thérémin sensors, custom-built by Robert Moog, the distance of his hands from the detectors providing control signals for regulating the course of the performance program.[6]

Appleton himself wrote a number of works for Synclavier, including *Prelude* (1978), *Untitled* (1979), and *Brush Canyon* (1986), in each case seeking to extend the musical possibilities of keyboard-controlled performance programs. The release of an upgraded version in 1980, the Synclavier II, stimulated further sales, the sounds of this instrument soon becoming familiar through their widespread use in advertising jingles and film soundtracks. The continuing high cost of this system, however, was eventually to seal the fate of this synthesizer in the face of increasing competition from newer and cheaper alternatives. Notwithstanding a diversification into other digital audio products, including an equally pioneering direct-to-disk multitrack recording system known as PostPro (1986), the parent company, NED, ran into financial difficulties and ceased trading in 1992. Rescue came in the first instance from a number of influential owners who formed a consortium to purchase the assets of the company, and also the entrepreneur Brian George who established a new company DEMAS to provide technical and hardware support. In 1995 all the assets and rights finally passed to DEMAS, and the Synclavier was given a new lease of life with an ongoing program of software development, initiated by Cameron Jones.

Notwithstanding its exceptional cost and exclusivity in marketing terms, the Synclavier was soon to have a major rival. In 1975, two Australians, Peter Vogel and Kim Ryrie, established a company called Fairlight in Rushcutters Bay, New South Wales. Having previously experimented with analog equipment, their initial proposal to manufacture digital audio effects units for film studios quickly evolved to the design of a complete, all-digital synthesizer, to be known as the Fairlight Computer Music Instrument, otherwise known as the Fairlight or the CMI.

Their original objective was to design a real-time synthesis engine that would generate sounds entirely from first principles, thereby emulating very closely the principles employed in the Synclavier. Faced with the complexities involved in meeting such a challenge, not least in creating sounds that were both realistic and easily controllable, the two pioneers turned their attention initially to the notion of acoustic modeling. The proposition here is that the physical principles involved in activating a conventional musical instrument such as the violin or trumpet may be directly simulated as a series of computational functions. With assistance from Tony Furze, a computer consultant, a prototype eight-voice synthesizer, known as the Qasar M8, was accordingly completed in 1976.

Unfortunately, the technology at their disposal could not adequately satisfy the real-time requirements of such a complex synthesis method with any satisfactory degree of refinement. As a result, the sounds produced were crude and inflexible, and with considerable reluctance this line of investigation was abandoned. Had these pioneers been better placed to succeed, their work would have led directly to an interesting method of sound synthesis that was to gain considerable importance during the 1980s and 1990s.[7]

It was thus more as a matter of last resort than original intention that they turned to the technology of sampling, in which sound is resynthesized from naturally generated waveform sources, captured in the first instance via an analog-to-digital converter. Manipulating natural sound material in a manner similar to that employed in the tape loops of the Mellotron offers a number of practical advantages, not least the fact that the sound sources, if carefully chosen, are intrinsically interesting in ways that cannot easily be synthesized from first principles.[8] There are, however, a number of technical hurdles to be surmounted before the true potential of this particular technique can be realized, and the designers of the Fairlight had to accept some major operational constraints in the earlier versions of their product.

Unlike the Synclavier, which made extensive use of custom-designed hardware, the control section of the Fairlight was based on standard microprocessor architectures, starting with the eight-bit Motorola 6800 that powered both Fairlight Series I, released in 1979, and also the Fairlight Series II, released in 1982. Although the quality of resynthesis, especially in the case of the Series I, was barely adequate as a result of using relatively low sampling rates and a resolution of only eight-bits, the novelty of sampled sounds caught the public imagination. The notion of a computerized orchestra led a number of leading pop and rock musicians, such as John Paul Jones, Kate Bush, Peter Gabriel, the Pet Shop Boys, and Stevie Wonder, to use Fairlight sounds extensively in their works. For a time these high-profile activities stimulated a campaign by trade unions to have the technology banned, on the grounds that it potentially threatened the livelihoods of their performing members.

Externally, the Fairlight I and II are very similar in appearance. The user is provided with one or optionally a pair of six-octave keyboards, an interactive graphics unit using a light pen system, and an alphanumeric keyboard, with the further possibility of adding up to three foot-pedals as auxiliary performance aids. Source sounds may either be sampled direct by attaching a microphone to the analog-to-digital converter port, or loaded from factory or user-generated libraries stored externally on floppy disks. Voicing specifications, such as the control of dynamics or timbre, may either be entered in a mnemonic code using the alphanumeric keyboard, or edited interactively in a graphical form using the light pen. In hardware terms polyphonic synthesis is achieved via a bank of eight individual audio cards, the operation of the entire system being controlled via a pair of eight-bit 6800 microprocessors.

Although the primary method of sound production is based on sampling technology, the Fairlight also provides some limited facilities for direct waveform synthesis via the light pen. These involve either directly drawn wave functions that may be shaped dynamically and combined with other sounds to generate more complex timbres, or the mapping of up to thirty-two frequency components as functions of individual amplitudes with respect to time.

Technical shortcomings such as the variable quality of sound reproduction and practical limitations on the number and length of individual samples that may be in use simultaneously were finally addressed with the Fairlight Series III, introduced in 1985. Although functionally very similar to its predecessors, this third and last version was substantially redesigned internally to take full advantage of its new computing engine, the sixteen-bit Motorola 68000 microprocessor.

Although the historical significance of the Fairlight lies primarily in the pioneering of sampling technology, its standing in this context is further strengthened by the development of another feature, included as a optional tool from the Series II models onwards. Known as the Real Time Composer interface or RTC, this provides the user with a sophisticated pattern-based event sequencer, anticipating resources that were subsequently to become an integral part of MIDI sequencing software programs. Basic facilities for registering and storing basic sequences of individual note/events were provided as a matter of course as part of the system software, but the RTC interface introduced an important new layer of performance control.

In RTC mode the timings of note/events are displayed as rhythmic patterns that may be directly interrogated and edited using the light pen or tablet. Although the duration of each note is indicated using standard music notation symbols, the neumes are spaced in a straight line across the screen, voice by voice according to the actual time interval that elapses between each successive note/event, this use of proportional spacing eliminating the need for rests. The actual duration, and ancillary information such as the pitch and volume of each note/event may then be accessed and modified by clicking on each note in turn to display the values of these parameters.

Like the Synclavier, the Fairlight was to suffer a similar downturn of fortunes as a proliferation of more competitively priced alternatives during the 1980s diminished the attraction of such an expensive system. By 1987 sales were rapidly declining and production finally ceased in 1988. Rescue came in 1989 from Amber Technology, which revived the fortunes of Fairlight with a new range of products, including a hard disk digital recording system, known as MFX. It was in the latter context that aspects of the Fairlight synthesizer architecture found a new lease of life in the form of signal processing tools for postproduction work in the recording and film industries. These commenced with the MFX2, released in 1991, and were developed further with the MFX3, released in 1994.[9]

As landmark developments, albeit focused exclusively at the high end of the market, these two pioneering systems clearly established the credentials of digital synthesis and signal processing systems as successors to their analog counterparts. In so doing they also established some very important operational criteria that have influenced the development of commercial computer music systems to the present day. Primary among these are the practical consequences of insulating the user from many of the internal processor functions by a hidden layer of proprietary software, which cannot easily be penetrated.

In the case of analog systems, the very nature of the technology ensures that with very few exceptions all internal functions are transparent and accessible. As a consequence, the component signal and control functions can be readily intercepted and monitored. Even at the level of servicing and repair, device faults can usually be identified and rectified using little more than a test probe and meter, and a collection of standard electronic spares such as transistors, capacitors, and resistors. In the digital domain an entirely new level of complexity is encountered. Complex logic analyzers are required to identify hardware faults in devices such as microprocessors, and compiled software programs can only be disassembled into source code with extreme difficulty and not always successfully. The use of proprietary hardware with embedded software components in ROM (sometimes referred to as firmware) effectively guarantees that selected design features can remain permanently hidden from the user.

From a manufacturer's point of view the use of such techniques to protect its commercial interests is both legitimate and essential. Nevertheless, these restrictions have proved a major source of frustration for those users who seek a degree of programming flexibility similar to that afforded by mature, open-architecture software synthesis systems such as CSOUND, where accessibility extends to the source code itself. As a result, many users have been able to use their programming skills to develop and embed new synthesis and signal processing functions of their own, and in so doing extended the range and scope of the available facilities for the broader community.

The markets specifically targeted by the Fairlight and the Synclavier encouraged other manufacturers to seek their fortunes with rival mixed digital systems, notably the Con Brio ADS 200, the Crumar General Development System (GDS) and the Synergy from the United States, and the PPG Wave 2.2 from Germany. PPG (Palm Productions GmbH) was founded in Hamburg in 1975 by Wolfgang Palm, partially in response to an association with members of Tangerine Dream, who at the time were actively seeking new resources for the production of electronic material. Having built an analog voltage-controlled synthesizer, the Model 300, Palm turned his attention to the digital domain, producing a prototype digital wave-table synthesizer in 1980, known as the Wave Computer 360.

Although this synthesizer used digital wave-table oscillators, it had no filters or other signal processing resources. Palm had intended to include digital filters, but the technology of the time was still not sufficiently advanced to allow him to fabricate such a facility without adding significantly to the manufacturing costs. Accordingly, in designing the PPG Wave 2.2, which followed in 1982, he adopted a mixed design approach, combining digital oscillators with an array of analog filters. The data for the oscillator wave-tables is selected from a library of almost two thousand waveforms stored in ROM. Once loaded, these waveforms can be manipulated using a bank of control knobs that allow the specification of envelopes and frequency and filtering modifications in a manner that closely approximates to the procedures used to operate the ADSR functions of a conventional voltage-controlled synthesizer.[10] Direct control of the digital functions such as voice selection and loading of data into memory is accomplished via a simple keypad, and a five-octave music keyboard serves as the performing interface.

In due course, the PPG Wave 2.2 was replaced by the Wave 2.3 and augmented by the PPG Waveterm (versions A and B). These were much improved modules that allow the direct sampling of externally generated sounds via an analog-to-digital converter as an alternative to sounds extracted from the factory-supplied wave-table bank. The computer interface is also upgraded with a graphics screen, which may be used to display sound parameters. Like the Fairlight and the Synclavier, the PPG attracted an enthusiastic and influential group of users from the rock and pop industries, including Chris Franke and Edgar Froese from Tangerine Dream, Trevor Horn of Frankie Goes to Hollywood, Jean Michel Jarre, and Stevie Wonder. It also achieved some success in penetrating the upper end of the educational market, especially in Europe, before also becoming a casualty of the MIDI revolution. Production of the PPG finally ceased in 1987.

Back in the United States, Con Brio entered the synthesizer market in 1978 with an upmarket hybrid product, known as the ADS 100. Although few production models were sold, the distinctive repertory of sounds became well known to the general public as a result of extensive use in creating the background sound material for the 1979 cult science fiction film *Star Trek: The Motion Picture*. Recognizing the need to penetrate the markets dominated by Fairlight and Synclavier, Con Brio replaced the ADS 100 with an all-digital synthesizer, the ADS 200, in 1980.

In technical terms, the ADS 200 synthesizer was possibly the most advanced mixed digital design to achieve commercial production during the early 1980s. The user interface includes of a pair of five octave keyboards, a video display monitor, and a panel of pushbuttons and rotary knobs for the entry of timbre and dynamic specifications. The synthesis facilities consist of a bank of sixty-four digital multiwaveform oscillators (expandable to 256 oscillators), each individually controllable in terms of frequency and amplitude via sixteen-segment function generators. In addition to additive synthesis, the ADS 200 may be programmed to apply both frequency and phase modulation techniques, supported by a four-track sequencing facility. The complexity of the system required an internal network of five microprocessors to control its various functions, supported by a floppy disk drive for loading and storing software and sequencing data.

A modified version, the ADS 200-R, was released in 1982. The primary differences were the provision of just a single music keyboard, but supported by an improved, sixteen-track polyphonic sequencer. Market forces, however, were already conspiring against the future prosperity of Con Brio. The company had entered the market too late to capitalize on the limited customer base for high-cost products already secured by Fairlight and Synclavier, and it ceased trading in 1983.

The Crumar General Development System (GDS) and the Synergy started out as research projects working from a prototype design for a bank of digital oscillators first suggested by Hal Alles of Bell Telephone Laboratories in 1979. Mario Crucianelli founded this Italian synthesizer company in 1977, in the first instance to manufacture electric pianos and analog synthesizers. In 1978, recognizing the potential of digital technology, Crucianelli formed a research and development partnership with Digital Keyboards Inc., a new but fast-growing company in New York, to develop state-of-the-art digital synthesizers with assistance from leading institutional researchers, notably S. Jerrold Kaplan at Stanford University.

The GDS was originally intended as an intermediate test bed for the Synergy, but such was the interest shown in its functional characteristics that it was manufactured as a product in its own right in 1980, some time before the production design for the Synergy had been completed. The basic architecture consists of a Z-80 microprocessor controlling a bank of thirty-two digital oscillators, of which up to sixteen at a time can be combined into a single voice. Each oscillator may be independently controlled in terms of frequency, amplitude, and basic waveform, thus creating a powerful and versatile resource for generating different timbres.

The commercial version is equipped with a single velocity-sensing five-octave keyboard, a video display monitor, an alphanumeric keyboard, and a bank of sixty-five rotary knobs, sliders, and joysticks for the control of individual synthesis parameters. A pair of floppy disk drive units provides facilities for loading and storing both system software and user data. The GDS differed from many of its commercial competitors in providing direct access to the underlying control language via a FORTRAN compiler, thus making it possible to program all the synthesis functions directly in computer code. This freedom to migrate between the manually controlled interface and the mathematical environment of software-generated functions made the system especially suitable for compositional research and development in a studio environment.

The Synergy, which followed in 1981, differs from the GDS in a number of respects, reflecting the specific objective of its architects to produce a performance instrument. The design is much more compact with a rationalized control panel of knobs and pushbuttons, and no support from a VDU or alphanumeric keyboard. The music keyboard, however, is extended to six octaves. Particular care was taken to ensure that this simplified user interface can sustain a significant degree of operational versatility when the synthesizer is used live on stage, anticipating design principles that were subsequently to become a standard feature of the MIDI environment. The inclusion of a pair of sensitivity controls, one for amplitude and one for timbre, is one notable example of this philosophy, allowing these voicing characteristics to be continuously varied during a performance.

In addition to twenty-four factory-generated timbres stored internally in ROM, a cartridge slot is also provided, allowing additional voice configurations to be loaded and directly accessed. As well as being fully polyphonic, the Synergy also generates a stereo output, allowing the component timbres to be distributed between the two channels to create an enriched spatial landscape. Facilities are also provided for active panning of these timbres between the outputs, along with other useful features such as the control of portamento, vibrato, and pitch transposition, fully anticipating many of the characteristics that have subsequently become standard features in modern digital synthesizers.

What really set this product apart from its immediate rivals was the highly competitive retail price, undercutting products such as the Fairlight and Synclavier by several orders of magnitude. Even so, initially healthy initial sales to educational institutions and leading artists with popular musical interests such as Wendy Carlos were soon to decline dramatically in the face of increasing competition from yet cheaper mass-produced alternatives associated with a new generation of MIDI synthesizer manufacturers.[11] Production of the synthesizer ceased in 1985, and Crumar stopped trading altogether in 1987.

With the possible exception of the GDS, which was never intended to be a commercial product, all of the mixed-digital systems just described are linked by two common attributes. These are: (1) strictly regulated access to key design features in order to ensure the protection of proprietary rights, and (2) a distinct emphasis on addressing the interests of high revenue-earning sectors of the music industry. The latter include rock and pop music, and film, television, and radio, not least the production of background material for advertising. The imperative to maintain substantial profit margins also ensured the exclusivity of these systems. The requirements of institutions specializing in electronic and computer music were thus often regarded as of only secondary importance in the face of pressures from the commercial music sector, which clearly had other priorities.

An alternative approach to system design and development was thus required, where greater priority could be given to the needs of composers and researchers at the forefront of developments in contemporary music. A number of universities were to make useful early contributions in this regard. One such initiative was fostered at the University of Illinois. In 1976, James Beauchamp, Ken Pohlmann, and Louis Chapman constructed a prototype digital synthesizer, controlled by a small TI 980 computer with just 8 K of memory. On the other side of the Atlantic, Kurt Andersen and Mike Manthey used a slightly larger TI 960A computer to develop a mixed digital system known as the EGG synthesizer at the University of Århus, Denmark, during the period 1975–7. In both cases, the object was to develop mixed-digital architectures that could support more flexible uses of tried and tested synthesis functions such as wave-table synthesis and filtering in real time.

Pioneering ventures such as these were to establish the foundations for a series of more substantial developments in this context. Three of the most significant systems to emerge from this quarter were eventually released commercially. The fourth, although destined not to proceed any further than the research laboratory, was to establish interface design criteria that were to prove highly influential for the future development of the computer music.

The first of the systems to be considered here, SYTER (Système Temps Réel/ Realtime System) was initiated by the Groupe de Recherches Musicales (GRM) in 1974. Having inherited the mantle of Pierre Schaeffer's pioneering work in *musique concrète,* this group became preoccupied with the development of new technical resources, and their interests in the creative possibilities of digital technology were given a considerable impetus with the purchase of a PDP 11/60 computer.

Recognizing that even such a powerful minicomputer lacked the necessary processing power to handle other than relatively simple real-time synthesis and signal processing applications internally, and aware of the potential limitations of hybrid approaches, attention turned instead to the development of a mixed-digital system. Jean-François Allouis and Denis Valette pioneered the hardware development of SYTER with a series of prototypes produced during the late 1970s, leading in due course to the construction of a complete preproduction version in 1984. Commercial manufacture of this digital synthesizer commenced in 1985, and by the end of the decade a number of these systems had been sold to academic institutions.

Benedict Mailliard developed the original software for SYTER. By the end of the decade, however, it was becoming clear that the processing power of personal computers was escalating at such a rate that many of the SYTER functions could now be run in real-time using a purely software-driven environment. As a result, a selection of these were modified by Hughes Vinet to create a suite of stand-alone signal processing programs. Finally, in 1993, the commercial version of this software, GRM Tools, was released for use with the Apple Macintosh.

The prototypes for SYTER accommodated both synthesis and signal processing facilities, and additive synthesis facilities were retained for the hardware production versions of the system. The aims and objectives of GRM, however, were geared very much toward the processing of naturally generated source material. As a consequence, particular attention was paid to the development of signal processing tools, not only in terms of conventional filtering and reverberation facilities but also more novel techniques such as pitch shifting and time stretching. Works realized using SYTER include *Voilements* by Jean Claude Risset (1987), which combines live and processed saxophone sounds, and *Syrcus* by Daniel Teruggi (1992), which uses a variety of exotic percussion sounds as source material for a work based on the metaphors of air, water, fire, and earth.

Whereas SYTER, and its software derivative GRM Tools, were clearly targeted at the needs of institutional users, including the tertiary education sector, these products share one feature in common with the commercial mixed-digital systems described earlier. The inner detail of the underlying technology is deliberately hidden from the inquisitive user.

The reverse is true in the case of the DMX-1000 audio computer, manufactured in the United States by Digital Music Systems and released directly to the commercial market in 1979. This consists of a very fast purpose-built digital signal generation and processing system, assembled from special integrated circuits known as bit slices. Crucially, the chief designer, Dean Walraff, chose to adopt an entirely open hardware architecture that allows programmers access to all of its component functions directly on an instruction-by-instruction basis. As the system is optimized for the execution of synthesis and signal processing tasks, management of the control interfaces and the compilation of run-time programs is devolved to a host computer. This configuration provides another example of a true mixed digital environment, where general and application-specific digital architectures are linked together in an optimal manner to create a fully integrated facility.

When the DMX-1000 was first released, most general purpose microcomputers still lacked sufficient processing power adequately to control its system functions in real time, and for this reason a small PDP 11 minicomputer, the PDP 11/34, was chosen as the preferred host. Although the system was originally intended for those major institutional users already likely to have access to such a computer, the level of interest generated within the computer music community led Digital Music Systems to develop a special version known as the DMX-1010. This was an entirely self-contained product, incorporating a LSI version of the PDP 11, and a specially adapted version of the DMX-1000.[12] The MIT software synthesis program MUSIC 11 served as the model for the main control language, MUSIC 1000, but the freedom to program the system directly using its special instruction set soon led others to develop a number of alternative software packages. Barry Truax, for example, developed a suite of POD programs and derivatives specifically for the DMX-1000 from 1983 onward.

Perhaps the most significant project dating from this period, certainly in terms of hardware engineering design, was that directed by Giuseppi di Giugno at IRCAM between 1976 and 1987. This resulted in a sequence of four systems known respectively as the 4A, the 4B, the 4C, and the 4X, the last-mentioned being released as a commercial product by Techniques Numériques Advancées in 1984. Sales to the computer music sector, however, were very few given the high cost of the production system, and the 4X was subsequently repackaged as a high performance digital signal audio processor for the acoustical research division of the French navy.

Di Giugno's research into novel audio hardware architectures dates back to the early 1970s, when he founded the Acoustics and Electronics (ACEL) research group at the University of Naples. His initial project, developing a computer-controlled analog synthesizer, caught the attention of Luciano Berio. Well aware of the limitations of voltage-controlled hardware the composer encouraged him to develop an all-digital architecture, which would be fully programmable in terms of individual device control functions and also the interconnections between the devices themselves.

Having completed the construction of a prototype of the 4A at ACEL, Di Giugno transferred his work to IRCAM and quickly finished a fully operational version consisting of 256 digital oscillators and matching envelope generators. Under the control of a PDP 11 computer, the 4A could be configured as a powerful additive synthesizer, the timbre-generating opportunities being enhanced by the ability to use up to four different wave shapes at any one time. Power and versatility nevertheless came at a price in creative terms, because composers had to specify their synthesis tasks with a very high level of spectral detail. The 4B and the 4C versions that followed sought to address this problem by providing FM synthesis facilities from a smaller bank of sixty-four oscillators and thirty-two envelope generators, the latter model being controlled by a conventional PDP 11, the former by its newer, microprocessor version, the LSI 11.

The command language for the first three versions of the Di Giugno synthesizer was originally written directly in assembler code, placing heavy demands on the programming skills of the composer. By 1980, however, Curtis Abbott had developed a higher-level command language for the 4C version, known as 4CED, which permitted the use of more musically oriented procedures without any significant loss of flexibility or computational efficiency. As has been the case with all the mixed digital systems so far discussed, real-time performance was the primary design objective, requiring particular attention to be paid to the operational characteristics of the communications interface.

Much of the compositional work carried out at IRCAM using the Di Giugno synthesizers tended to favor a foreground/background approach, in which the user interacts with a basic program of operations, preprogrammed into the system before the performance starts. In such an environment it is possible to use an alphanumeric computer keyboard as the primary means of control, provided that the associated VDU monitors the evolution of key computational processes in a manner that can be readily understood by the operator. This mode of operation was nevertheless to prove a source of considerable frustration to those IRCAM composers and researchers who sought a totally interactive environment, well aware of the much more versatile and truly interactive tools becoming available as part of the personal computer revolution. It was thus only a matter of time before mouse-driven interactive graphics tools replaced the older style user interfaces. Moves in this direction were to highlight some interesting tensions between those who saw computer music as a performance art and those who saw a continuing role for precompositional processes, to be carried out away from the synthesis system itself.

Still, essentially non-real-time software tools such as MUSICn derivatives thus coexisted at IRCAM alongside the 4X, encouraging a debate in both philosophical and practical terms on desirable modes of working, which continues to the present day. In the case of the 4C, Abbott deliberately created an environment in which the preferred mode of working was entirely text-based. This required the performer to keep track of the inner detail of programming structures rather than rely on graphic displays or arrays of icons. Nevertheless, some direct interaction with the synthesis process was possible via an array of sixteen potentiometers, which could be freely assigned as control devices for individual performance parameters.

The 4X differed significantly from its predecessors in providing extensive facilities for digital signal processing as well as direct synthesis, allowing up to sixteen different channels of externally generated material to be processed simultaneously in real time. This version offers a number of features broadly similar to the DMX-1000, notably a well-developed programming language that allows the composer to assemble chains of devices from modular components and then manipulate these composite functions in a manner similar to those used by the MUSIC family of programs. It also supports graphically oriented modes of parameter control, an aspect that was extensively developed in the subsequent commercial version.

Notable compositions realized using the early Di Giugno synthesizers include *Antony* (1977) by David Wessel, based on the 4A, and *Light* (1979) by Tod Machover, based on both the 4A and the 4C systems. In 1980 Machover combined the facilities of the 4A and 4C with those offered by MUSIC 10 (a derivative of the MUSICn family) running on the PDP 10 mainframe computer at IRCAM to produce *Soft Morning, City!*, a work scored for tape, soprano, and double bass. Extensive use is made of digital signal-processing techniques pioneered by James Moorer at Stanford to manipulate material provided by the soprano Jane Manning and the bass player Barry Guy for use in the tape part of the work.

It was the 4X, however, which was destined to achieve the greatest publicity with *Répons* by Pierre Boulez, completed in 1981. Here the acoustical performances of six percussion soloists are subject to live treatment in a dialogue with a core instrumental ensemble of twenty-four players. The resources of the 4X are used primarily to extend the sound world of the percussion sources rather than compete with them, creating a continuum for the development of the musical argument. Live interactions of such a complex nature was still very much a novelty in 1981, and the work was subject to several revisions for its subsequent performances.

Répons is a significant milestone in terms of the pioneering frontiers of digital audio technology and the exploration of its creative potential at the time of composition, and it raises as many questions as it answers in this context. Indeed, there is little doubt that Boulez envisioned the work as a research venture in its own right. In particular it highlights the complex nature of the relationships that may be established between performers and their sound-producing agents in situations in which the acoustic results of their physical actions interact directly with external processes, preprogrammed to make context-dependent decisions of their own. These important issues will be looked at more closely in due course.

The fourth and last mixed digital synthesis system to be considered here is the SSSP synthesizer, a product of the Structured Sound Synthesis Project, initiated in 1977. The project was coordinated by William Buxton, who—like Barry Truax—had studied at the Institute of Sonology, Utrecht, earlier in the decade, and also become aware of the potential of real-time digital synthesis and signal processing techniques. Having conducted some preliminary experiments of his own, he quickly concluded that the primary key to progress lay not only in maximizing the potential of the processing power available but also the means by which musical ideas were formulated and communicated to the system. In particular, he recognized the potential of a graphics-driven mode of operation, and accordingly set out to establish the fundamental criteria necessary to develop a suitably interactive control interface. The only significant differences between these criteria and those encountered with modern computer desktop facilities are the use of a tablet instead of a mouse, and the inclusion of an additional hand-operated control surface.

On his return to Canada, the opportunity to explore these objectives came with an invitation to join a team within the Computer Systems Research Group at the University of Toronto. Under the guidance of Ron Baecker and Les Mezei, Buxton, Gustav Ciamaga, and K. C. Smith constructed a digital synthesizer, controlled by a PDP 11/45 computer with the enhancement of a high-definition graphics monitor. The prototype version was completed in 1978, numerous revisions and improvements being implemented over the next four years as part of an ongoing program of research and development.

At the heart of the synthesizer lay a bank of sixteen digital oscillators, which generated up to eight different waveforms. Four different synthesis modes were available: independent voice mode, bank mode, frequency modulation mode, and VOSIM mode.[13] In independent voice mode, each oscillator was treated as an individual voice, using a fixed timbre selected from one of the eight primary waveforms. In bank mode, any number of oscillators up to a maximum of sixteen could be used in parallel to create a single voice. If sinusoidal functions were selected, additive synthesis techniques could be employed with up to sixteen independently controlled partials.

In frequency modulation mode, pairs of oscillators could be coupled to produce complex spectra in accordance with Chowning's principles. VOSIM mode was a direct implementation of Kaegi's methods to create vowel-like sounds, a consequence of Buxton's study of the method during his time at Utrecht. Up to four output channels were available, for projection between a maximum of sixteen different loudspeakers.[14] An additional mixing system, inserted between the synthesizer and the channel-distribution network, allowed the addition of up to sixteen different external sources to the output, thus creating a particularly versatile performance system.

Perhaps the most interesting feature of the system concerns the nature of the facilities provided for interactive communications. At the most basic level of operation, commands could be entered using a conventional alphanumeric keyboard. The primary design objective, however, was to provide musically attractive methods of physical contact with the synthesizer. In place of traditional input aids such as knobs, sliders, and joysticks, all of which suffer from the limitations of a fixed mechanical travel, a series of continuous plastic bands was provided for the entry of data by means of physical hand movements. These allowed existing function values to be increased or decreased depending on the direction in which the bands were rotated, and these controllers were normally used in conjunction with the main input device, a specially designed graphics interface.

The facilities offered by the SSSP synthesizer in the latter regard established benchmark standards for composer/machine communications that were second to none. Although the resources for the display and control of parameters provided by systems such as the Fairlight and Synclavier were suitably functional, they were arguably deficient in their ability to establish well-defined links between different modes of data representation. In the case of the SSSP, careful attention was paid to the musical consequences of changing from one mode to another, in particular the need to ensure visual coherence.

Composers were thus able to enter and display control data in a number of formats. For example, if the intention was to produce a "note/event" type of piece using tempered pitches, the associated software allowed the use of traditional musical notation. The screen displayed a "window" of the score on a pair of staves in its upper part and a list of permissible operations such as "append," "change," and "delete" in the lower. Scrolling of the score in both directions was controlled by one of the band regulators, a simple but very effective improvement on conventional cursor control methods.

Access to display characteristics was achieved via a computer-generated tracking cross, which could be moved to any position by using a tablet. The latter device consists of a flat sensing panel and a small handheld device known as a cursor, movements of the latter producing matching movements of the tracking cross displayed on the monitor screen. Manipulation commenced with the selection of an editing mode. This involved moving the cross until it was positioned over the corresponding entry in the list and then clicking a button on the tablet itself to register the choice. The cross could then be moved to the score area and used to modify the displayed data in the manner selected.

In the case of the "append" mode, concerned with adding notes to an existing score, the cross was positioned over the desired point of entry and the mouse button clicked again. This caused the cross to disappear, to be replaced by a small marker and a linear display of note types, this palette of options, in the interests of clarity, being displaced towards the right of the screen. The cursor was then used to manipulate the note-type display, the desired neume being positioned over the marker. Depressing another control button on the mouse caused the neume to be entered into the score, and a restoration of the tracking cross pointer to allow selection of the next editing function.

This level of flexibility extended to the other modes of data entry and display. These permitted the specification of acoustical data such as frequency, timbre, and envelope via similar processes of visual manipulation. The graphics software offered a variety of display methods, the choice depending on the intended action. Sound envelopes, for example, could be drawn directly onto a supplied grid, the software attempting to rectify obvious mistakes such as envelopes that do not progress continuously in a left-to-right direction when measured along the horizontal time axis.

Other actions, such as the entry of data for FM sounds, led to a portioning of the screen into segments, each concerned with a specific variable, for example, the waveform of each oscillator, the duration of the sound, the frequency of the carrier, or the modulation index. This mixture of numerical and graphical data was easily manipulated using the mouse in association with the rotary band regulators. If so desired, numerical data could be displayed in the form of slider settings, shown as crossbars on vertical lines that moved up and down in response to the physical movement of the regulators. Yet another display mode offered a perceptual model of the sound, of particular use in evaluating elements such as vowel formants, generated by means of the VOSIM option.

What made the SSSP so significant in historical terms was the clear structuring of links between the processes that describe the inner nature of the sounds themselves, the musical structures that determine their application, and the basic control data that determines the evolution of the work, event by event. Notwithstanding the ever-increasing sophistication of the MIDI-based systems that subsequently have come to dominate the world of computer music, relatively few of these have ever achieved such a high degree of functional integration.

One of the most distinctive features to be associated with microcomputers and personal computers has been their use of increasingly sophisticated and inter-active graphical user interfaces. It has already been noted that traditional computer manufacturers paid little attention to improving the performance of the standard terminal interface during the 1970s, assuming that the alphanumeric code pro-vided by the traditional teletypewriter was perfectly adequate for the majority of applications. Even the early visual display units were for the most part restricted to simple character displays, providing little more than an illuminated alternative to the conventional text output produced by a typewriter terminal. High-resolution graphics facilities such as those used for the development of the SSSP were for the most part bulky and exceedingly expensive. The laser printer was also still in its infancy, and the only practical means of reproducing such information accurately in hardcopy was the slow and often cumbersome graph plotter.

In their search for a cheap and convenient means of visual communication some microcomputer manufacturers, for example, Acorn, turned to the domestic television, developing special modulators that translate computer data into analog broadcast picture signals for display via a standard aerial socket. Although the resulting picture quality is relatively poor when compared with that obtainable from a modern high-definition computer monitor, this widely available domestic medium provided a cheap and easily programmable means of displaying both text and graphics simultaneously, with the added dimension of color.

The impact of such initiatives finally penetrated the very core of the computer industry, stimulating a number of hardware manufacturers to invest in the devel-opment of digital monitors with bit-mapped graphics capabilities, first in mono-chrome and then subsequently color. By the mid-1980s, high-definition VDUs had become the rule rather than the exception, forming an integral part of what has become the standard WIMPS-based computing environment.[15]

The development of complementary audio facilities for microcomputers pro-ceeded at a much more leisurely pace. The starting point for a number of initia-tives was the small internal loudspeaker provided as a standard facility for many first-generation microcomputers as an alert for certain important conditions, for example, that the machine has switched on and booted successfully, or that a se-rious system or user error has occurred. The most basic and in most cases the only possible method of sound production involved the application of on/off voltage pulses from a simple one-bit digital function generator direct to the speaker coil. No digital-to-analog converters are required for such a procedure, and sound pro-duction is thus limited to patterns of pulses with fixed amplitude.

Despite the severe practical limitations of such a resource, a number of enthu-siasts developed programs that play tunes or even simple chords in this manner. Ingenuity knows no bounds and some programmers managed to synthesize short extracts of recognizable speech using pulse trains, leading to the production of one or two elementary "speak and spell" programs for the educational sector. Although such material is of limited value for any serious compositional purposes, some dedicated software developers managed to use this technique to support musical applications such as aural training or the teaching of elementary harmony.

Commodore and Atari took the possibilities of generating sound a stage further by incorporating simple hardware circuits specifically for audio synthesis in their early microcomputers. Although such resources were still far from refined, they represented a marked improvement over the crude direct speaker modulation technique described above. The sound system for the Commodore 64, for example, was of a hybrid nature, comprising three digitally controlled analog oscillators that offer a choice of three basic waveforms, and the facility to program the pitch, duration, amplitude, and overall envelope of each note/event. In the case of the Atari 800, a special eight-bit digital sound chip facilitated the generation of up to four simultaneous tones.

Given the availability of such microcomputers with built-in facilities for tone generation, the emergence of the Apple II as an especially popular host for music applications toward the end of the 1970s might appear a little strange, given its lack of any sound resources other than a one-bit loudspeaker signaling system. The attraction lay in a unique combination of features that were to prove especially attractive to system developers. First, in terms of visual communications, the graphics capabilities of this Apple II were significantly superior to those offered by its immediate rivals. Second, even the earliest models allowed incremental memory expansion from a basic 4 K up to 48 K, at a time when other microcomputers such as the Commodore 64 had a fixed memory capacity of just 4 K. Third, and most important, Apple had been far-sighted enough to provide a bank of spare slots within the machine for the insertion of additional computer cards, the design and purpose of which was left entirely open to the ingenuity of third-party hardware developers.

Thus it was the possibilities of mixed digital synthesis technology became available to the fast-developing microcomputer market some time before the development of MIDI, and at a fraction of the cost of upmarket systems such as the Fairlight or Synclavier. One of the earliest of these products, known as the Mountain Computer Music System, was released commercially in 1980. This consisted of a pair of plug-in cards that provide sixteen individually programmable digital oscillators, linked to a stereo eight-bit digital-to-analog converter.

Although by modern standards the fidelity of this system leaves much to be desired, it nevertheless posed a credible threat to the prevailing notion that commercial digital synthesizers were by their very nature destined to be expensive products. Other manufacturers, notably ALF with its nine-voice MC1 audio card, and Sweet Micro Systems with its six-voice Mockingbird card, were soon competing for a share of this new market, albeit with products that were for the most part functionally less versatile that the Mountain Computer Music System. The ALF card, for example, only generates square wave functions, which are manipulated in the manner of an impulse generator to create distinctive timbres.

The problems encountered in programming these audio cards highlighted the shortcomings of the early user interfaces. In 1980, the earlier-mentioned graphics revolution was still very much in a formative stage. Nevertheless, computers such as the Apple II were able to support the visual display of music notation, and it was thus possible to develop software that would allow music data to be displayed prior to synthesis. Interactive WIMPs editing of music notation in the manner of the SSSP project, however, still lay some way into the future, and the conventional computer keyboard remained the primary means of data entry, using an alpha-numeric coding system.

Given these difficulties attention gravitated toward the possibility of attaching a music keyboard as an alternative input facility, requiring in this pre-MIDI era the development of special interfaces to link an electronic keyboard and computer functionally together. Accordingly, in 1981 a system known as the alphaSyntauri appeared on the market comprising a four-octave keyboard, a pair of foot pedals and a plug-in interface card, packaged together with a matching set of Mountain Computer boards for an Apple II. The software for this system, known as Music Master, includes an editor for the synthesizer voices and also a sequencing package that stores performance data on floppy disk. In addition, various performance functions can be controlled using either the foot-pedals or the games paddles provided as standard accessories for the computer.

The publicity material for the alphaSyntauri system cites its suitability as a teaching aid, performance instrument, compositional tool, and programmable synthesizer, thus clearly indicating the all-inclusive range of applications envisaged for this new generation of personal computing resources. Through extremely competitive pricing this product indeed left its mark on the educational sector during the relatively brief window of opportunity that existed before the advent of MIDI-based technology and the new generation of WIMPs-based personal computers. It also made a lasting impression on the very territory targeted by the Fairlight and Synclavier, the high-end of the popular music sector, featuring in works by artists such as Stevie Wonder and Herbie Hancock.

Rival plug-in systems include the Soundchaser from Passport Designs, a company subsequently to invest heavily in the design and marketing of software programs for MIDI-based computer music systems. This system also was based on the Mountain Computer cards, hosted by an Apple II, with accessories such as a music keyboard and sound editing and sequencing software. The basis for the sought-after middle ground between self-contained hardware architectures and all-software synthesis systems hosted by standard computers was thus becoming firmly established.

The launch of MIDI in 1983 provides a timely opportunity to take stock of the true nature of the underlying technology that supported the development of the medium at this time, in particular the quality of the music material generated by these various systems, large and small. The key to success lay only in part with the operational enhancements made possible through the use of computer hardware and software. The potential of new sound-producing and sound-processing methodologies could only be fully realized if the resulting sounds achieved the highest expectations in terms of their intrinsic fidelity. Even as late as the early 1980s, fundamental issues to do with both the sampling and the quantizing of audio signals had not been fully addressed by the majority of commercial systems. It was to take until the end of the decade, if not arguably several years beyond, before minimum benchmark standards in these critical areas were to become the rule rather than the exception.

In order to understand the true significance of fidelity in the context of digital audio, it is now necessary to return to the basic physical principles involved in its production and examine more fully their practical application in the context of computer music systems, both past and present.

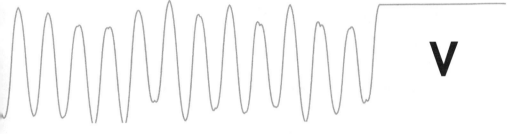

V

Digital Audio

13

The Characteristics of Digital Audio

The evolution of electronic and computer music has been shaped by two fundamental considerations: the creativity of the individuals who have engaged in the composition and performance of new works, and the functional characteristics of the resources used in the course of their production. Studying the nature of these interactions between artists and their tools is fundamental to understanding the development of the medium as a whole, from the earliest experiments with simple analog devices to the sophisticated applications of today, requiring the very latest digital technology. One factor of paramount importance is the intrinsic fidelity of these resources, bearing in mind that they often are deployed in conditions that are technically very demanding, and there are few practitioners who have not encountered significant difficulties in this context from time to time. Major advances have been made in recent years toward eliminating such deficiencies, but there are a number of quality issues that have yet to be fully resolved.

In tracing the antecedents of electronic music in chapter 1, it was shown how the foundations for this new medium were inextricably bound to the evolution of the audio industry as a whole. The development of recording and broadcasting prior to the Second World War established the core tools necessary for the wealth of creative activity that was to follow, but the processes of refinement, not least in terms of achieving acceptable levels of audio fidelity, had still to run their course.

During the early 1950s, magnetic tape became the primary medium for studio recording, and with the birth of the long-playing record important new benchmark standards could be established for the design of both professional and domestic audio equipment. Paramount among these standards was the accurate reproduction of the frequency and the dynamic response characteristics of the human ear.

Matching the frequency response of the ear requires an audio bandwidth extending to about 20 kHz. In terms of domestic listening, the 78 rpm phonograph record offered a limited fidelity of about 4 or 5 kHz, and in most countries AM radio transmissions have fared little better.[1] Such conditions provided little incentive for significantly higher standards within the professional recording industry during the first half of the twentieth century. The introduction of the long-playing record in 1948 offering bandwidths that extended to 18 kHz or thereabouts set major new benchmarks for the industry. These developments stimulated the manufacture of high-quality domestic listening systems, and in turn a demand for matching improvements in the quality of broadcast sound, using the extended bandwidths facilitated by the introduction of FM transmissions.

Unfortunately, external considerations, notably the need to regulate the allocation of radio frequencies, prevented full audio bandwidth broadcasting in most countries, the transmission of FM radio and television broadcasts generally limited to about 14 or 15 kHz, and in some instances no more than about 12 kHz. Although this degree of fidelity represented a significant improvement on that of AM radio, it still excluded the reproduction of potentially important spectral detail in higher frequency regions, and it was not until the advent of digital broadcasting that these bandwidth restrictions were finally overcome.

The dynamic response of the human ear has proved a much more difficult characteristic to reproduce. In order to understand the nature of these difficulties, it is necessary to study some key issues in more depth than hitherto. In earlier discussions, it has been shown that the volume of a sound is a function of its amplitude. This quantity is usually expressed in terms of the resulting pressure level of the acoustic sound wave, which is mathematically proportional to the square of the average amplitude.[2] This pressure level may be measured directly as a flow of energy per unit time across a unit area, and this rate is usually expressed in terms of watts per square meter. For example, at a frequency of 1 kHz, the pressure associated with our threshold of hearing corresponds to about 10^{-12} watts per square meter and our threshold of pain to about 1 watt per square meter, representing a physical pressure ratio of about 1,000,000,000,000 to 1.

In order to make the measurement of sound pressure levels (SPL) more manageable in numerical terms, the logarithmic unit of the decibel has been adopted for this purpose, where a tenfold change in sound pressure is equated to 10 dB. A hundredfold change equates to 20 dB, a thousandfold change to 30 dB, and so on. If the threshold of hearing at a frequency of 1 kHz is assigned a SPL of 0 dB, the threshold of pain equates to a SPL of about 120 dB.

The decibel scale of measurement is more understandable in the current context for another reason. In subjective terms, it is possible to establish an approximate correlation between a 1 decibel change in SPL and what subjectively may be identified as the minimum detectable change in the volume of an acoustic signal, sometimes referred to as the "just noticeable difference" or JND.[3] Although this correlation is only accurate at about 1 kHz, and prone to increasing errors outside a frequency range of approximately 400–2000 Hertz, it provides a useful point of reference for the following discussion.

Fortunately, it is rarely—if ever—the case that we encounter the extremities of our auditory thresholds in everyday listening. In terms of the threshold of hearing our neural responses are significantly influenced by the noise levels associated with the ambient surroundings, which are never completely quiet even on a calm night in the depths of the countryside. As a result, we automatically adjust our short-term threshold of hearing to a background SPL level that is perhaps 20 or 30 dB above the absolute threshold. At the other end of the dynamic scale, sustained SPL levels of 110 to 120 dB will permanently damage our ears, and most people prefer a listening environment in which the loudest sounds will not exceed a SPL level of about 100 dB. On this basis, the target requirements for audio systems in terms of their minimum acceptable dynamic range may be significantly reduced. In listening to an orchestral performance in a concert hall, for example, the following approximations may be taken as broadly representative:

Music Dynamic	Sound Pressure Level (dB)
ppp	30
pp	40
p	50
mp	55
mf	60
f	70
ff	80
fff	90

These figures suggest that audio systems capable of handling a dynamic range of about 50–55 dB should meet the minimum criteria for high quality music reproduction. Unfortunately, there are a number of other factors that have to be taken into consideration in arriving at a suitable specification. In the case of analog systems, the most significant of these is the presence of background noise and other low-level sources of interference within the system itself. Experience has shown that for these components to remain undetected subjectively when listening to recordings at normal playback levels, this ambient noise level needs to be at least 65–70 dB below the maximum playback level.

The quality of an audio system is ultimately constrained by the weakest component in the device chain. Steady improvements in electronic design ensured that by the end of the 1950s almost all of the primary items of equipment associated with a professional studio, for example, microphones, mixers, and amplifiers, could meet, or indeed exceed, the above specification. Within little more than a decade even higher signal-to-noise ratios of 90 dB or greater were being regularly attained, and today the minimum benchmark standard for most professional analog equipment is in the order of 120 to 130 dB.

The problems of residual noise arising directly from the use of analog tape recording technology, however, proved rather more problematic. Here the primary impediment to progress was the physical properties of the magnetic coating on the tape itself, because those particles that remain unaffected by the recording process automatically generate random signals, reproduced as background noise or hiss. Whenever the signal is loud, most of the magnetic particles are contributing to the registration of signal information, which itself masks any low-level noise. When the signal is soft, this underlying noise "floor" is entirely exposed.

Initially the signal-to-noise ratio of the medium, measured here as the difference between the maximum amplitude that can be recorded without overloading the tape and the residual hiss level generated by the magnetic medium itself, rarely exceeded about 55 dB, an inadequate margin for high quality classical music recordings. By the early 1960s, as a result of improved magnetic coatings, typical signal-to-noise ratios had steadily improved to about 60–65 dB, and by the dawn of the MIDI era in 1983 a new generation of high output tapes had extended these ratios by a further 10 dB. Although these specifications now met the minimum criteria for high fidelity recording, they left little margin for any error in regulating studio levels. A continuing interest in analog recording, notwithstanding the impact of the digital revolution, encouraged manufacturers to continue their quest for even better recording media, and by the end of the century a number of professional analog recording systems could deliver basic signal-to-noise ratios in excess of 85 dB.

It was a growing concern over residual hiss levels that inspired the development of electronic tape noise reduction systems during the 1960s for both professional and domestic applications. These generally consisted of a matching pair of inverted compressors and expanders, the former being applied to boost progressively lower signal levels by an increasing degree prior to recording, and the latter to restore the overall dynamic range on playback by reversing the process.[4] Because the expander operates on all the magnetic signals stored on the tape, including the residual tape hiss, the net effect on playback is a significant drop in the perceived hiss level, while at the same time restoring the dynamic profile of the original signal.

The leading pioneer in this field, Ray Dolby, launched his highly successful Dolby A noise reduction system for professional recording in 1965. In this design, the audio frequency spectrum is partitioned into four segments, each serviced by its own compressor and expander, the combined circuits achieving an overall improvement in the signal-to-noise ratio of about 10 dB. Its successor, the professional Dolby SR system, increased this margin to 20 dB. The domestic version of his system, Dolby B, developed specifically for use with cassette tapes, was released in 1968. This simplified version uses a single, variable tuning compressor/expander system, designed to provide a maximum improvement of 10 dB in the signal-to-noise ratio when measured above 4 kHz, targeting the middle to upper areas of the frequency spectrum where noise components are subjectively most prominent. Subsequent domestic derivatives, such as Dolby C, parallel the improvement of 20 dB associated with Dolby SR.

The crucial consideration here, as in all data compression methods, analog or digital, is the extent to which the integrity of the signals themselves is compromised by any side-effects resulting from this electronic processing. In the case of Dolby A and to a slightly lesser extent Dolby B, such distortions are generally so small that even the most discerning listener is rarely able to detect any loss in sound quality. Unfortunately, some rival noise reduction systems dating from the same period were not as well engineered, resulting in the generation of spurious and often highly undesirable artifacts in certain recording situations. The characteristics of electronic music were especially prone to the generation of such distortions, and a number of works dating from the 1970s and early 1980s suffer from unfortunate side-effects such as breathlike noise components superimposed on low frequency sounds, or irregular attack and decay envelopes.

The advent of digital recording heralded a new era of sound technology that aspired to eliminate all the perceived shortcomings of analog recording systems and set new standards of audio fidelity, capable of satisfying the most exacting requirements. Unfortunately, some other factors, not least an imperative from the fast-growing world of global communications to limit the amount of information actually transmitted across digital networks such as the Internet, has raised some other important issues concerning the growing use of data compression in the digital domain.

It will be recalled that a fundamental characteristic of computer-based synthesis programs is the use of a fixed sampling rate for generating, storing, and retrieving audio data.[5] Although this technique has implications for the generation of timbres at different frequencies, it ensures that all the elements contributing to a musical texture are developed synchronously and, if necessary, quite independently, the sample values associated with the individual sonic components being added together to create a composite digital audio function. Exactly the same operating conditions apply if sounds are imported from an external source, for example, an acoustic performance captured in the first instance as an analog signal via a conventional microphone and then digitized using an analog-to-digital converter.

In practical terms there is little to distinguish the basic principles of data conversion used for a software synthesis program such as CSOUND from those used for digital recording and broadcasting applications, where for broadly similar reasons fixed sampling rates are also employed. It will be recalled from chapter 6 that a digital representation of an analog function consists of a series of numbers, each representing the instantaneous value of the function at regular time intervals. If these numbers are passed to a digital-to-analog converter at the appropriate rate, a stepped approximation to the wave will be generated, the accuracy of the approximation being dependent both on the number of samples used per second, and the numerical accuracy of the approximations themselves. Both these factors affect the quality of reproduction, but in rather different ways.

With a fixed sampling rate, the number of samples available to represent one complete cycle of a wave steadily diminishes as its frequency is raised. If, for example, the sampling rate is set at 20 kHz (twenty thousand samples per second), each cycle of a 50 Hz sine wave will be represented by four hundred samples. This will reduce to forty samples at a frequency of 500 Hz, and only four samples at a frequency of 5000 Hz. In mathematical terms a critical point is reached, in this instance at 10000 Hz, exactly half the sampling rate, where just two samples are available to represent each cycle. This point is known as the Nyquist frequency, first identified by Harry Nyquist in 1928. His pioneering work on the mathematics of sampling led to an important theorem, which states that a periodic function can be represented as a regular succession of samples, provided that the sampling rate employed is at least twice the highest frequency component present in the waveform. Thus, at 20000 samples per second, the upper frequency limit for audio signals will be 10000 Hz.

This bandwidth restriction must not be breached under any circumstances; otherwise a potentially very unpleasant type of distortion will occur as the result of an effect known as "foldover," or aliasing. A number of circumstances may give rise to such errors, typically a synthesis procedure that generates spectral components that lie above the Nyquist frequency or the presence of similar transients in an externally sampled sound. Under such conditions, each cycle of any frequency component higher than the Nyquist will have completed before two samples can register its periodicity. As a result, a reflected or beat frequency wave is generated from successive samples, numerically equal to the sampling frequency minus the source frequency.

If, for example, a 14000 Hz sine wave is synthesized using just 20000 samples per second, the result in acoustic terms will be a folded frequency of 20000 − 14000 = 6000 Hz. Similarly, if a glissando is attempted using a sine wave that moves from 0 Hz to 20 Hz in such conditions, the result will be a tone that ascends as expected to 10 kHz, but then immediately changes direction to descend, as a reflection, back down to 0 Hz again. Further reflections will occur if the generated frequency exceeds the sample rate itself, a glissando from 20 kHz to 40 kHz resulting in a tone that once again moves from 0 Hz to 10 kHz and then back to 0 Hz.

The pioneers of software synthesis faced many obstacles in their quest for high fidelity, not least in terms of securing an adequate bandwidth. In computational terms, higher sampling rates require proportionally more CPU time per second of sound generated, and in the case of early mainframe computers this was an expensive commodity that had to be strictly rationed. The design of digital-to-analog and analog-to-digital converters also was still very much in its infancy, and there were further practical constraints concerning the maximum speed at which audio data files could be read from tape or computer disk. As a consequence, most early composers of computer music were restricted to sampling rates as low as 20 kHz, the corresponding Nyquist frequency of 10 kHz providing a audio bandwidth noticeably better than that generally associated with AM radio, but still significantly short of even the lowest FM broadcast standards.

In the same way that integrated circuits facilitated the microprocessor revolution, so the same technology was eventually to facilitate the development of chip-based audio converters that were faster, more accurate, cheaper, and more reliable. The primary market for such products was an embryonic digital audio industry, one of the first landmarks being the demonstration of a digital tape recorder by NHK Industries in 1967 that sampled at 30 kHz. Not to be outdone, two years later Sony demonstrated a rival system that sampled at 47.25 kHz, providing an audio bandwidth comfortably in excess of 20 kHz. It was to take another decade, however, for the notion of a domestic market for digital audio to become a practical reality. Initial attempts to develop digital sound tracks for videodiscs during the early 1970s encountered serious technical problems, but the vision and perseverance of pioneering companies such as Phillips and Sony led to new technologies that overcame these difficulties, for the most part concerned with the reliability of optical coding. Thus it was that the compact disc was launched in 1981, signaling the demise of the long-playing record within the decade.

The slightly unusual sampling rate of 44.1 kHz per channel adopted for the compact disc was derived from conventions already developed for the digital coding of video signals. Although this was the first sampling rate standard to impact directly on the domestic sector of the digital audio industry, listeners in some countries were already experiencing sometimes quite unwittingly the characteristics of another sampling rate standard, 32 kHz, established during the late 1960s specifically for use in broadcasting applications. This lower rate accommodated the audio bandwidths of 12 to 15 kHz required for FM radio, and the BBC, a major pioneer in digital broadcasting, made extensive use of this sampling rate for communicating program information between studios and radio transmitters in an intermediate digital format. A third industry sampling rate, that of 48 kHz, emerged during the 1980s, in the first instance for use with digital audio tape (DAT). Although this particular recording system only penetrated the domestic market to a very limited extent, its popularity in more specialist and professional contexts led to the adoption of the 48 kHz sampling rate standard as a widely used alternative to 44.1 kHz.

The application of full audio bandwidth sampling rates will reduce the risks of aliasing but will not eliminate them. Many natural sounds contain transient information lying at frequencies above our upper limit of audition, and unchecked all components above the Nyquist frequency will therefore be subject to aliasing. On the input side, therefore, the only way of ensuring that sampled signals in a conventional converter are not subject to such distortion is to insert a steep low-pass filter in the signal path specifically to eliminate such spectral elements before they reach the converter itself. Providing the frequency spectrum of these sampled signals is not subsequently extended as the result of internal signal processing routines, it might be concluded that the risks of any aliasing at the output side have also been eliminated. Unfortunately, this is not the case, for the small irregularities in stepped wave approximations automatically generate high frequency copies of the original spectrum, some components of which may fold back into the audio spectrum or interfere electronically with analog equipment to create other types of audible distortion. It has thus become standard practice to include low-pass filters as an integral design feature of both analog-to-digital and digital-to-analog converters.

These precautionary add-on devices, unfortunately, affect the operational bandwidth of the converters themselves. In discussing the characteristics of filters for analog synthesizers it was noted that even the sharpest filters do not cut off signals exactly at a specified frequency.[6] This attenuation takes place over a spread of frequencies at a rate that may vary from perhaps just 3 dB per octave for a gentle roll-off to about 80 or 90 dB per octave for the best "brick wall" filters. Indeed, any steeper response will introduce its own set of distortion components, typically the superimposition of a "ringing" quality to certain sound spectra. For this reason, low-pass filters for converters are usually designed to start the processes of attenuation at a point no higher than about 90 percent of the Nyquist frequency, to ensure adequate suppression is applied at the Nyquist frequency itself. The effective bandwidth of a digital audio system operating at 32 kHz, for example, will thus be reduced from 16 to about 14.5 kHz. The consequences for converters operating at 44.1 or 48 kHz are fortunately less severe, the resulting bandwidths of about 19.85 and 21.6 kHz still proving adequate for capturing all the spectral components that lie directly within the normal range of hearing.

Whereas the chosen sampling rate regulates the bandwidth of a digital audio signal, the resolution of the individual samples not only determines the overall dynamic range but also directly affects the quality of the sound information itself. It will be recalled that the total number of values that may be coded in a binary format depends on the number of bits available for each item of data. Thus, eight-bit samples offer a range of $2^8 = 256$ values, twelve-bit samples a range of $2^{12} = 4096$ values, and sixteen-bit samples a range of $2^{16} = 65\,536$ values. Since audio signals are bipolar, that is, they fluctuate symmetrically around a central point, the binary values are mapped as integers, providing a range of positive and negative values either side of zero. The integer range associated with eight-bit signal values thus extends from -128 to $+127$, the value zero being treated as a positive value for the purposes of symmetry. In a similar vein, the integer range for sixteen-bit signal values extends from $-32\,768$ to $+32\,767$.

In discussing the measurement of sound pressure levels it was noted that the SPL level is proportional to the square of the amplitude of a signal. In a digital context each extra bit provided for sampling an audio function doubles the range of amplitude values that can be registered, corresponding to an increase of about 6 dB. The maximum dynamic range for a sinusoidal wave function in the digital domain may be calculated as approximately $6.02*N + 1.76$, where N is the number of bits. Thus, an eight-bit system can accommodate a dynamic range of about 50 dB, a twelve-bit system a range of about 74 dB, and a sixteen-bit system a range of about 98 dB. When these values are compared with the signal-to-noise ratios of typical analog systems, it would appear that a twelve-bit coding format satisfies the minimum criteria here. Such a simple numerical comparison, however, overlooks the issue of the subjective quality of audio signals in digital systems when operating at lower dynamic levels.

In analog systems, dynamic range is usually measured in terms of the signal-to-noise ratio, defined it will be recalled as the difference in amplitude between the residual noise level of a system, and the level at which the electronic circuits begin to overload. Even in situations in which listeners become aware of some background hiss components, especially during quiet passages of music, the signals themselves will usually retain their underlying clarity. The same circumstances do not hold true in the case of digital audio systems. Here there is no such quantity as residual noise. If a digital signal is reduced to zero amplitude it produces a null string of samples and thus no output. This conclusion, however, overlooks the fact that the processes involved in quantizing signals introduce an error factor of its own. This results from the need to use integer approximations for the instantaneous values of a continuous function, where the significance of this error in percentage terms increases proportionally as the amplitude of the signal decreases.

In the case of an eight-bit system, the samples for a signal at maximum amplitude will be quantized to the nearest value on an integer scale that accommodates a bipolar range of 256 steps. If, however, the signal is attenuated by as little as 30 dB, the range of integer equivalents available from peak to peak reduces to just eight steps, thus increasing the crudeness of the approximation relative to the wave itself. Although the signal itself is much quieter, these physical distortions of the signal itself are subjectively far more unpleasant than low-level noise in an otherwise completely pure analog signal. The fundamental key to reducing these quantizing errors lies in maximizing the number of data bits available to quantize amplitude values. It is for this reason that digital systems generally require an extended dynamic range in order to compete favorably with their analog counterparts. As an indicative guide the dynamic range of 98 dB provided by a conventional sixteen-bit system is often compared qualitatively with analog systems offering signal-to-noise ratios in the region of 70–75 dB.

In the pioneering era of computer music, when audio converters had to be built from discrete components, it was rarely possible to achieve quantizing resolutions greater than about eleven or twelve bits. By the time integrated circuits were facilitating the fabrication of more accurate and reliable converters using silicon chips, other considerations were influencing the processes of audio engineering, in particular the transition to byte- rather than word-orientated computer architectures.[7] This fundamental change in hardware design had important implications for time-critical applications such as live synthesis, because a minimum of two bytes had to be allocated for sample values requiring resolutions greater than eight bits. During the early stages of the microprocessor revolution the implications of this additional processing overhead were quite significant, and for this reason many early commercial digital synthesizers, samplers, and computer audio cards were limited to eight-bit architectures. The consequential deficiencies in the audio quality of such products contrasted sharply with the sixteen-bit environment of pioneering designs such as the Synclavier, which utilized the maximum resolution that can be generated from two-byte samples.

Although sixteen-bit audio converters were still relatively expensive items at the start of the 1980s, the introduction of compact disc technology and the consequential need for mass production soon drove prices sharply downward. There were, however, a number of other engineering considerations that were to militate against the immediate implementation of higher-order sample resolutions within the computer music sector, and these issues will be considered further in due course. The pace of development might have been even more protracted were it not for a growing interest in the possibilities of professional digital recording and broadcasting, which soon demanded even higher standards of fidelity than that offered by the compact disc.

The launch of the compact disc as the digital replacement for the long-playing record stimulated a fierce controversy as to the relative merits of the two technologies. From a manufacturing point of view, the use of a sixteen-bit sample resolution at 44.1 kHz met all the basic criteria for high quality reproduction. At the same time, many more discerning listeners still preferred the results produced by the older analog technology, on the grounds that digital sound seemed to lack warmth and depth, and at times could appear harsh and brittle. With hindsight it can now be shown that these criticisms had some substance, and it is now generally recognized that the suppression of all possible digital artifacts requires the engineering of digital audio systems to much higher operational standards than those traditionally associated with the world of analog audio.

This quality debate forced manufacturers to look more closely at the design of converters, with a view to reducing still further the potential for both aliasing and quantizing errors. It was quickly discovered that the side effects resulting from both sources of distortion could be significantly reduced by using a data processing technique known as oversampling. This involves running the converter at a multiple of the basic sampling rate, typically times four, eight, or sixteen. More recent designs have sometimes used even higher multiples, for example, times 64 or times 128. On the input side, the extraction and conversion of intermediate sample values provides a more detailed analysis of the spectral content of the sampled wave, this additional information acquiring a particular significance for the accurate representation of components situated toward the upper end of the frequency spectrum. Once converted, each group of oversampled values is then averaged to produce normalized data at the expected sampling rate. On the output side, intermediate values are generated before their conversion using the technique of linear interpolation. Such normalized gradients lack the accuracy of genuine intermediate samples, but the process can improve the overall fidelity in a number of ways.

First, since the processes of analog-to-digital and digital-to-analog data conversion take place at a multiple of the true sampling rate, the Nyquist frequency is similarly transposed, reducing further the risk of aliased or reflected components entering the audio spectrum. Second, in terms of quantizing, the use of intermediate sample values increases the numerical accuracy of the lowest order bits, which in mathematical terms is comparable to an increase in the underlying bit resolution.

A third benefit relates to another feature of converter design that has not yet been considered. Manufacturers were well aware of the need to reduce the unpleasant side effects of low-level quantizing errors in conventional converters. As a consequence, it had become common practice since the late 1970s to add an electronic circuit that deliberately adds a small noiselike error signal to "dither" the actual value of the least significant bit of each sample. This has the effect of broadening the sharply focused frequency spectrum of spurious signals resulting from quantizing errors in order to give them a more noiselike quality. In subjective terms, this enhanced spectral dissipation significantly reduces the perceived distortion. Oversampling not only reduces the numerical significance of these errors but also usefully dissipates them in a similar manner across a much broader frequency spectrum, thus reducing their perceived significance still further.

In quantitative terms, quadrupling the sampling rate by means of oversampling increases the theoretical accuracy of resolution by one bit, equivalent to increasing the overall dynamic range by about 6 dB. Applying the same principles of proportionality, oversampling a sixteen-bit converter by a factor of sixteen increases the resolution from sixteen to eighteen bits, giving an overall dynamic range of about 110 dB. Even greater improvements have been achieved by using a triangle wave dither signal instead of conventional white noise when oversampling, in the latter instance increasing the theoretical resolution to nineteen bits and the dynamic range to about 116 dB. This particular technique has its origins in a principle known as Delta-Sigma modulation, which has been applied as a radical alternative to the conventional principles of sampling described above. Here, instead of converting sample values directly as absolute quantities, the conversion process proceeds by estimating the change from one sample value to the next, thus in effect following the trajectory of the wave. The primary advantage put forward for this approach is that it has distinct advantages when converting noncontinuous signals such as transients, the effects of gentle smoothing being preferable subjectively to the possible discontinuities resulting from approximating successive samples entirely from first principles.

In manufacturing terms, oversampling has proved a relatively straightforward and extremely cost-effective means of improving the quality of analog-to-digital and digital-to-analog converters. Modifying the hardware to produce genuine resolutions greater than sixteen bits proved a much greater challenge. Commercial eighteen-bit converters became available toward the end of the 1980s, and were quickly adopted by both the professional and the higher end of the domestic manufacturing sectors as superior alternatives to oversampled sixteen-bit converters. These converters were also subject to the use of oversampling in the quest for even higher resolutions, but it soon became clear that such extra definition was of only limited value if the underlying resolution of the data within the digital audio system itself could not exceed sixteen bits.

With the prospect of genuine twenty-bit converters by the mid-1990s and twenty-four-bit converters before the end of the century, the need for upgraded digital audio formats soon became overwhelming. Although existing sixteen-bit formats for well-established products such as the compact disc or the DAT recorder could not easily be modified, the professional audio industry was prepared to invest in new hardware technologies capable of handling higher resolution audio samples. By the dawn of the new millennium, a further set of industry standards had been established for digital audio architectures. These accommodate the use of twenty-four-bit or thirty-two sample values and an extended set of sampling rates based on multiples of 44.1 kHz and 48 kHz, for example, 88.2 kHz, 96 kHz, 176.4 kHz, and 196 kHz.

So far, this study of quality issues in digital audio has focused on what are essentially passive processes of exact data conversion and recovery. There is, however, another dimension that needs taken into account, concerning the implications of applying any signal processing function that changes the amplitudes of audio data within a digital environment.

In considering the principles of sampling and quantizing it has been established how the number of bits available to quantize each sample limit both the quality and the overall dynamic range of a digital system. If a digitized signal is attenuated, one important consequence is that each 6 dB reduction in amplitude has the practical effect of moving the lowest order bit of each sample value out of the active data register. In a simple integer-coding environment these values are discarded and cannot thus be subsequently recovered.

Consider now the implications of first attenuating and then boosting a full range signal, initially quantized and stored with a resolution of sixteen bits, by 24 dB. In computational terms the first stage of this process involves shifting the binary code four steps to the right within the data register, discarding the four lowest order bits in the process. Although the effective bit resolution is now only twelve bits, this is now associated with a playback sound level that is correspondingly quieter. As a result, the effects of any quantizing errors on immediate reaudition at this stage will be no different to those associated with the unprocessed coding and decoding of the same source signal, having first reduced the input amplitude to the same level via a simple analog gain control.

Potentially serious problems start as soon as any form of amplification is applied to these attenuated signals. As the associated bit patterns are progressively manipulated back up into vacant higher order locations in the data register there is no longer any information to map back into the lower-order bits, which as a consequence will simply fill up with null (= zero) values. Although the overall volume will be restored, the quality of the sound will remain permanently degraded, with the quantizing errors proportionally boosted as if this sound had been sampled with a twelve-bit resolution in the first place.

It thus follows that any digital audio environment that introduces changes in amplitude as the result of signal processing must have the capacity to retain the quantizing accuracy of the original signal if the overall fidelity is not to be compromised. Although the precise technical procedures applied to secure the retention of such information vary according to the architecture of the system, the basic principles that have to be observed are essentially the same.

There are two primary methods employed for coding numerical data within a computer. The first, known as a fixed-point format, represents numbers purely as integers in the manner described earlier. The most common solution that has been adopted here is to extend the internal data space available for registering each sample value by at least one byte. If sixteen-bit samples are mapped into the upper two bytes of an expanded register of twenty-four bits, a reserve of eight bits is available at the lower end of the register to store the lower order bits of any intermediate attenuation process that does not exceed about 50 dB. This same principle of enhanced coding is extensively used for a number of specialist computing architectures such as digital signal processors or DSPs, which have suitably extended internal hardware registers to accommodate and manipulate these higher order resolutions.

The alternative numeric data coding method for computer data is known as a floating-point format, and this mode of representation is employed extensively for scientific purposes. Here each data value is split up into two components, known respectively as the mantissa and the exponent. The mantissa consists of the basic numerical value, which unlike purely integer coding formats may include fractional values. Thus, the mantissas for the numbers 32 367, 3236.7, 323.67, 32.367, and so on, will all be coded identically as a raw integer, 32 367, the position of the decimal point being identified in terms of an associated exponent value. By this means the basic resolution of numerical values can be accurately preserved during processing operations that may involve amplitude changes of several orders of magnitude. Although floating point calculations carry additional computing overheads, this coding method ensures that the basic resolution offered by the mantissa, typically twelve to eighteen bits is preserved at all times.

An extended debate developed during the 1980s concerning the relative merits of fixed and floating-point data representations. Advocates of the latter approach argued for the development of floating-point digital-to-analog and analog-to-digital converters to eliminate the need for internal data format conversion, and a number of prototype versions where fabricated. The mainstream digital audio industry, however, has generally opted for extended precision integer formats. With the exception of the inner workings of sophisticated software synthesis programs such as CSOUND, floating-point point representations of digital audio are thus still relatively rare.

In charting the development of digital audio it has been shown that the ultimate constraints to fidelity are determined by two primary factors: first, the sampling rate, which determines the audio bandwidth, and, second, the quantizing accuracy of the individual samples, which determines the signal purity in terms of audible distortion. The consequences of increasing the specifications on either count are a proportional increase in the amount of digital data that is required to code this higher resolution information. Quality, thus, is only achieved at a price.

This escalation in the requirements of digital audio can be illustrated by comparing the data flow of an early monophonic eight-bit computer audio card, sampling at 20 kHz, with the equivalent data flow of a modern professional equivalent, offering perhaps twenty-four bit stereo output at 192 kHz. In the former case, the data flow is just 20 kilobytes/sec. In the latter case the data flow is 1152 kilobytes/sec, an increase in throughput of about 500 to 1.

In terms of general computer storage facilities such as the standard internal hard disk drive attached to a conventional personal computer, rapid improvements in computer technology have arguably kept pace with the general requirements of computer music, both in terms of overall capacity and also speed of access. As will be seen in due course, a typical IBM PC or Apple II computer dating from the early 1980s, for example, was equipped with a relatively slow hard drive, offering perhaps no more than 40 megabytes of storage. Within less than twenty years, the basic disk capacities of desktop computers were exceeding 20 gigabytes (20,000 megabytes), this improvement coincidentally also representing an increase in data storage facilities of 500 to 1.

One of the earliest examples of a high capacity digital storage medium suitable for the storage and retrieval of high-quality audio data was none other than the compact disc, its nominal capacity of 680 Megabytes offering in excess of an hour's recording in stereo at 44.1 kHz. The more recent DVD (Digital Versatile Disc),[8] through a combination of higher density recording and the use of up to four recording layers provides a maximum capacity slightly in excess of 17 gigabytes. Furthermore, unlike the conventional CD this newer recording medium accommodates a variety of data formats for both video and audio signals, in the latter context the protocol allowing approximately nine hours of stereo or two hours of eight-channel recording at 44.1 kHz. Alternatively, slightly in excess of an hour of stereo audio can be recorded on a DVD with a resolution of twenty-four bits and a sampling rate 192 kHz.

Notwithstanding the capacity of digital media to keep pace with the demands of the audio industry, concerns over the escalating data requirements of such applications were being voiced almost from the birth of the CD itself. Matters were finally to come to a head with the burgeoning of multimedia computing applications and the increasing use of the Internet to transmit information electronically. Thus it was that the development of sampling and quantizing technologies specifically designed to code and reproduce acoustic information with the minimum possible alteration to its detail came into conflict with a very different set of ideals that actively seek to compress the content of both video and audio data.

There is an important distinction to be made here between "lossless" compression, where the reduced data flow contains all the components necessary to restore the original signal, and "lossy" compression, where elements of the signal are permanently lost. It was quickly discovered that completely lossless methods of data compression in the digital domain could only achieve relatively modest efficiency gains. Attention was therefore focused increasingly on the design of lossy systems, engineered specifically to remove any video and audio information that in subjective terms can be regarded as redundant. Engineers prefer to refer to this technique as perceptual rather than lossy coding, on the grounds that the intention is to resynthesize images that appear to be identical, and suffer from no consequential artifacts. An early example of this type of data compression technology is the digital compact cassette (DCC), which was initially marketed as a rival to the DAT and specifically targeted at the domestic consumer market. This was followed in due course by other products based on similar principles such as the Sony MiniDisc. More recent examples include the data compression formats that have been developed specifically for digital radio, and the MP3 format (MPEG-1 Audio Layer-3), a derivative of the widely used MPEG (Motion Pictures Experts Group) digital signal compression protocol, which has proved especially popular for transmitting music information over the Internet.

The basis for these techniques is the hypothesis that the brain focuses on certain features in both aural and visual images and ignores others, and it is sometimes possible to remove some subsidiary information without its absence being noticed. Turning theory into practice, however, has not proved particularly straightforward, especially in the audio domain, and whereas some of the more sophisticated techniques are proving increasingly viable for many domestic listening applications, others are not so robust. The facility to vary the degree and nature of data compression, especially in Internet applications, has unfortunately resulted in a very variable quality of digital audio transmissions via this medium. MP3, for example, allows compression ratios that range from 96:1 for telephone quality sound, to a maximum of 12:1 for near CD-quality sound, and there is no absolute guarantee that the latter standard can be reliably assured in all situations.

The conflicting pressures of ever higher standards of digital audio fidelity and the need to reduce the amount of information actually transmitted over increasingly overloaded Internet networks thus create a curious paradox. It is expected that in due course the quality of lossy compression techniques will improve to the point at which processed sound material will become to all intents and purposes indistinguishable from the original. Progress toward this goal, however, can be measured in years rather than months, indicative of the increasingly complex world of digital communications associated with the new millennium. It is against this background of change and unresolved quality issues that the focus of attention returns to the 1970s, and the circumstances that gave birth to the MIDI synthesizer.

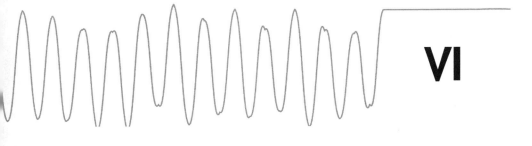

MIDI

VI

14

The Development of the MIDI Communications Protocol

The development of MIDI as an industry standard communications protocol for the control of synthesizers fundamentally changed the working environment for the commercial sector. By the end of the 1970s, the latter had expanded to embrace three primary areas of activity. In the digital domain, products such as the Fairlight and the Synclavier were exploring new and potentially very lucrative opportunities at the high end of the market, counterbalanced by a modest but steadily growing repertory of synthesis devices that could be attached to the new generation of microcomputers. In the middle of this spectrum lay the core of the third and largest market, devoted to the manufacture of voltage-controlled analog synthesizers. Many of the products of pioneers such as Moog, Buchla, ARP, and EMS (London) were still available, but now increasingly overshadowed by those being marketed by a new generation of companies that were to play a key role in the design revolution that was to follow. Several of these second-generation manufacturers were to become the market leaders in the new MIDI era, maintaining this status to the present day. Others were to prosper for only a limited period of time, becoming victims of increasingly intense commercial competition.

The entry of Japan was to prove especially significant in this regard. Yamaha had been manufacturing acoustic musical instruments since 1887, and during the

1960s the company became increasingly interested in the possibilities of electronic sound production. In 1973 Yamaha released its first analog synthesizer, known as the GX1. In commercial terms it was not a marketing success, as it was relatively expensive and users found its facilities cumbersome both to configure and operate. Useful lessons, however, were learned from this venture, and many of its more notable features were successfully reengineered in the CS80, released in 1977 and used extensively by a number of leading artists and groups, including Paul McCartney, the Electric Light Orchestra, and Kraftwerk. Interest at the lower-cost end of the market was also stimulated by two compact and highly portable synthesizers, the SY1 and the SY2 (1976), which offered a more limited choice of analog sounds.

Yamaha faced major competition from other quarters. The Roland Corporation, established in 1972, became the first manufacturer of analog keyboard synthesizers in Japan with the release of the SH-1000. Other models soon emerged from the production line, notably the SH-2000 (1973), the Jupiter-4 (1978), and the Jupiter-8 (1980), which found special favor with groups such as Duran Duran, Tangerine Dream, and Ultravox. Korg, having started as a company producing devices for electronic effects, such as rhythm generators, in the mid-1960s, steadily expanded its activities during the 1970s to embrace both electronic organs and synthesizers. The latter ranged from expensive systems such as the PS-3200 (1978), used by artists such as Jean Michel Jarre and Emerson, Lake, and Palmer, to budget-priced models such as the M500 (1977) and the MS-series, starting with the MS-10 and MS-20 in 1978. The MS-20 proved especially popular as a portable analog synthesizer, its use of patch-chords to interconnect voltage-controlled modules showing a strong affinity with the designs of ARP. Kawai, like Yamaha, started out as a manufacturer of acoustic instruments in 1927, but was also subsequently to diversify into the world of electronics. Trading in the first instance under the name Teisco, the company entered the synthesizer market during the late 1970s, producing a range of small but versatile keyboard models, including the S100P (1979) and the SX400 (1980).

Back in America developments became no less prolific. Two engineering students, Dave Rossum and Scott Wedge, started to design experimental analog synthesizer modules during the late 1960s, designing their first prototype model, the E-mu 25, in 1971. In 1972, they commenced the manufacture of a range of voltage-controlled modules for the growing numbers of individuals keen to assemble synthesizers to their own specifications, and a year later began production of fully assembled modular systems. In 1976, they started a series of pioneering developments based on the Zilog Z80 microprocessor, subsequently used as a control resource for a range of products, including the 4060 polyphonic keyboard and sequencer, released in1977. Although E-mu retained an interest in analog synthesizers producing the Audity Level I in 1977 and the Audity Level II in 1980 these large-scale ventures failed to achieve their commercial potential. Attention turned to a new line of development, leading to their first digital synthesizer, the Emulator I in 1981. This product was an important precursor of the MIDI sampler, and its operational features will be studied more closely in due course.[1] Early users included Stevie Wonder, David Bowie, Genesis, Herbie Hancock, and Philip Glass.

Dave Smith, John Bowen, and Barbara Fairhurst established Sequential Circuits in the mid-1970s. The earliest products consisted of a digital sequencer, known as the Model 800, and some ancillary programming tools, but attention soon turned to the manufacture of synthesizers. The Prophet 5 and Prophet 10, released in 1978, followed by the smaller but extremely versatile Pro-One in 1980, established the company as an influential market leader, attracting such diverse artists as Duran Duran, Peter Gabriel, Genesis, Tangerine Dream, The Who, and Rick Wakeman. Success, however, was not to prove a lasting legacy, for in 1987 the company was taken over by Yamaha, and as a consequence its distinctive range of synthesizers was abruptly discontinued.

Oberheim started out as a manufacturer of peripheral synthesis equipment during the early 1970s, starting with electronic effects units, and proceeding to the production of elementary digital sequencers for larger analog synthesizers, notably the pioneering DS-2. Attention soon turned to the manufacture of modular synthesizer components, in the first instance designing a range of add-on voice modules for existing systems. Known as Synthesizer Expander Modules or SEMs, their success encouraged Oberheim to develop the technology further, packaging various configurations of synthesis and processing modules as self-contained systems such as the Eight Voice (1974) and the OB-1 (1978). Like Sequential, Oberheim was also to suffer from Japanese competition. In 1985, its founder Tom Oberheim was bought out by a consortium, which renamed the company ECC Oberheim, and against the prevailing trend toward all-digital synthesizers continued manufacturing analog synthesizers continued to produce a range of distinctive models, starting with the Matrix-12 (1985).[2]

Competition within the analog synthesizer industry was further intensified when Carmine J. Bonanno, a gifted young electronics engineer with a keen interest in synthesizers, established Voyetra Technologies in 1975, trading as Octave Electronics. Early products such as the Cat (1977) were designed specifically to compete with established entry-level synthesizers such as the Minimoog and the ARP Odyssey, and did much to undermine the market position of these pioneering companies. In 1973 Moog had been bought by a large trading company, known as Norlin, and after several years struggling against the increasing competition ceased production in 1985, leaving Robert Moog free to continue his design activities elsewhere. ARP failed four years earlier, in 1981, for broadly similar reasons.

The marketing strength of Octave was considerably enhanced as a result of a subsequent merger with an electronic repair company in 1979 to form Octave-Plateau Electronics. This new partnership led to the Voyetra Eight, a keyboard synthesizer announced in 1981 and finally released in 1983. Unlike some of its contemporaries, this company was to survive and prosper in the new era of MIDI, but not as it turned out as a manufacturer of synthesizers. In 1986, Voyetra switched from MIDI hardware to the production of MIDI software, developing its product range to become a market leader in what was to prove an important new area of computer-based applications.[3]

This veritable explosion of manufacturing activity highlighted a fundamental drawback of the underlying technology: At the control level, the products of one manufacturer were totally incompatible with those of any other. Attaching a Buchla keyboard to a Moog synthesizer, for example, would result in some quite bizarre results as a result of their very different voltage-to-pitch laws. Matters finally came to a head when manufacturers began to design experimental digital control interfaces at the start of the 1980s. Although connecting unmatched voltage-controlled devices together will usually produce some form of response, any mismatch in a digital system will usually produce no response at all. Prototype systems of this type from this period such as the Key Code System of Yamaha and the SCI Digital Interface of Sequential Circuits were thus totally unable to communicate with each other. Given the growing desire of computer manufacturers to establish common communications standards throughout the industry, such a situation became rapidly untenable.

The idea of establishing an industry-standard digital protocol for connecting synthesizers and associated peripherals together at the control level was first put forward informally at a meeting of the National Association of Music Merchants (NAMM) in the early summer of 1981. This American organization had become an important international forum for the music industry, and its meetings attracted representatives from companies across the world, including most of those specifically involved in the design and manufacture of electronic musical instruments and synthesizers.

The initiative for a universal communications system came from Dave Smith, the president of Sequential Circuits, who persuaded I. Kakehashi from Roland, and Tom Oberheim to participate in a joint feasibility study with Chet Wood, one of his own design engineers. Progress was swift, and within a matter of months Smith was in a position to call a meeting with a larger group of interested manufacturers, which now included Kawai, Korg, and Yamaha. The outcome of discussions was positive and encouraging, and at an Audio and Engineering Society (AES) convention held just a few weeks later Smith and Wood formally presented their proposal for a USI (Universal Synthesizer Interface). Although this constituted little more than an outline description of a protocol to transmit note/event information between synthesizers, it was an important first step.

With the AES presentation the debate finally entered the public arena. A more detailed proposal was presented to a meeting of NAMM in January 1982, attended by representatives from CBS/Rhodes, E-mu, Kawai, Music Technology Inc. (Crumar), Oberheim, Octave Plateau, Passport Designs, Roland, Sequential Circuits,

Syntauri, Unichord (Korg), and Yamaha. Despite some improvements to the engineering specification, the suggested communications protocol was still at this stage restricted to the transmission of basic "on/off" note/event information. A number of companies objected to this limitation on the grounds that any universal protocol should be capable of carrying a far more comprehensive range of data, including information that might be used to configure the synthesis devices themselves. Arguments also developed over the hardware specification for the interface itself, and as a result agreement on an industry standard was only reached in principle, pending further discussions on its precise details.

During the summer of 1982, the initiative passed largely to the Japanese, leaving just Sequential Circuits to represent American interests. The collective enthusiasm of this new grouping of companies quickly paid dividends, and by September the draft of a considerably expanded specification was complete, including the final choice of an acronym, the Musical Instrument Digital Interface, or MIDI. This development was finally announced to the world in the form of an article that appeared in the October edition of the magazine *Keyboard,* written by Robert Moog. This personal seal of approval from such a respected pioneer had a significant impact on the more traditional and generally skeptical sectors of the music industry.

By the end of the year, both Sequential Circuits and Roland were producing synthesizers with MIDI-compatible interfaces, and a demonstration at the January 1983 meeting of NAMM finally persuaded manufacturers that this was a development that had to be taken seriously. The newly formed International MIDI Association published what was to become the definitive MIDI specification, Version 1.0, in the spring of 1983, and by the end of the year most synthesizer manufacturers had started to include a MIDI interface as a standard communications feature.[4]

Although an exhaustive description of MIDI is beyond the scope of this book, a number of its basic features need to be considered here, as they provide important clues to the significance of the protocol for the many systems that rely on its control, in both technical and musical terms. Such has been its impact that it is now very rare to encounter either hardware or software synthesis facilities that do not support or indeed depend on its use. What has changed markedly over the years is the nature of the working relationship between composers and performers and the various functional characteristics of MIDI. This has not come about from any material changes to MIDI itself, but instead the development of higher-level control facilities designed to insulate users from the more mundane aspects of its operation. Whereas these developments are clearly to be welcomed, it is still the case that situations will arise where a more thorough understanding of the underlying technology will prove invaluable in tracing the limitations of MIDI systems, the causes of operational difficulties, and the opportunities that exist for achieving workable solutions.

The expansion of the acronym MIDI is very misleading and has been the cause of much misunderstanding through its use of the word "interface." In computing terms an interface is usually defined as a hardware device that translates one form of data representation into another. By this definition digital-to-analog and analog-to-digital converters are clearly interfaces, as are the various ports fitted to computers to allow communication with external disk drives, printers, or other resources such as the Internet. MIDI requires special hardware interfaces to translate information from one format into another, but the MIDI specification itself is primarily a detailed description of a communications protocol for the transmission and reception of music data. Aside from one or two basic electrical features, the physical design of a MIDI interface and how the information is represented and interpreted internally are matters for individual manufacturers to resolve.

In the case of a digital synthesizer, this interface is merely required to convert data from one digital format into another. An analog synthesizer requires a completely different type of interface, incorporating digital-to-analog and analog-to-digital converters to translate suitable MIDI information into control voltages and vice versa. These so-called retrofit kits proved very popular with owners of older synthesizers from manufacturers such as Moog, Buchla, and ARP, as they neatly circumvent the problems of compatibility discussed earlier.

MIDI is a serial communications protocol, whereby all information is channeled into a single stream of bits, transmitted between devices via a single data cable. A parallel communications system was considered, but this option was rejected on the grounds that the multicore cabling required to transmit information would have proved bulky, relatively expensive, vulnerable to accidental damage, and also particularly susceptible to electrical interference if more than a meter or so in length. Artists were also quick to point out the practicalities of performing live on a stage, not least the requirement to locate synthesizers and keyboards some distance apart. In such situations, a fully screened serial communications network offered the only reliable medium for the transfer of digital information.

There are some important electrical differences between a MIDI system and the more traditional serial communications systems used extensively by the computing industry from the earliest days. Essentially, the former senses interruptions in current flow, whereas the latter usually detects voltage pulses. Conversion from one mode of operation to the other fortunately requires little more than a simple electronic circuit, and it thus has proved relatively straightforward to design basic MIDI interfaces that will work directly with computers. The MIDI specification makes one important stipulation in this context, that optical-isolators must be used on the data lines of all MIDI ports to protect equipment. An optical-isolator is a combination of a light emitting diode that can be switched on and off to represent equivalent binary conditions and a corresponding photoelectric cell that detects these changes. By using light as a buffering mechanism some major electronic problems can be avoided, for example, the unintentional creation of ground loops between equipment, which can sometimes upset digital data, or the accidental transmission of large voltage spikes, which might damage sensitive items of equipment.

There are three types of MIDI port: MIDI IN, MIDI OUT, and MIDI THRU. In each case, the electronic circuitry terminates in a conventional 5-pin DIN socket, allowing the use of screened connecting cables with a DIN plug at either end. Just two pins are required for MIDI transmissions, any radiation being suppressed via a third pin that is used to connect the cable sheathing to earth. As MIDI signals are transmitted in one direction only, the purpose of MIDI IN and MIDI OUT ports is for the most part self-explanatory. Whereas a device that only transmits MIDI signals, for example a simple master keyboard, will only require a MIDI OUT port, many items of equipment such as synthesizers and samplers that both send and receive MIDI signals will require access to both types of ports. Connecting two such devices together to achieve full bidirectional communications thus usually involves just a simple pair of MIDI cables, connecting each MIDI OUT port to the matching MIDI IN port.

More complex configurations require careful planning. At first sight, it might appear that all that is necessary to link three or more synthesizers together is a simple chain of connections, the output port on the last synthesizer being looped back to the input port on the first to complete an entirely circular communications chain. Unfortunately, this arrangement will rarely work, for there is no requirement in the MIDI specification for the MIDI IN port on a device to echo all incoming signals at the MIDI OUT port. Although some devices support this modified mode of operation, others will not, and in the latter circumstances incoming signals intended for a device further down the chain will not be passed on. The onward transmission of such material is the function assigned to the MIDI THRU port, but potential cabling difficulties do not stop here, because a number of cheaper synthesizers have omitted this port altogether on the grounds that it is only classified as optional in the original specification.

In the case of MIDI interfaces for computers, the lack of a THRU port is fortunately far less serious. All modern MIDI software is designed to use the MIDI OUT port in a suitably intelligent fashion, combining any incoming signals for onward transmission with new information generated by the computer itself to form a composite stream of data. Early books on MIDI offered numerous suggestions on how best to connect complex networks of devices together, but there are a number of situations in which an entirely satisfactory solution cannot be found in terms of direct device-to-device cabling. The primary key to solving this configuration difficulty lay in the design of electronically driven MIDI MERGE and MIDI THRU boxes, providing what are in effect programmable digital exchanges for the management of complex interconnections. Over the years these data link devices have become highly sophisticated, often supporting both manual and computer-controlled operation of their routing functions.

The quantity and nature of the data transmitted by MIDI varies significantly according to the context. At the heart of the various categories of MIDI commands lie the codes used to control the performance of a synthesizer, known collectively as channel voice messages. These are used to transmit data for individual note/ events, for example the activation of a voice in a synthesizer in response to a keystroke made on a music keyboard. The "note on" (sometimes referred to as "key on") message consists of three bytes, containing three separate items of information. The first byte, known as the status byte or instruction code, signals the start of a new MIDI message, and also identifies its purpose. The second byte identifies the pitch of the note as a simple numerical value. This value must lie in the range 0 to 127, for MIDI only allows the use of seven bits per byte for the storage of data.

In normal use, each of these numbers is identified with a specific key on an equal tempered keyboard, for example middle C corresponds to a value of 60, and Concert A, nine semitones above, corresponds to a value of 69. Some synthesizers allow this data to be modified internally to produce other temperaments, or transposed up or down a specified number of semitones. While the former facility has some value for playing ancient music and the latter can be a bonus for a keyboard player seeking easy transposition, there are important implications arising from the underlying requirement that all frequency information must be rationalized in terms of fixed pitch specifications. This limitation, for example, is of particular significance for the more demanding composer who may wish to work outside the constraints of the conventional twelve-note system of Western music.

The third byte in a "note on" message is reserved for keyboard velocity information. This function is used to denote the volume level based on the proposition that the faster a key is struck on a conventional keyboard instrument the louder it will sound. It is thus necessary to quantize this velocity as a value in the range 0 to 127. Not all MIDI keyboards can sense this performance characteristic, in which case a default value of 64 is automatically transmitted instead. While this method of dynamic control relates well to traditional keyboard skills associated with instruments such as the piano, the correlation is less obvious when controlling sounds that require continuous regulation of both pitch and dynamics, for example, strings or woodwind. In these circumstances, merely sensing the initial key velocity will provide insufficient information with regard to articulation, necessitating the use of supplementary channel voice messages that may be used for the registration of additional performance characteristics.

Some degree of variable pitch tuning can be achieved by using a three-byte channel voice message known as "pitch bend," which modifies the basic pitch setting in discrete steps. In this case both the second and third bytes are read together as a single item of data, allowing very fine gradations of control with a maximum resolution of fourteen bits (16,384 discrete steps). MIDI does not specify what range of pitch detuning this range of numbers should correspond to, and the usefulness of this feature thus depends very much on the functional characteristics of the specific synthesizer or voice module in terms of possible adjustments to the sensitivity of this control function. Because the usual device for controlling pitch bend is a hand-operated bidirectional wheel, designed to return to its median position as soon as it is released, accurate regulation of pitch variations in this manner can become a highly speculative operation.

Two other channel voice messages, one a more sophisticated version of the other, are provided to allow further modification of the primary "note on" data. Referred to as "key pressure" or "after-touch" messages, these codes allow subsequent changes in key pressure to be transmitted as a sequence of values that may be used to alter pitch or volume settings dynamically. Although this information is clearly useful for adding performance nuances, basic MIDI keyboards are often unable to provide this function. Similarly, many synthesizers will only respond to the simpler of the two messages and most entry-level models cannot respond to either.

The basic "key pressure" message is a single parameter that reflects an average value for all the keys currently depressed. Only two bytes are required, the status byte and a second byte that contains the overall pressure value on a scale from 0 (no pressure) to 127 (maximum pressure). The more elaborate "polyphonic key pressure" message monitors the depression of keys individually. Three bytes are required for this command, a status byte, a second byte containing the note number, and a third byte containing its pressure, once again measured on a scale from 0 to 127. Continuous control functions such as "pitch bend" and "key pressure" considerably increase the amount of MIDI data that has to be transmitted, for they actively sense any change in the device settings and immediately generate an updated message. This situation contrasts sharply with the much lower data rates associated with basic "note on" messages, and—as will be seen later—has some important implications for the overall traffic management of more complex MIDI information.

Because the duration of a note is not transmitted (in a live performance situation this would require knowledge of the future), an equivalent "note off" message has to be sent when the key is released. MIDI allows two means of achieving this. The first method uses a matching three-byte message but with a different status byte that tags it as a "note off" command. The second byte, as before, identifies which note is to be switched off, and the third byte the release velocity to be applied. In many systems the latter information is entirely redundant, although a few synthesizers can use this information to modify the decay of the note's envelope. The second method, which has become the preferred method over the years, simply sends another "note on" message for the note with a velocity of zero.

Two further channel voice messages are provided: "program change" and "control change," concerned respectively with directing the flow of information and the configuration of the hardware. "Program change" is designed to signal to the synthesizer that a different voice is to be selected. Only two bytes are required for this command, a status byte, and a data byte that represents a program (= voice) number in the range 0 to 127. To add an element of confusion, some synthesizer manufacturers automatically add one to this number when interpreting the binary code that is transmitted, so that the messages correspond to actual voice numbers in the range 1 to 128. Furthermore, the interpretation of the program number depends entirely on the configuration of the voices within the synthesizer itself at the time of transmission. Accidental loading of the wrong bank can result in unexpected and quite grotesque results, a situation all too familiar to composers who regularly use sequencing programs to store their works for later performance and then forget to log the precise specifications for the associated voice bank.

The value of this opportunity to choose from up to 128 different voices is tempered slightly by some practical considerations. In particular, many older synthesizers were only able to store a maximum of sixty-four different voices in a voice bank at any one time and some basic models could only manage thirty-two, or as few as sixteen. A further overriding restraint is the fact that a single MIDI routing can only handle a maximum of sixteen different channels of voice data at any one time. Fortunately, in a live performance situation, the ability to change a limited number of voices in a flexible manner is often a more important consideration than the capacity to indulge in orchestral textures that are more extensive than those associated with a late-nineteenth-century symphony or a grand opera. Within the confines of a studio, however, such a limitation can sometimes prove problematic.

As noted earlier, MIDI is a serial communications protocol, requiring all data information to be directed down a single data line. Voice messages intended for two or more separate channels have to be multiplexed together and then extracted correctly as the flow of MIDI information is passed down the chain to the various hardware devices. The key to differentiating between signals for different channels lies in the status byte that introduces each channel voice message. The first four bits in the status byte identify the type of command, and the second four bits identify the channel number. If so desired, channel information can be ignored altogether by receiving (but not transmitting) devices by disabling the internal number filter, in which case all channel voice messages will treated as relevant regardless of their number.

This particular feature forms one of a group of channel mode messages that are embedded as a special set of codes in the "control change" command that is otherwise used to modify the status of key hardware components within a MIDI configuration. The complete command requires three bytes; the usual status byte, a second byte to identify the control device to be altered, and a third byte to specify its new setting. The original MIDI specification identified the assignment of just two control device numbers, 0 and 1, leaving individual manufacturers to determine the designation (if any) of the others. The standard control number for a pitch bend regulator is 0, but this code became redundant with the introduction of the special "pitch bend" channel voice message described earlier. The standard control number for a modulation wheel, a device included in many synthesizers to regulate the amount of vibrato for voice if its synthesis algorithm requires this parameter, is 1.

As to the other control device numbers, many manufacturers have chosen to follow the allocations used by Yamaha, for example, 2 for a breath controller, 4 for an adjustable foot pedal control, 6 for a data entry knob or slider, and 64 for a sustain pedal. The original MIDI specification reserved numbers 0 to 63 for continuous controllers and numbers 64 to 95 for switches, but these designations have been subject to some change over the years. Numbers 91 to 95, for example, are now regularly used for variable control data such as depth of tremolo (92) and chorus effects (93).

Turning to the data itself, in the case of a switching device such as a sustain pedal, only two states need to be recognized, and as a result values in the range 0 to 63 are simply interpreted as "off," and values in the range 64 to 127 as "on." In the case of continuously variable controllers, however, there is an altogether more serious issue to be addressed. The limitation to just one data byte for a device control code severely restricts the attainable accuracy of the associated function. With hindsight, the simplest solution might have been provision of an additional data byte for these values in the message, allowing functions to be represented as 16,384 discrete steps, as is the case with the "pitch bend" channel voice message. Instead, the convention has been to divide up device codes 0 to 63 into pairs, 0 with 32, 1 with 33, and so on. By restricting the logical device numbers for variable controllers to the range 0 to 32, two messages can thus be sent for each higher resolution control change. The data value in the first element of the pair represents the most significant byte and the data value in the second element the least significant byte of a composite fourteen-bit MIDI data value. The requirement to send six bytes for each change of value rather than four is nevertheless an undesirable overhead in terms of data density, especially if a number of controllers are simultaneously active.

Channel numbers 121 to 127 are specially set aside for the channel mode messages. In ascending order their designations are as follows: "reset all controls," "local control," "all notes off," "omni mode off," "omni mode on," "mono mode on," and "poly mode on." As in the case of channel voice messages the same three-byte format is used, although only "local control" and "mono mode on" require use of the third byte to convey associated data values. The mode commands "reset all controls" and "all notes off" are self-explanatory. "Local control" affects the relationship between a keyboard and the associated voice banks in a synthesizer where both components are physically part of the same design. As in the case of the device control codes for switches, if the third byte contains a value of between 64 and 127, "local control" is switched on. In this operational mode the keyboard will drive both the internal voices and also any external devices that have been connected by MIDI to the appropriate channel. If instead the third byte contains a value between 0 and 63 local control is switched off, in which case MIDI information is still transmitted to external devices but the connection from the keyboard to all internal voices is disabled.

"Omni off" and "omni on" are the channel mode commands that determine whether a synthesizer voice will recognize a single designated channel message, or instead recognize all voice messages regardless of their channel number. The "mono mode on" and "poly mode on" commands determine whether a voice is to be monophonic, or polyphonic up to the maximum number of notes the hardware will allow to be generated simultaneously (typically eight , sixteen, or thirty-two). If two or more notes are activated simultaneously in the former mode, only one will actually appear at the output, usually the highest in terms of MIDI pitch value. If the third byte of the "mono mode on" command is set to zero then alternate transmission of the "mono" and "poly" messages will simply switch all the voices on all channels between the two modes. If the third byte of the "mono mode command" is non-zero, however, its numerical value will signal how many channels, numbered in ascending order from channel 1, will be set to mono, the prevailing status of the other channels remaining unaltered.

The possible combinations of the above commands are rationalized as four standard operating modes that are defined as follows: MODE 1; "omni on/poly," MODE 2; "omni on/mono," MODE 3; "omni off/poly," and MODE 4; "omni off/mono." MODE 1 is the default mode that every item of MIDI hardware should support. MODE 2 is particularly applicable to voltage-controlled synthesizers that have been retrofitted with MIDI, as they are generally only capable of generating monophonic sounds and lack the additional hardware necessary to decode information for different channels. MODE 3 is potentially the most powerful, because it allows polyphonic operation of up to sixteen different voices, each controlled on a different channel. MODE 4 is essentially a monophonic version of MODE 3 for use with solo voices on individual channels.

It is clear from the above discussion a considerable amount of MIDI information can be generated and transmitted in certain performance conditions. It has been shown that the registration of even a single note requires a minimum of six bytes of information, three to switch it on and three to switch it off. Although the basic sequence of "note on" and "note off" messages required to generate a slow monophonic melody will be relatively modest, the density of traffic will increase substantially if any active sensing channel commands such as key pressure are used to refine the pitch or amplitude characteristics. Playing notes faster will increase the data flow, as will the transmission of polyphonic, as opposed to monophonic data. Under extreme conditions the density of traffic can indeed increase to the point where MIDI itself reaches its operational limit. What then happens is a situation similar to a traffic jam, with delays in transmission as channel commands are forced to queue. This condition is sometimes referred to as "MIDI choke." Once these delays begin to exceed about 50 to 100 milliseconds the ear may well become aware of a lack of precision when an attempt is made to activate large clusters of notes on several channels simultaneously. To understand the nature and extent of this problem it is necessary to look more closely at the electronic specification of MIDI.

During the early 1980s, the standard operating speeds for serial transmission between computers and peripheral devices such as printers and VDUs were still relatively slow. The origins of this data communications mode go back to the early 1950s when manufacturers began to tackle the problems of connecting keyboard terminals to computers in situations demanding the use of significant lengths of cabling. The earliest operating speeds were very modest, typically 110 bits of digital information per second (110 baud), sufficient to drive standard mechanical teletypewriters at about 11 characters per second. With the advent of more modern terminals the need arose for higher speeds of transmission. 300 baud soon replaced 110 baud as an option, and in due course successively higher multiples became possible, starting with 1200 baud. By the time MIDI was first being discussed, 9600 baud had become the normal maximum baud rate for serial communications, and the next highest multiple, 19200 baud, was about to be implemented.

Although synthesizer manufacturers could only guess what densities of control information might be demanded in the future, they deduced correctly that even a transmission rate of 19200 baud was likely to prove too slow for the flow of control data in some circumstances. Present-day users of the Internet via conventional telephone links will still be only too aware of the limitations of serial modems when accessing large quantities of data, even when operated at relatively high rates such as 56000 baud.[5] In the event, the Committee preparing the specification of MIDI chose a fixed speed of 31250 baud for all control applications, which happens to be an exact division (1/32nd) of 1 Megahertz, the basic clock speed used by many first-generation microprocessors.

Each byte of MIDI information consists of eight bits, the first bit being used as a flag to indicate whether or not the byte is a status byte (set to 1), or a data byte (set to 0). This explains why only seven bits can be used for data in a single byte, and fourteen bits for data in a double byte, representing a total of 128 and 16,384 integers, respectively. In transmission terms, however, each MIDI byte requires ten bits, since both a start bit and a stop bit are added to allow for error checking. At a rate of 31250 baud, therefore, a maximum of 3125 bytes of MIDI information can be transmitted per second, or, viewed another way, a typical three-byte channel voice message takes about 1 millisecond to complete. Because all MIDI data has to be multiplexed as a single data stream, it can now be seen how the margin between detectable and nondetectable delays in response is of some significance, this boundary lying theoretically somewhere between 50 and 100 supposedly simultaneous messages.

When the continuous flow of data from active sensing devices is taken into account, it becomes clear that saturation of the transmission line is more than just a possibility. In practice, electrical considerations such as the internal buffering of MIDI messages and the physical routing of the MIDI cables will also add to the delays that are likely to occur. Fortunately, the introduction of MIDI signal merging and splitting devices has helped considerably to minimize the effects of latency in larger networks.

In addition to the basic channel messages described here, MIDI provides an additional set of commands known as system messages, used to send global information to the system as a whole. One in particular, known as a "system exclusive" message, holds the key to what has proved to be one of MIDI's most powerful features. By means of just a single status command it is possible to switch to a special mode of operation that allows the transfer information of any type from one device to another. The only basic requirement is strict adherence to the MIDI data format, which as already noted prohibits any use of the highest order bit in each byte for any data. The primary purpose of this mode is to provide individual synthesizer manufacturers with a facility for transmitting their own special system set-up messages between devices via MIDI, for example, the detailed specifications of voice algorithms.

Each participating manufacturer is allocated a special version of the two-byte command, the first byte containing the standard "system exclusive," status byte and the second byte a unique identifying number. This message ensures that other devices do not erroneously intercept the ensuing data flow. Once this command has been issued, the manufacturer is entirely responsible for determining the use of the data bytes that follow, with no restriction as to the number of bytes actually transmitted. This mode remains in force until the status byte of any other MIDI command is transmitted, at which point normal MIDI operation is resumed.

Perhaps the most unexpected use of "system exclusive" mode has been as a communications channel for transferring audio samples between synthesis devices. It is particularly unfortunate in this respect that MIDI limits data to seven bits per byte, for as a result eight-bit sound samples require two bytes instead of one, and sixteen-bit samples three bytes instead of two, introducing a significant element of redundancy into the transmission process. As will be seen in due course, much faster interfaces subsequently became available for the transfer of digital audio data from one item of MIDI equipment to another. This special use of MIDI, however, provided a basic solution to a difficult communications problem encountered with early digital samplers.[6] As sampling techniques gained in popularity, it was quickly recognized that without any established guidelines audio information would be transmitted in a variety of incompatible formats. To overcome this, the Sample Dump Standard or SDS was introduced in 1986, imposing a strict set of rules for the coding and transmission of audio data files.

A number of other system messages are available, principally concerned with the transmission and synchronization of timing information. In live performance, such information is not generally required, as each new event is manually activated by an action such as depressing a new key. If, however, the sequence of commands thus generated is to be recorded digitally for subsequent replay, then timing information has also to be registered. In the case of a MIDI system serviced by a single sequencer, all timing information can be generated internally by the latter device and it is not necessary to access the MIDI clock. When two or more sequencers are to be used together synchronization is only possible using a common clock counter, in which case the simplest solution is to use MIDI timing messages that have been specially developed for this purpose. The most fundamental of these is the MIDI SYNC message, which consists of a special status byte transmitted twenty-four times per quarter-note. More sophisticated sequencers subdivide this message by a factor of twenty to produce a much finer resolution of 480 timing points per quarter-note.

Timing information is also important whenever MIDI devices are used with other equipment that uses different synchronization facilities. The most common code to be encountered in this context is SMPTE, an acronym for the Society of Motion PicTure Engineers, developed in 1967 for the synchronization of video and audio information, and still widely used in the recording industry. Here time is measured in terms of "frames per second," necessitating a conversion facility if standard MIDI time codes are to be translated into SMPTE, and vice versa. To assist in this process, in 1987 MIDI adopted an alternative timing protocol known as MIDI Time Code, or MTC, with a new set of messages that recognize the use of SMPTE frames per second as a unit of time. Here each SMPTE frame is associated with four frames of MTC, the MIDI information being updated on average 120 times per second.

Apart from the above additions and some relatively minor modifications MIDI has hardly altered from its original specification. Perhaps the biggest cause of contention has been the fixed rate of 32150 baud, which by modern transmission standards for networked devices is exceedingly slow. Reference has already been made to the consequences of overloading MIDI, and even when sophisticated routing facilities are deployed opportunities still abound for data bottlenecks and consequential timing delays. Over the years, a number of attempts have been made to raise the speed of MIDI, but such has been the investment in synthesizer technology engineered to the current standard that at the time of writing none of these ventures has yet succeeded in convincing the industry as a whole. Perhaps the closest to achieving a possible success has been the ZIPI protocol, devised by Keith McMillen, David Wessel and Matthew Wright during the early 1990s, and first presented to the public in 1993. This was not so much an enhancement for MIDI but in effect a complete replacement, incorporating not only much higher transmission speeds but also an extended protocol for handling more sophisticated data control information. Manufacturers, however, have shown little interest in pursuing such initiatives, and the future of MIDI seems well assured.

Possibly the most significant enhancement of MIDI from the users' points of view has been the introduction of a General MIDI specification for voice alloca-tion. Prior to this initiative relatively little thought had been given to any form of general conventions in this context. As a result, the allocation of voice types, even in the most general of contexts, to specific voice numbers in a standard 128 ele-ment bank differed significantly from one manufacturer to another. In perform-ance situations, this can result in serious problems if it becomes necessary to sub-stitute one synthesizer with that of another manufacturer, especially where voice allocations have been preprogrammed into sequencing software.

Initial proposals for a General MIDI standard were not greeted with much en-thusiasm by a number of manufacturers, who could see no reason to reengineer the configuration of their own banks simply to comply with such a specification. The Music Manufacturers Association (MMA), the controlling body for the syn-thesizer industry, nonetheless agreed to adopt a generic format in 1991, known as General MIDI Level 1. Roland immediately responded with its own version, known as GS, and in 1995 Yamaha followed suit with a version known as XG. The underlying significance of General MIDI, however, was not seriously undermined by these breakaway developments, as both versions were designed as extensions to the basic format, albeit specific to the manufacturers' own products. The pur-pose of General MIDI is not so much to proscribe the inner characteristics of in-dividual instrumental sounds so that all synthesizers will sound exactly the same, but to provide instrumental families, and constituent members thereof that offer reasonable coherence in terms of voice typologies from one manufacturer to an-other. In 1999, General MIDI 2 was launched, offering a number of extensions both to the repertory of sounds and also the range of control facilities available for voice editing and performance.

MIDI is best suited as a control protocol for more popular genres of music, which although extensive in scope are by no means representative of the electronic medium as a whole. Given the success of MIDI as the universal standard for the medium, however, even designers of more specialist systems at the frontiers of technical and musical research have come to realize the importance of providing interfaces to accommodate this universal means of data communication. Having thus traced the early development of the microcomputer and the evolution of digi-tal synthesis techniques up to the birth of MIDI the stage is now set for a study of the MIDI-based products that followed.

From Analog to Digital:
The Evolution of MIDI Hardware

The Pioneering Phase, to 1983

In discussing the circumstances that led to the birth of the MIDI communications protocol a number of key features were identified concerning the concurrent state of the manufacturing sector. By 1980 innovative products such as the Synclavier and the Fairlight had signaled the dawn of a new era of digital hardware, but the full impact of such developments was still only being felt at the high cost end of the market. The core of the synthesizer industry was still dominated by architectures based upon voltage control technology. The necessary conditions for change were nevertheless being fostered by an expanding group of manufacturers, progressively and successfully undermining the market share of pioneering companies such as Moog and Buchla. This increase in competition led to a fundamental reappraisal of the technologies available for developing synthesis and signal processing hardware. The key initiative in terms of low cost digital technology was to come unexpectedly from a new entrant to the synthesizer market.

In 1981 the Japanese electronics manufacturer Casio launched a miniature all-digital synthesizer known as the VL-1, costing less than $100. This consists of a tiny keyboard of just over two octaves, a bank of five voices controlled by a set of pushbuttons, a one-hundred-note sequencer, and a rhythm unit offering a choice of ten different patterns. Some commentators dismissed the VL-1 as little more than a mass-produced toy, citing the rudimentary nature of the synthesis facilities and the limited audio fidelity. Others, however, quickly came to realize the underlying significance of a system that embodied the essential elements of a programmable digital music synthesizer for little more than the price of an upmarket scientific calculator. It is interesting to note in this context that by far the greatest proportion of the manufacturing costs of the VL-1 were associated with ancillary items such as the case, the keyboard, and the pushbuttons. All the synthesis processes are carried out via a single, specially fabricated microchip, using the same VLSI technology used to design microprocessors.

The VL-1 provided a major stimulus to two other manufacturing sectors with broadly similar interests. The first of these concentrated on the design of basic electronic keyboards, products that use an electronic means of sound production but are specifically engineered to function as simple instruments with a fixed repertory of voices. The second provided sound resources for a rapidly developing video games market, characterized by products that ranged from self-contained systems, complete with control paddles plugged directly into the aerial socket of a domestic television, to sophisticated arcade machines designed for the purposes of gambling. All three sectors became linked by a common mission to develop low-cost, high-performance sound chips offering a range of functional characteristics from sound effects to a programmable repertory of musical timbres.

Inspired by the success of the VL-1, Casio launched the CT series of digital synthesizers early in 1982, starting with the CT-701. Although these products were still targeted specifically at the low-cost end of the market, the relative sophistication of their resources posed a serious challenge to traditional analog designs. The original CT-701, for example, provided a five-octave keyboard, twenty preset voices, a rhythm box, and a sequencer. Moreover, it was polyphonic, allowing up to eight notes to be generated simultaneously, and also incorporated a light-pen facility for reading in music information from scores previously transcribed into a bar code format, using strips similar to those used to mark goods in a supermarket. Although this input method could only be used with specially precoded scores provided with the synthesizer, it clearly demonstrated the potential of a music data input technique that uses digital rather than analog technology.

Yamaha's first steps into the digital arena were in 1981, with the launch of the GS1 and GS2 synthesizers. These were relatively expensive products (the GS1 cost as much as a small Synclavier), but they served as important prototypes for the highly successful and influential DX series of all-digital MIDI synthesizers that were to follow. Strictly speaking, the GS synthesizers are of a hybrid construction, as analog circuits are used extensively for the last stages of synthesis to modify the tone quality by means of filtering and tremolo or chorus effects. The heart of the voice generation system nonetheless is entirely digital, and the design of this section merits closer scrutiny.

The complex arrays of chips and wiring interconnections to be found inside the GS1 and GS2 give a clue as to the experimental nature of these products. They were constructed to look outwardly like small grand pianos, the hammers, strings, and sound board section being replaced by a network of electronic circuits. The quantity of individual components used in these synthesizers and the generous layout of the circuit boards themselves indicates clearly that Yamaha's own development of VLSI chip technology was still at a relatively early stage. Nonetheless, these products offered the company a valuable opportunity to obtain useful feedback from customers concerning the strengths and weaknesses of this new approach to synthesizer design before fabricating circuits fully in silicon for the purposes of mass-production.

As regards the digital circuits themselves, a significant feature is the use of frequency modulation techniques to generate timbres rather than conventional additive methods. Yamaha had the foresight to patent a series of hardware algorithms for FM synthesis, thus effectively preventing any other manufacturer from developing rival FM systems. As noted earlier, this manufacturer had established close links with Stanford University, leading to a long and fruitful partnership with John Chowning and his associates.[1] This linking of advanced institutional research and commercial expertise for the mass-production of new musical products was to reap rich rewards for the company.

Although the implementation of Chowning's FM techniques in the GS1 and GS2 was far simpler than that subsequently adopted for the DX series, these early keyboard synthesizers clearly demonstrated the power and versatility of such algorithms as a method for generating a range of musical sounds. Furthermore, the instantaneous response of the specially designed hardware contrasted sharply with the non-real-time environment of most software-based computer music systems at this time. As products of a pre-MIDI era, however, with no facilities for directly accessing synthesis algorithms or performance data, the scope for experimentation beyond the factory-supplied preset voices was very limited.

Many of these functional restrictions were eliminated in the design of the DX series of synthesizers, launched in 1983. In contrast to the earlier GS models, these are compact, portable, and—most important—based on the MIDI control environment. The initial product range was entirely keyboard-based, the flagship DX7 providing the point of reference for a number of derivatives. These ranged from the large DX1 (essentially two DX7s combined as a single unit) providing thirty-two voices, to the entry level DX21 offering just eight voices, these differences of scale also being reflected in the number and sophistication of the FM algorithms provided. The latter may be programmed either directly in the manner described later or indirectly using a MIDI-based voice-editing program hosted on an associated microcomputer.[2]

Other models include voice-only systems such as the TX816 and TX802, designed for remote operation via MIDI either from a master keyboard such as the Yamaha KX88 or another keyboard synthesizer such as a DX7. Whereas the functional characteristics of a TX802 correspond closely to those offered by a single DX7 the TX816 is an altogether more powerful device, consisting of eight DX7 voice modules mounted in a single rack.

In terms of marketing strategies, the DX7 series, like many of the new generation of MIDI synthesizers, was targeted at a broad spectrum of potential users, from the pop and rock sector and educational users to the burgeoning domestic market. Prominent users of the DX7 have included Genesis, Kraftwerk, Brian Eno, Enya, Herbie Hancock, U2, Underworld, and Stevie Wonder.

The sound generation system for each voice in a DX7 consists of six oscillators that can be arranged in different configurations by selecting from a table of thirty-two basic algorithms. One algorithm specially configures all the generators as a parallel bank of six individually programmable audio oscillators, the outputs being directly mixed to produce a simple blend of timbres in an additive manner without any frequency modulation. The other algorithms comprise a mixture of parallel and serial connections, in some instances creating a sequence of three or even four oscillators within a single FM chain. These carefully researched extensions of the basic two-oscillator FM principle greatly expanded the variety of timbres that can be generated by this means. A further enhancement consists of a feedback facility for one of the oscillators, which can be used to introduce an element of resonance to the sound.

Considerable thought was given to facilities for controlling the frequency and amplitude settings for each oscillator. Because a fundamental characteristic of most synthesizer voices is a distinctive timbre that will transpose consistently up or down in pitch, the basic frequency settings for each oscillator are normally specified in the form of ratios of the chosen key selection. These can either be limited to simple multiples or submultiples to create spectra that are related harmonically or include fractional ratios to create more complex sounds. Alternatively, the oscillators can be individually assigned a specific fixed frequency value that is retained regardless of the key selection. Suitable combinations of fixed and frequency mode oscillators for the various algorithms may then be used to introduce a variety of effects, for example, timbres that vary according to the key selection or include a range of noiselike components.

The provision of separate envelope generators for each oscillator allows for considerable flexibility in determining the evolution of both timbre and volume. Additional function generators permit other characteristics to be superimposed on the resulting sound such as frequency or amplitude vibrato. The specifications for up to thirty-two different sounds are stored in the internal voice bank of the synthesizer (expanded to sixty-four in later versions), this information being loaded either from a special plug-in cartridge or input from an external source using MIDI in its "system exclusive" mode.[3] The internal bank provides the primary working area for voice development and performance, a battery backup ensuring that the information is not lost whenever the synthesizer is switched off. A library of 128 factory-produced voices can be accessed via a special ROM cartridge and erasable RAM cartridges are available for the storage of user-defined voices.

The general performance characteristics of the DX7 are further extended by the availability of keyboard sensing circuitry that takes advantage of the special options offered by MIDI in this regard. These include the ability to measure the velocity with which individual keys are depressed. This information may be used to modify the amplitude settings of selected oscillators to varying degrees, thus providing a powerful tool for controlling both the amplitude and the timbre of FM sounds in performance. In addition, the pressure exerted on individual keys after the initial stroke can be actively sensed and used to modify a selection of control settings. This facility is very useful for generating the subtle pitch variations that are associated with key actions on an acoustic instrument such as the clavichord, or for introducing a variable pitch or amplitude vibrato. Another enhancement consists of a comprehensive range of micro-tuning facilities to create different scaling systems as locally applied modifications to the standard equal temperament scaling of the standard MIDI pitch codes.

In the case of the early DX synthesizers only one voice can be active at a time. Later versions, such as the DX7 Mark II launched in 1985, allow two voices to be active to expand the timbre-generating possibilities of the system. In this model the user has the option either of mixing the two output signals together to create a blend or splitting the voices so that one voice responds to notes below a selected breakpoint on the keyboard and the other to notes above. Other enhancements include facilities for panning the voices stereophonically across two output channels and independent control of locally applied modifications such as the transposition of pitch data up or down by a specified number of semitone steps. Yamaha also produced an enhanced version of this synthesizer that incorporates a floppy disk unit for the storage of data, a useful alternative to the plug-in RAM cartridge.

Direct voice editing may be carried out using the alphanumeric display screen, a data entry slider, and a series of pushbuttons, many of which have a dual function as voice selection buttons when the synthesizer is used in performance mode. Here the problems to be faced by many manufacturers in devising screen-based editing facilities for digital synthesizers are clearly illustrated. On the original DX7 the display is so small that only one control parameter can be viewed at a time. Although the control panel is well organized and relatively simple to operate, with the effects of any alterations instantly audible, the inability to cross-reference other parameter settings at the same time or to view envelope functions graphically is a major practical drawback. The enlarged display facilities provided for the DX7

Mark II were a marked improvement, because they allow a number of related parameters to be viewed at a time, but they still lacked any graphics capabilities for the display of key functions such as the characteristics of an envelope shaper

Attention has already been drawn to the acoustical deficiencies that can result from inadequate sampling rates, too few bits to represent each sample, and shortcomings in the synthesis process itself. When compared with all-digital products of the same era, from the Mark II Synclavier to more modest systems based on the Mountain Computer boards, the perceived audio quality of the DX7 is as impressive as the versatility of its operation. Although its full technical specification has never been officially disclosed external measurements by a number of independent reviewers have generally confirmed the generally favorable verdict of such subjective assessments. It appears, for example, that the original DX7 achieves noise and distortion figures comparable to those associated with a twelve-bit sampling standard, a frequency response in the order of 18 kHz, and a purity of waveform generation that matches that of well-designed interpolating wave-table oscillators. Although the technical specifications of more basic members of the DX range of synthesizers reveal some design economies, the audio characteristics of later versions such as the DX7 Mark II approach those associated with the compact disc player.

The launch of such a high quality all-digital product in 1983 was an important landmark, not only for its inclusion of MIDI but also in finally establishing the credibility of digital rather than analog methods of synthesizer design at the very heart of the industry. Although today synthesizers of this vintage are more likely to be found in a museum than in active use on stage or in the studio, the particular importance of the DX7 in launching the era of the MIDI synthesizer must not be underestimated. Indeed, the Yamaha FM patents proved remarkably effective in restraining direct commercial competition for a number of years. As a result, other manufacturers were forced to turn to alternative synthesis methods for the development of competitive products.

The Development of the MIDI Sampler

A fundamental disadvantage of most conventional synthesis methods, including that of frequency modulation, is the lack of any direct connection with the natural sound world, and the processes of acoustic sound production. In due course, reference will be made to digital synthesis techniques that are modeled directly on acoustic principles, but back in the 1980s the most obvious solution for many manufacturers lay in the design of systems that capture and manipulate the characteristics of the natural sound world itself.

Fairlight had already pioneered the technique of digital sampling in 1979. Nonetheless, the high costs of the associated technology in terms of memory requirements and data processing power were significant obstacles to further development. A major breakthrough, however, occurred only two years later with the launch of the Emulator I by E-mu. Although still a relatively expensive product, this innovative device was only about a quarter of the price of a Fairlight.

The operational heart of the Emulator I consists of a Z-80 microprocessor, operating software permanently stored in ROM, and an associated 120 kilobytes of memory for the storage of sound samples, accessed by voice modules that allow the generation of polyphonic textures containing up to eight notes. Although the analog-to-digital and digital-to-analog converters only provide eight-bit resolution, special circuitry was incorporated to compress the dynamic range of sound material on the input side, and expand it again on the output. As noted in the earlier discussion of digital audio, such a nonlinear method of sampling and internal data compression introduces the possibility of data modifications, that may in some circumstances cause audible distortion.[4] From a commercial point of view, however, this drawback was considered less important than the considerable savings in costs resulting from a reduced memory requirement, and the benefits of an enhanced dynamic range approaching that of a conventional twelve-bit sampling system.

The sampling rate is fixed at 30 kHz, only slightly below the 32 kHz maximum used by the original Fairlight, but the low-pass filters in the Emulator restrict the effective bandwidth to just 10 kHz, which is well below the Nyquist frequency (15 kHz). Eight kilobytes of the 128K memory are reserved for the operating, leaving 120 kilobytes free for the storage of sound samples, normally divided equally to allow two different sounds to be resident at a time. Each sound in this format occupies a maximum of 60 kilobytes, one allocated to the upper two octaves and the other to the lower two octaves of the four-octave keyboard. At a sampling rate of 30 kHz, this restricts the maximum length of each sound to only 2 seconds, illustrating how critical the factor of memory size becomes when evaluating the functional characteristics of a sampler.

The original Fairlight suffered particularly badly in this respect, only permitting sounds with a maximum duration of 1.2 seconds to be sampled at maximum fidelity. The solution here was the inclusion of a facility to sample at lower rates whenever the duration of the sound is of overriding importance. Unfortunately, lowering the sampling rate also reduces the maximum attainable bandwidth in direct proportion, with potentially devastating consequences for the audio fidelity, especially if the source happens to be a sound with a rich timbre. Much care was therefore required in such instances, balancing the benefits of extra sampling time with the consequences for the resulting bandwidth.

The choice of sampling rate provides only an initial point of reference for assessing the performance characteristics of a sampler. How this information is then reproduced at different pitches is equally critical. A common practice in early designs involved varying the rate at which the voice modules read the sample data, for example, doubling the rate for output one octave higher and halving the rate for output one octave lower. Suitable divisions and multiples thereof will then produce the equal-tempered frequency steps required for a conventional music keyboard. As the basic bit-pattern of the sound is preserved throughout these processes of data extraction, no additional degradation in quality will normally occur when the material is resynthesized.

The principle disadvantage of this methodology is the need to supply individual digital-to-analog converters for each voice in a polyphonic texture, adding considerably to the overall manufacturing costs. An alternative approach that soon became the rule rather than the exception involves the use of a resampling algorithm to produce an equivalent pattern of samples, but converted to a fixed sampling rate.[5] Under these conditions, all the constituent sound components may be digitally added together to produce a composite function for output via a single digital-to analog converter, or in the case of a stereo format via a pair of converters.

Although the specific technical details of these internal design features are usually of little interest to the user, the subjective effects of such transpositions are highly significant, because they involve processes essentially no different to those associated with varying the speed of a conventional tape recording. Changes in pitch effected by these basic methods result in proportional changes in prominent characteristics such as the attack and decay times, and other time-varying features such as vibrato will be similarly modified. In the case of the Emulator I, the effects of excessive transposition can be minimized by using an optional multisampling facility that allows the memory to be partitioned into eight segments instead of simply two, each assigned to a specific half-octave of keys. If the sound source is an instrument such as a piano, a reasonable consistency of timbre can indeed be achieved by sampling notes at eight different pitches, suitably spaced half an octave apart. Unfortunately, a price has to be paid in terms of the memory available for the individual samples, with a maximum average duration of 0.5 seconds in this particular context. An alternative use of this partitioning facility involves sampling a different sound for each group of keys to create a structured set of textures or a set of individual instruments such as the components of a small percussion kit.

Sampling sounds at one pitch for reproduction at a number of different pitches is a technique employed by all samplers to varying degrees, and one important measure of their overall versatility is the number of different voices and samples that can be handled at any one time. Another is the capacity to edit and process sampled sounds before using them as voices for resynthesis. Modern samplers with large memories are capable of a variety of sophisticated editing procedures such as the reordering of user-defined sound segments in memory or the dynamic blending of two different sounds to create a new composite sound, that can sometimes be resampled for yet further processing.

Early non-MIDI samplers, such as the Emulator I, were usually restricted to features such as a simple looping facility to allow the sound to be artificially sustained for shaping via a simple envelope. Designing a good looping system is no easy task, because some sounds are not amenable to such a technique. The basic process starts with the selection of suitable start and end points for a loop within the time span of the sampled sound. The sampler is then programmed to read through the sound samples until the end point is encountered, at which point the sample pointer jumps back to the starting point for the loop and commences a second pass through the intervening samples. Depending on the setting of any associated envelope function the sound either: (1) terminates abruptly at this point, (2) continues through the remaining portion of the sample, or (3) simply continues to recycle through the loop until the envelope has completed its decay segment. More sophisticated samplers allow two or more loop segments to be created, with the possibility of selecting one segment as the primary sustain loop, linked to a fixed number of repeats of the others.

The greatest problem encountered in creating smooth loops concerns the breakpoint in the loop itself. Any discontinuity in the waveform will result in an audible click and it is thus very important to be able to move either the start or the end point of the loop segment sample by sample until the smoothest possible transition is achieved. All but the most basic architectures offer an automatic detection process, whereby the sampler itself seeks what it considers to be a suitable loop point. Although such a facility can sometimes prove very effective, it cannot always be relied on to achieve the best possible results in every situation. Wherever such a failure occurs it becomes necessary to override the automatic looping facility and make fine adjustments to the parameters manually, an option that is unfortunately not supported by every commercial MIDI sampler.

There is a further factor to be taken into account, for even the smoothest join will not remove the subjective effects of any significant differences in the nature of the sound material either side of the loop. The smallest change in overall amplitude of the sound between the start and end points can readily result in audible discontinuities and any step change in pitch and/or timbre is likely to be even more noticeable. Such problems are well known to those familiar with tape looping procedures, where a satisfactory solution can sometimes be effected by joining the ends of the loop together with a long diagonal splice, thus creating a physically engineered transition rather than a direct cut. The majority of samplers offer an electronic means of cross fading in a similar manner, but even the most sophisticated techniques currently available cannot fully overcome any significant discontinuities either side of the breakpoint.

Facilities to superimpose basic attack and decay characteristics and other modulation characteristics on recorded sounds to create new envelopes are very desirable, as they allow sound sources to be dynamically shaped in a consistent manner, regardless of their transposition. To this end, the Emulator I provides an adjustable three-stage attack/sustain/delay envelope shaper, augmented by a number of ancillary performance aids. The latter include a pair of modulation wheels to bend the pitch and introduce varying degrees of vibrato, a variable low-pass filter, and a special foot-pedal switch. This allows notes played in the lower half of the keyboard to be automatically doubled by corresponding notes in the upper half of the range.

The use of volatile RAM memory by a conventional sampler necessitates the provision of auxiliary data storage facilities both for the storage and retrieval of sampled sounds and also the system software required to operate the sampler. In the case of the latter, some manufacturers permanently encode this information in ROM, supplying any subsequent upgrades to registered users in the form of a conventional software program update that has to be loaded from a floppy disk every time the sampler is switched on. More sophisticated designs use Flash ROMs or EPROMs (Erasable Programmable Read Only Memory). These are special nonvolatile memory chips that can be specially reprogrammed by the user when new software releases become available.

Because the system software has to be resident in memory when the sampler is in use, its presence will reduce the amount of memory available for the samples themselves. In the early 1980s, these losses could be fairly significant, and a cause of discrepancies between the theoretical and the actual capacity of otherwise identical sampler specifications. It will be recalled, for example, that 8 K of the 128 K memory of the Emulator I was required for system software, more than 6 percent of the overall memory capacity. Fortunately, as sampler memory banks progressively increased in size the impact of this requirement steadily reduced, and by the end of the decade the effects on sampling capacity had become negligible.

One other issue, which still has yet to be fully resolved, concerns the compatibility of data formats for sampled sounds and their associated control parameters. Here manufacturers have been particularly concerned to protect their commercial interests by developing special formats to inhibit the transfer of propriety samples to other machines. In due course, software developers were to find partial solutions to such difficulties by writing sample conversion programs, albeit with a potential loss of some fidelity, but this continuing lack of a universally accepted format remains a major impediment to the exchange of sampled sounds from one architecture to another.

The storage capacity of floppy disks was to prove critical in constraining the functionality of early samplers such as the Emulator I, where each basic 2-second sound sample requires 60 kilobytes of storage space. In the case of a modern sampler sampling at the compact disc standard of $44,100 \times 16$ bit samples per second in stereo rather than mono, the same 2 seconds of sampled sound requires 176.4 kilobytes. Early 5.25" floppy disks, including the type used in the Emulator I, recorded at a low density and only made use of one side of the magnetic media. As a result, the maximum data capacity was little more than about 180 kilobytes. As the technology improved double-sided drives and higher recording densities were introduced, leading eventually to the modern 3.5" standard, offering data capacities of up to 1440 kilobytes (1.44 megabytes). Such disks, however, can still only store about 8 seconds of CD quality sound unless some form of electronic data compression is used, and the requirement for alternative facilities with much higher storage capacities thus becomes self-evident. This issue will be returned to in due course.

As a product dating from 1981, the Emulator I sampler predates the MIDI era, and therefore lacks the control facilities of a modern MIDI sampler. Although the original model made no provision for recording the performance of events either internally or externally, a special nine-hundred-note sequencer section was introduced in 1982 as an upgrade, creating a versatile and entirely self-contained system for both composition and performance.

The flexibility of the Emulator in the latter context focuses attention on a fundamental set of issues that needs to be revisited at this point. In considering the evolution of the medium as a whole it has become clear that the breadth of creative applications served by the emerging technologies over the years is remarkably broad. At one end of the spectrum, a lineage can be traced from the early electronic musical instruments of the 1920s and 1930s to what is now a formidable array of modern equivalents. These are for the most part keyboard-based, and designed specifically to imitate as realistically as possible the sounds of conventional musical instruments via a series of preset voices. At the other end of the spectrum, a desire to explore the potential of sound worlds beyond those associated with the natural acoustic environment opened up new horizons of opportunity for the serious composer, supported by an increasingly sophisticated set of resources for synthesis and signal processing. In providing a means of capturing and resynthesizing material of acoustic origin, it soon became clear that sampling technology was well suited to both areas of application. As a result, a parallel line of development to that targeted by the Emulator was soon established, concerned in the first instance with purely imitative applications.

In 1983, Kurzweil Music Systems, originally founded by Raymond Kurzweil to manufacture a text scanning and voice synthesis system for the visually impaired, responded to a challenge from Stevie Wonder to produce a keyboard synthesizer that could accurately reproduce to order the sounds of acoustic instruments. The resulting product, the Kurzweil 250, was released in early 1984 as an upmarket sampling keyboard, offering the performer a completely fixed repertory of sounds. The realism of these reproductions posed a major challenge to the designers of rival instruments based on all-electronic waveform generation techniques. Within two years the architecture of the Kurzweil also had been modified to provide a more flexible environment for the user through the addition of voice editing facilities, and also a sound digitizer for sampling external sounds captured via a microphone.

In design terms, the Kurzweil 250 was distinctive for its use of a floating-point format for the internal representation of samples, based on an eighteen-bit word length. Ten bits are assigned to the fractional value of each sample, leaving eight bits for the exponent. The former constraint limits the maximum signal-to-noise ratio to just 60 dB at full amplitude, but the overall performance is significantly better than that obtained from a conventional ten-bit integer system, especially at lower amplitudes, since the signal-to-noise ratio remains constant throughout the exponent range.[6]

The entire Kurzweil is controlled by a single sixteen-bit 68000 microprocessor, which supervises all processing and communications operations. The operating system and control software is stored in a special read-only memory, additional ROMs providing an extensive library of factory-supplied voices. Instead of storing a representative selection of perhaps six or eight sampled sounds, up to fifty separate recordings are digitized for each voice, thus ensuring that no sample has to be used more than twice in servicing the eighty-eight notes on the full-length keyboard. This intensive multisampling overcomes most of the problems of transposition discussed earlier and is matched by a facility to perform up to twelve voices at a time. Conventional storage of such information, however, would have required a prohibitive amount of memory space, so an analysis of the functional characteristics of each sound is stored instead, reducing the size of the basic sound library to little more than two megabytes.[7]

The digitizing facility of the Kurzweil 250 is not capable of reducing externally sampled sounds into such convenient components. This type of data is handled in a more conventional manner, converting the samples into a floating-point format before loading them into memory. The equivalent of 512 K samples are available for this purpose and the sampling rate may be adjusted in ten steps from 50 kHz down to 5 kHz, the maximum sampling times increasing proportionally from 10 seconds at the highest rate to 100 seconds at the lowest. For the reasons already outlined, however, the lowest sampling rates are of little practical value since the associated fidelity is very poor. This limitation is encountered with most variable sampling rate architectures dating from this period, and discerning users soon concluded that only a limited tradeoff between loss of quality and an enhanced sampling time was viable except in a very limited set of circumstances. As the cost of memory started to spiral downward, so variable sampling rates were generally abandoned in favor of fixed sampling rates, typically but by no means exclusively drawn from the developing industry standards of 16, 44.1, and 48 kHz.

The absence of any ancillary disk-based sample storage and editing facilities for the Kurzweil proved a major drawback when using the digitizer and this necessitated the services of an associated microcomputer. The company encountered significant difficulties in selecting a suitable host machine for this purpose, because none of the machines initially available proved sufficiently fast and powerful for their needs.

The launch of the Apple Macintosh in 1984 fortunately provided a timely and potentially attractive solution, and a high-speed interface known as the MacAttach was quickly developed for use with this computer.[8] In the case of the factory-generated voices, the main control panel of pushbuttons and sliders on the Kurz-weil itself provides basic editing facilities and also controls access to the internal sequencer, which has a capacity of about seventy-nine hundred notes. MIDI is supported via built-in ports, and many users have found this facility useful for accessing a wider range of sequencing and notation programs.

The marketing of such a powerful sampling keyboard in 1983 provided a major stimulus to other manufacturers seeking to exploit the potential of MIDI in a similar manner. None of these, however, chose to invest in the floating-point technology of the Kurzweil, concentrating instead on improving the performance of systems based on integer data architectures.

In 1984, E-mu replaced the Emulator I with the Emulator II. This added facilities for MIDI control, expanded the memory to 512 kilobytes, and upgraded the capacity of the integral floppy disk drive to a full megabyte. In terms of quantizing accuracy, this version achieves a performance equivalent to that of a conventional fourteen-bit digital audio system by using a type of Delta-Sigma modulation, where, it will be recalled, the changes in sample values are recorded instead of the absolute numerical value of each sample.[9] Instead of converting this information internally into conventional samples the data is kept in a Delta-Sigma format, dramatically reducing the data storage requirements for sampled sounds to just eight bits per sample.

The various improvements to the Emulator II were accompanied by a significant increase in price, reflecting, interestingly, a similar marketing strategy on the part of E-mu to that adopted by both Synclavier and Fairlight on the release of their own Mark II systems. Any notion that the sampler industry was destined to become the exclusive preserve of those willing to pay ever higher prices for the privilege, however, was dealt a mortal blow at the start of 1985 with the release of the Ensoniq Mirage. This keyboard-controlled sampler offered an attractive range of facilities and performance specifications for a fraction of the price of an Emulator II, and quickly captured an important sector of the MIDI market, forcing prices downward yet again.

The Mirage was the first commercial product to be manufactured by Ensoniq, a company originally launched in 1981 by a group of former Commodore engineers to design custom VLSI chips for digital synthesizers. Its features include 128 kilobytes of memory, and use of a variable sampling rate with an operational upper limit of 29.4 kHz. A nonlinear, eight-bit analog-to-digital and digital-to-analog conversion system is used, very similar to that employed by the Emulator I, and an internal sequencer is also provided, capable of registering 333 event sequences for each of eight polyphonic voices. A further refinement is the inclusion of an analog signal processing section, which provides facilities for filtering, enveloping, and modulating the sampled sounds prior to final audition. By the time production ceased in 1988, over thirty thousand models of the Mirage had been sold around the world.

Akai's first MIDI sampler, the S612, appeared in 1985, heralding a range of models from this manufacturer that have been distinguished by the lack of an integral keyboard. This design philosophy, subsequently adopted by a number of other sampler manufacturers, was a conscious attempt to establish a family of products that stood apart from the emerging sector of "plug and play" synthesizers, thus justifying a more upmarket but still strongly competitive pricing policy. The relative sophistication of this sampler was in no small part due to the imagination of its designer, David Cockerell, who had earlier been responsible for the design of Peter Zinovieff's pioneering mixed digital systems during the late 1960s and early 1970s.[10] Despite a number of practical drawbacks, in particular a maximum of only six simultaneous voices for the purposes of polyphony, limited editing facilities and a memory restricted to just 48 kilobytes of samples, the S612 set new standards of fidelity for the industry with the use of genuine twelve-bit converters. The variable sampling rate of between 4 and 32 kHz allows up to 1 second of sound in mono at the highest setting and up to 8 seconds at the lowest. In recognition of the growing expectation on the part of users for more advanced sound shaping facilities, the A612 also includes a low frequency oscillator for generating vibrato effects and an analog filter section to modify the resulting timbres.

Sequential Circuits responded with the Prophet 2000 (1985), a keyboard sampler offering an equivalent true twelve-bit resolution, but a much larger 256 kilobyte memory (expandable to 512 kilobytes). The latter is split into two banks, supporting eight-part polyphony and the choice of three fixed sampling rates (16, 32, and 42 kHz), sufficient at the highest setting for full audio bandwidth sampling. Each memory bank may be partitioned into eight subareas for multisampling, and the editing facilities allow two separate loops to be set up within each sound.

These enhancements marked a quantum leap forward in operational versatility. In particular the ability to partition the memory to sample and resynthesize two different sounds across the entire pitch range raised the prospect of true multitimbral operation, whereby a range of different voices can performed simultaneously using different MIDI voice channels. Each of these voices may be independently processed using an associated analog ADSR envelope shaper and voltage-controlled filter, thus offering considerable flexibility and refinement in the shaping of sounds.

Later in the same year Korg introduced the DSS-1, a keyboard sampler. Like the Prophet 2000 it also offers twelve-bit sampling and a memory of 256 kilobytes, but differs in its provision of a better range of sampling rates, including both the 32 and the 48 kHz audio industry standards. In addition, the DSS-1 also incorporates waveform synthesis facilities more usually associated with a traditional synthesizer, heralding a mixed sampling and resynthesis design technology that became popular in the late 1980s with the emergence of products such as the Yamaha SY77, to be considered later. In the case of the Korg, the user can sample external sounds, draw wave-shapes directly, or use additive synthesis to generate timbres with up to 128 individual harmonics. The ability to assign two digital oscillators to each note and the provision of a comprehensive effects unit in addition to ADSR envelope shaping facilities signaled a further expansion in the range of processing facilities to be associated with sampler architectures as the technology attained early maturity.

Roland entered the sampler market in 1986 with two keyboard samplers, the S-10 and the S-50, followed a year later by matching nonkeyboard versions, respectively the S-220 and the S-330. The S-10 and the S-220 offer eight-part polyphony, and sample at a fixed rate of 30 kHz with twelve-bit resolution. Whereas the 256 kilobytes of memory provided by these samplers might have appeared generous had they been released perhaps two or three years earlier, it was by this time barely adequate to service the growing desire of many composers and performers to work with multiple timbres. Both models allow the memory to be divided into four equal segments to support four different voices, but as a consequence the maximum length of sound that can actually be sampled reduces from about 4.4 seconds to little more than 1 second per voice. It is important to acknowledge, however, that these products were very competitively priced, thus appealing directly to those with a more limited budget.

The S-50, and its nonkeyboard relation the S-330, were engineered for the more demanding user. Although still restricted to just four independent voices, the polyphonic capability is increased to sixteen simultaneous notes and there is an option of sampling at either 15 or 30 kHz. The overall memory capacity is a more useful 750 kilobytes, expanded further to 1.5 megabytes in the S-550, an upgraded version of the S-330 released in 1988. One important design feature that characterizes the entire S series of samplers is the use of digital rather than an analog technology for the now customary audio processing section, which provides an attractive range of enveloping, filtering, and modulation facilities.

Akai responded to the growing competition from manufacturers such as Roland with the S900 released in 1986, a substantially reengineered version of the S612 supporting 750 kilobytes of memory, eight-part polyphony, twelve-bit resolution, and a maximum sampling rate of 40 kHz. A year later, Ensoniq announced the Ensoniq Performance Sampler or EPS, production starting early in 1988. This sampler uses expandable memory slots for easy upgrading from a basic 480 kilobytes to a maximum of 2.1 megabytes. No less than forty sampling rates are available, ranging from 6.25 to an impressive 52.1 kHz. In addition, up to eight different voices can be resident in memory at any one time, producing up to sixteen-part polyphony at higher sampling rates and twenty-part polyphony at lower sampling rates. Both the envelope shaping and filtering stages are of an all-digital design, offering a very versatile set of operating parameters. Internally, samples are stored in a sixteen-bit integer format as two-byte memory words, the extra bits allowing an extended integer scaling of dynamic levels internally without loss of resolution. Oversampling conventional twelve-bit converters achieves a maximum effective resolution of thirteen bits.

Although Yamaha was to concentrate its activities primarily on developing products for the synthesizer market it made one significant excursion into the sampler sector during the late 1980s, with the release of the TX16W in 1988. It is interesting to note here that in marked contrast to the fabrication of proprietary hardware for synthesizers such as the DX7 and its successors, the TX16W is based around a standard digital signal processor, the Motorola 56000.[11] In engineering terms, this product reflects an intermediate specification in terms of audio quality and performance, offering sixteen-part polyphony at a sampling rate of 48 kHz, delivered via twelve-bit converters. Although the basic memory capacity is only 1.5 megabytes, additional chips could be purchased to expand this to 6 megabytes.

The progressive increases in memory capacity offered by successive generations of samplers highlighted a further problem. This concerns the adequacy of the facilities that are provided for the input, output, and storage of samples. As sampler memory sizes started to exceed the storage capacity that can be provided by a single floppy disk, the need for alternative facilities became only too evident. By the mid-1980s, most personal computers were being fitted as a matter of course with hard disk drives, and this technology offered a convenient and increasingly affordable solution. Although by modern standards the capacities of such drives were exceedingly modest, they were sufficient to store a comprehensive set of sampled sound banks and the associated control parameters.[12]

Hard disk drives could be added to a sampler in two ways, either as an integral facility or as an external unit, connected via a suitable interface and cable. Although a few samplers of the period were manufactured with built-in hard drives, the external mode of connection soon became the preferred option, allowing the drive to be replaced or upgraded as and when required. Hard disk technology, however, still suffered from one potentially serious disadvantage. This concerned the lack of any truly practical means of removing the data completely from the system for safe-keeping, short of physically disconnecting the drive itself on each occasion, a practice that was firmly discouraged given the fragility of the connecting cable.

In terms of the electronic transfer of sample data to and from other destinations, an extension of MIDI provided one possible way around this impasse in the form of the MIDI Sample Dump Standard (SDS), discussed in the previous chapter. This protocol, it will be recalled, allows MIDI samplers to communicate samples with other MIDI-supported devices, using the "system exclusive" mode to transmit the data via a simple cable connection. Although some early samplers, such as the E-mu Emulator II, provided an alternative data link through a standard serial computer port, the relatively slow speeds of data transfer made all such options, including the MIDI SDS facility, very slow and cumbersome. This factor had serious implications for the development of sample-editing programs for use with an associated personal computer.[13] Eventually newer data storage technologies came to the rescue, for example, removable optical disks, which first appeared in the late 1980s, followed nearly a decade later by JAZ and ZIP cartridge drives, offering capacities that range upward from about 100 megabytes to orders of gigabytes.[14] The compact disc also has become a popular medium for storing and distributing sampled sound libraries, and the Internet now provides an attractive all-electronic alternative for downloading and uploading sample data via a personal computer.

By the mid-1980s, MIDI sampler technology was reaching the first stages of maturity, and already posing a major challenge to the market sector based on traditional synthesis methods. Issues of audio quality, however were still not fully resolved, in particular the deficiencies resulting from the use of low sampling rates and inferior bit resolutions, well short of the benchmark standards offered by the compact disc. The increasing popularity of the latter medium had brought a dramatic fall in the price of sixteen-bit digital-to-analog converters, and the pressure on sampler manufacturers to take advantage of these soon became overwhelming.

The initiative in this regard came from Greengate, a small enterprise working very much in the tradition of earlier companies such as Mountain Computer. Having developed the DS3, a modest twelve-bit sampler module specifically for use with the Apple II computer, a full sixteen-bit sampler known as the DS4 was released toward the end of 1986. Casio quickly followed with the sixteen-bit FZ-1 keyboard sampler, released early in 1987. The FZ-1 aroused particular interest in view of its extremely competitive price and the fact that such a high-quality product came from a manufacturer that hitherto had built its reputation principally on products more likely to be used for home entertainment rather than serious composition or performance. Other notable features include a basic memory capacity of 1 megabyte, expandable to 2 megabytes, and a comprehensive range of editing and processing facilities. The latter incorporate a graphics window, especially useful for locating suitable start and end points for loops, and a digital audio processing section that provides facilities for envelope shaping and filtering. The maximum sampling rate is 33 kHz, and polyphonic textures can be generated in up to eight parts. Of particular significance is the inclusion of a traditional synthesis section offering both additive and direct wave-function input facilities, much in the manner of the earlier Korg DSS-1.

The FZ-1 was soon to have a rival, the Prophet 3000 from Sequential. This sampler offers two megabytes of memory, sixteen-bit converters, and the three industry standard sampling rates of 32, 44.1, and 48 kHz. Initially, like most samplers dating from this period, it suffered from the limitations of a floppy disk drive as the only means of storing and retrieving samples. Within a matter of months, however, a hard disk option was released using the Small Computers System Interface (SCSI), a fast communications link developed by the computer industry especially for use with high-speed peripherals such as disks.[15] Within two years, almost all the leading sampler manufacturers had also introduced SCSI-based hard disk systems either as options or standard features. For Sequential Circuits, however, the Prophet-3000 was to be its final sampler.

Roland retained a twelve-bit format for its S series as late as the S-550 model, released in 1988 and its first sixteen-bit sampler, the S-330 released later the same year only achieves this specification at the output stage by oversampling the twelve-bit samples generated by the main processor. In a similar vein, E-mu retained its special data compression technology for new versions of the Emulator II, the Emax and the Emax SE. Here the primary technical improvements were a SCSI hard disk option, an increase in the maximum sampling rate to 42 kHz, and an expanded library of factory-supplied sounds. In addition, a series of software utilities were developed to enable audio data files obtained from other sources via the MIDI sample dump facility or SCSI to be converted to E-mu's special format.

In 1988, E-mu finally achieved true compact disc quality in terms of audio fidelity with the release of the Emulator III, a keyboard sampler that delivers a genuine sixteen-bit resolution, in stereo or mono, at 44.1 kHz. Four megabytes of memory are provided as standard, the extra slots allowing expansion to 8 or 16 megabytes. Further facilities include an integral hard disk with support for SCSI and a comprehensive suite of voice editing and audio processing facilities, supported by a liquid crystal display panel with graphics capabilities. A SMPTE port is also provided, allowing the timings of events to be accurately synchronized with audio-video devices.[16]

Akai responded with the S1000, released in 1988, offering very similar operational characteristics, for example, sixteen-bit sampling in mono or stereo at 44.1 kHz, up to 32 megabytes of memory, SCSI, and a comparable suite of editing and processing resources. One feature distinguishing this sampler from its immediate rivals concerns the use of full twenty-four-bit internal processing to ensure that losses of quality as a result of amplitude changes are kept to a minimum. With this development, the modern sampler had finally come of age, and with the release of an upgraded Ensoniq EPS and EPS-16+ in 1990, the migration of leading manufacturers to these upgraded operating standards was all but complete.

New Directions in Synthesizer Architectures

The influence of sampling technology was to extend to the very kernel of the mainstream synthesizer industry, but not before a number of alternatives to techniques such as Yamaha's FM synthesis had also made their mark. Despite the relentless advance of digital engineering, a number of manufacturers continued to make extensive use of analog circuits until the late 1980s, and even then the technology was not entirely abandoned.[17]

In many cases the processes of conversion were progressive, leading to number of interesting products along the way that combine elements of both technologies. A number of the design principles pursued here were derived from hybrid techniques successfully developed for systems such as EMS in Stockholm and MUSYS in London during the late 1960s and early 1970s. The principal advantage lay in the ability to control the functional characteristics of analog devices accurately in a digital domain without incurring the processing overheads associated with real-time, all-digital synthesis.

Antecedents from the pre-MIDI era include the eight-voice Trident from Korg, the OB series from Oberheim, the Jupiter series from Roland, the Prophet series from Sequential Circuits, and—from the dawn of the MIDI era itself—the sixteen-voice Rhodes Chroma (1982). One noticeable difference between these machines and their voltage-controlled counterparts is the replacement of patch chords or shorting pin connectors with electronic routing facilities, making it possible to store settings in a small memory bank for instant recall at the press of a button. With the introduction of MIDI, the momentum to replace voltage-controlled oscillators with digitally controlled equivalents gathered pace. Similar engineering changes were also applied in some instances to associated signal processing devices such as filters and envelope shapers, but this was by no means a universal practice. Other manufacturers introduced all-digital oscillators with integral digital-to-analog converters, but retained analog circuits for signal processing functions.

Such details are not always clear to the casual observer and commercial considerations often conspire to obscure the true nature of the underlying technology. In the case of a manufacturer such as Roland, however, the hybrid nature of its MIDI synthesizer designs at this time is well documented and can be clearly traced. During the early 1980s Roland increasingly employed a combination of digitally controlled analog oscillators (DCOs) with a selection of voltage-controlled processors such as filters, amplifiers, modulators, and envelope generators. This configuration forms the basis of the Juno series of synthesizers that followed the earlier Jupiter series. This range started with non-MIDI models such as the Juno 6 (1982) and Juno 60 (1983), progressing to MIDI versions such as the Juno 106 (1984), which proved especially popular with artists such as Vince Clarke, Frankie Goes to Hollywood, Tangerine Dream, Underworld, and Vangelis. The hybrid architecture supports six-voice polyphony, with two DCOs per voice, each voice being linked to its own voltage-controlled filter. The Juno range is also distinctive for being one of the last mainstream synthesizers to be equipped with a comprehensive range of the traditional manual control features associated with the voltage control era, notably banks of knobs and sliders. Production of the Juno ceased in 1988.

Roland used a similar combination of analog and digital electronics for the JX series of synthesizers, albeit with a greater emphasis on the latter technology at the control level. These models were developed in parallel with the Juno, the primary distinction from the user's point of view being the use of pushbuttons and a small display screen as the primary control interfaces. Roland, however, unlike many competitors, remained to be fully convinced that the latter mode of programming internal functions would prove universally popular. As a consequence, they provided a matching series of plug-in control units, starting with the PG-200 and progressing to the PG-800, offering a traditional control interface with knobs and sliders, much in the manner of the Juno series.

The JX-3P, introduced in 1983, was the first MIDI synthesizer to be manufactured by Roland. The MIDI implementation was very basic, limited to the processing of simple "note on" and "note off" messages. Later models such as the JX-8P (1986) make comprehensive use of the MIDI protocol, the keyboard, for example, providing both velocity and after-touch response characteristics. The largest, and by far the most successful JX, the JX-10 or Super JX (1986) is essentially two JX8-P synthesizers combined as a single instrument, with additional support from a built-in digital sequencer, using plug-in cartridges to store performance data. Each voice consists of a pair of DCOs, offering a choice of four basic waveforms: sawtooth, square, pulse, and noise. These functions are then spectrally shaped using matching voltage-controlled filters. A full ADSR envelope shaper is provided for each subgrouping of six voices, and the resulting signals can either be mixed directly or cross-modulated.

Modulation of pitch is also possible either via a low frequency oscillator or by using function patterns generated by an envelope shaper. Keyboard velocities can be sensed and applied as control functions and up to one hundred preset voices can be stored in the internal memory. These Roland synthesizers integrated readily into many performance situations during the 1980s. Functionally, however, they are representative of a very different design philosophy to that associated with an all-digital synthesizer such as the DX7, and their growing popularity as the decade advanced eventually forced Yamaha to rethink the merits of an architecture based solely on the principles of frequency modulation. By the mid-1980s, an ever-widening circle of performers were using Roland synthesizers, including Jean Michel Jarre, the Pet Shop Boys, and Pink Floyd.

The achievements of Casio again merit special attention at this point, not least for the production of a versatile range of all-digital synthesizers at very low cost during the mid-1980s. This CZ series, like the FZ-1 sixteen-bit sampler, took some commentators by surprise. From the original CZ-101 (1985) and its larger keyboard version the CZ-1000 (1985) to the more sophisticated but far from expensive CZ-5000 (1985), CZ-3000 (1986), and CZ-1 (1986) the key to success lay in the use of a synthesis technique that is potentially no less powerful than that of FM. As in the latter case, the secret lies not so much in the individuality of the technique itself, known in this case as phase distortion synthesis, but in the method of implementation.

The principles of phase distortion synthesis as implemented by Casio are essentially very simple. The basic technique of digital wave-table synthesis has already been described in connection with the MUSIC family of direct synthesis programs. In this context it has been shown how calculating a single cycle of a selected waveform as a table of values and then scanning it cyclically to extract a continuous function is computationally far more efficient than repetitively calculating each value in turn from first principles. Different frequencies at a chosen sample rate can be generated by varying the incremental value, and for the highest quality of output, interpolating samples that lie at points between the values stored in the table, rather than simply rounding to the nearest stored value. Providing the incremental value is constant on a cycle-by-cycle basis, then the resulting function will accurately reflect the stored function.

In the case of phase distortion synthesis, instead of extracting samples at a constant increment per cycle, the incremental step is varied during the course of each cycle. As a result, the extrapolated function is distorted in a controllable manner. In some respects, this technique has much in common with the analog pulse width modulation techniques described in connection with the early Cologne studio, but the use of ramp, triangle, or sinusoidal functions rather than just square waves greatly expands the degree of flexibility in terms of generating different timbres.[18]

Superficially, this also would appear to satisfy the underlying principle of FM modulation, where the frequency input to one oscillator is modulated by the output from a second oscillator. In functional terms, however, there are important differences in the ways in which control is exercised over the generation and variation of timbres. In the case of the CZ series of synthesizers, this control is segmented into three distinct stages each regulated by an eight-stage envelope function generator. The first of these manipulates the extraction of frequency information, the second the phase angle, and the third the overall amplitude of the envelope. Eight basic waveforms are provided for the phase distortion process itself; saw-tooth, square, pulse, a double sine consisting of two asymmetric cycles, a hybrid between a saw-tooth and a pulse, and three resonated versions of saw-tooth, triangle, and a trapezoid waveforms.

More complex waveforms can be produced by pairing any two of these component functions, and, with the exception of the CZ-101 and CZ-1000, two oscillators are automatically assigned to each voice, supporting in turn up to sixteen-voice polyphony. Control over timbre is exercised by the second-stage envelope function generator. Here modifications to the phase result in effects very similar to those associated with conventional filtering techniques.

Notwithstanding the relative sophistication of these synthesizers, the reputation of Casio as a manufacturer of products for domestic consumption resulted in a relatively low level of penetration into the core sector of the medium. Whereas the CZ-5000 included an integral sequencer its keyboard does not sense velocity information, a feature crucial to any serious performer. Conversely, the CZ-1 sensed keyboard velocity, but was not equipped with any sequencing facilities. Within a year of launching a new series of synthesizers, the VZ series, which combined elements of both FM and phase distortion synthesis, Casio abandoned the manufacture of both samplers and synthesizers to concentrate on keyboard products based almost entirely on a fixed range of presets.

Casio, however, was not alone in seeking out new synthesis methods and implementations during the mid-1980s. As noted earlier, it was the pioneering spirit of Sequential Circuits that had led to the development of the very first MIDI synthesizer, the Prophet 600, in late 1982. This derivative of the Prophet 5 retained voltage control technology for both synthesis and signal processing stages, offering five-voice polyphony with two oscillators per voice. As in case of other entirely analog synthesizers, however, problems of frequency drift and overall stability were greatly accentuated in the precise control environment of MIDI, and it was for this reason that Sequential turned their attention to sampling technology, leading to the Prophet 2000 and Prophet 3000. A continuing interest in synthesis methods, however, led in due course to the development of a simple but highly versatile means of generating compound waveforms, known as vector synthesis.

In essence, this technique is based on the principle of mediation between two or more different waveforms, where the user is free to determine the influence of each function on the composite output. For the pioneering Prophet VS (1986), Sequential designed a synthesis engine that accommodates up to four different waveforms, mixed together via a joystick that dynamically controls the relative strengths of each component. The intuitive nature of this technique contrasts sharply with the complexities of FM algorithms, and its ease of use proved very popular in some quarters, especially among those users who normally would venture no further than the basic bank of preset voices provided by the manufacturer. Further refinements include separate envelope shaping and filtering facilities for each waveform generator.

Considerable interest was shown in the Prophet VS by a number of leading performers, including Vince Clarke, Brian Eno, and Kraftwerk. Unfortunately, within less than a year, the VS suffered the same fate as that of the 3000 sampler, as a result of the acquisition of Sequential by Yamaha. The technique of vector synthesis, however, was to survive, for many members of the original research team were retained to design new synthesizers for Yamaha and also Korg, another recently acquired company. By this time Yamaha was becoming well aware of the need to replace the DX series, and in this case a strategic decision was taken to retain both the name and the associated manufacturing base of Korg for an alternative range of products.

Although Korg eventually ventured into the world of sampling with the DSS-1, which in effect doubled as a keyboard synthesizer and a sampler, the primary interests of the company remained firmly rooted in analog synthesis for many years. One of its most successful series of products, the Trident (1980), followed by the Trident Mark II (1982), not only sustained interest in voltage control technology, but also completely ignored the introduction of MIDI, right to the end of the production period in 1985. This growing isolation from mainstream developments was finally rectified at this point with the launch of its KW series of synthesizers in the same year, which in a manner very similar to the DSS-1 adopt the hybrid approach of digitally sampled waveforms, processed via voltage-controlled filters and envelope shapers.

This blurring of the distinction between sampler and synthesizer technology heralded a fundamental change in design philosophy as an increasing number of manufacturers turned to sampling as a means of providing a core repertory of voices for their synthesizers. Whereas true samplers continued to offer a comprehensive range of tools for capturing and shaping externally generated sound material, an array of sampling and resynthesis technologies emerged, each characterized by a specific set of operational characteristics, to ensure that the internal architectures used by individual manufacturers could thus be patented. Korg, for example, registered its own particular implementation of resynthesis technology as AI (later AI^2) synthesis. In essence, however, all these architectures are based on Pulse Code Modulation or PCM technology, whereby basic spectral information is extracted by directly sampling a conventionally digitized waveform. The original Korg KW-6000 (1985) relies entirely on a fixed repertoire of just eight sampled waveforms, permanently stored in ROM, and it is also restricted to just six-voice polyphony. Its larger relation, the KW-8000, released a few months later, expanded this repertoire to sixteen sampled waveforms and improved the polyphonic capacity to eight voices.

The purchase of Korg by Yamaha led to some major new developments in synthesis technology, which proceeded in parallel on three fronts. The first of these transformed the hybrid sampling and synthesis technology of the KW series into an all-digital product, the Korg M1 synthesizer, released in 1988. In addition to an expanded bank of sampled waveforms, now processed via digital filters and envelope shapers, the MI supports sixteen-voice polyphony. In multitimbral terms, up to eight different voices may be in use at any one time, with the possibility of further processing of the sounds via a comprehensive effects section that offers such treatments as echo, reverberation, flanging, and chorus effects.[19]

Further banks of waveforms may be imported using special data cards, inserted into a slot on the rear of the synthesizer. In addition the system incorporates a sophisticated eight- (later sixteen-) track sequencer that can store up to seventy-seven hundred individual note-events. Although a number of other synthesizers predating the M1 also incorporated advanced signal processing and sequencing facilities, the scale of the implementation here truly merits for the first time the use of the term "workstation" rather than simply "synthesizer."[20] Over the years a number of leading artists have used the Korg M1, including Depeche Mode, Fluke, Robert Miles, and 808 State.

The second area of development took Korg into the domain of FM synthesis, taking advantage of the patents established by Yamaha at the start of the decade. The result was the Korg DS-8, released in 1987. This eight-voice/eight-part multi-timbral synthesizer offers a less complicated user interface for manipulating the synthesis algorithms, which are in turn restricted to two-oscillator pairings rather than the four- or six-oscillator groupings used in the Yamaha DX series. Richness of timbre is achieved by offering a choice of basic oscillator wave-shapes that are already rich in harmonic content, for example, saw-tooth, square, bright saw-tooth, and bright square, the degree of modulation being regulated via an envelope shaper that directly manipulates the modulation index.

The third area of development was based on vector synthesis technology, taking direct advantage of the expertise imported from Sequential under the leadership of Dave Smith, the original founder of the company and a leading pioneer of MIDI. This led to the Korg Wavestation (1990), and in due course a series of upgraded versions, starting with the Wavestation EX (1992).[21] This was very much a design for the new decade, offering thirty-two-voice polyphony, which in multitimbral terms can make use of sixteen different voices simultaneously. Although primarily based on the four waveform matrix used in the Sequential Prophet VS, now called advanced vector synthesis (AVS), the Wavestation also incorporates elements of the Korg AI and AI^2 methods of extracting and sequencing composite segments of wave information, in an implementation identified as wave sequencing synthesis (WSS).

In many respects the Korg Wavestation highlights what was fast becoming a curious paradox at the end of the 1980s. On the one hand, the extensive range of resources available for manipulating and processing voice information had opened up rich opportunities for users to generate a variety of sound material from the basic bank of waveforms, easily augmented by means of plug-in PCM sample cards. On the other hand, the sheer complexity of the functions available for programming was a powerful disincentive to many performers and composers who were becoming increasingly to rely on presets, rather than go to the trouble of shaping new sounds.

Kawai added further to this debate in 1986 with the release of the K3 digital wave memory synthesizer, demonstrating very clearly that combining sampling and resynthesis with traditional waveform synthesis techniques could greatly expand the possibilities of sound production. In electronic terms, there is no material distinction to be made between generating sound material from a function table by cyclic extraction and reading though a stored file of sound samples. The basic issue here is that, whereas the core of many acoustic sounds can be effectively synthesized from first principles, key features such as the associated attack transients often lack suitable realism.

An effective compromise, pursued here, is to blend sampled attacks of a natural sound with a synthetic extension, leading in turn to more elaborate combinations of natural and synthetic elements. The K3 includes a bank of thirty-two preset waveforms including several composite timbres that blend material of both natural and synthetic origin. Waveforms also can be generated by means of additive synthesis either internally or by importing suitable data from an external source. In addition, both factory-supplied and user-defined waveforms can be directly accessed via two individually programmable digital oscillators, allowing the construction of a wide variety of composite waveforms.

The processing of voices is largely of an analog nature in the case of the K3. The facilities include voltage-controlled filters, envelope shapers, and a stereo chorus effects unit. With the K1, released in 1988, the facilities were expanded still further with a resident library of 256 sounds of both natural and sampled origin. Any four of these can be blended together to create new voices, which may be refined further using an extended range of all-digital signal processing facilities. In addition, the polyphonic capabilities are substantially enhanced from just six voices in the case of the K3 to sixteen voices in the case of the K1.

Kawai soon faced fierce competition from Roland, with the release of the D series of synthesizers, starting with the D-50 (1987) and D-10 (1988). Known as linear arithmetic or LA synthesis, this particular implementation of sampling and resynthesis technology allowed a sophisticated range of voicing possibilities, supported in the case of the D-10 by a full thirty-two voice/nine-part multitimbral capacity. The D series remained popular well into the 1990s, used extensively by musicians such as Eric Clapton, Vince Clarke, Enya, Fluke, Jean Michel Jarre, and Gary Numan.

Roland's decision to introduce the D series of synthesizers alongside its S series of samplers echoed a similar strategy adopted by Ensoniq, which within a year of releasing the Mirage launched an all-digital wave synthesizer, the ESQ-1 (1986). In the case of the ESQ-1 no less than three oscillators are assigned to each voice, drawing on an internal bank of thirty-two sampled and synthetic waveforms. The basic repertory of forty voices may be augmented by using plug-in cartridges, each supplying a further eighty preprogrammed voices. Two years later, Ensoniq released almost simultaneously the EPS sampler and the SQ-80 synthesizer, an upgraded version of the ESQ-1 based on an expanded repertory of sounds drawn from seventy-five synthetic and sampled waveforms. It was the top-of-the range VFX, however, released in 1990, which was to realize the full potential of this particular architecture.

The VFX offers no less than twenty-one independently programmable oscillators drawing on a bank of 109 basic waveforms, which can be modified to generate a total resource of eighteen hundred variants. These comprise strings, brass, breath, bass, tuned and nontuned percussion sounds, both sampled and synthesized, as well as an extensive array of more basic electronic sounds that include many single-cycle waveforms of varying complexity. Up to six oscillators can be assigned to each voice, allowing the production of rich and varied polyphonic textures in a multitimbral environment. Voice modification facilities include three six-stage envelope shapers, two independent dynamic digital filters, and a variety of modulation sources including a low frequency modulator offering seven different wave-shapes and a programmable delay. The integral effects unit provides fifteen different configurations including several types of reverberation as well as echo, delay, and chorus effects.

Yamaha's initial response to this growing competition was a pair of FM synthesizers, the YS-100 and the YS-200, released in 1989. In essence, these are little more that scaled down versions of the DX series with a simplified user interface. These products, however, were an interim measure pending the launch of a new all-digital SY series in 1990.[22] Two new models were released almost simultaneously, the SY22 and the SY77. Whereas it might be expected that one version would simply be an expanded or contracted version of the other, there are some interesting differences that can be identified at a more fundamental design level.

The SY22 combines the techniques of FM and vector synthesis, the latter implementation being derived from the Prophet VS with a joystick facility to vary the relative strengths of the component waveforms. In the case of the SY77, the vector synthesis part of this synthesis engine is replaced by wave-shaping facilities. These operate on single waveforms, albeit with an expanded range of processing facilities and also the possibility of using various combinations of up to four FM or sampled components for each voice. To distinguish these implementations from the former DX series and rival sampling architectures, Yamaha identify the two techniques as advanced frequency modulation (AFM) and advanced wave modulation (AWM, later AWM2) respectively.

AFM is an extension of the FM system used in the DX7, still relying on groupings of six oscillators but with a choice of forty-five rather than thirty-two algorithms. Although voices developed using a DX7 can be converted to run on the SY77, the true potential of the new system can only be realized by exploring its extended range of FM facilities. The most notable differences are a choice of sixteen different waveforms rather than just a simple sine wave, and the ability to tap three oscillators rather than one to generate feedback signals for enriching the timbre by means of resonance. The AWM facility is a full sixteen-bit 48 kHz sampling system, drawing on an extensive bank of factory-supplied sounds. From these two sources a number of different synthesis chains can be constructed. Both modulation facilities can be used independently, with their voices routed directly to the stereo output amplifiers either separately or as a simple audio mix. Alternatively, AWM waves can be used as control signals for selected operators of an AFM generator, thus producing a variety of complex and dynamically varying modulations.

Two banks of presets are permanently stored in read-only memory, each offering a repertory of sixty-four voices. Two of these voices are sampled percussion kits with individual instruments assigned to specific keys. A further sixty-four user-defined voices can be created in a programmable memory bank, supported by a floppy disk facility that also can be used to save data from the integral sixteen-track sequencer. The SY77 is fully multitimbral, supporting the use of up to sixteen independent voices on different MIDI channels, and between sixteen- and thirty-two-note polyphony is possible, depending on the distribution of AFM and AWM components. The credentials of this sophisticated synthesizer are further secured by the provision of a comprehensive stereo effects unit. Although additional factory-produced voices may be imported via a plug-in cartridge, the SY77 does not provide any other facility for importing sampled sounds. This drawback was rectified in the SY99, an upgraded version of the SY77 released in 1991.

Such combinations of waveform and sampling synthesis facilities supported by a digital processing section and an integral sequencer result in a remarkably self-sufficient system for the composition and performance of music, and this workstation concept was to achieve further prominence during the 1990s. The integration of so many different functions is particularly interesting, as for many users it conveniently circumvents the need to understand the intricacies of MIDI communications. This aspect was to become particularly important in performance situations in which synthesizers are essentially treated as instruments that draw on a preprogrammed repertory of sounds. In studio-based environments, however, the limitations of the simplified control interfaces that result from the use of small display screens and an associated set of pushbuttons become all too apparent, especially in situations in which sequencing resources are used to assemble and edit complete multitimbral performances. It is in this context that the development of computer-based MIDI software has achieved particular significance, and the characteristics of these supporting products will be discussed in the next chapter.

Beyond the Keyboard: Alternative Performance Controllers

So far this chapter has concentrated almost exclusively on the development of MIDI samplers and synthesizers during the formative years, circa 1983 to 1990. There are, however, a number of MIDI devices dating from this period that cannot be so conveniently subsumed into a single keyboard-controlled system without a significant loss of intrinsic functionality. For example, with the advantage of hindsight, it is now clear that one of the most unfortunate developments of this period in musical terms was the introduction of keyboard-based percussion facilities. Whereas these tools undoubtedly allowed rock and pop musicians easy access to such resources as a simple extension of keyboard technique, they also completely destroyed any practical link to the art of percussion playing.

The controversy that ensued was not entirely new; an earlier example was the development of keyboard-based string synthesizers during the 1970s, which proved especially popular with German rock and pop groups such as Tangerine Dream. The musical consequences of using repetitive "beat" patterns, however, generated by merely triggering unaltered reproductions of sampled percussive sounds, were of far greater significance in terms of their dehumanizing impact. One solution to this problem lay in the design of special drum machines, equipped with electronic sensing pads, activated either by a drumstick or a finger.

Devices such as these were in existence long before 1983, but the lack of a unified communication system to link the various components that constitute a percussion set created major problems of compatibility. With the advent of MIDI the integration of such facilities became a practical proposition. Although a number of leading synthesizer manufacturers added basic drum machines to their repertory of products, this market sector created opportunities for interests of a more specialist nature. Two such companies achieved particular prominence during the 1980s: Simmons, who produced the first complete electronic drum kit, and Roger Linn, generally recognized as being the inventor of the digital drum with the LM-1 (1979), followed by the Linn Drum (1982).

Simmons enjoyed a lasting success for many years, the pioneering all-analog SD55 system leading directly to the popular SDS series, ranging from early non-MIDI models such as the hybrid SDS7 to later versions such as the SDS1000. The concern for the performer is particularly evident in the well-crafted design of the drum pads. These found favor with many professional percussionists who continued to use them long after the company ceased trading later in 1988. Linn achieved particular prominence with the MIDI-controlled 9000 model (1984), combining a versatile sequencer with a sophisticated high quality drum synthesizer. Unfortunately, within months of the release of this product, Linn ran into financial difficulties and withdrew from the market. Akai, however, recognizing the potential of Linn, acquired the rights to its products and took Roger Linn on as a consultant. The result was a fruitful partnership that was to last for several years.

The first product of this collaboration was the Akai ADR15, released in 1987. This combines a sampling system for the direct capture of new sounds with a sequencer, which can be driven either by pressure or velocity sensitive buttons or by external drum pads, thus creating a powerful facility for live and/or sequence-assisted performance. The influence of the Linn 9000 is very evident in the design of this product, and these characteristics are also to found in the Akai MPC60, which replaced the ADR15 in 1988. The use of twelve-bit samples and a sampling rate of up to 40 kHz in the case of both models compares favorably with the general sampling standards of the time. Even here, however, sixteen-bit sampling was already making its presence felt with products such as the Alesis HR16 drum machine (1987). The latter provides forty-eight sixteen-bit velocity-sensitive programming pads and an extensive library of both acoustically sampled and electronically generated sound sources.

Roland's DDR30 and its associated set of six drum pads, introduced in 1985, is representative of a first-generation MIDI drum kit from a mainstream synthesizer manufacturer. The voices are configured by first selecting up to four basic sounds and then applying modifications to the pitch, timbre, and envelope characteristics. Up to eight variations can be specified for each drum pad and a working repertory is assembled and stored in memory as a complete kit. Up to thirty-two of these kits can be resident in memory at any time, allowing access to an extensive library of material at the push of a button. The DDR30 was designed specifically as a performance tool for a live percussionist, and thus lacks any facility for generating or recording performance patterns.

Roland initially saw rhythm generation as a quite separate application, regarding it as a by-product of the basic accompaniment presets that had become a standard feature of keyboards designed specifically for the home entertainment market. Such facilities are provided by the TR505 rhythm box, released in the same year. This offers a basic repertory of percussion sounds and programmable patterns that are accessed via a simple pusgbutton panel. The device was replaced by the TR626 in 1987, offering an expanded range of thirty digital voices, eight individual audio outputs, forty-eight presets, and forty-eight programmable patterns.

By 1988, firms such as Yamaha and Korg had added drum machines to their product ranges. Yamaha's RX7 offers a basic library of one hundred sampled sounds using sixteen-bit resolution, foreshadowing the AWM facility incorporated in the SY77. These sounds range from electric bass, marimba, and orchestral sounds to a comprehensive collection of drum and cymbal sounds that includes nine different bass drum samples, ten different snare samples, two rim shots, seventeen tom-toms, four cymbals, and four hi-hats. Although the machine can be operated using external drum pads, it is better suited to preprogrammed modes of operation that use the internal sequencer. The facilities for direct performance, for example, consist of a standard set of twenty-four press keys that are neither pressure- nor velocity-sensitive. The system, nonetheless, is capable of sixteen-note polyphony, and the sequencer, memory permitting, allows up to one hundred patterns to be stored of between one and ninety-nine bars in length. Simple programming procedures allow any one of the one hundred factory voices to be assigned to any key or any combination of keys thereof. In addition each sound can be edited in terms of its basic pitch, overall amplitude, decay, and stereo pan position.

In common with so many of Yamaha's products the RX series of drum machines are not so much components to form part of a system but a complete set of performance tools. A rather different philosophy is encountered with Korg's DRM-1 digital rhythm module, which also dates from this period. Here the emphasis is clearly biased toward the performer with the inclusion of a built-in pad-to-MIDI converter. The sequencer section is also rationalized to allow efficient interaction under performance conditions, the emphasis being on the direct recording of backing patterns for a complete song rather than the overlay of basic patterns to be pre-programmed into the system. The voice section consists of a small bank of internal sounds and four ROM cartridge slots on the front panel that will also accept sound cards from Korg's earlier DDD-1 and DDD-5 drum machines. When fully populated the system library can hold up to fifty-five different sounds, accessed by sixteen drum kit programs, each of which can contain up to sixteen variants.

The basic differences between the characteristics of a drum machine and those of a rhythm generator can be further illustrated by comparing the Korg DRM-1 with products such as the Roland R-8 Human Rhythm Composer, which appeared in 1989. The latter is specifically designed for the generation of automated rhythm tracks, combining an internal library of sixty-eight percussion sounds with a sophisticated multitrack sequencing facility, operated via a pushbutton editing panel. Drum pads or other performance aids are clearly of no relevance here, and the R-5 is best suited for compositional applications that specifically require the construction of elaborate rhythmic patterns.

Although by 1990 drum pads had come to represent perhaps the most significant development of MIDI-based performance tools aside from the MIDI keyboard, a number of other instrumental transducers were making their presence felt in this rapidly developing area of alternative controllers. One notable instrument to have been targeted in this respect was none other than the electric guitar, leading to products such as the Yamaha G10 MIDI guitar system and the Casio PG380 MIDI Synth guitar.

The G10, which appeared in 1988, was one of the first products of this type successfully to overcome the technical problems encountered in converting guitar pitches into equivalent MIDI codes. Although the fingerboard and frets very closely resemble the equivalent parts of a conventional guitar the similarities end here, as there is no guitarlike body, the latter being replaced by a small box underneath the playing area, which contains the electronics. The device is simply a controller, producing basic electronic signals that are converted into MIDI data by an associated device known as the G10C guitar-to-MIDI converter, which in turn has to be connected to an associated synthesizer before any sounds can be produced. In contrast, the Casio PG380 combines a MIDI-based pick-up system with an integral synthesizer module that offers sixty-four preset sounds, supported by plug-in ROM cards that expand the repertory to over one thousand sounds. In all other respects, this product looks and plays like a conventional instrument, the natural profile of the guitar sound box providing ample storage space for all the electronics.

In terms of entirely new areas of development for MIDI-based controllers it was the wind and brass families of instruments that attracted the attention of both Akai and Yamaha during these formative years. In 1987 Akai introduced two special MIDI controllers, the EVI (Electronic Valve Instrument) and the EWI (Electronic Wind Instrument). Both are designed in the first instance for use with an EV2000 voicing unit, which contains special synthesis modules for these instrumental families, but the controllers also can be connected directly via MIDI to any suitable synthesizer.

The EVI is closely modeled on the acoustic trumpet, consisting of a rectangular tube with three valvelike press switches, a mouthpiece, and what appears to be a small bell. In reality, the latter disguises a fourth valve and a set of roller sensors that control octave switching across a range of seven octaves. Two other sensors are provided on the opposite side of the tube to the main valves, one controlling pitch bend, the other affecting the subtleties of pitch that occur when a trumpeter alters the lip pressure on an acoustic instrument. The EWI has no bell and offers a simplified wind fingering system using press keypads in association with a roller-based octave switching system on the underside for the left thumb, matched with pitch bend sensors for the right thumb. Although key and octave selections determine the basic MIDI pitch information to be generated, overall dynamic and expressive control information is obtained by detecting wind and lip pressure respectively.

Yahama introduced a rival wind controller, the WX7, in the same year. As with the EVI and EWI, MIDI performance data is generated by a combination of key selections and wind and lip pressure. Conventional woodwind fingering is used to produce a basic chromatic scale, transposition over a six-octave range being controlled by thumb-operated buttons. Particular care has been taken with this controller to provide facilities for customizing its response to the requirements of the individual user. To this end, the plastic mouthpiece can be set to emulate the response of a recorder, or alternatively a saxophone or clarinet. In addition, the instrument's sensitivity to changes in wind pressure can be adjusted, as well as the point at which it will start to "speak." Commercial products such as the WX7 or the EWI and EVI have important links with a number of performance transducers, which have been developed by the institutional research sector, and several of these will be studied later.[23]

Other MIDI-related Hardware

It has already been noted how the Ensoniq VFX, the Korg Wavestation, and the Yamaha SY77 were indicative of a growing trend to combine comprehensive and versatile signal processing facilities with the core synthesis and voice shaping facilities associated with a conventional synthesizer. Such resources, however, were by no means new to MIDI. Self-contained "effects" units had proved popular especially with performing groups long before the era of MIDI, and although the range of functions that could actually be controlled via MIDI was strictly limited, many manufacturers saw the value of producing complementary products of this type for sale alongside synthesizers and samplers.

Yamaha released a sixteen-bit reverberation unit, the REV1, in 1984, followed early in 1985 by a cheaper but in many respects no less versatile version known as the REV7, the main difference being a reduced sampling rate of 31.25 kHz rather the 44.1 kHz used by the REV1. Over thirty different factory-generated preset programs are offered by the REV7, ranging from room and hall types of reverberation to simple chorus and flanging effects. Rival products from the same period offering similar facilities include the Lexicon 224X and the Alesis XT Digital Reverb.

By far the most popular Yamaha effects unit to emerge from this period, however, were members of the SPX series, starting with the SPX90 in 1986, updated as the SPX900 and then the SPX1000 (1990). The SPX90 significantly extends the facilities of the REV7, resulting in a versatile multieffects processor that offers other features such as pitch shifting and multiple delay echoes. The versatility of the SPX processors, not least the freedom to choose and program the individual effects, inspired other manufacturers to follow suit, leading to products such as the Alesis MidiVerb and QuadraVerb, the Eventide H3000 Ultra-Harmonizer, and the Korg A3 signal processor. A notable design feature of the A3 is the use of rotary knobs to adjust parameter settings rather than the usual array of buttons. These greatly speed up the process of adjusting parameter values, an important consideration when working in a performance environment. Forty-one different effects are available on the A3, the number in use at any one time (up to a maximum of six) and the order of chaining being determined by a preset connection patch, which is selected from a bank of twenty different configurations. The Eventide H3000 Ultra-Harmonizer is a more specialist effects processor, a development of earlier models such as the H910 and H949 and primarily intended for applications such as multiple pitch shifting, enhanced by associated effects such as delay, flanging, and reverberation.

The significance of MIDI as regards the dynamic operation of these effects units varies considerably from one product to another. In the case of a machine such as the Eventide H3000 Ultra-Harmonizer, special care has been taken to integrate the various processing control parameters with the performance characteristics of a MIDI keyboard such as note range and key pressure, velocity, and release. Most systems of this type, however, restrict the use of MIDI to program change commands and no more than perhaps one or two performance parameters. It is thus quite normal to use such facilities without any reference to MIDI whatsoever, and there are still a number of high-quality signal processors in regular use in both synthesis and recording studios that do not support MIDI at all.

This growing degree of choice between independent MIDI devices and the self-contained workstation also extended to hardware-based MIDI sequencing facilities. Early products such as the Roland MSQ-100 (1985), Akai ASQ-10 (1986), Korg SQD-1 (1986), or the Yamaha QX7 (1986) were quickly followed by a profusion of products with expanded functionality. These included the Kawai Q-80 (1988) and Roland MC-50 (1990), both capable of controlling up to thirty-two separate voice tracks, and the Yamaha QX3, which offers a comprehensive suite of editing facilities, the latter supported by an enlarged data display screen.

By the end of the 1980s, it was becoming clear that the future prosperity of hardware manufacturers would be increasingly dependent on their ability to maintain a competitive edge in terms of price, functionality, and ease of use in the face of growing competition from the computing sector. Whereas at the start of the decade the true significance of the microprocessor revolution could not have been predicted with any certainty, there was now little doubt that the burgeoning personal computer industry would soon pose a serious challenge to their autonomy.

In the same way that the minicomputer progressed from a studio control facility to a synthesis tool its own right, so it was that the prospect of using the increasingly affordable and ever more powerful personal computer for real-time software synthesis became a practical reality during the early 1990s.

Although, as will be seen in due course, hardware manufacturers were able to retain a firm grasp on the commercial MIDI market throughout the 1990s and into the new millennium, the impact of developments within the computing sector was ultimately to prove highly significant. It is therefore appropriate at this point to return to the start of the 1980s and chart the development of the personal computer as a musical resource during the latter part of the twentieth century.

16

From Microcomputer to Music Computer: The MIDI Dimension

At the start of the 1980s, the microcomputer was regarded by many sectors of the computing industry as little more than a tool for hobbyists. Large and expensive computers dominated the market and their future prosperity at the core of the industry seemed well assured. Few could have anticipated that by the end of the decade the centre of gravity would have changed so dramatically in favor of increasingly powerful personal computers, providing processing facilities for many applications that were equal or superior to those offered by traditional third-generation mainframe computers.

The early years of the microcomputer were characterized by a rapid proliferation of different machine architectures, each being associated with a unique set of operating characteristics. As a result, many models enjoyed a relatively short production life, which in turn militated against the development of suitably robust and well-crafted software tools, especially in more specialist areas of activity such as music. By the dawn of the MIDI era, however, the design and development of such computers was proceeding on a more rational basis. Manufacturers had started to concentrate on generic approaches to the production of new models, in many instances designed specifically to accommodate applications developed for earlier technologies. This new climate of stability provided an important stimulus to the computer industry as a whole, leading to a substantial investment in the development of software resources, targeted at the business, scientific, and leisure communities. Although the launch of the IBM PC in 1981 established the concept of the personal computer, it was the Apple Macintosh that pioneered the key feature for the future success of this product, the graphics-oriented user interface. This innovative computer was to transform the fortunes of Apple at a crucial time in the company's history. The company had entered a period of rapid decline in sales after the failure of the Apple III, the immediate successor to the Apple II, released in 1980, followed by a similarly unsuccessful launch of an expensive precursor of the Macintosh in 1983, known as the Lisa.

The potential value of a Graphics Universal Interface (GUI) environment for music applications, based on a basic set of windows, icons, mouse, and pointers tools (WIMPS) had been clearly demonstrated by the SSSP project back in 1977.[1] Six years later, the technology necessary to exploit such innovative ideas still attracted little interest from the mainstream computing industry, which continued to view such facilities as irrelevant to its primary markets in business and commerce. Apple recognized the significance of this overlooked opportunity, and having learned some important lessons from the deficiencies of the Lisa finally achieved the long-awaited revolution in computer design.

The GUI/WIMPS environment demanded an entirely different approach to the writing of software and fundamentally changed the operating characteristics of the computer itself. An important key to the success of the Macintosh lay with the decision to develop the computer almost entirely from first principles using the recently introduced sixteen-bit Motorola 68000 processor, thus abandoning the aging architecture of the Apple II.[2] Although the original Macintosh suffered from some practical drawbacks pending the launch of the much improved Macintosh II series in 1987, its impact on personal computer users was immediate and far-reaching.

The II series was powered by faster, upgraded versions of the 68000 processor, early models using the 68020 and later ones the 68030. This family of processors sustained the Macintosh range, including a number of important derivatives such as the Quadra, until the introduction of the PowerMac in 1994. In hardware terms, the PowerMac marked yet another major engineering feat, for it introduced a new series of Macintosh computers based on an entirely different processor known as the PowerPC 601, developed jointly by Apple, IBM, and Motorola in 1992–3. A fundamental reason for the improved performance delivered by this processor is the use of a Reduced Instruction Set Computing (RISC) architecture, which streamlines and greatly simplifies internal computing operations.[3]

In order to ensure continuity in terms of Macintosh software written prior to the PowerPC, Apple included a facility that allows programs written for the older processor to run in an emulation mode, where 68000 machine instructions are automatically translated into equivalent PowerPC instructions. The full potential of the new processor, however, could only be realized by writing programs that directly made use of the "native" machine instruction set, and in due course many applications were converted and updated using compilers that produced the required code. The steadily improving performance of successive PowerPC processors led the company to redesign the PowerMac first as the G3, released in 1997, the G4, released in 2000, and the G5, released in 2003.

Although the GUI/WIMPS interface has long since become the standard means of direct communication with personal computers, it is important to appreciate the significance of the late conversion of the IBM PC to this operating environment. The key impediment to progress in this regard lay with long-standing deficiencies intrinsic to the design concept of the original IBM PC. The user interface had been based on the traditional mainframe VDU terminal, consisting of a basic keyboard and a simple monochrome screen, used for the input and display of alphanumeric data and instructions. The imaging facilities left a great deal to be desired, and in many situations the TV monitor associated with an entry level microcomputer would produce a superior quality of image, especially if the intention was to display data in a graphical format.

The subsequent XT version of the IBM PC, released in early 1983, added a hard disk drive to the basic system, but still no serviceable GUI. Developers were led to believe that the AT version, scheduled for late 1984 and based on the first of the new 80 × 86 series of processors from Intel, the 80286, would allow Microsoft to develop a suitable graphics-based environment. IBM, however, was still far from convinced at this stage that such a radical change to the basic user interface was commercially advantageous, and as it transpired the AT proved less than adequate for the task.

As a consequence, the first version of Microsoft Windows, launched in 1985, only provided a very limited set of user functions. The majority of users continued to use the older DOS operating system, leaving Microsoft and Apple to engage in a long legal battle over proprietary rights for the GUI/WIMPS environment. Although Windows 2, released in 1987, was an improvement, it, too, received an equally lukewarm reception from PC users. Events began to gather pace with the release of the next generation of Intel-based PCs in the same year, based on the faster and more versatile 80386 processor. Market forces, however, were to move the goal posts for Microsoft with the rapid growth of a manufacturing sector concerned with the production of cheaper IBM PC clones. Given the consequential loss of proprietary rights over the future of the architecture, the IBM label became increasingly redundant as an identifying trademark, and it is for this reason that it is more relevant to refer to subsequent machines simply as Intel-based PCs.

Microsoft was finally able to establish the credibility of its product with the release of Windows 3.0 in 1990. Windows 3.0, however, was still far from the ideal, especially when compared with the now highly sophisticated GUI provided by the Macintosh II. The release of the 80486 processor in 1989 had provided useful improvements in the basic performance of Intel-based PCs, but Microsoft still faced major problems in developing a suitably versatile graphics environment. Moreover, the market was further confused by the development of an alternative system, OS/2, by IBM with some assistance from Microsoft. At this point, Microsoft and IBM finally went their own ways, each concentrating on its own version of the GUI. Although IBM continued to support and develop OS/2 and its derivative OS/2 Warp, neither versions of this GUI resulted in music applications of any significance that are not also fully represented in Windows versions.

The root cause of Microsoft's difficulties was the underlying design principles of the PC itself, which had remained basically unaltered since 1981. Furthermore, the rapid proliferation of PC clones made it impossible to contemplate any fundamental changes to the basic architecture, improvements being largely restricted to the design of the supporting graphics facilities. The release of Windows 3.1 in 1992 offered some marginal improvements in performance and versatility, but it was by now abundantly clear that Microsoft had to invest heavily in the design of new software that could work more effectively around these hardware limitations. This only become a commercial proposition with the introduction of a yet more powerful generation of Intel processors.

Thus it was that the Intel Pentium was born in 1993, still using the same basic instruction set as the original 80 × 86, but with expanded and much faster internal processing and addressing capabilities. By 1995 the Pentium I was sufficiently well established for the PC market to underpin the launch of Microsoft Windows 95 for individual PCs, providing a GUI that met the essential requirements of modern personal computing. For the first time, developers of WIMPS-based music software for the PC could compete on more or less equal terms with those creating equivalent products for the Apple Macintosh, in some instances producing versions for both architectures.

Further improvements in processing power led to the Pentium II in 1997, followed by the Pentium III released in 1999, and the Pentium 4 released in 2001.[4] In a similar vein, Microsoft made further improvements to Windows with the release of Windows 98 in 1998, followed in turn by Windows Millennium Edition (ME) in 2001, along with related versions such as Windows NT and its derivative Windows 2000, intended primarily for use in networked computing environments. In order finally to consolidate its position as the leading provider of operating systems for the Intel-based PC, Microsoft released a significant upgrade, Windows XP, in 2001, incorporating a number of radical changes to the WIMPS environment. In many respects Windows XP was Microsoft's answer to Apple's own major upgrade of its GUI operating system, known as OS X, released a year earlier.[5]

By the mid-1990s it had become abundantly clear that the future of personal computing in key sectors such as business, commerce, education, and home computing would be controlled to a significant extent by Microsoft, supplying both system and applications software primarily for its preferred platform, the Intel-based PC. Apple Computer, nevertheless, still retained a small but significant share of the overall market, and in some areas of activity, including those specifically concerned with music applications, the company was well placed to retain a major profile.

The 1990s saw the end of the road for the other personal computer architectures that had secured a share of the embryonic market during the 1980s, including both Atari and Commodore. It is important, nevertheless, to note that both companies developed GUI-based personal computers that were materially to influence the evolution of music applications during the intervening years, and these achievements merit closer scrutiny.

In 1985 Atari launched three personal computer models in quick succession, the 130 ST, the 520 ST, and the 1040 ST, all based on a 68000 processor and offering a high resolution interactive graphics environment very similar to that of the Macintosh. Subsequent versions included the Mega ST, with a detachable rather than an integral keyboard and also memory expansion facilities, followed by the Mega STE, which introduced further enhancements such as additional input/output facilities and an improved sound system.

Although these computers were to become very popular as alternatives to the Macintosh in the music and games sectors of the market, mainstream users in business and commerce took little interest. In an attempt to rectify this situation, Atari launched the TT030 in 1990, a much faster machine based on a 68030 processor, with the specific intention of developing a fully integrated business software environment. Unfortunately, this objective was never completed, and production of the TT030 was abruptly terminated in 1992. Its successor, the Falcon 030, quickly went into production as a replacement, but despite some encouraging initial sales it become clear that major software houses had lost interest in Atari as a computer manufacturer. The company accordingly withdrew from the computer market in 1993 to concentrate on a much more successful range of products, designed specifically for the games sector.

Not to be outdone, Commodore launched the Amiga family of personal computers in late 1985, starting with the 1000 model, based like the Macintosh on a 68000 processor and supported by a graphics user interface. In 1987, two further versions were released. The smaller 500 model was designed for the home entertainment market and the larger 2000 for the scientific, business, and commercial markets. A much more powerful version based on the 68030 processor, known as the 3000, followed in 1990. Unfortunately, the fortunes of Commodore were then to follow a very similar path to that of Atari. Despite the release of two further 68030-based machines, the A600 in 1992 and the A1200 in 1993, sales rapidly declined, and one year later Commodore also withdrew from the computer market. After a number of years of uncertainty, the rights to the Amiga passed first to Gateway in 1997, and then to Amino, in 2000, subsequently renamed as the Amiga Corp.

Notwithstanding the success of the Macintosh, Apple continued to market the Apple II for a number of years, introducing a substantially upgraded version known as the Apple II GS in 1986.[6] This used a special sixteen-bit processor known as the 65C816, which not only emulates all the functions of the original 6502 for compatibility with earlier Apple II models but also provides a high resolution GUI/WIMPS environment, very similar to that of the Macintosh. By 1990, however, the manufacturing era of the Apple II had finally came to an end.

The facilities provided by early personal computers for synthesizing sounds directly are of some historical interest. In the case of the Intel-based PC such opportunities were exceedingly limited, since the standard sound resource in all pre-Pentium models consists of no more than a single bit output register that directly drives a small internal loudspeaker. In this regard, no progress had been made since the first generation of microcomputers associated with the late 1970s.[7] In contrast, both Atari and Commodore had long since grasped the value of including more sophisticated sound resources as a standard feature.[8]

The Atari ST computers incorporate a basic three-voice synthesizer chip manufactured by Yamaha, capable of generating elementary tone sequences and a limited range of sound effects. Ingenuity, however, led to some interesting uses of this facility. Microdeal, for example, developed Quartet, a software package that allows short extracts of sampled sounds held in memory to be output via the synthesizer chip. Up to four different sounds can be generated simultaneously, with eight-bit resolution, but only 64 kilobytes of RAM can be accessed in total at a maximum sampling rate of 16 kHz. As a result, the audio bandwidth is less than 8 kHz. With the STE machines Atari upgraded the sound system to allow the output of sampled sounds direct from memory in a stereo format.

The sound resources of the Commodore Amiga went a stage further, providing facilities for the synthesis of both music and speech, the latter being aided by the inclusion of special synthesis chip and associated software that will generate recognizable speech as words are successively typed into the computer. For music or sound effects an eight-bit synthesizer with stereo outputs is provided. Although the audio bandwidth is only 7.5 kHz, up to four voices may be synthesized simultaneously, either using wave-table synthesis or synthesis from sampled sounds held in memory.

From the current perspective, the sound systems for both the Apple Macintosh and the Apple IIGS are of particular interest, because they set new standards of versatility and general fidelity for audio for the personal computer industry. In the case of the IIGS, Apple used a special eight-bit digital oscillator chip (DOC). Ensoniq manufactured this chip, using a version of the audio processor originally developed for the Mirage synthesizer.[9] Although many key functions are implemented, for example wave-table synthesis with up to thirty-two oscillators, or the multiple sampling of sounds direct from memory, the analog-to-digital input and stereo output facilities were not used, allowing only mono reproduction. Further, although the sampling rate is a respectable 31.25 kHz, the output filters limit the audio bandwidth to about 11 kHz.

The design of the sound system for the Apple Macintosh was radically different to that of the IIGS, consisting of discrete components to an Apple design in the early versions, replaced in due course by custom chips manufactured by Sony for the Macintosh II series. The sampling rate is 22.05 kHz, which is exactly half the 44.1 kHz industry standard used for compact discs, but the output filters reduce the bandwidth to only 7.5 kHz. Three basic forms of synthesis are provided: (1) a square wave generator for the production of "alert" signals, (2) sampling direct from memory, and (3) wave-table synthesis with up to four voices, in the latter two cases with an eight-bit resolution.

The functionality provided by these chips provided a major stimulus for those concerned with developing the audio capabilities of personal computers, and this subject will be returned to in due course.[10] Back in the mid-1980s, however, the primary interest of the commercial music sector lay with applications that ignored the internal sound circuitry altogether, in particular the control of external synthesizers and samplers via a MIDI port.

It will be recalled that there are some important differences between a MIDI interface and a conventional serial port. These concern both the physical nature of the electrical signals and also the data transmission speed of 31250 baud, which as already been noted does not conform to any of the standard baud rates developed by the computer industry for serial communications. In practical terms these difficulties can be overcome in two ways, the choice depending to a significant extent on the architecture of the computer itself.

The first solution requires the services of an external MIDI-to-serial data converter inserted between the MIDI network and a spare serial port on the computer. Although the electrical conversion of the associated signals only requires a relatively simple electronic circuit, arbitrating between the MIDI data rate and the speed of a typical serial port has not always proved so straightforward. During the 1980s, many personal computers were unable to sustain serial transmission speeds equal to or greater that the MIDI rate.[11] The serial ports for the original Apple Macintosh, for example, were restricted to just 19200 baud. Similarly it was not until the introduction of Windows 3.1 in 1992 that the operating system for the Intel-based PC would allow applications to use any of the serial ports at rates higher than 28800 baud.

In these circumstances, the only possible solution lies in the provision of some form of buffering, inserted between the port and the MIDI data converter. This technique will only work reliably if the density of MIDI traffic is sufficiently light or intermittent for the buffer to absorb any possible data overrun. If continuous MIDI information such as pitch bend messages is transmitted, the buffer will quickly overflow, resulting in loss or corruption of the data.

Early designs, such as the module manufactured by Sound Composition Systems (SCS), were based typically on an eight-kilobyte memory buffer. To reduce the chances of data overflow, the SCS unit incorporated special circuits to filter out active sensing information, but such a solution inevitably degrades the usefulness of such an interface. Furthermore, the buffer itself introduces an element of latency in the communication of data, which has potentially serious implications in performance situations.

The second solution requires a special MIDI interface card fitted directly to the main control bus of the microcomputer itself, bypassing the conventional ports. The electronics are necessarily more complicated in this case, because the card has to communicate directly with the CPU. Although inherently more expensive, this method neatly circumvents the compatibility problems described above in the case of add-on modules for serial ports. Roland pioneered this type of interface for the Intel-based PC with the MPU-401 card, which established a universal standard for the design of MIDI-to-PC interfaces, widely used for a number of years.

Atari and Yamaha both went a step further and produced personal computers with integral MIDI interfaces. In the case of Atari, all models from the ST-series onwards included a pair of MIDI IN and MIDI OUT ports as a standard feature, making these personal computers particularly attractive for MIDI-based music applications. The first Yamaha music computer, the CX5M, was manufactured as an extension of the DX range of MIDI equipment, designed in the first instance as a self-contained workstation that combined facilities for FM synthesis with the programmable features of a control computer. When the system first appeared in 1985, products such as the DX7 synthesizer and the QX7 sequencer already provided the primary tools for a programmable MIDI system, but Yamaha was aware of the growing attraction of graphics-driven facilities for advanced editing and sequencing applications.

Unfortunately, Yamaha based the computer on outdated hardware using MSX, a computing environment developed by Microsoft for the eight-bit Z-80 microprocessor. This provided an operating system, a BASIC language interpreter stored in a small ROM of only 32 K, an equivalent amount of RAM for general programming, and support for peripherals such as a keyboard and printer. By the time the CX5M appeared on the market, interest was already firmly focused on more modern sixteen-bit architectures, and the computer was withdrawn in 1988.

Although the MSX specification permits the addition of a disk-based operating system, the CX5M does not support this facility, using instead a set of ROM cartridges to provide the basic software and RAM cartridges of rather limited capacity for the storing user data from one session to another. Three further components complete the basic system: a VDU display to match the integral alphanumeric keyboard; a MIDI music keyboard; and a special plug-in module, a complete FM synthesizer designed to interface directly to the MSX system. Known as the SFG01, this is basically a scaled-down version of a DX9 with just four operators and eight algorithms, the associated software consisting of a voice editor, a sequencer, and a special program that allows the user to compose and synthesize scores using conventional music notation.

Yamaha's second music computer, the C1, released in 1989, proved more successful initially since it uses a conventional 80286 PC AT architecture. The MIDI facilities are comprehensive, consisting of two MIDI IN, one MIDI THRU, and eight MIDI OUT ports, all separately programmable. Unfortunately, these ports were not MPU-401 compatible, restricting the use of third party MIDI software, and with the advent of the Pentium I processor the company withdrew the system in 1993.

The major rationalization of personal computer architectures during the early 1990s suggests an outcome solely concerned with the relative merits of the Intel-based PC and the Apple Macintosh. Such an analysis, however, is a little too simplistic, especially in the specific context of music applications. Here some important differences arose of a geographical nature, largely the result of some marked variations in the marketing strategies adopted by key contributors just prior to this major rationalization of the industry.

During the 1980s, Apple aggressively marketed its personal computers within the United States at very competitive prices, and as a result significant sales were achieved for the Apple Macintosh, and to a lesser extent the Apple IIGS. As both Commodore and Atari also were developing products specifically to compete with the GUI/WIMPS environment, Apple went to considerable lengths to undermine their attempts to penetrate its primary markets, seeing Atari as a particularly significant threat.

In Europe and Asia, however, the situation was radically different. Apple demanded much higher prices for its products, in part to offset the effects of heavy discounting in the American market, and this policy severely restrained the development of these key market sectors. In the case of music-specific applications, these circumstances strongly favored the most immediate competitors, in particular Atari. As a consequence, the ST series became the most popular computing platform for MIDI in a number of countries, including both Germany and the United Kingdom. The subsequent withdrawal by Atari from the manufacture of computers resulted in a strong European-led movement to maintain its products and develop new software, notwithstanding the fact that the technology would no longer be supported. For this reason, Atari computers were still being used by significant numbers of composers and performers almost a decade after production ceased.

Although the development of MIDI has been subject to major change and rationalization in terms of the characteristics of the underlying hardware over the years, considerable benefits have accrued from the retention of the original 1983 MIDI protocol, Version 1.0, as the basis of all applications. The resulting repertory of software dating from the first decade of MIDI can be usefully divided into a number of categories, notably composition, music notation and score printing, sequencing, and voice editing.

The use of the computer as an aid to composition has already been cited in connection with the work of Hiller and Xenakis during the 1950s and 1960s and Chadabe during the 1970s.[12] The continuing work of Chadabe and his associates led to three pioneering MIDI programs from Intelligent Music for the Macintosh: Upbeat, Jam Factory, and M. The first of these is a rhythmic programming system that allows patterns to be generated and edited using a graphics interface. What distinguishes Upbeat from a conventional sequencing program is the availability of extended editing facilities that allow data such as key velocities, duration values, or the density of events to be modified using computer-generated probability functions. In addition, it is possible to change performance data dynamically, allowing alterations to be made intuitively via the mouse.

The notion of "Jamming" lies at the heart of Jam Factory, an improvisation program in which the performer first defines basic ideas in terms of fields of pitch data, selects an initial set of computer-driven performance algorithms, and then proceeds to modify their operation using the mouse as a master controller. At the heart of the process lie four performing instruments, each of which has to be initialized with a basic note pattern, usually input from a MIDI keyboard. This data is then analyzed to produce a set of probability tables that record how often a particular note follows: (1) a single note, (2) a two-note sequence, and (3) three-note sequences, in a manner reminiscent of the Olson and Belar composing machine.[13] Resynthesis proceeds by random or pseudorandom selection of pitch and duration values, suitably weighted according to these tables. The ability to alter the course of events using the mouse results in a remarkably flexible performing tool that permits the generation and shaping of a variety of textures of varying complexity and density in a "top down" manner similar to that of the POD programs of Barry Truax and the PROJECT programs of Gottfried Michael Koenig, in which control over the course of events is exercised on a macro rather than a micro level.[14]

In some respects, M has much in common with both Jam Factory in terms of the interactive processes of its operation and also Upbeat in terms of the number of different tracks that can be manipulated simultaneously. The arrangement of the graphical desktop, however, reveals a much stronger emphasis on compositional processes that have to be worked out in advance rather than interactively during the course of a performance. These require the user to input a basic set of note patterns via MIDI and then provide control data for an associated set of resynthesis algorithms that allow regulation of parameters such as event density, duration, and repetition. A number of layers can be specified in this manner, allowing the composer to build up rich textures using a selection of different voices.

Music notation programs have varied considerably both in terms of their sophistication and also emphasis over the years, a reflection of their dependence on the quality of the practical resources available for viewing and printing the results and also the breadth of interests that are thus encompassed. Although these various polarities have been subject to considerable convergence, even by the mid-1990s this process of consolidation was still far from complete. A primary driving force at one end of the spectrum has been the development of advanced typesetting packages purely for the production of printed music scores of the highest quality.

One of the earliest music notation programs for the personal computer, SCORE, can be traced back to the 1972 program of the same name developed by Leland Smith as a composing tool.[15] This program, originally developed for use with MUSIC V, provided the starting point for the development of MS, a general-purpose score writing program. In due course, Passport Designs took an interest in the program and used it as the basis of SCORE, first released in 1983. This was a nongraphics program for the IBM PC, limited to an alphanumeric coding language for the entry of music data. Another drawback was the lack of support for MIDI, which could have provided an alternative and much quicker means of basic data entry via a music keyboard, with the additional possibility of audio proofing the results by translating the score data back into time-sequenced note-events. Subsequent versions of the program accommodated interactive editing of data onscreen and also supported the use of an associated MIDI-based transcription program, known as Escort.

The lack of MIDI support for SCORE itself was rectified in its replacement Encore, phased in by Passport Designs during the 1990s, and later upgrades were made available in versions for both Apple and Intel-based PC computing platforms. Continuing support for SCORE, however, especially from institutional users, encouraged Leland Smith to continue its development as a PC-only notation program, management of the product subsequently passing to the San Andreas Press.

Personal Composer was the very first commercial MIDI-based music notation program, developed by Jim Miller in 1983 specifically for the IBM PC, subsequently revised and updated to take full advantage of the evolving graphics capabilities of the Microsoft Windows environment. Two of the earliest high quality notation programs for the Macintosh were Finale from Coda Music Technology, and HB Music Engraver, both released in 1987. These differed from SCORE in being designed from the outset as a fully interactive menu-driven graphics systems, the user accessing a series of dialogue boxes to change the functions of the mouse and also select the symbols to be used in pasting up the score. Audio proofing was also supported using either the internal synthesis facilities of the Macintosh or an external synthesizer, accessed via MIDI. Although HB Music Engraver only remained in production until the early 1990s, Coda continued to support and develop Finale, versions becoming available in due course for both the Intel-based PC and the Macintosh.

By the mid-1990s, other specialist notation programs were becoming available, notably Mosaic from Mark Of The Unicorn (MOTU) for the Apple Macintosh, and Sibelius, written in the first instance exclusively for the Acorn Archimedes. In due course, increasing demand from users of the two primary computing platforms led to versions of Sibelius for both Apple and Intel-based PC architectures, both allowing MIDI data entry and audio proofing.

What distinguishes these programs from other MIDI-based software with notational capabilities is the priority given to the provision of tools that can meet the most demanding expectations of the music publishing industry. This has proved to be no mean challenge given the diversity of views on issues such as the precise shape and position of individual neumes, the trajectory of expression marks, and the subtleties of context-driven considerations such as the horizontal spacing between individual notes. Here the limitations of MIDI as a data entry tool for constructing scores in Common Music Notation (CMN) become of material importance.

It will be recalled that a basic MIDI note message consists of just two components, the tempered pitch value, and its amplitude, measured in terms of the associated key velocity. In constructing a musical score from a MIDI keyboard transcription, the latter component is rarely, if ever used. In principle, it is possible to quantize and grade these velocity values in terms of a series of dynamic equivalents in common music notation, for example, *ppp*, *pp*, *p*, *mp*, *mf*, and so on. Other factors, however, such as the acoustic nature of the associated sounds, and the vagaries of performance practice make it almost impossible to classify these dynamics with any degree of certainty. Furthermore, most musical scores only give very selective indications of the intended dynamic level, often linked by transitional indicators such as *crescendo* and *decrescendo*. Given the nature and significance of these difficulties, most programs restrict their data capture routines for the display of conventional music notation to the tempered pitch values associated with each keystroke, registered as a pair of time-stamped MIDI "note on" and "note off" messages.

Although the pitch content of this data can converted into common music notation equivalents with relative ease, the automatic transcription of timing information is a much more complicated process. Here an important distinction has to be made between using a keyboard to register MIDI data for the purposes of sequencing, and using it specifically for music transcription. In the former case, preservation of all the nuances of event timing is highly desirable. In the latter case, "note on" and "note off" keystrokes have to be synchronized as accurately as possible with a metronome pulse, so that residual timing errors can be reliably corrected via a suitable software routine before the data is converted into notational symbols and mapped graphically onto music staves.

Here again, other practical issues can lead to less than perfect automatic transcriptions. In terms of pitch values, MIDI does not distinguish between chromatic alternatives, for example G-sharp and A-flat. Thus, whenever the associated pitch value of 68 is encountered, the notation software has to make a contextual decision, seeking clues from other data, for example, the key signature. Although such resources can be designed to work well in many situations, they cannot be totally relied on. Similarly, even the most intelligent software routines for transcribing note timing information into exact note lengths can never be wholly context-sensitive.

Visual proofing is thus always an essential component of all MIDI-based data entry systems designed specifically for the production of definitive musical scores. Indeed, this graphical verification process only constitutes the first stage in the preparation of a fully notated musical score. All the additional descriptors such as phrasing and articulation marks, or textual underlay in the case of vocal scores, have to be added manually using WIMPS-based tools.

A growing recognition of the limitations of MIDI as a protocol for encoding score data in common music notation led to the development of Notation Interchange File Format (NIFF) in 1995. As the acronym suggests, NIFF is a special music data format that sets out to encapsulate all the aspects of common music notation with minimal additional graphical information. The intention is to create a comprehensive specification that would allow the transfer of music scores between different notation programs without any loss of score data. This initiative was supported by a number of music software companies, including Passport Designs, MOTU, Opcode Systems, and Cakewalk Software, but unlike MIDI it has not achieved universal acceptance from manufacturers and is thus unfortunately of only limited practical value.

Although many of the transcription problems described above remain to be satisfactorily resolved, some improvements have been made in the MIDI output facilities associated with music notation software for the purposes of audio proofing. Translating dynamic markings such as *pp* or *mf* into suitably graded MIDI velocity values, or even interpolating transitional indicators such as *crescendo* are quantifiable procedures, and these can be extended to more complex features such as articulation and phrasing.

From a very early stage in the development of MIDI software, the boundary between notation and sequencing programs has been blurred by a number of products that support both areas of application with arguably equivalent proficiency. By 1990, for example, the market was already offering a number of dual-purpose applications, including Notator from C-Lab for the Atari ST, Personal Composer from Jim Miller for the Intel-based PC, and Concertware+MIDI from Great Wave Software for the Macintosh. C-Lab and Personal Composer combine powerful score writing facilities (up to thirty-two staves per page in the case of C-Lab) with multitrack sequencing facilities (sixty-four tracks in the case of C-Lab, thirty-two in the case of Personal Composer).

The original Concertware program was primarily a score-writing program, with a synthesis option, which allows material to be checked aurally using the internal sound system of the Macintosh. Its immediate derivative, Concertware+, extended these functions to provide a fully integrated music writing, synthesis and performance system with an internal sequencer. The addition of MIDI software drivers led in turn to Concertware+MIDI, which allows the sequencer to operate as the master control facility for an external synthesizer.

Crossing the boundary between these applications to view matters from the other side of the equation, it soon becomes clear why sequencing applications have provided the starting point for so many MIDI software programs that provide a broader range of editing and performance facilities. Here, as already noted, tools for the display and editing of data in common music notation are generally included as a matter of course, but until quite recently they have generally lacked the sophistication normally expected of a specialist engraving program. Some sequencing programs have been designed specifically to complement notation programs available from the same software manufacturer. MOTU, for example, designed the original version of Performer as a companion program for Professional Composer, the predecessor of Mosaic. Subsequently, Cakewalk developed Overture 2 (not be confused with an earlier program Overture, from Opcode) as a score writing companion to its primary suite of sequencing software.

In terms of methodologies for editing MIDI data, its visual representation in CMN format has only limited value, as so much detail has either been stripped out completely or quantized. Whereas it is possible quickly to identify and correct basic "wrong" notes or duration values, alternative facilities are required if more subtle changes are to be made to individual "note on" and "note off" timings or key velocity information. The most detailed mode of editing, universally supported by all but the most basic of sequencing programs, takes the form of time-sequenced event listings, where each MIDI event is recorded in terms of the individual MIDI values associated with each parameter, and its associated timestamp. To assist readability, pitch information is usually translated into a pitch class format, and the timestamp represented in terms of the beat and the subdivision thereof, referenced within the associated basic timeframe of a bar. This latter reference unit is established by the metronome speed and time signature specified by the performer before the associated MIDI track is recorded. Other MIDI data, such as velocity information is usually represented directly as a numerical value.

Some sequencing programs support other modes of visual representation, where the MIDI data values are displayed graphically using a vertical series of display grids for each component, time values providing a common parameter on the horizontal axis. Here aspects of common music notation (such as stave lines) are often combined with numerical components to create a hybrid mode of data representation. As an adjunct to direct data editing, more sophisticated sequencing programs provide facilities to shape the performance characteristics at a higher level of creative control. One of the most common techniques employed is known as a "groove" facility, which will adjust either the event timings or the velocity values, or in many cases both, to vary the overall "swing" or emphasis, according to taste. Many programs supply a comprehensive library of grooving options, representing the characteristics of well-known styles of popular music as well as some more exotic effects.

All modern sequencing programs will accommodate the registration of many thousands of individual MIDI events, sufficient for even the most substantial of MIDI-based works. A basic capacity of up to sixteen individual MIDI tracks is a standard feature, and many programs will accommodate up to twenty-four, thirty-two, or even sixty-four different tracks. This extra capacity not only allows a number of subtracks to be used for individual voices but also the use of multiple MIDI controllers, suitably synchronized together.[16]

The evolution of MIDI sequencing software over the years has to a large extent reflected the contemporary state of the personal computing industry in terms of the choice of different platforms and their associated characteristics. At the end of the 1980s the market leaders, measured in terms of choice of software, were the Atari ST and the Macintosh, with a small but nevertheless significant advantage in favor of the former in Europe, but not America. In contrast, relatively few MIDI sequencing programs had yet been developed for the Intel-based PC, the continuing lack of good graphics support at this time proving a major disincentive.

Commodore attracted some limited support from mainstream software manufacturers, but for the most part these were derivatives of programs written in the first instance for other computing platforms. A notable example of this was Steinberg's pioneering Pro-24 sequencing package, written originally for the Atari ST but subsequently released in a version for the Commodore Amiga. Steinberg's interest in supporting different platforms was taken a stage further with Cubase, originally released in versions for the Atari ST and the Macintosh, and subsequently augmented by a version for the Intel-based PC. In a similar vein, Passport Designs released its early sequencing program Mastertracks Pro in versions for the Apple IIGS, the Commodore 64, 128 and Amiga, the Atari ST, the Intel-based PC, and the Macintosh.

Such initiatives, however, did not receive universal support from the other manufacturers, and further progress in this regard was slow. Although the introduction of Windows 95, to be followed in turn by Windows 98, materially redressed the balance in terms of graphics functionality between the Apple Macintosh and the Intel-based PC, several manufacturers retained distinct preferences for one or other architecture. Whereas Steinberg and Emagic entered the new millennium with cross-platform sequencing software such as Cubase and Logic, both MOTU and Opcode remained primarily committed to the Macintosh with products such as Performer and Studio Vision. In a similar vein, Voyetra continued to manufacture exclusively for the Intel-based PC with products such as MIDI Orchestrator, in the company of other PC music software companies such as Cakewalk.

MIDI voice editing software involves the manipulation of synthesizer characteristics peculiar to specific architectures, accessed in System Exclusive mode. As noted earlier, the manipulation of voice parameters via miniature display panels built into the hardware itself can prove cumbersome and error-prone, since only a limited number of parameters van be viewed and changed at any one time. The option of using a WIMPS/GUI environment in association with a full-sized computer monitor is thus very attractive for those who wish to spend time crafting new voices or refining the characteristics of existing ones. During the early years of MIDI, a limited repertory of software emerged for voicing synthesizers, for the most part developed by third-party manufacturers.

The primary drawback to this approach was the need to buy a separate software package for each item of equipment. This situation was to change in 1989 with the release of Dr. T's eXclusive ORchestrator program (X-OR). This replaced an entire repertory of voice editors with a single integrated facility and also supplied a comprehensive library of new voices for a number of popular synthesizers, giving rise to the generic term editor/librarian. Furthermore, the program was released in versions for all the primary personal computer architectures in use at the time, specifically Amiga, Atari ST, Macintosh, and Intel-based PC. Two years later, Opcode entered this universal editor market with Galaxy, a comprehensive patch librarian program, followed by Galaxy Plus, which added voice-editing facilities.

In 1993, Dr. T sold the X-OR program to MOTU, which rereleased it in a new version known as Unisyn. Although initially available only for the Macintosh, a PC version was to follow in 1995. In the same year, Sound Quest released MIDI Quest another comprehensive editor/librarian for the Intel-based PC, soon to be followed by SoundDiver from Emagic, available for both Macintosh and PC.

During the second half of the 1990s, the market for MIDI software started to change in nature, largely as a result of a growing interest in the use of audio software, both for synthesis and also recording and editing. As will be seen in chapter 18, this development led to a fruitful integration of audio and MIDI applications, allowing both processes to operate side by side within a unified working environment. By the dawn of the new millennium, the status of the Intel-based PC also had been secured in this context, with a repertory of software finally to rival that available for the Apple Macintosh. This particular fight for supremacy, however, does not yet have a certain winner. In 2002, for example, Apple purchased Emagic in order to further its own interests in the development of music applications for OS X, all further support for Intel-based PC versions of Emagic software being abruptly discontinued. What is beyond reasonable doubt is importance that is now attached right across the spectrum to software, as opposed to hardware resources for the medium as a whole.

This burgeoning of MIDI software applications during the 1990s indeed posed major challenges for hardware manufacturers, anxious to preserve their investment in proprietary products. As the power of personal computers inexorably increased, so the superior performance of hardware synthesizers, samplers, and signal processors could no longer be assured. Whereas software synthesis systems had previously been confined to non-real-time modes of operation, by the mid-1990s it was becoming clear that a personal computer was rapidly acquiring a processing capacity that could rival that of a hardware MIDI synthesizer or sampler. Manufacturers thus faced a growing threat to their future prosperity, and their response to this challenge provides an interesting subject for discussion in the next chapter.

17

New Horizons for MIDI-based Technologies

The early 1990s signaled a period of consolidation in the design of MIDI synthesizers and samplers. In the case of samplers, the issue of fidelity had become primarily a matter of refinement and standardization, allowing greater attention to be paid to practical enhancements. The distinctions previously made between the characteristics of the sampler and the sampling synthesizer also became increasingly blurred as users of the former relied increasingly on the contents of imported sample libraries, rather than engaging directly in the processes of sampling and shaping new sounds.

Roland introduced the S-770 sampler in 1990, finally abandoning variable rate sampling techniques in favor of a fixed rate approach, providing the user with the options of 44.1, 24, and 22.05 kHz, serviced by stereo converters that deliver an enhanced resolution of twenty bits by means of oversampling. Although the samples are stored in memory in a conventional sixteen-bit format, twenty-four bit registers are used for all data processing tasks in order to preserve the maximum possible sample resolution.[1] A 40-megabyte hard disk is augmented by a CD-ROM facility for importing externally generated sample libraries, and the maximum memory size of 16 megabytes supports the use of twenty-four different voices. Perhaps the most distinctive feature is the provision of a video data port for the display of control parameters via an external television monitor, augmenting and bypassing the necessarily restricted display area of the built-in LED screen.

The CD-ROM has proved to be an extremely useful medium for the storage and transfer of digital audio data, not only for applications involving samplers but also more generally for multimedia personal computers. This device was developed during the late 1980s initially as a high-capacity, read-only alternative to the floppy disk. The introduction of CD recorders during the mid-1990s greatly extended the versatility of this cheap and reliable means of data storage as an alternative to more expensive optical, ZIP, and JAZ drives. Based on the technology of the conventional audio CD, the CD-ROM allows the structured storage of large quantities of digital information on a single disc, ranging from system and applications software to interactive educational packages that make full use of both audio extracts and video imaging.

An early proliferation of different formats devised by manufacturers for importing and exporting conventional audio data files impeded the development of a universal industry-wide standard for digital recording media, further compounding the transmission difficulties already noted in the case of sampler data formats. The rationalization of audio data file formats has been a slow process, the two most commonly used today being the WAV format introduced originally for the Intel-based PC, and the AIFF format favored by Apple software developers for the Macintosh.[2] In addition, the development of the Internet as a means of bulk data transfer has created further problems of compatibility in this context as a result of several new formats that have come into use, based on different data compression techniques.[3]

Akai's response to the Roland S-770 was the production of two new samplers, the S3000 and the S2800, released in 1993 as replacements for the aging but still very popular S1000 series. Although still not supporting use of the industry-standard 48 kHz sampling rate as an alternative to 44.1 and 22.05 kHz, the maximum memory capacity of 32 megabytes provided by the S3000 allows up to thirty-two voices to be configured. Akai also replaced the internal hard drive with an external unit, connected to the sampler via a SCSI port.

By the early 1990s, the basic capacity of hard drive systems was starting to increase markedly as a result of developments spearheaded by the personal computer industry. Akai's own external SCSI drive for the S3000, for example, offered a capacity of 105 megabytes, more than twice that of the Roland S770, augmented if required by an external CD-ROM option, also connected via the SCSI port. The latter technology was taken a stage further with the CD3000 model released in the same year, a playback-only version of the S3000 with an integral CD-ROM drive. Both the S3000 and the S2800 include an enhanced set of processing tools, including facilities for flanging, delay, chorus, and pitch shift.

E-mu released an upgraded version of the Emulator III, the EIIIXP in 1993, accompanied by an expanded range of processing options that include features such as simple time compression and expansion, allowing subtle changes in duration to be introduced without affecting the pitch of the material.[4] Further utilities are provided to support a CD-ROM drive as an alternative facility to the standard hard disk drive and the attachment of a Macintosh as a host computer for a software editor/librarian program.[5] In the case of the EIIIXP, the MIDI port is used to communicate control parameters in System Exclusive mode, and a SCSI port for the rapid transfer of the sample data itself.

At the start of 1993, Ensoniq replaced the EPS sampler with the ASR10 sampling keyboard, adding a number of additional signal processing effects and also a sequencer. An upgraded version, the ASR88, followed in 1995. In the same year E-mu introduced an alternative and less expensive range of samplers, the ESI series, starting with the ESI-32. It also replaced the flagship Emulator IIIXP with the upgraded E4, offering a maximum of 128 megabytes of memory, 128 voices, and improved sample processing facilities. Following a merger between E-mu and Ensoniq in 1988, the overall range of MIDI products produced by the new company was consolidated, leading to a revised series of samplers that include the ESI-2000 and the E4 Platinum, both released in 2000.

In 1997 Yamaha reentered the mainstream sampler market, almost a decade after the introduction of its only other true sampler, the TX16W. Although the new model, the A3000, faced stiff competition from Akai and E-mu, it was engineered to an attractive specification. With a memory capacity of up to 128 megabytes, capable of supporting sixty-four voices in sixteen multitimbral groupings, the basic performance of this sampler fully matched its rivals. It was, however, the design of the signal processing section that placed it in a class of its own, with the provision of no less than sixty different options to shape and enhance the basic voicings. After an intermediate upgrade, Yamaha released two new models in 2000, the A4000 and the flagship A5000, the latter providing 128 voices and an improved control interface with an enlarged LED display panel.

In the case of Roland, the S-770 sampler was to remain its primary model for almost the entire decade. Its successor, the VP-9000, released in 2000, signaled another milestone in sampler design with the use of an upgraded control architecture that allows real-time manipulation of the voicing control settings via MIDI. Supported by a 250 megabytes ZIP drive, two SCSI ports, and expansion slots that accommodate up to 136 megabytes of memory, this sampler is indicative of the significantly enhanced specifications that had become the rule rather than the exception by the start of the new millennium. Curiously, though, the VP-9000 only supports a maximum of six independent voices, far fewer than most of its immediate competitors.

Reflecting the general trend toward the development of entirely self-contained facilities, Roland introduced a sampler-based system known as the SP808 Groove Sampling Workstation in 1998, followed by the SP808EX Sampling Workstation in 2000. One unusual feature in both cases is the complete absence of any internal memory for the retention of active sample data, the latter facilities being provided entirely externally via a fast access 100-megabyte ZIP disk. The Workstation also doubles as an eight-track digital recorder, signaling another integration of technologies in the growing quest for self-contained systems based on proprietary hardware.

One issue that began to inhibit the design of both samplers and synthesizers during the early 1990s was the basic limitation of MIDI to just sixteen independently controlled voice channels. The growing interest in multitimbral applications highlighted the growing inadequacy of this feature, which could not be renegotiated industry-wide without a fundamental change to MIDI itself. Having concluded that such a modification was not a practical proposition, manufacturers realized that the only practical solution was to add a second MIDI port. This permits a second layer of sixteen voice channels to operate in parallel with the first, control data being communicated between twin port devices via an auxiliary MIDI cable.

Such a facility was provided as an option for the E-mu E4 sampler, and became a standard feature for later upgrades such as the E4XT Ultra. Akai users had to wait for the S5000 and S6000 series for the inclusion of this second port; these samplers were introduced as replacements for the S3000 and S2800 in 1998. Yamaha followed suit in 2000, adding a similar facility for the A5000. In addition to supplying twin MIDI ports Akai also signaled a long overdue recognition of the value of audio data standardization by providing support for samples that are coded in the WAV format, while at the same time maintaining backward compatibility with its previous manufacturer-specific sample formats. Further improvements with these new models include an expanded memory capacity of 255 megabytes, 128 voices, and twin multieffects facilities designed specifically to enhance the stereo capabilities of the sampler. In a further attempt to maintain the appeal of hardware-based devices in the face of growing competition from software-based alternatives, the user interface also was completely redesigned, using icons as navigation aids in association with a larger display screen.

Whereas samplers, by their very nature, are based on a basic underlying architecture more suited to processes of refinement and consolidation than innovation, a very different perspective emerges if the field of study is now broadened to include the evolution of synthesizers during the 1990s. A superficial study of this market sector suggests a continuing high level of activity in terms of the production of new models, not only from the established manufacturers but also some new entrants. A closer examination, however, reveals a decade of considerable flux in terms of architectures, fermented by the growing struggle of many companies to make their products more attractive in the face of competition and a declining market.

Many synthesizer manufacturers, having just emerged from a period of highly competitive and rapid development associated with the transition from entirely analog to all-digital architectures, were anxious to recover their development costs by merely repackaging existing products rather than designing new ones. It soon became clear, however, that ultimately such a strategy was not sustainable, forcing a resurgence of research and development activities in many quarters seeking new or significantly improved architectures. These included, ironically, a revival of interest in analog synthesis methods and their associated control techniques. Far from being a temporary or transitional phenomenon, this desire to revisit the characteristics of older technologies gathered pace as the decade advanced.

Roland took an early initiative in this regard with the release of the JD-800. This provides an array of sliders as dedicated operator controls, much in the same manner as analog synthesizers are traditionally programmed via a control surface populated with knobs. Introduced in 1991, this ROM-based waveform synthesizer proved especially popular with several long-established pop and rock composers and performers, including Emerson, Lake, and Palmer, Tangerine Dream, and Jean Michel Jarre.

It was the JP-8000, however, introduced by Roland in 1997 that signaled a more fundamental reintroduction of practical facilities capable of simulating many of the functional characteristics of these older synthesizers. No less than thirty-eight knobs and sliders are provided to control a bank of digital oscillators, offering saw-tooth, square, and triangle waveforms that are then shaped by resonating filters offering low-pass, high-pass, and band-pass characteristics. The inclusion of a ring modulator, a low frequency oscillator (LFO), and classic delay and chorus effects adds to the analog feel of a synthesizer that has proved attractive to artists such as Gary Numan, Orbital, and the Pet Shop Boys. Roland augmented the JP-8000 with a rack-mountable version, the JP-8080, introduced in 1998. This increases the polyphony from eight to ten voices and adds a sampling facility for importing external sounds, a morphing facility that allows the progressive transformation from one voice characteristic to another, and a classic twelve-band vocoder.

These excursions into a design area now known generally as "retro-synthesis" were nevertheless largely peripheral to the development of Roland's primary range of products, which were indeed to be sustained for a number of years by further refinements to its well-tested combination of sampling and resynthesis techniques. A new JV series of products was launched in 1991, starting with the JV-80, a 28-voice keyboard synthesizer. A number of both keyboard and nonkeyboard versions were to follow, including the JV-2080, a large sixty-four-voice, rack-mountable synthesizer released in 1997. In parallel with the JV series, Roland introduced several workstation versions complete with sequencers, for example, the XP-10 released in 1994, and the flagship XP-80, released in 1996. The JV series was itself further upgraded in 2000 with the release of a new XV series. The XV-5080 model is of particular interest, as it not only offers an additional range of sounds derived from a number of earlier architectures, notably the JD-800, but also allows voices to be imported from both the standard Roland and the Akai sample libraries. Users of this continuing product range have included groups such as Faithless, Hardfloor, and Apollo 440. The special requirements of performers were addressed further in 2001 with the release of the XV-88 keyboard synthesizer, offering 128-note polyphony and a full length weighted piano keyboard. Two expansion boards are available for this synthesizer, the SRX01 providing an extensive drum kit and the SRX02 an emulation of a concert grand piano.

Kurzweil, having established their commitment to sampling keyboards with the Kurzweil 250, made one notable excursion into the all-synthesis domain before moving on to pastures new, with the release of the K150 in 1988. This is an additive synthesizer based on a bank of 240 sine wave oscillators, each of which may be regulated in terms of both pitch and amplitude, via individual envelope generators. Twenty-two preset voices are provided, and polyphonic textures can be generated in up to sixteen parts, with full sixteen-channel MIDI support. The use of all-digital oscillators ensures the high degree of pitch stability necessary for the accurate synthesis of timbres using Fourier principles, albeit with an audio bandwidth limited to just 10 kHz.

It was the earlier-mentioned convergence between sampling and synthesis technologies, however, which underpinned the development of Kurzweil's main product range during the new decade, starting with K2000 series, released in 1991. The standard keyboard-based version of the K2000 extracts all its sounds from samples stored in ROM, with no facilities for external sampling. The latter possibility, however, is addressed via an upgrade option that is in essence an add-on, self-contained sampler with SCSI-based communication facilities. The K2000 synthesis engine provides an array of feature extraction options based on a patented design principle known as Variable Architecture Synthesis Technology (VAST). These options are organized into two hundred different programs, with a choice of treatments and effects ranging from vibrato, resonant filters, chorus, and reverberation to multiple delays and movement-based simulations of rotary loudspeakers. This synthesizer and its derivatives became popular with many major bands and individual artists, including Pink Floyd, Stevie Wonder, and Nine Inch Nails.

The K2500 series, released in 1996, added a sequencer as a standard feature, built-in sampling capabilities for both the K2500S and K2500XS versions, and no less than sixty different signal processing algorithms. The power and versatility of the K2500 series is reflected in their prices, placing these products very much at the upper end of the main manufacturing sector. This upmarket trend was taken a stage further with the K2600 series, released in 1999, which incorporates facilities for further expansion in terms of both memory and processing capabilities.

E-mu, notwithstanding its primary reputation as a manufacturer of samplers, made a number of successful excursions into the synthesizer market during the decade with a range of rack-mountable products, starting with the Proteus. No less than three different models of this synthesizer were produced during the period

1989 to 1996, based on read-only versions of the EIII sampler library. Whereas the Proteus 1 offers a general library of synthesizer sounds, augmented with a percussion section for popular music applications, the Proteus 2 concentrates on purely orchestral sounds. Conversely, the Proteus 3 provides a range of more exotic sounds drawn primarily from non-Western cultures.

After a short break in production, the Proteus series was relaunched in 1999 with the Proteus 2000, which offers 128 voices, twin MIDI control ports, and a greatly expanded and comprehensive set of sampled sound sources with over one thousand factory-provided presets. Not content with this all-embracing product, E-mu went a stage further with the Virtuoso, released in 2000, which was a comprehensive orchestral synthesizer with a similarly extensive array of voice presets. E-mu's interest in new applications was taken a step further in 2001 with the release of the table top MP7 and XL7 series of 128-voice synthesizers, designed specifically for the dance music sector of the market.

The E-mu Morpheus, released in 1994 is a more unusual product, based on a synthesis technique known as Z-plane synthesis, whereby the processes of sampling are manipulated by means of "morphing" between two or more distinct sounds. These carefully computed processes of transition between different sound sources are augmented by the use of high-resolution filters to modify the spectral content. Such techniques, if carefully applied, can be very effective in simulating acoustic methods of synthesis, creating a heightened sense of realism. Groups that have taken a particular interest in the performance characteristics of the Morpheus include Astral Projection, Fluke, and Orbital.

E-mu's interest in exploring less mainstream territories was taken a stage further with the Vintage Keys synthesizer, released in the same year. As the name suggests, this product recreates the sounds of a traditional analog voltage-controlled synthesizer, anticipating the earlier-mentioned JP series from Roland. The source waveforms are sampled simulations of analog synthesizer sounds, which may be treated to articulation effects such as portamento and the addition of tracking filters, the latter recalling the high "Q" resonant features of their analog ancestors. E-mu's repertory of simulations is extensive, including classic sounds derived from several leading synthesizers, including the ARP 2600, the Oberheim OB-series, the Fairlight, the Minimoog, the Sequential Prophet 5, and the Mellotron.

This growing interest in retro-synthesis was to be further underpinned by Yamaha as part of a general quest for new and improved architectures, precipitated in the first instance by a decision to discontinue the production of hardware synthesizers offering the distinctive FM technology, pioneered with the DX7. The self-styled AWM2 technique of sampling sounds, introduced with the SY series, was retained instead as the primary architecture for several models including the W-5 and W-7 workstations, launched in 1994 and subsequently discontinued in 1998.

This technique, however, was also to serve as the basis of some interesting new implementations, for example, the Yamaha CS1x (1996). This synthesizer is functionally similar to the E-Mu Vintage Keys, emulating the characteristics of a voltage-controlled synthesizer via a control panel that provides six knobs to regulate envelope attack, envelope release, filter cutoff frequency, filter resonance, and two further user-selectable functions. Based on AWM2 principles, this new family of synthesis algorithms creates voices in Yamaha's XG format, which greatly extends the possibilities of the basic voice bank specifications laid down by the General MIDI (GM) standard.[6] With 128 voices and presets supported by thirty-two note polyphony and a sixteen-voice multitimbral capacity, this synthesizer has proved especially popular with a number of concert and dance musicians, including David Bowie, Jamiroquai, and Underworld.

Yamaha's interest in retro-synthesis was taken a stage further in 1997 with the release of the AN1x, which extends the functionality of the CS1x by extending the range of parameters controlled by the console knobs and also allowing the user to morph between two sounds via the modulation wheel. The change of name, however, arises from the use of a novel means of voice generation that merits closer attention. Instead of using a modified AWM2 sampling and resynthesis architecture to simulate analog waveforms the AN1x reproduces these characteristics in a much more direct manner by directly modeling the electronic oscillator functions, leading to an altogether more realistic analog sound. Other facilities of note include a ring modulator and a ribbon controller.

Yamaha recognized that, as it had produced such a variety of synthesizer architectures, it faced a number of strategic decisions in shaping the future of its now extensive product range. The solutions included embedding AN (ANalog modeling) technology in a much expanded, fully integrated synthesizer architecture, the EX series, while at the same time sustaining the CS-series with the release of two further models in 1999, the CS2x and the flagship CS6x. The latter offers a sampling facility as an additional feature and no less than thirteen voltage-controlled filters with upgraded specifications, derived in part from the filter section of the AN1x.

Before the functional characteristics of the EX synthesizers are considered in detail, attention must turn to another important hardware development fostered by Yamaha during the mid-1990s. Although the development of the XG format was a major step forward, the company continued to seek genuinely new synthesis architectures. In the same way that it had developed FM technology from pioneering research carried out by John Chowning at Stanford University, so the company continued to keep a close eye on the activities of institutional research centers, with a view to identifying innovative projects that might bear commercial fruit.

The establishment of CCRMA in 1975 as a major research center for computer music was helped to no small extent by the substantial financial support it received from Yamaha by way of royalties. It thus far from surprising that having carefully evaluated the alternatives Yamaha should return to Stanford, with a view to establishing a new research partnership in its quest for new synthesis methods. A research program initiated by Julius Smith at Stanford in the mid-1980s became the primary focus of attention, where instead of attempting to simulate instrumental sounds by some means of waveform synthesis, the computer is used to simulate the acoustic functions of the instrument itself by means of physical modeling.[7]

In terms of realism, physical modeling has the capacity to replicate most if not all of the complexities of instrumental sounds in ways that are not practical in terms of basic waveform generation and manipulation, whether by means of sampling or synthesis from first principles. It also offers the possibilities of a performance environment that closely relates to conventional music practices. Unfortunately, as will be seen in due course, the technique is necessarily complex and often hard to implement in practical terms, either as hardware or software, or a combination of both.

Yamaha entered into a contract with CCRMA in 1989 to develop a commercial synthesizer based on acoustic modeling, and accordingly in 1994 it launched the VL1 Virtual Acoustic Synthesizer.[8] Although marketed as a keyboard synthesizer, the full potential of the VL1 requires the use of external MIDI controllers to provide continuous regulation of key performance parameters, and to this end both a breath controller and a foot controller pedal are supplied as standard accessories. Another distinctive feature of the VL1, seen by some as a major drawback, is the limitation to a monophonic mode of operation, the synthesis capabilities thus being concentrated on the production of a single melodic voice.

The control functions themselves represent almost the antithesis of those to be found in a FM synthesizer, where, it will be recalled, the basic parameters regulating the frequency and amplitude settings of the constituent oscillators bear no obvious relation to the resulting timbres. Depending on the chosen instrumental simulation, the user encounters a specific set of readily identifiable performance variables, for example, wind pressure or bow speed, embouchure measured in terms of the tightness of the lips engaging with a mouthpiece, or the pressure of a bow on a string. In the case of vocal sounds, the characteristics of the constituent formants can be regulated in terms of the tension or relaxation of the vocal chords and the mouth.

Although sales of the VL1 fell short of expectations, the distinctive characteristics of physical modeling were to reappear in 1999 embedded in the architecture of its new EX series, starting with the EX-5 and its smaller relation, the EX-7. With these products Yamaha was able to provide a comprehensive repertory of synthesis methods (with the notable exception of FM) within a single operating environment that accommodates a full complement of 128 voices, as well as an integral sequencer. Voices may be constructed from sampled waveforms using one or a combination of the following: (1 AWM2 technology, (2) analog synthesis modeling (AN), (3) VL physical modeling, and (4) Formulated Digital Sound Processing (FDSP), which superimposes a range of digital signal processing control options on AWM2 sounds.

This adaptation of VL modeling provides an interesting example of the en-

hanced potential of many synthesis technologies when their distinctive characteristics are combined as part of an integrated environment. Parallels may be drawn
here with the ways in which sampling synthesizers often store electronic waveforms alongside those sampled from the acoustic domain within the same voice
bank, allowing the construction of sounds that combine elements of the natural
sound world with those of the synthetic.

The activities of Korg during the 1990s provide an interesting parallel to those
associated with Yamaha, bearing in mind the earlier acquisition of the former company by the latter. It would appear that considerable freedom was given to the
Korg design team retained by Yamaha in terms of exploring new ideas, albeit with
the underlying expectation that the resulting products should complement rather
than compete with those of the parent company. After a period devoted primarily
to the continuing manufacture of established products such as the M1 and the
DS-8, Korg started to diversify and innovate in a distinctive manner, starting with
the Trinity workstation, which was released in 1995. The basic synthesis section
consists of 24 megabytes of sampled sounds and over one hundred effects. These
can be organized into thirty-two independent voices and controlled by an internal
sequencer. This further contribution to the general convergence between samplers
and synthesizers is taken a stage further with the option of an add-on sample playback module, designed to read and convert both Akai and Korg sample library formats. The latter facility is extended to provide full sampling capabilities in the
Korg Triton, which followed in 1999, with the added bonus of sixty-four independent voices, and the smaller Karma (Kay Algorithmic Real-time Music Architecture) workstation, released in 2001.

Connections also can be established between Yamaha's work with analog and
physical modeling, which led to products such as the AN1x and the VL1, and the
use of similar techniques to model the sounds of analog synthesizers in both the
Korg Prophecy (1996), and the Korg Z1 (1997). This use of retro-engineering,
playing to the strengths of older Korg synthesizers, was taken a stage further with
the MS-2000, released in 2000, which models a comprehensive repertory of analog sounds including those of the earlier MS series, dating from the early 1980s.
Korg's AI^2 technology for re-synthesizing sampled sounds was also given a new
lease of life in the same year with the release of the X5D. This product recreates
the characteristics of a number of Korg synthesizers dating from the late 1980s and
early 1990s, including the KW series and the Korg Wavestation.

During the early part of the 1990s Ensoniq continued to manufacture the VFX
digital synthesizer and also introduced the SQ series of synthesizers, starting with
the SQ-1 in 1991 and continuing with the SQ-2, released in 1992, essentially
ROM-based versions of the keyboard-based EPS-16+ sampler. Like other manufacturers, Ensoniq had become engrossed in the dilemma of consolidation or
innovation, and 1993 saw a transitional TS series consisting of two models, the
TS-10 and TS-12. Although these synthesizers were still based on the same basic

sampling and resynthesis architecture used in earlier models, with only limited processing options in terms of both filters and effects, the voicing characteristics were enhanced by the provision of a morphing facility to allow dynamic transitions between different waveforms.

By the mid-1990s it was becoming clear to Ensoniq that the greatest financial rewards could be reaped from the growing market for performance keyboards with comprehensive arrays of fixed presets, rather than synthesizer architectures geared more significantly toward a more interactive voicing environment. As a consequence, the boundary between synthesizers and keyboards became increasingly blurred, in turn taking the general convergence between samplers and synthesizers a stage further. Ensoniq's next series of synthesizer/keyboards clearly illustrates this trend. Launched in 1994, the KT-76, and its larger companion the KT-88, were clearly designed as performance instruments, with sixty-four voice polyphony and an extensive repertory of sampled piano, organ and instrumental sounds, available at the touch of a button and supported by a flexible high capacity sequencer. At the same time, it is hard to fault the extensive voicing capabilities provided for more demanding users, supported by a comprehensive range of editing functions.

This uncertainty as to the most advantageous operational characteristics lies beneath the surface of many MIDI-based products dating from the 1990s, and Ensoniq's apparent ambivalence in this regard is symptomatic of the problems facing manufacturers at this time in sustaining their markets. Two years later, Ensoniq was to address the requirements of serious composers with the MR-61 and the MR-76, both offering an enhanced set of console tools for manipulating the control parameters for individual voices. The year prior to the company's merger with E-mu, 1997, saw developments advance in yet a further direction with the release of the ASR-X, followed by the ASR-X Pro in 1998. In essence, the ASR series are resampling workstations that combine all the primary functions of a sampler, synthesizer, sequencer and effects unit as part of a unified editing suite, controlled via a set of velocity-sensitive touch pads.

The similarity between this control interface and the touch pads traditionally associated with more specialist drum machines is no coincidence, since the ASR-X was specifically targeted at this more discerning performance market. Ensoniq, however, was not the first manufacturer to introduce improvements to the user interface for the benefit of this particular market sector. It will be recalled how Akai's partnership with Roger Linn led to the manufacture of sampling/sequencer devices such as the MPC60 during the late 1980s. In 1994, Akai released the MPC3000, a significantly improved version of the MPC that is closely modeled on the S3000 sampler with full sixteen-bit stereo sampling at 44.1 kHz, a memory capacity of sixteen megabytes, and an effects unit, integrated with a high capacity hardware sequencing facility. This was followed by an upgraded version, the MPC2000 in 1997, which supports sixty-four-track sequencing.

Notwithstanding the merger with E-mu, the distinctive nature of Ensoniq products was sustained with release of the Fizmo in 1998. This forty-eight-voice synthesizer uses an upgraded version of the morphing technology first used in the TS series and now patented as second-generation Transwave technology. This allows the flexible and dynamic control of resampled timbres, which are then processed shaped using an extensive repertory of digital effects.

Kawai continued to maintain a presence in the synthesizer market during the 1990s. The synthesis-plus-sampling architecture of the K1 was followed by a sampling-only version, the K4, released toward the end of 1989, with the added facility of a digital filtering section and the option of either a keyboard or a rack-mountable version. In 1996 Kawai released a new synthesizer, the K5000, and a workstation version the K5000W, complete with built-in sequencer. Drawing on the architectures used in earlier K-series models, the K5000 offers a combination of additive and sampling technologies in a manner similar to that used for the K5, but with a comprehensive processing section that offers a full range of filter options and a choice of thirty-two different effects.

Although the 1990s have been identified as a period of considerable rationalization within the synthesizer industry, leading to a number of mergers and realignments of marketing strategies, opportunities still existed for new entrants and design philosophies. The history of the Swedish firm Clavia DMI provides a notable example of the success that can accrue from diversification into new types of products. Founded in 1983 by Hans Nordelius and Mikael Carlsson, this company started by manufacturing a range of digital percussion plates and drums, pioneering the techniques of sampled sounds that were to become central to this whole area of applications. By the end of the 1980s, Clavia had developed this early series of experimental devices into a comprehensive range of MIDI tools for percussionist and drummers, and continued to establish the credentials of the company in this relatively specialist market during the early 1990s.

The breakthrough in terms of the mainstream synthesizer market came in 1995 with the release of the Clavia Nord synthesizer. Designed as a digital simulation of an analog synthesizer, this competitively priced product attracted interest from performers such as Fatboy Slim, Cirrus, Fluke, and Underworld. The ability to revisit the sound worlds of Moog, Buchla, ARP, and even some of the early Roland synthesizers was attractive to many enthusiasts, and provided a strong incentive for other retro-synthesizers such as the Yamaha CS1x and the Roland JP-8000.

The resources provided by the original Nord Lead were relatively modest, consisting of just two oscillators and a single voltage-controlled filter for basic voicing and timbre shaping, supported by a single ADSR envelope generator and low-frequency oscillator (LFO). The synthesizer, however, was polyphonic, offering between four and twelve voices. The Nord Lead 2, released in 1997, added a ring modulator, a second LFO, and some additional functionality to the two oscillators. The Nord Lead 3, released in 2000, provides a more comprehensive layout of knobs for the user control surface and a redesigned oscillator section, with a choice of six basic waveforms. Further voicing flexibility is possible via a morphing facility that allows continuous control of parameters in four different groupings.

A similar pattern of diversification can be identified in the case of Alesis. As noted earlier, this company established its reputation in the first instance as a manufacturer of effects units during the early years of MIDI.[9] The history of the company can be traced back further, to the 1970s, when its founder, Keith Barr, established a small company known as MXR in California to market a range of signal processors for the audio industry. Recognizing a growing market for competitively priced effects units, he sought capital for a much larger enterprise, launched as Alesis in 1984.

Following his success with the MidiVerb, the HR-16 drum machine and the QuadraVerb, Barr started to manufacture a new series of products, including a multitrack digital tape recorder.[10] His entry into the synthesizer market came in 1993 with the launch of the Alesis QuadraSynth, available both in a keyboard and a rack-mountable version, known as the S4. This sampling synthesizer offers full sixty-four-voice polyphony and a comprehensive signal processing section, and quickly established itself in the mainstream commercial market. Upgraded versions of both synthesizers followed in 1995, with larger ROM memories, leading in turn to the QS-6 later the same year and the QS-8 in 1996, which became the flagship model for the series, complete with a full-sized 88-note keyboard. Diversity in terms of specifications then led to an expanded range of products including the QS-6.1, released in 1999, which offers a library of 640 different voice samples and four hundred factory presets for different mixes of timbre.

Notwithstanding the success of these products, Alesis was to strike out again into pastures new in 2001 with the launch of the A6 Andromeda. This is a hybrid analog synthesizer designed to challenge the growing market for retro-technology, dominated by products that simulate analog devices in a wholly digital environment. Whereas these simulations have become remarkably realistic in recent years, it is still very hard to replicate the true warmth and expressiveness of analog circuits in this domain. By using digitally controlled analog oscillators and filters Alesis managed to achieve a genuine analog sound and at the same time secure a high degree of operational stability. Another drawback of traditional voltage-controlled synthesizers is their general restriction to a purely monophonic mode of operation. Products such as the Andromeda, which supports full sixteen-voice multitimbral polyphony, demonstrate that a return to analog engineering does not necessarily involve revisiting such major operational limitations and provide a useful stimulus for those interested in developing the principles of retro-engineering still further.

This return to the world of analog engineering, however, was not as pioneering a venture as it might at first seem, for in truth the world of electronic music had never totally succumbed to the all-embracing aspirations of digital engineering.

One company above all others must take the credit for remaining committed to the technology throughout the 1980s and the 1990s: Oberheim. Despite encountering trading difficulties during the late 1980s that resulted in its purchase by the electric guitar manufacturer Gibson, the company successfully relaunched itself with the release of the Oberheim OB-Mx synthesizer module in 1994. This repackaged many of the most useful features associated with earlier members of the OB series as a single, fully integrated system offering a comprehensive user control panel and ample capacity for expansion and subsequent upgrading.

The most distinctive feature of the OB-Mx is its synthesis engine, which in audio terms is wholly analog, resulting in a particularly authentic repertory of sounds. The control circuitry, however, like the Andromeda, is digital, thus largely avoiding the problems of frequency drift associated with a direct implementation of voltage-control technology and facilitating polyphonic rather than purely monophonic operation. Two oscillators, two multifunction filters, three LFOs, and four envelope generators provide a powerful and flexible synthesis facility, accessed by a control surface that is almost identical to that used for the original OB models. Given this long-standing commitment to analog technology, it is somewhat ironic to note that with its next model, the OB-12, Oberheim finally abandoned this domain for the world of all-digital simulation. Released in 2000, this entirely redesigned synthesizer provides an expanded control surface, richly populated with twenty-two knobs, twenty-four sliders, and thirty-three buttons, and an enhanced LED screen for the display for control parameters.

The growing popularity of analog retro-synthesis during the1990s encouraged new entrants to this manufacturing sector, notably Novation from England, Quasimidi from Germany, and FutureRetro from the United States. Novation's first product was a small portable MIDI controller keyboard with a two-octave range, the MM10, launched in 1992. The company, after securing a foothold in the market, turned its attention to the manufacture of analog synthesizers, starting with the Novation Bass Station Keyboard, released in 1995. This portable bass synthesizer uses dual VCOs and a VCF to generate and shape the basic sawtooth and pulse waveforms, a classic ADSR and LFO completing the configuration of this genuine MIDI-controllable, voltage-control synthesizer. The success of this synthesizer led to the rack-mountable Bass Station, released in 1995 and subsequently Super Bass Station, released in 1997. The latter model adds separate ADSRs for the oscillator and filter sections, a noise generator, a second LFO and a ring modulator.

In 1996, the company diversified further with the release of the Novation Drum Station, a complementary unit that uses analog sound modeling techniques to shape the characteristics of digitally sampled drum and percussion sounds. By 1998 the design team was ready to launch the Novation SuperNova, a sixteen-voice analog synthesizer designed to rival the Oberheim OB-Mx. In expanding the architecture of the Super Bass Station to meet the requirements of a full range system, Novation added a third VCO to the synthesis section, a facility to create classic analog FM sounds, a range of effects such as flange, chorus and reverb, and a forty-two-channel vocoder. Other models were to follow the SuperNova, notably the Novation Nova (1999) a desktop performance version, and the SuperNova II released in 2000. A smaller version, known as the Novation A-Station, was released in 2001.

Quasimidi entered the market in 1996 with the RaveOlution 309, in essence an analog drum and percussion machine with integral sequencer, which found a particular market within the dance sector. A keyboard-based version, the Sirius, followed in 1998, with additional effects including a vocoder. In a similar manner to Novation, the product range was subsequently expanded to include a complete analog synthesizer, the Polymorph, released in 1999. Like the Super Nova, this synthesizer uses three VCOs per voice, but with the addition of a morphing facility to allow up to four independently controlled synthesis components to be dynamically varied via a sequencing facility.

This increasingly worldwide interest in establishing new companies for retro-synthesis took another step forward in 1998, when FutureRetro made its debut with the FutureRetro FR777, a monophonic analog synthesizer with integral sequencer, once again following the classic design principles used for rival products such as the Novation Super Bass Station.

The growing interest in retro-synthesis was not confined purely to reproducing the sounds of analog synthesizers, for by this stage the digital revolution had already discarded many distinctive products of an earlier era. It will be recalled that, even as early as 1994, a product such as E-mu's Vintage Keys synthesizer included the sounds of the Fairlight in its repertory of voices, and this quest to recreate the sounds of earlier digital technologies was taken a stage further by Waldorf. In chapter 12, attention was drawn to the pioneering work of Wolfgang Palm during the late 1970s in developing real-time digital oscillators, resulting in the innovative PPG Wave 2.2 and 2.3 synthesizers, and the PPG Waveterm.[11] With the demise of PPG in 1987, the rights to these products passed to Waldorf, a new company founded by Wolfgang Düren, who with assistance from Palm incorporated the technology into a new range of products, starting with the Microwave I, a rack-mountable synthesizer, released in 1990.

The significance of this product and its immediate successors lies in their ability to emulate so many different analog electronic sounds by means of digital wave-table synthesis. As other manufacturers continued the quest for new synthesis methods in the digital domain, so synthesizers such as the Microwave I and its successor the Microwave II made a virtue of the techniques of retro-synthesis, in so doing achieving increasing prominence. The real legacy of the PPG era, however, came to fruition in the design of the synthesizer that followed, the Waldorf Wave, released in 1993. Here the potential of digital wavetable synthesis is explored to the full, resulting in a sixteen-voice synthesizer that may be expanded to a maximum capacity of forty-eight voices. The power and versatility of this product came at a price, placing it in the same league as the Kurzweil 2000, and its distinctive sound has proved popular with many leading performers, including Eat Static and Enya.

Toward the middle of the decade Waldorf started to diversify its technology, resulting in an expanded range of products designed to satisfy the growing retromarket. The first of these, the Waldorf Pulse, was introduced in 1996. This monophonic synthesizer provides three audio oscillators offering saw-tooth, triangle and pulse waveforms, and a voltage-controlled filter, with independent ADSRs and two LFOs. Three years later, the company produced two compact versions of the Microwave II, the XT, and the XTk, and also launched the Waldorf Q synthesizer. The latter model, available in both keyboard and rack-mountable versions, emulates the characteristics of the voltage-controlled synthesizer via comprehensively equipped control surfaces, well populated with knobs and sliders for regulating individual functions. In 2000 the Micro Q was added to the range, taking the form of a more basic version of the rack-mountable option.

It would thus seem from the sheer scale and scope of the developments described above that the MIDI manufacturing sector entered the new millennium with an assured future in terms of the continuing production of proprietary hardware. Indeed, the continuing enthusiasm for self-contained performance devices from many quarters, not least the all-important rock and pop music industries, adds further weight to such a view. Such a conclusion, however, may be premature, because it fails to take account of even more fundamental changes in the nature and scope of digital technology that have been gathering significant momentum since the mid-1990s. In order to place these in an appropriate context it is necessary to complete yet another piece of this increasingly complex jigsaw puzzle by taking a further look at the evolution of the personal computer, this time in the context of its audio rather than its MIDI capabilities.

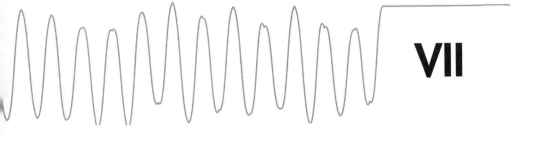

VII

Desktop Synthesis and Signal Processing

18

Personal Computers and Sound Processing

In considering the development of the personal computer as a musical tool, attention has so far focused primarily on applications that make relatively modest demands on the underlying technology, for example the development of software for editing and regulating control data within the MIDI environment. Tasks such as audio synthesis and signal processing were to prove a far more challenging prospect, in many instances requiring the services of additional hardware.

In the same way that the minicomputer was initially regarded as the poor relation of its mainframe parent, so for a number of years the personal computer was to remain overshadowed by an alternative, and initially much more powerful computer architecture, the UNIX computer workstation. Back in the early 1980s, it was still far from evident that the personal computer would become the primary technology for the industry as a whole. Moreover, there was an influential market sector, primarily associated with the work of research institutions that urgently required suitably powerful replacements for minicomputers such as the PDP 11. With the emphasis on performance rather than popular appeal a small group of independent manufacturers grasped this opportunity to invest in a new generation of compact, high-performance computer workstations to meet these criteria.

Achieving continuity for existing projects was of paramount importance, and the primary consideration here was the need to preserve and enhance UNIX, a special operating system and programming environment for writing applications that had become the industry standard for the sector. Bell Telephone Laboratories originally developed UNIX during the late 1960s as a time-sharing system for the PDP 11, using structures written almost entirely in the programming language C.[1] This decision was visionary in the sense that complete portability to other computers was anticipated from the outset. Although a version of UNIX, known as LINUX, was developed in due course specifically for the Intel-based PC, issues of software compatibility and the dominance of the primary Microsoft operating system has severely limited its impact. As a result, most personal computer users have not been able to benefit directly from the development of UNIX-based computer music facilities.

This situation was to have material consequences for the medium. To a certain extent, this institutional exclusivity was fostered by the prevailing culture of the UNIX community itself, which for many years ensured that the personal computer was dismissed as an inferior product, ill-equipped to cope with the special demands of scientific research. This attitude, however, was eventually to prove unsustainable. Although UNIX-based workstations remained at the leading edge of computing technology throughout the 1980s, the justification for their superior status and premium cost was progressively eroded. By the mid-1990s, high-end personal computers could already match the performance of entry-level UNIX workstations, and by the start of the new millennium the differences were more to do with the characteristics of the operating systems than issues of relative power and versatility.

The matrix of activities to be studied here is complex, not only in terms of the diversity of techniques and applications to be covered but also the nature and impact of the different facilities. Although many developments remained exclusive to the institution concerned, some were released in due course for wider consumption within the UNIX community. It was largely because of the vision of IRCAM during the early 1990s that advanced facilities of this type finally became available to a much wider constituency, with the release of non-UNIX versions of IRCAM software in a format suitable for the Apple Macintosh, in the first instance. As a result of this initiative, other leading computer music research institutions began to take a more positive interest in personal computers, leading to a highly beneficial convergence of interests as the millennium approached.

It is against this background that attention now turns to key features of the underlying technology. In this chapter, the primary focus of attention is the evolution of audio processing systems based on the personal computer, taking into account some interesting institutional research programs dating from the pre-MIDI era that directly influenced these developments. Chapter 19 studies the parallel developments that are associated with the evolution of UNIX-based workstations.

It will be recalled that until the mid-1980s the development of audio resources for computers was not a high priority for the computer industry. The introduction of the Apple Macintosh in 1984 was thus a significant landmark in this regard, as it incorporated a digital-to-analog converter and associated hardware that allowed audio data to be output directly from memory.[2] Although, it will be recalled, the fidelity was limited (mono only, with an eight-bit resolution at 22.05 kHz), the provision of such a facility stimulated a growing interest in the use of small computers to generate and process sound information.

A further impetus in this direction came from the MIDI community itself, notably the rapidly expanding sector concerned with developing the possibilities of sampling. Although MIDI samplers provided integrated editing facilities as a matter of course, frustration with the practical limitations of these features focused attention on the superior WIMPS-based resources provided by personal computers. Accordingly, a number of MIDI software manufacturers added sample editing programs to their list of products toward the end of the 1980s, including Blank Software (Alchemy), Dr. T, Steinberg, and Turtle Beach. Unfortunately, these applications generated their own problems, because the computer cannot directly manipulate audio data within the sampler. Instead, this information has to be transferred from the sampler to the computer for editing and then returned for use.

The most common means of data transfer during the early years of MIDI required the use of the special "system exclusive" mode provided by MIDI itself. The low data speed, however, severely impedes the transmission of high bandwidth audio data in this manner, resulting in significant delays in the transfer of data.[3] These range typically from about 20 seconds to about 90 seconds for a single second of sound, depending on the sampling rate, the mode (mono/stereo), and the associated bit resolution.

A further and in many ways more fundamental problem concerned the capacity of the CPU itself to process the data. It is important here to refine the distinction already made between applications that apply a computer simply to control low bandwidth functions, using for example conventional MIDI "note/event" messages, and those that engage directly with the audio data itself. Although the basic technology of these early machines was still not powerful enough to handle audio synthesis and signal processing tasks in real time, it occurred to some system developers that they might be used instead to control more powerful custom-designed audio processors.

It was with this prospect in mind that an important research initiative was launched at IRCAM in 1984. It had become increasingly clear to the institution that it required a central file server for handling the increasing number of audio data files created by composers. Aside from special audio processors such as the 4X, the core computing resources of the institution were now based around a VAX computer, essentially an upgraded thirty-two-bit version of the PDP minicomputer manufactured by DEC, and an early series of UNIX workstations manufactured by SUN.[4]

The announcement of the Apple Macintosh caught the attention of David Wessel and Adrian Freed, who persuaded Apple Computer to lend IRCAM a number of machines. It soon became apparent to Freed that the WIMPS environment of the Macintosh made the computer an attractive proposition as a control interface for the file server, and in 1985 the first version of a program known as MacMix appeared. Although communications between the Macintosh and the VAX were restricted to a single serial connection offering a relatively low bandwidth, this was still fast enough to allow interactive editing of soundfiles, the VAX computer translating the graphic control data directly into equivalent audio processing functions.

The range of facilities offered was extensive. The overall amplitude envelopes of sounds could be displayed and edited, and different audio segments selected and mixed or spliced together. An additional attraction was the ability to display different aspects of the editing process in separate windows. Thus, the inner detail of a complex editing function could be viewed in one window, while keeping an eye on the overall effect of any changes in another. The success of the venture led to a reworking of the software to produce a version for the SUN Workstations, known as SunMix.

The release of MacMix coincided with another important commercial development. In 1985 two computer designers, Peter Gotcher and Evan Brooks, established a company called Digidesign to manufacture Sound Designer, a Macintosh-based sample editing program designed in the first instance for use with the E-mu Emulator II sampler. Support for the data formats of other leading samplers such as the Sequential Prophet 2000 and the Akai S612 soon followed, with further additions in due course as the market steadily expanded. In 1986 Digidesign introduced a software synthesis package, Softsynth, offering a bank of thirty-two oscillators with a choice of waveforms, each controllable by a forty-stage envelope shaper and a fifteen-stage frequency envelope, with the option of configuring the arrangement for FM synthesis. In due course a more powerful version known as Turbosynth was released, providing a comprehensive range of synthesis and signal processing functions that include modulation, filtering, delay, pitch shifting, and looping, as well as a program to process externally sampled sounds.

Despite steady improvements in the design of the Macintosh, notably the introduction of the Macintosh II series in 1987, it was clear to Gotcher and Brooks that the computer still did not have the capacity to realize the true potential of Digidesign's growing repertory of software. Neither of the synthesis programs, for example, could operate in real time and the computer had difficulty in coping with long sounds. In addition, any direct sound output from these computers still suffered from the limited fidelity of the internal digital-to-analog converter.

Fortunately, recent developments in microchip technology now offered attractive solutions to both problems. In the case of the latter, the development of the compact disc player had stimulated the production of high-quality audio converter chips at increasingly competitive prices. In the case of the former, the processing bottlenecks encountered in manipulating large quantities of video and audio data provided an incentive for manufacturers to design a new family of microprocessors specifically engineered for the purpose, known as Digital Signal Processors or DSPs.

In the field of digital audio the concept of the DSP had been foreshadowed in the late 1970s and early 1980s by a number of pioneering systems built at various research institutions from discrete components. Examples already highlighted include the 4X developed at IRCAM, and the digital oscillator bank designed by Hal Alles at Bell Telephone Laboratories.[5] Two further systems dating from this period merit particular attention in this context, the Samson Box (otherwise known as the Systems Concepts Digital Synthesizer) and the Lucasfilm Digital Audio Processor.

The Samson Box was designed by Jim Samson and installed at CCRMA, Stanford, in 1977. Like the 4X, the synthesis hardware was built from arrays of logic gates, optimized for the tasks of audio signal generation and processing. Extensive use was made of instruction sequencing, known as pipelining, to speed up chains of signal processing steps, anticipating hardware techniques that were to feature prominently in the subsequent development of DSPs. The synthesizer's real time resources included 256 oscillators, 128 signal modifiers providing treatments such as modulation and filtering, and thirty-two delay units, supporting a variety of conventional and more innovative synthesis and signal processing functions, including FM and wave-shaping. Real-time control of the Samson Box was exercised by a small PDP 6 computer, which was linked to the main PDP 10 using shared data storage facilities.

The primary operating program, MUSICBOX, was closely modeled on the characteristics of MUSIC 10, allowing the user to specify instrumental specifications and performance data in advance. This allowed real-time synthesis of a predetermined list of events, but not as yet a fully interactive performance mode of operation. The challenges faced by programmers in developing suitable tools for composers within MUSICBOX were nonetheless considerable, as the Samson Box required many functions to be controlled simultaneously, and the control computer could only provide data sequentially. The solution lay in the construction of these tools via SAIL, a low-level language developed in 1976 by the Stanford Artificial Intelligence Laboratory specifically to simulate parallel control environments.

William Schottstaedt subsequently developed PLA as an alternative to MUSICBOX. Instead of generating a "note/event" type of score, this program directly engaged with the inner workings of SAIL to produce structures that were built on the notion of message passing between individual synthesis functions. The result was a much more interactive environment for composers, anticipating some important developments at IRCAM to be discussed in the next chapter.[6]

The Lucasfilm Digital Audio Processor is of special interest since its digital signal processing section, although built largely from discrete components, used principles of design that are remarkably similar to those associated with the internal construction of the modern DSP fabricated on a single silicon chip. This system was the brainchild of James Moorer, who moved to Lucasfilm from Stanford soon after completing his work on MUSIC 10 in the mid-1970s.[7] Assisted by James Snell, he began work on the project in early 1980, and by 1983 the system was fully operational.

Although designed specifically for the needs of the film industry, which had not been previously noted for particularly good standards of audio fidelity, the system was engineered to the highest specifications. A total of sixty-four channels of sound information could be processed at a 50 kHz sampling rate, mapped across a bank of eight processing modules controlled in turn by a 68000-based microcomputer. Each module offered a wide variety of functions, ranging from filtering and pitch shifting for individual channels to multitrack editing and mixing, accessed via a series of consoles that linked sound and vision for the purposes of film production.

Systems such as the Lucasfilm Digital Audio Processor clearly demonstrated the potential of audio signal processing to the recording industry. In 1984 AMS launched the Audiofile, an entirely self-contained digital recording system using computer disks to record tracks in place of conventional analog tape. Most broadcasting and recording companies were still very suspicious of the personal computer, and such market conditions stimulated the development of expensive products such as the PostPro recording system from New England Digital (NED) in 1986, and MFX from Fairlight in 1989. Further competition in this sector was stimulated by other entrants to this potentially very lucrative high-end market, for example WaveFrame, which started to manufacture multitrack digital recording and editing systems in 1986. The invention of the DSP, however, was eventually to undermine the exclusivity of such products, allowing the development of much more affordable facilities for the industry as a whole.

In the same way as Intel is credited with the manufacture of the first microprocessor in 1972, a similar distinction can be cited for the company's production of the first general purpose DSP chip in 1978, the 2920. As a novel and untested architecture attempting to penetrate an established market for conventional microprocessors, its impact was fairly modest, a disappointing speed of computation serving to mask the underlying significance of the special technology. In 1980 NEC introduced a faster and more powerful DSP known as the muPD7720. This inspired a number of leading microprocessor manufacturers to start developing rival products to an even higher specification, notably Texas Instruments with the release of the TMS 32000 in 1983.

The special characteristics of these digital signal processors require some qualification since it follows that any computing architecture that is optimized for a specific mode of operation will inevitably prove more efficient for some types of data processing and less so for others. As a result, there often are major differences between the functional characteristics of one DSP and those of another. The TMS 32000, for example, was designed specifically for applications such as computer graphics and the online control of industrial processes. Nevertheless, the architecture was sufficiently attractive to persuade several research groups to investigate its use for audio applications, in particular the possibility of using the processor for real-time synthesis applications. Such developments were helped significantly by the subsequent introduction of faster versions as part of a new 32020 series of processors, notably the 320C25, which provided a considerably improved instruction set for programmers. Rival products of a similar specification included the MB87064 from Fujitsu and the WE DSP16A from AT & T.

One notable feature of these early DSPs was the use of fixed-point data formats for internal processing. In discussing the relative merits of fixed-point and floating-point formats, attention has been drawn to the problems encountered whenever data is processed in a fixed-point format, in particular the loss of fidelity if amplitudes are attenuated and then subsequently boosted in value. DSPs such as the above generally operated at a maximum resolution of sixteen bits, which left no margin at all for processing high resolution audio signals. A major breakthrough came in 1985 with the release of the 56000 series of DSPs from Motorola. Here this problem is addressed by using twenty-four-bit rather than sixteen-bit registers for the processing of data, a feature it will be recalled that subsequently solved similar problems in the design of high quality samplers.[8]

It was a variant of the 56000, the 56001, which provided Digidesign with an attractive answer to the processing limitations of the Apple Macintosh. In 1988 it released a plug-in card known as the Sound Accelerator, consisting of a 56001 DSP and a sixteen-bit CD-quality digital-to-analog converter that outputs data at 44.1 kHz. Because the card is directly linked to the main data bus of the computer the DSP becomes in effect a co-processor, able to communicate at high speed with the Macintosh and its peripherals.

A further hardware upgrade soon followed, taking the form of a second plug-in card that communicates directly with an external interface box, the latter providing sixteen-bit stereo input and output facilities operating at a maximum rate of 48 kHz. In addition, the interface box incorporated digital input and output facilities for the growing number of commercial audio products that allowed the direct transfer of data in a digital format. These included professional quality CD players and the newer DAT recorder, already becoming popular in studios as a digital replacement for the traditional reel-to-reel analog stereo tape recorder.

One important consequence of this rapid growth in digital audio applications during the 1980s was an agreement throughout the recording industry to adopt just two primary protocols for the transfer of digital data at audio rates between individual devices. These are known as S/PDIF, and AES/EBU, the former essentially a simplified version of the latter, still widely regarded as the primary industry standard.[9]

In 1989 Digidesign released Sound Tools for the Macintosh, a version for the Atari ST following in 1990. This product consisted of two components, the Sound Accelerator card system described above, and an updated version of Sound Designer, known as Sound Designer II, which allows complete stereo digital audio files to be edited. In addition a range of signal processing options are provided. These include ten-band graphic equalization, time compression/expansion, and the superimposition of simple fade-in and fade-out envelopes, all of these functions being handled by the 56001 processor. A further program, DEC, was provided to allow four rather than two channels of audio information to be processed simultaneously.

In terms of the existing repertory of Digidesign software, programs such as Turbosynth could now operate in real time, the resulting output being simultaneously recorded in a data file for future use. Although Sound Designer II could still be used for editing voice data imported from MIDI samplers, Digidesign recognized that the requirements of this increasingly important group of users could be better served by designing a special plug-in DSP card and associated software. Known as Sample Cell, this facility is in effect a self-contained sampler, capable of addressing up to eight megabytes of memory.

By the time Sound Tools had become commercially available, Digidesign was already facing competition from other manufacturers, eager to capitalize on the signal processing opportunities provided by the Motorola 56000 series of DSPs. In 1987 the Swiss firm Studer-EdiTech released Dyaxis, a hard disk-based recording system based on the 56001 processor, and controlled by an Apple Macintosh. Although this was a relatively expensive product, targeted at the middle of the market between Sound Tools and systems such as PostPro, the fact that it was controlled by a personal computer impressed the recording industry, which regarded Studer as one of its most established and respected members. Moreover, the controlling software was none other than an updated version of MacMix, from IRCAM.

Sonic Solutions introduced a plug-in system using four 56000 processors in 1989, once again controlled by an Apple Macintosh. Offering very similar facilities to Sound Tools, this product was specifically intended for postproduction work in the burgeoning CD market, preparing recordings for mass duplication. Sound Tools already had the capacity to prepare CD sound files at the required sample rate of 44.1 kHz. Sonic Solutions, however, went one step further by including a special processing tool called NoNoise, which could be used to clean up defects in older analog recordings prior to their rerelease on CD. Later versions of Digidesign incorporated a number of operational improvements and refinements. The Audiomedia card, for example, which replaced Sound Designer in the early 1990s, provides audio processing, S/PDIF digital input/output and analog input/ output facilities on a single plug-in card.

In contrast to the growing popularity of the Apple Macintosh, the outlook for the Intel-based PC as a host for digital audio applications was still far from certain at this time. No sound facilities other than the basic one-bit signaling system were routinely provided by any of the manufacturers of these IBM clones, and the lack of an adequate graphics user interface made the architecture singularly unattractive for audio editing. Some important foundations for a change to this apparent impasse were nevertheless already in place, the incentive coming in the first instance from the games industry.

In 1985 Creative Labs introduced the GameBlaster, a plug-in card for the Intel-based PC that could be programmed to produce elementary sound effects. Three years later, this was replaced by the SoundBlaster, an improved card with the added facility of a digital-to-analog converter that could output sound in mono from memory at 22.05 kHz, with a resolution of eight bits. Thus, in essence, an Intel-based PC, when fitted with a SoundBlaster Card, could at last offer similar audio facilities to those provided by the original Apple Macintosh.

Another important milestone occurred a year later when Digigram introduced a sixteen-bit stereo audio card for the Intel-based PC, soon to be followed by a rival product, CardD, developed by Digital Audio Laboratories. The latter provides a full range of analog and S/PDIF input/output facilities, operating at 48, 44.1, 32, or 22.05 kHz. Although none of these cards directly support any co-processor hardware for synthesis and/or signal processing, their functionality transformed the Intel-based PC into a computer suitable for a range of basic digital audio applications.

Although Creative Labs still regarded the games industry as the primary market for its products, the company recognized the importance of developing high quality audio facilities. Accordingly, in 1993 it released the SoundBlaster 16, an upgraded version of the original SoundBlaster that offers CD-quality audio output at 44.1 kHz. With the release of the Windows 95 operating system in 1995, the Intel-based PC was at last ready to compete directly with Macintosh II-based systems. Both of these personal computer environments could now provide high-quality audio input and output and WIMPs-based editing on a comparable basis, and several manufacturers were engaged in the manufacture of rival plug-in audio cards to even higher specifications. SADiE, for example, had already released a stereo digital audio-processing card for the Intel-based PC, known as the XS, in 1991 and took full advantage of the improved Windows environment to develop a series of professional multitrack recording and editing systems.

Longstanding issues of hardware compatibility across these two computing platforms were resolved to a significant extent as the result of an important decision taken by Apple within a year of introducing the Power Macintosh in 1994 to redesign the internal communications bus architecture. As a consequence, the existing architecture, known as Nubus, was changed to conform to the PCI architecture that had become the universal standard for the Intel-based PC. Identical plug-in cards could often be used with both hosts, the differences confined to the operating characteristics of the controlling software in each case. Companies such as Digidesign quickly capitalized on the opportunities for cross-platform marketing with a new PCI version of its Audiomedia card and associated software, followed by compatible versions of Protools, its flagship fully professional digital multitrack recording and editing system, based on a system of plug-in DSP cards.

Technology was to change the goalposts yet again as the decade progressed. By the end of the 1990s, it was clear that improvements in the speed and processing power of personal computers had all but eliminated the need for any additional DSP support in the case of less demanding applications such as simple audio recording and sound file editing. This stimulated a market for programs requiring no additional processing hardware, for example, Peak for the Macintosh and Sound Forge for the Intel-based PC, and also encouraged manufacturers such as Protools to release software-only versions of their systems, albeit offering reduced specifications to those of their DSP-supported counterparts.

Notwithstanding the growing significance of the personal computer in this context, a major market still existed for self-contained digital recording systems of a more conventional nature. The success of the DAT recorder encouraged manufacturers to develop cheaper alternatives, targeted initially at the consumer market but again demonstrating the potential to satisfy more professional requirements. Philips and Sony, having collaborated over the development of the CD-ROM for the personal computer, decided to develop technologies directly in competition during the early 1990s. The digital compact cassette (DCC) recorder, developed by Philips, was released in 1992 as a replacement for the conventional analog cassette, the digital technology incorporating a facility to playback recordings in both formats.

Sony swiftly followed with the MiniDisc, a portable recorder based on the magneto-optical principles used for computer optical disks. One feature common to both systems is the use of lossy compression techniques to reduce the amount of information actually recorded. As early examples of data reduction technologies the quality issues already raised in this context are especially relevant.[10] Both systems deliver a near-CD quality but fall some way short of the noncompressed standards of fidelity provided by conventional DAT recorders.

The early 1990s also were notable for the development of two competitively priced digital multitrack recorders to challenge high-end systems such as PostPro, MFX, or Waveframe. These recorders provide eight channels of audio recording, multiplexed in a digital format onto a videotape cassette. Sixteen or even twenty-four channels of recording can be achieved by connecting and synchronizing two or three recorders together to create a single unit.

The first system, ADAT, was pioneered by Alesis and released in 1992. The recording media consists of a conventional VHS videotape that runs at three times the normal speed, using a special helical scan head to multiplex eight channels of digital audio as a continuous bit stream of data. Although the standard sampling rate is 48 kHz, this is adjustable on playback between 49.4 and 50.8 kHz, allowing a limited application of variable speed processing. Samples are stored with a resolution of sixteen bits, and each audio channel is assigned its own matching pair of analog-to-digital and digital-to-analog converters. Alesis replaced the ADAT with an improved version the ADAT XT in 1996, and in 1998 released the ADAT XT20, which upgrades the sample resolution from sixteen to twenty bits, serviced by oversampled converters that deliver an effective resolution of twenty-four bits.

The ADAT was soon to face direct competition from another quarter. At the end of 1992 Tascam released the DA88, an eight-track digital recorder that uses a more compact Hi-8 tape cassette, commonly used by portable video recorders. As with the ADAT a helical scanning system is used to record the multiplexed channels at either 44.1 or 48 kHz with a resolution of sixteen bits.

Two further models based on the same format were released in the mid-1990s, the DA38 and the DA98, an upgraded version that provides a comprehensive range of cueing and basic track editing features. In 2000 the entire series was upgraded to full twenty-four-bit sampling with the release of the DA78 and the DA98 HR. Backward compatibility for the playback of earlier recordings is provided and the recorders can also be set to record in the original sixteen-bit format if so desired. Whereas the DA78 provides eight channels of audio at either 44.1 or 48 kHz in a twenty-four bit format, the DA98 also can be set to record four channels of audio at 96 kHz, or two channels of audio at 192 kHz. Tascam took the use of twenty-four-bit technology a stage further in the same year with the release of the first DAT recorder capable or recording at this higher resolution, the DA 45.

In the same way that, during the 1990s, software-based audio recording systems for personal computers began to occupy the ground hitherto requiring the support of DSP technology, so the prospects for implementing real-time software synthesis and signal processing programs steadily improved. One program proved to be of particular significance in this context: Barry Vercoe's MUSICn derivative, CSOUND.[11] Although this was originally written for a UNIX-based workstation, the fact that it was written in the programming language C made it possible to develop versions suitable for both the Macintosh and the Intel-based PC. Real-time synthesis, using CSOUND, however, was still not a practical proposition for personal computer users at this time, and even high-performance workstations lacked adequate processing capacity. The orders of the delay generally encountered in generating audio data, however, were no worse than those encountered by direct synthesis composers using mainframe computers in the 1970s, and with each upgrade in processor speed this time interval steadily reduced.

It was Vercoe himself who pioneered the first truly real-time system for CSOUND in the late 1980s, using a specially constructed audio processor based on the Motorola 56x DSP series. Controlled by an Apple Macintosh, this system allowed the instant synthesis of a useful repertory of CSOUND functions, shifting the emphasis from the precomposed score to the world of performance, where events are directly triggered by suitable keystrokes on a keyboard.

By the middle of the 1990s, the standard processor speeds of personal computers had increased to the point where a similar performance could be achieved without the aid of DSP-based co-processors, thus increasing the overall accessibility of real-time CSOUND to the wider composing community. With the introduction of even faster and powerful personal computers such as the Apple Macintosh G4 and the Pentium 4-based PC almost the entire repertory of CSOUND facilities could at last be used in live performance.

One interesting result of this progression was the forging of useful links between CSOUND and MIDI in situations in which the performance control parameters for a CSOUND program are associated with the conventional note/event articulation of pitch and amplitude. In so doing, yet another applications boundary was crossed, as CSOUND, in effect, becomes a fully programmable, software-based MIDI synthesizer. Activities in this regard have taken on yet another dimension as a result of a growing interest in the characteristics of older synthesis technologies, associated in the first instance with voltage control and first-generation digital synthesizers.[12] Although investment in renewed hardware production is rarely viable, software simulations have proved an increasingly attractive alternative, using techniques pioneered commercially by Steinberg as Virtual Studio Technology or VST.

This initiative was underpinned by the development of a new family of software that combines MIDI sequencing facilities with multitrack audio recording facilities, allowing a mixture of MIDI control and audio tracks within a single program. Examples of this hybrid software include Digital Performer from MOTU, Pro Audio from Cakewalk, and Logic Audio from Emagic. The engagement of traditional MIDI software houses with the world of digital audio applications was thus met by similar developments proceeding in the opposite direction, extending the functionality of digital audio software to include the control of MIDI channels. A notable example of such a product is Protools from Digidesign, which now fully integrates both aspects.

Steinberg recognized the potential of this mixed environment for creating a new repertory of software synthesizers that could be used alongside the traditional hardware-based systems. This resulted in the release of Cubase VST, which adds a facility to include custom-designed "plug-in" devices, starting with modules such as the Pro-Five, which simulates the Sequential Prophet 5, and the Model E, which simulates the Minimoog. Later examples include the Waldorf PPG 2.V, released in 2000, recreating the functional characteristics of the original PPG synthesizers.[12]

An important feature of VST technology in this context is the intention not merely to recreate the sounds of these classic products but also simulate the original control surface using WIMPS. Unfortunately, the inherent limitations of a mouse-driven environment, where only one function component can be adjusted at a time, poses some major practical constraints on these virtual synthesizers. As a result, some hardware manufacturers decided to develop external control panels that incorporate a suitable range of sliders and knobs.

A major impetus for this new departure came from the professional audio industry. Although the WIMPS-based control structure of products such as Protools proved suitable for postproduction work, where the primary emphasis is on editing functions, many engineers found this situation less than ideal, especially when engaged with live recording rather than post-production editing. Here there is a particular need to monitor and regulate a number of control parameters in real time, relying on the dexterity of the operator's fingers to select and carefully adjust the console settings.

Recognizing the significance of this drawback to its software, Digidesign responded with its own physical control surface, ProControl, released in 1998 specifically to control Protools, followed by Control|24, released in 2001. In addition to managing the primary digital links direct to the computer, Control|24 provides a comprehensive set of analog input and output channels in the manner of a traditional mixer. In a similar vein, Steinberg introduced a hardware interface for its growing repertory of VST modules in 2001. Known as Houston, this control panel provides users with groups of physical sliders, rotary control knobs and push-buttons, each of which may be freely assigned to any of the functions associated with the chosen virtual module.

By the end of the 1990s, it had become clear that this conflation of computer-based technologies was indeed posing a major challenge to the traditional hardware synthesizer industry, notwithstanding the notable initiatives being pursued within the latter manufacturing sector. On the one hand, the convenience of a self-contained unit is self-evident, particularly in the context of live performance. On the other hand, the opportunities for gaining access to an expanding repertory of software synthesizer modules via a single command and control system were proving increasingly attractive, not least on the grounds of flexibility and the much lower costs involved in adding new modules. This trend toward an integrated environment also allowed an almost seamless integration of technologies right across the computer music spectrum. The plug-in VST environment, indeed, has expanded to embrace not only software simulations of older commercial synthesizers but also products of institutional research, for example, the signal processing resources of GRM Tools.[13]

Further indications of the far-reaching impact of these changes are provided by the widening activities of Yamaha. Although the MIDI synthesizer market remained central to the overall manufacturing strategy of this company, its interests have become increasingly focussed on other aspects of digital audio, in particular the recording sector. In 1987 Yamaha released the DMP7 audio mixer, a product in its own terms just as innovative as the DX7 synthesizer. This is a MIDI-controlled digital mixer, providing eight input channels and two output channels complete with motorized controls and built-in DSP facilities for equalization and audio effects. Although the audio fidelity of this product did not quite match the CD specification in terms of bit resolution, the ability to program its functions via MIDI anticipated the functionality of hybrid MIDI/audio sequencing systems by several years.

Building on the success of this product, Yamaha released an improved and expanded sixteen-channel version, the ProMix 01, in 1993, followed by the twenty-four-channel 02R, released in 1997. Although clearly intended to meet professional studio requirements, the price of the 02R proved sufficiently attractive to guarantee it a much larger customer base. Yamaha, however, was to take the technology a stage further. Well aware of the growing interest in computer sound cards it introduced a plug-in DSP synthesis module, for the Intel-based PC, the DB50XG, in 1995. In essence this provides a complete software-controlled XG-series synthesizer engine, which uses AWM2 wave-table synthesis to generate a total of 676 voices. The module, however, does not reproduce sound directly, and early users required the services of third-party audio converters such as those provided by the SoundBlaster 16 or Digidesign's Audiomedia card.

Realizing the significance of this shortcoming, Yamaha designed an advanced audio mixing system complete with converters that could compete directly with Digidesign's Protools. The result, a personal computer-based version of the 02R mixer, known as the DS2416, was released in 1998. Like Protools, the system is based on a special plug-in DSP processor card hosted by either an Intel-based PC or a Macintosh, and the output of an associated DB50XG synthesizer module can also be routed via its converters. Yamaha, however, recognized the added value of developing a single product at a lower overall cost, and within a matter of months released the SW1000XG. This provides an audio recording system complete with converters, hosting a plug-in card offering synthesizer and multieffects facilities. In due course a series of alternative plug-in cards were released, covering an extensive spectrum of Yamaha's analog and digital synthesis architectures, from the original DX7 to physical modeling.

By the dawn of the new millennium, it had become clear that a world previously dominated by self-contained hardware products was fast becoming a mixed economy, increasingly supportive of computer-based systems that offer more open structures and enhanced opportunities for developing new facilities based on software rather than new hardware. Before issues such as these can be considered in more detail, it is necessary to complete the perspective by considering the final element of this complex equation, the development of the UNIX-based computer workstation, and its subsequent impact on institutional computer music research.

19

Music Workstations and
Related Computing Architectures

The benefits of linking together a range of computer music tools to create an integrated environment for the composer or performer have already been highlighted in the context of commercial MIDI workstations.[1] Such products, however, are essentially restricted access, hardware-engineered systems, designed to offer a fixed repertory of synthesis and sequencing facilities determined by the manufacturer. The modern computer offers an alternative strategy, based on a more open and extensible architecture that allows different music applications from a variety of sources to be integrated within a single command and control environment. Such facilities often can be customized to meet the specific requirements of different users, taking advantage of new features as the underlying technology continues to develop.

Several features of the UNIX-based workstations have already been highlighted in the previous chapter, and the ground has been prepared for a more detailed study of their evolution in the specific context of computer music. Central to this discussion are the interesting and productive partnerships that evolved between a number of commercial and institutional interests, in many instances resulting in major advances at the leading edge of computer music research and development. Although a number of different activities have to considered here, a useful starting point is provided by the circumstances that led to the birth of a revolutionary computer during the late 1980s designed specifically for multimedia applications, known as the NeXT. What makes the development particularly interesting is that this computer was designed to bridge the gap that had opened up between personal computers and computer workstations, drawing on key aspects of both architectures. In so doing, it effectively upstaged both.

The origins of the NeXT can be traced back almost to the dawn of the microcomputer industry itself, specifically the birth of Apple Computer in 1976. Apple was the brainchild of two pioneers, Steve Wozniak and Steve Jobs, who together developed the company in partnership until 1981. At this point, the two founders parted company, with the departure of Wozniak to pursue other interests. For the next four years Jobs worked intensively directing the development of the Macintosh, concentrating specifically on the design of its innovative graphics user interface and associated WIMPS-based operating system. Although the release of the Macintosh I in 1984 attracted considerable media attention, from a commercial point of view early sales unfortunately fell short of expectations.[2] This precipitated a boardroom crisis in 1985, which isolated Jobs from the cutting edge of research and development within the company and precipitated his resignation from Apple, ironically just before the launch of the much more successful Macintosh II.

Jobs recognized the potential of developing an alternative to the Macintosh, targeted specifically at extending the upper end of the personal computer sector to embrace multimedia applications. Accordingly, he established a rival company to Apple, known as NeXT. The resulting computer, the NeXT Cube, was launched in 1988 and continued in production until 1993, at which point the company ran into financial difficulties, having failed to secure a viable share of the computer market. As a consequence, production of the Cube was abruptly terminated, and the company decided instead to concentrate on the more profitable development of software applications for other computer platforms, notably the Intel-based PC and UNIX-based workstations such as the Sun. In 1997 matters took another dramatic turn when Apple bought NeXT and Jobs returned to the fold, taking over as acting chairman in 1997, and his position back in command of Apple was confirmed within a matter of months.

The legacy of NeXT is to be found clearly embedded in the design of the Apple OS X operating system for the Macintosh, released in 2000, incorporating many features that can be directly traced back to the NeXT Cube. One other consequence of this interesting sequence of events is that many of the distinctive characteristics associated with early NeXT-based music applications could be revisited by system developers with relative ease, underpinning a new family of music software products designed specifically for the Macintosh G4 and its successors.

The NeXT computer was to prove a remarkable machine, offering many features that were not only years ahead of its time but also of particular value to the computer music research community. One of the most significant of these was the integration of microprocessor and DSP technology as part of the core architecture of the Cube itself. Three different processors were employed for this hybrid design. The first two consisted of a 68030 main processor and a 68882 math co-processor, delivering a basic computing performance that outclassed contemporary versions of both the Macintosh and also the Intel-based PC. The third processor, a 56001 DSP, was dedicated to vision and sound processing, in the latter context controlling the flow of data to a pair of integral sixteen-bit digital-to-analog converters, operating at a sampling rate of 44.1 kHz. Accessories such as a high-resolution laser printer, MIDI interface, a matching pair of analog-to-digital converters, and a bidirectional digital interface for a DAT recorder secured the credentials of the NeXT Cube as a particularly attractive resource for many of the more advanced computer music applications developed during the early 1990s.

The graphics user interface of the Cube is of particular interest, because it provided a working environment that was superior to any of its immediate rivals. A key aspect is the use of object-oriented processing or OOP techniques, which allow multiple tasks to be run within a single working environment. Several different processes may thus be initiated concurrently, monitored, and independently controlled via a series of graphics windows. Two basic software kits were provided for the handling of audio. The Sound Kit, developed by Lee Boynton, was specifically designed to control the recording, editing, and playback of sound data via the graphical editing resources, allowing traditional synthesis programs such as CSOUND to be installed with the minimum of difficulty. The Music Kit, designed by David Jaffe, provided a basic set of programming tools for the development of new music applications.

The fundamental characteristic that set the NeXT clearly apart from both the Macintosh and the Intel-based PC, fulfilling the basic criteria to be classed as a computer workstation, was the use of an operating system derived directly from UNIX. For all the perceived power and versatility, traditional UNIX workstations lacked many of the facilities necessary to create a user-friendly environment for multimedia applications. Indeed, until the early 1990s, very little attention was paid to developing resources specifically for either video or audio applications. This deficiency impeded the installation of audio converters for software synthesis programs such as MUSIC 11 in situations were the host computer was programmed for the UNIX environment. Difficulties were frequently encountered in ensuring that random glitches in the input and output of analog audio data were eliminated, a consequence of intermittent interruptions to the flow of data arising from complex task scheduling procedures intrinsic to UNIX itself.[3]

By combining the power of UNIX with the WIMPS environment associated with the Macintosh, while at the same time greatly simplifying the software routines necessary to operate the system, Jobs created NEXTSTEP, a special operating system for the NeXT that successfully addressed these specific issues. It was this product, subsequently developed in partnership with Sun Microsystems in 1994 as a reworked, platform-independent version known as OPENSTEP, that was to sustain the fortunes of NeXT as a software company, pending its subsequent purchase by Apple.

The NeXT computer quickly found favor with leading members of the computer music research community, not least those based at IRCAM. Considerable effort had previously been expended on hardware-based projects such as the 4X, but even this expensive and highly sophisticated resource suffered from a number of practical limitations. By the mid-1980s, the technology was also beginning suffer from the passage of time. Attention thus turned to the possibility of designing an advanced music workstation, using a NeXT Cube as the host computer for a custom-designed, high performance audio processor.

Before the characteristics of the resulting workstation are considered more closely, it is advantageous to give further consideration to the evolution of processor technologies during the late 1980s and early 1990s. Although significant progress was being made improving the basic performance of traditional processors such as the Motorola 680xx and the Intel 80x86 through a combination of faster clock speeds and some minor internal engineering changes, it was becoming clear that more radical design changes would soon be required.

It was with this prospect in mind that the concept of the reduced instruction set computing (RISC) architecture entered the arena for the first time, leading, for example, to the PowerPC 601 processor and the new PowerMac range of Macintosh computers released in 1994.[4] Intel quickly realized that the long-term future of the Intel-based PC required an equally radical processor upgrade, but the Intel design team faced a major problem. Whereas Apple had little difficulty persuading software developers to rewrite applications in order to take advantage of the superior power accessed by using native processor code, practical considerations made it impossible for Intel to pursue a similar strategy.

The problem here was the very nature of the Intel-based PC, a product that had been directly cloned from the original IBM PC and manufactured to the same basic specification by a formidable array of independent manufacturers worldwide. This situation made it impracticable to introduce any fundamental changes to the functional characteristics of the processor itself. In essence, therefore, Intel had no option but to develop special processors that were externally functionally identical to their predecessors, but internally redesigned to take advantage of the RISC environment. These design requirements were extremely complex and their full potential could not be realized overnight. Whereas the renamed successor to the 80486, the Pentium I, incorporated some RISC features, it was not until the introduction of the Pentium 4 that the true benefits of RISC processing were being significantly reflected in the internal architecture.

One feature common to all the computers so far discussed is the traditional concept of a central processing unit, based on a single processor. Many computational tasks encountered in audio signal processing require several processes to be executed in parallel, for example, the synthesis of a polyphonic texture from several independent voices, or the filtering of individual input channels within a digital mixer. In the case of a conventional CPU, such parallelism has to be simulated by cyclically processing small packets of data, drawn from each of the audio channels in turn. This requirement explains why, for example, the time taken to process a CSOUND score when using a conventional computer depends not only on the complexity of each CSOUND instrument but also how many instruments and how many notes are active concurrently.

If there is no further scope for increasing the power of a specific processor, a possible hardware solution is to connect two or more processors together in parallel. This requires the development of a special control system that can dynamically schedule concurrent tasks between the component processors in a suitably efficient manner. Unfortunately, this approach cannot be taken very far with conventional processors, because the proportion of time consumed in managing the system as a whole rises rapidly in proportion to the number of processors active within the network. Typically, adding a second processor will only increase the overall computational performance by about 50 percent. By the time a sixth processor is added to an existing network of five, a situation often has been reached in which the additional overheads required to manage the extra processor actually reduce the performance delivered by the system as a whole.

Hardware designers soon realized that solutions to the interprocessor communication problems encountered in constructing parallel computing systems required a fundamental reappraisal of the ways in which such processing engines are assembled. One solution, which attracted particular interest from those engaged in developing audio applications during the early 1990s, involves the construction of massively parallel processing systems from hundreds or even thousands of simple logic gates.

This engineering initiative also facilitated important research into the creative possibilities of exploring neural networks, specifically those that explore aspects of artificial intelligence by simulating the operation of the human brain. A major incentive was the need to develop more intuitive interfaces for communicating with the computer itself. An early and especially notable example of such a massively parallel resource was the Connection Machine, built at MIT in 1987–8 as a high-performance signal-processing tool for both video and audio applications.

Another major focus of interest during the 1980s, albeit associated mainly with European rather than American research initiatives, was the Transputer, designed by Inmos.[5] This is a RISC microcomputer fabricated on a single chip, incorporating a processor, memory, and a set of special high speed input/output communication links that allow two- or even three-dimensional networks of tens or even hundreds of these devices to be assembled and programmed with relative ease. Although this technology had been largely superseded by alternative processor architectures by the mid-1990s, many of its unique features are to be found embedded in the design of more recent high performance RISC-based processors, including, interestingly, the Pentium 4.

Manufacturers of computer workstations such as Sun and Silicon Graphics were especially keen to distance themselves from generic processors such as Intel x86 and the Motorola 68000 series, and accordingly began to develop special processors for their own UNIX-based systems. One notable consequence was the development of a Scalable Processor ARChitecture (SPARC) by Sun, which in turn generated a major new manufacturing sector devoted specifically to exploiting the potential of this technology. Although many of these initiatives were inspired in the first instance by a desire to develop high-performance graphics tools, such resources also offered opportunities for developing new audio applications, duly capitalized on by a number of music research groups.

Given this growing diversity of processor technologies, the system designers at IRCAM, in common with their contemporaries at other research institutions, faced a considerable dilemma in deciding precisely which design path to pursue. Although UNIX-based workstations from companies such as Sun and Silicon Graphics offered a potentially superior performance to the NeXT in raw computing terms, none of these computers could adequately meet the IRCAM's overall requirements.

The choice of the NeXT Cube for the host computer provided one part of the equation. The strategy to be adopted in designing the architecture for the real-time signal processing section was far less clear-cut. A primary consideration in choosing a suitable co-processor was the ease with which it could be programmed. Most of the high-speed DSPs available for system developers at this time lacked the support of mainstream compilers such as C, forcing programmers to work at a much lower programming level. Although this method of working is even today by no means redundant, the additional time and effort that is required to write robust and effective programs create major disincentives for system developers.

Conventional DSPs suffer from another disadvantage. In seeking an optimal performance in terms of signal processing efficiency, the tradeoff is usually a significantly reduced performance from the DSP if it is also required to cope with more general system monitoring and housekeeping tasks. As a result, these tasks are usually delegated to the host computer, operating as an external control device. The success of such an arrangement depends not only on the performance of the host computer itself but also the efficiency of the communication links that are established between the host computer and the signal processing section.

Fortunately for IRCAM, an attractive solution to both difficulties emerged in 1989, when Intel introduced a revolutionary new processor, the i860. This processor combines an extended RISC architecture with the streamlined construction of a DSP, allowing the downloading of many control functions from the i860 host to the i860 itself. Both integer and floating point data representations are supported for signal processing applications, which also can be written in higher-level programming languages such as C.

The prototype system, known as the IRCAM Music Workstation, consisted of a modular configuration of i860 processor boards with the option of combining one, two, or three identical units in a parallel configuration, controlled by the NeXT. Each unit incorporated two i860 processors, linked to a high-speed memory bank with shared processor access, and an associated network of control and communications hardware. Renamed as the ISPW, the system was launched as a commercial product by Ariel, in 1991.

Although the withdrawal of the NeXT computer in 1993 was to deal a fatal blow to the long-term future of this particular enterprise, the time and effort that had already been invested in developing applications was by no means lost to posterity. IRCAM, and a select group of co-researchers in other institutions, continued to use the existing workstations as a key platform for a further five years, transferring the results stage by stage to workstations such as the Sun, and also, interestingly, the Apple Macintosh. In the early 2000s, the transition to the personal computer became complete as IRCAM finally started to develop software specifically for the this environment, including some products specifically designed for the Intel-based PC.[6]

The legacy of software resources originating from the ISPW is extensive. One of the most significant outcomes can be traced back even further to an earlier research initiative directed by Miller Puckette. This project, based on an Apple Macintosh, set out to develop a graphical, real-time control environment for configuring and operating MIDI devices. Known initially as Patcher, a commercial version, MAX (named after Max Mathews), was developed and refined by David Zicarelli at Opcode for the Apple Macintosh, and released in 1988.

The MAX environment is predicated on the notion of a patchwork of devices and connections, represented graphically as a matrix of boxes and connecting lines. In effect each box is an "object," which receives and transmits messages to other objects via input and output links or tags that are located on the top or the bottom of each box, according to type. Each patch operates in either a "run" or an "edit" mode, the latter being used to configure the patch, the former to operate it in real time. The problems of complexity in mapping configurations, especially where connecting lines have to be overlaid, given the constraints of a two-dimensional display, are greatly reduced by the ability to create subpatches. These can be exploded for editing purposes and then hidden from view within a shell object that indicates all the external connections.

With the construction of the IRCAM Music Workstation, Puckette turned his attention to the possibility of adapting MAX not only to control MIDI functions but also the component procedures of audio processing. Here the intention was not to control external hardware, but to simulate synthesis and signal processing operations written entirely in software, much in the manner of MUSICn programs such as CSOUND. Similarities with this MUSICn derivative, however, can only be argued so far, as MAX is an object-oriented program, and traditional synthesis programs such as the former involve an essentially serially organized system of command and data flow. Whereas a number of graphics-based control interfaces have been developed for programs such as CSOUND, for example, Cecilia, developed by Jean Piché and Alexander Burton in 1997,[7] the MAX environment is very different, requiring the components of the synthesis process to operate as self-contained agents within an OOP-oriented hierarchy.

For MAX to work with real-time audio processes a special operating system had to be written for the ISPW. Known as "faster than sound" or FTS, this system distributed tasks between the i860s using the processing time intervals between samples quite independently from the host computer, run-time communications from the latter being limited to user-initiated control actions via the WIMPS interface. Although MAX was to prove the more significant performance tool, IRCAM's understanding of real-time synthesis and event processing environments during the early 1990s also was influenced by the work of Eric Lindemann and Murizio de Cecco, leading to a program called Animal (ANIMAted Language). This incorporated special facilities for representing and manipulating networks of objects that were to prove highly influential in the design of a number of subsequent IRCAM programs, including later versions of MAX itself.

For a number of years, those without access to an ISPW were unable to use the audio facilities provided by the IRCAM version of MAX. The commercial MIDI-only version, however, continued to evolve in the hands of Zicarelli with support from Puckette. An important development here was the introduction of a toolkit that allowed users to build and incorporate their own MAX objects. By 1994 it was becoming clear that the future lay in more portable software that could be used on general purpose computing platforms, and in anticipation of this work began on converting the ISPW program into processor-independent code.

The first version in this new format, known as MAX/FTS, was released in 1995 specifically for the Silicon Graphics workstation.[8] Zicarelli subsequently was able to adapt further work by Puckette to produce a version known as MSP (Max Signal Processing) for the Macintosh PowerMac, first released as a commercial product in 1997. Although the nature and complexity of real-time audio patches that could be successfully created using MSP were limited by the processing capabilities of the early PowerMacs, these operational restrictions steadily reduced as successively more powerful versions of the computer became available. With the introduction of the G3, parity with the original ISPW was all but achieved, and with the advent of the G4 series this important benchmark was finally surpassed.

Puckette was to add yet another perspective to this growing family of MAX-related software. His real-time prototype for Zicarelli evolved into Pd (Pure Data), essentially a simplified version of MSP designed for a real-time computer animation and computer audio software suite that runs under Windows for the Intel-based PC and also IRIX, a widely used operating environment for Silicon Graphics workstations. The story, however, does not end here, for in 1996 work started at IRCAM on yet another version of MAX. Known as jMAX, this has been written entirely in Java, a cross-platform general-purpose language that has evolved rapidly, largely as a result of the development of the Internet.[9] This program was finally released to the computer music community in 1998.

The IRCAM ISPW is widely regarded as one of the most innovative systems to have emerged from the formative years associated with the development of music workstations. Its importance, however, must be seen within a broader context that takes fully into account important initiatives associated with other institutions.

The concept of the self-contained computer music workstation can be traced back many years prior to the ISPW, and some examples of earlier systems that fit the general criteria have already been studied. These include the SSSP system pioneered by Bill Buxton and the commercial DMX-1010 system pioneered by Dean Walraff, dating from the late 1970s.[10] Another example from an earlier era is a special version of the UNIX-based Cadmus 9000 workstation, an early commercial rival to the Sun. The prototype for this adaptation was developed by Stephen Travis Pope at Cadmus, Munich, during 1983–4, in the first instance to provide a self-contained platform for the CMUSIC system that had been developed at CARL, University of California, San Diego. A commercial version, known as the PCS/Cadmus Music System, followed in 1985.

Although the PCS version greatly expanded the functionality of the Cadmus 9000 as a desktop music workstation, specifically designed to run CARL-based software, its performance was ultimately constrained by the basic processing capabilities of the Cadmus 9000. The only additional hardware facilities consisted of an interface to drive external digital-to-analog converters, manufactured by Sony, and the system lacked the processing power necessary for real-time performance applications. As in the case of the ISPW, the future lay in the development of music workstations incorporating high performance co-processors specifically designed for such demanding tasks.

One notable commercial product to emerge in direct competition to the ISPW, used by a number of institutions to create custom-designed music workstations, was the Quint processor, manufactured by Ariel as its own in-house product and marketed in parallel with the ISPW during the early 1990s. This consists of a bank of five Motorola 56001 DSP processors, fabricated on a single plug-in card, complete with local memory and control hardware for the host computer, the preferred choice being the NeXT. As in the case of the i860 boards used by the ISPW, two or three Quint processor cards can be linked together to increase the overall processing power of the system.

One major institution to make extensive use of the NeXT/Quint system was CCRMA, at Stanford. With the impeding withdrawal of the aging Samson Box in

1992, CCRMA urgently needed a new hardware platform. In 1990 System Concepts, designers of the original Samson Box, produced a specification for a replacement system of workstation proportions. With the preproduction ISPW and the NeXT/Quint already available for evaluation, however, CCRMA decided to invest in the latter technology for its primary music workstations, purchasing an additional ISPW for those who wished specifically to use IRCAM's MAX. Porting software that had been originally developed for the Samson Box to the NeXT/Quint posed significant challenges for the research team. PLA, for example, had to be completely rewritten in Lisp by Richard Taube. The new workstations provided the springboard for a number of Lisp-based software developments at CCRMA during the 1990s including a CCRMA version of the NeXT Music Kit, developed by David Jaffe and Julius Smith.

In addition to the Quint processor, Ariel manufactured a number of other specialist digital audio processing cards for system developers, for example, the S56X card, based on a single Motorola 56001 processor and the S32C card, based on the AT & T DSP32C processor. The architecture of the latter is of particular interest, because, unlike conventional DSPs such as the Motorola 560x0 series, it uses a thirty-two-bit floating-point architecture, especially suitable for preserving the accuracy of data in highly complex audio processing applications.[11]

Steven Travis Pope used both the fixed-point S56X card and the floating-point S-32C card as the audio processing engines for his second music workstation, the Interim DynaPiano or IDP, completed in 1991. Like the earlier PCS/Cadmus Music system, this also relies on a UNIX-based workstation, a SUN SPARCstation-2.

An interesting link can be traced directly from IRCAM to the development of another computer music workstation that dates from this time, in this instance designed entirely by a commercial company. When Giuseppi di Giugno left IRCAM in 1987, he returned to Italy to work for the electronic instrument maker Bontempi-Farfisa to head a new research and development division known as IRIS, investigating new technologies for digital synthesis and signal processing. Central to this venture was the development of a workstation known as MARS (Musical Audio Research Station), first released in 1991. This consists of three basic hardware components: a digital signal processor, a control processor and a host computer, the latter providing a graphical user interface. The DSP board, the SM1000, uses a pair of X20 custom-designed processors linked to a multipurpose MIDI/digital-to-analog/analog-to-digital, input/output board. A conventional Motorola processor handles communications between the DSP board and the input/output stage, and also between the DSP and the host computer, originally an Atari.

In software terms the original environment, known as EDIT20, was derived in the first instance from MUSIC V, abstracting and developing the synthesis and processing components from this program to develop a fully interactive set of tools. In due course the Atari computer was replaced with an Intel-based PC, and further improvements to the DSP board led subsequently to a new version of the

MARS workstation, released in 1997, which offers an open and extensible object-oriented working environment.

An important issue to be raised here, common to the design of all modern music workstations, is the nature of the programming toolkit provided for the development of music software applications, especially those that are intended for use in interactive performance situations. Whereas the suitability of C has significantly improved over the years as its characteristics have gradually expanded to embrace important functional extensions such as object-oriented constructs, it has not provided a universal solution to the requirements of music software developers.

Reference has already been made to Lisp in connection with the NeXT/Quint workstation. Another important language with useful multiple process control characteristics is Smalltalk-80, chosen by Pope to create the MODE object-oriented software environment for the IDP workstation. This handles all data representations, ranging from audio data to musical parameters, and the WIMPS user interface, complete with all the iconic tools necessary to develop processing applications, input/output data flow, and the overall scheduling of events. In addition to supporting the development of object-oriented software, MODE also accommodates more traditionally structured programs such as CMUSIC and CSOUND.

Smalltalk-80 also was used to create the programming environment for the Kyma/Platypus, an early computer music workstation developed by members of the Construction and Engineering Research Laboratory (CERL) at the University of Illinois in the mid-1980s. The use of a custom-engineered digital signal processing system anticipated the design philosophy of the IRCAM Music Workstation by several years. In engineering terms it is also notable for its use of RISC-based hardware. The Platypus workstation was designed and built by Lippold Haken and Kurt Hebel in 1984, and Kyma, the associated object-oriented programming environment, was completed a year later by Carla Scaletti.

Although many object-oriented applications were designed specifically for a particular workstation, others were conceived with more portable, generic applications in mind, facilitating their installation on a number of computing platforms. FORMES, written by Xavier Rodet and Pierre Cointe at IRCAM in the early 1980s, is a case in point. This environment, written in Lisp, was specifically designed to work on all the computing platforms supported at IRCAM at the time, including the VAX, the Sun workstations, and in due course the Apple Macintosh. Here, as with most OOP-based music environments, the primary imperative is to provide the composer or performer with an interactive interface that reflects as closely as possible the external musical structures and events that are used in ways that clearly relate to the underlying creative process.

A similar intention underpins the development of Artic by Roger Dannenberg, Paul McAvinney and Dean Rubine, which also dates from the early 1980s. Described as a functional language for real-time systems, this is a programming environment developed entirely from first principles, borrowing features from languages such as Lisp. Here the components of a real-time task are regarded as responses to individual events or functions, very much in the manner of GROOVE, where all the constituent processes are treated as functions of time.

The general trend toward generic cross-platform applications during the 1990s and early 2000s has proved very helpful in underpinning the development and broader dissemination of several of the music programs discussed earlier in this chapter. CCRMA's Lisp-based Music Kit, for example, has been ported from NEXT-STEP to OPENSTEP, Apple Macintosh OS X, Microsoft Windows, and LINUX. A similar recognition of the need to address issues of portability in a world of changing technology was significantly to extend the life of another music workstation, the Composers Desktop Project (CDP), established by a group of composers in York, England, during the mid-1980s.

The CDP was a remarkable initiative for two reasons. First, it was not underpinned by large institutional grants on the scale associated with research centres such as IRCAM or CCRMA. Although receiving limited support in the early years from the University of York it soon became a self-financing collective of enthusiasts, willing to give their time free of charge to the development of software tools. Second, in recognition of its mission to bring computer music facilities to individuals of limited means, affordability was always to remain a primary consideration.

Whereas the Apple Macintosh might in other circumstances have proved the most suitable platform for this initiative, cost considerations ruled it out.[12] This situation led the CDP to reject the Macintosh in favor of the significantly cheaper Atari ST 1040. This computer was then transformed into a versatile music workstation by adding an external hard disk drive for storing sound files, and a special interface developed by the CDP itself for high speed data communications between the Atari and a conventional digital audio tape (DAT) recorder. The latter provided the analog-to-digital and digital-to-analog converters necessary for the input and output of sound material, and also served as a general-purpose recording facility.

Although the CDP system lacked the much more sophisticated facilities associated with many of its rivals, it was a relatively cheap and versatile music workstation. A number of CPD developers contributed to the development of an extensive library of software applications, including Richard Dobson, Archer Endrich, Richard Orton, and Trevor Wishart. In addition, support was provided for the installation of CSOUND and a range of applications originating from leading research centers, including CARL. The declining fortunes of Atari during the early 1990s forced the CDP to consider alternative platforms, and the system was eventually released in versions for the Intel-based PC and also the Silicon Graphics workstation.

One further computer music workstation merits particular attention in the current context: UPIC. This system was the brainchild of Iannis Xenakis, who—with assistance from Guy Medique and a team of volunteers—was to foster it through many transformations from its initial conception during the early 1970s until his death in 2001. As noted in chapter 11, in 1966 Xenakis had established EMAMu (later CEMAMu) in Paris with the object of stimulating interdisciplinary research between the arts and the sciences. His own work in the early 1950s, using the computer to produce data structures for instrumental compositions, generated an early interest in the relationship between graphic representations and music notation, and this soon extended to the possibilities of using graphics directly for the purposes of sound generation and manipulation.

During the early 1970s, CEMAMu started to assemble the first of a series of UPICs (Unité Polyagogique Informatique CEMAMu), known as UPIC-A. This used a special graphics tablet and stylus to draw music functions, displayed on a simple graphics display unit. Although the sound quality obtained via the custom-designed digital-to-analog converter was exceptional for this pioneering era (up to fifty-two thousand samples per second, delivered with a resolution of sixteen bits) the system, based on a Solar 16-65 minicomputer, could not synthesize sound material in real time. By the late 1970s, the faster computing technology available for UPIC-B greatly reduced the latency between the input of functions and auditioning the results. The new system also allowed the external input of sounds via an analog-to-digital converter, but the response was still not fully interactive. Nor was this goal achieved with UPIC-C, which followed in the early 1980s, a situation that was all the more frustrating for its users, given the availability of improved graphics for kinetic picture manipulation.

This feedback loop between the actions of the composer/performer and the processes of synthesis was finally closed in 1988 by transferring sound generation from the host studio computer to a much faster custom-designed sixty-four-voice synthesizer. In 1991 this process of upgrading was completed with the release of a commercially available version of UPIC, using an Intel-based PC to control the synthesizer. Although the graphics environment was Windows-based, key features of the original design were retained, in particular the use of a digitizer table and scribe, rather than the conventional WIMPS mouse. By this time CEMAMu had been renamed Les Ateliers UPIC, and in 2000 the name of the organization changed yet again to CCMIX (the Center for the Composition of Music Iannis Xenakis).

Xenakis was particularly concerned to make his UPIC systems accessible to children, and devoted considerable time and effort to exploring ways of introducing UPICs to the education system in France. The powerful simplicity of the graphics interface distinguishes this workstation from many of its contemporaries, the immediacy of contact being further reinforced by the use of a large digitizer table (typically 75 × 60 centimeters) for the scribe, many times the more modest dimensions of a typical mouse pad.

This arrangement transformed the table into an interactive sound blackboard, allowing the physical crafting of sound components and processes with an intimacy that is rarely possible using standard WIMPS tools. Synthesis proceeds in four stages: (1) the drawing of wave-shapes (timbres), (2) the drawing of amplitude envelopes, (3) the composition of a score page of sound events using these shaped sound sources, and (4) the mixing of these sonic components. Although functions can be drawn entirely from first principles, it is often advantageous to start with one of a series of preset functions provided by the software and then subsequently modify its characteristics interactively.

The later versions of the UPIC facilitated the organization of the digitizer and associated display into a very special type of score, essentially a map of sound pictures assembled in a manner analogous to that used by artists when selecting colors from their palettes of paints. These pictures and their associated performance characteristics can be ordered into regions, for example, the basic repertory of source timbres and envelopes, the choice of sound patterns, and the direction and speed at which the material is to be accessed and synthesized. Performance of an UPIC score can thus be rehearsed or be entirely intuitive in nature, this flexibility allowing the user to establish a very personal working relationship with the system.

The use of an enlarged drawing surface for the input of music data to the UPIC highlights once again the practical limitations of the traditional WIMPS environment for many computer music applications, especially those that are performance-based. Although the MIDI keyboard has become the most widely used facility for the input of music data, a number of alternative controllers have been developed over the years. These include an interesting family of devices that exploit the potential of physical gesture as a means of regulating the processes of synthesis and signal processing. This area of activity merits closer scrutiny, and forms the subject of the next chapter.

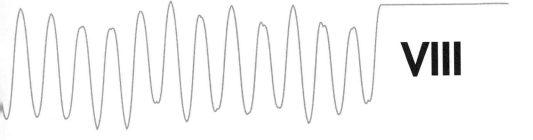

VIII

The Expanding Perspective

20

Performance Controllers

The adoption of the keyboard as the primary input and control device for commercial electronic and computer music systems has had a material influence on the processes of composition and performance within the electronic medium. In the acoustic domain, the conventional music keyboard is associated with a well-defined repertory of musical instruments, notably the piano, harpsichord, and organ. This practical link with traditional performance practice, however, does not extend to the use of a MIDI keyboard to control the functional characteristics of other instrumental sounds such as strings or woodwind, or those of the human voice.

True sensing of instrumental performance features requires a much closer correlation between the physical characteristics of acoustic instruments and the means employed to capture these in an electronic form, whether for the purposes of imitation or the execution of more elaborate synthesis tasks. In the commercial sector, the development of MIDI drum sensor pads was inspired at least in part by a realization that the use of a MIDI keyboard to trigger such events was a poor substitute for the art and craft of the performing percussionist.[1]

Yamaha, mainly as a result of its continuing interests as a manufacturer of conventional acoustic instruments, has taken a particular interest in the development of performance sensing devices. There is perhaps a certain philosophical significance to be attached in this context to the physical appearance of its early pre-MIDI GS1 and GS2 synthesizers, which look to all intents and purposes like small grand pianos. In 1988 Yamaha released the Disclavier, a conventional grand piano complete with hammer action and strings, with added sensors to measure the timing and velocity of keystrokes. This data is coded in a MIDI format and communications are bidirectional, allowing conventional performances to be recorded and then reproduced acoustically.

The EWI, the EVI, and the WX7 MIDI controllers also date from the late 1980s, the latter attempting to replicate and capture as closely as possible the physical performance characteristics of a woodwind performer. This particular technique was taken a stage further with Yamaha's range of Silent String instruments, dating from the early 1990s. These provide the traditional physical performance surface of the instrument complete with strings and bow, but without the acoustic resonator normally used to amplify the sounds. Instead, the vibrations are registered by sensors and reproduced electronically. Another manufacturer, Zeta Music, had already anticipated this design principle in the mid-1980s with a similar range of MIDI-based string instrument controllers, starting with the ZETA violin.

The issues to be dealt with here are potentially quite complex, as the physical sensing of instrumental performance characteristics via MIDI cannot always provide all the information that may be required for comprehensive and accurate data capture, particularly in terms of the nuances of expression. A MIDI keyboard is used primarily to activate discrete "on/off" note/events, any additional performance data being registered in terms of pitch velocities and key pressures. MIDI wind controllers such as the Yamaha WX7, or more recently the WX11, are able to capture other types of performance information, including such subtleties as wind pressure variations, using additional transducers to send continuous MIDI messages. Gary Lee Nelson carried out important pioneering work in this context during the 1980s at Oberlin College, Ohio, leading to the construction of his MIDI Horn by John Talbert in 1987. This involved a radical reengineering of its acoustic relative, reducing the device to a handheld rectangular box with valves, a set of additional controller keys, and a conventional horn mouthpiece.

Such extensive modifications highlight an interesting continuum between sensor-equipped acoustic instruments that otherwise function normally, intermediate instruments that replicate most or all of the performance functions in a reengineered fashion, and what are arguably new tools that facilitate the registration of a variety of human gestures. It is in this context that the adequacy of MIDI has been called seriously into question by some researchers, especially in situations where the data capture requirements are particularly demanding. Avoidance of the protocol, however, comes at a price in terms of the practical problems that have to be solved in applying alternative higher resolution data formats to synthesis engines. One solution that has found favor with some designers, albeit as a compromise, is the use of higher resolution techniques purely for the initial sensing stage, an intermediate processor being then deployed to interpret and rationalize the information into a standard MIDI format.

The MIDI Thérémin, manufactured by Robert Moog's company Big Briar is an example of a simple gesture capture controller that has proved popular with a number of composers and performers.[2] Another is the MIDI baton, developed by David Keane, Gino Smecca, and Kevin Wood at Queen's University, Canada, in 1990. This consists of a brass tube containing a simple accelerometer that provides a one-dimensional measurement of the speed at which the baton is moved through the air. Buchla's Lightning wand (1991) works on similar principles. Other devices, however, take motion-sensing techniques much further. Not for the first time, credit for pioneering research in this regard must be given to Max Mathews for a series of inventions that have significantly advanced both theory and practice in terms of gesture-based performance control.

In 1975, in response to a request from Pierre Boulez, Mathews began work on more advanced software for his GROOVE system, leading to an early version of the Conductor program, designed to interpret and apply control data generated via a handheld sensor. As the name of the program suggests, his preferred controller at this time was a handheld rod, used in the manner of a conductor's baton to provide the basic beat and also the nuances of expression within the beat. The practicalities of developing such a device, however, led to a number of modifications, and the Conductor program was developed to accept gesture-based information from other physical controllers, including joysticks.

A growing dissatisfaction with these devices led Mathews to start work on a series of custom-designed sensors, starting with the Sequential Drum, developed at IRCAM in 1980. This consists of a grid of horizontal and vertical wires and an associated handheld beater. When the latter is used to strike the grid a pair of wires is forced into contact, generating coordinates that are analyzed by the Conductor program. What distinguishes this sensor system from devices such as the mouse or computer tablet and scribe is the use of contact sensors to record the strength of each hit, rather than merely its position within the grid. Practical difficulties with the wire grid, however, soon led Mathews to develop another type of surface, the Daton. This consists of a solid but partially tactile skin in the form of a square, supported in each corner by a strain gauge. Drum strokes on different parts of the playing surface thus produce different responses from each of the gauges, the resulting information being decoded to produce the corresponding event coordinates in terms of both position and the force of impact.

Although the Daton proved more reliable, it still suffered from a number of practical shortcomings. Whereas it could accurately record the positioning and force of individual drum strokes as discrete events, it could not track movements of the drumstick across the surface, or for that matter in the air above. The problems were finally solved by Robert Boie, an engineer at Bell Telephone Laboratories, who developed the prototype for a new device, originally called the Radio Baton, during 1985–7, soon to be followed by an enhanced version, the Radio Drum, completed at CCRMA in 1989.

The standard arrangement for both devices consists of two handheld batons that emit radio frequencies from their tips, detected by a flat sensor plate immediately below. Whereas the convention Thérémin simply detects proximity, the Mathews/Boie devices register spatial positioning in three dimensions. Specific events are triggered by lowering a baton below an invisible trigger plane, situated a small distance above the detection plate. The Radio Drum extends this sensing arrangement to include measuring the impact of the baton on the sensor plate itself. The original versions of both devices did not directly support MIDI, requiring an alternative, much higher resolution serial protocol to send performance data direct to the associated computer for input to the Conductor program. MIDI data could then be generated within the computer for onward transmission to a MIDI synthesizer or signal processor. Later versions, developed during the 1990s, however, include the additional circuits necessary to generate MIDI signals directly.

In 1986, Tod Machover established the Hyperinstruments research group at MIT, with the specific goal of developing an expanded repertory of computer-assisted musical instruments that would allow performers to explore an expanded range of expressive performance skills. These have ranged from percussion, keyboard, and string instruments, for example, the Hypercello (1991), to devices that will track hand or even body gestures, for example, the Sensor Chair (1994), the Sensor Frame (1995), and the Digital Baton (1996). The latter device consists of a hand-held wand with an infrared transmitter at the tip, and a motion sensor camera. The pod end of the baton is molded to fit a hand grip, and incorporates five pressure sensors that measure movements within the hand of individual fingers and the palm of the hand itself.

In terms of generating multiple control functions from a physical gesture, the hand offers the greatest range of possibilities to be concentrated in a single limb. Buchla's Thunder MIDI controller (1990) is an example of a device that extends the drum pad principle to create a performance surface populated with thirty-six independent plate sensor areas, each of which can respond to individual finger movements. The first patented device for sensing hand movements was developed by Gary Grimes at Bell Telephone Laboratories in 1983. Known as the Digital Data Entry Glove, it incorporates sensors to detect finger flexing, fingertip pressure, general orientation, and wrist movements. It was originally intended as an alternative means of data entry to the conventional alphanumeric keyboard, but researchers quickly realized the potential of using such a highly versatile sensor to generate other types of control information.

An important initiative in this context came from members of the STudio for Electronics and Interactive Musicians (STEIM), Amsterdam, an independent studio founded by students of Henk Baadings in 1969. With support from the Dutch Ministry of Culture this enterprising collective took a particular interest in the development of small and portable performance systems, and, in the early 1980s, one of its leading members, Michael Waisvisz, started work on the development of handheld controllers. This led to the construction of The Hands in 1984, a complex but versatile pair of controllers that are strapped to the wrists, allowing the fingers to manipulate a set of key sensors, mounted on two miniature keyboards. Additional sensors monitor the physical movement of the hands and arms themselves. The Hands were subsequently rebuilt and modified, Hands II (1989) being followed by a much-improved version, Hands III in1997, the latter incorporating more accurate movement sensors.

The design of such controllers presupposes a performance environment that can make meaningful use of the resulting data. In the case of The Hands, the complexity of the information generated demands some form of intermediate processing and cross-correlation before the data can be usefully applied in a MIDI-driven context. Waisvisz spent considerable time developing and refining software for the management of his own devices during the 1980s, generally taking the form of extensions to a sophisticated general-purpose performance program developed at STEIM known as the Lick Machine.

In 1988, Waisvisz started work on another gesture controller known as the Web. This consists of a wire lattice, similar to a spider's web, which is manipulated by finger movements, sensors detecting the resulting changes in tension within the segments. The inspiration for this touch-based system can be traced back to the early 1970s, when Waisvisz discovered that it was possible to destabilize the synthesis functions of a voltage-controlled synthesizer, with some times quite unpredictable results, by removing the cover and touching the exposed voltage control circuits.[3] This led to the design of a series of Crackle Boxes, essentially simple synthesis devices with finger sensor pads on the top of the box directly connected to the internal control circuitry. Between 1976 and 1983, a number of Crackle Synthesizers were built by linking a number of Crackle Boxes together. In 1996, Waisvisz produced a new and more compact version of the Web known as the Small Web, or Belly Web, consisting of an oval frame mounted on a base control panel that provides an array of performance function switches and sliders.

The notion of using a glove fitted with sensors caught the attention of the games industry during the 1980s, leading to the development of the patented VPL Data-Glove by Thomas Zimmerman, released in 1987 by Nissho Electronics, Japan. The original version uses ten fiber-optic sensors to measure finger movements. An improved version released in 1995, known as the SuperGlove, uses special bend sensors to register the variations in pressure that occur when fingers are flexed within the glove. Mattel/Nintendo took a keen interest in the DataGlove and developed a prototype low-cost alternative known as the Z-Glove. Patent considerations, however, forced the company to come to a commercial arrangement with Nissho Electronics, leading to the production of the PowerGlove. Cost considerations prevented the use of fiber-optic sensors, and as a result a less accurate ultrasound tracking system was used, with sensors only on the first four fingers. Unfortunately, this product had a limited production span, and was withdrawn from sale in 1991. A subsequent revival of interest, however, led to the release of an improved version, known as the PC-PowerGlove, in 1995.

Optical sensing techniques also have proved a productive line of research in the development of gesture-driven controllers. John Cage had demonstrated the possibilities of detecting physical movement by means of light beams and optical sensors during the 1960s,[4] but the true potential of optics only became apparent with the development of digital transducers. This technology was used to construct the Videoharp, developed by Dean Rubine and Paul McAvinney at Carnegie Mellon in 1988. The device is a MIDI controller that optically tracks the movement of individual fingers on a sheet of glass, illuminated at one end by a neon striplight source. The sensor at the other end consists of a bank of memory cells with a transparent cover, making them sensitive to variations in the intensity of light. This bank functions as a sophisticated lens with a 60-degree line of vision across the glass to the illuminated opposite edge, creating a triangular detection area. When a finger touches the glass surface in the detection area the light beam is partially blocked, the memory cell system allowing detection of both the angle and also the apparent thickness of the interruption. Because the thickness of the finger relative to the total width of the light beam it is interrupting increases the closer it is placed to the sensor, this information can be used to map the movement of fingers in a two-dimensional playing area. In a later, improved version completed in 1990, two sheets of glass are used, allowing detection of finger movements from both hands, positioned one on each side.

Although the majority of gesture-based sensors involve the measurement of physical actions or other performance features such as the variations of wind pressure in a mouthpiece, some researchers have taken the capture process a stage further to embrace the acoustic content of the sound itself. A number of sensor systems have been developed that incorporate elements of both capture methods, the most usual approach being the construction of a facility to detect and analyze the acoustic pitch of notes being generated by a conventional instrument.

Pitch tracking devices were first explored commercially during the era of voltage control synthesizers, with varying degrees of success. A common technique involves passing the acoustic signal through a constantly sweeping band-pass filter, where the output is monitored to identify the peak amplitude associated with the fundamental frequency. The voltage level associated with this filter frequency setting is then registered and made available as a control input signal for an associated synthesizer. With the dawn of the MIDI era it became possible to extend this process and develop pitch-to-MIDI converters, in many instances using digital rather than analog processes of signal analysis. The MIDI trumpet developed by Dexter Morrill and Perry Cook at CCRMA in 1990 incorporates just such a converter, where the acoustic signal from a small transducer is passed to a NeXT computer for instant pitch analysis.

The problems encountered in designing devices of this type are far from trivial, because the accuracy of these detection processes cannot be guaranteed, especially in circumstances where the fundamental frequency is weak or intermittent as a result of any breaks in the continuous flow of notes. In the case of polyphonic textures, the difficulties of pitch detection escalate by several orders of magnitude. An important initiative emerged from a research area concerned in the first instance with the development of automatic accompanying systems for solo performers. In this situation a synthesizer, voiced usually as a piano, is required to track a soloist using a preprogrammed score of the complete work.

Reproducing the skills of a professional accompanist raises a number of interesting issues that have to be suitably resolved, given the subtle variations in tempo and other aspects of articulation that arise between the performance of one soloist and that of another. In addition, the unpredictability of the rehearsal environment as mistakes are made and different passages played again places additional burdens on the accompanying system as it works out what the performer is trying to play and how best to respond.

The most formidable challenge concerns how best to capture those characteristics of the soloist's own performance that are necessary to ensure both accurate synchronization and also a suitably matching interpretation. There are many subtleties to be addressed here. In a conventional rehearsal situation, for example, a human accompanist will invariably carry on playing for a few beats after the soloist suddenly stops without warning. A similar response must be built into the software if an equivalent working relationship is to be established between the performer and the synthetic accompanist.

It is clear from previous discussions that the problems encountered in acquiring performance control data from conventional orchestral instruments are very much more complex than those associated with pseudo-instrumental controllers with built-in sensors. Although it is possible to fit mechanisms to detect mechanical key movements, or in the case of fretted instruments such as the guitars the direct contact of strings with the fingerboard, the only comprehensive source of performance information is ultimately the acoustic sound itself. Among the various institutional projects that have addressed these issues, the pioneering work of two researchers merits special attention, Barry Vercoe and Roger Dannenberg.

Vercoe's interest in the relationship between control data and the interactive processes of synthesis and interpretation dates back to the early 1980s. During a period of research at IRCAM, funded by a Guggenheim Fellowship, he encountered a project using optical sensors attached to a conventional flute in order to track accurately the movements of fingers on the keys. He extended the scope of the project to include parallel acoustic tracking of the resulting notes, using the key movements to control real-time analysis software, hosted by the 4X. In functional terms, pitch selection and key press and release timing data were thus combined with detailed analyses of the resulting sounds, internal variations in terms of both pitch and amplitude providing a rich and comprehensive source of additional performance information. The resulting data was then used to control an automatic accompanying program, called Synthetic Performer.

Optical tracking had to be abandoned for the next project to make use of Synthetic Performer, based this time on a violin. The complete dependence on acoustic tracking placed additional demands on the analysis software, and as a consequence the program had to be considerably refined and upgraded. Work on score-following software continued at IRCAM long after Vercoe had returned to MIT. In 1990, work transferred from the 4X to the IRCAM ISPW, allowing new programs to be written using the IRCAM version of MAX. To assist in this development, Miller Puckette wrote a special graphical sequencer editor, EXPLODE, which works as an object within MAX itself.

Roger Dannenberg's work at Carnegie Mellon University in this area also dates from the early 1980s. His initial idea was to develop software that could track the visual movements of a conductor's baton and translate these gestures directly into control functions for an associated synthesizer, performing the score. In this respect, similarities can be identified with the performance facilities provided by Mathews for GROOVE. Dannenberg's attention, however, soon turned to the development of tracking systems for instrumental performers, in the first instance based on the trumpet. For this purpose, he used a small transducer inserted in the mouthpiece of the trumpet to convert the acoustic signal into a digital function, passed to a real-time pitch analysis program. The results of this analysis process were then used to control an associated software-based accompaniment program, driving a MIDI synthesizer.

In terms of commercial exploitation, much still remains to be done in terms of capitalizing on the innovative research that has been carried in this area in recent years. It is important in this context also to take account of the meteoric rise of the computer games console, leading to its own legacy of handheld controllers. Given the scale of investment that has been associated with these mass-produced projects, there are useful lessons to be learned from the nuances of engineering that have been incorporated in the design of such products. There are, however, major obstacles to be faced here, given that such controllers are for the most part designed for use with self-contained systems developed by particular manufacturers and as a result cannot easily be adapted for computer music applications.

Whereas in the 1980s and early 1990s the games industry was willing to develop products for the personal computer market, by the dawn of the new millennium the latter sector had been all but sidelined by manufacturers seeking to maximize their profits through the design of exclusive products. A growing interest in virtual reality during the 1990s stimulated renewed interest in performance controllers, but again investment became increasingly directed toward the development of fully integrated systems for the games market.

These developments raise some interesting issues about the long-term future of the personal computer, not least in the context of music applications. In considering the development of the MIDI synthesizer, it has been shown how the growing threat of desktop computer music systems led manufacturers to respond with the design of sophisticated workstations, offering many of the features associated with a software environment. Several features associated with the other side of the equation have now been studied, but one crucial area remains to be discussed. This is the legacy of innovative software-based applications that has emerged to underpin developments in the new millennium. Many of these are the fruits of institutional research, exploring new techniques of synthesis and signal processing, including the spatial projection of sound in different acoustic environments, and their importance for the future of the medium must not be underestimated.

New Horizons in Synthesis
and Signal Processing Software

Over the years, electronic and computer music has embraced a steadily expanding repertory of synthesis and signal processing technologies. An important factor
in shaping the course of these developments has been the changing nature of the
relationships fostered between the composers and performers, and those responsible for the technical development of the medium.

   During the pioneering years of electronic music, responsibility for shaping the
technology for electronic music lay almost exclusively with a handful of pioneering
studios, for the most part linked to institutions. Although—with the notable exception of the RCA synthesizer—the design of new tools was to remain relatively
limited, the interdisciplinary nature of many of these working environments encouraged a productive symbiosis. The many distinctive features of the Milan studio,
for example, illustrate the tangible benefits to be derived from such an association.[1]

   The advent of the voltage-controlled synthesizer dramatically altered this perspective. At a stroke, the ongoing dialogue between musicians and technologists
working in the leading "classical" studios was disrupted by a competitive manufacturing sector engaged in the production of commercial systems to serve a mass-
market culture. As a consequence, this important development of the technology

became isolated from the greatly expanded community of composers and performers seeking to use it, with little opportunity for any interactive dialogue.

This imbalance was partially redressed by a new generation of pioneers, for the most part attached to educational and scientific institutions that were well positioned to provide resources for research and development without the pressures of commerce. Indeed, computer music owes its origins to the pioneering work of these developers, exploring the creative potential of mainframe computers in ways that would have been completely impossible in a market-driven context.

Opportunities for a wider participation in the production of new facilities for the medium were relatively few and far between during the 1960s and 1970s, although due credit must be given to the activities of a growing number of hobbyists, keen to assemble their own electronic devices. With the introduction of the microprocessor, accessibility to digital engineering at the design level became increasingly affordable, laying the foundations of the mixed economy that has flourished in recent years, involving a broad spectrum of stakeholders, engaged at different levels with the potential of computer music technology. These stakeholders range from manufacturers and research institutions to home enthusiasts, investigating the possibilities of their own computers.

The primary key to this wider empowerment lies in the expanding repertory of software-based resources for computer music that has become available in recent years. Whereas a number of these have already been discussed in detail, the emphasis has for the most part been given to products that have become directly associated with the commercial market. As noted at the end of the previous chapter, this perspective masks the significance of some other important initiatives, and it is to these that attention is now turned.

The character of individual sounds, whether natural or synthetic, is crucially dependent on their spectral content and the ways in which the constituent frequency and amplitude components evolve as functions of time. During the pioneering era of electronic music the generation of such sounds entirely from first principles by means of Fourier synthesis was extremely time-consuming and subject to the vagaries of the underlying analog technology. Whereas some pioneers, notably those working at Cologne, were prepared to develop complex tone mixtures by recording and overlaying single sine waves of different frequencies and amplitudes, such a working environment was far from ideal.

Synthesis by this means, using individual sinusoidal components, is a challenging proposition even when working in the digital domain. Research carried out by Risset at Bell Telephone Laboratories during the late 1960s unmasked the magnitude of the challenges to be faced here in synthesizing the sounds of acoustic instruments from first principles.[2] He discovered, for example, that the simulation of just the attack transient of a single trumpet sound in this manner requires at least sixty different sinusoids, each individually crafted in terms of frequency and amplitude.

It is practical drawbacks such as these that encouraged researchers to investigate alternative synthesis methods, with a view to generating a rich and varied repertory of sound material from a rationalized and much more manageable set of control parameters. John Chowning's celebrated work on FM synthesis represents one of the earliest and most successful developments in this context, and it is for this reason that the associated scientific principles were discussed earlier in some depth.

It has already been noted, however, that this particular method of synthesis suffers from one major drawback, of particular relevance for those who wish to develop an extensive repertory of new sounds. This difficulty arises from the lack of any direct correlation between the values used to control the characteristics of a FM voice and the acoustical result. Mastery of this synthesis technique requires the detailed study of the complex interactions that occur in the management of the modulation process and the development of suitable strategies to regulate their use.

The commercial development of the digital synthesizer encouraged manufacturers to develop their own proprietary synthesis techniques, for example, the phase distortion synthesis method patented by Casio or the linear arithmetic synthesis method patented by Roland.[3] The distinctive characteristics of such products, however, could only be explored within the operational limits determined by the manufacturer and specifically embedded in the hardware design. Those who seek the maximum possible flexibility in exploring the possibilities of digital sound synthesis and signal processing require a software toolbox without hidden compartments, offering full and open access to a comprehensive range of resources. This vacuum has been filled at least in part by easily extensible programs such as CSOUND, and the significance of this particular tool will be reinforced further in due course.

A number of innovative synthesis methods merit particular attention in this context. The first of these, already alluded to in earlier chapters, embraces a family of synthesis algorithms that simulate the physical processes involved in the acoustic generation of musical sounds. Whereas traditional synthesis methods such as additive synthesis and FM synthesis use entirely artificial means of generating sound spectra, a technique such as physical modeling, sometimes referred to as synthesis by rule, sets out instead to replicate the physical means of sound production associated with acoustic instruments.

Kevin Karplus and Alex Strong carried out pioneering work in this context during the late 1970s, involving the modeling of plucked strings. This led to a synthesis algorithm of considerable versatility. The basic model takes the form of a variable length, digital delay line, energized by noise and incorporating a feedback path consisting of an attenuator and an adjustable low-pass filter, the resulting circuit inducing resonant frequencies akin to those of a vibrating string. Suitable adjustments to these parameters alter the decay of the string sound from a plucked characteristic to a sustained one, with the added possibility of changing pitch not only in discrete steps but also in an articulated manner by means of glissandi and slurring. Further adjustments allow the percussive characteristics of plucked string sounds to be transformed into drumlike timbres.

One major advantage of acoustic modeling techniques is their ability not only to reproduce the sounds of existing instruments with remarkable accuracy but also to create entirely new instruments based on different physical properties, where even these attributes are varied as part of the synthesis process itself. Although the models themselves can sometimes be inherently complex, only a relatively small number of control parameters are usually required to regulate their functional characteristics.

In scientific terms, the Karplus-Strong algorithm is regarded as a special case of acoustic modeling, because it replicates the physical vibration of strings, rather than the complete mechanical/acoustic process of a particular instrument. It is important to appreciate that the intention here is not necessarily to model the entire response characteristics of an acoustic instrument. Interesting and remarkably realistic simulations can often be achieved just by modeling those characteristics that are directly associated with the physical processes of excitation. This way, the underlying algorithm and its associated control parameters become much more manageable quantities, leaving ample opportunity to develop more elaborate synthesis models, should these be required.

Lejaren Hiller and James Beauchamp established the basic principles of physical modeling during the late 1960s.[4] These involve three components: (1) the physical characteristics of instruments in terms of the length and tension of strings, vibrating reeds, or columns of air; (2) the initial state of these characteristics; and (3) the boundary conditions that limit the possible degrees of variation. Useful parallels can be drawn with the elements of an analog circuit, where electric currents flow through a network of components, their progress being assisted or impeded by the characteristics of the components themselves. This differential regulation of data flow is a crucial part of the physical model, and has to be managed very carefully between the extreme conditions of zero flow and unregulated flow or short circuit, at which point the model becomes unstable with unpredictable aural consequences.

Of the various different models that have been developed over the years, the most successful have often been based on the principles of waveguide synthesis. Here the model is constructed in terms of the physical path along which the acoustic vibrations travel, whether in terms of solid media such as strings, or gaseous media such as air columns. Digital delay lines are often an important component in such processes and it can thus be seen that the Karplus-Strong algorithm has a strong affinity with this particular type of synthesis. Wind instruments such as horns, clarinets, and trumpets have been successfully modeled in the manner, along with a number of useful extensions to Karplus-Strong that take fuller account of the characteristics of acoustic propagation.

The work of David Jaffe and Julius Smith at CCRMA from the early 1980s onwards is of particular note in this context. Indeed, it was this acoustic modeling research project that inspired Yahama to explore the technique commercially, starting with the VL1 in 1994.[5] The particular advantages of physical modeling over more traditional methods of sound production lie principally in the capacity to create a significant degree of realism, not simply in terms of the basic timbre of the individual sounds but also the manner of their articulation. Subtle but important details such as the varying nature of attack transients or the interaction between the lips of a trumpet player and the standing waves set up in associated air column are very much context-dependent and therefore not easily reproduced using conventional techniques of sampling or synthesis.

Once again, we encounter with the VL1 yet another example of the tensions that developed between the designers of hardware-based products and those who prefer software-based alternatives. As the performance of personal computers continued to improve the latter option became increasingly attractive. IRCAM, for example, developed a physical modeling software program known as Modalys during the late 1990s, providing a comprehensive repertory of functions for simulating existing instruments and also designing new models.[6]

Synthesis of the vocal tract generates a very special set of problems that are especially challenging in the context of acoustic modeling. An alternative approach involves a technique known as formant synthesis, which follows the spirit of acoustic modeling but employs a slightly different methodology. Following on from Kaegi's exploratory work at Utrecht in the early 1970s developing VOSIM, Xavier Rodet, Yves Potard, and Jean Baptiste Barrière carried out further pioneering work at IRCAM during the early 1980s, resulting in a modeling process known as Fonction d' Onde Formantique (FOF). This was originally developed as the core algorithm for CHANT, a software program that allows composers to simulate the characteristics of the singing voice, later reworked as a synthesis resource for other programs such as MAX/MSP. As in the case of other popular algorithms such as Karplus-Strong, FOF also was developed as a unit generator for CSOUND.[8]

Modeling the singing voice requires the use of four or five FOF generators connected in parallel, each assigned to one of the primary formants or frequency clusters that are generated by the vocal tract. These formants are created by means of sinusoidal impulses, individually enveloped to create a band-limited response similar in characteristics to that which may be obtained by applying a pulse train to a conventional band-pass filter. The FOF algorithm, however, produces far more accurate approximations to the characteristics of the human voice, and may be readily manipulated to generate elaborate transformations such as bells, gongs, filtered noise effects, or wood percussion sounds. Although the technique provides a realistic spectrum of vowels, it is not, however, well suited to the production of consonants.

Waveguide techniques have been used for other voice synthesis algorithms, a notable example being SPASM, developed by Perry Cook at CCRMA in 1992. The user interface for this software program is especially interesting since it is based on a visual model of the vocal tract, represented on the computer screen as a cross-section of the human head. Graphic sliders are used to vary the physical dimensions of the tract, replicating its movements in regulating the flow of air from the lungs. The model is transformed into a performance tool using a control program known as Singer, and unlike FOF can handle the synthesis of both vowels and consonants.

One other potentially very powerful technique, granular synthesis, has already been touched on in the context of the POD programs developed by Barry Truax during the early1970s at Utrecht and Simon Fraser University, British Columbia.[9] The notion of breaking up the audio spectrum into minute grains of acoustic quanta was first proposed by Dennis Gabor in 1947, and indeed had a direct bearing on the research that led to the principles of the *Mathematical Theory of Communication*, published by Shannon and Weaver in 1949.[10]

It also has transpired that other synthesis methods have the capacity to exhibit granular characteristics under certain operating conditions. The parameters of FOF, for example, can be adjusted to produce granulated formants, opening up a rich new spectrum of sounds for use in composition or performance, and similar procedures may be applied to VOSIM. In a related context, it has already been shown in the earlier study of the POD programs that the application of stochastic distribution principles such as Poisson can result in granular structures, and indeed it was these characteristics that inspired Truax to develop his own algorithms. The earlier contributions of Xenakis during the 1960s should also be acknowledged here, in particular the application of his stochastic theories to the ordering of recorded fragments of sound, intricately spliced together using the medium of magnetic tape.

The true potential of granular synthesis, however, requires the processing capacity of the computer, and Truax was not alone in investigating its possibilities. Curtis Roads, for example, developed his own principles of granular synthesis at UCSD, starting in 1974. It was Truax, however, who transformed the technique from a synthesis-only technique, to a much more powerful analysis and resynthesis technique, manipulating the characteristics of existing sounds, in particular material drawn from the natural world. Known as GSAMX, this pioneering program became operational in 1994, running in real time on the DMX-1000. It has subsequently been ported to a number of general-purpose computing platforms including the Apple Macintosh.

The most notable feature of granular synthesis is the ability to explore the inner spectral detail of sounds by stretching their evolution in time from perhaps a fraction of a second to many orders of seconds. The resulting transformation from transient to continuously evolving spectra results in rich new textures that can be projected spatially in a stereo or a multichannel environment.

In many respects, the technique provides the most sophisticated and flexible example of a family of algorithms designed specifically to stretch events in time without necessarily altering their intrinsic pitch. All are based on principles of analysis and re-synthesis, and arguably can be classified as examples of digital signal processing techniques rather than those of synthesis. This blurring of the boundary between synthesis and processing illustrates the extent to which such applications have become part of an extended continuum of digital audio applications.

One of the earliest examples of this family of algorithms is based on the principle of linear predictive synthesis, or LPC, which owes its origins at least in part to the analog vocoder. This device, it will be recalled, was developed in the first instance to analyze the characteristics of speech, with the possibility of subsequently reversing the process to create an artificial talker.[11] Composers, however, were soon to recognize its potential as a processing and resynthesis tool for a much broader spectrum of sound material, leading to techniques such as cross-synthesis, in which the characteristics of one source can be superimposed on those of another. The development of LPC-based derivatives was pioneered by James Moorer at Stanford in the early 1970s and soon explored by others, for example, Paul Lansky and Charles Dodge at Princeton.

A particularly powerful feature of LPC is the ability to edit the data extracted from an initial analysis of an input signal in order to effect particular changes on subsequent processes of resynthesis. One benefit of using digital rather than analog filters to analyze spectral information is that it becomes possible to divide up the characteristics into separate components, using very short and usually overlapping segments or frames of sampled sound data. These consist of (1) the pitch of the sound, (2) its amplitude, (3) its timbre in terms of a spectrum of partials, and (4) whether or not the sound is actually pitched or instead primarily composed of noise.

The need to make a "yes/no" decision in the latter context regarding the status of each frame is a limiting consideration in the use of LPC for the purposes of resynthesis. Whereas the inevitable errors at the boundary of the two states is usually of little consequence for speech synthesis, it can sometimes prove disastrous when dealing with pitched material, resulting in unexpected and sometimes quite dramatic spectral instability. This practical drawback is generally less of a problem with an alternative technique, based on the principles of the phase vocoder.

In essence, the phase vocoder is a significant step back from the advanced mathematics of LPC toward the functional characteristics of the analog vocoder, where the analysis filters simply divide the spectrum into narrow bands and provide amplitude and phase data concerning the spectral energy recorded in each band. The biggest practical advantage of LPC is its ability to reduce analysis and resynthesis data to manageable quantities, whereas the raw data produced by the phase vocoder is invariably many orders of magnitude greater. This factor greatly increases the amount of computation that has to be carried out during the processes of resynthesis.

Whereas the phase vocoder generally performs better than LPC in handling pitched material, the reverse is usually true in the case of nonpitched material, making it a less suitable method for processing speech. The former attribute, however, has made the technique especially useful to composers, not least in facilitating a range of useful transformations during the resynthesis process. These include the accurate transposition of the harmonic spectra without altering the temporal evolution of the constituent events, the stretching of material in time without affecting its pitch, or a combination of both. Several researchers have contributed to the development of the phase vocoder over the years. Pioneering work by James Moorer during the late 1970s led to a number of implementations during the early 1980s, one of earliest and most influential versions being developed by Mark Dolson at CARL. During the 1990s, IRCAM developed a graphics-controlled extension of the phase vocoder, AudioSculpt, which allows the user to manipulate the evolution of timbre with respect to time by graphically editing the associated spectrogram display.[12]

Although the repertory of software synthesis and signal processing software algorithms continues to expand, increasing emphasis has been placed on modifications to existing techniques rather than the pursuit of entirely new concepts. There is always the possibility that a revolutionary new algorithm will become a necessary addendum to this account in due course, but the primary focus of attention has become the environment within which such tools are constructed and functionally linked together. These considerations apply both within applications, where the object is to construct a cognate set of synthesis and processing tools, and also across applications, where such connections are to be made at a higher operational level.

A number of these activities have already been highlighted in earlier discussions, for example, FORMES and Artic.[13] What distinguishes these environments from more conventional programs such as CSOUND is the fact that they are language-based, thus allowing the development of constructs that are syntactically flexible and also capable of communicating with one another at different operational levels. The various unit generators and operators in CSOUND provide a powerful set of building blocks for the construction of complex instruments, but these remain discrete entities that have to be individually regulated at the command level. Similar restrictions apply to a program such as CMUSIC, although in this instance somewhat greater use has been made of the constructs available within the C language itself to allow a greater degree of functional integration.[14]

Similar attributes apply to CMIX (1982) created by Paul Lansky at Princeton.

This is essentially a library of signal processing routines, which may be linked together using C-based constructs to create a powerful set of editing tools for audio files. The real key to a fully integrated environment, however, lies in the availability of facilities for composers to integrate both compositional and synthesis procedures as part of the same process of specification. Here, as has already been noted, programming languages other than C have sometimes been preferred, especially in situations that require a more object-oriented approach. Common Lisp Music (1991), written by William Schottstaedt at CCRMA specifically for the NeXT computer, is an example of this approach. The world of computing, however, soon realized the importance of extending the functionality of C to meet such requirements, and an object-oriented variant known as C++ has been available since 1986.

The transition from non-real-time to real-time modes of software synthesis and signal processing has highlighted the need for designing tools that are not only efficient in the use of resources but also engineered specifically for interactive working. Such features are evident in SuperCollider, a programming language designed by James McCartney in 1996. Whereas this program has its roots firmly in the MUSICn tradition, sustained and developed by both CMUSIC and CSOUND, it incorporates many features that facilitate the interactive design and performance of software instruments within a fully integrated environment. This has been achieved by allowing conventional list-based functions to be embedded inside real-time objects, which are then linked in a manner very similar to that used in programs such as MAX. Elements of two programming languages are combined here to optimize the efficiency of this hybrid approach, C++ for constructing the synthesis and processing functions, and Smalltalk-80 for the real-time management of the resulting objects.

The objectives of SuperCollider have been taken a stage further with the development of Structured Audio Orchestra Language (SAOL), the fruits of a research project based at MIT, launched in 1998. What makes this venture especially significant is that it creates an environment that seamlessly integrates with two of the primary audio formats used for the Internet. In so doing, SAOL engages directly with the underlying problems of audio quality when using the Internet, a problem discussed in chapter 13.

It will be recalled how MP3, widely used for the transmission of audio files across the Internet, is a lossy compression method, in which the degree of data compression may be varied according to context. At its highest resolution, equated with the lowest degree of compression, it has been argued that the resulting audio quality is equivalent to that of a conventional CD. MP3, however, has another practical disadvantage in that it cannot be used to stream music quality audio continuously over conventional modems. As a result, MP3 soundfiles have to be downloaded complete before they can be auditioned, a process that may take upward of three or four times the duration of the recording.

In order to facilitate real-time audio transmission, other lossy compression techniques have been developed that ensure that audio data can streamed continuously, no matter how severe the resulting effects on the quality of the signal. A widely used example of this is RealAudio. A fundamental imperative for the research team at MIT, was to develop a method that could stream music quality audio live across the Internet, and then embed this within a language for software synthesis and signal processing. This required a rather different approach to the mathematics of data reduction, where instead of directly compressing audio signals, their characteristics are described using CSOUND parameters, hence the use of the term Structured Audio.

Developments such as SAOL are indicative of what may be expected in future systems for computer music, where the facilities for data communication between users are becoming as significant as the tools available for composition and performance. The increasing emphasis on individual activity, based around the personal computer, has major implications for the ways in which computer music is created and disseminated to a wider audience. The traditional concert environment has always proved especially challenging for composers of electronic and computer music, especially in situations where the compositions are entirely prerecorded. The lack of a human performance element when listening to such works via loudspeakers leads to a fundamental questioning of the value, beyond a purely social one, of sitting in a concert hall as opposed to the comfort of one's own home. The artistic justification lies primarily in the effective use of acoustic space.

Interest in the spatial projection of sound is by no means a new phenomenon, nor for that matter is this issue specific to the medium of electronic and computer music. The idea of dividing instrumental and choral resources both by type and also physical location can be traced back to early Christian times, although it was not until the mid-sixteenth century that the practice began to be explored in large buildings such as St. Marks, Venice. Even during the formative pre-Second World War period, pioneers such as Varèse had grasped the creative significance of projecting sound from different parts of an auditorium using loudspeakers, and within a few years Poullin was developing his *potentiomètre d'espace*. Other early examples include the use of five- and four-channel diffusion configurations by Stockhausen for *Gesang der Jünglinge* and *Kontakte* respectively, and the use of multiple loudspeaker arrays by Varèse for the performances of *Poème électronique* in the Philips Pavilion in 1958.

It is important to bear in mind that the diffusion of sound in an acoustic space may involve either a fixed relationship or a variable relationship between the source sound material and the loudspeakers available for diffusion. In the case of *Kontake*, for example, the relationship is fixed, requiring a unique routing of each of the four tape channels to a designated loudspeaker. The location and movement of sounds within the listening area has thus been entirely predetermined by the composer in advance of the performance. Moreover, the projection of images is in essence only two-dimensional, as all the loudspeakers are to be mounted at the same height.

Poullin's *potentiomètre d'espace* was designed with a different performing environment in mind.[14] Here a fixed relationship between four primary audio source channels and directly associated loudspeakers is augmented by the variable distribution of sound from the fifth audio channel, regulated by the physical gestures of the operator during the performance. Moreover, the system provides a three-dimensional acoustic space as a result of the positioning of one loudspeaker in the ceiling. Multitrack tape recorders, however, were extremely rare even in professional recording studios until the late 1960s, and it is still the case that the majority of electronic and computer music works are mixed down to a stereo format. As a result, over the years relatively few works have been composed specifically for multichannel playback systems.

The restriction to just two source audio channels, however, does not preclude the possibility of projecting the material dynamically across multiple loudspeaker channels, and this has led to the construction of a number of performance systems specifically designed for this purpose. One of the first, known as the Gmebaphone, was designed by the Groupe de Musique Expérimental de Bourges (GMEB) in 1973 for its annual festival of electronic music. One year later, the Groupe de Recherches Musicales (GRM) completed the Acousmonium, a concert hall sound projection system allowing the diffusion of sound using up to forty-eight channels, distributed across eighty loudspeakers. Perhaps more than any other composing and performing group, the GRM have developed the art and craft of spatial projection from a limited number of source channels, serving as a model for other systems such as BEAST (Birmingham ElectroAcoustic Sound Theatre), established in the United Kingdom by Jonty Harrison in 1982.

As computer technology became increasingly accessible, a number of research groups started to investigate the possibilities of computer-controlled sound imaging and sound diffusion. Although systems based on the physical manipulation of signals via conventional mixing desks continue to flourish, there is an increasing realization that such techniques do not address some important issues, for example, the acoustic characteristics of sounds that move in space, a phenomenon known as the Doppler effect. On an even more fundamental level, the control of sound positioning, in which the images are created as an extension of stereophony, involves complex mathematical control of relative sound levels, and even in certain circumstances manipulation of characteristics within the sounds themselves.

In 1969 Salvatore Martirano, working with a group of composers and computer scientists started work on an elaborate synthesis and performance system, known as the Sal-Mar Construction. By 1971 it had become fully operational, allowing the diffusion of sound material generated by an array of analog synthesizer and signal processing modules to be distributed under digital control across a twenty-four channel array of loudspeakers, using a control panel of 291 touch-sensitive switches. By the mid-1980s the system had embraced MIDI, and on the control side a Macintosh computer, leading in turn to the construction of the YahaSALmaMAC orchestra and a sound diffusion system involving up to 250 individual loudspeakers. The latter is controlled by a program known as SAL (Sound And Logic), written in LeLisp, a version of Lisp especially suitable for interactive computer applications.

Martirano's pioneering work during the 1970s soon inspired others to investigate computer-controlled sound diffusion, for example, Edward Kobrin in Berlin, who in 1977 created a sixteen-channel system known as HYBRID IV. In 1978 members of the Structured Sound Synthesis Project (SSSP) in Toronto developed a similar programmable Sound Distribution System in conjunction with the SSSP synthesizer. IRCAM's initial involvement in developing software for spatial projection can be traced back to the work carried out for *Répons* in the early 1980s. Boulez was particularly concerned to create an acoustic space that encapsulated both the directional sounds of the instrumental players physically located on the periphery of the listening area, and also the distribution of the electronically processed material via the banks of loudspeakers mounted directly above. The software specially written for the 4X thus included the vectors necessary to direct these sounds dynamically via the multichannel playback system.

By the end of the 1980s, a growing interest in spatial projection had led to the construction of a number of computer-controlled sound projection systems, for example the thirty-two channel Trails system developed at the Tempo Real studio in Florence.[16] The majority of these systems, however, still did not fully address the underlying acoustic issues of accurate sound imaging. It was nearly another decade before research into these special characteristics began to produce fruitful results.

The projection of sound in large spaces involves complexities of sound reflection and reverberation that are very different from those generally encountered in a domestic listening environment. Providing clear constraints are imposed on the nature and use of sound imaging techniques it is sometimes possible to achieve interesting effects with a suitable degree of realism. It has, for example, proved possible to simulate the special characteristics of the Dolby cinema surround sound system in the home using a suitable decoder and additional loudspeakers.

It is important in this context to appreciate that the Dolby cinema system is restricted to a very special kind of spatial projection, and its functional characteristics are thus not all embracing. The primary digital music format, known as 5.1, requires a minimum of five speakers. Three are used for the primary sound projection spaced across the front of the listening area and two for associated surround sound effects, positioned to the rear. In the cinema the surround effect is often widened by chaining several speakers together for each surround channel, spaced along the sides and back of the auditorium. In addition, a sixth channel is often added, providing low frequency sounds fed to a special subwoofer speaker at the front. In the late 1990s, a modified version known as Surround EX was introduced, providing a third surround channel. This has considerably improved the spatial characteristics of the Dolby system, allowing independent loudspeaker channels for the rear sides and the back.

One spatial positioning technique that has particular potential for domestic listening environments, especially when auditioned via headphones, is known as Ambisonics. The technique was originally developed for the recording industry during the 1970s, using a special microphone designed to replicate the way in which sound images are captured and decoded by listeners via the ears and the brain. This process involves a mathematical method of coding that takes into account the shape of the head and the physical characteristics of the ears themselves, resulting in what is known as the head related transfer function or HRTF.

Researchers soon realized that if electronically generated sound images could be coded in HRTF and transferred directly to the ears of the listener, the brain will correctly decode the intended spatial characteristics. Once again, the development of computer-based sound coding techniques has facilitated the use of Ambisonics for a number of sound imaging applications; however, it has to be borne in mind that the very nature of the technique favors the use of headphones, as they directly engage with the ear. If loudspeakers are used instead, complications result from the inevitable presence of an intermediate acoustic space and the different position of individual listeners relative to the loudspeakers themselves. These difficulties are unfortunately compounded when the listening space is especially large, for example, in a concert hall.

Challenges such as these permeate all large-scale sound projection systems, and during the 1990s several research centers took an increasing interest in spatial imaging issues. In 1998, for example, the Center for New Music and Audio Technologies (CNMAT) at Berkeley established a flexible environment for investigating the characteristics of multichannel audio, under the direction of David Wessel. Further up the coast and into Canada, Barry Truax also became particularly interested in spatial imaging at Simon Fraser University. Starting in 1995, he collaborated with Tim Bartoo and Chris Rolfe over the design of first an eight- and then subsequently a sixteen-channel diffusion system known as the Richmond Audio Box. This uses sound imaging principles based on vectored coordinates to control the location of sounds, managed via the WIMPs interface of an associated Macintosh computer.

The last spatial imaging system to be considered in this context is the product of a research project carried out at IRCAM. Known as the *Spatialisateur* or SPAT, this software is the legacy of work originally pioneered using the 4X, taking the form of an application that can be embedded in both MAX/MSP and jMAX. In addition, a version has been produced for use with MPEG-4. What sets the SPAT apart from many other approaches is the intention that it should be integrated directly with the compositional processes of synthesis and signal processing, rather than simply applied to the results. Considerable thought has been given to the subtleties of sound projection in acoustic space, including the simulation of larger acoustic spaces in smaller listening environments in a variety of formats, ranging from stereo to multi-channel playback systems.

One final area of discussion in this context also holds a particularly important key to the future development of the medium. It is also in many respects the most problematic to address. The development of the Internet has transformed the world of communications, not least in terms of its capacity to distribute audio and video information in a multimedia environment. First and foremost this is facilitating the dissemination and exchange of electronic and computer music, both in terms of complete works and extracts thereof, thus increasing the accessibility of the medium for practitioners and audiences alike. Given the specialist nature of the discipline, embracing many minority interests, this powerful gateway to the world at large is of major significance for its future, and this issue will be returned to in chapter 22.

There are, however, some important considerations that cannot simply be ignored. Whereas a number of composers are prepared to allow the free distribution of their music via the Internet, others have commercial interests to protect, and in this context the situation is no different to that associated with commercial recordings right across the music industry. Issues of copyright and ownership abound, and the fluidity of this situation makes it impossible to predict the precise outcome of this engagement of conflicting interests. The same situation applies to the production and free distribution of music software via the Internet, an activity that is especially relevant to the current discussion. Whereas the distribution of licensed software in return for payment will undoubtedly continue to secure the interests of commercial and institutional software houses, there is nonetheless strong evidence of a rival shareware culture, fostered by a growing number of extremely able enthusiasts.

The implications of the latter development must not be underestimated, nor indeed the extent of activities in this regard before the dawn of the new millennium, let alone since. It will be recalled, for example, how CSOUND became available as free shareware during the early 1990s, and will continue to be for the foreseeable future. Perhaps more surprising has been the decision of commercial companies such as Protools to make software versions of their systems freely available to prospective users via the Internet from time to time, albeit offering a reduced set of specifications. More recently, the growing interest in "plug-ins" to increase the functionality of existing software has spawned considerable shareware activity, notably in the context of VST technology. Thus, the concept of the freely extensible, modular, software environment has taken root, raising the possibility of individuals custom-designing their own integrated desktop environment for computer music, drawing on an ever extending repertory of tried and tested techniques. These lie beyond the timeline that can be charted by this book, and will be monitored with considerable interest. It is hoped that the reader will be well placed to form critical judgments on the course of events, whether as a participant or an observer, drawing on the rich legacy of knowledge and experience that has been identified in this account.

22

Conclusion

In 1962, the Groupe de Recherches Musicales (GRM) compiled a provisional catalog of electronic music, listing the works produced by eighteen major electronic music studios from their birth to the date of census (1961). In 1968, an updated version of this catalogue was published in association with the Independent Electronic Music Center, New York. Compiled by Hugh Davies, the *International Electronic Music Catalog* set out to register every electronic work that had been realized up until the end of 1967, from concert pieces to live compositions, film tracks, and radio and television output.[1] The only data deliberately excluded from the listings were sound effects and other similar electronic trivia.

The exponential growth of creative activity during the intervening years is clearly demonstrated by the statistics. Over five thousand works are listed, with additional references to approximately another twenty-five hundred works for which the information was incomplete. The records of over 150 major studios are augmented by references to a similar number of smaller-scale enterprises, providing yet further evidence of the ever-widening involvement of composers and performers. Notwithstanding the remarkable thoroughness of this survey, Davies notes in the preface that the contents can only be regarded as a representative rather than definitive of the global production of electronic music up to that point. Indeed, events were already conspiring to undermine the prospects of attempting such an all-embracing catalog ever again, specifically the birth of the commercial voltage-controlled synthesizer and the explosion of activity that followed.

This broadening of perspective created new challenges for those wishing to study the development of the musical repertory, and by the early 1980s activities were so diverse that the output of works from traditional studios could no longer be regarded as even representative of the medium as a whole. It is largely for this reason that with just a few exceptions discussion of the associated repertory does not extend beyond the dawn of the MIDI era. Such a task is a major undertaking, and as noted in the introduction it requires a companion book devoted specifically to this subject area.

One of the biggest challenges to be faced in attempting such a survey is that of accessibility to the creative output itself. In terms of traditional means of dissemination through recordings and broadcasts, commercially marketed compact discs devoted to electronic music are few and far between outside the sphere of rock and pop music, and almost invariably linked to small companies with limited sales outlets. It is also the case that radio stations, even those with a special interest in promoting contemporary music, still show little or no interest in broadcasting works from the medium as a whole.

The withdrawal of the long-playing record during the late1980s resulted in the loss of an important legacy of recordings that had hitherto been retained by many recording companies in secondary lists, often obtainable by special order. In the case of electronic and computer music, an additional factor has always militated against the retention of recordings in current catalogues. Whereas works involving live performers have sometimes been given a new lease of life with a new interpretation, there are no such incentives for reissuing purely studio-generated works, in which the content has been fixed once and for all at the point of production.

The onward march of technology, however, has provided some solutions to this slow descent into obscurity. The migration from record to compact disc, for example, stimulated some notable revivals of older electronic works in the new format, and more recently there has a growth in the number of specialist associations and collectives seeking to promote the repertory of the medium through special compilations.[2] In a similar vein, the growth of the Internet as a means of disseminating music output has stimulated a variety of promotional activities both by record companies and individuals that range from excerpts from works to complete recordings.[3]

Such optimism, however, cannot completely compensate for the reality of the situation as regards securing easy and comprehensive access to the repertory as a whole. The retention of long-playing record listings from earlier editions of the book in the accompanying discography provides information now more for the benefit of the specialist archivist than that of the general reader, but without access to this information the task for those seeking such recordings becomes even harder. Even the compact disc section inevitably contains some entries that will no longer be current as the list of deletions continues to grow. Accessibility is further impeded by the fact that major retailers will not stock many of these recordings on a regular basis, requiring purchasers to place special orders or employ the services of a specialist supplier.

In contrast, the technology itself has become increasingly accessible, to the extent that in many countries the majority of readers will have direct access to a comprehensive range of resources via the personal computer and the Internet. Some also may own or at least have access to a MIDI synthesizer and allied equipment. Such firsthand experiences, however, can only provide a partial perspective on the true capabilities of the medium. The fuller picture requires an informed knowledge of the larger context, both technical and musical, that has underpinned and ultimately shaped the development of the medium. It is the latter aspect that has been central to the structure of this book, and this conclusion highlights some underlying issues that still need to be fully addressed.

One fundamental consideration that remains to be satisfactorily resolved is the terminology used to describe key characteristics of the medium. Particular contention in this context has arisen over the generic descriptors used to describe the various ways in which the technology has been used to create new music. Here there is no broad measure of agreement despite powerful advocacy from several quarters, and this highlights the widely differing perceptions of composers, performers, and—not least—the public at large.

A useful starting point is the title of this book. On the evidence that has been put forward there is a strong argument to the effect that it is no longer relevant to distinguish between "electronic" and "computer" music in considering present day activities. If this view is accepted, the question then arises: Which is the more appropriate descriptor, or is it the case that neither can now usefully serve this generic purpose?

In tracing the history of the medium, intrinsic differences between analog and digital systems have been of crucial importance in shaping the course of events. Until the late 1970s, the two technologies and their associated musical repertories developed along very different paths, and their subsequent convergence within an increasingly digital domain became a necessarily complex and protracted process. These processes of change, and their significance for the modes of description employed, were recognized during the 1970s by an initially small but steadily growing group of practitioners in Europe who favored a new term, "electroacoustic" or, more accurately, "electro-acoustic" music. In academic terms, there is much to commend this particular definition, because it does not attempt to partition the medium in terms of the techniques by which sound material is generated, processed, and organized. Instead, it focuses attention on the very special nature of the acoustic results, taking account of the fact that these will always be reproduced via loudspeakers or headphones. It thus follows from this line of argument that any critical evaluation of electroacoustic works should be based in the first instance on the perceived results and not in terms of the technical means by which they have been achieved.

This approach has led advocates to divide electroacoustic music into two distinct typologies. The first of these, identified as "acousmatic" music, embraces works that only exist in a recorded form, for direct reproduction. The second of these, identified as "live electronic" music, embraces works that involve instrumental performers and/or live synthesis and signal processing. Here the use of the descriptor "electronic" is seen as representing all possibilities in terms of the actual technology employed in their production, digital or analog.

These definitions of "electroacoustic" and "acousmatic," however, present very real problems to a wider public, as, unlike terms such as "electronic" or "computer," they have no obvious roots in the experiences of everyday life. As a result, they represent for many a vision of an art form that is both elitist and inaccessible. Whereas there are indeed many electroacoustic composers and performers who seek exclusivity in such a perspective, within the broader picture such attributes are unhelpful and indeed misleading. In the same way that common usage ultimately determines the evolution of language, so any attempt to force unfamiliar terminology in the current context is ultimately counterproductive to a better understanding of the medium. The case has yet to be made convincingly to the wider constituency, and this requires a greater willingness to engage in constructive debate.

One indicator of current perceptions can be obtained from any comprehensive Internet search engine simply by entering the phrases "electronic music," "computer music," and " electroacoustic music" in turn and observing the number of Web pages found for each descriptor. Although a number of objections can be raised regarding the veracity of this measure, the differences in terms of orders of magnitude provide powerful evidence to support the above view. In many respects interesting alternatives such as "electric music" have a stronger claim as a generic descriptor on grounds that both analog and digital circuits require electricity to activate them.[4]

This quest for more appropriate descriptors begs the question as to why any qualification of the term "music" should be necessary in the first place. To many nowadays, devices such as guitars, synthesizers, and audio processors are the primary agents for making music, and to their way of thinking it is acoustic instruments that require a special label rather than their electronic counterparts. Although such a contrary outlook will seem outrageous to the classical music lover, it is one that has been robustly championed by many writers of popular books and articles on MIDI, and cannot simply be ignored.

A more considered perspective seeks a reconciliation of these philosophical differences, perhaps by recognizing the diversity of sound-producing agents that may be used to generate music, and the ability of many of these tools to serve both serious and more popular applications alike. This in turn highlights yet again the importance of an informed understanding of the musical and the technical characteristics of the various tools that have been developed over the years, and the extent to which they have succeeded in enhancing the working environment for the composer and performer.

One of the most disappointing characteristics of the medium has been the reluctance of both composers and technologists to reflect on and learn from the experiences of their predecessors. In a number of instances, the search for new techniques of generating and manipulating sound in a creative context has at worst led to bitter frustration and disillusionment and at best wasted time and effort, in effect reinventing the wheel. A vital key here, which has still to be fully recognized in many quarters, is the need for a greater understanding of the intrinsic nature of sounds in a musical, as opposed to a purely technical, context. Contrast, for example, the slow pace of development in the development of genuinely new commercial products in recent years with the truly innovative ideas that have emerged from many institutional research projects over the same period, still awaiting full realization of their creative potential in the wider public domain.

Attention has already been drawn to the constraints that are often imposed by the underlying technology on the creative use of studio or performance equipment. Indeed, during the early years of electronic music, these constraints invariably dictated the methods of working. Schaeffer's *musique concrète*, for example, evolved in terms of the analyses and transformations of *objets sonores* obtained almost exclusively by the physical manipulation of source recordings, in the first instance using 78 rpm disc cutting facilities.[5] The creative bond with the latter recording medium became so intimate that the subsequent introduction of the tape recorder as a direct replacement was initially viewed with considerable misgivings.

At Cologne, too, the initial desire to synthesize material entirely from first principles, using a single sine-wave generator, resulted in its own methodology.[6] The desire to expand the range of techniques employed in these classical studios fermented quite naturally from a growing curiosity with the new medium, searching for new horizons in the pursuit of originality. Although progress was slow at this time, it was generally fruitful, in no small part attributable to the significance that was attached to detailed research and critical evaluation at each new step. In studying the growing problems of communication that confronted the composer as the complexity of the technology continued to grow it became quickly apparent that suitable modifications to conventional concepts of notation and instrumentation would require a fundamental reappraisal of the ways in which we describe musical sounds.[7]

As previously noted, the true significance of these shortcomings first became widely evident with the introduction of the commercial voltage-controlled synthesizer. With few exceptions these synthesizers provided little or no support for the novice practitioner beyond a basic set of operating instructions. Beyond the world of purely imitative "note/event" applications, individual users were simply left to experiment for themselves. These voyages of discovery rarely intersected, for in the absence of an environment conducive to the sharing of acquired knowledge and experiences the composition of electronic music remained a highly individual and often remote occupation. A crucial consideration here was the development of studios within the educational sector, and in most countries this revolution only started to gather momentum during the 1970s.

Some of the worst operational problems encountered with voltage-controlled synthesizers were eased by the introduction of sequencer control facilities, but this was but the first step toward the increased power and versatility offered by the world of computing, which unfortunately at the same time generated its own set of problems. In musical terms the birth of the digital medium was less than auspicious. The early pioneers, of necessity, were mainly scientists, and as a result artistic achievements in this domain were for many years overshadowed the work of more accomplished composers working in analog studios. The credibility of the new technology was not widely appreciated until the early 1980s when, ironically, the initiative was to be seized once again by the commercial sector.

This turn of events was to be subject to yet another twist. Whereas voltage-controlled synthesizers were indeed initially targeted at the all-important educational sector, the introduction of MIDI saw a marked change in emphasis toward servicing the requirements of the rock and pop industries. This is a reflection not only of the remarkable progress that had been made in developing newer and more versatile technologies but also the changing perception of commercial manufacturers as to the nature of their primary markets.

Perhaps the greatest source of frustration to system designers in this regard has been the reluctance of many users to engage directly with the underlying functional characteristics of the tools that are placed at their disposal. Educating a wider circle of users to the benefits to be gained from exploring these to the full is crucial to the musical development of the medium, and much work remains to be done in this area. Service engineers have been known to remark how few products returned to manufacturers for repair show any evidence of more than a superficial investigation of their features beyond those stored in factory presets. For many users of samplers, for example, access to a library of standard orchestral sounds, augmented perhaps by other samples of more exotic nature, is an accurate measure of the true extent of their interests.

This approach is entirely consistent with the craft of the traditional composer working with an ensemble of tried and tested acoustic instruments but it nevertheless passes up the opportunity to explore the true potential of these powerful synthesis and signal processing resources. It is only by unlocking the door to new sound worlds and techniques that such perspectives can be profitably extended. These processes of education and discovery are impaired by the continuing shortcomings of the various software and hardware interfaces used to link these technologies to their users. It is thus especially reassuring that both institutional and commercial research has concentrated increasingly on resolving these particular issues in recent years.

In the final analysis, it is the response of the listener that determines whether or not the inspiration of the composer has been successfully communicated, whether via a recording or a live performance. The variety of material that may be incorporated in an electroacoustic work creates a freedom of choice unprecedented in traditional music. This very diversity introduces its own problems, for in experiencing the unfamiliar there is an instinctive desire to identify features that relate to known phenomena, drawn from the experiences of everyday life. The pioneers at Cologne, for example, were to discover only too clearly that there were major hurdles to be surmounted in creating a musical language based exclusively on the attributes of synthetic sound.[8] Although some composers have remained committed to the pursuit of this particular objective, the majority have come to place a higher priority on the refinement of links between the synthetic and natural sound worlds, seeking a musical language that is common to both.

With the arrival and early maturity of the new millennium it is reasonable to suggest that digital technology now has the capacity to meet almost any creative requirement that might be placed on it.[9] There is of course considerable scope for refining further the ways in which existing techniques are applied for the benefit of composers and performers, but the real challenges lie in the artistic domain. Opportunities for composers and performers, professional or amateur, have never been so extensive and rewarding in this exciting medium of artistic expression. In this respect at least, the aspirations of the Futurists at the dawn of the twentieth century in seeking a means of sound production that reflects the day-to-day characteristics of an increasingly technical age have now been fully realized.[10] Time will show how profitably they are applied.

Notes

Chapter 1

1. Ferruccio Busoni, *Entwurf einer Neuen Aesthetic der Tonkunst* (Trieste, 1907; 2nd enlarged ed., Leipzig, 1910), English version, trans. Theodore Baker, *Sketch of a New Esthetic of Music* (New York: Schirmer, 1911), repr. "Sketch of a New Esthetic in Music," in *Three Classics in the Aesthetic of Music* (New York: Dover, 1962), 73–102.

2. Ibid., 95.

3. Filippo Tommaso Marinetti, *Le Figaro* (Paris, 12 February 1909).

4. Balilla Pratella, "Manifesto of Futurist Musicians" (open statement, Milan, 11 October1910).

5. Balilla Pratella, "Technical Manifesto of Futurist Music" (open statement, Milan, 11 March 1911).

6. Luigi Russolo, "The Art of Noises" (open statement to Balilla Pratella, Milan, 11 March 1913).

7. Ibid.

8. Ibid.

9. Ferrucio Busoni, trans. Theodore Baker, *Sketch of a New Esthetic in Music*, 95.

10. *New York Telegraph* (16 March 1916).

11. Ibid.

12. It was Betrand who was subsequently to construct the Dynaphone.

13. *Christian Science Monitor* (8 July 1922).

14. Joseph Schillinger, "Electricity, A Musical Liberator," *Modern Music*, 8 (1931): 26–31.

15. Joseph Schillinger, *The Schillinger System of Musical Composition: A Scientific Technique of Composing Music* (New York: Carl Fisher, 1946).

16. Joseph Schillinger, *The Mathematical Basis of the Arts* (New York: Philosophical Library, 1948, rep. New York: Da Capo Press, 1976).

17. Fernand Ouellette, *Edgard Varèse*, trans. Derek Coltman (London: Caldar and Boyars, 1973), 102–03.

18. Ibid., 129.

19. Ibid., 129.

20. See chapter 10.

21. Paul Hindemith, *Unterweisung im Tonsatz* (Mainz: AMP, 1937), English version, *The Craft of Musical Composition*, trans. Arthur Mendel and Otto Ortmann (London: Schott, 1945).

22. Leopold Stowkowski, "New Horizons in Music," *Journal of the Acoustical Society of America*, 4 (1932–3): 11–19.

23. Ibid., 14–15.

24. See also: John Whitney, "Moving Pictures and Electronic Music," *Die Reihe*, 7 (Vienna: Universal Edition, 1960), English version (Bryn Mawr, Penn.: Theodore Presser, 1965): 61–71.

25. Also quoted in: Fernand Ouellette, *Edgard Varèse*, 146–47.

26. John Cage, "The Future of Music: Credo" (1937), reproduced in *Silence* (London: Caldar and Boyars, 1968), 3–6.

Chapter 2

1. Renamed Westdeutscher Rundfunk in 1955.

2. Robert Richard, *Combat* (*Le Journal de Paris*, 11 July 1950).

3. A more detailed account of this technique, known as tape-head echo, will be given in the next chapter.

4. See Jacques Poullin, "Son et Espace," in *Vers une musique expérimentale* (Paris: La Revue Musicale, 1953), 105–14.

5. A description of the *Potentiomètre d'espace* is included in Jacques Poullin, "L'apport des techniques d'enregistrement dans la fabrication de matières des formes musicales nouvelles. Applications à la musique concrète," *L'Onde Electrique*, 34 (1954): 282–91, English version, "The Application of Recording Techniques to the Production of New Musical Materials and Forms. Application to Musique Concrète," trans. David Sinclair, *National Research Council of Canada*, TT 646 (1957).

6. Pierre Henry completed another version, *Le voile d'Orphée* in 1953. The work was subsequently reworked in his own studio, Apsome, and rereleased in 1966.

7. *La structure physique du signal en musique microphonique.*

8. Pierre Schaeffer, *À la recherche d'une musique concrète* (Paris: Éditions du Seuil, 1952).

9. These brief extracts from the treatise are translated by the author.

10. Pierre Schaeffer, *Traité des objets musicaux* (Paris: Éditions du Seuil, 1966).

Chapter 3

1. Werner Meyer-Eppler, *Elektrische Klangerzeugung* (Bonn: Dümmler, 1949).

2. Robert Beyer, "Das Problem der 'kommenden Musik,'" *Die Musik*, 20/12 (1928): 861–66.

3. Quoted in Otto Luening, "An Unfinished History of Electronic Music," *Music Education Journal*, 55/3 (November 1986): 46.

4. Pierre Schaeffer presented a concert of *musique concrète* during the same festival.

5. Karlheinz Stockhausen had become acquainted with Eimert during 1951, and on his suggestion paid his first visit to the Darmstadt Summer School that year.

6. Herbert Eimert, "What is Electronic Music?" *Die Reihe,* 1 (Vienna: Universal Edition, 1955), English version (Bryn Mawr, Penn.: Theodore Presser, 1958): 8–9.

7. H. H. Stuckenschmidt, "The Third Stage," *Die Reihe*, 1: 11–12.

8. Herbert Eimert, "The Place of Electronic Music in the Musical Situation," *Technische Hausmitteilungen des Nordwestdeutschen Rundfunks*, 6 (1954), English version, trans. David. A Sinclair, *National Research Council of Canada*, TT 610 (1956): 7.

9. Fourier's theorem states that any motion that recurs at a definite frequency can be built up from a number of simple vibrations whose frequencies are integral multiples of the fundamental recurrence frequency.

10. Nonetheless, the tracking filter, shaping the spectral content of a harmonic wave-shape, was to prove a fundamental design feature of the voltage-controlled synthesizer. See discussion in chapter 6.

11. The decibel is a logarithmic measurement of relative sound intensity. Its functional characteristics are considered further in chapter 13.

12. See Karl-Heinz Adams, "Filter Circuits for Electronic Sound Production," *Technische Hausmitteilungen des Nordwestdeutschen Rundfunks*, 6 (1954), English version, trans. David. A Sinclair, *National Research Council of Canada*, TT 605 (1956): 12,

13. Pierre Boulez, "'At the ends of fruitful land . . . '," *Die Reihe*, 1: 20–21.

14. More sophisticated electronic techniques for positioning sounds will be discussed in chapter 6 and again in chapter 21.

Chapter 4

1. Luciano Berio, "The Studio di Fonologia Musicale," *Score*, 15 (March 1956): 83.

2. James Joyce, *Ulysses* (London: Bodley Head, 1937).

3. Alfredo Lietti, "Gli implanti technici della studio di fonologia musicale di radio Milano," *Elettronica*, 5/3 (1956), English version, trans. David A. Sinclair, "The Technical Equipment of the Electronic Music Studio of Radio Milan," *National Research Council of Canada*, TT 859 (1957).

4. Manufactured by Eltro, Heidelberg, Germany.

Chapter 5

1. Although purely coincidental, it might be noted that this demonstration preceded Meyer-Eppler's pioneering series of lectures at the 1952 Darmstadt Summer School by just a matter of weeks.

2. Henry Cowell, "Current Chronicle: New York," *Musical Quarterly*, 37/4 (October 1952): 597.

3. "Ours" is a reference to *musique concrète*.

4. Schaeffer, *À la recherche*, 80.

5. Schaeffer was later to remark "I didn't like the work . . . ," see *Les Lettres Françaises* (16 June 1965).

6. See chapter 1.

7. See chapter 11. Hiller and Isaacson used the computer to write the *Illiac Suite for String Quartet* (1956).

8. See chapter 10.

9. A description of the constructional principles employed in this piece is given in Vladimir Ussachevsky, "Notes on a Piece for Tape Recorder," *Musical Quarterly*, 46/2 (April 1960): 202–09.

10. Claude E. Shannon and Warren Weaver, *The Mathematical Theory of Communication* (Urbana: University of Illinois Press, 1949).

11. See Harry F. Olson and Herbert Belar, "Aid to Musical Composition Employing a Random Probability System," *Journal of the Acoustical Society of America*, 33/9 (September 1961): 1163–70.

12. For a full version of this treatise, see Iannis Xenakis, *Musiques formelles: nouveaux principes formels de composition/Iannis Xenakis* (Paris: Richard-Masse, 1963), English version, *Formalized Music: Thought and Mathematics in Composition? Iannis Xenakis* (Bloomington: Indiana University Press, 1971; revised. ed., New York: Pendragon Press, 1992).

13. Leonard B. Meyer, "On the Nature and Limits of Critical Analysis," in *Explaining Music*: Essays and Explorations (Berkeley: University of California Press, 1973), 19–20.

Chapter 6

1. Harald Bode, "European Electronic Musical Instrument Design," *Journal of the Audio Engineering Society*, 9 (1961): 267.

2. Robert Moog, "Voltage-Controlled Electronic Music Modules," *Sixteenth Annual Fall Convention of the Audio Engineering Society* (14 October 1962).

3. See chapter 10.

4. Named after its inventor, Otto H. Schmitt (1913–98). It consists essentially of an amplitude-sensitive switch that closes to create an "on" state only when a signal applied to its input reaches or exceeds a preset level. This state is then maintained until the signal strength falls back again below the threshold point, whereupon the switch opens again.

5. The basic technique of polling through a cyclic sequence of digital waveform values to create a continuous function is known as wave-table synthesis, discussed in chapter 10. Although initially requiring the services of a computer, the advent of the microprocessor made it possible to transfer the technology to the self-contained hardware synthesizer in due course.

6. The principle described here is used in the design of digital-to-analog and analog-to-digital converters for both audio and control applications.

7. A comprehensive discussion of both sampling and quantizing is to be found in chapter 13 in the context of digital audio.

8. Further details of Oramics can be found in Daphne Oram, *An Individual Note: of Music, Sound, and Electronics* (London: Galliard; New York: Galaxy Music, 1972).

9. See chapter 1.

Chapter 7

1. From the RTF Berio moved first to IRCAM as head of the electroacoustic department (see chapter 11) from 1973–80, and then to Florence, where he founded his own research studio, Tempo Reale, in 1987.

2. See Iannis Xenakis, *Formalized Music: Thought and Mathematics in Composition? Iannis Xenakis* (Bloomington: Indiana University Press, 1971, rev. ed., New York: Pendragon Press, 1992).

3. For example Varèse's ill-fated project *Espace* (see chapter 1).

4. Starting with the integers 0 and 1, the Fibonacci series is created by adding together the most recent two numbers in a conventional integer sequence to provide the next number, and then repeating the operation, producing thus 0 1 1 2 3 5 8 13 21 34 55 89, and so on.

5. Prior to the reunification of Germany.

6. Later to become a significant center for the development of hybrid synthesis techniques (see chapter 12).

7 The Institute of Sonology transferred to the Royal Conservatory in The Hague in the early 1980s.

Chapter 8

1. Stockhausen's use of the tam-tam is strongly reminiscent of techniques employed for *musique concrète*, inspired in part by the work of Pierre Henry.

2. See discussion of *Gesang der Jünglinge* in chapter 3.

3. The Electronium (not to be confused with the Electronium Scott) is an electronic keyboard instrument with an accordion-like sound, manufactured by Hohner during the 1950s and 1960s.

4. The passage of time and the advance of technology have been particularly cruel for this piece. The abandonment of Morse code by international agreement in 2000 has transformed the nature of short wave radio signals, and the true character of this piece can no longer be realized using live sounds from the ether.

5. The VCS3 was the first commercial synthesizer to be manufactured by EMS London, launched in 1969.

6. Lejaren Hiller's use of composing algorithms for works such as HPSCHD is discussed in chapter 11.

7. This embryonic use of the technique predated the modern digital sampler by more than a decade.

Chapter 9

1. See chapter 1.

2. The Copycat, manufactured by Watkins Electric Music, proved a very popular portable echo unit with U.K. groups during the 1960s and 1970s, becoming obsolete with the emergence of more sophisticated digital effects units during the 1980s.

3. The Mellotron or Chamberlin, briefly referred to in chapter 2, is a keyboard instrument that reproduces sounds previously recorded on an array of tape loops, each of the latter being assigned to a specific key.

4. The closing section of Stockhausen's *Hymnen* provides a striking example of this technique.

Chapter 10

1. The teletypewriter was a modified electric typewriter, allowing electronic data to be manually keyed in and reproduced.

2. A more familiar present day analogy to batch processing is the spooling of printing tasks to a shared printer.

3. A particular problem was encountered in streaming digital audio data to and from converters without any breaks in the data flow. This is discussed further in chapter 19 in the context of UNIX-based workstations.

4. The characteristics of digital audio are studied in chapter 13.

5. Spooling from one end of a 2400′ magnetic tape to the other, for example, could take up to a minute or more.

6. This includes important derivatives such as C++. The subject of computer languages will be returned to in later chapters.

7. See chapter 1 for a discussion of Varèse's ill-fated attempts to gain access to these laboratories during the 1920s and 1930s.

8. The development of these leading research institutions will be studied further in due course.

9. The problems of additive synthesis in the analog domain are discussed in chapter 6.

10. A number of commercial digital synthesizers have used variable sampling rates to control the pitch of individual notes. This option, however, was not open to the designers of MUSICn programs in view of the need to synchronize the processes of component addition with a fixed rate of sampling.

11. See chapter 6 for a more detailed account of the functional characteristics of digital-to-analog and analog-to-digital converters.

12. Chapter 21 looks at a number of these algorithms in some detail.

13. Yamaha took an early interest in the commercial possibilities of FM synthesis, buying the patents from Stanford University for hardware implementations of FM and producing the first all-digital MIDI synthesizer, the DX7, in 1983. These developments are discussed further in chapter 14.

Chapter 11

1. SCORE was subsequently developed as a music notation program for the Intel-based PC. See chapter 16.

2. Vercoe's graphic input facility consisted of a special light pen and oscilloscope display

unit attached to a PDP11 allowing the input of simple music notation representations. This was soon eclipsed by the development of a powerful music graphics interface for the SSSP system developed by William Buxton and his associates at the University of Toronto, starting in 1977. See chapter 12.

3. This situation was to change dramatically with the development of the personal computer. See chapter 16.

4. The functional characteristics of the Tempophon are discussed in chapter 4.

5. For a further discussion of this technique and its derivatives, see chapter 21.

6. This work was subsequently withdrawn.

7. It will be recalled that Luening and Ussachevsky came across this pioneering venture when investigating the state of studio facilities at home and abroad in 1955. See chapter 5.

8. Work on this project commenced in 1967. See chapter 8.

9. Also known as the *Fourth String Quartet*.

10. The score data for this work including the text for the singer, was generated using MUSICOMP, a fully developed algorithmic composing program based on Hiller's theories.

11. Xenakis is referring here to Risset's work synthesizing acoustic instrument sounds.

12. Iannis Xenakis, "New Proposals in Microsound Structure," *Formalized Music: Thought and Mathematics in Composition* (Bloomington: Indiana University Press, 1971), 243–44.

13. This issue is returned to in chapter 22.

14. For a discussion of his later work developing UPIC, see chapter 19.

15. Truax's work with granular synthesis is discussed further in chapter 21.

16. See the discussion of Rodet's CHANT program in chapter 21.

17. Subsequently published as Max Mathews, "The Electronic Music Sound Studio of the 1970s," *Le Revue Musicale* (Paris: UNESCO, 1971): 129–41.

18. The development of the WIMPs environment is discussed in chapter 16.

19. Mathews, "The Electronic Music Sound Studio," 138.

20: The problems of digital sequencer design are discussed in chapter 6.

21. It was the PDP 8 that launched the era of the minicomputer.

22. "Pink" noise, as opposed to "white" noise, distributes energy on a logarithmic basis throughout the frequency spectrum, thus ensuring that if it is filtered down to a specified musical interval at any pitch center, such as a tone or a semitone, the energy throughput will be constant.

23. Essentially two VCS3s connected together.

24. This association resulted in the revolutionary DX7 MIDI synthesizer, released in 1983.

Chapter 12

1. Applications Specific Integrated Circuit.

2. Beginner's All-purpose Symbolic Instruction Code.

3. Zinovieff had fully grasped the significance of digital technology and was far-sighted enough to invest in his own research program. Unfortunately, his commercial company, EMS London, collapsed before he could exploit the full potential of this pioneering work.

4. See chapter 11.

5. See chapter 1.

6. Moog was subsequently to market his Thérémins commercially, taking advantage of the new MIDI environment that emerged in 1983.

7. This concept anticipated important research and development carried out by a number of research institutions, in the case of Stanford in association with Yamaha. See chapter 21.

8. See chapter 2.

9. Hard disk recording systems are considered further in chapter 18.

10. Attack-Decay-Sustain-Release.

11. The MIDI revolution is discussed from chapter 14 onward.

12. LSI stands for Large Scale Integrated, indicating in this context the use of micro-processor technology in place of older computer architectures.

13. See the discussion of VOSIM in chapter 11.

14. The subject of computer-controlled sound projection is returned to in chapter 21.

15. The evolution of this environment is considered more fully in chapter 16.

Chapter 13

1. Some AM European stations transmit on the maximum permitted bandwidth of about 8 kHz, but this still falls well short of an acceptable benchmark for high fidelity.

2. A sine wave, for example, fluctuates positively and negatively with respect to time. Taking a simple numerical average of the function thus produces a value of zero no matter what the amplitude. In order to work around this mathematical anomaly, the function is squared to make both segments of the wave positive. The mean value is then calculated and normalized by taking its square root, hence the expression "root-mean-square" or "rms" value. For sine waves, this average value can be approximated to 0.707 times the maximum amplitude.

3. A typical method of measuring this subjective feature is to place a listener in an ane-choic (completely dead) chamber and play an alternating sequence of two tones at the same frequency, starting of both tones at the same amplitude. The amplitude of one tone is then changed step by step until a point is reached where the listener indicates that there is a per-ceptible difference between the two.

4. The functional characteristics of compressors and expanders are discussed in chapter 6.

5. The basic principles involved in representing a continuous voltage function as a series of discrete numerical approximations are outlined in chapter 6, and further consideration is given to these principles in the discussion of MUSICn programs in chapter 10.

6. See chapter 6.

7. See chapter 10.

8. This is sometimes called a Digital Video Disc.

Chapter 14

1. See chapter 15.

2. The continuing production of analog synthesizers to the end of the twentieth century by Oberheim against the prevailing digital trends is discussed in chapter 17.

3. The development of MIDI software is discussed in chapter 16.

4. The actual publication date was 1984. Over the years the 1.0 definitive specification has been re-released a number of times, by the International MIDI Association with appendices listing supplementary features such as the characteristics of General MIDI, to be discussed later in this chapter. In the early 1990s the International MIDI Association changed its name to the MIDI Manufacturers Association (MMA). For a recent release of the MIDI specification, see *The Complete MIDI 1.0 Detailed Specification*, version 96.1, second ed. (Los Angeles: MIDI Manufacturers Association, 2001).

5. 56 Kbaud marks the highest permissible speed of conventional data transmission along standard voice lines in many countries. It is for this reason that dedicated high bandwidth digital lines using special protocols such as ISDN (Integrated Services Digital Network) are becoming increasingly common for domestic as well as commercial connections.

6. This aspect is discussed further in chapter 18.

Chapter 15

1. It might be noted at this point that Yamaha first made contact with Stanford as far back as 1971. Unlike many commercial companies, it was prepared to foster relationships with a leading research institution over a number of years before seeking to reap the commercial benefits. Such patience clearly paid off.

2. For a more general discussion of voice-editing software, see chapter 16.

3. See chapter 14.

4. See the discussion of digital audio in chapter 13.

5. It will be recalled that this mode of operation is invariably required for software synthesis using a computer.

6. See the discussion of floating-point formats in the context of digital signal processing in chapter 13.

7. This technique of data compression involves the use of "lossy" techniques, discussed in chapter 14.

8. The characteristics of the Apple Macintosh are discussed in chapter 16.

9. This technique was discussed in chapter 13.

10. See the discussion of VOCOM in chapter 12.

11. The characteristics of the 56000 DSP are discussed in chapter 16.

12. The relationship between computer disk storage capacity and the development of digital audio has already been discussed in chapter 13. Here, however, the context is slightly different since we are concerned with the storage of individually sampled sounds, rather than complete digital audio files.

13. See chapter 16.

14. ZIP and JAZ drives are designed and manufactured by Iomega. They are essentially high volume alternatives to the conventional floppy disk.

15. During the early 2000s, SCSI was increasingly replaced by alternative high-speed digital communication links such as USB and Firewire.

16. SMPTE is discussed in chapter 14.

17. Oberheim was not alone in this respect. See chapter 17.

18. See chapter 3.

19. The term "multitimbral" refers to the ability to synthesize more than one voice at a time, a feature that became increasingly significant as the age of MIDI advanced. There is thus a distinction to be made between polyphonic characteristics, that is the number of different notes that may sound simultaneously, and multitimbral characteristics, that is the number of different voices that may form part as part of a polyphonic texture. This subject will be studied more closely in chapter 17.

20. As will be seen in due course, the concept of the self-contained workstation became increasingly important to hardware synthesizer manufacturers as the personal computer gained in significance, not only as a control resource for MIDI but also in due course a synthesizer in its own right.

21. This product anticipates a discussion of more recent MIDI hardware developments in chapter 17.

22. The SY prefix had already been used for the SY1 and SY2 analog synthesizers manufactured by Yamaha during the late 1970s.

23. Several of these more innovative MIDI controllers are discussed in chapter 20.

Chapter 16

1. See chapter 12.

2. The Apple II processor, a 6502, was only eight-bit.

3. RISC architectures are considered further in chapter 19.

4. Some internal features of the Pentium are also RISC based.

5. The provenance of Apple's OS X is also discussed in chapter 19.

6. Although widely sold in the United States, very few models were sold in Europe.

7. See chapter 12 for a discussion of single-bit sound production.

8. The sound facilities provided by the Atari 800 and the Commodore 64 are described in chapter 12.

9. See chapter 15.

10. This subject is studied in chapter 18.

11. See chapter 14.

12. See chapters 5 and 12.

13. See chapter 5.

14. See chapter 11.

15. See chapter 11.

16. This use of multiple MIDI connections to increase the number of active voices is discussed further in chapter 17.

Chapter 17

1. See chapter 13 for a more detailed technical explanation of oversampling and extended processor bit resolutions.

2. WAV is an abbreviation for WAVe and AIFF is derived from Audio Interchange File Format.

3. See discussion in chapter13.

4. The use of techniques such as phase vocoding for time compression and expansion is discussed in chapter 21.

5. The use of a personal computer to edit samples is considered in chapter 18 as part of more detailed study of audio data processing techniques.

6. See chapter 14. It should be noted that Yamaha's XG bank specifications, introduced in 1995, are even more comprehensive than those eventually specified for General MIDI Level 2 (1999).

7. The technology of physical modeling is discussed in chapter 21.

8. Not to be confused with the Casio VL-1.

9. See chapter 15.

10. This recording system, known as ADAT, is discussed in chapter 18.

11. See chapter 12.

Chapter 18

1. C was developed from a prototype language known as BCPL (Binary Coded Programming Language). See *The Bell System Technical Journal*, 57/6/2 (July–August 1978).

2. See discussion in chapter 16.

3. See chapter 14.

4. See chapter 19.

5. Discussed in chapter 12.

6. See the IRCAM Music Workstation in chapter 19.

7. The migration of several leading researchers to Lucasfilm, in the first instance to work on the *Star Wars* series of films, had a significant short-term impact on developments in computer music.

8. This aspect of signal data processing is discussed in chapter 13.

9. The domestic industry adopted S/PDIF, taking advantage of its simpler electronic connections and the fact that it was possible to embed moderately robust "copy/protect" features in the digital data. Such codes could be easily ignored when using AES/EBU, the professional format.

10. See chapter 13.

11. See discussion in chapter 17.

12. In due course, the concept of VST expanded to include new synthesis technologies as well as the modeling of older ones. The development of the Plex Restructuring VST Synthesizer in 2002 by Steinberg and Wolfgang Palm is a striking example.

13. See chapter 12.

Chapter 19

1. See chapters 15 and 17.

2. The background to this course of events is outlined in chapter 16.

3. UNIX is essentially a time-sharing environment, and these process control features remain embedded in the software even when the system is restricted to a single user.

4. See chapter 16.

5. Inmos was subsequently taken over by SGS-Thomson Microelectronics.

6. For example, StarSync, used for synchronizing audio soundtracks with film.

7. Developed at the University of Montreal.

8. Silicon Graphics emerged as a major competitor to the Sun, leading the way in terms of developing advanced WIMPs-based tools for UNIX computer workstations during the early 1990s.

9. Java (originally known as Oak) was developed into a commercial product by Sun, in partnership with Netscape. During the late 1990s this alliance expanded to include many of the key developers of Internet software, with the notable exception of Microsoft.

10. See chapter 12.

11. The initiative for developing floating-point DSPs dates back to the late 1980s, when TMS adopted this alternative architecture for the design of a special version of the 32000 series, known as the TMS 32030. Motorola responded to this initiative with by launching the 96000 series of DSPs, similarly based on a floating-point architecture.

12. See discussion of Apple's global trading policy at this time in chapter 16.

Chapter 20

1. See discussion of non-keyboard MIDI controllers in chapter 15.

2. Joel Chadabe's use of Thërémins with the Synclavier 1 provides an interesting precedent for this type of gestural controller. See chapter 12.

3. Although the voltages involved are very small, these experiments were potentially very dangerous, given the proximity of exposed power supply terminals in many synthesizers dating from this era.

4. See chapter 8.

Chapter 21

1. See the discussion of the Milan studio in chapter 4.

2. See Jean Claude Risset and Max V. Mathews, "Analysis of Musical-Instrumental Tones," *Physics Today*, 22 (1969): 23–30.

3. See chapter 15.

4. This research formed part of an extended project into both analog and digital modeling of instrumental sounds, carried out at Illinois.

5. See chapter 17.

6. This program is specifically designed for the Apple Macintosh. See chapter 18.

7. See chapter 10.

8. Michael Clarke developed this CSOUND version of the algorithm at the universities of Durham and Huddersfield in the United Kingdom.

9. See chapter 11.

10. This publication also inspired the construction of the Olson and Belar composing machine at RCA. See chapter 5.

11. See chapter 3.

12. This program is also designed for the Apple Macintosh.

13. See chapter 19.

14. See chapter 10.

15. See chapter 3.

16. Directed by Berio.

Chapter 22

1. Hugh Davies, *Répertoire international des musiques electroacoustiques: International Electronic Music Catalog* (Paris: Groupe de Recherches Musicales de l'ORTF, and New York: Independent Electronic Music Center, 1968).

2. The Electronic Music Foundation, New York, was established during the mid-1990s specifically to foster the wider dissemination of electronic and computer music, both in terms of new recordings and also rereleases of established classics.

3. An interesting trend is this regard is the publication of some works exclusively on the Internet, thus relying entirely on this electronic means of communication.

4. See, for example, Joel Chadabe, *Electric Sound: The Past and Promise of Electronic Music* (Upper Saddle River, N.J.: Prentice Hall, 1997).

5. See chapter 2.

6. See chapter 2. The technical significance of this philosophy was discussed further in chapter 22.

7. Schaeffer's work in establishing a morphology for *musique concrète* is now largely forgotten. Nothing remotely similar in terms of scale and depth has been attempted since.

8. See chapter 3.

9. At the time of writing the first edition of this book, published in 1985, this state of technological development still lay far in the future.

10. See chapter 1.

Bibliography

The following suggestions for further reading are selected from a wide repertory of material dealing with aspects of electronic and computer music. One or two additional items have been included dealing with more general aspects of the art and practice of music that have a particular significance for the medium as a whole.

Catalogues and Periodicals

Bartle, Barton K. *Computer Software in Music and Music Education: A Guide*. Metuchen, N.J.: Scarecrow Press, 1987.

The Computer Music Journal (Cambridge, Mass.: MIT Press) 1– (1977–).

Contemporary Music Review (Chur, Switzerland: Harwood Academic Press) 1– (1984–).

Cross, Lowell. *A Bibliography of Electronic Music*. Toronto: University of Toronto Press, 1967.

Davies, Hugh. *Répertoire international des musiques electroacoustiques/International Electronic Music Catalog*. Paris: Groupe de Recherches Musicales de l'O.R.T.F, and New York: Independent Electronic Music Center, 1968.

Electronic Music Reports (Utrecht: Institute for Sonology) 1–4 (1969–71).

Electronic Music Review (Trumansberg, N.Y.: Independent Electronic Music Center) 1–7 (1967–9).

Interface (Amsterdam: Swets und Zeitlinger) 1–22 (1972–93).

Journal of Music Theory (New Haven, Conn.: Yale School of Music) 1–(1957–).

Organised Sound (Cambridge, England: Cambridge University Press) 1–(1996–).

Perspectives of New Music (Princeton, N.J. : Princeton University Press) 1–(1962–).

Die Reihe (Vienna: Universal Edition) 1–8 (1955–62). English Translations: (Bryn Mawr, Penn.: Theodore Presser).

Risset, Jean C. *An Introductory Catalog of Computer Synthesized Sounds* (Murray Hill, N.J.: Bell Telephone Laboratories) 1970.

Tjepkema, Sandra. *A Bibliography of Computer Music: A Reference for Composers* (Iowa: University of Iowa Press) 1981.

Books

Appleton, Jon H., and Ronald C. Perara, eds. *The Development and Practice of Electronic Music.* Englewood Cliffs, N.J.: Prentice Hall, 1975.

Backus, John. *The Acoustical Foundations of Music.* New York: Norton, 1969.

Bateman, Wayne. *Introduction to Computer Music.* New York: Wiley, 1980.

Boulanger, Richard. C., ed. *The Csound Book: Perspectives in Software Synthesis, Sound Design, Signal Processing and Programming.* Cambridge, Mass.: MIT Press, 1999.

Busoni, Ferruccio. *Sketch of a New Esthetic in Music.* Trans. Theodore Baker. New York: Schirmer, 1911.

Cage, John. *Silence.* London: Caldar and Boyars, 1968.

Chadabe, Joel. *Electronic Sound: The Past and Promise of Electronic Music.* Upper Saddle River, N.J.: Prentice Hall, 1997.

Deutsch, Herbert A. *Synthesis: An Introduction to the History, Theory and Practice of Electronic Music.* New York: Alfred Publishing Co., 1976.

Dobson, Richard. *A Dictionary of Electronic and Computer Music Technology.* Oxford: Oxford University Press, 1992.

Dodge, Charles, and Thomas A. Jerse. *Computer Music, Synthesis, Composition and Performance.* 2nd ed. London and New York: Schirmer, 1997.

Emmerson, Simon, ed. *The Language of Electroacoustic Music.* London: Macmillan, 1986.

Ernst, David. *The Evolution of Electronic Music.* New York: Schirmer, 1977.

Griffiths, Paul. *A Guide to Electronic Music.* London: Thames and Hudson, 1979.

Harvey, Jonathan. *The Music of Stockhausen.* London: Faber and Faber, 1976.

Hiller, Lejaren, and Leonard Isaacson. *Experimental Music.* New York: McGraw-Hill, 1959.

Holmes, Thomas. *Electronic and Experimental Music.* New York: Macmillan, 1986.

Howe, Hubert S. *Electronic Music Synthesis.* London and New York: Dent, 1975.

Judd, Frederick C. *Electronic Music and Musique Concrète.* London: Neville Spearman, 1961.

Keane, David. *Tape Music Composition.* London: Oxford University Press, 1980.

Lincoln, Barry B., ed. *The Computer and Music.* Ithaca, N.Y.: Cornell University Press, 1970.

Maconie, Robin. *The Works of Karlheinz Stockhuasen.* 2nd ed. Oxford: Oxford University Press, 1990.

Mathews, Max V., and Joan E. Miller. *The Technology of Computer Music.* Cambridge, Mass.: MIT Press, 1969.

Mathews, Max V., and John D. Pierce, eds. *Current Directions in Computer Music Research.* Cambridge, Mass.: MIT Press, 1989.

Meyer, Leonard B. *Explaining Music: Essays and Exploration.* Chicago: University of Chicago Press, 1978.

Moles, André A. *Information Theory and Aesthetic Perception.* Trans. Joel E. Cohen. Urbana: University of Illinois Press, 1966.

Moore, F. *Elements of Computer Music.* Englewood Cliffs, N.J.: Prentice Hall, 1989.

Nyman, Michael. *Experimental Music: Cage and Beyond.* London: Schirmer, 1974, rpt. 1981.

Olson, Harry F. *Music, Physics and Engineering.* New York: Dover, 1967.

Ouellette, Fernand. *Edgard Varèse.* London: Caldar and Boyars, 1973.

Paynter, John, Tim Howell, Richard Orton, and Peter Seymour, eds. *Companion to Contemporary Musical Thought.* London: Routledge, 1992.

Pressing, Jeff. *Synthesizer Performance and Real-Time Techniques.* Madison, Wisc.: A-R Editions, 1992.

Roads, Curtis. *Composers and the Computer.* Los Altos, California: W. Kaufmann, 1985.

Roads, Curtis, ed. *The Computer Music Tutorial.* Cambridge, Mass.: MIT Press, 1996.

Roads, Curtis, ed. *Music Machine.* Cambridge, Mass.: MIT Press, 1989.

Roads, Curtis, and John Strawn, eds. *Foundations of Computer Music.* Cambridge, Mass.: MIT Press, 1987.

Rothstein, Joseph. *MIDI: A Comprehensive Introduction.* Madison, Wisc.: A-R Editions, 1992.

Russolo, Luigi. *The Art of Noise.* Trans. Robert Filliou. New York: Something Else Press, 1967.

Schaeffer, Pierre. *À la recherche d'une musique concrète.* Paris: Éditions du Seuil, 1952.

Schaeffer, Pierre. *Traité des objets musicaux.* Paris: Éditions du Seuil, 1966.

Schillinger, Joseph. *The Mathematical Basis of the Arts.* Rpt. New York: Da Capo Press, 1976.

Schrader, Barry. *Introduction to Electro-Acoustic Music.* Englewood Cliffs, N.J.: Prentice Hall, 1982.

Schwartz, Elliott. *Electronic Music: A Listener's Guide.* New York: Prager, 1973.

Sear, Walter. *A Guide to Electronic Music and Synthesizers.* London: Omnibus, 1977.

Strange, Allen. *Electronic Music.* Dubique, Iowa: William C. Brown, 1972.

von Foerster, Heinz, and James W. Beauchamp, eds. *Music by Computers.* New York: Wiley, 1969.

Wells, Thomas H. *The Technique of Electronic Music.* New York: Schirmer, 1981.

Wick, Robert L. *Electronic and Computer Music: An Annotated Bibliography.* Westport, Conn.: Greenwood Press, 1997.

Winkel, Fritz. *Music, Sound and Sensation.* Trans. Thomas Binkley. New York: Dover, 1967.

Winkler, Tom. *Composing Interactive Music: Techniques and Ideas Using MAX.* Cambridge, Mass.: MIT Press, 1998.

Wörner, Karl H. *Stockhausen: Life and Work.* London: Faber and Faber, 1973.

Xenakis, Iannis. *Formalized Music: Thought and Mathematics in Composition? Iannis Xenakis.* Bloomington: Indiana University Press, 1971, rev. ed., New York: Pendragon Press, 1992.

Discography

Electronic and Computer Music

Records

AMM. *AMM Music* (1966). Elektra EUKS 7256.
    Live Electronic Music Improvised (1968). Mainstream MS 5002.
Anhalt, István. *Electronic Composition No. 4* (1961). Allied Record 17.
Appleton, Jon. *Zoetrope* (1974). Folkways FTS 3345.
    Mussem's Song (1976). Folkways FTS 3345.
    The Sydsing Camklang (1976). Folkways 3345.
    In Deserto (1977). Folkways FTS 3345.
    Syntrophia (1977). Folkways FTS 3345.
Arel, Bülent. *Electronic Music No 1* (1960). CRI S 356, Son Nova S 3.
    Stereo Electronic Music No. 1 (1960). Columbia MS 6566.
    Dramatic Fragment from "The Scapegoat" (1961). Son Nova S 3.
    Sacred Service: Prelude and Postlude (1961). CRI S 356, Son Nova S 3.
    Mimiana II: Freize (1969). CRI SD 300.
    Stereo Electronic Music No. 2 (1970). CRI SD 265, Finnada 9010 Q.
Ashley, Robert. *The Wolfman* (1964). ESP S 1009 (*Source Magazine* No. 4). Source 1.
    Untitled Mixes (1965). ESP S 1009.
    Accidents (1967). Source 2.
    Purposeful Lady Slow Afternoon (1968). Mainstream MS 5010.
Austin, Larry. *Hybrid Musics* (1980). IRIDA 0022, Broadway, New York: The New Music Distribution Center.
Babbitt, Milton. *Composition for Synthesizer* (1960–1). Columbia MS 6566.
    Vision and Prayer (1961). CRI SD 268, CRI S 268.

Philomel (1963–4). Acoustic Research AR 0654 083.

Ensembles for Synthesizer (1963). Columbia MS 7051, Finnadar 9010 Q.

Phonomena (1969–74). New World NW 209.

Reflections (1974–5). New World NW 209.

Badings, Henk. *Kaïn en Abel* (1956). Philips 400 036 AE, Philips ABE 10073.

Evolutionem (1957). Epic BC 1118, Philips 835 056 AY, Philips SABL 206.

Genese (1958). Epic BC 1118, Philips 835 056 AY, Philips SABL 206.

Capriccio (1959). Epic BC 1118, Limelight 86055, Philips 835 056 AY, Philips SABL 206.

Barraqué, Jean. *Étude* (1953). Barclay 89005.

Bayle, François. *Pluriel* (1962–3). Philips 836 894 DSY.

Archipel (1963). Philips 895 DSY.

Vapeur (1963). Boîte à Musique LD 072, Boîte à Musique 5072.

L'Oiseau-Chanteur (1964). Candide CE 31025, Philips 836 895 DSY, Varèse VS 81005.

Lignes et points (1966). Philips 836 895 DSY.

Espaces inhabitables (1966–7). Philips 836 895 DSY.

Jeïta ou Mumure des eaux (1970). Philips 6521 016.

Behrman, David. *Runthrough* (1966). Mainstream MS 5010.

Wavetrain (1966). (*Source Magazine* No. 3). Source 1.

Figure in a Clearing (1977). 325 Spring Street, New York: Lovely Music Ltd., LML 1041.

On the Other Ocean (1977). 325 Spring Street, New York: Lovely Music Ltd., LML 1041.

Berio, Luciano. *Mutazioni* (1955). RAI (Elettronica 1956 No. 3).

Perspectives (1957). Compagnia Generale del Disco ESZ 3.

Thema—Omaggio a Joyce (1958). Philips 836 897 DSY, Philips 835 485 AY, Turnabout N 34177 S.

Différences (1958–60). Mainstream MS 5004, Philips 839 323 DSY, Philips 6500 631.

Momenti (1960). Limelight LS 86047, Philips 836 897 DSY, Philips 835 485 AY.

Visage (1961). Candide CE 31027, Columbia OS 3320, RCA 61079, Turnabout TV 3406 S.

Laborintus II (1965). Harmonia Mundi HM 764.

Birtwistle, Harrison. *Four Interludes from a Tragedy* (1970). L'Oiseau-Lyre DSLO 17.

Chronometer (1971). Argo ZRG 790.

Boretz, Benjamin. *Group Variation II* (1973). CRI SD 300.

Boucourechliev, André. *Texte I* (1958). Mercury SR2 9123, Philips 835 486 AY

Texte II (1959). Boîte à Musique LD 071.

Boulez, Pierre. *Étude* (1952). Barclay 89005.

Brown, Earle. *Octet 1* (1953). CRI SD 330.

Four Systems (1954). Columbia MS 7139, EMI Electrola C 065 02469.

Times Five (1963). Boîte à Musique LD 072.

Brün, Herbert. *Anepigraphe* (1958). Amadeo AVRS 5006.

Klänge unterwegs (1961). Amadeo AVRS 5006.

Futility (1964). Heliodor HS 25047.

Cage, John. *Imaginary Landscape No. 1* (1939). Avakian JCS 1, EMI Electrola C 165 28954.

Credo in U.S. (1942). EMI Electrola C165 28954.

Radio Mix (1960). Cramps CRS LP 6101.

Williams Mix (1952). Avakian JCS 1.

Aria with Fontana Mix (1959). Mainstream MS 5005, Time S 8003.

Fontana Mix (1959). Turnabout RV 34046 S.

Cartridge Music (1960). Mainstream MS 5015, Time S 8009, DGG 137 009.

Music for Amplified Toy Pianos (1960). Cramps CRS LP 6101, EMI Electrola C 065 02469.

Solo for Voice 2 (1960). Odyssey 32 16 0156.

Rozart Mix (1963). EMI Electrola C 165 28954.

Variations II (1963). Columbia MS 7051, CBS France S 3461064.

Variations III (1963). DGG 139442, Wergo 60057.

Variations IV (1963). Everest 3130.

Fontana Mix-Feed (1964). Columbia MS 7139.

Sixty-Two Mesostics re Merce Cunningham (1971). Cramps CRS LP 6101 (extracts).

Cage, John, with Lejaren Hiller. *HPSCHD* (1967–9). Nonesuch H 71224.

Carlos, Walter. *Dialogues for Piano and Two Loudspeakers* (1963). Turnabout TV 34004 S.

Variations (1964). Turnabout TV 34004 S.

Switched on Bach (1968). Columbia MS 7194.

The Well Tempered Synthesizer (1969). Columbia MS 7286.

Sonic Seasonings (1971–2). Columbia PG 312234.

Clementi, Aldo. *Collage II* (1960). Compagnia Generale del Disco ESZ 3.

Davidovsky, Mario. *Electronic Study No. 1* (1960). Columbia MS 6566.

Electronic Study No. 2 (1962). CRI S 356, Son Nova S 3.

Synchronisms No. 1 (1963). CRI SD 204.

Synchronisms No. 2 (1964). CRI SD 204.

Synchronisms No. 3 (1964–5). CRI SD 204.

Electronic Study No. 3 (1965–6). Finnadar 9010 Q, Turnabout TV 34487 S.

Synchronisms No. 5 (1969). CRI SD 268, Turnabout TV 34487 S.

Synchronisms No. 6 (1970). Thurnabout TV 34487 S.

Dobrowolski, Andrej. *Music for Magnetic Tape and Oboe Solo* (1965). Muza Warsaw Fest 244.

Dodge, Charles. *Changes* (1969). Nonesuch H 71245.

Earth's Magnetic Field (1970). Nonesuch H 71250.

Extensions for Trumpet and Tape (1973). CRI SD 300.

Speech Songs (1973). CRI SD 348.

The Story of Our Lives (1974). CRI SD 348.

In Celebration (1975). CRI SD 348.

Druckman, Jacob. *Animus I* (1965). Turnabout TV 34177 S.

Animus II (1967–8). CRI SD 255.

Animus III (1969). Nonesuch H 71253.

Synapse → *Valentine* (1969–70). Nonesuch H 71253.

Eaton, John. *Piece for Solo Synket No. 3* (1965). Decca 710154.

Songs for R.P.B. (1965). Decca 710154.

    Concert Piece for Synket and Symphony Orchestra (1967). Turnabout TV 34428 S.

    Soliloquy (1967). Decca 710165.

    Thoughts in Rilke (1967). Decca 710165.

    Blind Man's Cry (1968). CRI SD 296.

    Duet for Synket and Moog (1968). Decca 710165.

    Mass (1970). CRI SD 296.

Eimert, Herbert. *Glockenspiel* (1953). DGG LP 16132.

    Étude über Tongemische (1953–4). DGG LP 16132.

    Fünf Stüke (1955–6). DGG LP 16132.

    Zu Ehren von Igor Stravinsky (1957). Wergo 60006.

    Variante einer Variation von Anton Webern (1958). Wergo 60006.

    Selektion 1 (1959–60). Mercury SR 2 9123, Philips 835 486 AY.

    Epitaph für Aikichi Kuboyama (1960–2). Wergo 60014.

    Sechs Studien (1962). Wergo 60014.

El-Dabh, Halim. *Leiyla and the Poet* (1961). Columbia MS 6566.

Ferrari, Luc. *Étude aux accidents* (1958). Boite à Musique LD 070.

    Étude aux sons tendus (1958). Boite à Musique LD 070.

    Visage V (1958–9). Limelight LS 86047, Philips 835 485 AY, Philips 6740 001.

    Tête et queue du dragon (1959–60). Candide CE 31025, Philips 835 487 AY, Varèse VS 81005.

    Tautologos I (1961). Boite à Musique LD 072.

    Tautologos II (1961). Boite à Musique LD 071.

    Composé-composite (1962–3). Philips 836 894 DSY.

    Hétérozygote (1963–4). Philips 836 885 DSY.

    Und so weiter (1966). Wergo 60046.

    J'ai été coupé (1969). Philips 836 855 DSY.

Gaburo, Kenneth. *Antiphony III* (1962). Nonesuch H 71199.

    Exit Music I: The Wasting of Lucrecetzia (1964). Nonesuch H 71199.

    Exit Music II: Fat Millie's Lament (1965). Nonesuch H 71199.

    Lemon Drops (1965). CRI S 356, Heliodor HS 25047.

    For Harry (1966). CRI S 356, Heliodor HS 25047.

    Antiphony IV (1967). Nonesuch H 71199.

Gerhard, Roberto. *Symphonie No. 3 'Collages'* (1960). Angel S 36558.

Ghent, Emanuel. *Brazen* (1975). New Direction in Music, Tulsa Studios Tulsa Oklahoma.

Glass, Philip. *Contrary Motion* (1969). Shandar 83 515.

    Music in Fifths (1969). Chatham Square LP 1003.

    Music in Similar Motion (1969). Chatham Square LP 1003.

    Two Pages (1969). Folkways 33902, Shandar 83 515.

    North Star (1977). Virgin V 2085.

Gruppo di Improvvisazione Nuove Consonanza: Cantata (1964). DGG 643 541, RCA Italiana MLDS 21243.

    Credo (1969). DGG 137 007.

Hambraeus, Bengt. *Konstellationer II* (1959). Limelight LS 86032, Philips 838 750
    Rota II (1963). Riks LP 7 S.
    Tetragon (1965). Ricks LP 7 S.
Henry, Pierre. *Concerto des ambiguïtés* (1950). Philips 6510 012, Ducretet-Thomson DUC
    8, London DTL 93090 (part).
    Batterie fugace (1950–1). Ducretet-Thomson DUC 8, London DTL 93090.
    Musique sans titre (1950–1). Ducretet-Thomson DUC 8.
    Tam-tam III (1950–1). Ducretet-Thomson DUC 8, London DTL 93090.
    Tam-tam IV (1950–1). Ducretet-Thompson DUC 9, London DTL 9321.
    Antiphonie (1952). Ducretet-Thomson DUC 9, London DTL 93121.
    Astrologie (1953). Ducretet-Thomson DUC 9, London DTL 93121.
    Vocalises (1953). Ducretet-Thomson DUC 9, London DTL 93121.
    Le Voile d'Orphée (1953 version). Ducrete-Thomson DUC 8, London DTL 93090,
        Philips 836 887 DSY.
    Orphée (1958 version). Philips 839 484 LY.
    Entité (1960). Limelight LS 86048, Philips 835 486 AY, Philips 836 887 DSY.
    Maléfices (1961). Philips 432 762 BE.
    La Noire à soixante (1961). Philips 836 892 DSY.
    Le Voyage (1961–2). Limelight LS 86049, Philips 836 899 DSY, Philips 6510 014. (part).
    La Reine verte (1963). Philips 6332 015 Philips 6510 014.
    Variations pour une porte et un soupir (1963). Philips 836 898 DSY, Philips 6510 014 (part).
    Le Voile d'Orphée (1966 version). Philips 680 201 NL.
    Granulométric (1962–7). Philips 836 892 DSY.
    Messe de Liverpool (1967). Philips 6501 0001.
    Apocalypse de Jean (1968). Philips C 3017, Philips 6521 001-3.
    Ceremony (1969). Philips 849 512.
    Messe pour le temps présent (1970). Philips 836 893.
    Mouvement-rhythme-étude (1970). Philips 6504 052.
    Mise en musique du cortical art (1971). Philips 6521 022.
    Musiques pout une fête (1971). Philips 6565 001.
    Cortical Art LLL (1973). Philips 6510 015.
    Machine Dance (1973). Philips 6510 013.
    Prismes (1973). Philips 6510 016.
Henry, Pierre, with Pierre Schaeffer. *Symphonie pour un himme seul* (1949–50). Ducretet-
    Thomson DUC 9, London DTL 93121.
    Bidule en ut (1950). Ducretet-Thomson DUC 8, London DTL 93090, Philips 6736 006.
Henze, Hans Werner. *Violin Concerto No. 2* (1971). ecca headline HEAD 5
    Tristan (1973). DGG 2530 834.
Hiller, Lejaren. *Nightmare Music from "Time of the Heathen"* (1961). Heliodor HS 2549 006.
    Vocalise (1962–3). Supraphon DV 6221.
    Computer Cantata (1963). CRI SD 310, Heliodor HS 25053.
    Music Machine (1964). Heliodor HS 25047.

Suite (1966). Heliodor HS 2549 006.

Algorithms 1 (1968). DGG 2543 005.

An Avalanche (1968). Heliodor HS 2549 006.

Computer Cantata for Percussion and Tape (1968). Heliodor HS 2549 006.

Hiller, Lejaren, with John Cage. *HPSCHD* (1967–9). Nonesuch H 71224.

Holliger, Heinz. *Siebengesang* (1967). DGG 2530 318.

Howe, Hubert S. *Three Studies in Timbre* (1970–3). Opus One, No. 47, New Music Distribution Service, 500 Broadway, NY.

Improvisation on the Overtone Series (1977). Opus One, No. 53, New Music Distribution Service.

Kagel, Mauricio. *Transición I* (1958–60). Limelight LS 86048, Philips 835 486 AY.

Transición II (1959). Mainstream MS 5003, Time S 8001.

Acustica (1968–70). DGG 2707 059.

Unter Storm (1969). DGG 2530 460.

Kayn, Roland. *Cybernetics III* (1969). DGG 2543 006.

Koenig, Gottfried Michael. *Klangfiguren II* (1955–6). DGG LP 16134.

Terminus II (1966–7). DGG 137 011.

Funktion Grün (1967). DGG 137 011.

Terminus X (1967). Philips 836 993 DSY.

Funktion Gelb (1968). Wergo 324.

Funktion Blau (1969). Philips 6736 006, Philips 6740 002.

Křenek, Ernst. *Pfingstoratorium—Spiritus Intelligentiae, Sanctus* (1955–6). DGG LP 16134.

Quintona (1966). Jornadas de Musica Experimental JME ME 2.

Lanksy, Paul. *Mild und leise* (1973–4). Odyssey Y 34239.

Le Caine, Hugh. *Dribsody* (1955). Folkways FMS 33436.

Ligeti, Györgu. *Artikulation* (1958). Limelight LS 86048, Philips 835 486 AY, Wergo 60059.

Glissandi (1957). Wergo 60076.

Lucia, Alvin. *North American Time Capsule* (1967). CBS France S 346 1066, Odyssey 32 16 0156.

Vespers (1968). Mainstream MS 5010.

I am Sitting in a Room (1970). (*Source Magazine* No. 7) Source 3.

Luening, Otto. *Fantasy in Space* (1952). Desto DC 6466, Folkways FX 6160, Innovation GB 1.

Rhapsodic Variations (1953–4). Louisville 545 5.

A Poem in Cycles and Bells (1954). CRI 112.

Carlsbad Caverns (1955). RCA Victor LPM 1280.

Suite from "King Lear" (1956). CRI 112.

Concerted Piece (1960). CRI SD 227.

Mâche, François-Bernard. *Volumes* (1960). Boîte à Musique LD 071.

Terre de feu (1963). Boîte à Musique LD 072, Candide CE 31025.

Maderna, Bruno. *Musica su due Dimensioni* (1952). Compagnia Generale de Disco ESZ 3.

Notturno (1956). RAI (*Elettronica* 1956 No. 3).

Continuo (1958). Limelight LS 86047, Philips 835 485 AY

Malec, Ivo. *Dahovi* (1961). Candide CE 31025, Philips 836 891 DSY, Philips 6740 001, Varèse VS 81005.

    Reflets (1961). Boîte à Musique LD 072, Boîte à Musique 5072.

    Tutti (1962–3). Philips 836 894 DSY.

    Canata pour elle (1966). Philips 836 891 DSY.

Martirano, Salvatore. *Underworld* (1964–5). Heliodor HS 25047.

    L's GA (1967–8). Polydor 245001.

Mathews, Max. *Bicycle Built for Two* (1962). Decca DL 79103.

Maxfield, Richard. *Night Music* (1960). Odyssey 32 16 0160.

Mayuzumi, Toshiro. *Campanology* (1959). Nippon Victor SJU 1515.

    Mandala (1969). Nippon Victor SJX 1004.

Messiaen, Olivier. *Fête des belles eaux* (1937). Erato LDE 3202, Erato STU 70102.

Mimaroğlu, İlhan. *Bowery Bum* (1964). Finnadar 9012, Turnabout TV 34004 S.

    Intermezzo (1964). Finnadar 9012, Turnabout TV 34004 S.

    Le Tombeau d'Edgar Poe (1964). Finnadar 9012, Turnabout TV 34004 S.

    Agony (1965). Finnadar 9012, Turnabout TV 34046 S.

    Anacolutha: Encounter and Episode II (1965). Finnadar SR 9001.

    White Cockatoo (1966). Finnadar SR 9001.

    Preludes I, II, VI, IX, XI, XIII (1966–7). Turnabout 34177 S.

    Piano Music for Performer and Composer (1967). Turnabout TV 34177 S.

    Prelude XII (1967). Finnadar SR 9001.

    Wings of the Derilious Demon (1969). Finnadar SR 9001.

    Sing Me a Song of Songmy (1970). Atlantic SD 1576, Finnadar SR 9001 (part).

    Hyperboles (1971). Finnadar SR 9001.

    Provocations (1971). Finnadar SR 9001.

    La Ruche (1972). Folkways 33951.

    To Kill a Sunrise (1974 Folkways 33951.

    Tract (1972–4). Folkways 33441.

Moroi, Makoto. *Shosange* (1968). Nippon Victor SJX 1004.

Mumma, Gordon. *Music for the Venezia Space Theatre* (1964). Advance FGR 5.

    Peasant Boy (1965). ESP S 1009.

    Mesa (1966). CBS France S 346 1065, Odyssey 32 16 0158.

    Hornpipe (1967). Mainstream MS 5010.

    Cybersonic Cantilevers (1973). Folkways FTS 33904.

Musica Elettronica Viva. *Spacecraft* (1967–8). Mainstream MS 5002.

    Sound Pool (1969). BYG 529 326.

Neuhaus, Max. Realization of Cage, *Fontana Mix-Feed* (1965). MASS ART M 133.

Nono, Luigi. *Omaggio a Emilio Vedova* (1960). Wergo 60067.

    La fabbrica illuminata (1964). Wergo 60038.

    Ricorda cosa ti hanno fatto in Auschwitz (1965). Wergo 60038.

    A floresta è jovem e cheia de vida (1966). Arcophon AC 6811, DGG 2531 004, Musique Vivante HM 30767.

Per Bastinia Tai-Yang Cheng (1967). Wergo 60067.

Contappunto dialettico alla mente (1967–8). DGG 2543 006.

Non consumiamo Mark (1969). I Dischi del Sole DS 182 4 CL.

Un volto, del mare (1969). I Dischi del Sole DS 182 4 CL.

Y entonces comprendió (1969–70). DGG 2530 436, Ricordi SAVC 501.

Como una ola de fuerza y luz (1971–2). DGG 2530 436, Ricordi SAVC 501.

Nordheim, Arne. *Epitaffio* (1963). Decca HEAD 23, Limelight LS 86061, Philips 839 250 AY.

Respons I (1966–7). Limelight LS 86061, Philips 839 250 AY.

Colorazione (1968). Philips 854 005 AY.

Solitaire (1968). Philips 6740 004, Philips 854 005 AY.

Five Osaka Fragments (1970). Philips 6507 034.

Oliveros, Pauline. *I of IV* (1966). Odyssey 32 16 0160.

Oram, Daphne. *Electronic Sound Patterns* (1962). HMV 7EG 8762.

Penderecki, Krzstof. *Psalmus* (1961). Superaphon DV 6221.

Phillipot, Michel. *Étude I* (1952). Ducrtete-Thomson DUC 9, London DTL 93121.

Ambiance I (1959). Boîte à Musique LD 070.

Ambiance II—Toast funèbre (1959). Boîte à Musique LD 071.

Maldoror (1960). Boîte à Musique LD 075-6.

Rhinocéros (1960). Vega T 31 SP 8003.

Étude III (1962). Candide CE 31025, Varèse VS 81005.

Pierce, John. *Five Against Seven—Random Canon* (1961). Decca DL 79103.

Variations in Timbre and Attack (1961). Decca DL 79103.

Pousseur, Henry. *Scambi* (version 1). (1957). Limelight LS 86048, Philips 835 486 AY.

Rimes pour différentes source sonores (1958–9). RCA Victrola VICS 1239.

Trois Visages de Liège (1961). Columbia MS 7051.

Jeu de miroirs de Votre faust (1966). Heliodor 2549 021, Wergo 60026.

Electre (1969). Universal Edition UE 13500.

Randall, Jim. *Quartets in Pairs* (1964). Nonesuch H 71245.

Mudgett: Monologues by a Mass Murderer (1965). Nonesuch H 71245.

Lyric Variations (1968). Vanguard VCS 10057.

Quartersines (1969). Nonesuch H 71245.

Reich, Steve. *Its Gonna Rain* (1965). Columbia MS 7265.

Come Out (1966). Odyssey 32 16 0160.

Violin Phase (1967). Columbia MS 7265.

Four Organs (1970). Angel S 36059, Shandar 10005.

Phase Patterns (1970). Shandar 10005.

Reynolds, Roger. *Ping* (1968). CRI SD 285.

Traces (1968–9). CRI SD 285.

Riehn, Rainer. *Chants de Maldoror* (1965–6, rev. 1968–9). DGG 137011.

Riley, Terry. *Dorian Reeds* (1966). Mass Art M 131.

Poppy Nogood and the Phantom Band (1968). Columbia MS 7315.

A Rainbow in Curved Air (1969). Columbia MS 7315.

Persian Surgery Dervishes (1971). Shanti 83 501-2.

Risset, Jean Claude. *Little Boy* (1968). Decca 710180.

    Mutations (1969). Collection GRM AM 564 09, Turnabout 34427.

    Dialogues (1975). Collection GRM AM 564 09.

    Inharmonic Soundscapes (1977). Significant Contemporary Works, Tulsa: Tulsa Studios, Oklahoma.

    Inharmonique (1977). Collection GRM AM 564 09.

    Moments Newtoniens (1977). Collection GRM AM 564 09.

Salzman, Eric. *Helix* (1966). Finnadar 9005.

    Larynx Music (1967). Finnadar 9005.

    The Nude Paper Sermon (1968–9). Nonesuch H 71231.

Schaeffer, Myron. *Dance 4 : 3* (1959). Folkways FMS 33436.

Schaeffer, Myron, with Harvey Olnick and Arnold Walter. *Summer Idyll* (1960). Folkways FMS 33436.

Schaeffer, Pierre. *Étude au Piano II* (1948). Ducretet-Thomson DUC 8, and London DTL 93090.

    Étude aux casseroles (1948). Ducretet-Thomson DUC 8, London DTL 93090, Philips 6521 021.

    Étude aux chemins der fer (1948). Ducretet-Thomson DUC 8, London DTL 93090, Philips 6521 021.

    Étude aux tourniquets (1948). Ducretet-Thomson DUC 8, London DTL 93090, Philips 6521 021.

    Étude pathétique (1948). Philips 6521 021.

    Étude violette (1948). Philips 6521 021.

    Suite pour quatorze instruments (1949). Philips 6521 021.

    Variations sur une flûte mexicaine (1949). Ducretet-Thomson DUC 8, London DTL 93090.

    L'Oiseau RAI (1950). Ducretet-Thomson DUC 9, London DTL 9321, Philips 6521 021.

    Étude aux allures (1958). Boîte à Musique LD 070, Philips 6521 021.

    Étude aux sons animés (1958). Boîte à Musique LD 070, Philips 6521 021.

    Étude aux objets (1959 version). Philips 835 478 AY.

    Étude aux objets (1967 version). Candide CE 31025, Varèse VS 81005 (part).

Schaeffer, Pierre, with Pierre Henry. *Symphonie pour un homme seul* (1949–50). Ducretet-Thomson DUC 9, London DTL 93121.

    Bidule en ut (1950). Ducretet-Thomson DUC 8, London DTL 93090, Philips 6736 006.

Smalley, Denis. *Pentes* (1974). Norwich, England: Univ. of East Anglia, UEA 81063.

    Chanson de geste (1978). Norwich, England: Univ. of East Anglia, UEA 81063.

    Pulses of Time (1979). Norwich, England: Univ. of East Anglia, UEA 81063.

Souster, Tim. *Spectral* (1972). Transatlantic TRAG 343.

    Afghan Amplitudes (1976). Transatlantic TRAG 343.

    Arcane Artefact (1976). Transatlantic TRAG 343.

    Music From Afar (1976). Transatlantic TRAG 343.

Stockhausen, Karlheinz. *Studie I* (1953). DGG LP 16133.

    Studie II (1954). DGG LP 16133.

    Gesang der Jünglinge (1955–6). DGG 16133, DGG 138 811.

Kontakte (1959–60). (tape alone). DGG 138 811.

Kontakte (1959–60). (tape plus instruments). Candide CE 31022, Vox STGBY 638.

Mikrophonie 1 (1964). Columbia MS 7355, CBS 72647, CBS S 77230, CBS 32 11 0044, DGG 2530 583.

Mixtur (1964). DGG 137 012, DGG ST 643 546.

Mikrophonie II (1965). Columbia MS 7355, CBS 72647, CBS S 77230, CBS 32 11 0044, DGG 2530 583.

Solo (1966). DGG 137 005, DGG 104 992.

Telemusik (1966). DGG 137 012, DGG ST 643 546.

Ensemble (1967). Wergo 60065.

Hymnen (1967). DGG 2707 039, DGG ST 139 421-2.

Prozession (1967). Candide CE 31001, CBS S 77230, Vox STGBY 615, DGG 2530 582.

Aus den sieben Tagen (1968). DGG 270 073, Harmonia Mundi 300899M.

Kurzwellen (1968). DGG 139 451, DGG 139 461.

Spiral (1968). DGG 2561 109, EMI Electrola C 165 02 313-14, Wergo 325.

Mantra (1970). DGG 2530 208.

Pole (1969–70). EMI Electrola C 165 02 313.

Sternklang (1971). Polydor 2612 031.

Trans (1971). DGG 2530 726.

Momente (1961–72). Nonesuch H 71157, Wergo 60024, DGG 3709 055.

Ylem (1972). DGG 2530 442.

Subotnic, Morton. *Prelude No. 4* (1966). Avant 1008.

Silver Apples of the Moon (1967). Nonesuch H 71174.

The Wild Bull (1968). Nonesuch H 71208.

Touch (1969). Columbia MS 7316.

Laminations (1969–70). Turnabout TV 34428 S.

Sidewinder (1971). Columbia M 30683.

Takemitzu, Toru. *Vocalism A-I* (1955, revised 1965). RCA VOCS 1334.

Tenney, James. *Five Stochastics Studies* (1961). Decca 71080.

Noise Study (1961). Decca DL 79103.

Tomita, Isao. *Snowflakes are Dancing* (1974). RCA ARL 1 0488.

Truax, Barry. *Nautilus* (1976). Imperial Record Corporation, Vancouver SMLP 4033.

Sonic Landscapes (1978). Imperial Record Corporation, Vancouver SMLP 4033.

Ussachevsky, Vladimir. *Composition* (1951–2). Folkways FTX 6169.

Experiment (1951–2). Folkways FTX 6169.

Reverberation (1951–2). Folkways FTX 6169.

Underwater Valse (1951–2). Folkways FTX 6169.

Sonic Contours (1952). Desto DC 64666.

Piece For Tape Recorder (1956). CRI 112, Finnadar 9010 Q.

Metamorphoses (1957). CRI S 356, Son Nova 3.

Improvisation No. 4711 (1958). Son Nova S 3.

Linear Contrasts (1958). CRI S 356, Son Nova S 3.

Wireless Fantasy (1960). CRI SD 227.

Creation: Prologue (1960–1). Columbia MS 6566.

Of Wood and Brass (1964–5). CRI SD 227.

Computer Piece No. 1 (1968). CRI SD 268.

Two Sketches for a Computer Piece (1971). CRI SD 268.

Ussachevsy, Vladimir, with Otto Luening. *Incantation* (1953). Desto DC 6466, Innovation GB 1.

Rhapsodic Variations (1953–4). Louisville 545 5.

A Poem in Cycles and Bells (1954). CRI 112.

Carlsbad Caverns (1955). RCA Victor LP 1280.

Suite from "King Lear" (1956). CRI 112.

Concerted Piece (1960). CRI SD 227.

Varèse, Edgard. *Déserts* (1954). Angel S 36786, Columbia MS 6362, CRI SD 268.

Poème électronique (1958). Columbia MS 6146.

Vercoe, Barry. *Synthesism* (1969–70). Nonesuch H 71245.

Wessel, David. *Antony* (1977). Tulsa, Oklahoma: New Directions in Music, Tulsa Studios.

Wishart, Tevor. *Red Bird* (1973–7). York, England: Philip Martin Books YES 7.

Wuorinen, Charles. *Time's Encomium* (1969). Nonesuch H 71225.

Xenakis, Iannis. *Diamorphoses* (1957). Boîte à Musique LD 070, Erato STU 70530.

Concret PH (1958). Philips 835 487 AY, Erato STU 70530.

Analogique B (1958–9). Philips 835 487 AY.

Orient-Occident (1960). Limelight LS 86047, Philips 835 485 AY, Erato STU 70530.

Bohor (1962). Erato STU 70530, Nonesuch H 71246.

Concret PH (revised version, 1968). Nonesuch H 71246.

Diamorphoses (revised version, 1968). Erato STU 70530, Nonesuch H 72146.

Orient-Occident (revised version, 1968). Nonesuch H 71246.

Persepolis (1971). Philips 6521 045.

Young, La Monte. *13 I 73 5: 35-6: 14: 03 PM NYC* (1969–73). Shandar 83510.

14 VII 73 9: 27: 27-10: o6: 41 PM NYC (1973). Shandar 83510.

Compact Discs (Recommended Selection)

Albright, William. *Sphaera*. Wergo 2029-2.

Anats, Linda. *A River from the Walls*. CDCM Centaur CRC 2512.

Appleton, John. *Brush Canyon*. CDCM Centaur CRC 2052.

Degitaru Ongaku. CDCM Centaur 2052.

Homenaje a Milans. CDCM Centaur 2133.

Pacific Rimbombo. CDCM Centaur 2180.

Arfib, Daniel. *Le Souffle du Doux*. Wergo 2022-50.

Ascione, Patrick. *Lune noire*. empreints DIGITALes IMED 9522.

Sur champ d'azur. empreints DIGITALes IMED 9522.

Valeurs d'ombre. empreints DIGITALes IMED 9522.

Austin, Larry. *Accidents*. CDCM Centaur CRC 2219.

AccidentsTwo: Sound Projections for Piano with Computer Music. CDCM Centaur CRC 2219.

Beachcombers. CDCM Centaur CRC 2078.

Canadian Coastlines: Canonic Fractals for Musicians and Computer Band. CDCM Centaur CRC 2219.

La Barbara. CDCM Centaur CRC 2166

Life Pulse Prelude. CDCM Centaur CRC 2133.

Max Mathews Episode. CDCM Centaur CRC 2180.

Montage: Theme and Variations for Violin and Computer Music on Tape. CDCM Centaur CRC 2110.

Rompido! CDCM CE130.

Quadrants: Event Complex No. 1. CDCM Centaur CRC 2407.

Quadrants: Event Complex No. 4. CDCM Centaur CRC 2219.

Quadrants: Event Complex No. 9. CDCM Centaur CRC 2219.

Shin-Edo: Cityscape Set. CDCM Centaur CRC 2428.

Sinfonia Concertante: A Mozartean Episode. CDCM Centaur CRC 2029.

Sonata Concertante. CDCM Centaur CRC 2029.

SoundPoemSet. CDCM Centaur CRC 2192.

Variations . . . beyond Pierrot. CDCM Centaur CRC 2428.

Averill, Ron. painting legs on the snake. CDCM Centaur CRC 2512.

Babbitt, Milton. Philomel. Neuma NE103.

Baitz, Rick. Kaleidocycles. CDCM Centaur CRC 2029.

Barlow, Clarence. Relationships for Melody Instruments. Wergo WE100, Wergo 2010-50.

Barrett, Natasha. Displaced:Replaced. empreints DIGITALes IMED 0262.

Industrial Revelations. empreints DIGITALes IMED 0262.

Red Snow. empreints DIGITALes IMED 0262.

Three Fictions. empreints DIGITALes IMED 0262.

The Utility of Space. empreints DIGITALes IMED 0262.

Viva la Selva! empreints DIGITALes IMED 0262.

Barrière, Jean-Baptiste. Chreode I. Wergo 2024-50.

Battey, Bret. Pater Nosters Tricylcic Companion. CDCM Centaur CRC 2512.

Bayle, François. Les Couleurs de la Nuit. Harmonia Mundi INA C 1001.

Motion-Emotion. Harmonia Mundi INA C 1001.

Le Sommeil d'Euclide. Wergo 2025-50.

Behrman, David. Runthrough. CDCM Centaur CRC 2490.

Belet, Briam. [MUTE]ation. CDCM Centaur CRC 2404.

Bennett, Gerald. Kyotaku. Wergo 2029-2.

Berger, Jonathan. Diptych. CDCM Centaur CRC 2091.

Bishoff, John. The Glass Hand. CDCM Centaur CRC 2195.

Bodin, Lars-Gunner. Anima. Wergo 2027-2.

Boesch, Rainer. Clavirissima. Wergo 2028-2.

Bönn, Georg. Fallout. Wergo 2051-2.

Bonnet, Antonie. Epitaphe. IRCAM IR103-3.

Boulez, Pierre. Explosante-fixe. IRCAM IR103-3.

Braxton, Anthony. Composition No. 107. CDCM Centaur CRC 2110.

Bresnick, Martin. *Lady Neil's Dumpe*. CDCM Centaur CRC 2029.

Brown, Chris. *Chain Reaction*. CDCM Centaur CDC 2195.

Brümmer, Ludger. *Ambre*. Wergo 2051-2
　Lilac. Wergo 2051-2.

Brün, Herbert. *A Mere Ripple*. EMF Media EM112.
　Dust. EMF Media EM112.
　Dustiny. EMF Media EM112.
　i toLD You so! CDCM Centaur CRC 2045, EMF Media EM112.
　More Dustiny. EMF Media EM112.

Butler, Martin. *Night Machines*. CDCM Centaur CRC 2076.

Cage, John. *Imaginary Landscape No. 1*. Wergo WE145-4.
　Music for Carillon No. 1. Wergo WE145-4.
　Sonatas and Interludes. Wergo WE145-4.
　Williams Mix. Wergo WE145-4.
　The Wonderful Widow of Eighteen Springs. Wergo WE145-4.

Campion, Edmund J. *Losing Touch*. IRCAM IR103-3.

Chadabe, Joel. *Follow me Softly*. CDCM Centaur CRC 2310, CDCM CE130.
　Modalities. CDCM Centaur CRC 2047.

Chafe, Chris. *In a Word*. Wergo 2016-50.
　Quadro. CDCM Centaur CRC 2091.
　Solera. Wergo 2026-2.

Chafe, Chris, and Dexter Morrill. *Duo Improvisation*. CDCM Centaur CRC 2133.

Chatham, Rick. *Constellations*. CDCM Centaur CRC 2192.

Chion, Michel. *Le prisonnier du son*. empreints DIGITALes IMED 9523.
　Requiem. empreints DIGITALes IMED 9312.
　24 préludes à la vie. empreints DIGITALes IMED 9523.

Choi, Insook. *Lit*. CDCM Centaur CRC 2302.

Chowning, John. *Phoné*. Wergo WE102, Wergo 2012-50.
　Sabelithe. Wergo WE102, Wergo 2012-50.
　Stria. Wergo WE102, Wergo 2012-50.
　Turenas. Wergo WE102, Wergo 2012-50.

Clark, Thomas. *Lightforms 2: Star Spectra*. CDCM Centaur CRC 2407.
　Peninsular. CDCM Centaur CRC 2029.

Curran, Alvin. *Animal Behavior*. CDCM Centaur CRC 2195.

Dalbavire, Marc-André. *Seuils*. IRCAM IR103-3.

Daoust, Yves. *Bruits*. empreints DIGITALes IMED 0156.
　La gamme. empreints DIGITALes IMED 0156.
　Impromptu. empreints DIGITALes IMED 0156.
　Ouverture. empreints DIGITALes IMED 0156.

Dashow, James. *Archimedes*. Wergo 2018-50.
　Argento. Wergo 2018-50.
　Legno. Wergo 2018-50.
　Mnemonics and Oro. Wergo 2018-50.

Sequence Symbols. Wergo WE100, Wergo 2010-50.

Le Tracce di Kronos, i Passi. CDCM Centaur CRC 2310, CDCM CE130.

Daoust, Yves. *Fantaisie*. empreints DIGITALes IMED 9843.

Il était une fois . . . (conte sans paroles). empreints DIGITALes IMED 9843.

Impromptu. empreints DIGITALes IMED 9843.

Résonances. empreints *DIGITALes IMED 9843*.

Water Music. empreints DIGITALes IMED 9843.

Davidovsky, Mario. *Synchronisms No. 9*. Wergo 2022-50.

Decoust, Michel. *Interphone*. Wergo 2024-50.

Delio, Thomas. *Against the Silence*. Wergo 2029-2.

De Lisa, Gere. *Si' L'Fosse*. CDCM Centaur CRC 2192.

Derrick, Brad. *Odd Waves*. CDCM Centaur CRC 2454.

Dhomont, Francis. *AvatArsSon*. empreints DIGITALes IMED 0158.

Chiaroscuro. empreints DIGITALes IMED 9603.

Espace/Escape. empreints DIGITALes IMED 9607.

Météores. empreints DIGITALes IMED 9603.

Novars. empreints DIGITALes IMED 0158, IMED 9608.

Objets retrouvés. empreints DIGITALes IMED 0158.

Phonurgies. empreints DIGITALes IMED 0158.

Points de fuite. empreints DIGITALes IMED 9607.

Signé Dionysos. empreints DIGITALes IMED 9603.

Dodge, Charles. *Any Resemblance is Purely Concidental*. Wergo 2031-2.

In Celebration. CDCM Centaur CRC 2213.

Roundelay. Wego 2024-50.

Dufort, Louis. *Décap*. empreints DIGITALes IMED 0051.

Pointes-aux-Trembles. empreints DIGITALes IMED 0051.

Transit. empreints DIGITALes IMED 0051.

Zénith. empreints DIGITALes IMED 0051.

Erbe, Tom. *After a Day*. CDCM Centaur CRC 2195.

Farra, Ricardo D. *Tierra y sol*. CDCM Centaur CRC 2347.

Fedele, Ivan. *Richiamo*. IRCAM IR103-3.

Ferretti, Ercolino. *Pipe and Drum*. Wergo 2033-2.

Trio. Wergo 2033-2.

Floyd, J. B. *Tribute*. CDCM Centaur CRC 2213.

Francesconi, Luca. *Etymo*. IRCAM IR103-3.

Fredrics, Howard J. *The Tragedy of the Leaves*. CDCM Centaur CRC 2245.

Frengel, Michael. *Three Short Stories*. CDCM Centaur CRC 2407.

Fulton, Douglas. *Bowling for Blood*. Wergo WER 2031-2.

Furham, Pablo. *Synergy*. CDCM Centaur CRC 2404.

Garton, Brad. *Approximate Rhythms*. CDCM Centaur CRC 2076.

Wasting. CDCM Centaur 2076.

Ghent, Emmanuel. *Phosphons*. Wergo 2022-50.

Gibson, John. *Thrum*. CDCM Centaur CRC 2454

Goebel, Johannes. *Après les Grands Tours*. Wergo 2051-2.

    Von Übersetzen über den Fluss. Wergo 2025-50.

Gonzalez-Arroyo, Ramón. *De l'Infinito Universo et Mondi*. Wergo 2051-2.

Guttman, Newman. *The Silver Scale*. Wergo 2033-2.

    Pitch Variations. Wergo 2033-2.

Haines, Stanley. *Prisms*. Wergo 2028-2.

Harrison, Jonty. *Aria*. empreints DIGITALes IMED 9627.

    Hot Air. empreints DIGITALes IMED 9627.

    Klang. empreints DIGITALes IMED 0052.

    Pair/Impair. empreints DIGITALes IMED 9627.

    Sorties. empreints DIGITALes IMED 0052.

    Splintering. empreints DIGITALes IMED 0052.

    Streams. empreints DIGITALes IMED 0052.

    Surface Tension. empreints DIGITALes IMED 0052.

    Unsound Objects. empreints DIGITALes IMED 9627, CDCM Centaur CRC 2347.

Harvey, Jonathan. *Advaya*. IRCAM IR103-3.

    Mortuos Plango, Vivos Voco. Sargasso SG110, Wergo 2025-2.

    Ritual Melodies. Sargasso SG110.

    Tombeau de Messiaen. Sargasso SG110.

    4 Images After Yeats. Sargasso SG110.

Helms, Mickey. *Whispering Modulations*. CDCM Centaur CRC 2404.

Henry, Pierre. *Messe de Liverpool*. Mantra MNTR 023.

    Messe pour le temps présent. Philips 412 706-2.

    Variations pour une porte et un soupir. Harmonia Mundi HMC 905 200.

Hiller, Lejaren. *An Avalanche for Pitchman, Prima Donna, Player Piano, Percussionist and Pre-recorded Tape*. Wergo 60128-50.

    Circus Piece: A Cadential Process. Wergo 60128-50.

    Computer Music for Percussion and Tape. Wergo 60128-50.

    Expo '85 for Multiple Synthesizers. Wergo 60128-50.

    Illiac String Quartet. Wergo 60128-50.

    Mix or Match: A Time Generating Process. Wergo 60128-50.

    Persiflage for Flute, Oboe and Percussion. Wergo 60128-50.

    Toy Harmonium. A Statistical Process. Wergo 60128-50.

    Transitions. A Hierarchical Process. Wergo 60128-50.

Hoffman, Elizabeth. *Vim*. CDCM Centaur CRC 2512.

Hunt, Jerry. *Fluud*. CDCM Centaur CRC 2029.

Hurel, Philippe. *Lecon de choses*. IRCAM IR103-3.

Jaffe, David. *Silicon Valley Breakdown*. Wergo 2016-50.

    Telegram to the President. CDCM Centaur CRC 2091.

    Terra Non Firma. CDCM Centaur CRC 2180.

Jaffe, David, and Andrew Schloss. *Wildlife*. CDCM Centaur CRC 2180.

Jarret, Michael. *Cassandre*. IRCAM IR103-3.

Jones, David. *Still Life Dancing*. CDCM Centaur CRC 2052.

    Still Life in Wood and Metal. CDCM Centaur CRC 2052.

Jones, David E. *Scritto*. Wergo 2024-50.

Karbat, Julie. *Child and the Moon-Tree*. CDCM Centaur CRC 2047.

Karpen, Richard. *Denouement*. CDCM Centaur 2144.

    Eclipse. Wergo 2025-50.

    Il Nome. Wergo 2027-2.

    Sotto/Sopra. CDCM Centaur CRC 2512.

Kaske, Stephan. *Transition No. 2*. Wergo WE100, Wergo 2010-50.

Keefe, Robert. *The Ephemerides for Harp and Percussion: Moon, 1650-1657*. CDCM Centaur CRC 2078.

Kessler, Thomas. *Flute Control*. Wergo 2026-2.

Klein, Joseph. *Dog (after W. S. Merwin)*. CDCM Centaur CRC 2407.

Koenig, Gottfried Michael. *Three ASKO Pieces*. Wergo 2022-50.

Korte, Karl. *Colloquy*. CDCM Centaur CRC 2245.

Krupowicz, Stanislaw. *Farewell Variations on a Theme by Mozart*. Wergo 2031-2.

La Barbara, Joan. *The Tree of Blue Leaves*. CDCM Centaur CRC 2166.

Lanciano, Thierry. *Aloni*. Wergo 2032-2.

Lansky, Paul. *As if*. CDCM Centaur CRC 2110.

    as it grew dark. Wergo 2031-2.

    Guy's Harp. New Albion NA 030CD.

    idle chatter. Wergo WE100, Wergo 2010-50.

    just-more-idle-chatter. CDCM Centaur CRC 2076.

    Late August. New Albion NA 030CD.

    Not So Heavy Metal. New Albion NA 030CD.

    Smalltalk. New Albion NA 030CD.

    Stroll. CDCM Centaur CRC 2213.

    Wasting. CDCM Centaur CRC 2076.

Leroux, Philippe. *M.* IRCAM IR103-3.

Levinas, Michael. *Go-go!*. IRCAM IR103-3.

Lewin, David. *Study No. 1*. Wergo 2033-2.

    Study No. 2. Wergo 2033-2.

Lindberg, Magnus. *Related Rocks*. IRCAM IR103-3

Lindroth, Scott. *Syntax*. CDCM Centaur CRC 2029.

Lindwall, Christer. *Points*. Wergo 2021-50.

Lippe, Court. *Music for Clarinet and ISPW*. CDCM Centaur CRC 2310, CDCM CE130.

    Music for Guitar and Tape. CDCM Centaur CRC 2192.

    Music for Sextet and ISPW. CDCM Centaur CRC 2255.

Long, Michael. *there is a gray thing*. CDCM Centaur CRC 2454

Lorrain, Denis. *Black it Stood as Night*. Wergo 2022-50.

Loy, Gareth. *Blood from a Stone*. CDCM Centaur 2133.

    Nekyia. Wergo 2025-2.

Maiguashca, Mesias. *El Oro*. Wergo 2053-2.

    FM Melodies II. Wergo 2025-2.

    The Nagual. Wergo 2053-2.

    Sacateca's Dance. Wergo 2053-2.

    The Spirit Catcher. Wergo 2053-2.

    The Tonal. Wergo 2053-2.

    The Wings of Perception II. Wergo 2053-2.

Manoury, Philippe. *En echo*. IRCAM IR103-3.

Mey, Thierry. *Kinok*. IRCAM IR103-3.

Maresz, Yan. *Metallics*. IRCAM IR103-3.

Martirano, Salvatore. *Electronic Dance No. 1*. CDCM Centaur CRC 2266.

    L's G.A. CDCM Centaur CRC 2266.

    Look at the back of my head for awhile. CDCM Centaur CRC 2266.

    Sampler: Everything Goes when the Whistle Blows. CDCM Centaur CRC 2045.

    SATBehind Demo. CDCM Centaur CRC 2266.

    UIUS & Jest fa Laffs. CDCM Centaur CRC 2177.

    Underworld. CDCM Centaur CRC 2266.

Matalon, Martin. *Metropolis*. IRCAM IR103-3.

Mathes, Michael. *The First Sea*. CDCM Centaur 2192.

Mathews.Max. *Bicycle Built for Two*. Wergo 2033-2.

    International Lullaby. Wergo 2033-2.

    Masquerades. Wergo 2033-2.

    Numerology. Wergo 2033-2.

    The Second Law. Wergo 2033-2.

Matthews, Michael. *In Emptiness, Over Emptyness*. CDCM Centaur CRC 2347.

McLean, Barton. *Demons of the Night*. CDCM Centaur CRC 2047.

    A Little Night Music. CDCM Centaur CRC 2047.

    Visions of a Summer Night. CDCM Centaur CRC 2047.

McNabb, Michael. *City of Conguence*. Wergo 2015-50.

    City of Desire. Wergo 2015-50.

    City of No Resistance. Wergo 2015-50.

    City of Reflection. Wergo 2015-50.

    Dreamsong. Wergo 2020-2.

    Hidden City. Wergo 2015-50.

    Love in the Asylum. Wergo 2020-2.

    Mars Suite. Wergo 2020-2.

McTee, Cindy. *"M" Music*. CDCM Centaur CRC 2213.

    Metal Music. CDCM Centaur CRC 2078.

Melby, John. *Chor der Weisen*. CDCM Centaur CRC 2045.

    Concerto no. 1 for Flute and Computer-Synthesized Tape. CDCM Centaur CRC 2110.

Milburn, Andrew. *Elmore*. CDCM Centaur CRC 2076.

    Wasting. CDCM Centaur CRC 2076.

Montague, Stephen. *Silence: John, Yvar & Tim*. CDCM Centaur CRC 2347.

Moore, Adrian. *Dreamarena*. empreints DIGITALes IMED 0053.
   Foil-Counterfoil. empreints DIGITALes IMED 0053.
   Junky. empreints DIGITALes IMED 0053.
   Sieve. empreints DIGITALes IMED 0053.
   Study In Ink. empreints DIGITALes IMED 0053.
Moravec, Paul. *Devices and Desires*. CDCM Centaur CRC 2052.
Morrill, Dexter. *Quartet*. CDCM Centaur CRC 2091.
Motz, Wolfgang. *sotto pressione*. Wergo 2030-2.
Mowitz, Ira. *Kol Aharon*. CDCM Centaur CRC 2255.
Murail, Tristan. *L'éspirit des dunes*. IRCAM IR103-3.
Nagel, Jody. *Gandalf the Grey*. CDCM Centaur CRC 2245.
Nelson, Gary Lee. *Fractal Mountains*. Wergo 2030-2.
Nelson, Jon C. *the rain has a slap and a curve*. CDCM Centaur CRC 2407.
Normandeau, Robert. *Clair de terre*. empreints DIGITALes IMED 0157.
   Éclats de voix. empreints DIGITALes IMED 9419/20.
   Ellipse. empreints DIGITALes IMED 9944.
   Erinyes. empreints DIGITALes IMED 0157.
   Figures de rhétorique. empreints DIGITALes IMED 9944.
   Le renard et la rose. empreints DIGITALes IMED 9944.
   Malina. empreints DIGITALes IMED 0157.
   Spleen. empreints DIGITALes IMED 9419/20.
   Tangram. empreints DIGITALes IMED 9419/20.
   Tropes. empreints DIGITALes IMED 9419/20.
   Venture. empreints DIGITALes IMED 9944.
Nune, Emmanuael. *Lichtung I*. IRCAM IR103-3.
Obst, Michael. *Inferno—Ein Spiel von Menschen unserer Zeit*. IRCAM IR103-3.
Oliveros, Pauline. *Lion's Tale*. CDCM Centaur CRC 2047.
Oppenheim, Daniel V. *Round the Corners of Purgatory*. Wergo 2021-50.
Pape, Geraed. *Le Fleuve du Desir III*. Mode MO168-3
Paris, François. *Les confessions silencieuces*. IRCAM IR103-3.
Parmegiani, Bernard. *La Création du Monde*. Harmonia Mundi INA C 1002.
Pauset, Brice. *Perspectivae Sintagma I*. IRCAM IR103-3.
Payne, Maggie. *Resonant Places*. CDCM Centaur CRC 2195.
Petersen, Tracy L. *Digital Tantra I*. Wergo 2027-2.
Phelps, James. *Sax Houses*. CDCM Centaur 2302.
Piekaski, James. *Dreamfile*. CDCM Centaur CRC 2078.
Pierce, John. *Eight-Tone Canon*. Wergo 2033-2.
   Sea Sounds. Wergo 2033-2.
   Stochatta. Wergo 2033-2.
   Variations in Timbre and Attack. Wergo 2033-2.
Pinkston, Russell. *Don't Look Now*. CDCM Centaur CRC 2245.
Polanski, Larry. *And to Rule*. CDCM Centaur CRC 2133.
Pope, Stephen. *Kombination XI*. CDCM Centaur CRC 2166.

Radunskaya, Ami. *A Wild and Reckless Place*. CDCM Centaur CRC 2180.

Rai, Takayuki. *Five Inventions Accompanied by Computers*. Wergo 2028-2.

    The Vanity of Word. Wergo 2024-50.

    Three Inventions. CDCM Centaur CRC 2255.

Reynolds, Roger. *Odyssey*. IRCAM IR103-3

    Transfigured Wind IV. Neuma NE103, Neuma 450-73/74.

Risset, Jean-Claude. *Computer Suite from Little Boy*. Wergo WE103, Wergo 2013-50.

    Contours. Neuma New Music Series Vol 1.

    L'autre face. Wergo 2027-2.

    Passages. Wergo WE103, Wergo 2013-50.

    Saxatile. Mode MO168-3.

    Songes. Wergo WE103, Wergo 2013-50.

    Sud. Wergo WE103, Wergo 2013-50.

Robindore, Brigitte. *Comme Etrangers et Voyagers sur la Terre*. Mode MO168-3.

    L'Autel de la Perte et de la Transformation. Mode MO168-3.

Rodes, Curtis. *nscor*. Wergo WE100, Wergo 2010-50.

    Purity. Mode MO168-3.

    Sonal Atoms. Mode MO168-3.

Rogers, Rowell. *Centoph*. CDCM Centaur CRC 2078.

Rolnick, Neil. *A Robert Johnson Sampler*. CDCM Centaur CRC 2047.

    The Persistence of the Clave. CDCM Centaur CRC 2133.

    Vocal Chords. CDCM Centaur CEC 2047.

    What is the Use? CDCM Centaur CRC 2039.

Rosenboom, David. *A Precipice in Time*. CDCM Centaur CRC 2110.

    On Being Invisible II. CDCM Centaur 2490.

    Systems of Judgement. CDCM Centaur CRC 2077.

Rubin, Anna. *Crying for Laughing and Golden*. Neuma New Music Series Vol. 1.

Rush, Loren. *A Little Traveling Music*. Wergo 2022-50.

Saariaho, Kaija. *Jardin Secret*. Ondine IR105, Wergo 2025-2.

    Noanoa. Ondine IR105

    Pres. IRCAM IR103-3, Ondine IR105.

    Six Japanese Gardens. Ondine IR105.

Savouret, Alain. *Don Quixote Corporation*. Wergo 2021-50.

Scaletti, Carla. *sunSurgeAutomata*, CDCM Centaur CRC 2045.

Schaeffer, Pierre. *L'oeuvre musicale*. INA C1006–09

Schindler, Allan. *At the Edge*. CDCM Centaur CRC 2177.

    Tremor of Night and Day. CDCM Centaur CRC 2091.

Schoeller, Phillipe. *Vertigo Apocalypse*. IRCAM IR103-3.

Schottstaedt, William. *Dinosaur Music*. Wergo 2016-50.

    Leviathan. Wergo 2025-50.

    Water Music I. Wergo 2016-50.

    Water Music II. Wergo 2016-50.

Schrader, Barry. *Beyond*. CDCM Centaur CRC 2490.

Schultz, Mark. *Eùrendil*. CDCM Centaur CRC 2245.

Scott, Douglas. *Interlude and Fantasy*. CDCM Centaur CRC 2177.

Settel, Jack. *Hok Pwah*. CDCM Centaur CRC 2302.

Shatin, Judith. *Sea of Reeds*. CDCM Centaur CRC 2454.

　　Three Summers Heat. CDCM Centaur CRC 2454.

Smalley, Denis. *Base Metals*. empreints DIGITALes IMED 0054.

　　Clarinet Threads. empreints DIGITALes IMED 9209, Wergo 2026-2.

　　Darkness After Time's Colours. empreints DIGITALes IMED 9209.

　　Empty Vessels. empreints DIGITALes IMED 0054.

　　Pentes. empreints DIGITALes IMED 0054.

　　Piano Nets. empreints DIGITALes IMED 9209.

　　Tides. empreints DIGITALes IMED 0054.

　　Valley Flow. empreints DIGITALes IMED 9209.

　　Wind Chimes. empreints DIGITALes IMED 9209, Wergo 2025-2.

Smith, William O. *Transformations*. CDCM Centaur CRC 2512.

Spiegel, Laurie. *Cavis Muris*. CDCM Centaur CRC 2166.

Stockhausen, Karlheinz. *Étude*. Stockhausen-Verlag CD 3.

　　Gesang der Jünglinge. Stockhausen-Verlag CD 3.

　　Hymnen. Stockhausen-Verlag CD 10.

　　Kontakte (tape alone). Stockhausen-Verlag CD 3.

　　Kontakte (tape plus instruments). Wergo WE123, Wergo 6009-2.

　　Kurzwellen. Stockhausen-Verlag CD 13.

　　Mantra. Stockhausen-Verlag CD 16, Wergo 6267-2.

　　Mikrophonie I. Stockhausen-Verlag CD 9.

　　Mikrophonie II. Stockhausen-Verlag CD 9.

　　Mixtur. Stockhausen-Verlag CD 8.

　　Octophonie. Stockhausen-Verlag CD 41.

　　Prozession. Stockhausen-Verlag CD 11.

　　Solo. Stockhausen-Verlag. CD 45.

　　Spiral. Stockhausen-Verlag CD 15.

　　Studie I. Stockhausen-Verlag CD 3.

　　Studie II. Stockhausen-Verlag CD 3.

　　Telemusik. Stockhausen-Verlag CD 9.

Strange, Allen. *Shaman: Sisters of Dreamtime*. CDCM Centaur CRC 2404.

　　Sleeping Beauty. CDCDM Centaur CRC 2213.

Stroppa, Marco. *In cielo, in tera, in mare*. IRCAM IR103-3.

　　Traiettoria. Wergo 2030-2.

Subotnick, Morton. *Intimate Immensity (Prologue—Fire)*. CDCM Centaur CRC 2490.

　　Jacob's Room. Wergo 2014-50.

　　Silver Apples of the Moon. Wergo 2035-2.

　　Touch. Wergo 2014-50.

　　Trembling. CDCM Centaur CRC 2177.

　　The Wild Bull. Wergo 2035-2.

Tanaka, Karen. *Metallic Crystal*. IRCAM IR103-3.

Teitelbaum, Richard. *Golem 1*. CDCM Centaur CRC 2039.

    Run Some By You. Wergo 2028-2.

Tenney, James. *Analog #1: Noise Study*. Artifact AR106.

    Collage #1 ("Blue Suede"). Artifact AR106.

    Dialogue. Artifact AR106, Wergo 2033-2.

    Ergodos II (For John Cage). Artifact AR106.

    Fabric for Che. Artifact AR106.

    For Ann (Rising). Artifact AR106.

    Music for Player Piano. Artifact AR106.

    Phases (For Edgard Varèse). Artifact AR106.

Tepei, Sever. *Cuniculi*. CDCM Centaur CRC 2045.

Terrugi, Daniel. *E Cosi Via*. Wergo 2028-2.

Thibault, Alan. *Concerto pour piano MIDI*. empreints DIGITALes IMED 9003.

    ELVIS. empreints DIGITALes IMED 9003.

    OUT. empreints DIGITALes IMED 9003.

    Le Soleil et l'acier. empreints DIGITALes IMED 9003.

    Volt. empreints DIGITALes IMED 9003.

Thome, Diane. *The Ruins of the Heart*. CDCM Centaur CRC 2144.

Thompson, Michael. *Klank I, II, III, IV*. CDCM Centaur CRC 2407.

Trayle, Mark. *Primitive Still Life (with Pairs)*. CDCM Centaur CRC 2490.

Troum, Neal. *Organ Nose*. CDCM Centaur CRC 2454.

Truax, Barry. *Ariel*. Cambridge Street Records CG100, Wergo CSR-CD8701.

    The Blind Man. Cambridge Street Records CG100, Wergo CSR-CD8701.

    Riverrun. Cambridge Street Records CG100, Wergo CSR-CD8701.

    Solar Ellipse. Cambridge Street Records CG100, Wergo CSR-CD8701.

    Wave Edge. Cambridge Street Records CG100, Wergo CSR-CD8701.

Tseng, Yu-Chung. *A Little Ying Yang*. CDCM Centaur CRC 2407.

Ungvary, Tamas. *Gypsy Childern's Giant Dance with Ili Fourier*. Wergo 2032-2.

Vaggione, Horacio. *KITAB*. CDCM Centaur CRC 2255.

    Thema. Wergo 2026-2.

Varèse, Edgard. *Poème électronique*. Neuma CD 450-74, Neuma NE103.

Viñao, Alejandro. *Toccata del Mago*. Wergo 2031-2.

Waisvisz, Michael. *The Hands*. Wergo WE100, Wergo 2010-50.

Warren, Alicyn. *Contraption*. CDCM Centaur CRC 2076.

    Something Else Again. CDCM Centaur CRC 2454.

Waschka, Rodney. *At Night, however, it Creaks and Breaks*. CDCM Centaur CRC 2078.

    Help me Remember. CDCM Centaur CRC 2177

    Last Night. CDCM Centaur CRC 2133.

    Visions of Habakkuk. CDCM Centaur CRC 2310, CDCM CE130.

    Xuan Men. CDCM Centaur CRC 2192.

Wessell, David. *Antony*. Wergo 2030-2.

Westerkamp, Hildegard.

    Beneath the Forest Floor. empreints DIGITALes IMED 9631.

    Cricket Voice. empreints DIGITALes IMED 9631.

Fantasie for Horns II. empreints DIGITALes IMED 9631.

Kits Beach Soundwalk. empreints DIGITALes IMED 9631.

A Walk Through The City. empreints DIGITALes IMED 9631.

Wishart, Trevor. *Red Bird*. EMF Media EM122.

VOX-5. Wergo 2024-50.

White, Frances. *Birdwing*. CDCM Centaur CRC 2347.

Ogni pensiero cola. Wergo 2027-2.

Still Life with Piano. CDCM Centaur CRC 2076.

Trees. CDCM Centaur CRC 2302.

Wingate, Mark. *Ode to the South-Facing Form*. CDCM Centaur CRC 2245.

Winsor, Phil. *Anamorphoses*. CDCM Centaur CRC 2078.

Dulcimer Dream. CDCM Centaur CRC 2029.

Piaono Etudes. CDCM Centaur 2407.

Wishart, Trevor. *Vox 5*. Virgo VC7 91108-2.

Wolff, Christiam. *Mayday Materials*. CDCM Centaur CRC 2052.

Wolman, Amnon. *A Circle in Fire*. Wergo 2026-2.

Wyatt, Scott. *Still Hidden Laughs*. CDCM Centaur CRC 2029.

Wyman, Dan. *Through the Reed*. CDCM Centaur CRC 2404.

Xenakis, Iannis. *Bohor*. EMF Media EM102.

Concret PH. EMF Media EM102.

Diamorphoses. EMF Media EM102.

Hibiki-Hana-Ma. EMF Media EM102.

Mycenae Alpha. Mode MO168-3, Neuma 450-73/74.

Orient-Occident. EMF Media EM102.

Polytope de Cluny. Mode MO168-3.

S.109. EMF Media EM102.

Young, John. *Inner*. empreints DIGITALes IMED 0261.

Liquid Sky. empreints DIGITALes IMED 0261.

Pythagoras's Curtain. empreints DIGITALes IMED 0261.

Time, Motion and Memory. empreints DIGITALes IMED 0261.

Virtual. empreints DIGITALes IMED 0261.

Yuasa, Joji. *A Study in White*. Wergo 2027-2.

Towards 'The Midnight Sun' - Homage to Ze-Ami. Wergo 2029-2.

Rock and Popular Music

Records

The Beach Boys. *Good Vibrations* (1966). Reprise 2223.

Smiley Smile (1966–7). Capitol T 2891.

The Beatles. *Revolver* (1967). Parlophone PCS 7009.

Sgt. Pepper's Lonely Hearts Club Band (1967). Capitol MAS 2653, Parlophone PCS 7027.

Magical Mystery Tour (1967). Capitol MAL 2835.

Emerson, Lake, and Palmer. *Pictures at an Exhibition* (1971). Cotillion ELP 66666, Manticore K33501.

Brain Salad Surgery (1973). Manticore MS 66669.

Eno, Brian (Matching Moles, Roxy Music). *Another Green World* (1975). Island ILPS 9351.

Discreet Music (1975). Obscure 3.

Froese, Edgar. *Aqua* (1973–4). Virgin V 2016, Virgin VR 13 111.

The Grateful Dead: Anthem of the Sun (1967–8). Warner Brothers WS 1749.

Live/Dead (1968). Warner Brothers WS 1830.

Aoxomoxoa (1969). Warner Brothers WS 1790.

Hendrix, Jimi. *The Jimi Hendrix Experience* (1967–8). Polydor 2683 031, Reprise RS 6261.

Kraftwerk. *Trans-Europe Express*. Fopp SN16301.

Matching Moles. *Little Red Record* (1972). Columbia KC 32148.

Oldfield, Mike. *Tubular Bells* (1975). Virgin V 2001.

Pink Floyd. *Atom Heart Mother* (1970). EMI Harvest SHVL 781.

Dark Side of the Moon (1972–3). EMI Harvest SHVL 804.

Meddle (1971). EMI Harvest SHVL 795.

The Rolling Stones. *Their Satanic Majesties Request* (1967). London NPS 2.

Soft Machine. *Soft Machine* (1968). Probe CPLP 4500.

Soft Machine II (1969). Probe CPLP 4505.

Soft Machine VII (1973). Columbia KC 32716.

Tangerine Dream. *Rubycon* (1975). Virgin VR 13 116.

Cyclone (1978). Virgin V 2097.

Velvet Underground. *Andy Warhol's Velvet Underground Featuring Nico* (1967–9). MGM 2683 006, Verve V6 5008.

Yes (Rick Wakeman). *Close to the Edge* (1972). Atlantic K 50012, Atlantic SD 7244

Yessongs (1973). Atlantic SD 3 100.

Frank Zappa and the Mothers of Invention. *Uncle Meat* (1967–8). Bizarre 2024.

Roxy and Elsewhere (1974). Disc ZDS 2202, WEA K 69201.</R>

Compact Discs (Recommended Selection)

ABBA. *Waterloo*. Polydor 5499592, Universal 549959.

Africa Bambaata. *Don't Stop . . . Planet Rock*. Tommy Boy 1052.

Aphex Twin. *Classics*. R & S RS95035, Pias America 5.

Selected Ambient Works '85–'92. Apollo AMB3922, Pias America 4.

Atkins, Juan. *Wax Trax! Mastermix, Vol 1*. Imports TVT72542, Tee Vee Toons 7254

The Beach Boys. *Good Vibrations*. Capitol CDS 7812942.

Summer Love Vol 1. Rhino 71065.

The Beatles. *Sgt. Pepper's Lonely Hearts Club Band*. Capitol 46442, Apple CDP 7464422.

The Bee Gees. *Saturday Night Fever*. Polydor 8253892, Polygram 825389.

Their Greatest Hits: The Record. Polydor 5894492, Universal 589400.

Can. *Future Days*. Spoon SPOONCD9, Mute 69055.

Soon Over Babaluma. Spoon SPOONCD10, Mute 69065.

Tago Mago. Spoon SPOONCD67, Mute 69054.

The Chipmunks. *Greatest Hits*. Curb 77591.

Eno, Brian (Matching Moles, Roxy Music). *Another Green World*. EG/Virgin 21.
    Discreet Music. EG/Virgin 23.
    Roxy Music. Virgin 47447, ROXYCD1.

Froese, Edgar. *Aqua*. Caroline 1624, Virgin CDV2016.

Gaynor, Gloria. *I Will Survive: The Anthology*. Polydor 5572362, Polygram 557236.

Grandmaster Flash and The Furious Five. *Back To The Old School*. Sequel 305.
    Greatest Hits. Sequel 622.

Greatful Dead. *Aoxomoxoa*. Warner Bros 1790, WEA 7599271782.
    Anthem of the Sun. Warner Bros 1749, WEA 7599271732.

Hendrix, Jimi. *The Jimi Hendrix Experience*. MCA 1123162.

Kraftwerk. *Autobahn*. Capitol CD 7461532, EMI 46153.
    The Man Machine. Capitol 7460392.
    Trans-Europe Express. Capitol 46473.

May, Derrick. *Innovator*. R & S TMT2, Transmit Records 4.

Pink Floyd. *Atom Heart Mother*. Capitol 46034, EMI CDEMD1072.
    Dark Side of the Moon. Capitol 46001, EMI CDEMD1064.
    Meddle. Capitol 46032, EMI CDEMD 1061.

The Rolling Stones. *Their Satanic Majesties Request*. ABKCO 8002, DERAM 8444702.

Silvester. *You Make me Feel (Mighty Real)*. Unidisc 1457.

Soft Machine. *Soft Machine*. Dressed to Kill METRO 380.
    Soft Machine: Vols 1 and 2. Big Beat CDWIKD920.

Summer, Donna. *Love To Love You Baby*. Casablanca 8227922, Polygram 822792.

Tangerine Dream. *Cyclone*. Virgin TAND9.
    Rubycon. Virgin TAND6, Virgin 86091.

Velvet Underground. *The Velvet Underground and Nico*. Polygram 531250, Polydor 5312502.

Village People. *The Best of the Village People*. Universal 546558.

Yes (Rick Wakeman). *Close to the Edge*. Atlantic 82666.

Frank Zappa and the Mothers of Invention. *Roxy and Elsewhere*. RYKODISC 10520.
    Uncle Meat. RYKODISC 10506/7.

Index